UNIVERSITY CASEBOOK SERIES®

MEDIA LAW

CASES AND MATERIALS

NINTH EDITION

MARC A. FRANKLIN
Frederick I. Richman Professor of Law, Emeritus
Stanford University

DAVID A. ANDERSON
Fred and Emily Marshall Wulff Centennial Chair in Law
University of Texas

LYRISSA C. BARNETT LIDSKY
Stephen C. O'Connell Chair in Law
University of Florida

AMY GAJDA
Class of 1937 Professor of Law
Tulane University

FOUNDATION
PRESS

The publisher is not engaged in rendering legal or other professional advice, and this publication is not a substitute for the advice of an attorney. If you require legal or other expert advice, you should seek the services of a competent attorney or other professional.

University Casebook Series is a trademark registered in the U.S. Patent and Trademark Office.

© 1977, 1982, 1987, 1990, 1995, 2000, 2005 FOUNDATION PRESS
© 2011 By THOMSON REUTERS/FOUNDATION PRESS
© 2016 LEG, Inc. d/b/a West Academic
    444 Cedar Street, Suite 700
    St. Paul, MN 55101
    1-877-888-1330

Printed in the United States of America

ISBN: 978-1-60930-467-6

To the memory of Ruth K. Franklin
and
to Karen and Howard and Dave

PREFACE TO THE NINTH EDITION

This book aims to help students acquire the tools they will need to understand the media law world of the future. In a period of dramatic changes in journalism, the media industries, and the wider legal and political environments, this task is daunting. We have tried to select materials that are most likely to be relevant in resolving future media law issues. In some instances that has meant including subjects not previously considered central to media law, such as anonymous speech and foreign law, and considering issues from the perspective of non-traditional media actors, including both citizen journalists and online content providers. In other instances, we seek to provide students with tools to resolve future issues by distilling from familiar precedents the fundamental principles that will continue to be the major weapons against censorship, chilling effects, and suppression of information.

This edition retains the basic organizational framework of the previous edition. Part I deals primarily with First Amendment limits on governmental regulation of media. Part I separately addresses materials that single out electronic media for disparate treatment and questions whether such treatment will continue in the new media environment. Part II addresses private litigation that arises from media publication. Part III deals with legislation, regulations, and judicial actions that inhibit (or sometimes aid) newsgathering.

We have tried to resist the temptation to cram ever more detail into the textual material between principal cases. What remains is material we consider essential to understanding the subject.

MARC A. FRANKLIN
DAVID A. ANDERSON
LYRISSA BARNETT LIDSKY
AMY GAJDA

May 2016

ACKNOWLEDGMENTS

The authors wish to thank Rachael L. Jones, Linda Riedemann Norbut, Josef Ghosn, and Peter L. Rogers Jr. for their assistance in producing this edition. We are also grateful to readers of the previous editions for their criticisms and suggestions.

Thanks are also due to authors and copyright holders who permitted excerpts from the following words to be included in this book:

Emerson, Thomas I., *The System of Freedom of Expression*, copyright © 1970 by Thomas I. Emerson. Reprinted with permission of the author.

Meiklejohn, Alexander, "The First Amendment Is an Absolute," copyright © 1961 by The University of Chicago. All Rights Reserved. Reprinted by permission of The University of Chicago Press from *Supreme Court Review* (1961), 245, 255–262.

Ohlhausen, Maureen K., *The FCC's Knowledge Problem: How to Protect Consumers Online*, copyright © 2015. Reprinted by permission of Federal Communications Law Journal from 67 Fed. Comm. L.J. 203 (2015).

SUMMARY OF CONTENTS

PART I. THE FIRST AMENDMENT AND GOVERNMENT REGULATION

PART II. LEGAL ISSUES ARISING FROM PUBLICATION

PART III. LEGAL ISSUES ARISING
FROM NEWSGATHERING

TABLE OF CONTENTS

PART III. LEGAL ISSUES ARISING
FROM NEWSGATHERING

TABLE OF CASES

The principal cases are in bold type.

UNIVERSITY CASEBOOK SERIES®

MEDIA LAW

CASES AND MATERIALS

NINTH EDITION

The First Amendment and Government Regulation

CHAPTER I

FOUNDATIONS OF MEDIA LAW

A. THE ROLE OF THE FIRST AMENDMENT

This is a book about media law, not a book about the First Amendment. Media law has many sources other than the First Amendment. The law of defamation and invasion of privacy is largely common law. A reporter's privilege to refuse to disclose confidences is controlled in many states by statutes. Open-meetings and open-records statutes determine the outcome of most controversies over press access to governmental information. Broadcast regulation is largely accomplished by federal statutes and Federal Communications Commission regulations, which impose obligations and restrictions.

Conversely, many areas of First Amendment law have little to do with media. The religion, association, and petition clauses of that amendment rarely are invoked by the mass media. Even the speech clause generates much litigation that does not affect the media, although it can inform some media-related cases. Cases involving censorship of libraries and school materials, use of streets and parks as public forums, and picketing are First Amendment cases but not media law cases.

Nevertheless, the First Amendment does play a large role in nearly every area of media law. It limits the extent to which states may protect reputation and privacy. It gives the press the right to attend trials, to publish lawfully obtained information, and to protect sources. It protects the right to disseminate pornography and to advertise. It imposes limits on the government's ability to regulate broadcasting—limits that are shifting as technologies and attitudes toward broadcasting change. It affects what may be published on the Internet.

Because the influence of the First Amendment is so pervasive in media law, we begin with a brief and selective treatment of First Amendment history and theory. Our focus is on those portions of First Amendment jurisprudence that are likely to influence the outcome of media law issues. The media lawyer must not forget, however, that judges do not see media First Amendment issues in isolation from other kinds of First Amendment cases. A judge hearing a media law case may be influenced by a recently decided picketing case, for example. Conversely, while Supreme Court jurisprudence is key, a judge may find that fact differences in a newer lawsuit warrant a different outcome.

---

1. BEGINNINGS

The First Amendment reads:

Congress shall make no law respecting an establishment of religion, or prohibiting the free exercise thereof; or abridging the freedom of speech or of the press; or the right of the people peaceably to assemble, and to petition the government for a redress of grievances.

First Amendment jurisprudence as we know it was quite slow to develop. Not until 1925 did the Court apply the First Amendment to the states, and not until 1931 did it invalidate a statute on First Amendment grounds. For the first 100 years of U.S. history, controversies over freedom of speech and press were resolved as a matter of common law rather than First Amendment law. The American common law of free speech and free press began to diverge from its English heritage quite early and developed throughout the eighteenth and nineteenth centuries. Sir William Blackstone wrote in the 1760s that the English common law of freedom of the press consisted of nothing more than freedom from prior restraints, leaving the government free to punish after the fact "any dangerous or offensive writings." By that time, freedom of the press in the American colonies was somewhat broader, both in theory and in practice. The trial of printer John Peter Zenger in New York in 1735 established the practice of allowing the jury to return a general verdict of "not guilty" in seditious libel cases, in contrast to the practice in England where the jury was only allowed to decide whether the defendant had published the words in question. For this reason, and because of widespread public resistance to government prosecutions of speech,* the common law of seditious libel became generally ineffectual in America in the eighteenth century. The common law prohibition against prior restraints was widely accepted in both England and the United States.

The Sedition Act of 1798—enacted just seven years after the First Amendment was adopted—touched off a controversy that became a defining event in the history of freedom of expression. The Federalist Party passed this statute, together with the Alien Act, in an attempt to keep Thomas Jefferson's Republican Party from winning the election of 1800. The Act made it a crime to print any false, scandalous, and malicious writings about the federal government, the Congress, or the president. It conspicuously omitted the vice presidency, which Jefferson then held, and it expired by its own terms in 1801. The Act was enforced vigorously and effectively against Republican newspapers, which were already vastly outnumbered by the Federalist press. Three Republican editors were convicted and three leading Republican newspapers were

---

*   We, like courts and other commentators, sometimes use "speech" as shorthand for "freedom of expression" or "freedom of speech and press."

forced to cease publication. There were 15 indictments in all, leading to 10 convictions. Despite this virtual silencing of the newspapers that supported him, Jefferson won the election and there was no attempt to renew the Sedition Act.

The Sedition Act was never tested in the Supreme Court, but it touched off the first national debate over the meaning of press freedom. It prompted James Madison and Thomas Jefferson to write extended discourses on freedom of speech and press, in which both argued that the First Amendment had been intended to deny the federal government the power to punish seditious libel. In the course of making these arguments, they embraced more comprehensive visions of freedom of expression than had generally been expressed previously. Some contend these were post hoc constructions that cannot be trusted as accurate statements of the framers' intentions, but all agree that they were influential interpretations upon which much subsequent doctrine was based. Madison's exegesis was adopted by the Virginia legislature and is known as "The Virginia Report of 1799–80." Jefferson's contribution was "The Kentucky Resolutions of 1798." Both are excerpted in Leonard Levy (ed.), Freedom of the Press From Zenger to Jefferson (1966).

A related case from around the same the time, People v. Croswell, 3 Johns. Cas. 337 (N.Y. 1804), hints at inconsistencies in Jefferson's stance on seditious libel. A newspaper, The Wasp, published an article alleging that Jefferson had paid others to implicate George Washington and John Adams in crimes and other misdeeds. The court upheld the jury's verdict against the publisher, finding that the "virtuous" Jefferson should be protected from libels of private character, specifically those "expos[ing] to the public eye one's personal defects or misfortunes." "[T]he truth of the charge," the court wrote, "would rather aggravate than lessen the baseness and evil tendency of the publication."

There were additional free speech and free press controversies in the nineteenth century, principally over censorship of abolitionist publications in the southern states before the Civil War and censorship of "obscenity" in the industrial states after the war. For reasons that have yet to be fully explained, these conflicts did not generate much development of free speech jurisprudence. Courts seemed to acquiesce in generalizations such as "freedom of speech is protected but abuse of the right is not" and in broad definitions of concepts like obscenity. See generally David M. Rabban, The First Amendment in Its Forgotten Years, 90 Yale L.J. 514 (1981).

One reason the First Amendment played little role in the nineteenth century was that it applied only to the federal government. That was clear both from its language, which restricted only Congress, and from its legislative history, which explicitly rejected application to the states. Adoption of the Fourteenth Amendment in 1868 was not understood at the time to require any change in this thinking. Because the scope of federal governmental activity was vastly narrower in the nineteenth century than it is today, there were fewer occasions for federal suppression of speech or press. However, much of the suppression of abolitionist material was done by federal postal officials, and the Comstock Act of 1873, which allowed postal authorities to seize "obscenity" and prosecute its senders, was a federal statute.

In any event, the Supreme Court did not begin to develop a comprehensive First Amendment jurisprudence until World War I. Anti-war protesters, socialists, anarchists, and communists who made speeches, circulated leaflets, and led demonstrations were prosecuted under the Espionage Act of 1917, the Sedition Act of 1918, and various state statutes enacted in the face of the Red Scare that followed the war. Some raised First Amendment defenses, but the courts uniformly rejected them. The cases did, however, precipitate the Supreme Court's first serious attempts to interpret the First Amendment. In Schenck v. United States, 249 U.S. 47 (1919), the Court affirmed convictions for publishing a leaflet that urged young men to violate the military draft law. Justice Holmes wrote for the majority that expression could be punished when "the words used are used in such circumstances and are of such a nature as to create a clear and present danger that they will bring about the substantive evils that Congress has a right to prevent. It is a question of proximity and degree."

Even so, Holmes saw the danger of government censorship in such cases. He began dissenting, often holding that radical speech presented no "clear and present danger." He was often joined by Justice Brandeis, who himself had written of the dangers of media overreaching in a now-famous law review article on privacy. Their views gradually became more protective of speech, and in 1927 Brandeis articulated what has become a classic endorsement of free speech:

> Those who won our independence believed that the final end of the State was to make men free to develop their faculties; and that in its government the deliberative forces should prevail over the arbitrary. They valued liberty both as an end and as a means. They believed liberty to be the secret of happiness and courage to be the secret of liberty. They believed that freedom to think as you will and to speak as you think are means indispensable to the discovery and spread of political truth; that without free speech and assembly, discussion would be futile; that with them, discussion affords ordinarily adequate protection against the dissemination of noxious doctrine; that the greatest menace to freedom is an inert people; that public discussion is a political duty; and that this should be a fundamental principle of the American government. They recognized the risks to which all human institutions are subject. But they knew that order cannot be secured merely through fear

of punishment for its infraction; that it is hazardous to discourage thought, hope and imagination; that fear breeds repression; that repression breeds hate; that hate menaces stable government; that the path of safety lies in the opportunity to discuss freely supposed grievances and proposed remedies; and that the fitting remedy for evil counsels is good ones. Believing in the power of reason as applied through public discussion, they eschewed silence coerced by law—the argument of force in its worst form. Recognizing the occasional tyrannies of governing majorities, they amended the Constitution so that free speech and assembly should be guaranteed.

Fear of serious injury cannot alone justify suppression of free speech and assembly. Men feared witches and burnt women. It is the function of speech to free men from the bondage of irrational fears. To justify suppression of free speech there must be reasonable ground to fear that serious evil will result if free speech is practiced. There must be reasonable ground to believe that the danger apprehended is imminent. There must be reasonable ground to believe that the evil to be prevented is a serious one. Every denunciation of existing law tends in some measure to increase the probability that there will be violation of it. Condonation of a breach enhances the probability. Expressions of approval add to the probability. Propagation of the criminal state of mind by teaching syndicalism increases it. Advocacy of law-breaking heightens it still further. But even advocacy of violation, however reprehensible morally, is not a justification for denying free speech where the advocacy falls short of incitement and there is nothing to indicate that the advocacy would be immediately acted on. The wide difference between advocacy and incitement, between preparation and attempt, between assembling and conspiracy, must be borne in mind. In order to support a finding of clear and present danger it must be shown either that immediate serious violence was to be expected or was advocated, or that the past conduct furnished reason to believe that such advocacy was then contemplated.

Those who won our independence by revolution were not cowards. They did not fear political change. They did not exalt order at the cost of liberty. To courageous, self-reliant men, with confidence in the power of free and fearless reasoning applied through the processes of popular government, no danger flowing from speech can be deemed clear and present, unless the incidence of the evil apprehended is so imminent that it may befall before there is opportunity for full discussion. If there be time to expose through discussion the falsehood and fallacies, to avert the evil by the processes of education, the remedy to be applied is more speech, not enforced silence. Only an emergency can justify repression. Such must be the rule if authority is to be reconciled with freedom. Such, in my opinion, is the command of the Constitution. It is therefore always open to Americans to challenge a law abridging free speech and assembly by showing that there was no emergency justifying it.

Whitney v. California, 274 U.S. 357, 375–77 (1927) (Brandeis, J., concurring).

The Brandeis opinion in *Whitney* marked a turning point in First Amendment jurisprudence. Before 1927 the Supreme Court rejected all the First Amendment challenges it faced. From 1927 until the beginning of World War II, the Court sustained First Amendment claims fairly consistently, usually on the ground that the government had failed to show that the speech in question posed a clear and present danger.

---

2. INTERPRETING THE FIRST AMENDMENT

We begin by considering various views as to the values served by protecting speech.

a. FOSTERING A MARKETPLACE OF IDEAS

First Amendment jurisprudence often embraces the idea that the government should not pick winners and losers in the marketplace of ideas. One of the earliest uses of the "marketplace of ideas" concept came in 1644 in John Milton's Areopagitica, an essay against the English system of licensing publications: "And though all the winds of doctrine were let loose to play upon the earth, so Truth be in the field, we do injuriously by licensing and prohibiting to misdoubt her strength. Let her and Falsehood grapple; who ever knew Truth put to the worse, in a free and open encounter?"

Two hundred years later, the English philosopher and economist John Stuart Mill embraced the notion more broadly, as a reason for denying all government power to suppress speech, even though he recognized that truth sometimes loses:

[T]he peculiar evil of silencing the expression of an opinion is, that it is robbing the human race: posterity as well as the existing generation; those who dissent from the opinion, still more than those who hold it. If the opinion is right, they are deprived of the opportunity of exchanging error for truth; if wrong, they lose what is almost as great a benefit, the clearer perception and livelier impression of truth, produced by its collision with error.

. . .

> [T]he dictum that truth always triumphs over persecution is one of those pleasant falsehoods which men repeat after one another till they pass into commonplaces, but which all experience refutes. History teems with instances of truth put down by persecution. If not suppressed forever, it may be thrown back for centuries. . . . It is a piece of idle sentimentality that truth, merely as truth, has any inherent power denied to error of prevailing against the dungeon and the stake.

John Stuart Mill, On Liberty 20, 30–31 (S. Collini, ed. 1989).

The marketplace metaphor, envisioned by Milton and developed by Mill, entered First Amendment jurisprudence in Justice Holmes' dissenting opinion in Abrams v. United States, 250 U.S. 616 (1919). Abrams and four other socialist immigrants were convicted of sedition for publishing pamphlets that urged workers in munitions plants to strike to protest the deployment of American troops to help put down the Russian Revolution. A majority of the Supreme Court upheld the convictions, but Justice Holmes, joined by Justice Brandeis, argued in dissent that the pamphlets were not seditious because they did not attack the form of the U.S. government or cripple it in its war effort. More generally, Holmes wrote:

> Persecution for the expression of opinions seems to me perfectly logical. If you have no doubt of your premises or your power and want a certain result with all your heart you naturally express your wishes in law and sweep away all opposition. To allow opposition by speech seems to indicate that you think the speech impotent, as when a man says that he has squared the circle, or that you do not care whole-heartedly for the result, or that you doubt either your power or your premises. But when men have realized that time has upset many fighting faiths, they may come to believe even more than they believe the very foundations of their own conduct that *the ultimate good desired is better reached by free trade in ideas*—that the best test of truth is the power of the thought to get itself accepted in the competition of the market, and that truth is the only ground upon which their wishes safely can be carried out. That at any rate is the theory of our Constitution. It is an experiment, as all life is an experiment.

Holmes thus endorsed the notion that the government should largely avoid regulating speech, because regulation would hamper this type of critical discourse. Judge Learned Hand voiced a similar sentiment in an antitrust case brought against the Associated Press. He observed that one of the most "vital of all general interests" is "the dissemination of news from as many different sources, and with as many different facets and colors as is possible. That interest is closely akin to, if indeed it is not the same as, the interest protected by the First Amendment; it presupposes that right conclusions are more likely to be gathered out of a multitude of tongues, than through any kind of authoritative selection. To many this is, and always will be, folly; but we have staked upon it our all." United States v. Associated Press, 52 F. Supp. 362 (S.D.N.Y. 1943).

For an illuminating insight into the views of the First Amendment held by Justice Holmes, Judge Learned Hand, and the influential scholar Zechariah Chafee, see Gerald Gunther, "Learned Hand and the Origins of Modern First Amendment Doctrine: Some Fragments of History," 27 Stan. L. Rev. 719 (1975). See generally Stanley Ingber, The Marketplace of Ideas: A Legitimizing Myth, 15 Duke L.J. 1 (1984); G. Edward White, The Canonization of Holmes and Brandeis: Epistemology and Judicial Reputations, 70 N.Y.U. L. Rev. 576 (1995). For extensive analysis of the application of First Amendment principles during wartime, see Geoffrey Stone, Perilous Times: Free Speech in Wartime from the Sedition Act of 1798 to the War on Terrorism (2004).

Critics of the marketplace theory point to the fact that it is an ideal that has never been fully realized. Many citizens even in an Internet age have been barred from meaningful participation in the marketplace of ideas by poverty or inadequate education, and class, race, or gender may impair the ability of some speakers to make their voices heard. Media corporations sometimes set the parameters of public debate based on what sells rather than on what an informed citizenry needs to know. And even though the Internet gives many citizens widespread access to a medium of mass communication, the speakers whose voices are most influential online can be the same speakers whose voices dominate public debate in the conventional media. A more fundamental critique of the marketplace theory has to do with the limits of human nature. Even if the marketplace of ideas were functioning perfectly, there is still some question whether "Truth" would emerge, as human beings often adhere to irrational beliefs.

Several contemporary critics of the marketplace theory also argue that it prevents democratic reforms that would actually advance free speech interests. Professor Cass Sunstein argues, for example, that adherence to the marketplace metaphor has resulted in "safeguard[ing] speech that has little or no connection with democratic aspirations and that produces serious social harm." Sunstein argues that just as the federal government intervened in the economic marketplace to correct market failures during the New Deal, governmental intervention in the marketplace of ideas is sometimes warranted:

> [It is possible] that government controls on the broadcast media, designed to ensure diversity of view and attention to public affairs, would help the system of free expression. Such controls could promote both political deliberation and political equality. In such reforms, I contend, lies the best hope for keeping faith

with time-honored principles of democratic self-government under modern conditions.

Cass R. Sunstein, Democracy and the Problem of Free Speech xviii–xx, 18–19 (1993). Relatedly, as the marketplace has grown to include speech that directly inflicts profound emotional harm on individuals, such as hate speech or the unconsented publication of intimate photographs, it is more difficult for some to embrace an all-encompassing marketplace.

Despite these criticisms, the marketplace theory of free speech remains a powerful force in First Amendment jurisprudence. One explanation might be that judges, at least the Justices of the U.S. Supreme Court, are less dissatisfied than the critics with the results of marketplace-based jurisprudence. As Professor Sunstein acknowledges, that model has produced a great deal of freedom:

> Over the last forty years, the American law of freedom of speech experienced nothing short of a revolution. The revolution accomplished enormous good. It would be hard to argue that a return to the pre-1950 law of free speech would provide a better understanding of the free speech principle. . . .

> At the same time, a crucial part of that achievement is a dynamic and self-revising free speech tradition. Our liberty of expression owes much of its content to the capacity of each generation to rethink the understandings that were left to it. To the economists' plea that "the perfect is the enemy of the good," we should oppose John Dewey's suggestion that "the better is the enemy of the still better."

Id. at 250.

———

b.   FACILITATING SELF-GOVERNMENT

In his 1948 book, Free Speech and Its Relation to Self-Government, Professor Alexander Meiklejohn set forth the view that the First Amendment protects only "political" speech. There he argued that speech not relevant to self-government was protected only by the due process clause, not the First Amendment. The notion that "political speech" lies at the core of the First Amendment is now widely embraced, but the argument that the First Amendment protects nothing more has not been accepted. Indeed, Meiklejohn's own definition of "political" speech seemed to expand significantly between that book and his 1961 article excerpted below. Readers of the article were surprised to learn that speech of "governing" importance includes even obscenity. If the concept extends that far, what kinds of speech does it exclude?

The First Amendment Is an Absolute

Alexander Meiklejohn.
1961 Sup. Ct. Rev. 245, 255–262.

. . . The First Amendment does not protect a "freedom to speak." It protects the freedom of those activities of thought and communication by which we "govern." It is concerned, not with a private right, but with a public power, a governmental responsibility.

In the specific language of the Constitution, the governing activities of the people appear only in terms of casting a ballot. But in the deeper meaning of the Constitution, voting is merely the external expression of a wide and diverse number of activities by means of which citizens attempt to meet the responsibilities of making judgments, which that freedom to govern lays upon them. That freedom implies and requires what we call "the dignity of the individual." Self-government can exist only insofar as the voters acquire the intelligence, integrity, sensitivity, and generous devotion to the general welfare that, in theory, casting a ballot is assumed to express.

The responsibilities mentioned are of three kinds. We, the people who govern, must try to understand the issues which, incident by incident, face the nation. We must pass judgment upon the decisions which our agents make upon those issues. And, further, we must share in devising methods by which those decisions can be made wise and effective or, if need be, supplanted by others which promise greater wisdom and effectiveness. Now it is these activities, in all their diversity, whose freedom fills up "the scope of the First Amendment." These are the activities to whose freedom it gives its unqualified protection. . . .

. . .

. . . First of all, the freedom to "vote," the official expression of a self-governing man's judgment on issues of public policy, must be absolutely protected. None of his subordinate agencies may bring pressure upon him to drive his balloting this way or that. None of them may require him to tell how he has voted; none may inquire by compulsory process into his political beliefs or associations. In that area, the citizen has constitutional authority and his agents have not.

Second, there are many forms of thought and expression within the range of human communications from which the voter derives the knowledge, intelligence, sensitivity to human values: the capacity for sane and objective judgment which, so far as possible, a ballot should express. These, too, must suffer no abridgment of their freedom. I list four of them below.

1.   Education, in all its phases, is the attempt to so inform and cultivate the mind and will of a citizen that he shall have the wisdom, the independence, and, therefore, the dignity of a governing citizen.

Freedom of education is, thus, as we all recognize, a basic postulate in the planning of a free society.

2.   The achievements of philosophy and the sciences in creating knowledge and understanding of men and their world must be made available, without abridgment, to every citizen.

3.   Literature and the arts must be protected by the First Amendment. They lead the way toward sensitive and informed appreciation and response to the values out of which the riches of the general welfare are created.

4.   Public discussions of public issues, together with the spreading of information and opinion bearing on those issues, must have a freedom unabridged by our agents. Though they govern us, we, in a deeper sense, govern them. Over our governing, they have no power. Over their governing we have sovereign power.

. . .

. . . We must recognize that there are many forms of communication which, since they are not being used as activities of governing, are wholly outside the scope of the First Amendment. Mr. Justice Holmes has told us about these, giving such vivid illustrations as "persuasion to murder" and "falsely shouting fire in a theatre and causing a panic." And Mr. Justice Harlan, referring to Holmes and following his lead, gave a more extensive list: "libel, slander, misrepresentation, obscenity, perjury, false advertising, solicitation of crime, complicity by encouragement, conspiracy. . . ." Why are these communications not protected by the First Amendment? Mr. Justice Holmes suggested an explanation when he said of the First Amendment in *Schenck*: "It does not even protect a man from an injunction against uttering words that may have all the effect of force."

. . .

. . . In the current discussions as to whether or not "obscenity" in literature and the arts is protected by the First Amendment, the basic principle is, I think, that literature and the arts are protected because they have a "social importance" which I have called a "governing" importance. For example, the novel is at present a powerful determinative of our views of what human beings are, how they can be influenced, in what directions they should be influenced by many forces, including, especially, their own judgments and appreciations. But the novel, like all the other creations of literature and the arts, may be produced wisely or unwisely, sensitively or coarsely, for the building up of a way of life which we treasure or for tearing it down. Shall the government establish a censorship to distinguish between "good" novels and "bad" ones? And, more specifically, shall it forbid the publication of novels which portray sexual experiences with a frankness that, to the prevailing conventions of our society, seems "obscene"?

The First Amendment seems to me to answer that question with an unequivocal "no." Here, as elsewhere, the authority of citizens to decide what they shall write and, more fundamental, what they shall read and see, has not been delegated to any of the subordinate branches of government. It is "reserved to the people," each deciding for himself to whom he will listen, whom he will read, what portrayal of the human scene he finds worthy of his attention.

. . .

c.   BROADER PURPOSES

Professor Emerson articulated a broader view of the purposes of the First Amendment, one that is widely shared today.

The System of Freedom of Expression

Thomas I. Emerson.
6–9 (1970).

The system of freedom of expression in a democratic society rests upon four main premises. These may be stated, in capsule form, as follows:

First, freedom of expression is essential as a means of assuring individual self-fulfillment. The proper end of man is the realization of his character and potentialities as a human being. For the achievement of this self-realization the mind must be free. Hence suppression of belief, opinion, or other expression is an affront to the dignity of man, a negation of man's essential nature. Moreover, man in his capacity as a member of society has a right to share in the common decisions that affect him. To cut off his search for truth, or his expression of it, is to elevate society and the state to a despotic command over him and to place him under the arbitrary control of others.

Second, freedom of expression is an essential process for advancing knowledge and discovering truth. An individual who seeks knowledge and truth must hear all sides of the question, consider all alternatives, test his judgment by exposing it to opposition, and make full use of different minds. Discussion must be kept open no matter how certainly true an accepted opinion may seem to be; many of the most widely acknowledged truths have turned out to be erroneous. Conversely, the same principle applies no matter how false or pernicious the new opinion appears to be; for the unaccepted opinion may be true or partially true and, even if wholly false, its presentation and open discussion compel a rethinking and retesting of the accepted opinion. The reasons which make open discussion essential for an intelligent individual judgment likewise make it imperative for rational social judgment.

Third, freedom of expression is essential to provide for participation in decision making by all members of society. This is particularly significant for political decisions. Once one accepts the premise of the Declaration of Independence—that governments "derive their just powers from the consent of the governed"—it follows that the governed must, in order to exercise their right of consent, have full freedom of expression both in forming individual judgments and in forming the common judgment. The principle also carries beyond the political realm. It embraces the right to participate in the building of the whole culture, and includes freedom of expression in religion, literature, art, science, and all areas of human learning and knowledge.

Finally, freedom of expression is a method of achieving a more adaptable and hence a more stable community, of maintaining the precarious balance between healthy cleavage and necessary consensus. This follows because suppression of discussion makes a rational judgment impossible, substituting force for reason; because suppression promotes inflexibility and stultification, preventing society from adjusting to changing circumstances or developing new ideas; and because suppression conceals the real problems confronting a society, diverting public attention from the critical issues. At the same time the process of open discussion promotes greater cohesion in a society because people are more ready to accept decisions that go against them if they have a part in the decision-making process. Moreover, the state at all times retains adequate powers to promote unity and to suppress resort to force. Freedom of expression thus provides a framework in which the conflict necessary to the progress of society can take place without destroying the society. It is an essential mechanism for maintaining the balance between stability and change.

The validity of the foregoing premises has never been proved or disproved, and probably could not be. Nevertheless our society is based upon the faith that they hold true and, in maintaining a system of freedom of expression, we act upon that faith. . . .

NOTES AND QUESTIONS

1.   The four premises identified by Emerson are widely accepted. Is each of them equally important? Are there others that should be included?

2.   Consider how each of the authors above would respond to the freedom of publication on the Internet. Would each necessarily embrace such freedom of expression?

———————

Professor Ed Baker identified individual autonomy, self-fulfillment, participation in change, self-realization, and self-determination as the key First Amendment values. "[T]he assumption that respect for people's equality and autonomy is fundamental may . . . provide the best explanation for the basic commitments of actual liberal democratic states." In his view, the "foundational status" of these values helps explain "why utilitarian balancing does not justify limiting first amendment rights." C. Edwin Baker, Human Liberty and Freedom of Speech, 47–50 (1989).

Autonomy is invaded both when an individual is forbidden from speaking and when the individual is required to speak. The First Amendment sometimes seems to protect this autonomy-based interest. For example, it denies government the power to stop a protester from expressing his thoughts even in a way that others find offensive, see, e.g., Cohen v. California, 403 U.S. 15 (1971) (protecting the right to wear a jacket bearing the words "Fuck the Draft"). It also denies the state power to compel drivers to display on license plates a state motto they find repugnant, see Wooley v. Maynard, 430 U.S. 705 (1977), or to require religious objectors to recite the pledge of allegiance, West Virginia State Board of Education v. Barnette, 319 U.S. 624 (1943). Justice Robert Jackson explained the principle at stake in *Barnette* as follows:

> If there is any fixed star in our constitutional constellation, it is that no official, high or petty, can prescribe what shall be orthodox in politics, nationalism, religion, or other matters of opinion or force citizens to confess by word or act their faith therein. If there are any circumstances which permit an exception, they do not now occur to us.

Professor Jed Rubenfeld argues that the autonomy-based interest described by Justice Jackson—which he calls the anti-orthodoxy principle—is the bedrock of the First Amendment. Rubenfeld points out that the anti-orthodoxy principle is "absolutely incompatible with cost-benefit, balancing approaches to the First Amendment." Rubenfeld concedes, however, that "[t]he domain of speech to which the anti-orthodoxy principle applies is not all encompassing. There is a kind of orthodoxy that government can and does enforce every day, even in the sense of prescribing what people must and must not say. I refer to the orthodoxy of true and false facts. While it is true that 'there is no such thing as a false idea' under the First Amendment, there is clearly such a thing as a false fact. The laws of libel, fraud, perjury, and so on, all punish people for speaking falsely on matters of fact." The First Amendment's Purpose, 53 Stan. L. Rev. 767, 818–821 (2001). Is there a clear distinction between ideas and facts? A distinction workable enough to be useful? In 2012 the Supreme Court in U.S v. Alvarez, 132 S. Ct. 2537 (2012), held that a statute punishing those who lied about military medals was unconstitutional. Does the anti-orthodoxy principle dictate that the government may not punish the publication of false facts unless there is direct harm caused to an individual by the false speech?

Another aspect of autonomy involves the individual's right to receive information. Denying that right might be thought to interfere with the autonomous individual's right to learn, choose, and decide. This interest also seems to receive some First Amendment protection. For example, the Supreme Court held that consumers had standing to attack a state law forbidding price advertising by pharmacists, because they had a First Amendment right to receive that information in the interest of making informed consumer decisions. See Virginia State Board of Pharmacy v. Virginia Citizens Consumer Council, Inc., 425 U.S. 748 (1976) (the Court also recognized an instrumentalist interest in efficient operation of a free market economy).

A different function of free speech is identified by Professor Vincent Blasi in The Checking Value in First Amendment Theory, 1977 Am. B. Found. Res. J. 521, 527:

> ... This is the value that free speech, a free press, and free assembly can serve in checking the abuse of power by public officials. Consider the most important ways in which the First Amendment has made a difference in recent years. But for the peace marches and other protests, the Johnson administration might very well have escalated the war in Vietnam after the Tet offensive and the Nixon administration might have attempted to sustain a wider war after the Cambodian "incursion." But for the tradition of a free press, the crimes and abuses of Watergate might never have been uncovered. These incidents in our recent political experience are so familiar that it is easy to underestimate their importance. In the last decade, the First Amendment has had at least as much impact on American life by facilitating a process by which countervailing forces check the misuse of official power as by protecting the dignity of the individual, maintaining a diverse society in the face of conformist pressures, promoting the quest for scientific and philosophic truth, or fostering a regime of "self-government" in which large numbers of ordinary citizens take an active part in political affairs.

———

The theories discussed above suggest that speech must be protected because of its positive values. Another possibility is that speech is protected because of the *negative* effects of allowing government to regulate speech:

> ... Throughout history the process of regulating speech has been marked with what we now see to be fairly plain errors. Whether it be the condemnation of Galileo, religious persecution in the sixteenth and seventeenth centuries, the extensive history of prosecution for expressing seditious views of those now viewed as patriots, or the banning of numerous admittedly great works of art because someone thought them obscene, acts of suppression that have been proved erroneous seem to

represent a disproportionate percentage of the governmental mistakes of the past. . . .

. . .

Freedom of speech is based in large part on a distrust of the ability of government to make the necessary distinctions, a distrust of governmental determinations of truth and falsity, an appreciation of the fallibility of political leaders, and a somewhat deeper distrust of governmental power in a more general sense. . . .

Frederick Schauer, Free Speech: A Philosophical Enquiry 81–86 (1982).

————

d.   FIRST AMENDMENT ECLECTICISM

There is no necessity to choose one exclusive justification for protecting speech, of course. Some of those who espouse the self-realization justifications insist that all other arguments are derivative, but most First Amendment theorists are willing to accept a pluralistic notion of purposes. Professor Schauer suggests viewing the First Amendment as an umbrella for a number of more or less distinct principles, each with its own justification, and each directed towards a separate group of problems:

Under such a view . . . we might in fact have several first amendments. We might have one first amendment directed primarily to the problem of government suppression of its critics. The justifications for this first amendment might be largely of the democratic theory and abuse of governmental power varieties. . . . Another first amendment might be directed primarily towards the problem of open inquiry in the sciences and academic institutions, being based primarily on the heritage of Galileo and the search for truth/marketplace of ideas justifications for the principle of free speech. . . . A third first amendment might be a reaction to an excess of historical censorship of the arts . . . perhaps even based in part on notions of self-realization.

Frederick Schauer, Must Speech Be Special?, 78 Nw. U. L. Rev. 1284, 1303–04 (1983). See also Steven Shiffrin, The First Amendment and Economic Regulation: Away From a General Theory of the First Amendment, 78 Nw. U. L. Rev. 1212 (1983) (arguing that no "single theory could explain, or dictate helpful conclusions in, the vast terrain of speech regulation"). Is a multiplicity of theories a problem in itself? Should a need for judicial efficiency push toward consolidation of First Amendment theory?

For an insightful treatment of most of the major threads of First Amendment jurisprudence, see Daniel A. Farber, The First Amendment (3d ed. 2010).

————

B. EMERGENCE OF MEDIA LAW

Though the First Amendment has a rich history, First Amendment litigation by the mass media is a relatively recent phenomenon. The press did not win a First Amendment case in the Supreme Court until 1931, and not until 1964 did the Supreme Court hold that the First Amendment imposed any limitations on state tort actions such as libel. The first Supreme Court decision striking down a federal statute under the First Amendment was in 1965.

Thus, although the law of free speech and free press has been developing for centuries, First Amendment law has developed comparatively recently. In fact, only in the last half-century have the established media engaged regularly in constitutional confrontations with authorities. In part this reflects changes in journalism and the relationship of the press to the government. During World War II, virtually the entire American press voluntarily acquiesced in government censorship of military news. As recently as the late 1940s, the White House was covered only by a handful of reporters who sometimes played poker with President Truman. Reporters and government officials often acted as allies, the latter releasing information as a favor, and receiving favorable publicity in return. The investigation of wrongdoing was largely left to ambitious prosecutors and investigating committees; the press's role primarily was to report and comment upon the activities of government.

Media law emerged as a recognized field in the second half of the twentieth century. A few important cases involving newspapers and pamphlets were decided earlier, but not until the emergence of powerful newspapers and broadcast networks around mid-century was there enough media-specific litigation and legislation to spawn media law profession. In the 1970s and 1980s, publishers and broadcasters were strong financially and politically, and they aggressively attacked laws and practices that limited journalistic freedom.

The Supreme Court was an important factor in the growth of media law during this period. The Court accepted dozens of media law cases, and while the publishers and broadcasters did not always win, they did secure important advances in the protection of journalists from prior restraints, criminal punishment for disclosing matters of public interest, and liability for defamation and invasion of privacy. Media used their political clout to get Congress and state legislatures to pass laws guaranteeing access to governmental meetings and records, shielding journalists from subpoenas and newsroom searches, and repealing some restrictions that constrained broadcast journalism.

In the 1960s the relationship between the press and the government changed dramatically. It began with the civil rights movement, with the press often providing sympathetic coverage of the demonstrators' confrontations with governmental authority, first in the South, then in the cities of the North as the movement exploded across the nation. Hostility grew as the press began to join those challenging the government's pronouncements about the goals and progress of the war in Vietnam. In the meantime, changes in the law of defamation made it easier for the press to take on a role as investigator of government, in addition to its roles as reporter and commentator. Investigative journalism reached perhaps its apogee with the Watergate scandal, which began with disclosures by the Washington Post of White House activities that eventually forced President Nixon to resign.

From that point, investigations by the media themselves and enthusiastic media reporting of others' allegations of wrongdoing have played pivotal roles in many of the major events of the times. Media disclosures forced several presidential candidates to withdraw and led to the defeat of several nominees for high executive or judicial office. Journalistic revelations such as President Clinton's trysts with a White House intern, publication of photos of prisoner abuse at Abu Ghraib prison in Iraq, and disclosures about secret CIA prisons and warrantless electronic surveillance at times drove the discussion of national affairs. The media themselves frequently became a political issue, sometimes criticized for their aggressiveness and sometimes accused of being insufficiently critical of official information.

While the media were becoming more aggressive journalistically, they were also becoming more assertive in the legal system. Until the 1970s, there was no organized media bar. James Goodale, former general counsel of The New York Times, organized an annual media law seminar under the auspices of the Practising Law Institute in New York. This created a nucleus of experienced First Amendment lawyers who shared ideas and expertise among themselves and with other media lawyers across the country. About the same time, the Media Law Reporter was established, bringing important opinions and legislative developments from all jurisdictions to the attention of media lawyers in multiple locations.

Armed with more expertise, better information, and a support network, media lawyers began asserting new First Amendment arguments, not only defensively in response to libel suits and subpoenas, but also offensively, to gain access to courtrooms and governmental institutions, to gain new protections for commercial speech, to attack discriminatory taxation, and to force reconsideration of restrictions on broadcast journalism.

The last third of the twentieth century saw a dramatic increase in First Amendment litigation involving the mass media. More than half of all the press cases decided by the U.S. Supreme Court in its history were decided post-1970. This litigation changed the nature of American journalism and profoundly altered the relationship between the press and government at all levels. Those years saw a shift in the nature of First Amendment litigation away from defamation, where the constitutional principles were fairly well settled, to cases involving newsgathering, media liability for harmful (but not defamatory) content, media business activities, and the ownership and control of digital expression.

In the 1990s and the early years of the 21st century, the growth of media law slowed considerably. Traditional media companies became preoccupied with deregulation, acquisition of additional outlets, and the threats and opportunities presented by the rapid growth of the Internet. In the twenty years following 1990, the Supreme Court decided far fewer media law cases than in the preceding twenty years. Media seemed less eager to seek the Court's intervention, and the Court seemed less eager to offer it. If the development of media law was slowed by these developments, it was all but halted by the recession that began in 2008. Newspapers and broadcasters lost audience and advertisers, shrank the size of their product, closed bureaus, laid off journalists by the thousands, filed for bankruptcy, and in a few instances went out of business. The struggle to survive seriously dampened enthusiasm for spending money to advance journalistic freedom through litigation or legislation. At times, media-related corporations such as Google or push-the-envelope Internet-based publishers such as Gawker stepped in to further such interests, but as media lines and related ethics issues became murkier, those interests sometimes became for some uncomfortably aligned.

C. EVOLUTION OF THE NEWS MEDIA

1. EARLY HISTORY OF THE PRESS

When the First Amendment was ratified in 1790, the press consisted of about 100 newspapers, almost all produced by local printers who operated as sole proprietors. Their contents were chiefly advertisements, notices of auction sales, shipping news, short clippings from papers in other states, letters from places in the West and from the West India Islands, and extracts from European newspapers. They rarely published news of local events. See "A Century of Population Growth from the First Census of the United States to the Twelfth 1790–1900," Department of Commerce and Labor—Bureau of the Census, Government Printing Office (1909).

In the 1830s a few metropolitan newspapers began seeking mass audiences. They were known as "the penny press" because they sold their products for a penny. They hired reporters to cover local events and often took positions at odds with the local governing elites. As the nation grew, newspapers became boosters of western expansion and a newspaper was usually one of the first businesses established in frontier towns. By the time of the Civil War, many newspapers had become large commercial operations, and they devoted substantial resources to covering the war. In both the North and the Confederacy, governments tried with mixed success to censor news about the war. Magazines emerged in the 1850s, and after the Civil War their numbers increased from 700 in 1865 to 3,300 in 1885. By 1870 Harper's had a circulation of 150,000. Book publishing also flourished after the war.

In the late 19th century Joseph Pulitzer, William Randolph Hearst, and a few other publishing magnates established their newspaper empires. Efforts to professionalize the journalism occupation began, through adoption of journalistic standards, formation of press clubs, and initiation of journalism education programs in universities. Newspapers began to depend more on advertising revenue and less on circulation revenue; advertising provided 44 percent of print media revenue in 1879 and 66 percent in 1914.

Henry Luce launched Time, the first news magazine, in the 1920s. Radio emerged as an important source of news in the 1930s, with a boost from President Franklin Roosevelt who used radio to speak directly to the public during the Depression and World War II. Films became a powerful shaper of public opinion; during World War II the film industry willingly lent itself to the government's propaganda purposes.

Marketing of television sets began in 1938, but the war delayed the development of TV programming until the late 1940s. In the 1950s television rapidly became the public's preferred source of news. Gripping coverage of the civil rights movement, the Kennedy assassination, and the war in Vietnam solidified television's dominance in news.

In the last third of the 20th century, ownership of the news media consolidated in fewer and fewer hands. Chains bought up local independent newspapers. ABC, CBS, and NBC acquired television stations in major markets. A few large magazine publishers produced many different titles. Owners began to cross media lines, with print media groups acquiring broadcast and cable outlets and vice versa. Some of the resulting media conglomerates then became subsidiaries of nonmedia conglomerates such as General Electric and Disney. The consolidation became global when foreign media moguls like Rupert Murdoch and Conrad Black acquired major U.S. media holdings.

---

2. THE DECLINE OF OLD MEDIA AND THE RISE OF NEW

By the end of the twentieth century, newspapers, television, and magazines were among the most profitable industries in America and had grown considerably in a few short years. The New York Times Company in 1975 posted earnings of less than $13 million; in 1998 the company reported a profit of $521 million. The Washington Post Company's profits rose from $12 million in 1975 to $417 million in 1998. The average operating margin (defined as before-tax profit divided by revenue) for publicly traded newspaper companies in 1997 was 19.5 percent compared with 7.6 percent for all manufacturing industries. Television stations often enjoyed operating margins of more than 45 percent. See Newspapers Arrive at Economic Crossroads, Nieman Reports Summer 1999 (Special Issue) at 4.

The first decade of the twenty-first century, however, witnessed the most precipitous decline in the history of the print and broadcast media, as reflected in the annual reports on the state of the news media by the Pew Project for Excellence in Journalism. Daily newspaper circulation fell from 58 million in 2000 to 43.5 million in approximately a decade. The audience for TV networks' evening newscasts dropped from 32 million to 22 million in the same period. The number of Americans who regularly viewed local television news dropped from 64 percent to 52 percent. The circulation of Time magazine declined from 4.1 million to 3.3 million, and Newsweek magazine from 3.2 million to 2.3 million.

The loss of revenues was equally drastic. Newspaper advertising revenues fell from $48 billion in 2000 to $25 billion a decade later. Local television revenues dropped from around $20 billion to $16 billion. Total ad pages in magazines declined significantly as well.

These revenue losses led to the closing of a few newspapers; widespread closing of bureaus covering Washington, statehouses, and foreign capitals; and massive layoffs and buyouts of journalists. The Poynter Institute estimated that the newspaper industry had lost about 30 percent of its reporting and editing capacity in approximately ten years. Network television news resources declined by more than half from their peak in the 1980s. One-third of the newspaper jobs that existed in 2001 had disappeared by 2009. Employment by local television stations peaked in 2007, but 1,650 job losses followed just two years later.

The only segment of the conventional news media that was prospering at the start of the decade was cable television, though its audience numbers too would falter within five years. The audience for prime-time cable news had grown from 1.5 million in 2000 to 3.8 million in 2010, and total revenue had grown from $1.3 billion to $2.8 billion. Most of the growth was at Fox, which by then had passed CNN as the most watched news channel and had over half of the cable news audience. The three major cable news networks' investment in programming increased from $870 million to $1.6 billion, but the Pew Project noted that much of the new investment was in ideological talk shows rather than the gathering and presentation of news.

With regard to new media, by the start of 2010 there were at least 4,600 online news and information sites, and the number of unique visitors to those sites showed healthy growth each year. Sixty percent of Americans reported that they received some of their news from an online source. Most consulted other news sources as well, relying on two to five sites. Fifty-nine percent of Internet users used some kind of social media, such as Twitter or networking sites, and perhaps as a result, readership of blogs declined 26 percent. Three-fourths of Internet users reported that they received news forwarded through email or on networking sites. Classified advertising, once a major source of revenue for newspapers, mostly moved to Craigslist and other online services.

Also during these years, new practitioners of journalism emerged. Citizen journalism became a modest success, occasionally as a stand-alone news source, more often in collaboration with old media which began to encourage audiences to supply photos, videos, and eyewitness accounts of disasters, storms, and similar news events. Universities, foundations, and interest groups began to experiment with newsgathering operations of their own. Some of the journalists laid off by conventional media started online news operations, and some philanthropists helped to establish investigative reporting and other online journalistic ventures. To some extent, the losses in conventional media were merely the result of migration of audiences and advertisers from old media to new.

Some observers believed that the net loss of journalistic resources from the decline of old media was a transitional phenomenon, part of a process of "creative destruction" from which new and perhaps more democratic and energetic forms of journalism would evolve.

They were proved correct, in one sense, by 2015. The Pew Research Center's Journalism Project that year suggested that "a mobile majority" had emerged: the new majority of news readers who received news and information mostly from their phones. Of the top 50 news-related websites identified that year, 39 received more visitors on smartphones than desktop computers, and those publishers and others responded by creating websites and applications for such users.

At the same time, however, Pew noted that those who used smartphones to access news spent less time reading the information, thereby potentially affecting both public understanding of important issues and advertising revenue. While online news sharing continued and a majority of people suggested that they received news about government and politics from their Facebook accounts, Pew noted that such information would necessarily be driven mostly by computer algorithms and friends' posts, limiting broader news consumption. Moreover, the report suggested that while it was difficult to assess the viability of digital news in a collective sense, several new digital news outlets had had surprisingly "bumpy ride[s]" by 2015. Digital news in general showed no signs of slowing, but its collective financial viability remained uncertain. "[I]f news in the social space is more incidental and driven to a large degree by friends and algorithms," the report's authors wrote, "then gaining a foothold there may be even more elusive—or at least less in the industry's own hands—than a secure financial model."

In the meantime traditional newspapers continued to fare poorly. Pew reported in 2015 that weekday circulation had fallen by nearly 20 percent in a decade, and advertising revenue was down by half in ten years; it characterized an already troubled industry as "hard hit." Cable news, having reported gains in the 2010 Pew report, showed a decline of eight percent in viewership in the 2015 report. There was some better news for broadcast television, however: local newscasts showed small gains, as did network newscasts.

What remained unclear was whether the mix of new media and traditional media would continue to fully serve traditional news and information functions. The Pew Project concluded in its 2010 report that "[u]nless some system of financing the production of content is developed, it is difficult to see how reportorial journalism will not continue to shrink, regardless of the potential tools offered by technology." In 2015, at a time when audiences were shifting to mobile devices in significant numbers and when Facebook alone was reported to have pulled in 37 percent of mobile display ad revenue, worries about funding traditional journalism continued apace.

3. NEW MEDIA, NEW ISSUES

The very features of the online world that make it a vast, easily accessible marketplace of ideas also create significant issues. Most of media law developed at a time when it could be assumed that most public communications would be scrutinized by editors, producers or other trained intermediaries. In other words, media law developed at a time when there were editorial and ethics norms largely practiced by the same journalists fighting for First Amendment-based rights in the nation's courts. For better or worse, the vast majority of online expression is not subject to such editorial scrutiny and many online publishers do not follow a standardized ethics code. Internet access providers find it almost impossible to review the huge volume of electronic communication that flows through their servers, even if they desired to do so, and news websites are similarly deluged. Because the Internet facilitates anonymous and inexpensive communication, it may be difficult to identify the originator of a defamatory or otherwise harmful message. And communication flows effortlessly across state and national boundaries, so the state or nation in which the harm occurs may be unable to exercise jurisdiction.

New media, therefore, beget new legal questions: Is it possible to protect reputation or privacy from anonymous online attacks? Should media be responsible for outside commenters who post scandalous things on their websites? Is it impossible for the government to protect national security secrets from disclosure by websites over which American courts have no power, for either jurisdictional or practical reasons?

Consider in particular three interconnected matters, each of which has arisen as technology has advanced, and each of which will be explored in greater depth in later chapters.

First, consider the increasingly important question of who is a journalist. In the days of legacy or mainstream media, such an individual was easily identified. Today the answer is not so easy. If, for example, state reporter's shield laws protect journalists from being forced to reveal their sources, then delineating who is a journalist is necessary. Should all internet publishers be shielded, and if not, who should fall outside the protective shield? Are there legitimate reasons for giving members of "the press" special protections or access to government sources or sites denied to citizens generally?

Second, consider that a federal statute has been interpreted to protect most Internet publishers from liability for unaffiliated posts from readers. If a mainstream news website that opens its news articles to reader posts is not liable for readers' defamatory comments, should a new media publisher whose website solicits humiliating gossip about private individuals or their embarrassing photographs have similar protections? Is there a legitimate reason to delineate between the two, and if so, where should that line be drawn?

Third, consider the anonymous commenter who posts a defamatory or privacy-invading piece of information to another's website. Even if the website itself is not liable, should the anonymous commenter be unmasked, and if so, when? Returning to the first series of questions above, should all website publishers be able to protect such individuals as "sources," just as Washington Post reporters protected their so-called Deep Throat source while investigating the Watergate scandal, even if the publisher and the poster have no previous relationship?

These questions highlight issues, many of them quite complex, that are likely to generate the media law of the future. At this moment no one knows how media law will evolve, but the lawyers, judges, legislators, and regulators who will shape that law have a rich body of history, principles, and experience to draw upon. Great changes—technological, cultural, and economic—have confronted media law in the past. The materials in this book demonstrate the means by which media law has adapted, experimented, evolved, and improvised up to now. The principles and policies developed in these materials may not directly answer all future issues, but they are the starting point from which the new media law will evolve.

———

CHAPTER II

FIRST AMENDMENT PRINCIPLES THAT APPLY TO MEDIA GENERALLY

Most First Amendment principles apply to all media. For example, when Congress or a state legislature attempts to restrict speech on the ground that it is obscene, the courts apply the same set of precedents whether the material is presented in print, on television, in film, or on the Internet. But there are a few instances in which courts appear to apply different First Amendment principles based on the characteristics of the medium in which the speech appears. Courts apply different rules, for example, to statutes that restrict "indecent" speech depending on the medium in which the speech is presented; material that would be constitutionally protected if it appeared in a magazine may be unprotected when offered on television. The next chapter explores medium-specific First Amendment principles, whereas this chapter explores those that apply to all media equally.

Distinguishing between "medium-specific" First Amendment principles and those that apply to all media is only one of several useful ways of dividing up the universe of media law cases. Another important distinction is between direct government restrictions on media speech and those that arise as a result of private litigation. An injunction preventing a newspaper from publishing defamatory statements about a political figure is a direct governmental restriction on media speech, as is a statute forbidding broadcasters from declaring winners in elections until the polls have closed. A libel suit, on the other hand, represents a private litigant's attempt to use the legal process to restrict speech. The distinction between government restrictions and restrictions arising from "private" litigation is imperfect, of course. Direct governmental action to restrict speech may be instigated by a private person, as when a citizen's complaint leads the local prosecutor to initiate an obscenity prosecution. And the private lawsuit implicates governmental decisions, either by statute or judicial decision, to protect such interests as reputation and privacy.

Nonetheless, the distinction between direct and indirect restrictions is important because the Supreme Court typically applies a different First Amendment methodology to libel claims than it does to statutes restricting exit polling. In a few areas, the Court has borrowed some of the methodologies it applies to direct government restrictions for use in analyzing claims brought by private litigants. But despite these occasional mergings of methodologies, the assumption that direct governmental regulation poses different threats to a free press than private litigation is still important. This chapter and the next deal with direct governmental regulation; the following five chapters deal principally with private litigation.

A second important distinction within the sphere of direct governmental regulation is between content-based and content-neutral regulations. The dividing line between content-based and content-neutral regulations is so significant that it often has the effect of determining the constitutionality of the government's action, even though the classification of restrictions as content-based or content-neutral is not always easy or consistent. Content-based regulations invariably raise significant First Amendment issues; content-neutral restrictions, on the other hand, only occasionally involve First Amendment issues. For example, if city inspectors determine that a newspaper's business premises do not comply with the fire code, the First Amendment does not prevent the city from issuing a citation or shutting the building down to protect public safety, even if this has an effect on publication of the news. On the other hand, a heavy but content-neutral tax on newsprint may raise First Amendment concerns. Even when content-neutral regulations raise First Amendment concerns, they tend to be subject to less exacting review than content-based regulations. That said, there is a tremendous variation in how both categories of regulations are treated in various contexts, as you will see in the following materials.

A. PRIOR RESTRAINTS ON PUBLICATION

The invention of a commercially viable printing press in the late fifteenth century prompted many governments to attempt to control its use. In England, the government pursued a variety of strategies for controlling the press, including prohibiting printers from publishing works that had not been licensed by government officials, who could censor objectionable passages or deny a license altogether. The licensure requirement was codified by Parliament in a series of acts making it a criminal offense to print a work without a license; it was in response to the first of these that John Milton wrote *Areopagitica*, his highly influential essay opposing licensing and justifying protection of free expression, in 1644. The last licensing legislation expired in 1694 and was not renewed. Licensing requirements came to be known as "prior restraints." Even before the First Amendment was adopted, it was understood in both England and America that "prior restraints" were inconsistent with freedom of speech. The English jurist William Blackstone wrote in his influential treatise in 1769:

> The liberty of the press is indeed essential to the nature of a free state; but this consists in laying no previous restraints on publications, and not in freedom from censure for criminal

matter when published. Every freeman has an undoubted right to lay what sentiments he pleases before the public; to forbid this is to destroy the freedom of the press; but if he publishes what is improper, mischievous or illegal, he must take the consequence of his own temerity.

4 William Blackstone, Commentaries 151, 152. Some have argued that the framers of the First Amendment shared Blackstone's view that freedom of the press meant *only* freedom from prior restraint, but the historical evidence suggests that the framers saw that a free press would be essential to their vision of democracy and understood that it would have to mean more than freedom from prior restraint. See, e.g., David A. Anderson, The Origins of the Press Clause, 30 UCLA L. Rev. 455 (1983). Leonard Levy once held the contrary view but he retreated from that position. See Leonard Levy, Emergence of a Free Press xi (1985).

The Supreme Court embraced Blackstone's view for a brief time. In Patterson v. Colorado, 205 U.S. 454 (1907), the publisher of the Rocky Mountain News had been fined $1,000 for contempt for publishing articles and a cartoon attributing improper political motives to several members of the Colorado Supreme Court. When he appealed his conviction to the U.S. Supreme Court, the majority, in an opinion by Justice Holmes, held that the First Amendment was not violated because there was no prior restraint. Even if Patterson's statements were true, the First Amendment did not forbid punishing the publication. "The preliminary freedom extends to the false as well as the true; the subsequent punishment may extend as well to the true as to the false." The Court began to recede from this view after World War I. In cases involving criminal prosecutions of anarchists and other political radicals, the majority of the Court upheld the convictions, but not on the ground that the First Amendment forbade only prior restraints.

It has never been doubted that the First Amendment was intended *at least* to forbid prior restraints. The hostility to prior restraints grew out of the English experience with licensing of the press, and what Blackstone meant by "prior restraint" was an administrative system giving some agency of government power to grant or deny permission to publish. At early common law, however, the definition of prior restraints did not extend to injunctions. Only later, with the expansion of equity jurisdiction and the emergence of injunctive relief as a common remedy, was the concept of prior restraint applied to judicial prohibitions against publication.

The following case was the first case ever in which the Court invoked the First Amendment to invalidate any type of state restriction on the press.

1. THE PRESUMPTION OF UNCONSTITUTIONALITY

Near v. Minnesota

Supreme Court of the United States, 1931.
283 U.S. 697.

[A Minnesota law allowed authorities to close down a "malicious, scandalous and defamatory newspaper, or other periodical" on grounds it constituted a public nuisance, provided the publisher was permitted to defend on the ground "that the truth was published with good motives and for justifiable ends." The Saturday Press, a scandal sheet published by an anti-Semitic muckraker named Jay Near, published articles charging that law enforcement officers were permitting a Jewish gangster to control gambling, bootlegging and racketeering in Minneapolis. A Minneapolis prosecutor initiated a nuisance abatement proceeding and showed that the Press on nine occasions had published articles that "made serious accusations against the public officials named and others in connection with the prevalence of crimes and the failure to expose and punish them." Near offered no evidence but contended the statute authorizing the abatement was unconstitutional. The state court enjoined the Press from publishing or circulating "any publication whatsoever which is a malicious, scandalous or defamatory newspaper."

The state supreme court affirmed, adding that it saw no reason for "defendants to construe the judgment as restraining them from operating a newspaper in harmony with the public welfare, to which all must yield," and that defendants had not indicated a desire "to conduct their business in the usual and legitimate manner." Near's appeal to the Supreme Court was funded by Col. Robert McCormick, the legendary publisher of the Chicago Tribune, who shared some of Near's biases but also was a zealous promoter of press freedom.]

■ MR. CHIEF JUSTICE HUGHES delivered the opinion of the Court.

. . .

This statute, for the suppression as a public nuisance of a newspaper or periodical, is unusual, if not unique, and raises questions of grave importance transcending the local interests involved in the particular action. It is no longer open to doubt that the liberty of the press, and of speech, is within the liberty safeguarded by the due process clause of the Fourteenth Amendment from invasion by state action. . . . Liberty of speech, and of the press, is also not an absolute right, and the State may punish its abuse. Whitney v. California. [ ] Liberty, in each of its phases, has its history and connotation and, in the present instance, the inquiry is as to the historic conception of the liberty of the press and whether the statute under review violates the essential attributes of that liberty.

. . .

If we cut through mere details of procedure, the operation and effect of the statute in substance is that public authorities may bring the owner or publisher of a newspaper or periodical before a judge upon a charge of conducting a business of publishing scandalous and defamatory matter— in particular that the matter consists of charges against public officers of official dereliction—and unless the owner or publisher is able and disposed to bring competent evidence to satisfy the judge that the charges are true and are published with good motives and for justifiable ends, his newspaper or periodical is suppressed and further publication is made punishable as a contempt. This is of the essence of censorship.

The question is whether a statute authorizing such proceedings in restraint of publication is consistent with the conception of the liberty of the press as historically conceived and guaranteed. In determining the extent of the constitutional protection, it has been generally, if not universally, considered that it is the chief purpose of the guaranty to prevent previous restraints upon publication. The struggle in England, directed against the legislative power of the licenser, resulted in renunciation of the censorship of the press [citing Blackstone]. . . . The distinction was early pointed out between the extent of the freedom with respect to censorship under our constitutional system and that enjoyed in England. Here, as Madison said, "the great and essential rights of the people are secured against legislative as well as against executive ambition. They are secured, not by laws paramount to prerogative, but by constitutions paramount to laws. This security of the freedom of the press requires that it should be exempt not only from previous restraints by the Executive, as in Great Britain, but from legislative restraint also." Report on the Virginia Resolutions, Madison's Works, vol. IV, p. 543. . . .

The criticism upon Blackstone's statement has not been because immunity from previous restraint upon publication has not been regarded as deserving of special emphasis, but chiefly because that immunity cannot be deemed to exhaust the conception of the liberty guaranteed by state and federal constitutions. The point of criticism has been "that the mere exemption from previous restraint cannot be all that is secured by the constitutional provisions"; and that "the liberty of the press might be rendered a mockery and a delusion, and the phrase itself a by-word, if, while every man was at liberty to publish what he pleased, the public authorities might nevertheless punish him for harmless publications." 2 Cooley, Const. Lim., 8th ed., p. 885. But it is recognized that punishment for the abuse of the liberty accorded to the press is essential to the protection of the public, and that the common law rules that subject the libeler to responsibility for the public offense, as well as for the private injury, are not abolished by the protection extended in our constitutions. . . .

The objection has also been made that the principle as to immunity from previous restraint is stated too broadly, if every such restraint is deemed to be prohibited. That is undoubtedly true; the protection even as to previous restraint is not absolutely unlimited. But the limitation has been recognized only in exceptional cases: "When a nation is at war many things that might be said in time of peace are such a hindrance to its effort that their utterance will not be endured so long as men fight and that no Court could regard them as protected by any constitutional right." Schenck v. United States, 249 U.S. 47, 52. No one would question but that a government might prevent actual obstruction to its recruiting service or the publication of the sailing dates of transports or the number and location of troops. On similar grounds, the primary requirements of decency may be enforced against obscene publications. The security of the community life may be protected against incitements to acts of violence and the overthrow by force of orderly government. The constitutional guaranty of free speech does not "protect a man from an injunction against uttering words that may have all the effect of force. Gompers v. Bucks Stove & Range Co., 221 U.S. 418, 439." *Schenck* [ ] These limitations are not applicable here. Nor are we now concerned with questions as to the extent of authority to prevent publications in order to protect private rights according to the principles governing the exercise of the jurisdiction of courts of equity.

The exceptional nature of its limitations places in a strong light the general conception that liberty of the press, historically considered and taken up by the Federal Constitution, has meant, principally although not exclusively, immunity from previous restraints or censorship. The conception of the liberty of the press in this country had broadened with the exigencies of the colonial period and with the efforts to secure freedom from oppressive administration. That liberty was especially cherished for the immunity it afforded from previous restraint of the publication of censure of public officers and charges of official misconduct. . . . Madison, who was the leading spirit in the preparation of the First Amendment of the Federal Constitution, thus described the practice and sentiment which led to the guaranties of liberty of the press in state constitutions:

> "In every State, probably, in the Union, the press has exerted a freedom in canvassing the merits and measures of public men of every description which has not been confined to the strict limits of the common law. On this footing the freedom of the press has stood; on this footing it yet stands. . . . Some degree of abuse is inseparable from the proper use of everything, and in no instance is this more true than in that of the press. It has accordingly been decided by the practice of the States, that it is better to leave a few of its noxious branches to their luxuriant growth, than, by pruning them away, to injure the vigour of those yielding the proper fruits. . . ."[10]

---

[10] Report on the Virginia Resolutions, Madison's Works, vol. iv, 544.

The fact that for approximately one hundred and fifty years there has been almost an entire absence of attempts to impose previous restraints upon publications relating to the malfeasance of public officers is significant of the deep-seated conviction that such restraints would violate constitutional right. . . .

. . . Subsequent punishment for such abuses as may exist is the appropriate remedy, consistent with constitutional privilege.

. . .

[The Court said the provision allowing the newspaper to defend on the ground of truth published with good motives could not save the statute. "If such a statute, authorizing suppression and injunction on such a basis, is constitutionally valid, it would be equally permissible for the legislature to provide that at any time the publisher of any newspaper could be brought before a court, or even an administrative officer (as the constitutional protection may not be regarded as resting on mere procedural details) and required to produce proof of the truth of his publication, or of what he intended to publish, and of his motives, or stand enjoined."]

. . .

For these reasons we hold the statute, so far as it authorized the proceedings in this action . . . to be an infringement of the liberty of the press guaranteed by the Fourteenth Amendment . . .

■ MR. JUSTICE BUTLER, dissenting.

. . .

The Minnesota statute does not operate as a *previous* restraint on publication within the proper meaning of that phrase. It does not authorize administrative control in advance such as was formerly exercised by the licensers and censors but prescribes a remedy to be enforced by a suit in equity. In this case there was previous publication made in the course of the business of regularly producing malicious, scandalous and defamatory periodicals. The business and publications unquestionably constitute an abuse of the right of free press. The statute denounces the things done as a nuisance on the ground, as stated by the state supreme court, that they threaten morals, peace and good order. . . . It is fanciful to suggest similarity between the granting or enforcement of the decree authorized by this statute to prevent *further* publication of malicious, scandalous and defamatory articles and the *previous restraint* upon the press by licensers as referred to by Blackstone and described in the history of the times to which he alludes.

. . .

■ MR. JUSTICE VAN DEVANTER, MR. JUSTICE MCREYNOLDS, and MR. JUSTICE SUTHERLAND concur in this opinion.

NOTES AND QUESTIONS

1.   Some of the special hostility to prior restraints stems from the historical characteristics of licensing schemes, which conditioned publication on the approval of a professional censor who usually operated in secret and with broad discretion. *Near*, by contrast, involved a specific statute that required the government to apply to a court for an injunction and gave the publisher the opportunity to avoid being enjoined by showing that the material was true and "published with good motives and for justifiable ends." Was the Court justified in treating the *Near* injunction as if it were as objectionable as a licensing system?

2.   While the *Near* case was making its way from the Minnesota Supreme Court to the U.S. Supreme Court, Chief Justice Taft and Justice Sanford died. Both had usually voted with the group that dissented in *Near*. They were replaced by Chief Justice Hughes and Justice Roberts, both of whom joined Justices Holmes, Brandeis, and Stone in the majority. "If Taft was still Chief Justice and Sanford was still sitting, there would have been at least five votes, perhaps even six, for the Minnesota law." Fred Friendly, Minnesota Rag 119 (1981). Friendly's book is a lively account of the case, the politics and journalism of the time, and the personalities involved in the litigation.

3.   Note that the injunction in *Near* was issued only after it had been proved that the publisher had repeatedly published "malicious, scandalous and defamatory" material—a charge he did not attempt to refute. Suppose he had been convicted ten times previously on criminal charges arising from his publications. Would the First Amendment still preclude an injunction?

Tory v. Cochran. The Supreme Court did not mention the *Near* decision in a peculiar case that, like *Near*, involved an injunction against a continuing libel. In Tory v. Cochran, 544 U.S. 734 (2005), Johnnie Cochran, who gained fame as attorney for O.J. Simpson, obtained a judgment against Ulysses Tory for defamation. The California trial court found that Tory, together with Ruth Craft and others, had libeled and slandered Cochran to "coerce" Cochran to pay him money. The trial court noted that Tory "indicated that he would continue to engage in this activity in the absence of a court order." The court therefore issued a broad permanent injunction that "prohibited Tory, Craft and their agents or representatives from picketing, from displaying signs, placards, or other written or printed material, and from orally uttering statements about Johnnie L. Cochran, Jr., and about Cochran's law firm in any public forum."

After the California Court of Appeals affirmed the grant of the permanent injunction, the United States Supreme Court granted certiorari to resolve the following question: "Whether a permanent injunction as a remedy in a defamation action, preventing all future speech about an admitted public figure, violates the First Amendment." Johnnie Cochran died after the Court heard oral arguments in the case. The Court chose not to dismiss the case as moot, but did not think it appropriate to address the central question in the case—the validity of a permanent injunction in a defamation case brought by a public figure—in light of Cochran's death. The Court wrote that the "grounds for the injunction are much diminished, if they have not disappeared altogether," since Tory's behavior could no longer have any coercive effect on Cochran. "Consequently the injunction, as written, now amounts to an overly broad prior restraint upon speech, lacking plausible justification."

The Court vacated and remanded the case to the California Court of Appeals, noting: "If, as the Cochran supplemental brief suggests, injunctive relief may still be warranted, any appropriate party remains free to ask for such relief. We express no view on the constitutional validity of any such new relief, tailored to these changed circumstances, should it be entered." Justices Thomas and Scalia, dissenting, would have dismissed the Court's writ of certiorari as improvidently granted in light of Cochran's death. Does the Court's opinion in *Tory* imply that *Near* would not preclude a permanent injunction as a remedy for speech that had been adjudicated to be defamatory or otherwise unprotected?

In a Seventh Circuit case involving a permanent injunction issued after trial as a remedy for libel, Judge Richard Posner stated that a complete prohibition on enjoining defamation "would make an impecunious defamer undeterrable." McCarthy v. Fuller, 810 F.3d 456 (7th Cir. 2015) (holding that a permanent injunction entered against libelous speech was overbroad but remanding to permit the trial judge to craft narrower injunction). In concurrence, Judge Sykes questioned whether a permanent injunction against defamation would ever be appropriate, noting:

> Defamation by its nature is highly contextual. A statement that is defamatory in one circumstance, time, or place might not be defamatory in another circumstance, time, or place. A permanent injunction as a remedy for defamation does not account for constantly changing contextual factors that affect whether the speech is punishable or protected. If factual circumstances change in a way that affects the defamation calculus, the person enjoined must risk contempt or seek the court's permission to speak.

For cases approving the use of narrow and specific injunctions as a remedy for defamation, see Hill v. Petrotech Res. Corp., 325 S.W.3d 302 (Ky. 2010); Balboa Island Vill. Inn, Inc. v. Lemen, 156 P.3d 339 (Cal. 2007); Sid Dillon Chevrolet v. Sullivan, 559 N.W.2d 740 (Neb. 1997);

Advanced Training Sys., Inc. v. Caswell Equip. Co., 352 N.W.2d 1 (Minn. 1984); Retail Credit Co. v. Russell, 218 S.E.2d 54, 62–63 (Ga. 1975); O'Brien v. Univ. Cmty. Tenants Union, Inc., 327 N.E.2d 753 (Ohio 1975). If an injunction is narrow and specific, does it give an impecunious but clever defamer ample room to continue defaming a plaintiff who has won a judgment at trial?

2. DEFINING PRIOR RESTRAINT

Are injunctions like those in *Near* and *Tory* really prior restraints? What is it that distinguishes prior restraints from other kinds of prohibitions on speech? And what is the distinctively pernicious characteristic of prior restraints? Litigators, aware of the preemptive power of the phrase "this is a prior restraint," attempt to apply the label to many different kinds of disputes. One recurring argument might be called the "de facto prior restraint" argument: the restriction in question is not in form a licensing scheme or an injunction, but the challenger claims it will have the same effect.

The Supreme Court rejected such an argument in Alexander v. United States, 509 U.S. 544 (1993). Alexander, operator of numerous "adult entertainment" businesses in Minnesota, was convicted of transporting multiple copies of four obscene magazines and three videos in interstate commerce and engaging in the business of selling obscene material. Those convictions provided the basis for a finding that he had engaged in a "pattern of racketeering" for purposes of the Racketeer Influenced and Corrupt Organizations Act (RICO), and under the forfeiture provisions of RICO the government seized all of Alexander's thirty-one businesses, confiscated $9 million in profits, and destroyed all of the inventory found in his stores, which included books and videos worth millions, most of which had never been found to be legally obscene and were therefore presumptively protected by the First Amendment.

The Supreme Court held, 6–3, that the forfeiture should not be analyzed as a prior restraint. Viewing it as a subsequent punishment, the Court said the seizure was no more likely to chill speech than the six-year prison sentence and $100,000 fine that Alexander did not challenge on First Amendment grounds. The Court remanded, however, for further consideration of Alexander's claim that the forfeiture was an "excessive fine" under the Eighth Amendment. Excerpts from the majority and dissenting opinions on the prior restraint issue follow. Chief Justice Rehnquist, for the Court:

> [P]etitioner's proposed definition of the term "prior restraint" would undermine the time-honored distinction between barring speech in the future and penalizing past speech. The doctrine of prior restraint originated in the common law of England, where prior restraints of the press were not permitted, but punishment after publication was. This very limited application of the

principle of freedom of speech was held inconsistent with our First Amendment as long ago as Grosjean v. American Press Co., 297 U.S. 233, 246 (1936). While we may have given a broader definition to the term "prior restraint" than was given to it in English common law, our decisions have steadfastly preserved the distinction between prior restraints and subsequent punishments. Though petitioner tries to dismiss this distinction as "neither meaningful nor useful," [ ] we think it is critical to our First Amendment jurisprudence. Because we have interpreted the First Amendment as providing greater protection from prior restraints than from subsequent punishments, [ ] it is important for us to delineate with some precision the defining characteristics of a prior restraint. To hold that the forfeiture order in this case constituted a prior restraint would have the exact opposite effect: it would blur the line separating prior restraints from subsequent punishments to such a degree that it would be impossible to determine with any certainty whether a particular measure is a prior restraint or not.

Despite Chief Justice Rehnquist's statement that "it is important for us to delineate with some precision the defining characteristics of a prior restraint," his opinion contains nothing more specific than the excerpt quoted above.

■ JUSTICE KENNEDY, joined by JUSTICES BLACKMUN and STEVENS, dissented:

The majority tries to occupy the high ground by assuming the role of the defender of the doctrine of prior restraint. It warns that we disparage the doctrine if we reason from it. But as an analysis of our prior restraint cases reveals, our application of the First Amendment has adjusted to meet new threats to speech. The First Amendment is a rule of substantive protection, not an artifice of categories. The admitted design and the overt purpose of the forfeiture in this case are to destroy an entire speech business and all its protected titles, thus depriving the public of access to lawful expression. This is restraint in more than theory. It is censorship all too real.

. . .

As our First Amendment law has developed, we have not confined the application of the prior restraint doctrine to its simpler forms, outright licensing or censorship before speech takes place. In considering governmental measures deviating from the classic form of a prior restraint yet posing many of the same dangers to First Amendment freedoms, we have extended prior restraint protection with some latitude, toward the end of declaring certain governmental actions to fall within the presumption of invalidity. This approach is evident in *Near*. . . .

. . . In one sense the injunctive order [in *Near*], which paralleled the nuisance statute, did nothing more than announce the conditions under which some later punishment might be imposed, for one presumes that contempt could not be found until there was a further violation in contravention of the order. But in *Near* the publisher, because of past wrongs, was subjected to active state intervention for the control of future speech. We found that the scheme was a prior restraint because it embodied "the essence of censorship."

. . .

. . . As governments try new ways to subvert essential freedoms, legal and constitutional systems respond by making more explicit the nature and the extent of the liberty in question. First in *Near*, and later in [other cases], we were faced with official action which did not fall within the traditional meaning of the term prior restraint, yet posed many of the same censorship dangers. Our response was to hold that the doctrine not only includes licensing schemes requiring speech to be submitted to a censor for review prior to dissemination, but also encompasses injunctive systems which threaten or bar future speech based on some past infraction.

Although we consider today a new method of government control with unmistakable dangers of official censorship, the majority concludes that First Amendment freedoms are not endangered because forfeiture follows a lawful conviction for obscenity offenses. But this explanation does not suffice. The rights of free speech and press in their broad and legitimate sphere cannot be defeated by the simple expedient of punishing after in lieu of censoring before. [ ] This is so because in some instances the operation and effect of a particular enforcement scheme, though not in the form of a traditional prior restraint, may be to raise the same concerns which inform all of our prior restraint cases: the evils of state censorship and the unacceptable chilling of protected speech.

Does Justice Kennedy's opinion suggest that anything that "chills speech unacceptably" should be analyzed as a prior restraint?

3. OVERCOMING THE PRESUMPTION

The Pentagon Papers Case. Recall that the Supreme Court in *Near* stated that the First Amendment's prohibition against prior restraints could be overcome only in "exceptional cases," such as cases involving dire threats to national security. The first real test of the "national security" exception came in New York Times Co. v. United States, 403 U.S. 713 (1971), which is better known as the "Pentagon Papers" case.

While the war in Vietnam and the domestic controversy surrounding it were at their peak, The New York Times obtained a copy of a classified 47-volume government report that came to be popularly known as the "Pentagon Papers." After several months of intense and highly secret preparations, the Times began publishing a series of articles about the report. The Justice Department moved to enjoin publication. A district judge in New York denied the injunction, but publication was temporarily restrained pending appeal, and the Court of Appeals for the Second Circuit ordered the injunction granted.

While the Times' case was being litigated, the Washington Post began publishing material from the same report. The Justice Department also moved to enjoin the Post. A district judge in Washington refused to issue a preliminary injunction and the Court of Appeals for the District of Columbia affirmed. The Supreme Court issued stays to prevent publication in both cases, heard oral argument, and five days later issued its decision.

The Court issued a brief per curiam opinion dissolving the injunctions:

> Any system of prior restraints of expression comes to this Court bearing a heavy presumption against its constitutional validity." Bantam Books, Inc. v. Sullivan, 372 U.S. 58, 70 (1963); see also Near v. Minnesota, 283 U.S. 697 (1931). The Government "thus carries a heavy burden of showing justification for the imposition of such a restraint." Organization for a Better Austin v. Keefe, 402 U.S. 415, 419 (1971). The District Court for the Southern District of New York in the *New York Times* [ ] case and the District Court for the District of Columbia and the Court of Appeals for the District of Columbia Circuit [ ] in the *Washington Post* case held that the Government had not met that burden. We agree.

New York Times Co. v. United States, 403 U.S. 713 (1971).

Every member of the Court wrote a separate opinion. Justice Black, concurring, argued that the injunctions were so clearly unconstitutional that the Court should have vacated them without hearing oral argument. Justice Douglas, concurring, also believed the First Amendment was an absolute bar to enjoining publication. Justice Brennan, concurring, noted that the government had only offered "surmise or conjecture" of harmful consequences from publishing the documents and that such speculation did not rise to the level of demonstrating that this case fit within that "single, extremely narrow class of cases in which the First Amendment's ban on prior judicial restraint may be overridden," citing *Schenck* and *Near*. Justice Marshall, concurring, believed the executive branch had no power to ask the courts to enjoin publication when Congress had not authorized such a remedy. Justice Stewart, in a concurring opinion, stressed that "in the cases before us we are asked neither to construe specific regulations nor to apply specific laws. We are asked, instead, to perform a function that the Constitution gave to the Executive, not the Judiciary." Justice White, concurring, noted that Congress had enacted provisions of the Criminal Code that might apply to the newspapers' conduct, but that Congress had not authorized an injunctive remedy.

Chief Justice Burger, in a dissenting opinion, noted that although the Times had delayed publication for three or four months after it obtained the documents, the newspapers were insisting on such fast review that the Court did not know what it was acting on. He thought the *Times* case should go to trial in the district court before the Supreme Court decided anything on the merits. Justice Blackmun, in another dissent, said the case should be resolved by weighing "the broad right of the press to publish" against "the very narrow right of the government to prevent," but believed the Court had not had time to develop appropriate standards for that balancing.

Justice Harlan also dissented, arguing that "the Court has been almost irresponsibly feverish in dealing with these cases":

> Both the Court of Appeals for the Second Circuit and the Court of Appeals for the District of Columbia Circuit rendered judgment on June 23. The New York Times' petition for certiorari, its motion for accelerated consideration thereof, and its application for interim relief were filed in this Court on June 24 at about 11 a.m. The application of the United States for interim relief in the *Post* case was also filed here on June 24 at about 7:15 p.m. This Court's order setting a hearing before us on June 26 at 11 a.m., a course which I joined only to avoid the possibility of even more peremptory action by the Court, was issued less than 24 hours before. The record in the *Post* case was filed with the Clerk shortly before 1 p.m. on June 25; the record in the *Times* case did not arrive until 7 or 8 o'clock that same night. The briefs of the parties were received less than two hours before argument on June 26.

> This frenzied train of events took place in the name of the presumption against prior restraints created by the First Amendment. Due regard for the extraordinarily important and difficult questions involved in these litigations should have led the Court to shun such a precipitate timetable.

Justice Harlan ultimately dissented on the basis that the Court had exceeded its authority by doing more than assuring that "the subject matter of the dispute does lie within the proper compass of the President's foreign relations power" and that "the determination that disclosure of the subject matter would irreparably impair the national security be made by the head of the Executive Department concerned—

here the Secretary of State or the Secretary of Defense—after actual personal consideration by that officer."

Although the government never sought to invoke criminal sanctions against the media in the Pentagon Papers episode, it did file charges against Daniel Ellsberg and Anthony Russo for leaking the papers to the Times. The government dropped the prosecutions after it was revealed that the White House "plumbers," the same group responsible for the Watergate burglary, had burglarized the office and home of Ellsberg's psychiatrist looking for information to discredit him. The case is discussed in Melville G. Nimmer, National Security Secrets v. Free Speech: The Issues Left Undecided in the Ellsberg Case, 26 Stan. L. Rev. 311 (1974).

Might journalists be criminally prosecuted for soliciting leaks of classified information? The indictments in 2005 of two lobbyists for the American Israel Public Affairs Committee for violating the Espionage Act by conspiring with a Pentagon official who leaked classified information to the lobbyists raised that possibility. News organizations filed amicus curiae briefs urging dismissal of the indictments, arguing that under the government's interpretation of the Espionage Act, journalists could be successfully prosecuted for inducing leaks of classified information. The indictments were eventually dismissed after the Fourth Circuit ruled that the government would have to disclose certain classified information. See United States v. Rosen, 557 F.3d 192 (4th Cir. 2009). For a discussion of the dearth of First Amendment precedents to prevent such prosecutions, see William E. Lee, Probing Secrets: The Press and Inchoate Liability for Newsgathering Crimes, 36 Am. J. of Crim L. 129 (2009).

Although the government has not yet prosecuted traditional journalists under the Espionage Act, it has used the Act as the basis for obtaining a warrant to search a journalist's emails. In 2010, the FBI obtained a search warrant for the personal email of Fox News correspondent James Rosen based on showing probable cause that Rosen had violated the Espionage Act by soliciting classified information from State Department official Stephen Jin-Woo Kim. Ann E. Marimow, A Rare Peek Into a Justice Department Leak Probe, Wash. Post, May 19, 2013. After the warrant's existence came to light in May 2013, the Justice Department indicated it had little interest in actually prosecuting Rosen but had instead used the search warrant merely to bolster its investigation of the source of the leak. Ann E. Marimow, Justice Department's Scrutiny of Fox News Reporter James Rosen in Leak Case Draws Fire, Wash. Post, May 20, 2013. Stephen Jin-Woo Kim pleaded guilty to sharing national security information with Rosen. Merrill Knox, Former State Dept. Adviser Pleads Guilty in James Rosen Leak Case, MediaBistro, Feb. 7, 2014. Mr. Rosen stated that the incident "marked, by all accounts, the first time in American history that a reporter had been designated a criminal by the United States government simply for doing his job." Grant Pender, Journalist James Rosen Speaks About Press Freedoms Under Obama Administration, The Daily Northwestern, Apr. 12, 2015.

The Progressive Case. One of the few cases upholding a prior restraint on the press in the interest of national security is United States v. The Progressive, Inc., 467 F.Supp. 990 (W.D. Wis. 1979). There, the government sought an injunction under the Atomic Energy Act, 42 U.S.C. § 2011 et seq., prohibiting The Progressive magazine from publishing an article entitled "The H Bomb Secret: How We Got It, Why We're Telling It," by Howard Morland. The magazine contended that the projected article merely assembled data already in the public domain and readily available to any diligent seeker. It said it planned to publish the article to "alert the people of this country to the false illusion of security created by the government's futile efforts at secrecy." The government maintained that much of the information was not in the public domain, that the article contained a core of information that had never before been published, and that even if the specific information was in the public domain, publishing it all in one easily accessible article could help enemies who otherwise might not put all the pieces together. The judge wrote:

> Does the article provide a "do-it-yourself" guide for the hydrogen bomb? Probably not. A number of affidavits make quite clear that a *sine qua non* to thermonuclear capability is a large, sophisticated industrial capability coupled with a coterie of imaginative, resourceful scientists and technicians. One does not build a hydrogen bomb in the basement. However, the article could possibly provide sufficient information to allow a medium size nation to move faster in developing a hydrogen weapon. It could provide a ticket to by-pass blind alleys.
>
> . . .
>
> The Secretary of State states that publication will increase thermonuclear proliferation and that this would "irreparably impair the national security of the United States." The Secretary of Defense says that dissemination of the Morland paper will mean a substantial increase in the risk of thermonuclear proliferation and lead to use or threats that would "adversely affect the national security of the United States."
>
> . . .
>
> A mistake in ruling against The Progressive will seriously infringe cherished First Amendment rights. If a preliminary injunction is issued, it will constitute the first instance of prior restraint against a publication in this fashion in the history of this country, to this Court's knowledge. Such notoriety is not to

be sought. It will curtail defendants' First Amendment rights in a drastic and substantial fashion. It will infringe upon our right to know and to be informed as well.

A mistake in ruling against the United States could pave the way for thermonuclear annihilation for us all. In that event, our right to life is extinguished and the right to publish becomes moot.

In the *Near* case, the Supreme Court recognized that publication of troop movements in time of war would threaten national security and could therefore be restrained. Times have changed significantly since 1931 when *Near* was decided. Now war by foot soldiers has been replaced in large part by war by machines and bombs. No longer need there be any advance warning or any preparation time before a nuclear war could be commenced.

In light of these factors, this Court concludes that publication of the technical information on the hydrogen bomb contained in the article is analogous to publication of troop movements or locations in time of war and falls within the extremely narrow exception to the rule against prior restraint.

    . . .

The judge distinguished the *Pentagon Papers* case on the ground that it involved historical matters rather than a future threat to national security, and because in the Progressive case a statute, Section 2274 of the Atomic Energy Act, authorized injunctions against disclosure of restricted data pertaining to nuclear weapons by anyone with reason to believe such data will be used to secure an advantage to any foreign nation.

While the magazine's appeal of the preliminary injunction was pending, a newspaper in Madison, Wisconsin, published a letter containing the information that The Progressive had been enjoined from publishing, and the Chicago Tribune announced that it would publish the same letter. The government then withdrew its complaint and the case was dismissed. See United States v. Progressive, Inc., 467 F.Supp. 990 (W.D. Wis. 1979), dismissed as moot, 610 F.2d 819 (7th Cir. 1979). Although the government reserved its right to bring criminal charges, it did not do so.

Although the *Progressive* decision is a product of the Cold War era, it is easy to transpose its security concerns to a more modern context. After September 11, 2001, it is easy to imagine terrorists using information about weaknesses in the nation's critical infrastructure (such as nuclear power plants) or information about chemical or biological weapons materials to harm thousands, hundreds of thousands, or even millions of people.

Permissible Prior Restraints. In a few narrow areas of the law, prior restraints are imposed, if not routinely, at least without the rigorous scrutiny seen in the preceding cases. One such area is copyright infringement. Injunctions are expressly authorized by Section 502 of the Copyright Act and are not an uncommon remedy. Another is trade secret law, which permits a former employee to be enjoined from disclosing matters deemed confidential, either by virtue of the employment contract or the concept of fiduciary obligations imposed by law. See, e.g., Cherne Industrial, Inc. v. Grounds & Associates, Inc., 278 N.W.2d 81 (Minn. 1979) ("Given the public interest in preserving the ability of parties to freely enter contracts and to seek judicial enforcement of such contracts and in providing judicial remedies for breaches of fiduciary duties imposed by law, any infringement by the injunction on defendants' First Amendment rights is tolerable and justified.") But see State ex rel. Sports Management News, Inc. v. Nachtigal, 921 P.2d 1304 (Ore. 1996), in which the Oregon Supreme Court characterized a statute authorizing courts to require parties to obtain prior court approval before disclosing trade secrets as "a classic 'prior restraint' on publication" and held that the statute violated a state constitutional ban on laws "restraining the free expression of opinion." The court went on to hold that since there was no "historical exception for the prior-restraint protection of trade secrets from publication by a third-party publisher who receives information lawfully," the law was unconstitutional. See also Mark A. Lemley & Eugene Volokh, Freedom of Speech and Injunctions in Intellectual Property Cases, 48 Duke L.J. 147 (1998) (arguing that preliminary injunctions should be granted with the same reluctance in intellectual property cases as they are in defamation cases).

4. INJUNCTIONS TO PROTECT FAIR TRIAL RIGHTS

a. ENJOINING THE PRESS

Nebraska Press Association v. Stuart

Supreme Court of the United States, 1976.
427 U.S. 539.

[Six members of a family were found murdered in a small Nebraska town. Local, regional, and national media converged to cover the story. A suspect, Simants, was arrested, charged with committing the murders in the course of a sexual assault, and publicly arraigned. Two days after the arraignment, in preparation for a preliminary hearing to determine whether Simants should be bound over to district court for trial, his attorney and the county attorney jointly requested the county judge to restrict "matters that may or may not be publicly reported to the public" to protect Simants' right to a fair trial. The judge granted the request, prohibiting reporting of any testimony or evidence adduced at the hearing. He further ordered members of the press to observe the

Nebraska Bar-Press Guidelines, voluntary standards that had been adopted by the state bar and news media to protect suspects' fair trial rights. Reporters attended the preliminary hearing subject to this order. At the conclusion of the hearing the county judge bound Simants over to the district court.

Petitioners—several press and broadcast associations, publishers, and reporters—intervened the next day in the district court, asking Judge Stuart to vacate the county judge's order. He refused to do so, but narrowed the order to specifically prohibit petitioners from reporting five subjects: (1) the existence or contents of a confession Simants had made to law enforcement officers, which had been introduced in open court at arraignment; (2) the fact or nature of statements Simants had made to other persons; (3) the contents of a note he had written the night of the crime; (4) certain aspects of the medical testimony at the preliminary hearing; (5) the identity of the victims of the alleged sexual assault and the nature of the assault. He also forbade reporting the specific prohibitions of the restrictive order and ordered the petitioners to observe the Bar-Press Guidelines.

Petitioners applied to the Nebraska Supreme Court for a stay, a writ of mandamus, and an expedited appeal. They also sought a stay from the U.S. Supreme Court. When the Nebraska Supreme Court did not act promptly, Justice Blackmun, as Circuit Justice, granted a partial stay as to the Bar-Press Guidelines and reporting of some other matters but left in place the prohibition against reporting the confession and other facts "highly prejudicial" to Simants or "strongly implicative" of his guilt.

Six weeks after the order was first entered, the Nebraska Supreme Court upheld the order, but further narrowed it to prohibit only reporting of the existence and nature of confessions or admissions and other facts "strongly implicative" of the accused. The court remanded to the district court to consider whether further pretrial proceedings should be closed to the press and public. The U.S. Supreme Court granted certiorari but did not stay the order except to the extent that it had already been stayed by Justice Blackmun. In the meantime, Simants was convicted and sentenced to death.

The Supreme Court held that the controversy was not moot because the dispute otherwise was "capable of repetition, yet evading review."]

■ MR. CHIEF JUSTICE BURGER delivered the opinion of the Court.

. . .

In Sheppard v. Maxwell, 384 U.S. 333 (1966), the Court focused sharply on the impact of pretrial publicity and a trial court's duty to protect the defendant's constitutional right to a fair trial. With only Mr. Justice Black dissenting, and he without opinion, the Court ordered a new trial for the petitioner, even though the first trial had occurred 12 years before. Beyond doubt the press had shown no responsible concern for the constitutional guarantee of a fair trial; the community from which the jury was drawn had been inundated by publicity hostile to the defendant. But the trial judge "did not fulfill his duty to protect [the defendant] from the inherently prejudicial publicity which saturated the community and to control disruptive influences in the courtroom." [ ] The Court noted that "unfair and prejudicial news comment on pending trials has become increasingly prevalent," [ ] and issued a strong warning:

> "Due process requires that the accused receive a trial by an impartial jury free from outside influences. Given the pervasiveness of modern communications and the difficulty of effacing prejudicial publicity from the minds of the jurors, *the trial courts must take strong measures to ensure that the balance is never weighed against the accused.* . . . Of course, there is nothing that proscribes the press from reporting events that transpire in the courtroom. But where there is a reasonable likelihood that prejudicial news prior to trial will prevent a fair trial, the judge should *continue the case* until the threat abates, *or transfer it* to another county not so permeated with publicity. In addition, *sequestration of the jury* was something the judge should have raised *sua sponte* with counsel. If publicity during the proceedings threatens the fairness of the trial, a new trial should be ordered. But we must remember that reversals are but palliatives; the cure lies in those remedial measures that will prevent the prejudice at its inception. The courts must take such steps by rule and regulation that will protect their process from prejudicial outside interferences. *Neither prosecutors, counsel for defense, the accused, witnesses, court staff nor enforcement officers coming under the jurisdiction of the court should be permitted to frustrate its function.* Collaboration between counsel and the press as to information affecting the fairness of a criminal trial is not only subject to regulation, but is highly censurable and worthy of disciplinary measures." [ ] (emphasis added).

Because the trial court had failed to use even minimal efforts to insulate the trial and the jurors from the "deluge of publicity," [ ] the Court vacated the judgment of conviction and a new trial followed, in which the accused was acquitted.

> . . .

The state trial judge in the case before us acted responsibly, out of a legitimate concern, in an effort to protect the defendant's right to a fair trial. What we must decide is not simply whether the Nebraska courts erred in seeing the possibility of real danger to the defendant's rights, but whether in the circumstances of this case the means employed were foreclosed by another provision of the Constitution.

V.

The First Amendment provides that "Congress shall make no law ... abridging the freedom ... of the press," and it is "no longer open to doubt that the liberty of the press, and of speech, is within the liberty safeguarded by the due process clause of the Fourteenth Amendment from invasion by state action." [*Near*]. The Court has interpreted these guarantees to afford special protection against orders that prohibit the publication or broadcast of particular information or commentary— orders that impose a "previous" or "prior" restraint on speech. None of our decided cases on prior restraint involved restrictive orders entered to protect a defendant's right to a fair and impartial jury, but the opinions on prior restraint have a common thread relevant to this case.

[The Court reviewed its prior restraint cases, primarily *Near* and New York Times Co. v. United States.]

The thread running through all these cases is that prior restraints on speech and publication are the most serious and the least tolerable infringement on First Amendment rights. A criminal penalty or a judgment in a defamation case is subject to the whole panoply of protections afforded by deferring the impact of the judgment until all avenues of appellate review have been exhausted. Only after judgment has become final, correct or otherwise, does the law's sanction become fully operative.

A prior restraint, by contrast and by definition, has an immediate and irreversible sanction. If it can be said that a threat of criminal or civil sanctions after publication "chills" speech, prior restraint "freezes" it at least for the time.

The damage can be particularly great when the prior restraint falls upon the communication of news and commentary on current events. Truthful reports of public judicial proceedings have been afforded special protection against subsequent punishment. [ ] For the same reasons the protection against prior restraint should have particular force as applied to reporting of criminal proceedings, whether the crime in question is a single isolated act or a pattern of criminal conduct. . . . The extraordinary protections afforded by the First Amendment carry with them something in the nature of a fiduciary duty to exercise the protected rights responsibly—a duty widely acknowledged but not always observed by editors and publishers. It is not asking too much to suggest that those who exercise First Amendment rights in newspapers or broadcasting enterprises direct some effort to protect the rights of an accused to a fair trial by unbiased jurors.

Of course, the order at issue—like the order requested in *New York Times*—does not prohibit but only postpones publication. Some news can be delayed and most commentary can even more readily be delayed without serious injury, and there often is a self-imposed delay when responsible editors call for verification of information. But such delays are normally slight and they are self-imposed. Delays imposed by governmental authority are a different matter. . . . As a practical matter, moreover, the element of time is not unimportant if press coverage is to fulfill its traditional function of bringing news to the public promptly.

The authors of the Bill of Rights did not undertake to assign priorities as between First Amendment and Sixth Amendment rights, ranking one as superior to the other. In this case, the petitioners would have us declare the right of an accused subordinate to their right to publish in all circumstances. But if the authors of these guarantees, fully aware of the potential conflicts between them, were unwilling or unable to resolve the issue by assigning to one priority over the other, it is not for us to rewrite the Constitution by undertaking what they declined. It is unnecessary, after nearly two centuries, to establish a priority applicable in all circumstances. Yet it is nonetheless clear that the barriers to prior restraint remain high unless we are to abandon what the Court has said for nearly a quarter of our national existence and implied throughout all of it. . . .

. . .

VI.

We turn now to the record in this case to determine whether, as Learned Hand put it, "the gravity of the 'evil,' discounted by its improbability, justifies such invasion of free speech as is necessary to avoid the danger." United States v. Dennis, 183 F.2d 201, 212 (1950), aff'd, 341 U.S. 494 (1951); see also Learned Hand, The Bill of Rights 58–61 (1958). To do so, we must examine the evidence before the trial judge when the order was entered to determine (a) the nature and extent of pretrial news coverage; (b) whether other measures would be likely to mitigate the effects of unrestrained pretrial publicity; [and] (c) how effectively a restraining order would operate to prevent the threatened danger. The precise terms of the restraining order are also important. We must then consider whether the record supports the entry of a prior restraint on publication, one of the most extraordinary remedies known to our jurisprudence.

A.

In assessing the probable extent of publicity, the trial judge had before him newspapers demonstrating that the crime had already drawn intensive news coverage, and the testimony of the County Judge, who had entered the initial restraining order based on the local and national attention the case had attracted. The District Judge was required to assess the probable publicity that would be given these shocking crimes prior to the time a jury was selected and sequestered. He then had to examine the probable nature of the publicity and determine how it would affect prospective jurors.

Our review of the pretrial record persuades us that the trial judge was justified in concluding that there would be intense and pervasive pretrial publicity concerning this case. He could also reasonably conclude, based on common human experience, that publicity might impair the defendant's right to a fair trial. He did not purport to say more, for he found only "a clear and present danger that pretrial publicity *could* impinge upon the defendant's right to a fair trial." (Emphasis added.) His conclusion as to the impact of such publicity on prospective jurors was of necessity speculative, dealing as he was with factors unknown and unknowable.

B.

We find little in the record that goes to another aspect of our task, determining whether measures short of an order restraining all publication would have insured the defendant a fair trial. Although the entry of the order might be read as a judicial determination that other measures would not suffice, the trial court made no express findings to that effect; the Nebraska Supreme Court referred to the issue only by implication. [ ]

Most of the alternatives to prior restraint of publication in these circumstances were discussed with obvious approval in Sheppard v. Maxwell [ ]: (a) change of trial venue to a place less exposed to the intense publicity that seemed imminent in Lincoln County;[7] (b) postponement of the trial to allow public attention to subside; (c) searching questioning of prospective jurors . . . to screen out those with fixed opinions as to guilt or innocence; (d) the use of emphatic and clear instructions on the sworn duty of each juror to decide the issues only on evidence presented in open court. Sequestration of jurors is, of course, always available. Although that measure insulates jurors only after they are sworn, it also enhances the likelihood of dissipating the impact of pretrial publicity and emphasizes the elements of the jurors' oaths.

This Court has outlined other measures short of prior restraints on publication tending to blunt the impact of pretrial publicity. [ ]. Professional studies have filled out these suggestions, recommending that trial courts in appropriate cases limit what the contending lawyers, the police, and witnesses may say to anyone. See American Bar Association Project on Standards for Criminal Justice, Fair Trial and Free Press 2–15 (Approved Draft, 1968).[8]

---

[7] The respondent and intervenors argue here that a change of venue would not have helped, since Nebraska law permits a change only to adjacent counties, which had been as exposed to pretrial publicity in this case as Lincoln County. We have held that state laws restricting venue must on occasion yield to the constitutional requirement that the State afford a fair trial. *Groppi v. Wisconsin*, 400 U.S. 505 (1971). We note also that the combined population of Lincoln County and the adjacent counties is over 80,000, providing a substantial pool of prospective jurors.

[8] Closing of pretrial proceedings with the consent of the defendant when required is also recommended in guidelines that have emerged from various studies. At oral argument petitioners' counsel asserted that judicially imposed restraints on lawyers and others would be

We have noted earlier that pretrial publicity, even if pervasive and concentrated, cannot be regarded as leading automatically and in every kind of criminal case to an unfair trial. The decided cases "cannot be made to stand for the proposition that juror exposure to information about a state defendant's prior convictions or to news accounts of the crime with which he is charged alone presumptively deprives the defendant of due process." [ ] Appellate evaluations as to the impact of publicity take into account what other measures were used to mitigate the adverse effects of publicity. The more difficult prospective or predictive assessment that a trial judge must make also calls for a judgment as to whether other precautionary steps will suffice.

We have therefore examined this record to determine the probable efficacy of the measures short of prior restraint on the press and speech. There is no finding that alternative measures would not have protected Simants' rights, and the Nebraska Supreme Court did no more than imply that such measures might not be adequate. Moreover, the record is lacking in evidence to support such a finding.

C.

We must also assess the probable efficacy of prior restraint on publication as a workable method of protecting Simants' right to a fair trial, and we cannot ignore the reality of the problems of managing and enforcing pretrial restraining orders. The territorial jurisdiction of the issuing court is limited by concepts of sovereignty. [ ] The need for *in personam* jurisdiction also presents an obstacle to a restraining order that applies to publication at large as distinguished from restraining publication within a given jurisdiction. [ ]

The Nebraska Supreme Court narrowed the scope of the restrictive order, and its opinion reflects awareness of the tensions between the need to protect the accused as fully as possible and the need to restrict publication as little as possible. The dilemma posed underscores how difficult it is for trial judges to predict what information will in fact undermine the impartiality of jurors, and the difficulty of drafting an order that will effectively keep prejudicial information from prospective jurors. When a restrictive order is sought, a court can anticipate only part of what will develop that may injure the accused. But information not so obviously prejudicial may emerge, and what may properly be published in these "gray zone" circumstances may not violate the restrictive order and yet be prejudicial.

Finally, we note that the events disclosed by the record took place in a community of 850 people. It is reasonable to assume that, without any news accounts being printed or broadcast, rumors would travel swiftly by

---

subject to challenge as interfering with press rights to news sources. [ ] We are not now confronted with such issues. We note that in making its proposals, the American Bar Association recommended strongly against resort to direct restraints on the press to prohibit publication. ABA Standards, at 68–73. Other groups have reached similar conclusions. [ ]

word of mouth. One can only speculate on the accuracy of such reports, given the generative propensities of rumors; they could well be more damaging than reasonably accurate news accounts. But plainly a whole community cannot be restrained from discussing a subject intimately affecting life within it.

Given these practical problems, it is far from clear that prior restraint on publication would have protected Simants' rights.

D.

Finally, another feature of this case leads us to conclude that the restrictive order entered here is not supportable. At the outset the County Court entered a very broad restrictive order, the terms of which are not before us; it then held a preliminary hearing open to the public and the press. There was testimony concerning at least two incriminating statements made by Simants to private persons; the statement—evidently a confession—that he gave to law enforcement officials was also introduced. The State District Court's later order was entered after this public hearing and, as modified by the Nebraska Supreme Court, enjoined reporting of (1) "[c]onfessions or admissions against interests made by the accused to law enforcement officials"; (2) "[c]onfessions or admissions against interest, oral or written, if any, made by the accused to third parties, excepting any statements, if any, made by the accused to representatives of the news media"; and (3) all "[o]ther information strongly implicative of the accused as the perpetrator of the slayings." [ ]

To the extent that this order prohibited the reporting of evidence adduced at the open preliminary hearing, it plainly violated settled principles: "[T]here is nothing that proscribes the press from reporting events that transpire in the courtroom." Sheppard v. Maxwell [ ]. The County Court could not know that closure of the preliminary hearing was an alternative open to it until the Nebraska Supreme Court so construed state law; but once a public hearing had been held, what transpired there could not be subject to prior restraint.

The third prohibition of the order was defective in another respect as well. As part of a final order, entered after plenary review, this prohibition regarding "implicative" information is too vague and too broad to survive the scrutiny we have given to restraints on First Amendment rights. [ ] The third phase of the order entered falls outside permissible limits.

E.

. . . We cannot say on this record that alternatives to a prior restraint on petitioners would not have sufficiently mitigated the adverse effects of pretrial publicity so as to make prior restraint unnecessary. Nor can we conclude that the restraining order actually entered would serve its intended purpose. Reasonable minds can have few doubts about the gravity of the evil pretrial publicity can work, but the probability that it would do so here was not demonstrated with the degree of certainty our cases on prior restraint require.

Of necessity our holding is confined to the record before us. But our conclusion is not simply a result of assessing the adequacy of the showing made in this case; it results in part from the problems inherent in meeting the heavy burden of demonstrating, in advance of trial, that without prior restraint a fair trial will be denied. The practical problems of managing and enforcing restrictive orders will always be present. In this sense, the record now before us is illustrative rather than exceptional. It is significant that when this Court has reversed a state conviction, because of prejudicial publicity, it has carefully noted that some course of action short of prior restraint would have made a critical difference. [ ] However difficult it may be, we need not rule out the possibility of showing the kind of threat to fair trial rights that would possess the requisite degree of certainty to justify restraint. This Court has frequently denied that First Amendment rights are absolute and has consistently rejected the proposition that a prior restraint can never be employed. [ ]

. . . We hold that, with respect to the order entered in this case prohibiting reporting or commentary on judicial proceedings held in public, the barriers have not been overcome; to the extent that this order restrained publication of such material, it is clearly invalid. To the extent that it prohibited publication based on information gained from other sources, we conclude that the heavy burden imposed as a condition to securing a prior restraint was not met and the judgment of the Nebraska Supreme Court is therefore

Reversed.

[JUSTICES BRENNAN, STEWART, and MARSHALL concurred in the judgment. They would have held that prior restraints against the press are never a permissible method of protecting the right to a fair trial. JUSTICE STEVENS, concurring, said he might well join in this conclusion if forced to face the issue squarely, but preferred to leave open the possibility of enjoining publication of information improperly obtained. JUSTICE WHITE, concurring, doubted that such restraints would ever be permissible, and said that if the result "in case after case is to be similar to our judgment today, we should at some point announce a more general rule and avoid the interminable litigation that our failure to do so would necessarily entail." JUSTICE POWELL concurred separately, stating that a prior restraint should issue only when the publicity "poses a high likelihood of preventing, directly and irreparably," the impaneling of an impartial jury.]

NOTES AND QUESTIONS

1.   Taking into account the view of the concurring justices, under what circumstances would a prior restraint be permissible to protect fair trial

rights? Why might the barrier be lower here than in New York Times v. United States?

2.   Would the result be different if a statute made it a criminal offense for the media to publish specified facts considered by the legislature to be "highly prejudicial" to the defendant's right to a fair trial?

3.   Since *Nebraska Press Association*, decisions upholding restrictive orders against the press have been rare. One observer doubts that such orders can ever comply with the stringent requirements of that case: "As noted by Justice White in his concurring opinion, it should be highly unlikely that the 'heavy burden' of satisfying the three elements of the Burger test can ever be met." Floyd Abrams, "Prior Restraints," in 3 Communications Law 799, 814 (Practicing Law Institute 1993).

––––––––

Privileged Communications. Might the requirements of *Nebraska Press Association* be met if the media threatened to reveal privileged communications between a defendant and his attorney? The question has not been definitively answered, but some courts have indicated the answer might be yes. During the prosecution of Panamanian General Manuel Antonio Noriega on federal drug charges, CNN announced it would broadcast excerpts from tapes the government had made of telephone calls from Noriega to his defense counsel. At the request of Noriega's attorneys, a district judge issued a temporary restraining order prohibiting the broadcast of the tapes, and directed the network to turn the tapes over to him for in-camera review to determine whether they contained privileged communications. CNN refused to turn the tapes over, broadcast one of them, and sought emergency relief in the Court of Appeals. The network argued that under *Nebraska Press Association*, no prior restraint could be issued in the absence of a threshold finding that the information (a) would threaten Noriega's right to a fair trial, and (b) prohibiting broadcast was the only means of protecting that right. The Court of Appeals held that the network could not insist that such findings be made and, at the same time, deny the trial court access to the tapes:

> After review of such tapes, it is entirely conceivable that the District Court may determine that the disclosure of only portions of such tapes would threaten the Sixth Amendment rights of Noriega. Under such circumstances the accused's Sixth Amendment right to a fair trial is properly balanced against the First Amendment rights of the press and public. At this juncture, however, we are required to speculate as a result of CNN's refusal to produce the tape recordings.

United States v. Noriega, 917 F.2d 1543 (11th Cir. 1990). The Supreme Court denied CNN's application for stay and petition for certiorari, with Justices Marshall and O'Connor dissenting. 498 U.S. 976 (1990). CNN was eventually held in contempt for broadcasting the first tape in defiance of the temporary restraining order. To avoid paying a "substantial" fine, CNN broadcast an apology and paid $85,000 to cover the government's legal fees.

Does the refusal by the Eleventh Circuit and the Supreme Court to stay the order requiring CNN to turn the tapes over to the judge imply that *Nebraska Press Association* does not preclude enjoining publication of significant privileged communications?

For a wide range of views on *Nebraska Press Association*, see symposia in 20 St. Louis U. L.J. 654 (1976) and 29 Stan. L. Rev. 383 (1977).

––––––

b.   GAGGING TRIAL PARTICIPANTS

Beaufort County Board of Education v. Beaufort County Board of Commissioners

Court of Appeals of North Carolina, 2007.
645 S.E.2d 857.

■ TYSON, JUDGE.

[The Board of Education sued the County Commissioners alleging that they deliberately underfunded the public school system for improper reasons. The Board asked the trial court to order the Commissioners to appropriate the amount of money needed to maintain the public school system.

Before the trial began, the trial court, on its own motion, orally forbade the parties and their attorneys from communicating with members of the news media regarding the litigation. The owner of a local television station, Media General, moved for dissolution of the gag order. The trial court heard arguments from Media General's counsel but failed to rule on the motion prior to proceeding with the trial. After the suit was submitted to the jury, the trial court dissolved the gag order and stated, "Let the record show that the Court now terminates any restrictions that may have been imposed on anybody about speaking to anybody." Media General appealed, contending the gag order was unconstitutional.]

. . .

III. Mootness

. . .

Our Courts have long recognized an exception to dismissals for mootness and have held it is proper for the appellate courts to hear appeals where the issues are "capable of repetition, yet evading review." [ ] . . . There are two elements required for the exception to apply: (1) the challenged action [is] in its duration too short to be fully litigated prior to its cessation or expiration, and (2) there [is] a reasonable expectation that the same complaining party would be subjected to the same action again. Boney Publishers, Inc. v. Burlington City Council, 566 S.E.2d 701, 703–04 [(N.C. Ct. App. 2002)].

. . . In *Boney Publishers, Inc.*, the plaintiff, a newspaper publisher, alleged the Burlington City Council had violated the Open Meetings Law and Public Records Act, and sought declaratory and injunctive relief. [ ] We stated the appeal was "technically moot because the information sought by plaintiff ha[d] been fully disclosed." [ ] However, this Court applied an exception to dismissing the plaintiff's appeal as moot because: (1) all the requested information was disclosed in open session well before the controversy could be fully litigated and (2) there was a reasonable likelihood that the defendant, in considering the acquisition of other property for municipal purposes, could repeat the challenged conduct and subject the plaintiff to the same action and restrictions. [ ]

Here, as in *Boney Publishers, Inc.*, the gag order was lifted and the court proceedings completed before this controversy could be fully resolved. The trial court and this Court had not ruled upon Media General's motion and appeal prior to the completion of the trial. A reasonable likelihood remains that the trial court might attempt to repeat the conduct at issue in this case and subject Media General to the same or a similar action in another case. Due to the trial court's failure to rule upon Media General's motion, the short duration of the trial, and the elapsed time to obtain appellate review, Media General's allegations are "capable of repetition, yet evading review" and are properly before this Court. [ ]

IV. Constitutionality of the Gag Order

Media General argues the trial court erred by entering and then failing to dissolve the unconstitutional gag order. We agree.

. . .

In Sherrill v. Amerada Hess Corp., [504 S.E.2d 802, 807 (N.C. Ct. App. 1998)] this Court discussed controlling precedents concerning gag orders and unanimously stated:

"The issuance of gag orders prohibiting participants in judicial proceedings from speaking to the public or the press about those proceedings is a form of prior restraint." [ ] The phrase "prior restraint" refers to "judicial orders or administrative rules that operate to forbid expression before it takes place." [ ] "Prior restraints" are not unconstitutional per se, Southeastern Promotions, Ltd. v. Conrad, 420 U.S. 546 (1975), but are presumptively unconstitutional as violative of the First Amendment, New York Times Co. v. United States, 403 U.S. 713 (1971); [ ] Nebraska Press Ass'n v. Stuart, 427 U.S. 539, 558 (1976), and are "repugnant to the basic values of an open society." [ ]

As "prior restraints," gag orders are subject to strict and rigorous scrutiny under the First Amendment. [ ] The party asserting validity of the order must establish: (1) "a clear threat to the fairness of the trial;" (2) "such threat is posed by the actual publicity to be restrained;" and (3) "no less restrictive alternatives are available" to rebut the presumptive unconstitutionality of gag orders. [ ] "Furthermore, the record must reflect findings [of fact] by the trial court that it has considered each of the above factors ... and contain evidence to support [each] such finding[ ]." [ ] The trial court's findings of fact must support its conclusions of law in order to enter a lawful order. [ ] "Finally, [the gag order] must comply with the specificity requirements of the First Amendment." [ ]

In *Sherrill*, the trial court entered a gag order that prohibited the parties to a civil proceeding and their attorneys from communicating with the public and the press about the case. [ ] In support of this directive, the trial court found as a fact, "[T]hat communications concerning the [a]ctions with media representatives and with other persons not parties to this action by the parties and their counsel ... will be detrimental to the fair and impartial administration of justice in such [a]ctions." [ ] The plaintiffs argued the gag order constituted an unconstitutional prior restraint of their First Amendment right to free speech. [ ] A unanimous panel of this Court reversed the gag order and held:

> Although the record reflects a finding that communications concerning the action by the parties to persons not involved in the suit would "be detrimental to the fair and impartial administration of justice," there is no evidence in the record to support this finding. Furthermore, the trial court made no findings reflecting the consideration of less restrictive alternatives. [ ]

Here, the ... gag order utterly failed to meet any of the required standards set forth in *Sherrill*. The trial court neglected to enter findings of fact that either a "clear threat" existed to the "fairness of the trial" and that the threat was posed by the "publicity to be restrained," or that it considered "less restrictive alternatives." [ ] The gag order was not reduced to writing, signed by the judge, filed with or entered by the Clerk of Superior Court.

. . .

[The trial judge's order was vacated.]

NOTES AND QUESTIONS

1.   Note that the court did not question Media General's right to intervene. Whether media have standing to complain about orders not aimed at them directly may depend on the jurisdiction's procedural rules. In some instances, they may be required to institute a separate proceeding. See, e.g., United

States v. Sherman, 581 F.2d 1358 (9th Cir. 1978) (holding that a petition for a writ of mandamus was the proper remedy).

2.   In Gentile v. State Bar of Nevada, 501 U.S. 1030 (1991), the Supreme Court held that states may discipline lawyers for their comments about pending cases upon a showing that the comments pose a substantial likelihood of materially prejudicing the pending proceeding. It rejected an argument that Nebraska Press Association v. Stuart should apply to lawyer speech as well as press speech, and would require a showing of clear and present danger rather than substantial likelihood. The Court said lawyer speech could be more closely regulated because, as officers of the court, they surrender some of their speech rights, and because their special access to information makes their comments especially likely to cause prejudice. The case involved a bar association reprimand rather than a gag order.

Was the *Beaufort* court right to follow *Nebraska Press* rather than *Gentile*? If so, is it because the challenger was the press rather than a lawyer? Because the order in *Beaufort* was a prior restraint? Assuming it was a prior restraint as to the participants, should it be viewed as a prior restraint as to the television station?

5.   PRIOR RESTRAINTS AND THE INTERNET

In 2010 Wikileaks.com began releasing some 250,000 secret U.S. government documents. They were posted on Wikileaks' websites and some were also published by mainstream news outlets, including the Guardian in England and The New York Times, which obtained the documents through arrangements with Wikileaks. The documents included diplomatic cables, intelligence assessments, and confidential military information. The federal government began a criminal investigation of Wikileaks founder Julian Assange and pressured some U.S. companies to sever ties with Wikileaks. Secretary of State Hillary Clinton called the disclosures "an attack against the international community." But the government made no attempt to enjoin Wikileaks or the other media from disclosing the documents. The following case illustrates some of the obstacles that may have discouraged the government from pursuing a prior restraint in the age of the Internet.

Bank Julius Baer & Co. v. Wikileaks

United States District Court, Northern District of California, 2008.
535 F. Supp. 2d 980.

■ JEFFREY S. WHITE, DISTRICT JUDGE.

[Wikileaks.org, which said its mission was to provide "an uncensorable Wikipedia for untraceable mass document-leaking and analysis," invited people to post leaked documents revealing information about claimed wrongdoing by governments and businesses. Someone posted on the site confidential documents allegedly showing that Julius Baer Bank and Trust, based in the Cayman Islands, engaged in hiding assets, laundering money, and evading taxes. The bank filed suit against Wikileaks.org and Dynadot, the site's domain registrar, seeking to shut down the site. It described Wikileaks as a "fictitious entity of unknown type and origin." The judge issued a temporary restraining order forbidding further distribution of the documents. Dynadot, a company that leases domain names to website operators for a fee, agreed to the entry of an injunction requiring it to disable the Wikileaks website.

News of the order shutting down the website set off a furor on the Internet and among mainstream media. As part of its plan to avoid legal interference, Wikileaks maintained "mirror sites" (copies of itself) in Belgium, Germany, and the Christmas Islands, and registered with companies, other than Dynadot, for the purpose of evading jurisdiction. Fans of Wikileaks used the Internet to widely publicize the addresses of those sites and the fact that the material remained available there. Lawyers for public interest groups, Internet watchdogs, and mainstream news organizations filed motions to intervene or appear as amicus curiae, urging that the injunction be dissolved. They argued that the order was akin to closing down a newspaper, and that there was no precedent in prior restraint jurisprudence for shutting down an entire outlet because of one item it had published.]

. . . Plaintiffs allege that Defendants WikiLeaks, Wikileaks.org and Dynadot, LLC have unlawfully and wrongfully published on the website wikileaks.org confidential, as well as forged, bank documents belonging to Plaintiffs. Plaintiffs allege that such publication violates consumer banking and privacy protection law, under both foreign and American law.

On February 8, 2008, Plaintiffs filed an *ex parte* application for a temporary restraining order ("TRO") and order to show cause re preliminary injunction. . . . On February 14, 2008, this Court held a hearing at which Plaintiffs and Defendant Dynadot appeared and represented that they had reached an agreement. Per that agreement, Dynadot would (1) lock the wikileaks.org domain name and account in order to prevent access to and any changes from being made to the domain name and account information, and (2) disable the website such that the optional private who-is service for the domain name and account remained turned off. On February 15, 2008, the Court approved the parties' settlement agreement and issued the agreed-upon permanent injunction, pending further order of the Court. In addition, on February 15, 2008, the Court entered the unopposed amended TRO against WikiLeaks which restrained WikiLeaks, or its agents, from the display, use or dissemination of the property identified by the Plaintiffs as private, personal banking information of its clients.

. . . The Court set a hearing on the motion for a preliminary injunction for February 29, 2008 . . . [Before that hearing,] the Court received numerous filings from various interested parties seeking to be heard as *amicus curiae*, moving to intervene and moving to dismiss. The Court did not receive any submission from Defendant Dynadot and received only a notice to appear and joinder in the various *amicus* briefs by an individual, John Shipton, who claims to be the owner of the wikileaks.org domain name.

On February 29, 2008, this Court held a hearing on the motion for preliminary injunction and heard at length from all concerned parties, including Plaintiffs, Dynadot, Mr. Shipton, the website's domain name owner, Daniel Mathews, a user and potential officer of wikileaks.org, and the numerous *amicus curiae*.

The issues pending before this Court are whether the stipulated permanent injunction between Plaintiffs and Dynadot should be dissolved, whether Plaintiffs' motion for preliminary injunction against WikiLeaks should be granted, and how to proceed procedurally with the various interested parties before this Court. As addressed at the hearing on this matter, the Court sets out its reasons and final adjudication pertaining to those issues.

ANALYSIS

A.   Standards Applicable to Motions for Preliminary Injunction

The standards for obtaining a preliminary injunction are well established. It is appropriate to issue a preliminary injunction if the moving party establishes either (1) a combination of probable success on the merits and the possibility of irreparable injury, or (2) that serious questions are raised and the balance of hardships tips sharply in favor of the moving party. [ ]

... In addition, within the Ninth Circuit, the Court also must consider the public interest when it assesses the propriety of issuing an injunction. [ ]

B.   Concerns Before the Court

1.   Subject Matter Jurisdiction.

. . .

From the face of the Complaint, Plaintiffs have indicated that they are themselves foreign citizens and entities formed and operated under the laws of Switzerland and the Cayman Islands. [ ] In addition, Plaintiffs have alleged that although Dynadot is a citizen of California, other "Defendants are each citizens or subjects of a State or different States or foreign states, with some of them located in and residing within the State of California." [ ] Plaintiffs further allege that Defendant WikiLeaks is "a fictitious business name, alias and/or entity of unknown type and origin, with its principal place of business in the State of California." [ ] Although there is no firm evidence of the citizenship of the named defendants, except Dynadot, during the oral argument on the pending motion, counsel for Mr. Shipton appeared and represented that the owner of the domain name wikileaks.org is a citizen of Australia and a resident of Kenya.

From the founding of the federal courts, it has been unanimously held that "the courts of the United States have no jurisdiction of cases between aliens." . . . In order for the Court to exercise subject matter jurisdiction over this matter, complete diversity must be established under the original Complaint. [ ]

The Court is concerned that it may well lack subject matter jurisdiction over this matter in its entirety.

2.   Public Interest.

Within the Ninth Circuit, the Court must consider the public interest when it assesses the propriety of issuing an injunction. [ ] As made abundantly clear by the various submissions of the *amicus curiae*, the current request for an injunction, as well as the Court's original entry of a stipulated injunction, raises issues regarding possible infringement of protections afforded to the public by the First Amendment to the United States Constitution. The First Amendment encompasses the "right to receive information and ideas." Kleindienst v. Mandel, 408 U.S. 753 (1972) (citation omitted); see also Board of Education v. Pico, 457 U.S. 853 (1982) ("the right to receive ideas is a necessary predicate to the *recipient's* meaningful exercise of his own rights of speech, press, and political freedom") (emphasis in original).

Although the matter of the First Amendment implications of the permanent injunction against Dynadot or the more limited preliminary injunction Plaintiffs seek against WikiLeaks has not been fully briefed, it is clear that in all but the most exceptional circumstances, an injunction restricting speech pending final resolution of the constitutional concerns is impermissible. See Procter & Gamble Co. v. Bankers Trust Co., 78 F.3d 219, 226–27 (6th Cir. 1996).

3.   Efficacy of an Injunction.

The record currently before the Court indicates that even the broad injunction issued as to Dynadot had exactly the opposite effect as was intended. The private, stolen material was transmitted over the internet via mirror websites which are maintained in different countries all over the world. Further, the press generated by this Court's action increased public attention to the fact that such information was readily accessible online. The Court is not convinced that Plaintiffs have made an adequate showing that any restraining injunction in this case would serve its intended purpose. See Nebraska Press Association v. Stuart, 427 U.S. 539, 569, 96 S. Ct. 2791, 49 L.Ed.2d 683 (1976). In addition, there is evidence in the record that "the cat is out of the bag" and the issuance of an injunction would therefore be ineffective to protect the professed privacy rights of the bank's clients. [ ]

4.   Narrowly Tailored Remedy.

At the TRO hearing, the Court was concerned that because WikiLeaks failed to appear and no interested party appeared on their behalf, the only effective remedy to stop the leaking of personal banking information was the broad remedy it made available by signing the stipulated permanent injunction between Plaintiffs and Dynadot. However, now that the Court has the full panoply of parties and the interested entities before it, the Court is concerned that an injunctive remedy, if any, that may be available to Plaintiffs should be narrowly tailored and the least restrictive means to achieve the purpose of protecting banking clients from disclosure of their personal information. For example, given sufficient evidence that the Court has jurisdiction to hear the matter and that the restriction would be constitutionally valid, the Court might fashion an injunction requiring the limited redaction of identifying information on the leaked documents. Because the Court is not convinced that the existing permanent injunction is the least restrictive means to achieve Plaintiffs' goals, this additional reason counsels against maintaining the permanent injunction or issuing a preliminary injunction at this time.

CONCLUSION

For the above reasons, the Court DISSOLVES the stipulated permanent injunction between Plaintiffs and Dynadot. In addition, the Court DENIES Plaintiffs' motion for a preliminary injunction and DECLINES to extend the TRO. . . .

NOTES AND QUESTIONS

1.   The judge feared that he lacked subject matter jurisdiction because diversity jurisdiction does not extend to suits in which all parties are foreigners. That would not be a problem if only one of the parties was a foreigner, but there could be other difficulties. If the lawyer representing the owner of the Wikileaks domain name had not appeared, would the court have lacked personal jurisdiction to enter an injunction against Wikileaks? Whether posting Internet material that can be accessed in the forum state is enough to confer jurisdiction is unsettled, as we shall see in Chapter Four.

2.   Suppose the court determines that it has jurisdiction even though the foreign defendant makes no appearance and stays out of the United States. If the defendant ignores the injunction, how can the court enforce it?

3.   Most media cannot or would not avail themselves of the jurisdiction-evading tactics used by Wikileaks. But nearly all of them now publish online as well as in print or broadcast form, and that may make it easier for them to avoid being enjoined. Today the publishers of the Pentagon Papers or the article about the H-bomb would have the option of publishing instantly online. As the Wikileaks case indicates, once information has been published on the Internet, it may be difficult to show that an injunction can be effective.

Does that leave any circumstances in which prior restraints against media remain a viable threat?

4.   As noted above, the government did not enjoin Wikileaks after its 2010 publication of thousands of diplomatic cables and more than 700,000 battlefield reports from U.S. operations in Iraq and Afghanistan. Nor did the government enjoin the other news organizations with whom Julian Assange shared the documents from disclosing the classified information. The government did, however, criminally prosecute the soldier who gave Wikileaks the information. That soldier, Private Bradley Manning (now known as Chelsea Manning), was convicted of espionage and other charges and sentenced to 35 years in prison. Julie Tate, *Bradley Manning Sentenced to 35 Years in Wikileaks Case*, Wash. Post, Aug. 21, 2013. In the meantime Swedish prosecutors sought to question Julian Assange about sex assault claims, but Assange obtained asylum in the Ecuadorian embassy in London to avoid extradition to Sweden. As of 2015 the Justice Department was still "conducting an active, long-term criminal investigation into Wikileaks." Ed Pilkington, *U.S. Government Still Hunting Wikileaks as Obama Targets Whistleblowers*, The Guardian, March 5, 2015.

6.   DISOBEYING INJUNCTIONS

In *Near*, the Pentagon Papers case, *Progressive*, and *Nebraska Press*, the publishers opted to comply with the injunction while challenging it in court, instead of disobeying and challenging it when held in contempt for doing so. Media are sometimes unwilling to delay publication while the courts decide. For one thing, they fear that by the time the courts vindicate their right to publish, the matter will no longer be news because the public's attention will have turned to something else. Second, as soon as one media outlet is enjoined from publishing, its competitors usually attempt to get and publish the same information. As a result, the media do not acquiesce easily in prior restraints, even temporarily.

Of particular concern to media is the so-called "collateral bar." This rule, employed in most jurisdictions, holds that one charged with contempt for disobeying an injunction cannot defend on the ground that the injunction was unconstitutional. The theory is that although a statute may be ignored with impunity by one who successfully gambles that it will be held invalid, orderly judicial process requires that injunctions be obeyed until found to be invalid.

Most prior restraints are ultimately held to be unconstitutional. When a media organization is subjected to a prior restraint that it believes is unconstitutional, must it nevertheless defer publication until the matter is resolved by the courts? In states that recognize the collateral bar, the answer is yes, with some large exceptions.

The Providence Journal Case. The Providence Journal obtained from the FBI (through the federal Freedom of Information Act) logs of the FBI's electronic surveillance of Raymond Patriarca, a reputed mob leader who had recently died. Patriarca's son sued to enjoin publication on the ground that the FBI had wrongfully released the logs. Over the objections of the Journal and the government, the district court granted a temporary restraining order forbidding publication pending a hearing two days later. The next day the Journal published an article based on information from the logs, together with a statement by the newspaper saying that, although it respected the judge, "in this case we are convinced that his order would impose a prior restraint in violation of the Constitution. For that reason we have decided to publish in today's Journal Bulletin the first of a series of stories based on the Patriarca tapes."

The judge appointed a special prosecutor to press criminal contempt charges against the newspaper and its executive editor. The judge convicted them and sentenced the editor to 18 months in jail, which would be suspended on a condition that he performs 200 hours of community service. The Journal was fined $100,000.

The trial court relied on Walker v. City of Birmingham, 388 U.S. 307 (1967), which affirmed contempt convictions of Dr. Martin Luther King, Jr., and others for violating an injunction against parading without a permit, even though the injunction was ultimately held to be unconstitutional. The trial court also cited United States v. Dickinson, 465 F.2d 496 (5th Cir. 1972), upholding two reporters' convictions for contempt for publishing in violation of a judge's order, despite the fact that the appellate court found that order unconstitutional.

On appeal by the Journal, a panel of the Court of Appeals for the First Circuit reversed. It held that both *Walker* and *Dickinson* recognized an exception allowing the defendant to ignore a "transparently invalid" injunction. The TRO against the Journal came within this exception because (1) the Supreme Court precedents create a heavy presumption of unconstitutionality, (2) there was no statutory authorization for the injunction against the Journal, (3) the privacy interests invoked by Patriarca's son were not a sufficient basis for a prior restraint, and (4) the FBI had already disseminated the same information to other media outlets, making it unlikely that the injunction would be effective in preventing the alleged harm. "Because the order was transparently invalid, the appellants should have been allowed to challenge its constitutionality at the contempt proceedings." 820 F.2d 1342 (1st Cir. 1986).

At the request of the special prosecutor, the case was re-heard en banc. The full court did not vacate the panel opinion, but modified it with a brief additional opinion of its own:

> [I]t seems to us that some finer tuning is available to minimize the disharmony between respect for court orders and respect for free speech.

> It is not asking much, beyond some additional expense and time, to require a publisher, even when it thinks it is the subject of a transparently unconstitutional order of prior restraint, to make a good faith effort to seek emergency relief from the appellate court. If timely access to the appellate court is not available or if timely decision is not forthcoming, the publisher may then proceed to publish and challenge the constitutionality of the order in the contempt proceedings.

In re Providence Journal, 820 F.2d 1354 (1st Cir. 1987) (en banc).

After this decision, when would a prior restraint *not* be "transparently invalid"? If the appellate court immediately grants the defendant's request for review, but does not immediately decide the case, may the defendant safely disobey the injunction on the ground it is being denied a "timely decision"? Is proof that further delay would have caused the defendant to be "scooped" by a competitor sufficient to show that a "timely" decision was not forthcoming?

In *Dickinson*, the court wrote, "[I]n the absence of strong indications that the appellate process is being deliberately stalled—certainly not so in this record—violation with impunity does not occur simply because immediate decision is not forthcoming, even though the communication enjoined is 'news.'" If the appellate court agrees to review the restraint in accordance with its usual timetable, rather than grant expedited review, is the process being "deliberately stalled"? Is the defendant being denied a "timely decision"?

It was once suggested that the cases "may require no more than an attempt to appeal a void restraining order up to the time the constitutionally protected action is planned to take place." See James C. Goodale, The Press Ungagged: The Practical Effect on Gag Order Litigation of Nebraska Press Association v. Stuart, 29 Stan. L. Rev. 497, 509–10 (1977). That seemed plausible when news organizations in the normal course of business would not expect to publish or broadcast for at least a few hours. Now that most news is first reported online as soon as it can be prepared, is there any principled way to determine how much delay is too much?

Rule 65 of the Federal Rules of Civil Procedure permits courts to issue an ex parte temporary restraining order when the applicant shows that the TRO is necessary to prevent irreparable injury to the applicant. The Sixth Circuit held that a higher standard must be met when the order would enjoin publication. It said such orders against the press violate the First Amendment unless a "showing is made that it is impossible to serve or notify the opposing parties and give them an opportunity to participate." Substantively, the applicant must show not only that the order is necessary to prevent irreparable injury, but also that the interest threatened is "more fundamental than the First Amendment itself." Finally, such a restraint is to be reviewed de novo at the appellate level, rather than under the usual abuse-of-discretion standard. See Procter & Gamble Co. v. Bankers Trust Co., 78 F.3d 219 (6th Cir. 1996).

7. WHY ARE PRIOR RESTRAINTS BAD?

Once a court labels a restriction on speech a prior restraint, the court usually will pronounce it unconstitutional with little further analysis. In an influential law review article, Rethinking Prior Restraints, 92 Yale L.J. 409, 426–33 (1983), Professor John Jeffries searched for the "defining characteristics" that make prior restraints distinctively pernicious and concluded that they were hard to find, at least in the case of injunctions.

First, Jeffries noted the difference between historical prior restraints (e.g., requirements for administrative preclearance, such as licenses) and more modern prior restraints (e.g., injunctions):

> Under a regime of injunctions, there is no routine screening of speech and no administrative shortcut to suppression. The government has to shoulder the entire burden of identifying the case for suppression and of demonstrating in court a constitutionally acceptable basis for such action. Moreover, because an injunction must be sought in open court, the character of the government's claims remains subject to public scrutiny and debate. Most important, the decision to suppress is made by a court, not a censor. Of course, judges are not perfect; sometimes they may err on the side of suppression and enjoin speech without sufficient justification. But the fact remains that judges, unlike professional censors, have no vested interest in the suppression of speech. The institution of the judiciary is peculiarly well suited—in personnel, training, ideology, and institutional structure—to implement the ideals of the First Amendment. . . .
>
> Not only are injunctions unlike administrative preclearance, they are also far more like subsequent punishments than the conventional rhetoric would suggest. In both cases the *threat* of punishment comes before publication; in both cases the *fact* of punishment comes after. The apparent distinction in timing is actually only a shift in the focus of attention. The procedures in an action for criminal contempt— the enforcement phase of the injunctive process—are generally the same as those used in ordinary criminal prosecutions. Proof must be had beyond a reasonable doubt, and the right to trial by jury is guaranteed where the sentence exceeds imprisonment for six months.
>
> On examination, the chief difference between the two schemes turns out to be this: Under a system of injunctions, the

adjudication of illegality precedes publication; under a system of criminal prosecution, it comes later. This is a difference, and perhaps for some purposes it matters, but why the timing of the adjudication should affect the scope of First Amendment freedoms is not at all clear.

... [T]here is only one respect in which injunctions plausibly can be claimed to have a First Amendment impact significantly greater than the threat of subsequent punishment. That argument is based on the traditional rule that the legality of an injunction may not be challenged by disobeying its terms. In its most uncompromising form, the traditional approach would declare that the invalidity or even unconstitutionality of a court order would be no defense in a contempt proceeding based on violation of that order.

. . .

The reasons for the collateral bar rule are obvious and not unimportant. They include the preservation of judicial authority and the orderly settlement of disputes—values evoked by Justice Stewart's reference to "the civilizing hand of law." But it is also clear that, at least in the context of injunctions against speech, the collateral bar rule must be carefully circumscribed. The Supreme Court has recognized the point and limited the rule accordingly. Indeed, in Walker [v. City of Birmingham] itself the Court acknowledged that a different situation would be presented if an injunction were "transparently invalid" or if delay or frustration were encountered in the effort to contest its validity.

The first of these exceptions covers the case of an injunction so palpably contrary to authority that it falls under a kind of "plain error" rule. The limitation is not trivial, for existing First Amendment precedents would render "transparently invalid" a vast range of injunctions against speech. Nevertheless, this formulation does not address the truly close case, however occasionally it may arise. The second exception may be more to the point, for it speaks directly to the central problem of the collateral bar rule—the risk that an injunction against speech, even though ultimately invalidated, will so delay publication as to make the speech untimely and hence valueless for its purpose. The worst case would be an election-eve attempt by the party in power to enjoin publication of politically damaging information. In such circumstances, even the few days necessary to obtain expedited appellate review might prove seriously prejudicial to that system of representative government which the First Amendment, above all else, should be thought to undergird. In my view, therefore, the normal operation of the collateral bar rule can be sustained only so long as expedited appellate review allows an immediate opportunity to test the validity of an injunction against speech and only so long as that opportunity is genuinely effective to allow timely publication should the injunction ultimately be adjudged invalid. In any event, this is, as Professor Blasi put it, only a "controversy over the validity and scope of the collateral bar rule." It should be addressed in those terms and not, in my view, as a remote and usually unarticulated premise underlying a broad and uncritical acceptance of the conventional rhetoric of prior restraint.

. . .

The conclusion that I draw from all this is embarrassingly modest. It is not that injunctions are preferable to subsequent punishment as a mechanism for suppression of speech, though that may be true in some cases. Nor would I assert that there is never a case in which injunctive relief should be specially disfavored. In some situations (the election-eve gambit comes to mind) an injunction may be differentially destructive of First Amendment values, just as in others (perhaps regulation of obscenity) it may prove differentially protective. My only point is to question the broad and categorical condemnation of injunctions as a form of "prior restraint."

In my view, a rule of special hostility to administrative preclearance is fully justified, but a rule of special hostility to injunctive relief is not. Lumping both together under the name of "prior restraint" obscures rather than clarifies what is at stake in these cases. . . .

If the collateral bar is what makes prior restraints especially objectionable, what tenable objections might there be in states that reject the collateral bar rule and allow challenges to the validity of the injunction after its violation?

B. CONTEMPT

At common law, judges were permitted to use their contempt powers not merely as a sanction for disobedience to judicial orders, but also to prevent publication of matters they believed would interfere with the administration of justice, such as criticism of judges and commentary about pending cases. They were allowed to exercise the contempt power not only against parties before the court, but also against third parties such as newspapers. In England, vestiges of this broad contempt power still exist. The British press can be held in contempt for publications that create a substantial risk of seriously prejudicing an active judicial proceeding, even if no restrictive order has been issued and even if the publisher is unaware of the risk. In the United States, decisions holding such exercises of the contempt power unconstitutional were among the first important press victories in the Supreme Court after *Near*.

The key case was Bridges v. California, 314 U.S. 252 (1941). The Los Angeles Times was held in contempt for publishing a warning that a judge in a pending case would make "a serious mistake if he granted probation" to two Teamsters accused of assaulting non-union truck drivers. Controversial labor leader Harry Bridges was also held in contempt for making other statements about the case. The Court held, 5–4, that the contempt power could be used to punish comments made outside the courtroom only if they presented a "clear and present danger" of obstructing justice. The Times' statement did not meet that test because, given the newspaper's well-known hostility to unions, "it is inconceivable that any judge in Los Angeles would expect anything but adverse criticism from it in the event probation were granted." The dissenters thought such a danger existed because the judge was facing re-election and might be intimidated by the newspaper's editorial.

The Court later held that even misstatements of fact did not justify holding a newspaper in contempt if the clear-and-present-danger test was not met. See Pennekamp v. Florida, 328 U.S. 331 (1946). A much-quoted rationale for these decisions was articulated in Craig v. Harney, 331 U.S. 367 (1947):

> [The] law of contempt is not made for the protection of judges who may be sensitive to the winds of public opinion. Judges are supposed to be men of fortitude, able to thrive in a hardy climate.... Judges who stand for reelection run on their records.... Discussion of their conduct is appropriate, if not necessary. The fact that discussion at this particular point of time was not in good taste falls far short of meeting the clear and present danger test.

The decision was especially emphatic because the judge who had been criticized was a lay judge and it was argued that such judges might be more vulnerable to pressure than judges trained in the law.

In Wood v. Georgia, 370 U.S. 375 (1962), the Court extended the principle to criticism of a grand jury investigation, asserting that "a greater degree of disinterestedness and impartiality is assured by allowing free expression" of a sheriff's opinion that an investigation of racial bloc voting was improper.

Although *Bridges*, *Pennekamp*, and *Wood* left open the possibility that the contempt power could be used against out-of-court statements if the clear-and-present-danger test was met, the cases have proved to be a remarkably sturdy barrier against English-style use of the contempt power. The U.S. Supreme Court has never upheld a use of the criminal contempt power to suppress media publication.

C. DIRECT PROHIBITIONS

The cases dealing with prior restraints and contempt focused on the special characteristics of those remedies. They did not necessarily provide a framework for judging the constitutionality of punishing the press—or other speakers—after the fact for violating statutes forbidding certain disclosures. The Supreme Court's early approach to cases involving criminal punishment applied a clear-and-present-danger test. As we saw in Chapter One, that test failed to protect defendants in the World War I era, but became quite protective between 1927 and World War II. With the beginning of the Cold War, however, government efforts to suppress "subversive" speech multiplied, and the Court was often persuaded that the speakers presented a clear and present danger. In 1951, the Court held that the speeches and writings of leaders of the Communist Party of the United States presented such a danger. It upheld convictions under the Smith Act, which forbade advocating the overthrow of the government by force or violence. Dennis v. United States, 341 U.S. 494 (1951). That decision encouraged the widespread abuses of the McCarthy era and permitted convictions of more than 100 Communists during the next six years. Finally, in Yates v. United States, 354 U.S. 298 (1957), the Court put some teeth in the clear-and-present-danger test, holding that advocating the overthrow of the government does not meet the test unless it includes a call for specific, concrete action. That brought an end to the prosecution of Communists under the Smith Act, but by then, it was obvious that the clear-and-present-danger test was an unreliable means of protecting speech.

A more rigorous variation of the test was employed in Brandenburg v. Ohio, 395 U.S. 444 (1969), involving the prosecution of a Ku Klux Klan member for advocating racial and religious bigotry. The Court held that "[T]he constitutional guarantees of free speech and free press do not permit a State to forbid or proscribe advocacy of the use of force or of law violation except where such advocacy is directed to inciting or producing imminent lawless action and is likely to incite or produce such action." Since the statute permitted punishment of advocacy without a showing that imminent, lawless action was likely to follow, the convictions could not stand.

Clear-and-present-danger and incitement were concepts developed to evaluate restrictions aimed at preventing violence. Neither of them provided much guidance for judging the constitutionality of restrictions aimed at preventing some other kind of harm. The following cases illustrate the evolution of a more broadly applicable First Amendment methodology.

Mills v. Alabama

United States Supreme Court, 1966.
384 U.S. 214.

■ MR. JUSTICE BLACK delivered the opinion of the Court.

[The Alabama Corrupt Practices Act made it a crime to solicit votes for or against any ballot proposition on election day. The Birmingham Post-Herald carried an editorial urging voters to adopt a mayor-council form of government on the day that question was being voted upon. Its editor, James E. Mills, was arrested for violating the statute. The trial court held the statute unconstitutional and dismissed the complaint, but the Alabama Supreme Court reversed, holding that the law was a reasonable restriction imposing only a minor limitation on the press.]

I.

[The Supreme Court rejected the state's argument that there was no final judgment because Mills had not yet been convicted.]

II.

We come now to the merits. The First Amendment, which applies to the States through the Fourteenth, prohibits laws "abridging the freedom of speech, or of the press." The question here is whether it abridges freedom of the press for a State to punish a newspaper editor for doing no more than publishing an editorial on election day urging people to vote a particular way in the election. We should point out at once that this question in no way involves the extent of a State's power to regulate conduct in and around the polls in order to maintain peace, order and decorum there. The sole reason for the charge that Mills violated the law is that he wrote and published an editorial on election day urging Birmingham voters to cast their votes in favor of changing their form of government.

Whatever differences may exist about interpretations of the First Amendment, there is practically universal agreement that a major purpose of that Amendment was to protect the free discussion of governmental affairs. This of course includes discussions of candidates, structures and forms of government, the manner in which government is operated or should be operated, and all such matters relating to political processes. The Constitution specifically selected the press, which includes not only newspapers, books, and magazines, but also humble leaflets and circulars, see Lovell v. City of Griffin, 303 U.S. 444, to play an important role in the discussion of public affairs. Thus the press serves and was designed to serve as a powerful antidote to any abuses of power by governmental officials and as a constitutionally chosen means for keeping officials elected by the people responsible to all the people whom they were selected to serve. Suppression of the right of the press to praise or criticize governmental agents and to clamor and contend for or against change, which is all that this editorial did, muzzles one of the very agencies the Framers of our Constitution thoughtfully and deliberately selected to improve our society and keep it free. The Alabama Corrupt Practices Act by providing criminal penalties for publishing editorials such as the one here silences the press at a time it can be most effective. . . . [T]he Alabama Supreme Court nevertheless sustained the constitutionality of the law on the ground that the restrictions on the press were only 'reasonable restrictions' or at least 'within the field of reasonableness.' The court reached this conclusion because it thought the law imposed only a minor limitation on the press-restricting it only on election days-and because the court thought the law served a good purpose. It said:

> 'It is a salutary legislative enactment that protects the public from confusive last-minute charges and countercharges and the distribution of propaganda in an effort to influence voters on an election day; when as a practical matter, because of lack of time, such matters cannot be answered or their truth determined until after the election is over.' [ ]

This argument, even if it were relevant to the constitutionality of the law, has a fatal flaw. The state statute leaves people free to hurl their campaign charges up to the last minute of the day before election. The law held valid by the Alabama Supreme Court then goes on to make it a crime to answer those 'last-minute' charges on election day, the only time they can be effectively answered. Because the law prevents any adequate reply to these charges, it is wholly ineffective in protecting the electorate 'from confusive last-minute charges and countercharges.' We hold that no test of reasonableness can save a state law from invalidation as a violation of the First Amendment when that law makes it a crime for a newspaper editor to do no more than urge people to vote one way or another in a publicly held election.

The judgment of the Supreme Court of Alabama is reversed and the case is remanded for further proceedings not inconsistent with this opinion.

. . .

■ MR. JUSTICE DOUGLAS, with whom MR. JUSTICE BRENNAN joins, concurring.

. . .

The decision of the Alabama Supreme Court approved a law which, in my view, is a blatant violation of freedom of the press. The threat of penal sanctions has, we are told, already taken its toll in Alabama: the Alabama Press Association and the Southern Newspaper Publishers Association, as amici curiae, tell us that since November 1962 editorial comment on election day has been nonexistent in Alabama. The chilling effect of this prosecution is thus anything but hypothetical; it is currently being experienced by the newspapers and the people of Alabama.

We deal here with the rights of free speech and press in a basic form: the right to express views on matters before the electorate. In light of appellant's concession that he has no other defense to offer should the case go to trial, [ ] and considering the importance of the First Amendment rights at stake in this litigation, it would require regard for some remote, theoretical interests of federalism to conclude that this Court lacks jurisdiction because of the unlikely possibility that a jury might disregard a trial judge's instructions and acquit.

Indeed, even had appellant been unwilling to concede that he has no defense—apart from the constitutional question—to the charges against him, we would be warranted in reviewing this case. That result follows a fortiori from our holdings that where First Amendment rights are jeopardized by a state prosecution which, by its very nature, threatens to deter others from exercising their First Amendment rights, a federal court will take the extraordinary step of enjoining the state prosecution. Dombrowski v. Pfister, 380 U.S. 479; Cameron v. Johnson, 381 U.S. 74. As already noted, this case has brought editorial comment on election day to a halt throughout the State of Alabama.

. . .

For these reasons, and for the reasons stated in the opinion of the Court, I conclude that the judgment is final.

[Justice Harlan would have dismissed the appeal for want of a final judgment. On the merits, he would have held that the statute could not be applied to Mills because it did not give him fair warning that the editorial he published was illegal.]

NOTES AND QUESTIONS

1.   The Alabama Supreme Court apparently believed the appropriate constitutional inquiry was whether the statute was a reasonable restriction and whether the limitation it imposed was minor. What test does the U.S. Supreme Court apply?

2.   Justice Black describes the statute as a "flagrant abridgment of the constitutionally guaranteed freedom of the press," and his opinion emphasizes the press's constitutional role in the discussion of public affairs. Does that indicate that this is a press clause decision that would not necessarily apply to a non-press speaker? For example, would *Mills* preclude enforcement of a statute that forbade candidates from making last-minute accusations about their opponents?

———

At the time *Mills* was decided, numerous state and federal laws limited participation in politics by corporations and unions. In 1907 Congress prohibited corporations and unions from contributing directly to candidates for federal office, and in 1947 the law was broadened to prevent corporations and unions from exercising their influence indirectly by making expenditures (e.g., paying for ads) supporting or opposing federal candidates. Most states had similar laws. In Buckley v. Valeo, 424 U.S. 1 (1976), the Supreme Court held that independent expenditures supporting or opposing candidates were a form of speech protected by the First Amendment, but that direct contributions were more likely to corrupt the political process and therefore could be limited.

Invalidation of the restrictions on independent expenditures led to increased use of "soft money" (funds not controlled by the candidate), and that generated widespread concern about the dominance of corporate and union money in political campaigns. After many years of unsuccessful efforts, campaign reform advocates finally persuaded Congress in 2002 to pass the Bipartisan Campaign Reform Act, also known as the McCain-Feingold Act. That law aimed to close the loophole that allowed corporations and unions to spend money attempting to influence elections as long as they did not expressly advocate the election or defeat of specific candidates. The statute exempted news stories, editorials, and media commentary. In McConnell v. Federal Election Comm'n, 540 U.S. 93 (2003), the Court upheld the principal features of the BCRA, rejecting the argument that the exemption for news and commentary gave media corporations an unconstitutional advantage over other corporations.

In Citizens United v. Federal Election Comm'n, 558 U.S. 310 (2010), the Court overruled the main aspects of the *McConnell* decision, holding that the First Amendment does not permit Congress to restrict independent political expenditures of corporations and unions. The Court held, 5–4, that restrictions based on the identity of the speaker are impermissible unless they can survive strict scrutiny. The majority said the rationale that justified restriction of direct contributions did not suffice when applied to independent expenditures because the latter do not give rise to corruption or the appearance of corruption, even though they may buy the donor influence with elected officials. The argument that the vast wealth of corporations might distort politics failed because that rationale could just as easily justify restriction of speech by powerful media entities, in the majority's view.

In dissent, Justice Stevens, joined by Justices Sotomayor, Breyer, and Ginsburg, wrote, "The Court's ruling threatens to undermine the integrity of elected institutions across the nation." In their view, corporate domination of politics posed a threat to democracy that had been recognized since the inception of the Republic and was within Congress's power to prevent.

The dissent cited the Press Clause as proof that the framers of the First Amendment contemplated distinctions between different types of speakers, but the majority emphatically rejected the possibility that the First Amendment might treat the press differently than non-media speakers: "We have consistently rejected the proposition that the institutional press has any constitutional privilege beyond that of other speakers." The quotation was from a previous dissenting opinion by Justice Scalia, and the majority did not mention the Press Clause.

Mills v. Alabama was not cited in the *Citizens United* case. If it is true that nonmedia corporations enjoy no less First Amendment protection than the press, would *Mills* have been sufficient authority to strike down the BCRA limitations on corporate electioneering?

———

Landmark Communications, Inc. v. Virginia
Supreme Court of the United States, 1978.
435 U.S. 829.

[The Virginia constitution directed the legislature to create a commission to investigate charges against judges and decreed that proceedings before the commission "shall be confidential." A statute creating the commission declared that the proceedings were confidential "and shall not be divulged by any person to anyone except the Commission, except that the record of any proceeding filed with the Supreme Court shall lose its confidential character." A proceeding is filed with the Supreme Court only when the commission finds grounds for filing a formal complaint.

Landmark's newspaper, the Virginian Pilot, accurately reported that a named judge was under investigation by the Commission. Landmark was found guilty of a misdemeanor and fined $500 plus costs of prosecution. The Supreme Court of Virginia affirmed. It rejected Landmark's argument that the statute applied only to the participants in the proceedings or to initial disclosure of confidential information. Instead, it concluded that the paper's actions "clearly . . . violated" the statute.

On appeal, the Supreme Court of the United States noted that virtually every state had such a commission, and that all provided for confidentiality. The accepted reasons for confidentiality were (1) it is thought to encourage the filing of complaints and willing participation of witnesses; (2) judges are protected from injury by publication of unexamined complaints until the meritorious can be separated from the unjustified; and (3) confidence in the judiciary is maintained by avoiding announcement of groundless claims. In addition, when removal is justified judges are more likely to resign voluntarily or retire if publicity can be avoided.

But even accepting the value of confidentiality, the Court considered this "only the beginning of the inquiry." Landmark was not attacking the confidentiality requirement. It was objecting to making it a crime to divulge or publish the information—a step taken by only Virginia and Hawaii.]

■ MR. CHIEF JUSTICE BURGER delivered the opinion of the Court.

. . .

The narrow and limited question presented, then, is whether the First Amendment permits the criminal punishment of third persons who are strangers to the inquiry, including the news media, for divulging or publishing truthful information regarding confidential proceedings of the Judicial Inquiry and Review Commission. We are not here concerned with the possible applicability of the statute to one who secures the information by illegal means and thereafter divulges it. We do not have before us any constitutional challenge to a State's power to keep the Commission's proceedings confidential or to punish participants for breach of this mandate.[10] [ ] Nor does Landmark argue for any constitutionally compelled right of access for the press to those proceedings. [ ] Finally, as the Supreme Court of Virginia held, and appellant does not dispute, the challenged statute does not constitute a prior restraint or attempt by the State to censor the news media.

Landmark urges as the dispositive answer to the question presented that truthful reporting about public officials in connection with their public duties is always insulated from the imposition of criminal sanctions by the First Amendment. It points to the solicitude accorded even untruthful speech when public officials are its subjects, [ ], and the extension of First Amendment protection to the dissemination of truthful commercial information, [ ] to support its contention. We find it unnecessary to adopt this categorical approach to resolve the issue before us. We conclude that the publication Virginia seeks to punish under its statute lies near the core of the First Amendment, and the Commonwealth's interests advanced by the imposition of criminal sanctions are insufficient to justify the actual and potential encroachments on freedom of speech and of the press which follow therefrom. [ ]

A.

In Mills v. Alabama, 384 U.S. 214, 218 (1966), this Court observed: "Whatever differences may exist about interpretations of the First Amendment, there is practically universal agreement that a major purpose of that Amendment was to protect the free discussion of governmental affairs." . . . The operations of the courts and the judicial conduct of judges are matters of utmost public concern. . . .

. . .

The operation of the Virginia Commission, no less than the operation of the judicial system itself, is a matter of public interest, necessarily engaging the attention of the news media. The article published by

---

[10] At least two categories of "participants" come to mind: Commission members and staff employees, and witnesses or putative witnesses not officers or employees of the Commonwealth. No issue as to either of these categories is presented by this case.

Landmark provided accurate factual information about a legislatively authorized inquiry pending before the Judicial Review and Inquiry Commission, and in so doing clearly served those interests in public scrutiny and discussion of governmental affairs which the First Amendment was adopted to protect. [ ]

B.

. . .

The Commonwealth . . . focuses on what it perceives to be the pernicious effects of public discussion of Commission proceedings to support its argument. It contends that the public interest is not served by discussion of unfounded allegations of misconduct which defames honest judges and serves only to demean the administration of justice. The functioning of the Commission itself is also claimed to be impeded by premature disclosure of the complainant, witnesses, and the judge under investigation. Criminal sanctions minimize these harmful consequences, according to the Commonwealth, by ensuring that the guarantee of confidentiality is more than an empty promise.

It can be assumed for purposes of decision that confidentiality of Commission proceedings serves legitimate state interests. The question, however, is whether these interests are sufficient to justify the encroachment on First Amendment guarantees which the imposition of criminal sanctions entails with respect to nonparticipants such as Landmark. The Commonwealth has offered little more than assertion and conjecture to support its claim that without criminal sanctions the objectives of the statutory scheme would be seriously undermined. While not dispositive, we note that more than 40 States having similar commissions have not found it necessary to enforce confidentiality by use of criminal sanctions against nonparticipants.

Moreover, neither the Commonwealth's interest in protecting the reputation of its judges, nor its interest in maintaining the institutional integrity of its courts is sufficient to justify the subsequent punishment of speech at issue here, even on the assumption that criminal sanctions do in fact enhance the guarantee of confidentiality. Admittedly, the Commonwealth has an interest in protecting the good repute of its judges, like that of all other public officials. Our prior cases have firmly established, however, that injury to official reputation is an insufficient reason "for repressing speech that would otherwise be free." [ ]. The remaining interest sought to be protected, the institutional reputation of the courts, is entitled to no greater weight in the constitutional scales. . . . Mr. Justice Frankfurter, in his dissent in *Bridges,* [314 U.S. 252 (1941)] agreed that speech cannot be punished when the purpose is simply "to protect the court as a mystical entity or the judges as individuals or as anointed priests set apart from the community and spared the criticism to which in a democracy other public servants are exposed." [ ]

The Commonwealth has provided no sufficient reason for disregarding these well established principles. We find them controlling and, on this record, dispositive.

. . .

Accordingly, the judgment of the Supreme Court of Virginia is reversed, and the case remanded for further proceedings not inconsistent with this opinion.

■ MR. JUSTICE BRENNAN and MR. JUSTICE POWELL took no part in the consideration or decision of this case.

■ MR. JUSTICE STEWART, concurring in the judgment.

Virginia has enacted a law making it a criminal offense for "any person" to divulge confidential information about proceedings before its Judicial Inquiry and Review Commission. I cannot agree with the Court that this Virginia law violates the Constitution.

There could hardly be a higher governmental interest than a State's interest in the quality of its judiciary. Virginia's derivative interest in maintaining the confidentiality of the proceedings of its Judicial Inquiry and Review Commission seems equally clear. Only such confidentiality, the State has determined, will protect upright judges from unjustified harm and at the same time insure the full and fearless airing in Commission proceedings of every complaint of judicial misconduct. I find nothing in the Constitution to prevent Virginia from punishing those who violate this confidentiality. [ ]

But in this case Virginia has extended its law to punish a newspaper, and that it cannot constitutionally do. If the constitutional protection of a free press means anything, it means that government cannot take it upon itself to decide what a newspaper may and may not publish. Though government may deny access to information and punish its theft, government may not prohibit or punish the publication of that information once it falls into the hands of the press, unless the need for secrecy is manifestly overwhelming.

It is on this ground that I concur in the judgment of the Court.

NOTES AND QUESTIONS

1.   The Court concludes that protecting the reputations of judges and courts is not a sufficient reason to restrict the "public scrutiny and discussion of governmental affairs which the First Amendment was adopted to protect." Does that proposition offer any more guidance for the resolution of other cases than the methodology the Alabama Supreme Court employed in *Mills*?

2.   What is the "categorical" approach proposed by the newspaper in *Landmark*? Would that provide a more predictable basis for deciding future cases? Why does the majority decline to adopt it?

3.   Justice Stewart and the majority seem to agree that this decision does not necessarily preclude the state from prosecuting a commission employee for leaking information to the press. For Justice Stewart, this follows from his view that the First Amendment gives the press special protection. How would the majority justify the distinction? On the ground that the state's interests are stronger when the defendant is an employee? Because the employee's First Amendment claims are weaker?

Smith v. Daily Mail Publishing Co.
Supreme Court of the United States, 1979.
443 U.S. 97.

[A West Virginia statute made it a crime for a newspaper to publish the names of juveniles in connection with delinquency proceedings without a written order of the court. The respondent newspapers learned over a police radio about a killing at a junior high school. Reporters went to the scene and obtained the name of the suspect by asking witnesses, the police, and a prosecuting attorney. The name was revealed thereafter in the newspapers and over several broadcasting stations. After being indicted, the newspapers obtained an order from the state supreme court barring any prosecution on the ground that the statute was unconstitutional.]

■ MR. CHIEF JUSTICE BURGER delivered the opinion of the Court.

We granted certiorari to consider whether a West Virginia statute violates the First and Fourteenth Amendments of the United States Constitution by making it a crime for a newspaper to publish, without the written approval of the juvenile court, the name of any youth charged as a juvenile offender.

. . .

(2)

Respondents urge this Court to hold that because § 49–7–3 requires court approval prior to publication of the juvenile's name it operates as a "prior restraint" on speech. [ ] Respondents concede that this statute is not in the classic mold of prior restraint, there being no prior injunction against publication. Nonetheless, they contend that the prior approval requirement acts in "operation and effect" like a licensing scheme and thus is another form of prior restraint. See *Near v. Minnesota* [ ]. As such, respondents argue, the statute bears "a 'heavy presumption' against its constitutional validity." [ ] They claim that the State's interest in the anonymity of a juvenile offender is not sufficient to overcome that presumption.

. . .

Petitioners do not dispute that the statute amounts to a prior restraint on speech. Rather, they take the view that even if it is a prior restraint the statute is constitutional because of the significance of the State's interest in protecting the identity of juveniles.

(3)

The resolution of this case does not turn on whether the statutory grant of authority to the juvenile judge to permit publication of the juvenile's name is, in and of itself, a prior restraint. First Amendment protection reaches beyond prior restraints, [ ] and respondents acknowledge that the statutory provision for court approval of disclosure actually may have a less oppressive effect on freedom of the press than a total ban on the publication of the child's name.

Whether we view the statute as a prior restraint or as a penal sanction for publishing lawfully obtained, truthful information is not dispositive because even the latter action requires the highest form of state interest to sustain its validity. Prior restraints have been accorded the most exacting scrutiny in previous cases. [ ] However, even when a state attempts to punish publication after the event it must nevertheless demonstrate that its punitive action was necessary to further the state interests asserted. [*Landmark*]. Since we conclude that this statute cannot satisfy the constitutional standards defined in *Landmark Communications, Inc.,* we need not decide whether, as argued by respondents, it operated as a prior restraint.

Our recent decisions demonstrate that state action to punish the publication of truthful information seldom can satisfy constitutional standards. In *Landmark Communications* we declared unconstitutional a Virginia statute making it a crime to publish information regarding confidential proceedings before a state judicial review commission that heard complaints about alleged disabilities and misconduct of state-court judges. In declaring that statute unconstitutional, we concluded:

> "[T]he publication Virginia seeks to punish under its statute lies near the core of the First Amendment, and the Commonwealth's interests advanced by the imposition of criminal sanctions are insufficient to justify the actual and potential encroachments on freedom of speech and of the press which follow therefrom." 435 U.S., at 838.

In [Cox Broadcasting Corp. v. Cohn, 420 U.S. 469 (1975)], we held that damages could not be recovered against a newspaper for publishing the name of a rape victim. The suit had been based on a state statute that made it a crime to publish the name of the victim; the purpose of the statute was to protect the privacy right of the individual and the family. The name of the victim had become known to the public through official court records dealing with the trial of the rapist. In declaring the statute unconstitutional, the Court, speaking through Mr. Justice White, reasoned:

"By placing the information in the public domain on official court records, the State must be presumed to have concluded that the public interest was thereby being served. . . . States may not impose sanctions on the publication of truthful information contained in official court records open to public inspection." 420 U.S., at 495.

One case that involved a classic prior restraint is particularly relevant to our inquiry. In Oklahoma Publishing Co. v. District Court, 430 U.S. 308 (1977), we struck down a state court injunction prohibiting the news media from publishing the name or photograph of an 11-year-old boy who was being tried before a juvenile court. The juvenile judge had permitted reporters and other members of the public to attend a hearing in the case, notwithstanding a state statute closing such trials to the public. The court then attempted to halt publication of the information obtained from that hearing. We held that once the truthful information was "publicly revealed" or "in the public domain" the court could not constitutionally restrain its dissemination.

None of these opinions directly controls this case; however, all suggest strongly that if a newspaper lawfully obtains truthful information about a matter of public significance then state officials may not constitutionally punish publication of the information, absent a need to further a state interest of the highest order. These cases involved situations where the government itself provided or made possible press access to the information. That factor is not controlling. Here respondents relied upon routine newspaper reporting techniques to ascertain the identity of the alleged assailant. A free press cannot be made to rely solely upon the sufferance of government to supply it with information. See Houchins v. KQED, Inc., 438 U.S. 1, 11 (1978) (plurality opinion); Branzburg v. Hayes, 408 U.S. 665, 681 (1972). If the information is lawfully obtained, as it was here, the state may not punish its publication except when necessary to further an interest more substantial than is present here.

Rule

(4)

The sole interest advanced by the State to justify its criminal statute is to protect the anonymity of the juvenile offender. It is asserted that confidentiality will further his rehabilitation because publication of the name may encourage further antisocial conduct and also may cause the juvenile to lose future employment or suffer other consequences for this single offense. In Davis v. Alaska, 415 U.S. 308 (1974), similar arguments were advanced by the State to justify not permitting a criminal defendant to impeach a prosecution witness on the basis of his juvenile record. We said there that "[w]e do not and need not challenge the State's interest as a matter of its own policy in the administration of criminal justice to seek to preserve the anonymity of a juvenile offender." [ ] However, we concluded that the State's policy must be subordinated to the defendant's

Sixth Amendment right of confrontation. Ibid. The important rights created by the First Amendment must be considered along with the rights of defendants guaranteed by the Sixth Amendment. See Nebraska Press Assn. v. Stuart. [ ] Therefore, the reasoning of *Davis* that the constitutional right must prevail over the state's interest in protecting juveniles applies with equal force here.

The magnitude of the State's interest in this statute is not sufficient to justify application of a criminal penalty to respondents. Moreover, the statute's approach does not satisfy constitutional requirements. The statute does not restrict the electronic media or any form of publication, except "newspapers," from printing the names of youths charged in a juvenile proceeding. In this very case, three radio stations announced the alleged assailant's name before the Daily Mail decided to publish it. Thus, even assuming the statute served a state interest of the highest order, it does not accomplish its stated purpose.

In addition, there is no evidence to demonstrate that the imposition of criminal penalties is necessary to protect the confidentiality of juvenile proceedings. . . . [A]ll 50 states have statutes that provide in some way for confidentiality, but only five, including West Virginia, impose criminal penalties on nonparties for publication of the identity of the juvenile. Although every state has asserted a similar interest, all but a handful have found other ways of accomplishing the objective. See [*Landmark*].[3]

(5)

Our holding in this case is narrow. There is no issue before us of unlawful press access to confidential judicial proceedings, [ ]; there is no issue here of privacy or prejudicial pretrial publicity. At issue is simply the power of a state to punish the truthful publication of an alleged juvenile delinquent's name lawfully obtained by a newspaper.[4] The asserted state interest cannot justify the statute's imposition of criminal sanctions on this type of publication. Accordingly, the judgment of the West Virginia Supreme Court of Appeals is

Affirmed.

■ MR. JUSTICE POWELL took no part in the consideration or decision of this case.

[Justice Rehnquist, who concurred in the judgment, filed the only separate opinion. He believed that protecting juveniles in this type of

---

[3]   The approach advocated by the National Council of Juvenile Court Judges is based on cooperation between juvenile court personnel and newspaper editors. It is suggested that if the courts make clear their purpose and methods then the press will exercise discretion and generally decline to publish the juvenile's name without some prior consultation with the juvenile court judge.

[4]   In light of our disposition of the First and Fourteenth Amendment issue, we need not reach respondents' claim that the statute violates equal protection by being applicable only to newspapers but not other forms of journalistic expression.

case was an interest of the "highest order" and "far outweighs any minimal interference with freedom of the press. . . ." He also noted that the Court's decision "renders nugatory" state expungement laws, because a potential employer may now obtain information on juvenile offenses by visiting the morgue of the local newspaper. Also, in future cases the "press will still be able to obtain the child's name in the same manner as it was acquired in this case. [ ] Thus, the Court's reference to effective alternatives [other than criminal punishment] for accomplishing the State's goal is a mere chimera."

He did concur, however, because the state's statute did not accomplish its stated purpose. Since broadcasters could, and did, identify the juvenile, it was "difficult to take very seriously West Virginia's asserted need to preserve the anonymity of its youthful offenders when it permits other, equally, if not more, effective means of mass communication to distribute this information without fear of punishment."]

NOTES AND QUESTIONS

1.   Here, as in *Landmark*, the Court states the outcome as the result of a balancing process: "The asserted state interest cannot justify the statute's imposition of criminal sanctions on this type of publication." But that conclusion seems to flow from a more detailed proposition: "[I]f a newspaper lawfully obtains truthful information about a matter of public significance then state officials may not constitutionally punish publication of the information, absent a need to further a state interest of the highest order." This proposition has become known as the *Daily Mail* principle. We will see it employed in other cases in this book as a formula for judging not only criminal punishments of speech, but other types of limitations on speech as well.

2.   Under this principle, a threshold question is whether the information was lawfully obtained. Generally, courts construe that requirement generously. For example, they usually hold that the *Daily Mail* principle protects media defendants even when they receive the information from someone they know obtained it illegally. See, e.g., Bartnicki v. Vopper, a case discussed more fully in Chapter Eight.

3.   Justice Rehnquist thought the state's interest in protecting juveniles in this case was of the "highest order." The majority apparently did not share his view of the importance of the interest. How are judges supposed to determine whether state interests are sufficiently high to meet this standard? Should the constitutionality of the statute turn on the value assigned to the interest by the state, or by the reviewing judges?

4.   How exactly does the Court balance the interests at stake in this case? Consider the following:

> Someone says that the First Amendment "interests" associated with pornography are "outweighed" by the resultant violence to and subordination of women. Someone else replies that on the contrary,

as far as he is concerned, the First Amendment rights at stake outweigh the harms. Neither of these people will actually be engaged in anything like a real balancing of interests. They will be wholly unable to explain the "calculations" that supposedly went into their "balance." Neither will have the slightest actual idea of the real-world amounts of the "costs" or "benefits" involved, nor of how to measure them, nor even of what would count as a relevant cost or benefit. How then did they know which way, for them, the balance came out? The rhetoric of balancing is a disguise in such contexts. It serves as conclusory, obfuscatory language masking more fundamental, although frequently very poorly thought-through, instincts about the freedom of speech.

Jed Rubenfeld, *The First Amendment's Purpose*, 53 Stan. L. Rev. 767, 789 (2001).

Remedies for Unconstitutional Press Censorship by Public Officials. Public officials who use criminal law to suppress press criticism of their job performance may create additional First Amendment issues. In Lacey v. Maricopa County, 693 F.3d 896 (9th Cir. 2012) (en banc), the co-owners of a Phoenix newspaper filed a § 1983 claim against Maricopa County Sheriff Joseph Arpaio, "known as 'America's toughest sheriff,'" alleging that he caused them to be investigated and arrested for publishing articles critical of him. Plaintiffs also sued the Maricopa County Attorney, a special prosecutor appointed by the county attorney, and Maricopa County. The newspaper owners alleged that Sheriff Arpaio put intense pressure on the county attorney to prosecute them for publishing Sheriff Arpaio's publicly available home address. The newspaper published the address as part of a series of articles that were highly critical of the Sheriff's job performance. Although other newspapers had published the sheriff's address, the plaintiffs alleged that the sheriff singled them out for prosecution because their newspaper had criticized him. The county attorney removed himself from the charging decision, asserting that he had a conflict of interest because the newspaper had also criticized him, and instead appointed a special prosecutor to make the charging decision. The special prosecutor, who had close ties to Sheriff Arpaio, used his powers to investigate and arrest the newspaper owners. The complaint alleged that the special prosecutor:

> issued broad, invalid subpoenas demanding that the paper reveal its sources, disclose its reporters' notes, and reveal information about anyone who visited the *New Times's* website; [the special prosecutor also issued] motions for arrest warrants, contempt findings, and fines. . . . [However, h]e did not wait for the warrants or other official approval before authorizing Arpaio's "Selective Enforcement Unit" to arrest [both newspaper owners] at their homes.

The newspaper owners contended that the sheriff's and prosecutors' actions constituted false arrest, malicious prosecution, and violated their constitutional rights to freedom of expression and equal protection. A federal district court dismissed the claims against the sheriff and special prosecutor on grounds of qualified immunity.

The Ninth Circuit held that the newspaper owners had asserted facts that, if true, were sufficient to establish false arrest and violations of their constitutional rights. The court also held that the newspaper owners' constitutional rights were "clearly established" and the sheriff and special prosecutor therefore could not claim qualified immunity. With regard to plaintiffs' allegation that the defendants' actions violated the First Amendment, the court stated: "It is hard to conceive of a more direct assault on the First Amendment than public officials ordering the immediate arrests of their critics. And, in this case, there was nothing subtle about their efforts to stifle the New Times." The court also addressed plaintiffs' claims against the county attorney and held that his appointment of a special prosecutor was a "prosecutorial function for which immunity is vital." The court affirmed in part, reversed in part, and remanded to the district court. Subsequently, the Maricopa County Board of Supervisors approved a $3.75 million settlement of the lawsuit. Michelle Ye Hen Lee and Michael Kiefer, Maricopa County Supervisors Settle Lawsuits Filed by 'New Times' Founders, Stapley, The Ariz. Republic, Dec. 20, 2013.

Punishing Publication of False Speech. The statutes declared unconstitutional in *Landmark* and *Daily Mail* would have punished the publication of true information. May a statute punish the press for publishing false information that is not defamatory? The answer to that question is intimated by the Supreme Court's decision in United States v. Alvarez, 132 S.Ct. 2537 (2012), also noted in Chapter One.

Alvarez claimed he had played hockey for the Detroit Red Wings, married a starlet in Mexico, served 25 years in the Marine Corps, and won the Congressional Medal of Honor. He made these statements while introducing himself at his first meeting as a board member of local water district in California. All were lies: he had never even served in the military. He was convicted under the federal Stolen Valor Act, which makes it a misdemeanor to falsely claim to have received a military honor authorized by Congress. The Ninth Circuit held the statute unconstitutional, and the Supreme Court agreed in a 6–3 decision.

Justice Kennedy, writing for a plurality also including Justices Ginsburg, Sotomayor, and Chief Justice Roberts viewed the statute as a content-based restriction on speech and applied strict scrutiny. Their opinion proceeded from the proposition that there is no categorical rule exempting falsehoods from First Amendment protection. The plurality conceded that the government had compelling interests in protecting the integrity of the military honors system, but said there must be "a direct causal link between the restriction imposed and the injury to be prevented." They also stated that the government presented no evidence that public perception of military awards was diluted by false claims such as Alvarez's, and that the government presented no evidence that counterspeech could not refute the lie. "Only a weak society needs government protection or intervention before it pursues its resolve to preserve the truth," they wrote. "Truth needs neither handcuffs nor a badge for its vindication."

Justices Breyer and Kagan concurred in the judgment, but on the ground that the statute could not survive even intermediate scrutiny. They said laws restricting false speech about philosophy, religion, history, social sciences and the arts may require strict scrutiny, but restrictions on deliberate falsehoods about easily verifiable facts require only intermediate scrutiny. Even under intermediate scrutiny, the statute was unconstitutional because the government's objectives could be served by less restrictive means. Congress could tailor the act more narrowly, by requiring a showing that the lie caused actual harm, or limiting it to statements made in contexts where harm was likely.

Both the plurality opinion and the concurrence suggested that the government could protect the integrity of military honors by compiling a readily available database of legitimate honor winners so imposters could be easily exposed. In dissent, Justices Alito, Thomas, and Scalia questioned whether that alternative was workable, noting testimony that the Defense Department has been unable to compile a comprehensive list of recipients before 2001. The dissenters contended that false statements enjoy no First Amendment protection unless it is necessary to protect them to avoid chilling truthful speech. "[T]he Stolen Valor Act presents no risk at all that valuable speech will be suppressed."

———

D. INDIRECT BURDENS

The cases in the preceding section all involved criminal statutes; the consequence of violation was a fine or imprisonment. But legislatures often attempt to achieve their objectives through other types of sanctions. When those sanctions have the effect of penalizing the exercise of speech and press rights, the Supreme Court long ago recognized that they too raise First Amendment problems.

1. ACCESS

The marketplace-of-ideas theory of the First Amendment has long been questioned by people who believe that concentration of ownership in the media industries has destroyed whatever marketplace may have existed when the First Amendment was adopted. A leading modern proponent of that view is Professor Jerome Barron. He believes the marketplace of ideas is an antiquated concept because the media and society have changed so much since 1791. It is difficult for a person to begin a newspaper because of the prohibitive cost or to begin a broadcast service because of licensing restrictions. Barron sees the media as censors because they limit the views they disseminate and permit few new or unpopular ideas to be heard widely. Barron concludes that those who do not control media should be able to express their views through the mass media. "At the very minimum," Barron writes, "the creation of two remedies is essential—(1) a nondiscriminating right to purchase editorial advertisements in daily newspapers, and (2) a right of reply for public figures and public officers defamed in newspapers." Jerome A. Barron, *Freedom of the Press for Whom?* 6 (1975). See also Jerome A. Barron, *Access to the Press—A New First Amendment Right*, 80 Harv. L. Rev. 1641 (1967).

Barron had an opportunity to try to persuade the Supreme Court to make his ideas the law. He represented Pat Tornillo, the litigant seeking access to the press, in the case that follows.

Miami Herald Publishing Co. v. Tornillo
Supreme Court of the United States, 1974.
418 U.S. 241.

■ MR. CHIEF JUSTICE BURGER delivered the opinion of the Court.

The issue in this case is whether a state statute granting a political candidate a right to equal space to reply to criticism and attacks on his record by a newspaper, violates the guarantees of a free press.

I.

In the fall of 1972, appellee, Executive Director of the Classroom Teachers Association, apparently a teachers' collective bargaining agent, was a candidate for the Florida House of Representatives. On September 20, 1972, and again on September 29, 1972, appellant printed editorials critical of appellee's candidacy. In response to these editorials appellee demanded that appellant print verbatim his replies, defending the role of the Classroom Teachers Association and the organization's accomplishments for the citizens of Dade County. Appellant declined to print the appellee's replies, and appellee brought suit in Circuit Court, Dade County, seeking declaratory and injunctive relief and actual and punitive damages in excess of $5,000. The action was premised on Florida Statute § 104.38 (1973), a "right of reply" statute. . . .[2]

[Appellant sought a declaration that § 104.38 was unconstitutional. The Circuit Court held that the section violated both the state and federal constitutions. On direct appeal, the Florida Supreme Court reversed, holding that the statute furthered the "broad societal interest in the free flow of information to the public." It also held that the statute is not impermissibly vague because it informs "those who are subject to it as to

---

[2] "104.38 *Newspaper Assailing Candidate in an Election; Space for Reply.* If any newspaper in its columns assails the personal character of any candidate for nomination or for election in any election, or charges said candidate with malfeasance or misfeasance in office, or otherwise attacks his official record, or gives to another free space for such purpose, such newspaper shall upon request of such candidate immediately publish free of cost any reply he may make thereto in as conspicuous a place and in the same kind of type as the matter that calls for such reply, provided such reply does not take up more space than the matter replied to. Any person or firm failing to comply with the provisions of this section shall be guilty of a misdemeanor of the first degree, punishable as provided in § 775.082 or § 775.083."

what conduct on their part will render them liable to its penalties." Civil remedies, including damages, were held to be available under this statute. The Florida Supreme Court narrowed the statute by construing "any reply" to mean a reply "wholly responsive to the charge made," and said the reply must be "neither libelous nor slanderous of the publication nor anyone else, nor vulgar nor profane." The case was remanded for further proceedings accordingly.]

. . .

III.

A.

The challenged statute creates a right to reply to press criticism of a candidate for nomination or election. The statute was enacted in 1913, and this is only the second recorded case decided under its provisions.

Appellant contends the statute is void on its face because it purports to regulate the content of a newspaper in violation of the First Amendment. Alternatively it is urged that the statute is void for vagueness since no editor could know exactly what words would call the statute into operation. It is also contended that the statute fails to distinguish between critical comment which is and which is not defamatory.

B.

[In this section the Court "set out in some detail" virtually every argument made by proponents of access to the media. The Court noted that access advocates argued that in 1791 "[a] true marketplace of ideas existed in which there was relatively easy access to the channels of communication" but at the time *Tornillo* came before the Court concentration of ownership in the media industry, the "elimination of competing newspapers in most of our large cities," and other technological and economic developments had "place[d] in a few hands the power to inform the American people and shape public opinion." The increasing power and influence of the media had also deprived the public of meaningful participation in public debate. The Court summarized the historical and economic arguments of access advocates as follows:]

> It is urged that the claim of newspapers to be "surrogates for the public" carries with it a concomitant fiduciary obligation to account for that stewardship. From this premise it is reasoned that the only effective way to insure fairness and accuracy and to provide for some accountability is for government to take affirmative action.

[The Court then reviewed legal arguments supporting enforced access:

—Associated Press v. United States, 326 U.S. 1 (1945) (upholding enforcement of antitrust laws against news service, and noting that the First Amendment "rests on the assumption that the widest possible dissemination of information from diverse and antagonistic sources is essential to the welfare of the public;" freedom of the press "does not sanction repression of that freedom by private interests").

—New York Times Co. v. Sullivan, 376 U.S. 254 (1964) (in limiting state libel law the Court spoke of a "profound national commitment to the principle that debate on public issues should be uninhibited, robust, and wide-open").

—Rosenbloom v. Metromedia, Inc., 403 U.S. 29 (1971) (plurality opinion in libel case asserts that if states "fear that private citizens will not be able to respond adequately to publicity involving them, the solution lies in the direction of ensuring their ability to respond, rather than in stifling public discussion of matters of public concern"—and observing that "some states have adopted retraction statutes or right-of-reply statutes").

—Passages from books or articles by Justice Douglas (expressing "deep concern" regarding the effects of newspaper monopolies), Professor Barron (his previously cited writings) and Professor Emerson (contending that a "limited right of access to the press can be safely enforced," but preferring "[g]overnment measures to encourage a multiplicity of outlets, rather than compelling a few outlets to represent everybody").]

IV.

However much validity may be found in these arguments, at each point the implementation of a remedy such as an enforceable right of access necessarily calls for some mechanism, either governmental or consensual. If it is governmental coercion, this at once brings about a confrontation with the express provisions of the First Amendment and the judicial gloss on that Amendment developed over the years.

The Court foresaw the problems relating to government-enforced access as early as its decision in Associated Press v. United States. There it carefully contrasted the private "compulsion to print" called for by the Association's bylaws with the provisions of the District Court decree against appellants which "does not compel AP or its members to permit publication of anything which their 'reason' tells them should not be published." 326 U.S., at 20 n. 18. In Branzburg v. Hayes, 408 U.S. 665, 681 (1972), we emphasized that the cases then before us "involve no intrusions upon speech or assembly, no prior restraint or restriction on what the press may publish, and no express or implied command that the press publish what it prefers to withhold." In Columbia Broadcasting System, Inc. v. Democratic National Committee, 412 U.S. 94, 117 (1973), the plurality opinion as to Part III noted:

"The power of a privately owned newspaper to advance its own political, social, and economic views is bounded by only two factors: first, the acceptance of a sufficient number of readers—

and hence advertisers—to assure financial success; and, second, the journalistic integrity of its editors and publishers."

An attitude strongly adverse to any attempt to extend a right of access to newspapers was echoed by several Members of this Court in their separate opinions in that case. Id., at 145 (Stewart, J., concurring); id., at 182 n. 12 (Brennan, J., dissenting). Recently, while approving a bar against employment advertising specifying "male" or "female" preference, the Court's opinion in Pittsburgh Press Co. v. Human Relations Comm'n, 413 U.S. 376, 391 (1973), took pains to limit its holding within narrow bounds:

> "Nor, *a fortiori,* does our decision authorize any restriction whatever, whether of content or layout, on stories or commentary originated by Pittsburgh Press, its columnists, or its contributors. On the contrary, we reaffirm unequivocally the protection afforded to editorial judgment and to the free expression of views on these and other issues, however controversial."

Dissenting in *Pittsburgh Press*, Mr. Justice Stewart, joined by Mr. Justice Douglas, expressed the view that no "government agency—local, state, or federal—can tell a newspaper in advance what it can print and what it cannot." [ ]

We see that beginning with *Associated Press*, supra, the Court has expressed sensitivity as to whether a 'restriction or requirement constituted the compulsion exerted by government on a newspaper to print that which it would not otherwise print. The clear implication has been that any such compulsion to publish that which " 'reason' tells them should not be published" is unconstitutional. A responsible press is an undoubtedly desirable goal, but press responsibility is not mandated by the Constitution and like many other virtues it cannot be legislated.

Appellee's argument that the Florida statute does not amount to a restriction of appellant's right to speak because "the statute in question here has not prevented the Miami Herald from saying anything it wished" begs the core question. Compelling editors or publishers to publish that which " 'reason' tells them should not be published" is what is at issue in this case. The Florida statute operates as a command in the same sense as a statute or regulation forbidding appellant to publish specified matter. Governmental restraint on publishing need not fall into familiar or traditional patterns to be subject to constitutional limitations on governmental powers. Grosjean v. American Press Co., 297 U.S. 233, 244–45 (1936). The Florida statute exacts a penalty on the basis of the content of a newspaper. The first phase of the penalty resulting from the compelled printing of a reply is exacted in terms of the cost in printing and composing time and materials and in taking up space that could be devoted to other material the newspaper may have preferred to print. It is correct, as appellee contends, that a newspaper is not subject to the finite technological limitations of time that confront a broadcaster but it is not correct to say that, as an economic reality, a newspaper can proceed to infinite expansion of its column space to accommodate the replies that a government agency determines or a statute commands the readers should have available.

Faced with the penalties that would accrue to any newspaper that published news or commentary arguably within the reach of the right-of-access statute, editors might well conclude that the safe course is to avoid controversy. Therefore, under the operation of the Florida statute, political and electoral coverage would be blunted or reduced. Government-enforced right of access inescapably "dampens the vigor and limits the variety of public debate," New York Times Co. v. Sullivan, supra, 376 U.S. at 279. The Court, in Mills v. Alabama, 384 U.S. 214, 218 (1966) stated:

> "[T]here is practically universal agreement that a major purpose of [the First] Amendment was to protect the free discussion of governmental affairs. This of course includes discussions of candidates. . . ."

Even if a newspaper would face no additional costs to comply with a compulsory access law and would not be forced to forgo publication of news or opinion by the inclusion of a reply, the Florida statute fails to clear the barriers of the First Amendment because of its intrusion into the function of editors. A newspaper is more than a passive receptacle or conduit for news, comment, and advertising. The choice of material to go into a newspaper, and the decisions made as to limitations on the size and content of the paper, and treatment of public issues and public officials—whether fair or unfair—constitute the exercise of editorial control and judgment. It has yet to be demonstrated how governmental regulation of this crucial process can be exercised consistent with First Amendment guarantees of a free press as they have evolved to this time. Accordingly, the judgment of the Supreme Court of Florida is reversed.

It is so ordered.

■ MR. JUSTICE BRENNAN, with whom MR. JUSTICE REHNQUIST joins, concurring.

I join the Court's opinion which, as I understand it, addresses only "right of reply" statutes and implies no view upon the constitutionality of "retraction" statutes affording plaintiffs able to prove defamatory falsehoods a statutory action to require publication of a retraction. See generally Note, Vindication of the Reputation of a Public Official, 80 Harv. L. Rev. 1730, 1739–1747 (1967).

■ MR. JUSTICE WHITE, concurring.

. . . A newspaper or magazine is not a public utility subject to "reasonable" governmental regulation in matters affecting the exercise of journalistic judgment as to what shall be printed. [ ]. We have learned, and continue to learn, from what we view as the unhappy experiences of other nations where government has been allowed to meddle in the internal editorial affairs of newspapers. Regardless of how beneficent-sounding the purposes of controlling the press might be, we prefer "the power of reason as applied through public discussion" and remain intensely skeptical about those measures that would allow government to insinuate itself into the editorial rooms of this Nation's press.

. . .

To justify this statute, Florida advances a concededly important interest of ensuring free and fair elections by means of an electorate informed about the issues. But prior compulsion by government in matters going to the very nerve center of a newspaper—the decision as to what copy will or will not be included in any given edition—collides with the First Amendment. Woven into the fabric of the First Amendment is the unexceptionable, but nonetheless timeless, sentiment that "liberty of the press is in peril as soon as the government tries to compel what is to go into a newspaper." 2 Z. Chafee, Government and Mass Communications 633 (1947).

. . . [T]his law runs afoul of the elementary First Amendment proposition that government may not force a newspaper to print copy which, in its journalistic discretion, it chooses to leave on the newsroom floor. . . .

NOTES AND QUESTIONS

1.   The Court maintains that the statute penalizes newspapers that publish material that might trigger a right of reply. What is the penalty? Assume that the statute in *Tornillo* required the newspaper to accept Tornillo's reply as a paid advertisement at prevailing rates. Most papers try to maintain a certain ratio of advertising to news, so in the aggregate an increase in advertising generates an increase in news space. If the likely effect of the statute would be to increase the newspaper's revenues and allow it to increase the amount of space dedicated to news, would the statute still be unconstitutional? What if the statute required the newspaper to post Tornillo's reply only in the online version of its newspaper? Is the "intrusion into the function of editors" an independent ground of decision?

2.   Note that the Court does not ask whether Florida had a compelling interest in giving candidates a right of reply; the findings that the statute imposed a content-based penalty and interfered with the function of editors seem to have conclusively established its unconstitutionality. In this respect, it resembles Mills v. Alabama. Note that *Mills* and *Tornillo* both predated *Landmark* and *Daily Mail*, the cases in which the Court first applied something resembling the compelling interest test.

3.   Professor Sunstein suggests that claims for access are strengthened by recognition that a newspaper's power to exclude people who want to write for it is largely the result of legal entitlements, such as the law of trespass which

enables the newspaper to deny people access to its facilities. "The system [of protection for speech] in a regime of property rights may well be fine or even wonderful; but it should be assessed in terms of its consequences for speech." Cass R. Sunstein, Democracy and the Problem of Free Speech (Free Press 1995).

4.   Access proponents sometimes argue that a right of access to media can be implied from the First Amendment itself. In *Tornillo*, it was unnecessary to make that argument because the right had been created by the legislature, and the judiciary was being asked to uphold the statute rather than to create a new right at the constitutional level. Does the decision leave any room for the argument based on an implied First Amendment right?

———

2. FINANCIAL DISINCENTIVES

Simon & Schuster, Inc. v. New York State Crime Victims Board

Supreme Court of the United States, 1991.
502 U.S. 105.

■ JUSTICE O'CONNOR delivered the opinion of the Court:

[A New York statute required that an accused or convicted criminal's income from works describing his crime be deposited in an escrow account. These funds were then made available to the victims of the crime and the criminal's other creditors; if not claimed within five years the criminal could recover the funds. The statute had been inspired by fears that serial killer David Berkowitz, nicknamed "Son of Sam" by the press, might reap a windfall profit by selling his story. The statute, popularly known as the Son of Sam law, was one of several ways in which the state sought to obtain compensation for crime victims and their families.

Simon & Schuster published a book called "Wiseguy" about the criminal career of an organized crime figure named Henry Hill. The book sold over a million copies and was made into a movie called "Goodfellas." The Board invoked the Son of Sam statute and ordered Simon & Schuster to turn over all money payable to Hill. Instead, Simon & Schuster sought a declaration that the Son of Sam law violated the First Amendment and an injunction barring its enforcement. The district court found the statute to be consistent with the First Amendment and granted the Board's motion for summary judgment. The Court of Appeals affirmed.]

II.   [A.]

A statute is presumptively inconsistent with the First Amendment if it imposes a financial burden on speakers because of the content of their speech. . . .

This is a notion so engrained in our First Amendment jurisprudence that last Term we found it so "obvious" as to not require explanation. [ ]

It is but one manifestation of a far broader principle: "Regulations which permit the Government to discriminate on the basis of the content of the message cannot be tolerated under the First Amendment." . . . [T]he government's ability to impose content-based burdens on speech raises the specter that the government may effectively drive certain ideas or viewpoints from the marketplace. [ ]

The Son of Sam law is such a content-based statute. It singles out income derived from expressive activity for a burden the State places on no other income, and it is directed only at works with a specified content. Whether the First Amendment "speaker" is considered to be Henry Hill, whose income the statute places in escrow because of the story he has told, or Simon & Schuster, which can publish books about crime with the assistance of only those criminals willing to forgo remuneration for at least five years, the statute plainly imposes a financial disincentive only on speech of a particular content.

. . .

The Son of Sam law establishes a financial disincentive to create or publish works with a particular content. In order to justify such differential treatment, "the State must show that its regulation is necessary to serve a compelling state interest and is narrowly drawn to achieve that end." Arkansas Writers' Project [v. Ragland, 481 U.S. 221, 231 (1987)].

B

The Board disclaims, as it must, any state interest in suppressing descriptions of crime out of solicitude for the sensibilities of readers. [ ] As we have often had occasion to repeat: " '[T]he fact that society may find speech offensive is not a sufficient reason for suppressing it. Indeed, if it is the speaker's opinion that gives offense, that consequence is a reason for according it constitutional protection.' " . . . The Board thus does not assert any interest in limiting whatever anguish Henry Hill's victims may suffer from reliving their victimization.

There can be little doubt, on the other hand, that the State has a compelling interest in ensuring that victims of crime are compensated by those who harm them. Every State has a body of tort law serving exactly this interest. The State's interest in preventing wrongdoers from dissipating their assets before victims can recover explains the existence of the State's statutory provisions for prejudgment remedies and orders of restitution. . . .

The State likewise has an undisputed compelling interest in ensuring that criminals do not profit from their crimes. Like most if not all States, New York has long recognized the "fundamental equitable principle," [ ] that "[n]o one shall be permitted to profit by his own fraud, or to take advantage of his own wrong, or to found any claim upon his own iniquity, or to acquire property by his own crime." [ ] The force of this interest is evidenced by the State's statutory provisions for the forfeiture of the proceeds and instrumentalities of crime. [ ]

The parties debate whether book royalties can properly be termed the profits of crime, but that is a question we need not address here. For the purposes of this case, we can assume without deciding that the income escrowed by the Son of Sam law represents the fruits of crime. We need only conclude that the State has a compelling interest in depriving criminals of the profits of their crimes, and in using these funds to compensate victims.

The Board attempts to define the State's interest more narrowly, as "ensuring that criminals do not profit from storytelling about their crimes before their victims have a meaningful opportunity to be compensated for their injuries." [ ] Here the Board is on far shakier ground. The Board cannot explain why the State should have any greater interest in compensating victims from the proceeds of such "storytelling" than from any of the criminal's other assets. Nor can the Board offer any justification for a distinction between this expressive activity and any other activity in connection with its interest in transferring the fruits of crime from criminals to their victims. Thus even if the State can be said to have an interest in classifying a criminal's assets in this manner, that interest is hardly compelling.

    . . .

[T]he Board has taken the *effect* of the statute and posited that effect as the State's interest. If accepted, this sort of circular defense can sidestep judicial review of almost any statute, because it makes all statutes look narrowly tailored. As Judge Newman pointed out in his dissent from the opinion of the Court of Appeals, such an argument "eliminates the entire inquiry concerning the validity of content-based discriminations. Every content-based discrimination could be upheld by simply observing that the state is anxious to regulate the designated category of speech." [ ]

In short, the State has a compelling interest in compensating victims from the fruits of the crime, but little if any interest in limiting such compensation to the proceeds of the wrongdoer's speech about the crime. We must therefore determine whether the Son of Sam law is narrowly tailored to advance the former, not the latter, objective.

C

As a means of ensuring that victims are compensated from the proceeds of crime, the Son of Sam law is significantly overinclusive. As counsel for the Board conceded at oral argument, the statute applies to works on *any* subject, provided that they express the author's thoughts or recollections about his crime, however tangentially or incidentally. [ ] In addition, the statute's broad definition of "person convicted of a crime" enables the Board to escrow the income of any author who admits in his work to having committed a crime, whether or not the author was ever actually accused or convicted. [ ]

These two provisions combine to encompass a potentially very large number of works. Had the Son of Sam law been in effect at the time and place of publication, it would have escrowed payment for such works as The Autobiography of Malcolm X, which describes crimes committed by the civil rights leader before he became a public figure; Civil Disobedience, in which Thoreau acknowledges his refusal to pay taxes and recalls his experience in jail; and even the Confessions of Saint Augustine, in which the author laments "my past foulness and the carnal corruptions of my soul," one instance of which involved the theft of pears from a neighboring vineyard. [ ] *Amicus* Association of American Publishers, Inc., has submitted a sobering bibliography listing hundreds of works by American prisoners and ex-prisoners, many of which contain descriptions of the crimes for which the authors were incarcerated, including works by such authors as Emma Goldman and Martin Luther King, Jr. A list of prominent figures whose autobiographies would be subject to the statute if written is not difficult to construct: The list could include Sir Walter Raleigh, who was convicted of treason after a dubiously conducted 1603 trial; Jesse Jackson, who was arrested in 1963 for trespass and resisting arrest after attempting to be served at a lunch counter in North Carolina; and Bertrand Russell, who was jailed for seven days at the age of 89 for participating in a sit-down protest against nuclear weapons. The argument that a statute like the Son of Sam law would prevent publication of *all* of these works is hyperbole—some would have been written without compensation—but the Son of Sam law clearly reaches a wide range of literature that does not enable a criminal to profit from his crime while a victim remains uncompensated.

Should a prominent figure write his autobiography at the end of his career, and include in an early chapter a brief recollection of having stolen (in New York) a nearly worthless item as a youthful prank, the Board would control his entire income from the book for five years, and would make that income available to all of the author's creditors, despite the fact that the statute of limitations for this minor incident had long since run. That the Son of Sam law can produce such an outcome indicates that the statute is, to say the least, not narrowly tailored to achieve the State's objective of compensating crime victims from the profits of crime.

III

. . . The State's interest in compensating victims from the fruits of crime is a compelling one, but the Son of Sam law is not narrowly tailored to advance that objective. As a result, the statute is inconsistent with the First Amendment.

The judgment of the Court of Appeals is accordingly

Reversed.

■ JUSTICE KENNEDY, concurring in the judgment.

The New York statute we now consider imposes severe restrictions on authors and publishers, using as its sole criterion the content of what is written. The regulated content has the full protection of the First Amendment and this, I submit, is itself a full and sufficient reason for holding the statute unconstitutional. In my view it is both unnecessary and incorrect to ask whether the State can show that the statute " 'is necessary to serve a compelling state interest and is narrowly drawn to achieve that end.' " [ ] That test or formulation derives from our equal protection jurisprudence, [ ] and has no real or legitimate place when the Court considers the straightforward question whether the State may enact a burdensome restriction of speech based on content only, apart from any considerations of time, place, and manner or the use of public forums.

Here, a law is directed to speech alone where the speech in question is not obscene, not defamatory, not words tantamount to an act otherwise criminal, not an impairment of some other constitutional right, not an incitement to lawless action, and not calculated or likely to bring about imminent harm the State has the substantive power to prevent. No further inquiry is necessary to reject the State's argument that the statute should be upheld.

Borrowing the compelling interest and narrow tailoring analysis is ill advised when all that is at issue is a content-based restriction, for resort to the test might be read as a concession that States may censor speech whenever they believe there is a compelling justification for doing so. Our precedents and traditions allow no such inference.

This said, it must be acknowledged that the compelling interest inquiry has found its way into our First Amendment jurisprudence of late, even where the sole question is, or ought to be, whether the restriction is in fact content based. Although the notion that protected speech may be restricted on the basis of content if the restriction survives what has sometimes been termed " 'the most exacting scrutiny,' " [ ] may seem familiar, the Court appears to have adopted this formulation in First Amendment cases by accident rather than as the result of a considered judgment. . . .

. . .

The inapplicability of the compelling interest test to content-based restrictions on speech is demonstrated by our repeated statement that "above all else, the First Amendment means that government has no power to restrict expression because of its message, its ideas, its subject matter, or its content." [ ] These general statements about the government's lack of power to engage in content discrimination reflect a surer basis for protecting speech than does the test used by the Court today.

There are a few legal categories in which content-based regulation has been permitted or at least contemplated. These include obscenity, see, e.g., Miller v. California, defamation, see, e.g., Dun & Bradstreet, Inc. v. Greenmoss Builders, Inc. , incitement, see, e.g., Brandenburg v. Ohio, or situations presenting some grave and imminent danger the government has the power to prevent, see, *e.g., Near.* These are, however, historic and traditional categories long familiar to the bar, although with respect to the last category it is most difficult for the government to prevail. See New York Times Co. v. United States. While it cannot be said with certainty that the foregoing types of expression are or will remain the only ones that are without First Amendment protection . . . the use of these traditional legal categories is preferable to the sort of ad hoc balancing that the Court henceforth must perform in every case if the analysis here used becomes our standard test.

. . .

With these observations, I concur in the judgment of the Court holding the statute invalid.

[Justice Thomas did not participate. An opinion by Justice Blackmun concurring in the judgment is omitted.]

NOTES AND QUESTIONS

1.   The observation that the Son of Sam law was content-based looms large in the majority's analysis and even larger in the concurrence's. The term is used to distinguish restrictions that target the substance of the speech from those that target aspects of speech other than its substance; these are called "content neutral." We will explore this distinction in Chapter Three.

2.   Justice Kennedy says the determination that the regulation is content-based means it is unconstitutional except in "a few legal categories in which content-based regulation has been permitted." The majority says it only means that the regulation must survive the compelling-interest analysis. Which view is supported by *Daily Mail* and *Landmark*? Despite Justice Kennedy's objection, the approach employed by the majority has become the usual method of analyzing content-based restrictions.

3.   Is the compelling-interest test employed by the majority merely an elaboration of *Daily Mail*'s requirement that the state show "a need to further a state interest of the highest order"? Even if there is no appreciable difference between "an interest of the highest order" and "a compelling interest," might there be a substantial difference between proving "a need" and proving that the restriction is "narrowly drawn" to achieve the state's goal? Notwithstanding this possible difference, the compelling-interest test is sometimes called the *Daily Mail* test.

4.   The compelling-interest test is often described as "strict scrutiny." The test is so difficult to meet that it has been said (albeit in a different context) that it is " 'strict' in theory, and fatal in fact." Gerald Gunther, The Supreme Court 1971 Term—Foreword: In Search of Evolving Doctrine on a Changing

Court: A Model for a Newer Equal Protection, 86 Harv. L. Rev. 1, 8 (1972). If that is true, might Justice Kennedy's approach be preferred on the ground that it avoids the need for futile attempts by the state to meet the compelling-interest test?

———

3. TAXATION

Concern about taxation of the press has played a role in American constitutional thought from the beginning. The Stamp Act of 1765, imposed upon the colonies by Parliament to help pay the cost of maintaining a British army on American soil, levied a tax on newspapers, books, pamphlets, and documents. It was one of the most hated of all the measures imposed on the colonies by England, and helped to catalyze American demands for independence. It forced American printers to take sides in the growing conflict between Tories and Patriots and thus helped mold the press into a powerful voice for independence.

It cannot be said that the First Amendment was specifically intended to prevent special taxes on the press, because the Framers left no record that they ever discussed the matter. But it is clear that the First Amendment was enacted against a historical background that saw such taxes as a potential threat to freedom of the press. That history is fully developed in Randall P. Bezanson, Taxes on Knowledge in America (Univ. of Penn. Press 1994). Beginning in the 1980s, the Supreme Court decided a series of tax challenges by the media. The decisions are summarized in the case that follows.

Leathers v. Medlock
Supreme Court of the United States, 1991.
499 U.S. 439.

[Arkansas applied its general sales tax to cable television services but exempted newspapers, magazines, and home antenna satellite services. Cable interests challenged the tax on First Amendment grounds. While the litigation was pending, the legislature amended the tax statute to bring satellite services under the tax but continued to exempt newspapers and magazines. The Arkansas Supreme Court held that the discrimination that had existed between cable services and satellite services violated the First Amendment because those were substantially the same medium, but the continuing discrimination between different media, such as cable and print, was constitutional.

The Supreme Court granted both sides' petitions for certiorari and held that the tax system did not violate the First Amendment when it taxed only cable and satellite services, or even when it taxed cable alone. The case was remanded to the Arkansas Supreme Court, however, for consideration of the cable operators' claim that the tax statute violated the equal protection clause during the period when it taxed cable operators but exempted satellite services. (On remand, the Arkansas Supreme Court rejected the equal protection claim. 842 S.W.2d 428 (Ark. 1992).)]

■ JUSTICE O'CONNOR delivered the opinion of the Court.

. . .

Cable television provides to its subscribers news, information, and entertainment. It is engaged in "speech" under the First Amendment, and is, in much of its operation, part of the "press." [ ] That it is taxed differently from other media does not by itself, however, raise First Amendment concerns. Our cases have held that a tax that discriminates among speakers is constitutionally suspect only in certain circumstances.

In Grosjean v. American Press Co., 297 U.S. 233 (1936), the Court considered a First Amendment challenge to a Louisiana law that singled out publications with weekly circulations above 20,000 for a 2% tax on gross receipts from advertising. The tax fell exclusively on 13 newspapers. Four other daily newspapers and 120 weekly newspapers with weekly circulations of less than 20,000 were not taxed. The Court discussed at length the pre-First Amendment English and American tradition of taxes imposed exclusively on the press. This invidious form of censorship was intended to curtail the circulation of newspapers and thereby prevent the people from acquiring knowledge of government activities. [ ] The Court held that the tax at issue in *Grosjean* was of this type, and was therefore unconstitutional. [ ]

In Minneapolis Star & Tribune Co. v. Minnesota Comm'r of Revenue, 460 U.S. 575 (1983), we noted that it was unclear whether the result in *Grosjean* depended on our perception in that case that the State had imposed the tax with the intent to penalize a selected group of newspapers or whether the structure of the tax was sufficient to invalidate it. [ ] *Minneapolis Star* resolved any doubts about whether direct evidence of improper censorial motive is required in order to invalidate a differential tax on First Amendment grounds: "Illicit legislative intent is not the *sine qua non* of a violation of the First Amendment." [ ]

At issue in *Minneapolis Star* was a Minnesota special use tax on the cost of paper and ink consumed in the production of publications. The tax exempted the first $100,000 worth of paper and ink consumed annually. Eleven publishers, producing only 14 of the State's 388 paid circulation newspapers, incurred liability under the tax in its first year of operation. The Minneapolis Star and Tribune Company (Star Tribune) was responsible for roughly two-thirds of the total revenue raised by the tax. The following year, 13 publishers, producing only 16 of the State's 374 paid circulation papers, paid the tax. Again, the Star Tribune bore roughly two-thirds of the tax's burden. We found no evidence of impermissible legislative motive in the case apart from the structure of the tax itself.

We nevertheless held the Minnesota tax unconstitutional for two reasons. First, the tax singled out the press for special treatment. We noted that the general applicability of any burdensome tax law helps to ensure that it will be met with widespread opposition. When such a law applies only to a single constituency, however, it is insulated from this political constraint. [ ] Given "the basic assumption of our political system that the press will often serve as an important restraint on government," we feared that the threat of exclusive taxation of the press could operate "as effectively as a censor to check critical comment." [ ] "Differential taxation of the press, then, places such a burden on the interests protected by the First Amendment," that it is presumptively unconstitutional. [ ]

Beyond singling out the press, the Minnesota tax targeted a small group of newspapers—those so large that they remained subject to the tax despite its exemption for the first $100,000 of ink and paper consumed annually. The tax thus resembled a penalty for certain newspapers. Once again, the scheme appeared to have such potential for abuse that we concluded that it violated the First Amendment: "[W]hen the exemption selects such a narrowly defined group to bear the full burden of the tax, the tax begins to resemble more a penalty for a few of the largest newspapers than an attempt to favor struggling smaller enterprises." [ ]

Arkansas Writers' Project, Inc. v. Ragland, 481 U.S. 221 (1987), reaffirmed the rule that selective taxation of the press through the narrow targeting of individual members offends the First Amendment. In that case, Arkansas Writers' Project sought a refund of state taxes it had paid on sales of the Arkansas Times, a general interest magazine, under Arkansas' Gross Receipts Act of 1941. Exempt from the sales tax were receipts from sales of religious, professional, trade and sports magazines. [ ] We held that Arkansas' magazine exemption, which meant that only "a few Arkansas magazines pay any sales tax," operated in much the same way as did the $100,000 exemption in *Minneapolis Star* and therefore suffered from the same type of discrimination identified in that case. [ ] Moreover, the basis on which the tax differentiated among magazines depended entirely on their content. [ ]

These cases demonstrate that differential taxation of First Amendment speakers is constitutionally suspect when it threatens to suppress the expression of particular ideas or viewpoints. Absent a compelling justification, the government may not exercise its taxing power to single out the press. See *Grosjean*, [ ]; *Minneapolis Star*, [ ]. The press plays a unique role as a check on government abuse, and a tax limited to the press raises concerns about censorship of critical information and opinion. A tax is also suspect if it targets a small group of speakers. See *Minneapolis Star*, [ ]; *Arkansas Writers'*, [ ]. Again, the fear is censorship of particular ideas or viewpoints. Finally, for reasons that are obvious, a tax will trigger heightened scrutiny under the First Amendment if it discriminates on the basis of the content of taxpayer speech. [ ]

The Arkansas tax at issue here presents none of these types of discrimination. The Arkansas sales tax is a tax of general applicability. It applies to receipts from the sale of all tangible personal property and a broad range of services, unless within a group of specific exemptions. Among the services on which the tax is imposed are natural gas, electricity, water, ice, and steam utility services; telephone, telecommunications, and telegraph service; the furnishing of rooms by hotels, apartment hotels, lodging houses, and tourist camps; alteration, addition, cleaning, refinishing, replacement, and repair services; printing of all kinds; tickets for admission to places of amusement or athletic, entertainment, or recreational events; and fees for the privilege of having access to or use of amusement, entertainment, athletic, or recreational facilities. [ ] The tax does not single out the press and does not therefore threaten to hinder the press as a watchdog of government activity. We have said repeatedly that a State may impose on the press a generally applicable tax. [ ]

Furthermore, there is no indication in this case that Arkansas has targeted cable television in a purposeful attempt to interfere with its First Amendment activities. Nor is the tax one that is structured so as to raise suspicion that it was intended to do so. Unlike the taxes involved in *Grosjean* and *Minneapolis Star*, the Arkansas tax has not selected a narrow group to bear fully the burden of the tax.

The tax is also structurally dissimilar to the tax involved in *Arkansas Writers'*. In that case, only "a few" Arkansas magazines paid the State's sales tax. [ ] Arkansas Writers' Project maintained before the Court that the Arkansas Times was the only Arkansas publication that paid sales tax. The Commissioner contended that two additional periodicals also paid the tax. We responded that, "[w]hether there are three Arkansas magazines paying tax or only one, the burden of the tax clearly falls on a limited group of publishers." [ ] In contrast, [the statute in question] extended Arkansas' sales tax uniformly to the approximately 100 cable systems then operating in the State. [ ] While none of the seven scrambled satellite broadcast services then available in Arkansas [ ] was taxed until [the amendment] became effective, Arkansas' extension of its sales tax to cable television hardly resembles a "penalty for a few." [ ]

The danger from a tax scheme that targets a small number of speakers is the danger of censorship; a tax on a small number of speakers runs the risk of affecting only a limited range of views. The risk is similar to that from content-based regulation: it will distort the market for ideas. "The constitutional right of free expression is . . . intended to remove governmental restraints from the arena of public discussion, putting the decision as to what views shall be voiced largely into the hands of each of us . . . in the belief that no other approach would comport with the premise of individual dignity and choice upon which our political system rests." Cohen v. California, 403 U.S. 15, 24 (1971). There is no comparable danger from a tax on the services provided by a large number of cable operators offering a wide variety of programming throughout the State. That the Arkansas Supreme Court found cable and satellite television to be the same medium does not change this conclusion. Even if we accept this finding, the fact remains that the tax affected approximately 100 suppliers of cable television services. This is not a tax structure that resembles a penalty for particular speakers or particular ideas.

Finally, Arkansas' sales tax is not content based. There is nothing in the language of the statute that refers to the content of mass media communications. Moreover, the record establishes that cable television offers subscribers a variety of programming that presents a mixture of news, information, and entertainment. It contains no evidence, nor is it contended, that this material differs systematically in its message from that communicated by satellite broadcast programming, newspapers, or magazines.

Because the Arkansas sales tax presents none of the First Amendment difficulties that have led us to strike down differential taxation in the past, cable petitioners can prevail only if the Arkansas tax scheme presents "an additional basis" for concluding that the State has violated petitioners First Amendment rights. See *Arkansas Writers'*, [ ]. Petitioners argue that such a basis exists here: Arkansas' tax discriminates among media and, if the Arkansas Supreme Court's conclusion regarding cable and satellite television is accepted, discriminated for a time within a medium. Petitioners argue that such intermedia and intramedia discrimination, even in the absence of any evidence of intent to suppress speech or of any effect on the expression of particular ideas, violates the First Amendment. Our cases do not support such a rule.

. . .

[D]ifferential taxation of speakers, even members of the press, does not implicate the First Amendment unless the tax is directed at, or presents the danger of suppressing, particular ideas. That was the case in *Grosjean*, *Minneapolis Star*, and *Arkansas Writers'*, but it is not the case here. The Arkansas Legislature has chosen simply to exclude or exempt certain media from a generally applicable tax. Nothing about that choice has ever suggested an interest in censoring the expressive activities of cable television. Nor does anything in this record indicate that Arkansas' broad-based, content-neutral sales tax is likely to stifle the free exchange of ideas. We conclude that the State's extension of its generally applicable sales tax to cable television services alone, or to cable and satellite services, while exempting the print media, does not violate the First Amendment.

. . .

■ JUSTICE MARSHALL, with whom JUSTICE BLACKMUN joins, dissenting.

. . .

Our decisions on selective taxation establish a nondiscrimination principle for like-situated members of the press. Under this principle, "differential treatment, unless justified by some special characteristic of the press, . . . is presumptively unconstitutional," and must be struck down "unless the State asserts a counterbalancing interest of compelling importance that it cannot achieve without differential taxation." *Minneapolis Star*, [ ].

The nondiscrimination principle is an instance of government's general First Amendment obligation not to interfere with the press as an institution. As the Court explained in *Grosjean*, the purpose of the Free Press Clause "was to preserve an untrammeled press as a vital source of public information." [ ] Reviewing both the historical abuses associated with England's infamous " 'taxes on knowledge' " and the debates surrounding ratification of the Constitution, [ ] our decisions have recognized that the Framers viewed selective taxation as a distinctively potent "means of abridging the freedom of the press." [ ]

. . .

. . . If *Minneapolis Star, Arkansas Writers' Project*, and *Grosjean* stand for anything, it is that the "power to tax" does *not* include "the power to discriminate" when the press is involved. Nor is it the case under these decisions that a tax regime that singles out individual members of the press implicates the First Amendment *only* when it is "directed at, or presents the danger of suppressing, *particular* ideas." [ ] Even when structured in a manner that is content-neutral, a scheme that imposes differential burdens on like-situated members of the press violates the First Amendment because it poses *the risk* that the State might abuse this power. See *Minneapolis Star* [ ].

At a minimum, the majority incorrectly conflates our cases on selective taxation of the press and our cases on the selective taxation (or subsidization) of speech generally. *Regan* [v. Taxation With Representation, 461 U.S. 540 (1983)] holds that the government does not invariably violate the Free Speech Clause when it selectively subsidizes one group of speakers according to content-neutral criteria. This power, when exercised with appropriate restraint, inheres in government's legitimate authority to tap the energy of expressive activity to promote the public welfare. See Buckley v. Valeo [ ].

But our cases on the selective taxation of the *press* strike a different posture. Although the Free Press Clause does not guarantee the press a preferred position over other speakers, the Free Press Clause does "protec[t] [members of the press] from invidious discrimination." L. Tribe, American Constitutional Law § 12–20, p. 963 (2d ed. 1988). Selective taxation is precisely that. In light of the Framers' specific intent "to preserve an untrammeled press as a vital source of public information," [*Grosjean, Minneapolis Star*], our precedents recognize that the Free Press Clause imposes a special obligation on government to avoid disrupting the integrity of the information market. As Justice Stewart explained:

> "[T]he Free Press guarantee is, in essence, a *structural* provision of the Constitution. Most of the other provisions in the Bill of Rights protect specific liberties or specific rights of individuals: freedom of speech, freedom of worship, the right to counsel, the privilege against compulsory self-incrimination, to name a few. In contrast, the Free Press Clause extends protection to an institution." Stewart, "Or of the Press," [26 Hastings L.J. 631 (1975)]

Because they distort the competitive forces that animate this institution, tax differentials that fail to correspond to the social cost associated with different information media, and that are justified by nothing more than the State's desire for revenue, violate government's obligation of evenhandedness. Clearly, this is true of disproportionate taxation of cable television. Under the First Amendment, government simply has no business interfering with the process by which citizens' preferences for information formats evolve.

NOTES AND QUESTIONS

1. If a distinction between general interest magazines and sports magazines is content-based and a distinction between cable television and home satellite television is content-neutral, how would courts classify a statute that taxed newspapers distributed by home delivery and exempted those delivered by mail?

2. Why was it significant in *Minneapolis Star* that the tax targeted a few large newspapers? Is the potential for abuse greater there than where the tax targets a particular medium?

3. Would the cases preceding Leathers v. Medlock come out differently if the First Amendment contained the speech clause but no press clause? If they are press clause cases, how broadly does the concept of "press" reach? Would it reach discriminatory taxation of movies?

4. In an omitted portion of the majority opinion, Justice O'Connor writes that "Inherent in the power to tax is the power to discriminate." At least where speech is not involved, it is true that legislatures are allowed to discriminate without much explanation: railroads can be taxed differently than trucking companies, farm owners differently than small business owners, beer differently than wine. These differences unquestionably affect

the competitive positions of the taxpayers, and in some instances that is no doubt their purpose. May the legislature exempt a particular medium from taxation for the very purpose of enhancing its competitive position vis-à-vis competing media?

5.   Under the dissenters' "nondiscrimination principle for like-situated members of the press," which media would be considered like-situated? Might the state be required to justify such discrimination on the basis of differing social costs created by the media in question? Would the legislature be allowed to discriminate on the basis of asserted social costs or benefits that are content-related—for example, social costs and benefits of pornography as compared with those of news?

6.   In view of the Court's insistence in Citizens United v. FEC that the First Amendment offers no special protection to the press, should the taxation cases discussed in *Leathers* be viewed not as press-specific, but as applicable to any tax that treats some speakers differently than others? Since all taxpayers are speakers, is that principle unworkable?

Discrimination Among Different Types of Media. The most common form of intermedia tax discrimination is between newspapers, which often are exempted from sales taxes, and magazines, which usually are not. *Leathers* seems to permit that distinction, and some courts have so interpreted it. But just a few days after deciding *Leathers*, the Supreme Court denied certiorari in a Tennessee case, holding that it is unconstitutional to exempt newspapers from a sales tax but not magazines. See Newsweek, Inc. v. Celauro, 789 S.W.2d 247 (Tenn. 1990), cert. denied 499 U.S. 983 (1991) (Blackmun, J., dissenting).

The Pennsylvania Supreme Court, 4–2, affirmed a decision allowing magazines to be taxed when newspapers were not, but a dissenting opinion argued that the distinction violated the free press clause of the state constitution. The majority interpreted Leathers v. Medlock as permitting some media to be exempted from sales taxes when others are not, as long as the distinction is based on format rather than content. The dissenters did not address this First Amendment analysis, but said the Pennsylvania constitution provides broader protection for the press. That document, which was adopted in 1776 and thus predates the First Amendment, states that "the printing press shall be free to every person who may undertake to examine the proceedings of the Legislature or any branch of government, and no law shall ever be made to restrain the right thereof." The dissenters wrote that "[a] tax on magazines that discourages one form of expression, magazines, in favor of another, newspapers, clearly operates to restrain the use of the printing press to examine the proceedings of government." The majority, however, decided that because the distinction between magazines and newspapers is based on format rather than content, it satisfies the state constitution as well as *Leathers*. Magazine Publishers of America v. Commonwealth, 654 A.2d 519 (Pa. 1995).

Questions of this sort promise to become even more vexing as conventional means of delivery of media give way to technological change. If newspapers are delivered electronically, for example, will differential taxation of newspapers and cable be defensible then? In response to lobbying from Newsday, which planned to launch an electronic newspaper, the New York legislature redefined that state's sales tax exemption for newspapers. The language was carefully crafted in an attempt to avoid exempting other providers of on-line information services. See Jerome L. Wilson, New York gives a tax break to electronic newspapers, Editor and Publisher, Aug. 27, 1994. Is it possible to distinguish these kinds of information services sufficiently to avoid unconstitutionality?

———

E. DISFAVORED SPEECH

The "few legal categories in which content-based regulation has been permitted" that Justice Kennedy referred to in *Simon & Schuster* were at one time thought of as categories of unprotected speech. Their existence was first asserted in Chaplinsky v. New Hampshire, 315 U.S. 568 (1942):

> There are certain well-defined and narrowly limited classes of speech, the prevention and punishment of which have never been thought to raise any Constitutional problem. These include the lewd and obscene, the profane, the libelous, and the insulting or "fighting" words—those, which by their very utterance inflict injury or tend to incite an immediate breach of the peace. It has been well observed that such utterances are no essential part of any exposition of ideas, and are of such slight social value as a step to truth that any benefit that may be derived from them is clearly outweighed by the social interest in order and morality.

Today, most of these categories of speech are no longer thought to be wholly outside the protection of the First Amendment. Categorization is used not to deny protection altogether, but to single out certain kinds of speech for more or less protection. For example, advertising, once treated as an unprotected category, is now treated as a species of speech entitled to some protection, but less than the full protection of the First Amendment. Libel is no longer considered unprotected speech; instead, a special set of First Amendment rules governs defamatory speech, as we shall see in Chapter Four. In R.A.V. v. City of St. Paul, 505 U.S. 377 (1992), the Court attempted to explain:

> . . . Our decisions since the 1960s have narrowed the scope of the traditional categorical exceptions for defamation, [ ], and for obscenity, [ ], but a limited categorical approach has remained an important part of our First Amendment jurisprudence.

We have sometimes said that these categories of expression are "not within the area of constitutionally protected speech," [ ] or that the "protection of the First Amendment does not extend" to them [ ]. Such statements must be taken in context, however, and are no more literally true than is the occasionally repeated shorthand characterizing obscenity "as not being speech at all," [ ]. What they mean is that these areas of speech can, consistently with the First Amendment, be regulated because of their constitutionally proscribable content (obscenity, defamation, etc.)—not that they are categories of speech entirely invisible to the Constitution, so that they may be made the vehicles for content discrimination unrelated to their distinctively proscribable content. Thus, the government may proscribe libel; but it may not make the further content discrimination of proscribing only libel critical of the government. . . .

In R.A.V. the Court held that even if cross-burning was within the category of "fighting words," a hate-speech ordinance could not single out cross-burning that arouses anger "on the basis of race, color, creed, religion, or gender" because that would punish fighting words that convey a particular message while leaving other fighting words unpunished.

Although the Court sometimes indicates that other categories of lesser-protected speech might be recognized, it has shown no eagerness to do so. In United States v. Stevens, 559 U.S. 460 (2010), the government urged the Court to create a new category for "crush videos." At issue was a federal statute making it a crime to make or distribute videos in which a living animal is illegally and intentionally "maimed, mutilated, tortured, wounded, or killed." The government argued that such videos, like the types of speech identified in *Chaplinsky*, "are no essential part of any exposition of ideas, and are of such slight social value as a step to truth that any benefit that may be derived from them is clearly outweighed by the social interest in order and morality." The Court seemed to reject not only the proposed new category, but also the premise articulated by *Chaplinsky*. Chief Justice Roberts, writing for an 8–1 majority, wrote "The First Amendment's guarantee of free speech does not extend only to categories of speech that survive an ad hoc balancing of relative social costs and benefits. The First Amendment itself reflects a judgment by the American people that the benefits of its restrictions on the Government outweigh the costs. Our Constitution forecloses any attempt to revise that judgment simply on the basis that some speech is not worth it."

The Court granted that its prior precedent seemed to employ "simple cost-benefit analysis" to recognize unprotected categories of speech such as obscenity, defamation, fraud, incitement, and speech integral to criminal conduct, but Chief Justice Roberts asserted that the recognized categories involved other factors as well; chiefly, the imprimatur of history and tradition on suppression. As Roberts wrote: "Maybe there are some categories of speech that have been historically unprotected, but have not yet been specifically identified or discussed as such on our case law. But if so, there is no evidence that 'depictions of animal cruelty' is among them."

The categories in which the First Amendment's protection is weakest are obscenity and child pornography. The mass media rarely run afoul of restrictions on these types of speech, but we treat them briefly to provide context.

1. OBSCENITY

Legislatures and the courts have long wrestled with how to protect public sensibilities about sexually explicit expression without violating the First Amendment. Much of the constitutional law of obscenity reflects a process of refining and elaborating the boundaries of the category. The first step was a narrowing of the concept from "immorality" to explicit sexual depictions. In Joseph Burstyn, Inc. v. Wilson, 343 U.S. 495, 1 Med. L. Rptr. 1357 (1952), the Court held that a movie could not be banned by the state on the ground that it was "sacrilegious." The film version of "Lady Chatterley's Lover" could not be banned on the ground that it endorsed adultery because the First Amendment "protects advocacy of the opinion that adultery may sometimes be proper, no less than advocacy of socialism or the single tax." Kingsley Int. Pictures Corp. v. Regents, 360 U.S. 684 (1959).

The Court first attempted to define obscenity in Roth v. United States, 354 U.S. 476 (1957): material was obscene if "to the average person, applying contemporary community standards, the dominant theme of the material taken as a whole appeals to prurient interest." It soon became apparent, however, that even members of the Court could not agree on the application of this definition to specific books or films, leading the late Justice Stewart to write in 1964 that an intelligent definition might be impossible, but "I know it when I see it." Jacobellis v. Ohio, 378 U.S. 184, 197 (1964) (Stewart, J., concurring). On 31 occasions, the Court reviewed purportedly obscene material and rendered judgment as to its permissibility. Justice Brennan complained that the examination of this material was "hardly a source of edification to the members of this Court," and Chief Justice Burger noted that the Court's case by case determination of obscenity had cast it in the "role of a supreme and unreviewable board of censorship for the 50 states." Paris Adult Theatre I v. Slaton, 413 U.S. 49, 92–93 (1973) (Brennan, J., dissenting); Walker v. Ohio, 398 U.S. 434, 434 (1970) (Burger, C.J., dissenting). In 1973 the Court, 5–4, articulated the definition that remains in effect today:

(a) [W]hether "the average person, applying contemporary community standards" would find that the work, taken as a whole, appeals to the prurient interest [ ], (b) whether the work depicts or describes, in a patently offensive way, sexual conduct specifically defined by the applicable state law; and (c) whether the work, taken as a whole, lacks serious literary, artistic, political, or scientific value.

Miller v. California, 413 U.S. 15 (1973). The Court held further that "contemporary standards" were to be determined by juries on the basis of their own perceptions, not by reference to nationwide standards. In *Paris Adult Theatre*, the Court held that as long as the *Miller* test was met, theaters could be enjoined from showing obscene films, even if the evidence showed that no one but consenting adults ever saw them, in the interests of "quality of life and the total community environment, the tone of commerce in the great city centers, and possibly, the public safety itself."

The result of this jurisprudence has been considerable diversity in the treatment of obscenity from one place to another. In some cities prosecutors have abandoned the effort to control hard-core pornography, presumably because they believe juries will not convict under local standards. In other cities authorities continue to prosecute, apparently with some success. In still others, adult theaters and other outlets for hard-core pornography are restricted by zoning ordinances to certain districts.

The distribution or public exhibition of sexually explicit expression that meets the *Miller* definition for obscenity may constitutionally be banned, whether it is printed, broadcast, mailed, distributed by telephone, or made available via the Internet. The medium may not, however, be irrelevant to the operation of obscenity regulations. There is some authority for the proposition that a national community standard, rather than local community standards, must be applied in regulating obscene speech on the Internet. See U.S. v. Kilbride, 584 F.3d 1240 (9th Cir. 2009). The argument is that use of local community standards would subject all Internet communicators to the standards of the most restrictive communities. But some courts suggest that Internet users, like other interstate communicators, can tailor their operations to steer clear of the least tolerant communities. See, e.g., United States v. Thomas, 74 F.3d 701 (6th Cir. 1996).

In Ashcroft v. ACLU [I], 535 U.S. 564 (2002), six Justices expressed the view that a national community standard, rather than local standards, may be required in regulating indecent speech on the Internet. The posture of the case did not require a decision on that point, but in concurring and dissenting opinions a majority of the Court suggested that the practical effects of subjecting online communicators to the potential of prosecution under most restrictive local standards would impose a burden on Internet speech that might be unconstitutional. As we shall soon see, indecency is treated differently than obscenity, so local standards might be permissible in regulation of obscenity even if they are impermissible in connection with indecency. The justices expressed no view on that.

Despite the Court's continued adherence to the categorical approach, there is much about the law of obscenity that does not seem categorical at all. Even obscene material receives some First Amendment protection. The state cannot require pre-screening, even of material that meets the test for obscenity, unless it provides special procedures to assure prompt decision and speedy judicial review, see Freedman v. Maryland, 1 Media L. Rep. 1126 (1965), and the state cannot punish a person for possessing obscene material in a private home, see Stanley v. Georgia, 394 U.S. 557 (1969). "If the First Amendment means anything," Justice Marshall wrote for the Court in *Stanley*, "it means that a State has no business telling a man, sitting alone in his own house, what books he may read or what films he may watch. Our whole constitutional heritage rebels at the thought of giving government the power to control men's minds."

The basis for regulating obscene content broadcast over radio and television has existed in Congressional legislation since the enactment of the Communications Act of 1934. The current version is now found in the general criminal law, 18 U.S.C. § 1464:

> Whoever utters any obscene, indecent, or profane language by means of radio communications shall be fined [up to $250,000] or imprisoned not more than two years, or both.

The same penalties apply to obscene programming on cable. See 47 U.S.C. § 559.

2. CHILD PORNOGRAPHY

Where children are involved in the creation or consumption of sexually explicit expression, the Supreme Court has permitted states to enact regulations without requiring that the material fit the *Miller* definition of obscenity. For example, the Supreme Court has found that states may not only criminalize the depiction of children in sexually explicit films and photographs, they may prohibit the distribution, and even the mere possession, of those films and photographs in an effort to eliminate the market for child pornography. See New York v. Ferber, 458 U.S. 747 (1982).

Once *Ferber* made clear that sexual depictions of actual minors would receive no constitutional protection, the battle shifted to digitally created "virtual" child pornography and pornography depicting adults who were made to look like children. Congress's first attempt to deal with this failed. The Child Pornography Protection Act of 1996, 18 U.S.C. § 2252A(a)(5)(b), criminalized the production or distribution of any image that "is, or appears to be, of a minor engaging in sexually explicit conduct" or that is "advertised, promoted, presented, described, or distributed in such a manner that conveys the impression" that it depicts a minor engaged in sexually explicit conduct. The government argued that the ban was necessary to prevent use of electronically-created child pornography to whet the appetites of pedophiles for the real thing, prevent them from using such material to seduce children, and avoid stimulating a market for images of real children.

But the Court, 6–3, held that "the Government may not suppress lawful speech as the means to suppress unlawful speech." It held the statute overbroad, noting that because it contained no "redeeming value" element in its definition of child pornography, it could be applied to mainstream movies if the fact-finder thought one of the actors "appeared to be" a minor. The Court distinguished *Ferber* on two grounds: first, that it involved material that created a permanent record of a child's abuse, the continued circulation of which would harm the child who had participated; and second, that banning material that uses actual children has a more "proximate link" to removing the economic motive that leads to its production. See Ashcroft v. The Free Speech Coalition, 535 U.S. 234 (2002).

Congress then took another approach to the matter. It passed a new statute making it a crime to knowingly "advertise[ ], promote[ ], present[ ], distribute[ ], or solicit[ ] . . . any material or purported material in a manner that reflects the belief, or is intended to cause another to believe," that it is "an obscene visual depiction of a minor [actual or virtual] engaging in sexually explicit conduct; or a visual depiction of an *actual* minor engaging in sexually explicit conduct." 18 U.S.C. § 2252A(a)(3)(B) (2000 ed., Supp. V) (emphasis added). The statute defined "sexually explicit conduct" as "actual or simulated sexual intercourse . . . , bestiality, masturbation, sadistic or masochistic abuse, or lascivious exhibition of the genitals or pubic area of any person." 18 U.S.C. § 2256(2)(A). The minimum sentence for violation is five years imprisonment. During deliberations in the House and Senate, this new statute was said to be aimed at "pandering and solicitation."

The Eleventh Circuit Court of Appeals held the new statute unconstitutional on the grounds that it was overbroad and vague, but the Supreme Court reversed on a 7–2 vote. United States v. Williams, 553 U.S. 285 (2008). The respondent in *Williams* was charged with pandering under the statute after uploading child pornography to an Internet chat room that he explicitly designated as "REAL."

The Court held that the statute was neither substantially overbroad nor vague. The Court construed the statute narrowly, limiting it to portrayals that would necessarily cause a reasonable viewer to believe that the actors actually engaged in sexual conduct on camera and excluding pandering of materials billed as virtual child pornography or "sex between youthful-looking adult actors." The Court said any over breadth was not substantial, because the statute only criminalized "knowingly" seeking to induce a transfer of child pornography in a manner that indicates the defendant believed, and intended to lead the recipient to believe, that the material being offered was child pornography.

Based on this narrow construction of the statute, the Court concluded that it did not criminalize "a substantial amount of protected expressive activity" because it banned only speech that is *categorically* excluded from First Amendment protection, namely "offers to provide or requests to obtain child pornography." Although the appellate court had worried that the statute would punish the "braggart, exaggerator, or outright liar" who offered child pornography without possessing it, the Supreme Court did not see this as an obstacle, since the First Amendment allows bans on both fraudulent offers and offers to provide illegal products. Moreover, the Court held that the appellate court had been mistaken in thinking it "unconstitutional to punish someone for mistakenly distributing virtual child pornography as real child pornography" because "[t]here is no First Amendment exception from the general principle of criminal law that a person attempting to commit a crime need not be exonerated because he has a mistaken view of the facts."

The Court also held that the statute was not vague because it clearly specified what facts must be proved in order to impose liability. The Court dismissed, as a "fanciful hypothetical" the concern that the statute might apply to a person who offered innocent photos of a baby in the bathtub with a slightly racy caption. The statutory phrases defining the "manner" in which the purported child pornography must be promoted or solicited make clear that liability only attaches when "the defendant hold[s], and make[s] a statement that reflects, the belief that the material is child pornography; or that he communicate[s] in a manner intended to cause another so to believe." The Court treated these issues as "clear questions of fact" of the sort that courts and juries deal with every day. "What renders a statute vague is not the possibility that it will sometimes be difficult to determine whether the incriminating fact it establishes has been proved; but rather the indeterminacy of precisely what that fact is."

In dissent, Justices Souter and Ginsburg said the statute attempted to evade the First Amendment protection of virtual child pornography recognized by *Free Speech Coalition* by punishing proposals to transact in it rather than the virtual child pornography itself. The result, they said, is that virtual or "fake" child pornography receives First Amendment protection, but proposals to transact in it do not. "We should hold that a transaction in what turns out to be fake pornography is better understood, not as an incomplete attempt to commit a crime," they wrote, "but as a completed series of intended acts that simply do not add up to a crime, owing to the privileged character of the material the parties were in fact about to deal in."

3. COMMERCIAL SPEECH

Advertising receives a great deal more First Amendment protection than obscenity and child pornography, but it is nevertheless disfavored, as compared to noncommercial speech.

Until the 1970s the Supreme Court refused to extend First Amendment protection to advertising. Since then it has decided many cases that together create a specialized First Amendment jurisprudence for what has come to be called "commercial speech." Media take a keen interest in these cases. For one thing, what happens here can affect media revenues. Supreme Court decisions holding that pharmacies, lawyers, and other professionals had a First Amendment right to advertise brought millions of dollars of new ad revenue to media. Decisions upholding federal laws banning broadcast cigarette advertising diverted millions of dollars of ad money from television to print, billboards, and sponsorship of sports events (until that was restricted too). For another, commercial speech jurisprudence may have implications for First Amendment theory generally. Commercial speech analysis often seems to call into question the assumption that courts may not discriminate among various types of protected speech based on judgments as to its value. For both of these reasons, media companies often may be found among the amici who file briefs in support of potential advertisers who argue that particular advertising restrictions are unconstitutional. Occasionally, as in the following case, media entities themselves challenge the restrictions.

Greater New Orleans Broadcasting Association, Inc. v. United States

Supreme Court of the United States, 1999.
527 U.S. 173.

■ JUSTICE STEVENS delivered the opinion of the Court.

Federal law prohibits some, but by no means all, broadcast advertising of lotteries and casino gambling. In United States v. Edge Broadcasting Co., 509 U.S. 418 (1993), we upheld the constitutionality of 18 U.S.C. § 1304 as applied to broadcast advertising of Virginia's lottery by a radio station located in North Carolina, where no such lottery was authorized. Today we hold that § 1304 may not be applied to advertisements of private casino gambling that are broadcast by radio or television stations located in Louisiana, where such gambling is legal.

. . .

II

Petitioners are an association of Louisiana broadcasters and its members who operate FCC-licensed radio and television stations in the New Orleans metropolitan area. But for the threat of sanctions pursuant to § 1304 and the FCC's companion regulation, petitioners would broadcast promotional advertisements for gaming available at private, for-profit casinos that are lawful and regulated in both Louisiana and neighboring Mississippi. According to an FCC official, however, "[u]nder appropriate conditions, some broadcast signals from Louisiana broadcasting stations may be heard in neighboring states including Texas and Arkansas," [ ] where private casino gambling is unlawful.

Petitioners brought this action against the United States and the FCC in the District Court for the Eastern District of Louisiana, praying for a declaration that § 1304 and the FCC's regulation violate the First Amendment as applied to them, and for an injunction preventing enforcement of the statute and the rule against them. [On cross-motions for summary judgment, the District Court and the Fifth Circuit upheld the constitutionality of the statute.]

III

In a number of cases involving restrictions on speech that is "commercial" in nature, we have employed [the four-part test outlined in Central Hudson Gas & Elec. Corp. v. Public Serv. Comm'n of N.Y., 447 U.S. 557 (1980)] to resolve First Amendment challenges:

> At the outset, we must determine whether the expression is protected by the First Amendment. For commercial speech to come within that provision, it at least must concern lawful activity and not be misleading. Next, we ask whether the asserted governmental interest is substantial. If both inquiries yield positive answers, we must determine whether the regulation directly advances the governmental interest asserted, and whether it is not more extensive than is necessary to serve that interest. [ ]

In this analysis, the Government bears the burden of identifying a substantial interest and justifying the challenged restriction. [ ]

The four parts of the *Central Hudson* test are not entirely discrete. All are important and, to a certain extent, interrelated: Each raises a relevant question that may not be dispositive to the First Amendment inquiry, but the answer to which may inform a judgment concerning the other three. Partly because of these intricacies, petitioners as well as certain judges, scholars, and *amici curiae* have advocated repudiation of the *Central Hudson* standard and implementation of a more straightforward and stringent test for assessing the validity of governmental restrictions on commercial speech. . . . In this case, there is no need to break new ground. *Central Hudson,* as applied in our more recent commercial speech cases, provides an adequate basis for decision.

IV

All parties to this case agree that the messages petitioners wish to broadcast constitute commercial speech, and that these broadcasts would satisfy the first part of the *Central Hudson* test: Their content is not misleading and concerns lawful activities, *i.e.,* private casino gambling in Louisiana and Mississippi. As well, the proposed commercial messages would convey information—whether taken favorably or unfavorably by the audience—about an activity that is the subject of intense public debate in many communities. In addition, petitioners' broadcasts presumably would disseminate accurate information as to the operation of market competitors, such as pay-out ratios, which can benefit listeners by informing their consumption choices and fostering price competition. Thus, even if the broadcasters' interest in conveying these messages is entirely pecuniary, the interests of, and benefit to, the audience may be broader. See Virginia Bd. of Pharmacy v. Virginia Citizens Consumer Council, Inc., 425 U.S. 748, 764–765 (1976); [ ]

The second part of the *Central Hudson* test asks whether the asserted governmental interest served by the speech restriction is substantial. The Solicitor General identifies two such interests: (1) reducing the social costs associated with "gambling" or "casino gambling," and (2) assisting States that "restrict gambling" or "prohibit casino gambling" within their own borders. Underlying Congress' statutory scheme, the Solicitor General contends, is the judgment that gambling contributes to corruption and organized crime; underwrites bribery, narcotics trafficking, and other illegal conduct; imposes a regressive tax on the poor; and "offers a false but sometimes irresistible hope of financial advancement." [ ] With respect to casino gambling, the Solicitor General states that many of the associated social costs stem from "pathological" or "compulsive" gambling by approximately 3 million Americans, whose behavior is primarily associated with "continuous play" games, such as slot machines. He also observes that compulsive gambling has grown along with the expansion of legalized gambling nationwide, leading to billions of dollars in economic costs; injury and loss to these gamblers as well as their families, communities, and government; and street, white-collar, and organized crime. [ ]

We can accept the characterization of these two interests as "substantial," [even though] the federal policy of discouraging gambling in general, and casino gambling in particular, is now decidedly equivocal.

. . .

V

The third part of the *Central Hudson* test asks whether the speech restriction directly and materially advances the asserted governmental interest. "This burden is not satisfied by mere speculation or conjecture; rather, a governmental body seeking to sustain a restriction on commercial speech must demonstrate that the harms it recites are real and that its restriction will in fact alleviate them to a material degree." [ ] Consequently, "the regulation may not be sustained if it provides only ineffective or remote support for the government's purpose." [ ] We have observed that "this requirement is critical; otherwise, 'a State could with ease restrict commercial speech in the service of other objectives that could not themselves justify a burden on commercial expression.' " [ ]

The fourth part of the test complements the direct-advancement inquiry of the third, asking whether the speech restriction is not more extensive than necessary to serve the interests that support it. The Government is not required to employ the least restrictive means conceivable, but it must demonstrate narrow tailoring of the challenged regulation to the asserted interest—"a fit that is not necessarily perfect, but reasonable; that represents not necessarily the single best disposition but one whose scope is in proportion to the interest served." [ ] On the whole, then, the challenged regulation should indicate that its proponent " 'carefully calculated' the costs and benefits associated with the burden on speech imposed by its prohibition." [ ]

As applied to petitioners' case, § 1304 cannot satisfy these standards. With regard to the first asserted interest—alleviating the social costs of casino gambling by limiting demand—the Government contends that its broadcasting restrictions directly advance that interest because "promotional" broadcast advertising concerning casino gambling increases demand for such gambling, which in turn increases the amount of casino gambling that produces those social costs. Additionally, the Government believes that compulsive gamblers are especially susceptible to the pervasiveness and potency of broadcast advertising. [ ] Assuming the accuracy of this causal chain, it does not necessarily follow that the Government's speech ban has directly and materially furthered the asserted interest. While it is no doubt fair to assume that more advertising would have some impact on overall demand for gambling, it is also reasonable to assume that much of that advertising would merely channel gamblers to one casino rather than another. More important, any measure of the effectiveness of the Government's attempt to minimize the social costs of gambling cannot ignore Congress' simultaneous encouragement of tribal casino gambling, which may well be growing at a rate exceeding any increase in gambling or compulsive gambling that private casino advertising could produce. [ ] And, as the Court of Appeals recognized, the Government fails to "connect casino gambling and compulsive gambling with broadcast advertising for casinos"—let alone broadcast advertising for non-Indian commercial casinos. [ ]

We need not resolve the question whether any lack of evidence in the record fails to satisfy the standard of proof under *Central Hudson*, however, because the flaw in the Government's case is more fundamental: The operation of § 1304 and its attendant regulatory regime is so pierced by exemptions and inconsistencies that the Government cannot hope to exonerate it. [ ] Under current law, a broadcaster may not carry advertising about privately operated commercial casino gambling, regardless of the location of the station or the casino. [ ] On the other hand, advertisements for tribal casino gambling authorized by state compacts—whether operated by the tribe or by a private party pursuant to a management contract—are subject to no such broadcast ban, even if the broadcaster is located in, or broadcasts to, a jurisdiction with the strictest of antigambling policies. [ ] Government-operated, nonprofit, and "occasional and ancillary" commercial casinos are likewise exempt. [ ]

. . .

Even putting aside the broadcast exemptions for arguably distinguishable sorts of gambling that might also give rise to social costs about which the Federal Government is concerned—such as state lotteries and pari-mutuel betting on horse and dog races, [ ]—the Government presents no convincing reason for pegging its speech ban to the identity of the owners or operators of the advertised casinos. The Government cites revenue needs of States and tribes that conduct casino gambling, and notes that net revenues generated by the tribal casinos are dedicated to the welfare of the tribes and their members. [ ] Yet the Government admits that tribal casinos offer precisely the same types of gambling as private casinos. Further, the Solicitor General does not maintain that government-operated casino gaming is any different, that States cannot derive revenue from taxing private casinos, or that any one class of casino operators is likely to advertise in a meaningfully distinct manner from the others. The Government's suggestion that Indian casinos are too isolated to warrant attention is belied by a quick review of tribal geography and the Government's own evidence regarding the financial success of tribal gaming. [ ] If distance were determinative, Las Vegas might have remained a relatively small community, or simply disappeared like a desert mirage.

. . .

. . . Considering the manner in which § 1304 and its exceptions operate and the scope of the speech it proscribes, the Government's second asserted interest provides no more convincing basis for upholding the regulation than the first.

VI

Accordingly, respondents cannot overcome the presumption that the speaker and the audience, not the Government, should be left to assess the value of accurate and nonmisleading information about lawful conduct. [ ] Had the Federal Government adopted a more coherent policy, or accommodated the rights of speakers in States that have legalized the underlying conduct, see *Edge,* [ ], this might be a different case. But under current federal law, as applied to petitioners and the messages that they wish to convey, the broadcast prohibition in 18 U.S.C. § 1304 and 47 CFR § 73.1211 (1998) violates the First Amendment. The judgment of the Court of Appeals is therefore

Reversed.

■ JUSTICE THOMAS, concurring in the judgment.

I continue to adhere to my view that "[i]n cases such as this, in which the government's asserted interest is to keep legal users of a product or service ignorant in order to manipulate their choices in the marketplace," the *Central Hudson* test should not be applied because "such an 'interest' is *per se* illegitimate and can no more justify regulation of 'commercial speech' than it can justify regulation of 'noncommercial' speech." 44 Liquormart, Inc. v. Rhode Island, 517 U.S. 484, 518 (1996) (opinion concurring in part and concurring in judgment). Accordingly, I concur only in the judgment.

[A concurring opinion by CHIEF JUSTICE REHNQUIST is omitted.]

NOTES AND QUESTIONS

1.   In justification of the distinction between commercial speech and other forms of speech, the Court has noted that commercial speech is "more easily verifiable by its disseminator" and less likely to be "chilled by proper regulation." Virginia Bd. of Pharmacy v. Virginia Citizens Consumer Council, Inc., 425 U.S. 748 (1976). Are those reasons persuasive?

2.   Justice Thomas has long contended that there is no valid reason for the distinction. In his opinion in the *44 Liquormart* case, which he cited above, he made the further argument that even if some regulation of commercial speech is permissible,

> Whatever power the State may have to regulate commercial speech, it may not use that power to limit the content of commercial speech, as it has done here [by forbidding liquor stores to advertise prices], "for reasons unrelated to the preservation of a fair bargaining process." Such content-discriminatory regulation—like all other content-based regulation of speech—must be subjected to strict scrutiny.

Justice Scalia sometimes voiced similar views. The Court continues to employ the *Central Hudson* analysis in commercial speech cases, but it sometimes hints, as it did in the principal case, that it might re-think that analysis if the *Central Hudson* approach failed to protect the speech in question.

3.   The *Central Hudson* test permits restrictions on commercial speech only if they directly advance a substantial governmental interest and are no more

extensive than necessary to serve that interest. As those criteria were applied in the principal case, are they appreciably less speech-protective than the analysis that would be applied under the *Daily Mail* line of cases?

4.   As we shall see in the next chapter, the Court sometimes permits restrictions on broadcasting that would not be permissible as to print media. Note that in *Greater New Orleans* the government did not invoke, and the Court did not apply, any broadcast-specific First Amendment analysis. Was that a mistake on the government's part? Is there any reason why broadcast advertising of casinos should enjoy less First Amendment protection than similar advertising on billboards or in newspapers?

5.   It is not always easy to distinguish commercial from non-commercial speech, especially with the growth of sophisticated kinds of advertisements such as "native advertising" and "image advertising." In Jordan v. Jewel Food Stores, Inc., 743 F.3d 509 (7th Cir. 2014), also discussed later in an appropriation context, the Seventh Circuit concluded that the grocery chain's advertisement congratulating Jordan on his Naismith Memorial Basketball Hall of Fame induction was commercial speech. The ad appeared in a contemporaneous "commemorative" Sports Illustrated issue devoted entirely to Michael Jordan's career. The grocery chain contended that the First Amendment shielded it from liability because the ad was not commercial speech, but the court looked behind the "text" of the image advertisement to uncover its "dominant" purpose as "a promotional device for the advertiser." The court noted that the text of the ad was a simple message of congratulations, but "considered in context, . . . [the] ad has an unmistakable commercial function: enhancing the [grocery chain's] brand in the minds of consumers." The court further stated: "This commercial message is implicit but easily inferred, and is the dominant one." The court rejected the grocery chain's argument that its message was "a benevolent act of good corporate citizenship," bolstering the conclusion by pointing to the ad's prominent use of the grocery chain's logo and slogan. The ad was "exploiting public affection for Jordan at an auspicious moment in his career," and its noncommercial and commercial aspects were not so intertwined that the court was persuaded it was worthy of the highest level of First Amendment protection. As a result, the court remanded to allow Jordan to pursue his claims and the case settled in 2015. In a separate case involving a similar congratulatory ad placed by a different Chicago grocery chain, a jury awarded Jordan nearly $9 million and, instead of an appeal, the case settled shortly thereafter. Kim Janssen, Michael Jordan Hands Court Settlement to 23 Chicago Nonprofits, Chi. Trib., Dec. 15, 2015.

6.   Journalists increasingly rely on sophisticated analysis of large volumes of computerized data, often found in publicly available data sets, to add richer context to news stories. The Supreme Court's decision in Sorrell v. IMS Health Inc., 131 S.Ct. 2653 (2011), likely bolstered journalists' ability to conduct data journalism. In *Sorrell*, the Court held unconstitutional a statute restricting the sale, disclosure and use of pharmacy records that disclosed the prescribing practices of doctors. The statute's aim, in large part, was to prevent pharmaceutical manufacturers from using the data to market

to doctors to encourage them to prescribe name-brand drugs. The statute's exceptions allowed for non-commercial uses of the data, such as health care research. The Court rejected the argument that the Vermont statute only regulated data as a commodity, noting that "[f]acts, after all, are the beginning point for much of the speech that is most essential to advance human knowledge and to conduct human affairs." The Court held that "[s]peech in aid of pharmaceutical marketing . . . is a form of expression protected by the Free Speech Clause of the First Amendment." Because the Vermont statute "burden[ed] disfavored speech by disfavored speakers," it was subject to heightened judicial scrutiny. Dissenting, Justices Breyer, Ginsburg, and Kagan argued against the application of "heightened scrutiny" and argued for upholding the Vermont statute under the *Central Hudson* test. Does the decision have implications for government attempts to protect privacy in the Big Data era?

CHAPTER III

DIFFERENT RULES FOR SOME MEDIA

In the cases discussed so far, there has been no suggestion that the First Amendment might apply differently to different media. Even in the *Wikileaks* case, where distribution via the Internet posed novel jurisdictional and enforcement issues, the judge applied standard First Amendment principles. In most contexts, that is the norm; courts apply the same doctrines to all media in cases involving prior restraint, libel, contempt, and privacy, for example. In some important respects, however, broadcasting and cable are restricted in ways that would not be permitted if applied to print media.

Our purpose in this chapter is not to survey the many regulations to which electronic media are subject; those are too numerous and detailed to be fully covered here. Rather, our purpose is to explore the various justifications that are given for refusing to apply general First Amendment principles to some media in some settings. The disparate treatment of electronic media is entrenched, and the affected industries to some extent have learned to live with their regulatory environments. But as new media emerge, courts must decide what First Amendment paradigm to apply to them. Understanding why courts have thought it appropriate to deny full First Amendment protection to some media in some contexts in the past may help us foresee how new media are likely to be treated.

A. BROADCASTING

1. FAIRNESS

In *Tornillo*, the Supreme Court insisted that the First Amendment prohibits the government from requiring a newspaper to give a right of reply to a person attacked in its pages. In the following case, the issue was whether the First Amendment permits the government to require a broadcaster to give a right of reply. The case represents perhaps the apogee in differential treatment of media.

Red Lion Broadcasting Co., Inc. v. Federal Communications Commission

Supreme Court of the United States, 1969.
395 U.S. 367.

■ MR. JUSTICE WHITE delivered the opinion of the Court.

The Federal Communications Commission has for many years imposed on radio and television broadcasters the requirement that discussion of public issues be presented on broadcast stations, and that each side of those issues must be given fair coverage. This is known as the fairness doctrine, which originated very early in the history of broadcasting and has maintained its present outlines for some time. It is an obligation whose content has been defined in a long series of FCC rulings in particular cases, and which is distinct from the statutory requirement of § 315 of the Communications Act that equal time be allotted all qualified candidates for public office. Two aspects of the fairness doctrine, relating to personal attacks in the context of controversial public issues and to political editorializing, were codified more precisely in the form of FCC regulations in 1967. The two cases before us now, which were decided separately below, challenge the constitutional and statutory bases of the doctrine and component rules. *Red Lion* involves the application of the fairness doctrine to a particular broadcast, and [ ] arises as an action to review the FCC's 1967 promulgation of the personal attack and political editorializing regulations, which were laid down after the *Red Lion* litigation had begun.

[A radio program broadcast on WGCB, a radio station in Red Lion, Pennsylvania, publicly attacked Fred J. Cook, author of a book entitled "Goldwater—Extremist on the Right." During the program, the host, the Rev. Billy James Hargis, said that Cook "had been fired by a newspaper for making false charges against city officials" and that "Cook has then worked for a Communist-affiliated publication." Hargis also claimed that Cook had "defended Alger Hiss and attacked J. Edgar Hoover." Cook asked WGCB to provide him a tape of the broadcast and free air time in which to respond to Hargis's personal attacks; WGCB refused to comply with this request. Cook then complained to the FCC, which ordered WGCB to provide Cook with a transcript or tape of the program and free air time to respond to Hargis's on-air attacks on Cook. The Court of Appeals affirmed the FCC order. 381 F.2d 908 (D.C. Cir. 1967). While that case was pending, the Commission promulgated more specific rules relating to personal attacks and political editorials. Those rules were held unconstitutional in FCC v. Radio Television News Directors Association, 400 F.2d 1002 (7th Cir. 1968). In the Supreme Court that case was consolidated with *Red Lion*.]

C.

Believing that the specific application of the fairness doctrine in *Red Lion*, and the promulgation of the regulations in *RTNDA*, are both authorized by Congress and enhance rather than abridge the freedoms of speech and press protected by the First Amendment, we hold them valid and constitutional, reversing the judgment below in *RTNDA* and affirming the judgment below in *Red Lion*.

II.

The history of the emergence of the fairness doctrine and of the related legislation shows that the Commission's action in the *Red Lion* case did not exceed its authority, and that in adopting the new regulations the Commission was implementing congressional policy rather than embarking on a frolic of its own. . . .

A.

. . .

There is a twofold duty laid down by the FCC's decisions and described by the 1949 Report on Editorializing by Broadcast Licensees, 13 F.C.C. 1246 (1949). The broadcaster must give adequate coverage to public issues, United Broadcasting Co., 10 F.C.C. 515 (1945), and coverage must be fair in that it accurately reflects the opposing views. New Broadcasting Co., 6 P & F Radio Reg. 258 (1950). . . .

When a personal attack has been made on a figure involved in a public issue, both the doctrine of cases such as *Red Lion* and Times-Mirror Broadcasting Co., 24 P & F Radio Reg. 404 (1962), and also the 1967 regulations at issue in *RTNDA* require that the individual attacked himself be offered an opportunity to respond. Likewise, where one candidate is endorsed in a political editorial, the other candidates must themselves be offered reply time to use personally or through a spokesman. These obligations differ from the general fairness requirement that issues be presented, and presented with coverage of competing views, in that the broadcaster does not have the option of presenting the attacked party's side himself or choosing a third party to represent that side. But insofar as there is an obligation of the broadcaster to see that both sides are presented, and insofar as that is an affirmative obligation, the personal attack doctrine and regulations do not differ from the preceding fairness doctrine. . . .

B.

[The Court rejected arguments that the Commission lacked power to impose the fairness requirements. It held that the Commission's statutory mandate to promulgate rules and regulations to serve the "public convenience, interest, or necessity," 47 U.S.C. § 303 and 303(r), was "broad enough to encompass these regulations."]

III.

The broadcasters challenge the fairness doctrine and its specific manifestations in the personal attack and political editorial rules on conventional First Amendment grounds, alleging that the rules abridge their freedom of speech and press. Their contention is that the First Amendment protects their desire to use their allotted frequencies continuously to broadcast whatever they choose, and to exclude whomever they choose from ever using that frequency. No man may be prevented from saying or publishing what he thinks, or from refusing in his speech or other utterances to give equal weight to the views of his opponents. This right, they say, applies equally to broadcasters.

A.

Although broadcasting is clearly a medium affected by a First Amendment interest, United States v. Paramount Pictures, Inc., 334 U.S. 131, 166 (1948), differences in the characteristics of new media justify differences in the First Amendment standards applied to them. Joseph Burstyn, Inc. v. Wilson, 343 U.S. 495, 503 (1952). For example, the ability of new technology to produce sounds more raucous than those of the human voice justifies restrictions on the sound level, and on the hours and places of use, of sound trucks so long as the restrictions are reasonable and applied without discrimination. Kovacs v. Cooper, 336 U.S. 77 (1949). . . .

Where there are substantially more individuals who want to broadcast than there are frequencies to allocate, it is idle to posit an unabridgeable First Amendment right to broadcast comparable to the right of every individual to speak, write, or publish. If 100 persons want broadcast licenses but there are only 10 frequencies to allocate, all of them may have the same "right" to a license; but if there is to be any effective communication by radio, only a few can be licensed and the rest must be barred from the airwaves. It would be strange if the First Amendment, aimed at protecting and furthering communications, prevented the Government from making radio communication possible by requiring licenses to broadcast and by limiting the number of licenses so as not to overcrowd the spectrum.

This has been the consistent view of the Court. Congress unquestionably has the power to grant and deny licenses and to eliminate existing stations. [ ] No one has a First Amendment right to a license or to monopolize a radio frequency; to deny a station license because "the public interest" requires it "is not a denial of free speech." National Broadcasting Co. v. United States, 319 U.S. 190, 227 (1943).

By the same token, as far as the First Amendment is concerned those who are licensed stand no better than those to whom licenses are refused. A license permits broadcasting, but the licensee has no constitutional right to be the one who holds the license or to monopolize a radio frequency to the exclusion of his fellow citizens. There is nothing in the

First Amendment which prevents the Government from requiring a licensee to share his frequency with others and to conduct himself as a proxy or fiduciary with obligations to present those views and voices which are representative of his community and which would otherwise, by necessity, be barred from the airwaves.

This is not to say that the First Amendment is irrelevant to public broadcasting. On the contrary, it has a major role to play as the Congress itself recognized in § 326, which forbids FCC interference with "the right of free speech by means of radio communication." Because of the scarcity of radio frequencies, the Government is permitted to put restraints on licensees in favor of others whose views should be expressed on this unique medium. But the people as a whole retain their interest in free speech by radio and their collective right to have the medium function consistently with the ends and purposes of the First Amendment. It is the right of the viewers and listeners, not the right of the broadcasters, which is paramount. [ ] It is the purpose of the First Amendment to preserve an uninhibited market-place of ideas in which truth will ultimately prevail, rather than to countenance monopolization of that market, whether it be by the Government itself or a private licensee. [ ] It is the right of the public to receive suitable access to social, political, esthetic, moral, and other ideas and experiences which is crucial here. That right may not constitutionally be abridged either by Congress or by the FCC.

B.

Rather than confer frequency monopolies on a relatively small number of licensees, in a Nation of 200,000,000, the Government could surely have decreed that each frequency should be shared among all or some of those who wish to use it, each being assigned a portion of the broadcast day or the broadcast week. The ruling and regulations at issue here do not go quite so far. They assert that under specified circumstances, a licensee must offer to make available a reasonable amount of broadcast time to those who have a view different from that which has already been expressed on his station. The expression of a political endorsement, or of a personal attack while dealing with a controversial public issue, simply triggers this time sharing. As we have said, the First Amendment confers no right on licensees to prevent others from broadcasting on "their" frequencies and no right to an unconditional monopoly of a scarce resource which the Government has denied others the right to use.

In terms of constitutional principle, and as enforced sharing of a scarce resource, the personal attack and political editorial rules are indistinguishable from the equal-time provision of § 315, a specific enactment of Congress requiring stations to set aside reply time under specified circumstances and to which the fairness doctrine and these constituent regulations are important complements. That provision, which has been part of the law since 1927, Radio Act of 1927, § 18, 44 Stat. 1170, has been held valid by this Court as an obligation of the licensee relieving him of any power in any way to prevent or censor the broadcast, and thus insulating him from liability for defamation. The constitutionality of the statute under the First Amendment was unquestioned. Farmers Educ. & Co-op. Union v. WDAY, 360 U.S. 525 (1959).

Nor can we say that it is inconsistent with the First Amendment goal of producing an informed public capable of conducting its own affairs to require a broadcaster to permit answers to personal attacks occurring in the course of discussing controversial issues, or to require that the political opponents of those endorsed by the station be given a chance to communicate with the public. Otherwise, station owners and a few networks would have unfettered power to make time available only to the highest bidders, to communicate only their own views on public issues, people and candidates, and to permit on the air only those with whom they agreed. There is no sanctuary in the First Amendment for unlimited private censorship operating in a medium not open to all. "Freedom of the press from governmental interference under the First Amendment does not sanction repression of that freedom by private interests." Associated Press v. United States, 326 U.S. 1, 20 (1945).

C.

It is strenuously argued, however, that if political editorials or personal attacks will trigger an obligation in broadcasters to afford the opportunity for expression to speakers who need not pay for time and whose views are unpalatable to the licensees, then broadcasters will be irresistibly forced to self-censorship and their coverage of controversial public issues will be eliminated or at least rendered wholly ineffective. Such a result would indeed be a serious matter, for should licensees actually eliminate their coverage of controversial issues, the purposes of the doctrine would be stifled.

At this point, however, as the Federal Communications Commission has indicated, that possibility is at best speculative. The communications industry, and in particular the networks, have taken pains to present controversial issues in the past, and even now they do not assert that they intend to abandon their efforts in this regard. It would be better if the FCC's encouragement were never necessary to induce the broadcasters to meet their responsibility. And if experience with the administration of these doctrines indicates that they have the net effect of reducing rather than enhancing the volume and quality of coverage, there will be time enough to reconsider the constitutional implications. The fairness doctrine in the past has had no such overall effect.

That this will occur now seems unlikely, however, since if present licensees should suddenly prove timorous, the Commission is not powerless to insist that they give adequate and fair attention to public issues. It does not violate the First Amendment to treat licensees given the privilege of using scarce radio frequencies as proxies for the entire community, obligated to give suitable time and attention to matters of great public concern. To condition the granting or renewal of licenses on a willingness to present representative community views on controversial issues is consistent with the ends and purposes of those constitutional provisions forbidding the abridgment of freedom of speech and freedom of the press. Congress need not stand idly by and permit those with licenses to ignore the problems which beset the people or to exclude from the airways anything but their own views of fundamental questions. The statute, long administrative practice, and cases are to this effect. . . .

E.

In view of the scarcity of broadcast frequencies, the Government's role in allocating those frequencies, and the legitimate claims of those unable without governmental assistance to gain access to those frequencies for expression of their views, we hold the regulations and ruling at issue here are both authorized by statute and constitutional. . . .

NOTES AND QUESTIONS

1.   *Red Lion* was discussed extensively in Professor Barron's brief in the *Tornillo* case, but it was not mentioned in the Supreme Court's opinion. Is it self-evident that *Red Lion* is irrelevant as to newspapers? At the time of the *Tornillo* decision, the Miami Herald was one of two major daily newspapers in the Miami area. Is it plausible that WGCB had more control over the views and voices available to its listeners than the Herald had over those available to its readers?

2.   In 1969, cable television and UHF television were in their infancy. Not all radios were equipped to receive FM broadcasts. Satellite television, digital broadcasting, and the Internet were unheard of. However persuasive the scarcity-of-frequencies argument may have been then, the new technologies make it seem quaint today. See, e.g., Christopher S. Yoo, The Rise and Demise of the Technology—Specific Approach to the First Amendment, 91 GEO. L.J. 245 (2003); Thomas W. Hazlett, et al., The Overly Active Corpse of Red Lion, 9 Nw. J. Tech. & Intell. Prop. J. 51 (2015) ("There is literally no limit to the number of 'broadcast frequencies' given time sharing or frequency-splitting possibilities, e.g., or the creation of joint ownership interests in a license").

3.   The FCC no longer enforces the fairness doctrine or the personal attack or political editorial rules. See Syracuse Peace Council v. FCC, 867 F.2d 654 (D.C. Cir. 1989) (affirming the FCC's determination that the fairness doctrine no longer serves the public interest); Radio-Television News Directors Association v. FCC, 229 F.3d 269 (D.C. Cir. 2000) (ordering FCC to vacate the personal attack rule).

4.   The idea that different First Amendment standards might be appropriate for some media is far from dead. See, e.g., Ronald J. Krotoszynski, Jr., The Irrelevant Wasteland: An Exploration of Why *Red Lion* Doesn't Matter (Much) in 2008, the Crucial Importance of the Information Revolution, and the Continuing Relevance of the Public Interest Standard in Regulating Access to Spectrum, 60 Admin. L. Rev. 911 (2008), arguing that the public interest standard articulated in *Red Lion* should be used to mandate universal access to the Internet.

5.   Although the Court has not overruled *Red Lion*, courts rarely rely on it. One exception was Time Warner Entertainment Co. v. FCC, 93 F.3d 957 (D.C. Cir. 1996), in which the court found *Red Lion*'s "relaxed standard of scrutiny" appropriate in relation to direct broadcast satellite television because of the "finite number of satellite positions available for DBS use."

---

2.   POLITICAL BROADCASTS

Campaigns for elective office have been regulated differently over radio and television than in print media ever since the Radio Act of 1927. The demise of the fairness doctrine has not affected these special requirements, which apply only to over-the-air broadcasters and cablecasters who originate their own programming.

Section 315(b) of the federal Communications Act forbids stations from charging candidates more than their "lowest unit rate," i.e., the best rate they offer other advertisers. Section 315(e) has long required broadcasters to keep records of requests by political candidates to buy time as an aid in the enforcement of campaign spending regulations. The Bipartisan Campaign Reform Act of 2002 greatly expanded that record-keeping requirement, to include requests from any individual or group to buy time for any message relating to elections, national legislative issues, or any "political matter of national importance." Since 2014, stations must also make these records available online.

Equal Opportunities. The best-known restriction on broadcast speech about elections requires a station that makes time available to one candidate to offer an "equal opportunity" to all other candidates for the same office. This obligation, imposed by Section 315(a), applies to all candidates for public office. It is popularly known as the "equal time" requirement, but what it actually requires is an equal opportunity to persuade voters, not necessarily quantitative parity. The station may not censor the reply, and cannot be held liable if the reply defames someone. See Farmers Educ. & Co-op. Union v. WDAY, Inc., 360 U.S. 525 (1959).

Equal opportunity obligations are triggered by a candidate's "use" of airtime, which occurs when the candidate's name or likeness is aired. A candidate does not need to appear in an advertisement to trigger equal opportunity obligations. For example, during the primary campaign leading up to the 2016 presidential election, Republication candidate

Donald Trump's appearance on NBC's Saturday Night Live reportedly led the network to give free air time to five other candidates.

The equal opportunity rule does not apply to candidate appearances in bona fide newscasts, news interviews, news documentaries if the appearance is incidental to the subject, or on-the-spot coverage of news events, including political conventions. Presidential news conferences have been held to come within the "news events" exception. See Kennedy for President Comm. v. Federal Communications Comm'n, 636 F.2d 417 (D.C. Cir. 1980) (*Kennedy I*) (holding that supporters of Senator Edward M. Kennedy were not entitled to time to reply to statements President Carter made in a press conference carried by the networks on the evening before the New Hampshire primary in 1980).

Some television series focused on current events also have been deemed exempt from the equal opportunity rule. In In re GNH Productions Inc. (FCC Aug. 10, 2015), for example, the FCC found that a series entitled "Crime Watch Daily" was exempt, even though its coverage of trials might include interviews with or depictions of attorneys or judges running for office. Relevant factors in the determination of whether a series qualifies for the exemption for "bona fide news" include whether the series is regularly scheduled, whether producers retain control over format, content and participants, and whether programming choices are made based on newsworthiness rather than a desire to advance a particular candidate. See In re ANE Productions Inc., #DA 1101946 (FCC 2011). Because of exceptions such as this, the effects of the rule are confined largely to political advertising and broadcasting personalities who run for public office.

At one time, the FCC interpreted "candidate" to include supporters, so that a station that granted use of its facilities to supporters of one candidate had to treat supporters of the other candidates equally, essentially as it would have had to treat the candidates themselves. Letter to Nicholas Zapple, 23 F.C.C.2d 707 (1970) (the *Zapple* Doctrine). In 2014, however, the FCC determined that the demise of the Fairness Doctrine had left no basis for the enforcement of the Zapple Doctrine. In re Application of Capstar TX LLC, 29 F.C.C.R. 5010, 2014 WL 1871102 (May 8, 2014); In re Application of Journal Broadcast Corp., 29 F.C.C.R. 5014, 2014 WL 1871103 (May 8, 2014). See David Oxenford, FCC Decides That It Will No Longer Enforce the Zapple Doctrine—Killing the Last Remnant of the Fairness Doctrine, Broadcast Law Blog, May 8, 2014.

Candidates excluded from televised debates have had little success when they invoked § 315 in an effort to be included or to be given compensatory time; broadcasters may sponsor debates among major candidates without incurring obligations under Section 315(a). Petitions of Henry Geller, et al., 95 F.C.C.2d 1236 (1983), affirmed without opinion in League of Women Voters Educ. Fund v. Federal Communications Comm'n, 731 F.2d 995 (D.C. Cir. 1984).

In the 1996 election, third party candidate Ross Perot mounted several challenges to his exclusion from coverage of the two major party candidates. He was excluded from the debates between President Bill Clinton and Bob Dole on the basis of a determination by the nongovernmental Commission on Presidential Debates (CPD) that he did not have a realistic chance of winning. Finding that the equities and the public interest weighed against the court's interference, and holding that there was no state action to support Perot's constitutional claims, the district court denied relief. The court of appeals rejected a claim that the Federal Election Commission (FEC) had unconstitutionally delegated power to the CPD by permitting each debate-holding group to establish its own "pre-established objective criteria" to determine who may participate. Perot v. Federal Election Comm'n, 97 F.3d 553 (D.C. Cir. 1996).

Perot then argued to the FCC that he was entitled to equal opportunity time based on the major networks' coverage of the Democratic and Republican nominating conventions, the presidential debates, and other programming provided by the networks, including appearances by Clinton and Dole on the ABC program 20/20. The FCC denied Perot's complaint on the ground that all of the programs complained of qualified as bona fide news programming under Section 315(a). In re Complaint of Ross Perot v. ABC, CBS, NBC, and Fox Broadcasting Co., 11 FCC Rcd. 13109 (1996). In the last days of the campaign, several networks offered free time to the two major candidates and Perot again sought equal opportunity time. The FCC again ruled that the broadcasts fell within the bona fide news event exemption. In re Requests of Fox Broadcasting Co., Public Broadcasting Service, and Capital Cities/ABC, Inc., 11 FCC Rcd. 11101 (1996).

Requirements similar to the equal opportunities provision and the equivalent lowest-unit-rate provision are applicable to cable systems that originate their own programming. See 47 C.F.R. §§ 76.205, 76.209. Cable operators are not responsible under these rules for secondary transmissions or mandated access channels.

Reasonable Access. The second major statute imposing duties on broadcasters in connection with political campaigns applies only to campaigns for federal office—Congress and the presidency. Section 312(a)(7) of the Communications Act requires licensees to give federal candidates "reasonable access" to the airwaves. How to determine what that requires is the issue in the following case.

CBS, Inc. v. Federal Communications Commission

Supreme Court of the United States, 1981.
453 U.S. 367.

■ CHIEF JUSTICE BURGER delivered the opinion of the Court.

[In late 1979 the Carter-Mondale Committee sought to buy 30 minutes of prime time for use in December in order to begin the 1980 campaign. CBS feared that such a sale would require it to sell time under Section 315 to all other announced candidates. ABC responded that it had not yet decided when to begin selling time for the 1980 campaign. NBC responded that December 1979 was too early. The FCC, 4–3, held the networks in violation of Section 312(a)(7). The court of appeals affirmed. The Court agreed with the FCC and the court of appeals that Congress had intended to create "an affirmative, promptly enforceable right of reasonable access to the use of broadcast stations for individual candidates seeking Federal elective office," rather than simply to codify prior policies that the FCC had developed under the general public interest standards.]

III A

Although Congress provided in § 312(a)(7) for greater use of broadcasting stations by federal candidates, it did not give guidance on how the Commission should implement the statute's access requirement. Essentially, Congress adopted a "rule of reason" and charged the Commission with its enforcement. . . . The Commission has issued some general interpretative statements, but its standards implementing § 312(a)(7) have evolved principally on a case-by-case basis and are not embodied in formalized rules. . . .

Broadcasters are free to deny the sale of air time prior to the commencement of a campaign, but once a campaign has begun, they must give reasonable and good-faith attention to access requests from "legally qualified" candidates for federal elective office. Such requests must be considered on an individualized basis, and broadcasters are required to tailor their responses to accommodate, as much as reasonably possible, a candidate's stated purposes in seeking air time. . . . [T]o justify a negative response, the broadcaster must show a realistic danger of substantial program disruption—perhaps caused by insufficient notice to allow adjustments in the schedule—or of an excessive number of equal time requests. Further, in order to facilitate review by the Commission, broadcasters must explain their reasons for refusing time or making a more limited counteroffer. If broadcasters take the appropriate factors into account and act reasonably and in good faith, their decisions will be entitled to deference even if the Commission's analysis would have differed in the first instance. . . .

[The Court held that the Commission properly undertook to determine for itself when an election campaign had in fact commenced, without giving deference to the licensee's views on that subject. "Such a decision is not, and cannot be, purely one of editorial judgment."]

Petitioners also challenge the Commission's requirement that broadcasters evaluate and respond to access requests on an individualized basis. In petitioners' view, the agency has attached inordinate significance to candidates' needs, thereby precluding fair assessment of broadcasters' concerns and prohibiting the adoption of uniform policies regarding requests for access.

[The Court rejected the contention. Although the Commission has admonished broadcasters not to "second-guess" the candidate's wisdom or the effectiveness of the particular format, the request need not be honored. The Commission "mandates careful consideration of, not blind assent to, candidates' desires for air time." Even though uniform policies would be more convenient for broadcasters, that approach "would allow personal campaign strategies and the exigencies of the political process to be ignored." These ground rules were sufficiently clear in late 1979 to permit the FCC to rule that the networks had violated the statute by failing to grant "reasonable access."]

IV

Finally, petitioners assert that § 312(a)(7) as implemented by the Commission violates the First Amendment rights of broadcasters by unduly circumscribing their editorial discretion. In [*CBS v. DNC*, 412 U.S. 94 (1973)], we stated:

The role of the Government as an "overseer" and ultimate arbiter and guardian of the public interest and the role of the licensee as a journalistic "free agent" call for a delicate balancing of competing interests. The maintenance of this balance for more than 40 years has called on both the regulators and the licensees to walk a "tight-rope" to preserve the First Amendment values written into the Radio Act and its successor, the Communications Act.

Petitioners argue that the Commission's interpretation of § 312(a)(7)'s access requirement disrupts the "delicate balanc[e]" that broadcast regulation must achieve. We disagree.

A licensed broadcaster is "granted the free and exclusive use of a limited and valuable part of the public domain; when he accepts that franchise it is burdened by enforceable public obligations." [ ] This Court has noted the limits on a broadcast license:

A license permits broadcasting, but the licensee has no constitutional right to be the one who holds the license or to monopolize a . . . frequency to the exclusion of his fellow citizens. There is nothing in the First Amendment which prevents the Government from requiring a licensee to share his frequency with others. . . . [*Red Lion.*]

[ ]. Although the broadcasting industry is entitled under the First Amendment to exercise "the widest journalistic freedom consistent with its public [duties]," [*CBS v. DNC*], the Court has made clear that:

> *It is the right of the viewers and listeners, not the right of the broadcasters which is paramount.* It is the purpose of the First Amendment to preserve an uninhibited marketplace of ideas in which truth will ultimately prevail, rather than to countenance monopolization of that market. . . . It is the right of the public to receive suitable access to social, political, esthetic, moral, and other ideas and experience which is crucial here. [*Red Lion*] (emphasis added).

The First Amendment interests of candidates and voters, as well as broadcasters, are implicated by § 312(a)(7). We have recognized that "it is of particular importance that candidates have the . . . opportunity to make their views known so that the electorate may intelligently evaluate the candidates' personal qualities and their positions on vital public issues before choosing among them on election day." [Buckley v. Valeo] Indeed, "speech concerning public affairs is . . . the essence of self-government." [Garrison v. Louisiana] The First Amendment "has its fullest and most urgent application precisely to the conduct of campaigns for political office." [Monitor Patriot Co. v. Roy] Section 312(a)(7) thus makes a significant contribution to freedom of expression by enhancing the ability of candidates to present, and the public to receive, information necessary for the effective operation of the democratic process.

Petitioners are correct that the Court has never approved a *general* right of access to the media. [ ] Nor do we do so today. Section 312(a)(7) creates a *limited* right to "reasonable" access that pertains only to legally qualified federal candidates and may be invoked by them only for the purpose of advancing their candidacies once a campaign has commenced. The Commission has stated that in enforcing the statute, it will "provide leeway to broadcasters and not merely attempt *de novo* to determine the reasonableness of their judgments. . . ." If broadcasters have considered the relevant factors in good faith, the Commission will uphold their decisions. [ ] Further, § 312(a)(7) does not impair the discretion of broadcasters to present their views on any issue or to carry any particular type of programming.

Section 312(a)(7) represents an effort by Congress to assure that an important resource—the airwaves—will be used in the public interest. We hold that the statutory right of access, as defined by the Commission and applied in these cases, properly balances the First Amendment rights of federal candidates, the public, and broadcasters.

The judgment of the Court of Appeals is affirmed.

[Justice White, joined by Justices Rehnquist and Stevens, dissented on the ground that the Commission and the Court had failed to give sufficient weight to a "long-standing statutory policy of deferring to editorial judgments that are not destructive of the goals of the Act." As a result, the Commission had read Section 312(a)(7) much too broadly. Congress had intended only "to codify what it conceived to be the preexisting duty of the broadcasters to serve the public interest by presenting political broadcasts."]

[In a separate dissent, Justice Stevens argued that the result created "an impermissible risk that the Commission's evaluation of a given refusal by a licensee will be biased—or will appear to be biased—by the character of the office held by the candidate making the request." He noted that the four Democratic commissioners had voted for the Carter-Mondale request and the three Republicans had dissented.]

NOTES AND QUESTIONS

1.   Could the Court uphold a similar statute demanding that print media offer federal candidates reasonable access? In considering this, recall (a) the passage stating that the licensee is "granted the free and exclusive use of a limited and valuable part of the public domain;" and (b) the passage stating that the statute is an "effort by Congress to assure that an important resource—the airwaves—will be used in the public interest." Is it essential to the Court's reasoning that the airwaves be treated as a "public resource"?

2.   Newspapers and magazines are subject to no rules comparable to the requirements relating to political broadcasts. Most candidates probably have more options for communicating with voters through radio and television than they have through print media, so the scarcity rationale seems inadequate to explain the disparate treatment. Is the rationale offered in the principal case more persuasive?

3.   The Court's opinion refers at one point to the "First Amendment interests of candidates and voters." Later it refers to the "First Amendment rights of federal candidates, the public, and broadcasters." Do federal (or all) candidates have special constitutional speech rights that do not extend to members of the public generally? Is the Court suggesting that some types of speech should be accorded greater protection (here in the form of access) than others?

4.   In discussing the First Amendment's role in elections, the Court concludes that the statute "makes a significant contribution to freedom of expression by enhancing the ability of candidates to present, and the public to receive, information necessary for the effective operation of the democratic process." Might the same have been said of the statute in *Tornillo?*

Political Ads and the No-Censorship Provision. When anti-abortion candidates began using graphic displays of fetuses in their television spots, broadcasters were unclear whether these spots had to be aired at all under Section 312(a)(7) and, if so, whether the presentations had to be at times chosen by the candidate under Section 315. Becker, a congressional candidate in Georgia, ran a spot displaying images of aborted fetuses on a station in Atlanta. The station received many complaints from viewers and asked the FCC whether it could channel such commercials in the future to late-night hours. The Commission concluded (1) that Mr. Becker's initial advertisement was not indecent, (2) that there was evidence in the record "indicating that the graphic political advertisements at issue can be psychologically damaging to children," (3) that "nothing in 312(a)(7) precludes a broadcaster's exercise of some discretion with respect to placement of political advertisements so as to protect children," and (4) that channeling would not violate the no-censorship provision of Section 315(a). The court of appeals reversed, holding that the ruling violated both Section 312(a)(7) and Section 315(a). See Becker v. FCC, 95 F.3d 75 (D.C. Cir. 1996).

The court held that refusing to air Becker's commercials in prime time violated the no-censorship provision of Section 315 because it inhibited the manner in which he was able to discuss public issues and deprived him of the ability to convey his message when and how he saw fit by forcing him to either change its content or accept a time slot that deprived him of his preferred audience. The court concluded:

> Finally, section 315(a) not only prohibits censorship, it also requires that candidates be given "equal opportunities" to use a broadcaster's facilities. To satisfy this requirement, a broadcaster must "make available periods of approximately equal audience potential to competing candidates to the extent that this is possible." [ ] The FCC claims that the [ruling here] does not involve the equal opportunity provision because there was no equal opportunity request before it. Because the equal opportunity requirements "forbid any kind of discrimination by a station between competing candidates," however, channeling clearly implicates the equal opportunity provision of section 315(a).

> This is so because if a station channels one candidate's message but allows his opponent to broadcast his messages in prime time, the first candidate will have been denied the equal opportunity guaranteed by this section. On the other hand, if the station relegates the opponent's advertisements to the broadcasting Siberia to which the first candidate was assigned, it would be violating the opponent's right of reasonable access under section 312(a)(7). We agree with petitioners that these provisions may not be read to create such a tension.

3. OWNERSHIP

Broadcasters have historically been subject to restrictions on ownership designed to ensure the availability of local programming and maintain diversity of voices on the airwaves. The constitutional foundation for such regulation was National Broadcasting Co., Inc. v.

United States (1943), which approved a number of restrictions on broadcast networks, including restrictions on ownership. NBC argued that the regulations violated its First Amendment rights, but the Court rejected the argument on scarcity grounds:

> Freedom of utterance is abridged to many who wish to use the limited facilities of radio. Unlike other modes of expression, radio inherently is not available to all. That is its unique characteristic, and that is why, unlike other modes of expression, it is subject to governmental regulation. Because it cannot be used by all, some who wish to use it must be denied. . . . The licensing system established by Congress in the Communications Act of 1934 was a proper exercise of its power over commerce. The standard it provided for the licensing of stations was the "public interest, convenience, or necessity." Denial of a station license on that ground, if valid under the Act, is not a denial of free speech. . . .

Despite the vast changes in broadcasting since then, the Court has not revisited the constitutionality of ownership limits in the radio and television industries.

At their height, these limits were quite stringent. They included limits on the number of outlets a single entity could own in one market and nationally. A one-to-a-market rule restricted one person from owning or controlling more than one broadcast license in any geographic market, another rule prohibited cross-ownership of newspaper and broadcast facilities in the same market; and a national audience cap provided that no person could own or control TV stations reaching more than 25 percent of the U.S. population.

Beginning with passage of the Telecommunications Act of 1996, Pub. L. 104–104, 110 Stat. 56, many of these rules have been scrapped. Today, the national ownership limits for radio have been eliminated and the local limits have been significantly relaxed. The statutory limits on broadcast-cable cross-ownership in the same market have been eliminated. The FCC's local duopoly rule, which once prevented joint ownership of two VHF stations in the same market, has been relaxed to allow such combinations in many markets. The FCC also relaxed its radio-television cross-ownership rule to permit those combinations too.

In 2003 the FCC announced a massive relaxation of the remaining limits on media ownership, which set off a firestorm of protest among public interest groups and in Congress. As a result, some of the FCC's proposals were thwarted.

The FCC initially raised the national ownership cap from 12 television stations reaching 25 percent of the audience to 35 percent with no limit on the number of stations. Aggressive acquisition campaigns by Viacom and News Corp. soon bumped up against that new limit, however, and in 2003 the FCC proposed to raise it to 45 percent. (The limits are actually higher than stated because an owner's UHF stations count only fractionally.) The 45 percent limit encountered substantial public opposition and Congress intervened, forbidding the FCC to raise that limit higher than 39 percent, a figure that allowed Viacom and News Corp. to keep all the stations they had acquired.

Many of the other provisions in the 2003 FCC order were challenged by public interest and consumer groups in Prometheus Radio Project v. FCC, 373 F.3d 372 (3d Cir. 2004). The most significant of those was the provision relaxing the ban on cross-ownership of a newspaper and a television station in the same market. Media corporations have long owned newspapers and television stations in different markets, and most media conglomerates do. But the cross-ownership rule is a major obstacle to mergers among those conglomerates because the merged entity often would end up owning both in the same market. Under intense pressure from the media industry, the FCC proposed to abolish the ban on cross-ownership in markets with at least nine TV stations, retain it in markets with no more than three stations, and permit it on a case-by-case basis in medium-sized markets.

In the *Prometheus* case the Third Circuit held, 2–1, that the FCC's decision to permit cross-ownership employed several "irrational assumptions and inconsistencies." The majority said the FCC gave too much weight to the Internet as a media outlet and irrationally assumed that all media of the same type should count equally regardless of their actual contribution to diversity of viewpoints. The court agreed, however, that the complete ban on cross-ownership was no longer justified and that the FCC had authority to change it. The court remanded for further fact-finding and rule-making proceedings.

The 2003 FCC order also proposed to raise the number of television stations a single entity can own in a single market from two stations in the largest markets to three and from one to two in medium-sized markets, as long as no more than one of the commonly-owned stations was in the top four in local ratings. The Third Circuit approved the top-four limitation but remanded for reconsideration of the numerical limits.

The *Prometheus* case was unusual. The issue was not the FCC's power to regulate, but its power to deregulate, and it was the Commission arguing that its exercise of power to limit ownership was unjustified. Judge Ambro, writing for the majority, said "the Commission has long acted on the theory that diversification of mass media ownership serves the public interest by promoting diversity of program and service viewpoints, as well as by preventing undue concentration of economic power." The majority said the Commission could not reverse itself on that question without more adequately justifying the change of heart.

The *Prometheus* decision led to a long stalemate over questions of ownership limits. The Third Circuit stayed its order vacating the new rules and remanded to the FCC to either justify its 2003 relaxation of the ownership rules or adopt new regulations. The FCC began a review of ownership rules and asked the Third Circuit to extend the stay. In 2007 the FCC voted to relax the newspaper-broadcast station cross-ownership rules, but left intact other ownership rules. In 2011 the Third Circuit vacated the relaxed newspaper-broadcast cross-ownership rules as well as a rule designed to increase ownership diversity because the FCC had not complied with the Administrative Procedure Act's notice and comment requirements. Prometheus Radio Project v. FCC, 652 F.3d 431 (3d Cir. 2011). The court once again remanded the rules to the FCC. This meant that the stricter newspaper-broadcast station cross-ownership restrictions remained in place, but the debate over deregulation continued. In 2011 the FCC issued a Notice of Proposed Rule Making and in 2014 issued a Further Notice of Proposed Rule Making; in these proceedings, the FCC gathered data about market conditions designed to bolster eventual changes to the ownership rules. See FCC's Review of the Broadcast Ownership Rules, available at https://www.fcc.gov/consumers/guides/fccs-review-broadcast-ownership-rules.

The FCC's role is to promote competition, localism, and diversity. Does deregulation accomplish these goals? Are these goals in tension with one another? Does the development of the Internet and other communications technologies alleviate the risks of concentration of ownership in the conventional media? Has the fight for local ownership and diversity of viewpoints already been lost?

Cable Ownership. The FCC has twice attempted to prohibit a single entity from owning cable systems that reach more than 30 percent of the nation's subscribers, but each time the limit has been struck down by the courts on nonconstitutional grounds. The first decision was Time Warner Entertainment Co. v. FCC, 240 F.3d 1126 (D.C. Cir. 2001). In 2008 the Commission issued a revised version of the 30 percent limit, arguing that that limit is necessary to assure that programmers will have a viable market for their programs even if one of the major cable system owners declines to carry their programming. The Court of Appeals again struck down the limit, chastising the FCC for failing to heed the court's previous objections. The court said the FCC's calculations were faulty because they failed to take into account the availability of direct broadcast satellites and other delivery platforms in determining what share of cable ownership would threaten competition. Comcast Corp. v. FCC, 579 F.3d 1 (D.C. Cir. 2009).

In a different context the same court rejected a cable operator's First Amendment argument. It held that limitations on a cable provider's ability to fill its channels with programming in which it had a financial interest were not content based and therefore were subject only to intermediate scrutiny. See Time Warner Entertainment Co. L.P. v. U.S. 211 F.3d 1313 (D.C. Cir. 2000).

4. INDECENCY

The FCC's statutory authority to police indecency in broadcasting comes from 18 U.S.C. §1464, which provides that "[w]hoever utters any obscene, indecent, or profane language by means of radio communication shall be fined . . . or imprisoned not more than two years, or both." Protection of children looms large in the reasons given by Congress and the FCC for restricting indecency. Numerous Supreme Court opinions endorse the proposition that the State may suppress some speech to serve that interest, but the Court has made it clear that the effort to protect children cannot unduly restrict access by adults, who have a constitutional right to see and hear non-obscene but indecent material. "Regardless of the strength of the government's interest" in protecting children, the Court has written, "the level of discourse reaching the mailbox simply cannot be limited to that which would be suitable for a sandbox." Bolger v. Youngs Drug Products Corp., 463 U.S. 60, 74–75 (1983). As the following cases illustrate, the tension between those two objectives lies at the heart of much indecency litigation.

The Supreme Court's 1978 decision in FCC v. Pacifica Foundation, 438 U.S. 726 (1978), is the precedent supporting attempts by Congress and the FCC to police indecency on the airwaves and cable. *Pacifica* involved a 1973 broadcast by a noncommercial radio station of a now-famous monologue by comedian George Carlin entitled "Filthy Words." In the monologue (now available for viewing on YouTube), Carlin repeats various permutations of seven "words you couldn't say on the public airwaves." A man driving with his young son heard the 2 p.m. broadcast of the Carlin monologue and subsequently complained to the FCC. Pacifica responded that it had played the monologue during a program about contemporary society's attitude toward language, that immediately before the broadcast it had advised listeners that the program included "sensitive language which might be regarded as offensive to some," and that it had received no other complaints about the broadcast.

The FCC held that Pacifica "could have been the subject of administrative sanctions" but chose not to impose any penalty. The FCC nonetheless put the order in Pacifica's license file with the notation that if there were further complaints, punishment might follow. Pacifica appealed, and the Supreme Court held that the First Amendment allowed the FCC to prohibit broadcast of "indecent" programming. The Court acknowledged that such prohibitions would be unconstitutional if applied to books or magazines, but said broadcasting was different because (1) it is a "uniquely pervasive presence in the lives of all Americans," and (2) it is "uniquely accessible to children."

In the years since 1978, the FCC's efforts to rid the airwaves of indecent speech have spurred challenges from broadcasters on both constitutional and administrative law grounds. In the case below, which involves in part celebrities who used profanity on live broadcasts, the Supreme Court addresses the constitutionality of indecency regulation—but not on First Amendment grounds.

Federal Communications Commission v. Fox Television Stations, Inc.

Supreme Court of the United States, 2012.
132 S. Ct. 2307.

■ JUSTICE KENNEDY delivered the opinion of the Court.

In FCC v. Fox Television Stations, Inc., 556 U.S. 502, 529 (2009) *(Fox I)*, the Court held that the Federal Communication Commission's decision to modify its indecency enforcement regime to regulate so-called fleeting expletives was neither arbitrary nor capricious. The Court then declined to address the constitutionality of the policy, however, because the United States Court of Appeals for the Second Circuit had yet to do so. On remand, the Court of Appeals found the policy was vague and, as a result, unconstitutional. 613 F.3d 317 (2010). The case now returns to this Court for decision upon the constitutional question.

I

A.

Title 18 U. S. C. §1464 provides that "[w]hoever utters any obscene, indecent, or profane language by means of radio communication shall be fined . . . or imprisoned not more than two years, or both." The Federal Communications Commission (Commission) has been instructed by Congress to enforce §1464 between the hours of 6 a.m. and 10 p.m. [ ] And the Commission has applied its regulations to radio and television broadcasters alike [ ]. Although the Commission has had the authority to regulate indecent broadcasts under §1464 since 1948 (and its predecessor commission, the Federal Radio Commission, since 1927), it did not begin to enforce §1464 until the 1970's. [ ]

This Court first reviewed the Commission's indecency policy in FCC v. Pacifica Foundation, 438 U.S. 726 (1978). In *Pacifica*, the Commission determined that George Carlin's "Filthy Words" monologue was indecent. It contained " 'language that describes, in terms patently offensive as measured by contemporary community standards for the broadcast medium, sexual or excretory activities and organs, at times of the day when there is a reasonable risk that children may be in the audience.' " *Id.*, at 732 (quoting 56 F.C.C.2d 94, 98 (1975)). This Court upheld the Commission's ruling. The broadcaster's statutory challenge was rejected. The Court held the Commission was not engaged in impermissible censorship . . . and that §1464's definition of indecency was not confined to speech with an appeal to the prurient interest [ ]. Finding no First Amendment violation, the decision explained the constitutional standard under which regulations of broadcasters are assessed. It observed that "broadcast media have established a uniquely pervasive presence in the lives of all Americans," . . . and that "broadcasting is uniquely accessible to children, even those too young to read" [ ]. In light of these considerations, "broadcasting . . . has received the most limited First Amendment protection." [ ]. Under this standard the Commission's order passed constitutional scrutiny. The Court did note the narrowness of its holding, explaining that it was not deciding whether "an occasional expletive . . . would justify any sanction." [S]ee also *id.*, at 760–761 (Powell, J., concurring in part and concurring in judgment) ("[C]ertainly the Court's holding . . . does not speak to cases involving the isolated use of a potentially offensive word in the course of a radio broadcast, as distinguished from the verbal shock treatment administered by respondent here").

From 1978 to 1987, the Commission did not go beyond the narrow circumstances of *Pacifica* and brought no indecency enforcement actions. [ ] Recognizing that *Pacifica* provided "no general prerogative to intervene in any case where words similar or identical to those in *Pacifica* are broadcast over a licensed radio or television station," the Commission distinguished between the "repetitive occurrence of the 'indecent' words" (such as in the Carlin monologue) and an "isolated" or "occasional" expletive, that would not necessarily be actionable. [ ]

In 1987, the Commission determined it was applying the *Pacifica* standard in too narrow a way. It stated that in later cases its definition of indecent language would "appropriately includ[e] a broader range of material than the seven specific words at issue in [the Carlin monologue]." [ ] Thus, the Commission indicated it would use the "generic definition of indecency" articulated in its 1975 *Pacifica* order, [ ] and assess the full context of allegedly indecent broadcasts rather than limiting its regulation to a "comprehensive index . . . of indecent words or pictorial depictions" [ ].

. . .

In 2001, the Commission issued a policy statement intended "to provide guidance to the broadcast industry regarding [its] caselaw interpreting 18 U. S. C. §1464 and [its] enforcement policies with respect to broadcast indecency." [ ] In that document the Commission restated that for material to be indecent it must depict sexual or excretory organs or activities and be patently offensive as measured by contemporary community standards for the broadcast medium. [ ] Describing the framework of what it considered patently offensive, the Commission explained that three factors had proved significant:

"(1) [T]he explicitness or graphic nature of the description or depiction of sexual or excretory organs or activities; (2) whether the material dwells on or repeats at length descriptions of sexual or excretory organs or activities; (3) whether the material appears to pander or is used to titillate, or whether the material appears to have been presented for its shock value." [ ]

As regards the second of these factors, the Commission explained that "[r]epetition of and persistent focus on sexual or excretory material have been cited consistently as factors that exacerbate the potential offensiveness of broadcasts. In contrast, where sexual or excretory references have been made once or have been passing or fleeting in nature, this characteristic has tended to weigh against a finding of indecency." [ ] The Commission then gave examples of material that was not found indecent because it was fleeting and isolated, [citing one FCC ruling finding "a fleeting and isolated utterance" in the context of live and spontaneous programming not actionable and another finding that fleeting language referring to sexual activity with a child was patently offensive].

B.

It was against this regulatory background that the three incidents of alleged indecency at issue here took place. First, in the 2002 Billboard Music Awards, broadcast by respondent Fox Television Stations, Inc., the singer Cher exclaimed during an unscripted acceptance speech: "I've also had my critics for the last 40 years saying that I was on my way out every year. Right. So f*** 'em." [ ] Second, Fox broadcast the Billboard Music Awards again in 2003. There, a person named Nicole Richie made the following unscripted remark while presenting an award: "Have you ever tried to get cow s*** out of a Prada purse? It's not so f***ing simple." [ ] The third incident involved an episode of NYPD Blue, a regular television show broadcast by respondent ABC Television Network. The episode broadcast on February 25, 2003, showed the nude buttocks of an adult female character for approximately seven seconds and for a moment the side of her breast. During the scene, in which the character was preparing to take a shower, a child portraying her boyfriend's son entered the bathroom. A moment of awkwardness followed. [ ]

After these incidents, but before the Commission issued Notices of Apparent Liability to Fox and ABC, the Commission issued a decision sanctioning NBC for a comment made by the singer Bono during the 2003 Golden Globe Awards. Upon winning the award for Best Original Song, Bono exclaimed: " 'This is really, really, f***ing brilliant. Really, really great.' " [ ] Reversing a decision by its enforcement bureau, the Commission found the use of the F-word actionably indecent. [ ] The Commission held that the word was "one of the most vulgar, graphic and explicit descriptions of sexual activity in the English language," and thus found "any use of that word or a variation, in any context, inherently has a sexual connotation."[ ] Turning to the isolated nature of the expletive, the Commission reversed prior rulings that had found fleeting expletives not indecent. The Commission held "the mere fact that specific words or phrases are not sustained or repeated does not mandate a finding that material that is otherwise patently offensive to the broadcast medium is not indecent." [*Golden Globes Order*].

C.

[The Commission did not impose penalties on Fox or NBC on the ground that they did not have sufficient notice that such broadcasts would violate FCC policy regarding fleeting expletives, but imposed forfeitures of $27,500 on each of the 45 ABC affiliates that carried the NYPD Blue episode on the ground that the policy against nudity was sufficiently clear.]

[Fox appealed the FCC decision arguing, among other things, that the government may not punish broadcast speech that in any other medium would be protected by the First Amendment. Fox and other networks argued that changes in the media landscape, especially the growth of cable and the Internet, had made the rationale of *Pacifica* untenable. The Second Circuit did not decide the constitutional question, but vacated the rulings against Fox on the ground that the Commission's reversal of policy violated the Administrative Procedures Act. In *Fox I* the Supreme Court reversed that decision and did not consider the constitutional question because it had not been decided by the Court of Appeals. On remand from *Fox I*, the Court of Appeals again held the Commission's indecency policy unconstitutional, this time on the ground that the policy failed to give broadcasters sufficient notice of what would be considered indecent. The Court of Appeals found the vagueness inherent in the policy had forced broadcasters to "choose between not airing . . . controversial programs [or] risking massive fines or possibly even loss of their licenses." The Second Circuit then vacated the forfeiture order against ABC, determining that it was bound by its *Fox* decision striking down the entirety of the Commission's indecency policy.]

The Government sought review of both judgments. . . .

II

A fundamental principle in our legal system is that laws which regulate persons or entities must give fair notice of conduct that is forbidden or required. [ ] This requirement of clarity in regulation is essential to the protections provided by the Due Process Clause of the Fifth Amendment. [ ] It requires the invalidation of laws that are impermissibly vague. A conviction or punishment fails to comply with due process if the statute or regulation under which it is obtained "fails to provide a person of ordinary intelligence fair notice of what is prohibited, or is so standardless that it authorizes or encourages seriously discriminatory enforcement." [ ] As this Court has explained, a regulation is not vague because it may at times be difficult to prove an incriminating fact but rather because it is unclear as to what fact must be proved. [ ]

Even when speech is not at issue, the void for vagueness doctrine addresses at least two connected but discrete due process concerns: first, that regulated parties should know what is required of them so they may act accordingly; second, precision and guidance are necessary so that those enforcing the law do not act in an arbitrary or discriminatory way. [ ] When speech is involved, rigorous adherence to those requirements is necessary to ensure that ambiguity does not chill protected speech.

These concerns are implicated here because, at the outset, the broadcasters claim they did not have, and do not have, sufficient notice of what is proscribed. And leaving aside any concerns about facial invalidity, they contend that the lengthy procedural history set forth above shows that the broadcasters did not have fair notice of what was forbidden. Under the 2001 Guidelines in force when the broadcasts occurred, a key consideration was " 'whether the material dwell[ed] on or repeat[ed] at length' " the offending description or depiction. [ ]. In the 2004 *Golden Globes* Order, issued after the broadcasts, the Commission changed course and held that fleeting expletives could be a statutory violation. *Fox I* [ ]. In the challenged orders now under review the Commission applied the new principle promulgated in the *Golden Globes* Order and determined fleeting expletives and a brief moment of indecency were actionably indecent. This regulatory history, however, makes it apparent that the Commission policy in place at the time of the broadcasts gave no notice to Fox or ABC that a fleeting expletive or a brief shot of nudity could be actionably indecent; yet Fox and ABC were found to be in violation. The Commission's lack of notice to Fox and ABC that its interpretation had changed so the fleeting moments of indecency contained in their broadcasts were a violation of §1464 as interpreted and enforced by the agency "fail[ed] to provide a person of ordinary intelligence fair notice of what is prohibited." [ ]. This would be true with respect to a regulatory change this abrupt on any subject, but it is surely the case when applied to the regulations in question, regulations that touch upon "sensitive areas of basic First Amendment freedoms" [ ].

The Government raises two arguments in response, but neither is persuasive. As for the two fleeting expletives, the Government concedes [in its brief] that "Fox did not have reasonable notice at the time of the broadcasts that the Commission would consider non-repeated expletives indecent." The Government argues, nonetheless, that Fox "cannot establish unconstitutional vagueness on that basis . . . because the Commission did not impose a sanction where Fox lacked such notice." [ ] As the Court observed when the case was here three Terms ago, it is true that the Commission declined to impose any forfeiture on Fox . . . and in its order the Commission claimed that it would not consider the indecent broadcasts either when considering whether to renew stations' licenses or "in any other context"[ ]. This "policy of forbearance," as the Government calls it, does not suffice to make the issue moot. Though the Commission claims it will not consider the prior indecent broadcasts "in any context," it has the statutory power to take into account "any history of prior offenses" when setting the level of a forfeiture penalty. [ ] Just as in the First Amendment context, the due process protection against vague regulations "does not leave [regulated parties] . . . at the mercy of *noblesse oblige.*" [ ] Given that the Commission found it was "not inequitable to hold Fox responsible for [the 2003 broadcast]" . . . and that it has the statutory authority to use its finding to increase any future penalties, the Government's assurance it will elect not to do so is insufficient to remedy the constitutional violation.

In addition, when combined with the legal consequence described above, reputational injury provides further reason for granting relief to Fox. . . . [F]indings of wrongdoing can result in harm to a broadcaster's "reputation with viewers and advertisers." . . . [The challenged FCC orders] describe in strongly disapproving terms the indecent material broadcast by Fox, [ ] (noting the "explicit, graphic, vulgar, and shocking nature of Ms. Richie's comments"), and Fox's efforts to protect children from being exposed to it, [ ] (finding Fox had failed to exercise " 'reasonable judgment, responsibility, and sensitivity to the public's needs and tastes to avoid [a] patently offensive broadcas[t]' "). Commission sanctions on broadcasters for indecent material are widely publicized. [ ] The challenged orders could have an adverse impact on Fox's reputation that audiences and advertisers alike are entitled to take into account.

With respect to ABC, the Government with good reason does not argue no sanction was imposed. The fine against ABC and its network affiliates for the seven seconds of nudity was nearly $1.24 million. [ ] The Government argues instead that ABC had notice that the scene in NYPD Blue would be considered indecent in light of a 1960 decision where the Commission declared that the "televising of nudes might well raise a serious question of programming contrary to 18 U. S. C. §1464." [ ] This argument does not prevail. An isolated and ambiguous statement from a 1960 Commission decision does not suffice for the fair notice required when the Government intends to impose over a $1 million fine for allegedly impermissible speech. The Commission, furthermore, had released decisions before sanctioning ABC that declined to find isolated and brief moments of nudity actionably indecent. [The court cited an FCC decision finding full frontal nudity in Schindler's List was not indecent]. This is not to say, of course, that a graphic scene from Schindler's List involving nude concentration camp prisoners is the same as the shower scene from NYPD Blue. It does show, however, that the Government can point to nothing that would have given ABC affirmative notice that its broadcast would be considered actionably indecent. It is likewise not sufficient for the Commission to assert, as it did in its order, that though "the depiction [of nudity] here is not as lengthy or repeated" as in some cases, the shower scene nonetheless "does contain more shots or lengthier depictions of nudity" than in other broadcasts found not indecent. [ ] This broad language fails to demonstrate that ABC had fair notice that its broadcast could be found indecent. In fact, a Commission ruling prior to the airing of the NYPD Blue episode had deemed 30 seconds of nude buttocks "very brief" and not actionably indecent in the context of the broadcast. [ ] In light of this record of agency decisions, and the absence of any notice in the 2001 Guidance that seven seconds of nude buttocks would be found indecent, ABC lacked constitutionally sufficient notice prior to being sanctioned.

The Commission failed to give Fox or ABC fair notice prior to the broadcasts in question that fleeting expletives and momentary nudity could be found actionably indecent. Therefore, the Commission's standards as applied to these broadcasts were vague, and the Commission's orders must be set aside.

III

It is necessary to make three observations about the scope of this decision. First, because the Court resolves these cases on fair notice grounds under the Due Process Clause, it need not address the First Amendment implications of the Commission's indecency policy. It is argued that this Court's ruling in *Pacifica* (and the less rigorous standard of scrutiny it provided for the regulation of broadcasters, [ ]) should be overruled because the rationale of that case has been overtaken by technological change and the wide availability of multiple other choices for listeners and viewers. [ ] The Government for its part maintains that when it licenses a conventional broadcast spectrum, the public may assume that the Government has its own interest in setting certain standards.[ ] These arguments need not be addressed here. In light of the Court's holding that the Commission's policy failed to provide fair notice it is unnecessary to reconsider *Pacifica* at this time.

This leads to a second observation. Here, the Court rules that Fox and ABC lacked notice at the time of their broadcasts that the material they were broadcasting could be found actionably indecent under then-existing policies. Given this disposition, it is unnecessary for the Court to address the constitutionality of the current indecency policy as expressed in the *Golden Globes* Order and subsequent adjudications. The Court adheres to its normal practice of declining to decide cases not before it. [ ]

Third, this opinion leaves the Commission free to modify its current indecency policy in light of its determination of the public interest and applicable legal requirements. And it leaves the courts free to review the current policy or any modified policy in light of its content and application.

The judgments of the United States Court of Appeals for the Second Circuit are vacated, and the cases are remanded for further proceedings consistent with the principles set forth in this opinion.

■ JUSTICE GINSBURG, concurring in the judgment

In my view, the Court's decision in FCC v. Pacifica Foundation . . . was wrong when it issued. Time, technological advances, and the Commission's untenable rulings in the cases now before the Court show why *Pacifica* bears reconsideration. Cf. FCC v. Fox Television Stations, Inc., 556 U.S. 502–535 (2009) (Thomas, J., concurring).

■ JUSTICE SOTOMAYOR took no part in the consideration or decision of these cases.

NOTES AND QUESTIONS

1.   The question remains unanswered whether the First Amendment permits the FCC to punish the broadcast of fleeting expletives. The vagueness problem, as described by the Second Circuit, was that the FCC's policy "forced broadcasters to 'choose between not airing . . . controversial programs [or] risking massive fines or possibly even loss of their licenses.' " Is the uncertainty as to whether the FCC has any power to regulate broadcast indecency any less likely to put broadcasters to such a choice? At some point, does the Court's "normal practice of declining to decide cases not before it" become a First Amendment issue in itself?

2.   Can the FCC cure the vagueness problem by decreeing that any use of certain words, or any nude depiction of certain body parts, is a violation? Is there a more nuanced solution that would pass muster?

3.   The Supreme Court declined to hear the FCC's appeal of a Third Circuit decision vacating the Commission's $550,000 fine against CBS for Janet Jackson's bare breast making a sudden appearance due to a "wardrobe malfunction" during the 2004 Super Bowl halftime show. FCC v. CBS Corp., 132 S.Ct. 2677 (2012).

4.   In the present media environment, is broadcasting different than other media in terms of its pervasiveness and accessibility to children? If so, what is the appropriate response: free broadcasting from indecency restraints, or expand them to other media that are pervasive and accessible to children? Do online media fit that description?

5.   From the *Pacifica* decision in 1978 through 2015, every content restriction on nonbroadcast media that reached the Supreme Court was struck down. Does that suggest that *Pacifica*'s days are numbered?

6.   In 2013 the FCC announced that it had reduced the backlog of pending indecency complaints by 70 percent. The FCC continues to police indecency, however, as illustrated by a $325,000 fine issued against a Virginia televisions station for broadcasting "a video image of a hand stroking an erect penis" during a 6 p.m. newscast. The station that broadcast the image claimed that it appeared inadvertently during a story about a volunteer fire fighter who had previously been an adult film star. The station aired an image of the woman taken from a website sponsored by the distributor of adult films in which she had appeared. On the border of the website were small video images of other adult films. The airing of one of these small

images, which appeared for three seconds during the newscast, triggered the fine. Notice of Apparent Liability for Forfeiture, In the Matter of WDBJ Television, Inc., File Nos. EB–IHD–14–00016819 and EB–12–IH–1363, March 23, 2015. FCC15–32.

———

B. CABLE

1. INDECENCY ON CABLE TELEVISION

The cable industry has been engaged in a decades-long battle with regulators over indecent programming. In the 1980s several states attempted to regulate indecency on cable, but the courts struck down those efforts. In 1992 Congress tackled the issue, passing a statute that required cable operators to segregate indecent programming and block it from all except those who specifically ordered it. The Supreme Court held that unconstitutional on the ground that less restrictive means (such as scrambling laws and lockboxes) were available to restrict children's access. Denver Area Educ. Telecomm. Consortium, Inc. v. Federal Communications Comm'n, [*DAETC*], 518 U.S. 727 (1996). The Court upheld another provision of the statute that authorized cable operators to refuse to carry indecent programming on the channels they leased to others. Cable systems used that authority to insist that cable networks scramble indecent programming, which cable operators then made available to subscribers through unscrambling devices for an additional fee. Scrambling in that era was imprecise, however; and sometimes audio or visual portions of the scrambled programs could be heard or seen by nonsubscribers, a phenomenon known as "signal bleed."

United States v. Playboy
Entertainment Group, Inc.

Supreme Court of the United States, 2000.
529 U.S. 803.

[To shield children from hearing or seeing images resulting from signal bleed, Congress added Section 505 to the Telecommunications Act of 1996. It required cable television operators providing channels "primarily dedicated to sexually-oriented programming" either to "fully scramble or otherwise fully block" those channels or to limit their transmission to hours when children are unlikely to be viewing (set by the FCC as 10 p.m. to 6 a.m.). Because fool-proof scrambling was expensive in the pre-digital era, the majority of cable operators responded to § 505 by adopting the "time channeling" approach. That meant that, for two-thirds of the day, no viewers could receive the programming in question.

Playboy Entertainment Group, a supplier of much of the affected programming, challenged § 505's constitutionality. A three-judge District Court concluded that § 505's content-based restriction on speech violated the First Amendment because the Government might further its interests in less restrictive ways. The less restrictive alternative identified by the court was the provision in § 504 of the Act, which required cable operators to block any channel upon a subscriber's request. The evidence showed that less than one percent of subscribers requested such blocking. The government argued that it therefore was not an effective alternative, but the court said that might be because the option was not sufficiently publicized. The court said the government had the burden of proving the ineffectiveness of voluntary blocking by individual households, and had not discharged it.]

■ JUSTICE KENNEDY delivered the opinion of the Court.

. . .

Since § 505 is a content-based speech restriction, it can stand only if it satisfies strict scrutiny. Sable Communications of Cal., Inc. v. FCC, 492 U.S. 115, 126 (1989) [which held that the feasibility of a technological approach to controlling minors' access to "dial-a-porn" messages required invalidation of a complete statutory ban on telephonic pornography]. If a statute regulates speech based on its content, it must be narrowly tailored to promote a compelling Government interest. *Ibid.* If a less restrictive alternative would serve the Government's purpose, the legislature must use that alternative. [Reno v. ACLU.] To do otherwise would be to restrict speech without an adequate justification, a course the First Amendment does not permit.

Our precedents teach these principles. Where the designed benefit of a content-based speech restriction is to shield the sensibilities of listeners, the general rule is that the right of expression prevails, even where no less restrictive alternative exists. We are expected to protect our own sensibilities "simply by averting [our] eyes." Cohen v. California, 403 U.S. 15, 21 (1971); accord, Erznoznik v. Jacksonville, 422 U.S. 205, 210–211 (1975). Here, of course, we consider images transmitted to some homes where they are not wanted and where parents often are not present to give immediate guidance. Cable television, like broadcast media, presents unique problems, which inform our assessment of the interests at stake, and which may justify restrictions that would be unacceptable in other contexts. See [*DAETC, Pacifica*]. No one suggests the Government must be indifferent to unwanted, indecent speech that comes into the home without parental consent. The speech here, all agree, is protected speech; and the question is what standard the Government must meet in order to restrict it. As we consider a content-based regulation, the answer should be clear: The standard is strict scrutiny. This case involves speech alone; and even where speech is indecent and enters the home, the objective of shielding children does not suffice to support a blanket ban if the protection can be accomplished by a less restrictive alternative.

. . .

There is, moreover, a key difference between cable television and the broadcasting media, which is the point on which this case turns: Cable systems have the capacity to block unwanted channels on a household-by-household basis. The option to block reduces the likelihood, so concerning to the Court in *Pacifica* [ ], that traditional First Amendment scrutiny would deprive the Government of all authority to address this sort of problem. The corollary, of course, is that targeted blocking enables the Government to support parental authority without affecting the First Amendment interests of speakers and willing listeners—listeners for whom, if the speech is unpopular or indecent, the privacy of their own homes may be the optimal place of receipt. Simply put, targeted blocking is less restrictive than banning, and the Government cannot ban speech if targeted blocking is a feasible and effective means of furthering its compelling interests. This is not to say that the absence of an effective blocking mechanism will in all cases suffice to support a law restricting the speech in question; but if a less restrictive means is available for the Government to achieve its goals, the Government must use it.

. . .

When a student first encounters our free speech jurisprudence, he or she might think it is influenced by the philosophy that one idea is as good as any other, and that in art and literature objective standards of style, taste, decorum, beauty, and esthetics are deemed by the Constitution to be inappropriate, indeed unattainable. Quite the opposite is true. The Constitution no more enforces a relativistic philosophy or moral nihilism than it does any other point of view. The Constitution exists precisely so that opinions and judgments, including esthetic and moral judgments about art and literature, can be formed, tested, and expressed. What the Constitution says is that these judgments are for the individual to make, not for the Government to decree, even with the mandate or approval of a majority. Technology expands the capacity to choose; and it denies the potential of this revolution if we assume the Government is best positioned to make these choices for us.

. . .

There is little hard evidence of how widespread or how serious the problem of signal bleed is. Indeed, there is no proof as to how likely any child is to view a discernible explicit image, and no proof of the duration of the bleed or the quality of the pictures or sound. To say that millions of children are subject to a risk of viewing signal bleed is one thing; to avoid articulating the true nature and extent of the risk is quite another. Under § 505, sanctionable signal bleed can include instances as fleeting as an image appearing on a screen for just a few seconds. The First

Amendment requires a more careful assessment and characterization of an evil in order to justify a regulation as sweeping as this. Although the parties have taken the additional step of lodging with the Court an assortment of videotapes, some of which show quite explicit bleeding and some of which show television static or snow, there is no attempt at explanation or context; there is no discussion, for instance, of the extent to which any particular tape is representative of what appears on screens nationwide.

    . . .

It is no response that voluntary blocking requires a consumer to take action, or may be inconvenient, or may not go perfectly every time. A court should not assume a plausible, less restrictive alternative would be ineffective; and a court should not presume parents, given full information, will fail to act. If unresponsive operators are a concern, moreover, a notice statute could give cable operators ample incentive, through fines or other penalties for noncompliance, to respond to blocking requests in prompt and efficient fashion.

[The government argued that many parents would fail to order blocking even if § 504 were well publicized: "There would certainly be parents—perhaps a large number of parents—who out of inertia, indifference, or distraction, simply would take no action to block signal bleed, even if fully informed of the problem and even if offered a relatively easy solution." In those instances, "Section 505 would be the only means to protect society's independent interest."]

Even upon the assumption that the Government has an interest in substituting itself for informed and empowered parents, its interest is not sufficiently compelling to justify this widespread restriction on speech. The Government's argument stems from the idea that parents do not know their children are viewing the material on a scale or frequency to cause concern, or if so, that parents do not want to take affirmative steps to block it and their decisions are to be superseded. The assumptions have not been established; and in any event the assumptions apply only in a regime where the option of blocking has not been explained. The whole point of a publicized § 504 would be to advise parents that indecent material may be shown and to afford them an opportunity to block it at all times, even when they are not at home and even after 10 p.m. Time channeling does not offer this assistance. The regulatory alternative of a publicized § 504, which has the real possibility of promoting more open disclosure and the choice of an effective blocking system, would provide parents the information needed to engage in active supervision. The Government has not shown that this alternative, a regime of added communication and support, would be insufficient to secure its objective, or that any overriding harm justifies its intervention.

There can be little doubt, of course, that under a voluntary blocking regime, even with adequate notice, some children will be exposed to signal bleed; and we need not discount the possibility that a graphic image could have a negative impact on a young child. It must be remembered, however, that children will be exposed to signal bleed under time channeling as well. Time channeling, unlike blocking, does not eliminate signal bleed around the clock. Just as adolescents may be unsupervised outside of their own households, it is hardly unknown for them to be unsupervised in front of the television set after 10 p.m. The record is silent as to the comparative effectiveness of the two alternatives.

Basic speech principles are at stake in this case. When the purpose and design of a statute is to regulate speech by reason of its content, special consideration or latitude is not accorded to the Government merely because the law can somehow be described as a burden rather than outright suppression. We cannot be influenced, moreover, by the perception that the regulation in question is not a major one because the speech is not very important. The history of the law of free expression is one of vindication in cases involving speech that many citizens may find shabby, offensive, or even ugly. It follows that all content-based restrictions on speech must give us more than a moment's pause. If television broadcasts can expose children to the real risk of harmful exposure to indecent materials, even in their own home and without parental consent, there is a problem the Government can address. It must do so, however, in a way consistent with First Amendment principles. Here the Government has not met the burden the First Amendment imposes.

. . .

■ JUSTICE BREYER, with whom the CHIEF JUSTICE, JUSTICE O'CONNOR, and JUSTICE SCALIA join, dissenting.

. . .

The majority first concludes that the Government failed to prove the seriousness of the problem—receipt of adult channels by children whose parents did not request their broadcast. [ ] This claim is flat-out wrong. For one thing, the parties concede that basic . . . scrambling does not scramble the audio portion of the program. For another, Playboy itself conducted a survey of cable operators who were asked: "Is your system in full compliance with Section 505 (no discernible audio or video bleed)?" To this question, 75% of cable operators answered "no." [ ] Further, the Government's expert took the number of homes subscribing to Playboy or Spice, multiplied by the fraction of cable households with children and the average number of children per household, and found 29 million children are potentially exposed to audio and video bleed from adult programming. [ ] Even discounting by 25% for systems that might be considered in full compliance, this left 22 million children in homes with faulty scrambling systems. [ ] And, of course, the record contains additional anecdotal evidence and the concerns expressed by elected officials, probative of a larger problem. [ ]

. . . *If signal bleed is not a significant empirical problem, then why, in light of the cost of its cure, must so many cable operators switch to nighttime hours?* There is no realistic answer to this question. I do not think it realistic to imagine that signal bleed occurs just enough to make cable operators skittish, without also significantly exposing children to these images. [ ]

If, as the majority suggests, the signal bleed problem is not significant, then there is also no significant burden on speech created by § 505. The majority cannot have this evidence both ways. And if, given this logical difficulty and the quantity of empirical evidence, the majority still believes that the Government has not proved its case, then it imposes a burden upon the Government beyond that suggested in any other First Amendment case of which I am aware.

III

The majority's second claim—that the Government failed to demonstrate the absence of a "less restrictive alternative"—presents a closer question. The specific question is whether § 504's "opt-out" amounts to a "less restrictive," but *similarly* practical and *effective*, way to accomplish § 505's child-protecting objective. As *Reno* tells us, a "less restrictive alternativ[e]" must be "at least as effective in achieving the legitimate purpose that the statute was enacted to serve." [ ]

The words I have just emphasized, "similarly" and "effective," are critical. In an appropriate case they ask a judge not to apply First Amendment rules mechanically, but to decide whether, in light of the benefits and potential alternatives, the statute works speech-related harm (here to adult speech) out of proportion to the benefits that the statute seeks to provide (here, child protection).

These words imply a degree of leeway, however small, for the Legislature when it chooses among possible alternatives in light of predicted comparative effects. Without some such empirical leeway, the undoubted ability of lawyers and judges to imagine *some* kind of slightly less drastic or restrictive an approach would make it impossible to write laws that deal with the harm that called the statute into being. As Justice Blackmun pointed out, a "judge would be unimaginative indeed if he could not come up with something a little less 'drastic' or a little less 'restrictive' in almost any situation, and thereby enable himself to vote to strike legislation down." [ ] Used without a sense of the practical choices that face legislatures, "the test merely announces an inevitable [negative] result, and the test is no test at all." [ ]

I turn then to the major point of disagreement. Unlike the majority, I believe the record makes clear that § 504's opt-out is not a similarly effective alternative. Section 504 (opt-out) and § 505 (opt-in) work differently in order to achieve very different legislative objectives. Section 504 gives parents the power to tell cable operators to keep any channel out of their home. Section 505 does more. Unless parents explicitly consent, it inhibits the transmission of adult cable channels to children whose parents may be unaware of what they are watching, whose parents cannot easily supervise television viewing habits, whose parents do not know of their § 504 "opt-out" rights, or whose parents are simply unavailable at critical times. In this respect, § 505 serves the same interests as the laws that deny children access to adult cabarets or X-rated movies. [ ] These laws, and § 505, all act in the absence of direct parental supervision.

. . . I could not disagree more when the majority implies that the Government's independent interest in offering such protection—preventing, say, an 8-year-old child from watching virulent pornography without parental consent—might not be "compelling." [ ] No previous case in which the protection of children was at issue has suggested any such thing. Indeed, they all say precisely the opposite. [ ] They make clear that Government has a compelling interest in helping parents by preventing Minors from accessing sexually explicit materials in the absence of parental supervision. [ ]

. . .

IV

Section 505 raises the cost of adult channel broadcasting. In doing so, it restricts, but does not ban, adult speech. Adults may continue to watch adult channels, though less conveniently, by watching at night, recording programs with a VCR, or by subscribing to digital cable with better blocking systems. [ ] The Government's justification for imposing this restriction—limiting the access of children to channels that broadcast virtually 100% "sexually explicit" material—is "compelling." The record shows no similarly effective, less restrictive alternative. Consequently § 505's restriction, viewed in light of the proposed alternative, is proportionate to need. That is to say, it restricts speech no more than necessary to further that compelling need. Taken together, these considerations lead to the conclusion that § 505 is lawful.

I repeat that my disagreement with the majority lies in the fact that, in my view, the Government has satisfied its burden of proof. In particular, it has proved both the existence of a serious problem and the comparative ineffectiveness of § 504 in resolving that problem. This disagreement is not about allocation of First Amendment burdens of proof, basic First Amendment principle, nor the importance of that Amendment to our scheme of Government. First Amendment standards are rigorous. They safeguard speech. But they also permit Congress to enact a law that increases the costs associated with certain speech, where doing so serves a compelling interest that cannot be served through the adoption of a less restrictive, similarly effective alternative. Those standards at their strictest make it difficult for the Government to prevail. But they do not make it impossible for the Government to prevail.

. . .

Congress has taken seriously the importance of maintaining adult access to the sexually explicit channels here at issue. It has tailored the restrictions to minimize their impact upon adults while offering parents help in keeping unwanted transmissions from their children. By finding "adequate alternatives" where there are none, the Court reduces Congress' protective power to the vanishing point. That is not what the First Amendment demands.

I respectfully dissent.

[Concurring opinions of Justices Stevens and Thomas are omitted].

[In a separate dissenting opinion, Justice Scalia argued that § 505 could be sustained on the "simpler ground" that a business that offers hard-core sexual material as a constant and intentional objective of its business and promotes it as such is not protected by the First Amendment.]

> Thus, while I agree with Justice Breyer's child-protection analysis, it leaves me with the same feeling of true-but-inadequate as the conclusion that Al Capone did not accurately report his income. It is not only children who can be protected from occasional uninvited exposure to what appellee calls "adult-oriented programming"; we can all be. Section 505 covers only businesses that engage in the "commercial exploitation of erotica solely for the sake of their prurient appeal," [ ]—which, as Playboy's own advertisements make plain, is what "adult" programming is all about. In most contexts, contemporary American society has chosen to permit such commercial exploitation. That may be a wise democratic choice, if only because of the difficulty in many contexts (though not this one) of identifying the panderer to sex. It is, however, not a course compelled by the Constitution. Since the Government is entirely free to *block* these transmissions, it may certainly take the less drastic step of dictating how, and during what times, they may occur.

NOTES AND QUESTIONS

1. If Congress still believes that voluntary blocking at the customer's request does not sufficiently protect children, what legislative options does this decision leave open? Would the Court sustain a requirement similar to that of § 505 if Congress marshaled stronger evidence of the exposure of children to signal bleed and the ineffectiveness of voluntary blocking? What kind of evidence might suffice?

2.   Will regulation always fail the no-less-restrictive-alternative test if technology provides means by which parents can protect their children? Note that the means must also be "effective." Is regulation permissible if the means is ineffective only because of parental indifference? Does the government have an interest in protecting children whose parents do not protect them? Is it compelling?

3.   Justice Scalia long argued, as he did in his dissent here, that harm to children is not the only justification for regulation of indecency. What other interests might suffice? Preserving a set of attitudes about sex? Maintaining a level of decorum in public discourse? Regulating an industry that may create socially costly externalities? Would this approach be consistent with the choice that has been made between these values and speech through the narrow definition of obscenity?

4.   Does the First Amendment prevent the FCC from regulating indecency on cable television as it does broadcast television indecency?

_____

2. ACCESS

We have already seen that regulation of broadcasters (including the requirement that they obtain a license before broadcasting) has been justified largely as an attempt to ensure that a variety of voices have access to the spectrum. Congress and the Federal Communications Commission have attempted to achieve a similar objective in cable television. The following case provides the Supreme Court's most extensive consideration so far of government's role in promoting media diversity. The specific issue was the constitutionality of must-carry rules, which require cable operators to carry the signals of local over-the-air broadcasters. The rules had been relaxed for a time in the 1980s but were reinstated by Congress in 1992.

Turner Broadcasting System, Inc. v. Federal Communications Commission [*Turner I*]

Supreme Court of the United States, 1994.
512 U.S. 622.

■ JUSTICE KENNEDY announced the judgment of the Court and delivered the opinion of the Court, except as to Part III–B.

Sections 4 and 5 of the Cable Television Consumer Protection and Competition Act of 1992 require cable television systems to devote a portion of their channels to the transmission of local broadcast television stations. [Congress authorized a three-judge federal court to hear challenges to the law, with a direct appeal to the Supreme Court. Cable system operators and cable program providers brought such a challenge.] The case presents the question whether these provisions abridge the freedom of speech or of the press, in violation of the First Amendment.

The United States District Court for the District of Columbia granted summary judgment for the United States, holding that the challenged provisions are consistent with the First Amendment. Because issues of material fact remain unresolved in the record developed thus far, we vacate the District Court's judgment and remand the case for further proceedings.

[The Court reviewed the history and characteristics of cable television, discussed the 1992 Act in detail, and rejected the government's contention that regulation of cable should be analyzed under the same standard that applies to regulation of broadcast television.]

II [B]

[T]he First Amendment, subject only to narrow and well-understood exceptions, does not countenance governmental control over the content of messages expressed by private individuals. [*R.A.V.*]; Texas v. Johnson, 491 U.S. 397, 414 (1989). Our precedents thus apply the most exacting scrutiny to regulations that suppress, disadvantage, or impose differential burdens upon speech because of its content. [ ]. Laws that compel speakers to utter or distribute speech bearing a particular message are subject to the same rigorous scrutiny. [ ]. In contrast, regulations that are unrelated to the content of speech are subject to an intermediate level of scrutiny, [ ], because in most cases they pose a less substantial risk of excising certain ideas or viewpoints from the public dialogue.

Deciding whether a particular regulation is content based or content neutral is not always a simple task. We have said that the "principal inquiry in determining content neutrality . . . is whether the government has adopted a regulation of speech because of [agreement or] disagreement with the message it conveys." [ ] See *R.A.V.* [ ] ("The government may not regulate [speech] based on hostility—or favoritism—towards the underlying message expressed"). The purpose, or justification, of a regulation will often be evident on its face. [ ] But while a content-based purpose may be sufficient in certain circumstances to show that a regulation is content based, it is not necessary to such a showing in all cases. [ ] Nor will the mere assertion of a content-neutral purpose be enough to save a law which, on its face, discriminates based on content. [ ]

As a general rule, laws that by their terms distinguish favored speech from disfavored speech on the basis of the ideas or views expressed are content based. [ ] By contrast, laws that confer benefits or impose burdens on speech without reference to the ideas or views expressed are in most instances content neutral. [ ]

C

Insofar as they pertain to the carriage of full power broadcasters, the must-carry rules, on their face, impose burdens and confer benefits without reference to the content of speech. Although the provisions interfere with cable operators' editorial discretion by compelling them to offer carriage to a certain minimum number of broadcast stations, the extent of the interference does not depend upon the content of the cable operators' programming. The rules impose obligations upon all operators, save those with fewer than 300 subscribers, regardless of the programs or stations they now offer or have offered in the past. Nothing in the Act imposes a restriction, penalty, or burden by reason of the views, programs, or stations the cable operator has selected or will select. The number of channels a cable operator must set aside depends only on the operator's channel capacity [ ]; hence, an operator cannot avoid or mitigate its obligations under the Act by altering the programming it offers to subscribers. Cf. [*Tornillo*].

The must-carry provisions also burden cable programmers by reducing the number of channels for which they can compete. But, again, this burden is unrelated to content, for it extends to all cable programmers irrespective of the programming they choose to offer viewers. [ ] And finally, the privileges conferred by the must-carry provisions are also unrelated to content. The rules benefit all full power broadcasters who request carriage—be they commercial or noncommercial, independent or network-affiliated, English or Spanish language, religious or secular. The aggregate effect of the rules is thus to make every full power commercial and noncommercial broadcaster eligible for must-carry, provided only that the broadcaster operates within the same television market as a cable system.

It is true that the must-carry provisions distinguish between speakers in the television programming market. But they do so based only upon the manner in which speakers transmit their messages to viewers, and not upon the messages they carry: Broadcasters, which transmit over the airwaves, are favored, while cable programmers, which do not, are disfavored. Cable operators, too, are burdened by the carriage obligations, but only because they control access to the cable conduit. So long as they are not a subtle means of exercising a content preference, speaker distinctions of this nature are not presumed invalid under the First Amendment.

That the must-carry provisions, on their face, do not burden or benefit speech of a particular content does not end the inquiry. Our cases have recognized that even a regulation neutral on its face may be content-based if its manifest purpose is to regulate speech because of the message it conveys. [ ]

Appellants contend, in this regard, that the must-carry regulations are content-based because Congress' purpose in enacting them was to promote speech of a favored content. We do not agree. Our review of the Act and its various findings persuades us that Congress' overriding objective in enacting must-carry was not to favor programming of a particular subject matter, viewpoint, or format, but rather to preserve access to free television programming for the 40 percent of Americans without cable.

In unusually detailed statutory findings, [ ], Congress explained that because cable systems and broadcast stations compete for local advertising revenue, [ ], and because cable operators have a vested financial interest in favoring their affiliated programmers over broadcast stations, [ ], cable operators have a built-in "economic incentive . . . to delete, reposition, or not carry local broadcast signals." [ ]. Congress concluded that absent a requirement that cable systems carry the signals of local broadcast stations, the continued availability of free local broadcast television would be threatened. . . .

. . .

Appellants and the dissent make much of the fact that, in the course of describing the purposes behind the Act, Congress referred to the value of broadcast programming. In particular, Congress noted that broadcast television is "an important source of local news[,] public affairs programming and other local broadcast services critical to an informed electorate," [ ], and that noncommercial television "provides educational and informational programming to the Nation's citizens." [ ]. We do not think, however, that such references cast any material doubt on the content-neutral character of must-carry. That Congress acknowledged the local orientation of broadcast programming and the role that noncommercial stations have played in educating the public does not indicate that Congress regarded broadcast programming as more valuable than cable programming. Rather, it reflects nothing more than the recognition that the services provided by broadcast television have some intrinsic value and, thus, are worth preserving against the threats posed by cable. . . .

. . .

D

Appellants advance three additional arguments to support their view that the must-carry provisions warrant strict scrutiny. In brief, appellants contend that the provisions (1) compel speech by cable operators, (2) favor broadcast programmers over cable programmers, and (3) single out certain members of the press for disfavored treatment. None of these arguments suffices to require strict scrutiny in the present case.

1

. . .

Tornillo and *Pacific Gas & Electric* [Co. v. Public Utilities Comm'n of Cal., 475 U.S. 1, 11 (1986) (plurality opinion) (invalidating a rule requiring a privately owned utility to include with its bills "an editorial newsletter published by a consumer group critical of the utility's ratemaking practices")] do not control this case for the following reasons. First, unlike the access rules struck down in those cases, the must-carry rules are content-neutral in application. . . .

Second, appellants do not suggest, nor do we think it the case, that must-carry will force cable operators to alter their own messages to respond to the broadcast programming they are required to carry. [ ] Given cable's long history of serving as a conduit for broadcast signals, there appears little risk that cable viewers would assume that the broadcast stations carried on a cable system convey ideas or messages endorsed by the cable operator. . . .

Finally, the asserted analogy to *Tornillo* ignores an important technological difference between newspapers and cable television. Although a daily newspaper and a cable operator both may enjoy monopoly status in a given locale, the cable operator exercises far greater control over access to the relevant medium. A daily newspaper, no matter how secure its local monopoly, does not possess the power to obstruct readers' access to other competing publications—whether they be weekly local newspapers, or daily newspapers published in other cities. Thus, when a newspaper asserts exclusive control over its own news copy, it does not thereby prevent other newspapers from being distributed to willing recipients in the same locale.

The same is not true of cable. When an individual subscribes to cable, the physical connection between the television set and the cable network gives the cable operator bottleneck, or gatekeeper, control over most (if not all) of the television programming that is channeled into the subscriber's home. Hence, simply by virtue of its ownership of the essential pathway for cable speech, a cable operator can prevent its subscribers from obtaining access to programming it chooses to exclude. A cable operator, unlike speakers in other media, can thus silence the voice of competing speakers with a mere flick of the switch.

The potential for abuse of this private power over a central avenue of communication cannot be overlooked. [ ] The First Amendment's command that government not impede the freedom of speech does not disable the government from taking steps to ensure that private interests not restrict, through physical control of a critical pathway of communication, the free flow of information and ideas. . . .

2

Second, appellants urge us to apply strict scrutiny because the must-carry provisions favor one set of speakers (broadcast programmers) over another (cable programmers). Appellants maintain that as a consequence of this speaker preference, some cable programmers who would have secured carriage in the absence of must-carry may now be dropped. Relying on language in Buckley v. Valeo, appellants contend that such a regulation is presumed invalid under the First Amendment because the government may not "restrict the speech of some elements of our society in order to enhance the relative voice of others." [ ]

To the extent appellants' argument rests on the view that all regulations distinguishing between speakers warrant strict scrutiny, [ ], it is mistaken. . . .

Our holding in *Buckley* does not support appellants' broad assertion that all speaker-partial laws are presumed invalid. Rather, it stands for the proposition that speaker-based laws demand strict scrutiny when they reflect the Government's preference for the substance of what the favored speakers have to say (or aversion to what the disfavored speakers have to say). [ ] Because the expenditure limit in *Buckley* was designed to ensure that the political speech of the wealthy not drown out the speech of others, we found that it was concerned with the communicative impact of the regulated speech. . . .

The question here is whether Congress preferred broadcasters over cable programmers based on the content of programming each group offers. The answer, as we explained above, [ ], is no. Congress granted must-carry privileges to broadcast stations on the belief that the broadcast television industry is in economic peril due to the physical characteristics of cable transmission and the economic incentives facing the cable industry. Thus, the fact that the provisions benefit broadcasters and not cable programmers does not call for strict scrutiny under our precedents.

3

[The Court rejected the argument that strict scrutiny was required by the line of cases that apply strict scrutiny to taxation schemes that single out one medium or a subset thereof (see *Leathers*). Although the must-carry rules applied only to cable and not to other video delivery systems such as satellite systems, the Court said this discrimination against the cable medium was justified by the bottleneck monopoly power exercised by cable operators and the dangers this posed to the viability of broadcast television. It also said the must-carry provisions applied to all cable systems and therefore did not create as much risk of undermining First Amendment interests as narrowly targeted tax schemes.]

III [A]

In sum, the must-carry provisions do not pose such inherent dangers to free expression, or present such potential for censorship or manipulation, as to justify application of the most exacting level of First Amendment scrutiny. We agree with the District Court that the appropriate standard by which to evaluate the constitutionality of must-carry is the intermediate level of scrutiny applicable to content-neutral restrictions that impose an incidental burden on speech. See Ward v. Rock Against Racism, 491 U.S. 781 (1989); United States v. O'Brien, 391 U.S. 367 (1968).

Under *O'Brien*, a content-neutral regulation will be sustained if

"it furthers an important or substantial governmental interest; if the governmental interest is unrelated to the suppression of free expression; and if the incidental restriction on alleged First Amendment freedoms is no greater than is essential to the furtherance of that interest." [ ]

To satisfy this standard, a regulation need not be the least speech-restrictive means of advancing the Government's interests. "Rather, the requirement of narrow tailoring is satisfied 'so long as the . . . regulation promotes a substantial government interest that would be achieved less effectively absent the regulation.' " [ ] Narrow tailoring in this context requires, in other words, that the means chosen do not "burden substantially more speech than is necessary to further the government's legitimate interests." [ ]

Congress declared that the must-carry provisions serve three interrelated interests: (1) preserving the benefits of free, over-the-air local broadcast television, (2) promoting the widespread dissemination of information from a multiplicity of sources, and (3) promoting fair competition in the market for television programming. [ ] None of these interests is related to the "suppression of free expression," [ ], or to the content of any speakers' messages. And viewed in the abstract, we have no difficulty concluding that each of them is an important governmental interest. [ ]

. . . The interest in maintaining the local broadcasting structure does not evaporate simply because cable has come upon the scene. Although cable and other technologies have ushered in alternatives to broadcast television, nearly 40 percent of American households still rely on broadcast stations as their exclusive source of television programming. . . .

Likewise, assuring that the public has access to a multiplicity of information sources is a governmental purpose of the highest order, for it promotes values central to the First Amendment. . . . Finally, the Government's interest in eliminating restraints on fair competition is always substantial, even when the individuals or entities subject to particular regulations are engaged in expressive activity protected by the First Amendment. [ ]

B

That the Government's asserted interests are important in the abstract does not mean, however, that the must-carry rules will in fact advance those interests. When the Government defends a regulation on speech as a means to redress past harms or prevent anticipated harms, it must do more than simply "posit the existence of the disease sought to be cured." [ ] It must demonstrate that the recited harms are real, not merely conjectural, and that the regulation will in fact alleviate these harms in a direct and material way. [ ]

. . . On the state of the record developed thus far, and in the absence of findings of fact from the District Court, we are unable to conclude that the Government has [demonstrated either].

In sum, because there are genuine issues of material fact still to be resolved on this record, we hold that the District Court erred in granting summary judgment in favor of the Government. . . . [W]e think it necessary to permit the parties to develop a more thorough factual record, and to allow the District Court to resolve any factual disputes remaining, before passing upon the constitutional validity of the challenged provisions.

[The dissenters thought it clear that the provisions were content-based and that strict scrutiny was required. In the view of Justice O'Connor, joined by Justices Scalia, Ginsburg, and Thomas, the content-based nature of the regulation at issue was a congressional preference for the types of programs that broadcast stations provide to the public. She cited legislative findings that broadcast television stations continue to be an important source of local news and public affairs programming. This emphasis on localism amounted to legislative favoritism based on the content of broadcasters' speech. Since it was content-based, the regulation had to pass the exacting strict scrutiny standard and could not do so.]

NOTES AND QUESTIONS

1. *Tornillo* held that a newspaper's choice of material to publish constituted the exercise of editorial control and judgment that couldn't be regulated consistently with the First Amendment. Why doesn't that apply to a cable operator's choice of material to carry on its channels? Much of the material published by newspapers consists of material they choose from other sources, such as wire services and syndicates. And today some cable systems offer their own programming as well as material produced by others. Are there other bases for distinguishing cable from newspapers?

2. The Court suggests two additional distinctions. One is that viewers aren't likely to assume that cable operators endorse the programming of the local broadcasters they carry. Would newspaper readers be likely to believe

the Miami Herald endorsed Tornillo's response? The other suggested distinction is that "the cable operator exercises far greater control over access to the relevant medium." But that is true only if the relevant medium is the local cable system in the first case and all competing publications in the other. Is that the right comparison?

3.   Is the argument that must-carry rules are content-neutral a sufficient basis for distinguishing *Tornillo?* Would the Court sustain a requirement that newspapers devote a portion of their space to independent contributors?

4.   The Court acknowledges that one of Congress's purposes, in addition to preserving access to free television, was to protect local programming. Is the latter a content-based purpose? How can the Court know which was Congress's "overriding objective"? Is it meaningful to refer to the "benefits of free, over-the-air local broadcasting" without considering the content of that broadcasting? Is the "widespread dissemination of information from a multiplicity of sources" a worthy goal of government regulation if the content of that expression is similar or identical?

5.   Does the *Turner* Court's refusal to apply the editorial judgment rationale to cable narrow the applicability of *Tornillo* to instances in which the regulation operates as a content-based penalty?

6.   Justice Stevens did not join in Part III–B of Justice Kennedy's opinion because he thought the must-carry rules should be sustained without further proceedings. That left the Court evenly divided between the four dissenters who would have held the rules invalid without further proceedings and the four justices who voted to remand. Justice Stevens concurred in the judgment to remand in order to provide a disposition.

7.   On remand, the three-judge court again held the must-carry rules constitutional. The Supreme Court was again sharply divided, but five justices agreed that the *O'Brien* test was satisfied by evidence that the rules would be effective in "(1) preserving the benefits of free, over-the-air local broadcast television," and "(2) promoting the widespread dissemination of information from a multiplicity of sources." Turner Broadcasting System, Inc. v. Federal Communications Commission [*Turner II*], 520 U.S. 180 (1997).

———————

Content Neutrality. If a regulation is characterized as content-based, it must survive strict scrutiny; if it is content-neutral, only intermediate scrutiny is required. Because the latter test is relatively easy to satisfy and the former is quite rigorous, the characterization is often outcome-determinative. In *Turner I*, there was little doubt that the must-carry rules would be held unconstitutional if they were considered content-based.

How a restriction will be characterized is sometimes unpredictable. Consider, for example, United States v. O'Brien, 391 U.S. 367 (1968). That case involved the conviction of an anti-war protester for burning his draft card to protest the U.S. military establishment. The Court conceded that the act was symbolic speech protected by the First Amendment, but characterized the statute that prohibited it as content-neutral, even though it had been passed in reaction to public indignation over draft card burning by opponents of the war in Vietnam, and even though the report of the Senate Armed Services Committee said its purpose was to stop "the defiant destruction and mutilation of draft cards by dissident persons who disapprove of national policy." Professor Rodney Smolla has written, "For the Supreme Court to whitewash this law by pretending it was passed for reasons unrelated to expression was sheer hypocrisy— this was one of the most content-based laws the Congress had ever passed and the Court knew it." See Rodney A. Smolla, Free Speech in an Open Society 54–64 (1992).

For many years the must-carry rules at issue in *Turner I* were defended on a content-based ground: that they were necessary to assure the survival of local stations which, unlike cable channels, provided local news, weather, and public affairs programming. In the decision the Court minimized that purpose and emphasized the alternative aim of preserving "access to free television programming for the 40 percent of Americans without cable."

In *Turner I* the Court said laws that distinguish favored speech from disfavored speech on the basis of the ideas or views expressed are content-based, while laws that confer benefits or impose burdens on speech without reference to the ideas or views expressed are content-neutral. The Court does not consistently employ that test. For example, in Arkansas Writers' Project v. Ragland, 481 U.S. 221 (1987), the Court held that a state tax that applied to general interest magazines but exempted sports magazines was content-based because whether a particular publication was exempt could only be determined by looking at its content. There was no suggestion that the two types of magazines espoused different ideas or views.

More recently, in Reed v. Town of Gilbert, 135 S.Ct. 2218 (2015), the Supreme Court addressed a sign ordinance that regulated signs differently based on whether they were classified as "political," "ideologicial," or "temporary directional signs." In striking down the ordinance, the Court stated:

> Government regulation of speech is content based if a law applies to particular speech because of the topic discussed or the idea or message expressed. [ ]. This commonsense meaning of the phrase 'content based' requires a court to consider whether a regulation of speech 'on its face' draws distinctions based on the message a speaker conveys. [ ]. Some facial distinctions based on a message are obvious, defining regulated speech by particular subject matter, and others are more subtle, defining regulated speech by its function or purpose. Both are

distinctions drawn based on the message a speaker conveys, and, therefore, are subject to strict scrutiny.

Our precedents have also recognized a separate and additional category of laws that, though facially content neutral, will be considered content-based regulations of speech: laws that cannot be 'justified without reference to the content of the regulated speech,' or that were adopted by the government 'because of disagreement with the message [the speech] conveys' [ ]. Those laws, like those that are content based on their face, must also satisfy strict scrutiny.

The Court further stated that "an innocuous justification cannot transform a facially content-based law into one that is content neutral,"emphasizing that "whether a law is content neutral on its face" must be assessed "*before* turning to the law's justification or purpose." Was this the methodology employed by the majority in *Turner*?

Justice Kennedy's analysis in *Turner* did not distinguish between regulations that focus on the subject matter of the speech and regulations that focus on the viewpoint expressed. In other contexts the Court has recognized that viewpoint discrimination is a different—and more objectionable—phenomenon than content discrimination. It has said that a prohibition against fighting words might be permissible even though it singles out particular content (and is therefore content-based), but a prohibition against fighting words that express racial hostility is impermissible because that singles out a particular viewpoint within the larger category of fighting words (and is therefore viewpoint-based). See R.A.V. v. St. Paul, 505 U.S. 377 (1992). The Court has never upheld a restriction that it identified as viewpoint-based.

Professor Wojciech Sadurski says whether a restriction is characterized as content-based or content-neutral depends on the generality of the question asked. He cites as an example a regulation banning solicitation of political contributions near the entrance to a post office, which the Court upheld on the ground that it was content-neutral because it banned solicitation of money for any purpose. Dissenting, Justice Brennan considered it content-based: "If a person on postal premises says to members of the public, 'Please support my political advocacy group,' he cannot be punished. If he says 'Please contribute $10,' he is subject to criminal prosecution. His punishment depends entirely on what he says." See United States v. Kokinda, 497 U.S. 720, 753 (1990).

Professor Sadurski suggests that "the best way of making sense of the 'content-based' nature of the restriction is not by looking at the character of the speech restricted (because at this level, characterization depends crucially upon the level of generality), but rather at the rationale for the restriction, and whether the rationale refers to the content of the speech." Under this analysis, the restriction in *Kokinda* would be content-neutral if its purpose was to avoid impeding access to the post office, but content-based if the rationale was to spare patrons the possible annoyance of being asked for money. Wojciech Sadurski, Freedom of Speech and its Limits, 164–65 (1999).

As *Turner I* indicates, this analysis does not necessarily make the characterization more predictable, because there can be disagreement as to the restriction's real purpose.

————

C. THE INTERNET

1. PORNOGRAPHY AND CHILDREN

Reno v. ACLU
Supreme Court of the United States, 1997.
521 U.S. 844.

■ JUSTICE STEVENS delivered the opinion of the Court.

[A three-judge district court panel enjoined the government from enforcing the provisions of the Communications Decency Act (CDA) that made it a crime to knowingly transmit indecent material to a minor, 47 U.S.C. § 223(a), or make available to a minor "any comment, request, suggestion, proposal, image, or other communication that, in context, depicts or describes, in terms patently offensive as measured by contemporary community standards, sexual or excretory activities or organs." 47 U.S.C. § 223(d). The government appealed.

Justice Stevens recounted in some detail the history and growth of the Internet, the availability of sexually explicit material in that medium, and the difficulty of verifying ages of recipients of Internet communications. The government relied on *Pacifica* and other cases permitting suppression of speech in the interest of protecting children, but the Court said the regulations at issue in these cases were more narrowly tailored, suppressed less speech, and posed less of a burden to adult access than did the CDA.]

V

In Southeastern Promotions, Ltd. v. Conrad, 420 U.S. 546, 557 (1975), we observed that "[e]ach medium of expression . . . may present its own problems." Thus, some of our cases have recognized special justifications for regulation of the broadcast media that are not applicable to other speakers, see [*Red Lion, Pacifica*]. In these cases, the Court relied on the history of extensive government regulation of the broadcast medium, see, e.g., [*Red Lion*], the scarcity of available frequencies at its inception, see, e.g., Turner Broadcasting System, Inc. v. FCC, [*Turner I*]; and its "invasive" nature, see Sable Communications Inc. v. FCC, 492 U.S. 115, 128 (1989).

Those factors are not present in cyberspace. Neither before nor after the enactment of the CDA have the vast democratic fora of the Internet been subject to the type of government supervision and regulation that has attended the broadcast industry. Moreover, the Internet is not as "invasive" as radio or television. The District Court specifically found that "[c]ommunications over the Internet do not 'invade' an individual's home or appear on one's computer screen unbidden. Users seldom encounter content 'by accident.' " [ ] It also found that "[a]lmost all sexually explicit images are preceded by warnings as to the content," and cited testimony that " 'odds are slim' that a user would come across a sexually explicit sight by accident." *Ibid.*

We distinguished *Pacifica* in *Sable*, [ ] on just this basis. In *Sable*, a company engaged in the business of offering sexually oriented prerecorded telephone messages (popularly known as "dial a porn") challenged the constitutionality of an amendment to the Communications Act that imposed a blanket prohibition on indecent as well as obscene interstate commercial telephone messages. We held that the statute was constitutional insofar as it applied to obscene messages but invalid as applied to indecent messages. In attempting to justify the complete ban and criminalization of indecent commercial telephone messages, the Government relied on *Pacifica*, arguing that the ban was necessary to prevent children from gaining access to such messages. We agreed that "there is a compelling interest in protecting the physical and psychological well being of minors" which extended to shielding them from indecent messages that are not obscene by adult standards, [ ] but distinguished our "emphatically narrow holding" in *Pacifica* because it did not involve a complete ban and because it involved a different medium of communication, [ ]. We explained that "the dial it medium requires the listener to take affirmative steps to receive the communication." [ ] "Placing a telephone call," we continued, "is not the same as turning on a radio and being taken by surprise by an indecent message." [ ]

Finally, unlike the conditions that prevailed when Congress first authorized regulation of the broadcast spectrum, the Internet can hardly be considered a "scarce" expressive commodity. It provides relatively unlimited, low cost capacity for communication of all kinds. The Government estimates that "[a]s many as 40 million people use the Internet today, and that figure is expected to grow to 200 million by 1999." This dynamic, multifaceted category of communication includes not only traditional print and news services, but also audio, video, and still images, as well as interactive, real time dialogue. Through the use of chat rooms, any person with a phone line can become a town crier with a voice that resonates farther than it could from any soapbox. Through the use of Web pages, mail exploders, and newsgroups, the same individual can become a pamphleteer. As the District Court found, "the content on the Internet is as diverse as human thought." [ ] We agree with its conclusion that our cases provide no basis for qualifying the level of First Amendment scrutiny that should be applied to this medium.

VI

Regardless of whether the CDA is so vague that it violates the Fifth Amendment, the many ambiguities concerning the scope of its coverage render it problematic for purposes of the First Amendment. For instance, each of the two parts of the CDA uses a different linguistic form. The first uses the word "indecent," 47 U.S.C. § 223(a) (1994 ed. Supp. II), while the second speaks of material that "in context, depicts or describes, in terms patently offensive as measured by contemporary community standards, sexual or excretory activities or organs," § 223(d). Given the absence of a definition of either term, this difference in language will provoke uncertainty among speakers about how the two standards relate to each other and just what they mean. Could a speaker confidently assume that a serious discussion about birth control practices, homosexuality, the First Amendment issues raised by the Appendix to our *Pacifica* opinion, or the consequences of prison rape would not violate the CDA? This uncertainty undermines the likelihood that the CDA has been carefully tailored to the congressional goal of protecting minors from potentially harmful materials.

The vagueness of the CDA is a matter of special concern for two reasons. First, the CDA is a content based regulation of speech. The vagueness of such a regulation raises special First Amendment concerns because of its obvious chilling effect on free speech. [ ] Second, the CDA is a criminal statute. In addition to the opprobrium and stigma of a criminal conviction, the CDA threatens violators with penalties including up to two years in prison for each act of violation. The severity of criminal sanctions may well cause speakers to remain silent rather than communicate even arguably unlawful words, ideas, and images. [ ] As a practical matter, this increased deterrent effect, coupled with the "risk of discriminatory enforcement" of vague regulations, poses greater First Amendment concerns than those implicated by the civil regulation reviewed in [*DAETC*]. . . .

VII

We are persuaded that the CDA lacks the precision that the First Amendment requires when a statute regulates the content of speech. In order to deny minors access to potentially harmful speech, the CDA effectively suppresses a large amount of speech that adults have a constitutional right to receive and to address to one another. That burden on adult speech is unacceptable if less restrictive alternatives would be at least as effective in achieving the legitimate purpose that the statute was enacted to serve.

. . .

For the purposes of our decision, we need neither accept nor reject the Government's submission that the First Amendment does not forbid a blanket prohibition on all "indecent" and "patently offensive" messages communicated to a 17-year-old—no matter how much value the message may contain and regardless of parental approval. It is at least clear that the strength of the Government's interest in protecting minors is not equally strong throughout the coverage of this broad statute. Under the CDA, a parent allowing her 17-year-old to use the family computer to obtain information on the Internet that she, in her parental judgment, deems appropriate could face a lengthy prison term. [ ] Similarly, a parent who sent his 17-year-old college freshman information on birth control via e-mail could be incarcerated even though neither he, his child, nor anyone in their home community found the material "indecent" or "patently offensive," if the college town's community thought otherwise.

The breadth of this content-based restriction of speech imposes an especially heavy burden on the Government to explain why a less restrictive provision would not be as effective as the CDA. It has not done so. The arguments in this Court have referred to possible alternatives such as requiring that indecent material be "tagged" in a way that facilitates parental control of material coming into their homes, making exceptions for messages with artistic or educational value, providing some tolerance for parental choice, and regulating some portions of the Internet-such as commercial Web sites-differently from others, such as chat rooms. Particularly in the light of the absence of any detailed findings by the Congress, or even hearings addressing the special problems of the CDA, we are persuaded that the CDA is not narrowly tailored if that requirement has any meaning at all.

XI

. . .

For the foregoing reasons, the judgment of the District Court is affirmed.

[JUSTICE O'CONNOR'S concurring opinion is omitted.]

NOTES AND QUESTIONS

1. Citing the district court's finding that "[c]ommunications over the Internet do not 'invade' an individual's home or appear on one's computer screen unbidden," the Court said the Internet is not as "invasive" as radio or television. But today many messages do pop up on computer screens unbidden, and many children have not only computer access, but also smart phones and similar devices that offer instant web access and full browsing capability. A Pew Research Center survey in 2015 found that almost three-quarters of teens have smart phones. Ninety-two percent of teens go online daily, and 24 percent report being online almost constantly. Amanda Lenhart, Teens, Social Media & Technology Overview of 2015, http://www.

pewinternet.org/2015/04/09/teens-social-media-technology-2015/. Is the Internet still less invasive (or less pervasive) than radio or television?

2.   Are any of the rationales that have been used to justify regulation of broadcasting and cable applicable to the Internet? Is there *any* compelling reason to regulate the content of online communication?

3.   In Brown v. Entertainment Merchants Assn., 564 U.S. 786 (2011), the Supreme Court rejected the argument that the interactive and immersive nature of video games justified the application of "medium-specific" First Amendment principles. The case involved a constitutional challenge to a California statute prohibiting sale or rental of violent video games to minors. The state argued that the interactive graphic realism of such games justified the prohibition, but the Court struck down the California law as a content-based restriction on speech. The Court conceded that video games have little to do with protection of discourse on public matters, which it identified as the primary purpose of the First Amendment's free speech guarantee. The Court, however, said that "we have long recognized that it is difficult to distinguish politics from entertainment, and dangerous to try." The Court found no constitutionally relevant distinction between video games and the "books, plays, and movies that preceded them." Further, the Court observed that throughout American history, critics have accused new entertainment media enjoyed by minors of having pernicious effects, and it portrayed California's concern about video games as simply another misguided and moralistic attempt to censor children's media consumption. For further discussion of the Roberts Court's lack of receptiveness to arguments for "medium-specific" First Amendment protections, see Lyrissa Barnett Lidsky, Not A Free Press Court? 2012 B.Y.U. L. Rev. 1819 (2012).

The Child Online Protection Act. Congress responded to the Supreme Court's decision in Reno v. ACLU by enacting a more limited indecency provision, the Child Online Protection Act (COPA), 47 U.S.C. § 231. The new law applied only to persons "engaged in the business" of communicating "material that is harmful to minors," § 231(e)(6), and provided affirmative defenses if the defendant could show that in good faith it had restricted access by requiring use of a credit card, digital certificate that verifies age, or other reasonable available technology, § 231(c). Enforcement of COPA was immediately enjoined, however, and the Supreme Court upheld the preliminary injunction on the ground that it probably would ultimately be held unconstitutional for reasons similar to those in *Playboy* and *Reno*: use of filtering and blocking technologies by recipients was almost certain to be found effective and less restrictive than a ban directed at the purveyors of material "harmful to minors." See Ashcroft v. American Civil Liberties Union [II], 542 U.S. 656 (2004).

The 5–4 majority said filters impose restrictions at the receiving end instead of restricting speech at its source, thereby allowing adults to receive information they want without the inconvenience of going through identification procedures and without the chilling effect of criminalizing a particular species of speech. The fact that the government could not compel use of filters did not prevent that from being an effective alternative, the majority said, because the government could provide incentives for schools and libraries to use them and promote their acceptance by parents and industry. As in *Playboy*, the fact that some parents would not avail themselves of the opportunity did not necessarily make filtering an ineffective alternative.

In dissent, Justices Breyer, Rehnquist, and O'Connor argued that filtering could not properly be considered an alternative at all, because it was just the status quo that Congress had found to be an inadequate response to the issue of children's access to online pornography. They believed the majority had construed COPA unnecessarily broadly. Properly construed, it would reach only commercial pornography that is "close to obscene," they said, and therefore would impose only modest burdens on speech.

Dissenting separately, Justice Scalia again argued, as he did in *Playboy*, that the business of pornography enjoys no First Amendment protection. He said COPA applied only to that business and therefore was not unconstitutional.

The Court remanded for full consideration on the merits, and the district court again concluded that COPA was unconstitutionally vague, overbroad, and not narrowly tailored. The Court of Appeals affirmed, ACLU v. Mukasey, 534 F.3d 181 (3d Cir. 2008). The Third Circuit said the statute was not narrowly tailored:

> Given the vast quantity of speech that COPA does not cover but that filters do cover, it is apparent that filters are more effective in advancing Congress's interest. . . . Moreover, filters are more flexible than COPA because parents can tailor them to their own values and needs and to the age and maturity of their children and thus use an appropriate flexible approach differing from COPA's "one size fits all" approach. Finally, the evidence makes clear that, although not flawless, with proper use filters are highly effective in preventing minors from accessing sexually explicit material on the Web.

The court also concluded that the statute was impermissibly vague in several respects. It was unclear whether the scienter standard was "intentionally" or "with knowledge of the character of the material." The statutory phrase "engaged in the business" was not defined in such a way as to limit the act to commercial pornography. Web operators could not know whether the phrase "designed to appeal to the prurient interest of minors" should be interpreted with reference to four-year-olds or sixteen-year-olds. It was impossible to know whether the instruction that material was to be considered "as a whole" would refer to the whole image in question, the whole Web page, or the whole Web site. In addition, the statute was overbroad because it "effectively suppresses a large amount of speech that adults have a constitutional right to receive and to address to one another. . . ."

Do these decisions leave Congress with no way to prevent distribution of online pornography to children? If there are ways parents can protect their children at the receiving end, are all efforts to curtail indecency at the source doomed because parental controls will be considered less restrictive of adults' access? Is there still room, after *Playboy*, for an argument that the parental options are not effective?

———

2. OPEN ACCESS

Existing technology gives broadband providers the ability to control various aspects of subscribers' access to the Internet—for example, what websites and applications they can access, and the speed and reliability of various connections. In a few instances they have used this power to slow peer-to-peer communications or to levy surcharges on certain users. Congress and the FCC have been urged to adopt regulations to prevent providers from discriminating among subscribers who have paid for the same level of access. The goal of such regulations is known colloquially as "network neutrality," although there is little agreement as to exactly how much neutrality this should require. Providers say they need freedom to engage in such discrimination to make efficient use of their networks' capacities. Critics say the providers want to control the architecture of broadband, give preferential treatment to sites and services in which they have a financial interest, and emulate the model of the cable television industry's multiple tiers of service for which the subscriber pays extra fees.

Embedded in this controversy are many questions about the appropriate regulatory model (if any). The clearest nondiscrimination model is common carrier regulation. Traditional telephone companies, for example, are treated as common carriers who must offer service to all similarly situated customers on the same terms and at the same rates. Cable television offers another model; cable systems are required to offer a certain basic level of content (as we saw in *Turner I*), but beyond that they have considerable freedom to choose what to offer their customers, how to package it, and how to price it. As users of the electromagnetic spectrum (and possibly by virtue of their pervasiveness and intrusiveness), broadband providers might be thought to be subject to the broadcasting model of regulation. Or they might be thought to be as immune from regulation as booksellers or newspapers.

The FCC has attempted to regulate net neutrality to ensure an "open Internet," but, as of 2015, its efforts to do so have twice been rebuffed by the U.S. Court of Appeals for the D.C. Circuit on jurisdictional grounds. Comcast Corp. v. FCC, 600 F.3d 642 (D.C. Cir. 2010) (holding that FCC lacked ancillary jurisdiction to enforce net neutrality); Verizon v. FCC, 740 F.3d 623 (D.C. Cir. 2014). A summary of the tortuous path to net neutrality regulation, written by a Commissioner of the Federal Trade Commission, appears in the article excerpt below.

The FCC's Knowledge Problem:
How to Protect Consumers Online

Hon. Maureen K. Ohlhausen
67 Fed. Comm. L.J. 203 (2015).

. . .

II.   NET NEUTRALITY AND THE FCC: A CASE STUDY IN REGULATORY DIFFICULTY

. . . The FCC's history in addressing net neutrality concerns is a case study in the difficulties of regulating a dynamic industry through ex ante, prescriptive regulation.

A.   What is Net Neutrality?

The D.C. Circuit's [2014] decision in Verizon v. FCC is the latest judicial volley in a long-standing public policy debate over the neutrality of the Internet, or "net neutrality." Net neutrality as a policy goal is notoriously difficult to define, in part because the goal has evolved substantially over the course of the debate. . . . In broad terms, however, net neutrality is the concept that access to the Internet should be provided on equal, nondiscriminatory terms for all content providers and consumers. In 2007, as Director of the FTC's Office of Policy Planning, I led the FTC's inquiry into net neutrality and the release of the subsequent report, "Broadband Connectivity Competition Policy." Based in part on my experience in leading that effort, I will briefly explain the concerns that animate each side in this debate.

1.   Proponents of Net Neutrality Regulation

Net neutrality advocates focus on certain characteristics of the early Internet and express fears that the Internet of the future will be worse for lacking those characteristics. Specifically, they emphasize the Internet's "end-to-end architecture," which carries content between users and servers at the "edge" of the Internet on a "first-in, first-out" or "best efforts" basis. Advocates describe this approach as not just an engineering solution, but also a fundamental philosophical principle. Professors Mark Lemley and Lawrence Lessig explain this viewpoint as follows: "While the e2e [end-to-end] design principle was first adopted for technical reasons, it has important social and competitive features as well. E2e expands the competitive horizon by enabling a wider variety of applications to connect to and to use the network."

Network neutrality advocates see the success of content and applications providers like Google, Netflix, and Facebook as contingent on these fundamental design principles, and especially the Internet's end-to-end architecture. In particular, many successful "edge" providers are concerned that owners of the underlying infrastructure could engage in anticompetitive hold-up, either by cutting off access to users or to other networks, by charging high prices for transport, or by providing better services to one content provider instead of its competitor either for a fee or because of a business affiliation. As explained in the FTC broadband report, content providers worry about "(1) blockage, degradation, and prioritization of content and applications; (2) vertical integration by ISPs [Internet service providers] and other network operators into content and applications; . . . and (3) the diminution of political and other expression on the Internet." These concerns over vertical integration in the industry are the main force propelling the FCC's efforts toward prescriptive, rule-based net neutrality regulations.

Net neutrality advocates generally support a "strong presumption in favor of preserving the architectural features that have produced this extraordinary innovation." They want government to protect these core design attributes by prohibiting certain types of behavior by network infrastructure owners.

2. Opponents of Net Neutrality Regulation

Opponents of net neutrality regulation question the validity of the narrative told by advocates. They describe how the Internet has never really been "neutral" in the sense that advocates portray the concept. They also argue that "best-effort delivery" of information is not neutral in effect—certain types of services are harmed more than others by such a rubric. Furthermore, they argue, the end-to-end architecture and the other design principles were engineering solutions to specific historical problems; as the problems have changed, it is appropriate for engineering solutions also to change.

Opponents of net neutrality rules are concerned that regulation, by its nature, is inflexible and would penalize innovation in an attempt to maintain the original design principles of the Internet. They argue that Internet innovation has depended upon the latitude to experiment with new and different business models. They point out that many pioneering Internet businesses were vertically integrated and thus would arguably violate modern network neutrality regulation were they still in business today. They further argue that adopting rigid network neutrality rules would freeze the existing business environment in place and potentially prevent experimentation with different technologies and types of vertically-integrated businesses or business practices. Regulation could also reduce many of the efficiencies of vertical integration (like eliminating double marginalization problems) and skew investment incentives. Instead of allowing the market to guide investment dollars where needed and businesses to charge based on the best use of potentially scarce resources, like bandwidth, net neutrality opponents fear the effect of the government dictating many of these critical decisions. Thus, rather than prescriptive rules, opponents advocate more fact-intensive and flexible enforcement of widely acknowledged legal and economic norms, such as antitrust law and consumer protection law. They also question whether a systemic problem requiring expansive solutions even exists.

B. The FCC's History of Broadband Regulation: The Road to Reclassification

1.   Broadband as a Title I Information Service

The FCC's earliest regulatory approach to consumer Internet service was to treat it as a common carrier service. Telephone companies were not permitted to ban, tamper with, or differentiate between dial-up telephone ISPs, such as CompuServe or AOL. The FCC used a different approach for always-on cable broadband Internet services. In 2002, it issued the Cable Modem Order, which deemed cable modem service to be neither a separate "telecommunications service" under Title II nor "cable service" under Title VI, but instead a largely unregulated "information service" under Title I. The Supreme Court in 2005 upheld this decision and agreed that cable modem access is an interstate "information service" subject only to Title I. The FCC then extended similar treatment to broadband access over telephone-based digital subscriber or "DSL" lines.

These classifications permitted the FCC to, in essence, deregulate Internet access. To maintain the possibility of future regulatory action, the FCC asserted ancillary jurisdiction over broadband providers under provisions like Section 4(i) of the Act. In 2005, the FCC acted on this putative authority and issued an Internet Policy Statement outlining certain Internet freedoms "to ensure that broadband networks are widely deployed, open, affordable, and accessible to all consumers." In 2008, the Commission alleged Comcast had violated this policy by slowing customers' use of peer-to-peer networking applications and ordered Comcast to cease and desist from the practice. Comcast complied with the order but challenged the FCC's exercise of authority over network management practices. The D.C. Circuit sided with Comcast, concluding the FCC's actions were "flatly inconsistent" with the law, in large part because the agency had linked its ancillary jurisdiction over Comcast's actions to mere statements of policy in the Act rather than to sections of the Act expressly delegating authority.

With its authority to impose net neutrality requirements on broadband providers called into question, then-Chairman Genachowski proposed a "Third Way" to shore up the FCC's position. Under this approach, the agency would reclassify the transmission component of "broadband services" as "telecommunications services," allowing the FCC to exercise direct jurisdiction over network management under Title II. The FCC would then forebear from applying certain Title II obligations on broadband service to lighten the regulatory load. Congress expressed bipartisan, widespread concern with the Third Way proposal, which led the FCC to argue for yet other bases for its network neutrality jurisdiction—Section 706 of the Telecommunications Act of 1996 and ancillary jurisdiction related to additional specific sections of Titles II, III, and VI.

Based on this new theory of authority, the agency adopted the Open Internet Order in December 2010 with new network neutrality rules. Those rules provided that: (1) ISPs must be transparent and disclose their network management practices; (2) both wireless and fixed network owners may not block lawful applications or services, except for purposes of reasonable network management; and (3) fixed broadband providers may not unreasonably discriminate, including by degrading the quality or speed of a consumer's access or as to particular websites or services.

2. The *Verizon* Decision

Verizon and others challenged the Order before the U.S. Court of Appeals for the D.C. Circuit, which handed down its decision on January 14, 2014, striking the Order down in part. The court agreed that the FCC had the authority under Section 706 to regulate broadband traffic to promote broadband deployment. According to the court, the FCC reasonably interpreted the ambiguous texts of sections 706(a) and 706(b) as empowering it to establish rules governing how broadband providers treat Internet traffic. Although the FCC had previously decided that Section 706(a) "does not constitute an independent grant of authority," the court agreed that the Order had "offered a reasoned explanation for its changed understanding of Section 706(a)."

Having concluded that the FCC possesses authority to regulate broadband providers under Section 706, the court also held that section 706 authorized the particular rules adopted in the Open Internet Order because the FCC's rules applied directly to broadband providers and sought to promote the congressional goals of Section 706.

The court also found the FCC's conclusion that the Open Internet Order would encourage broadband deployment to be rational and supported by substantial evidence. The court thus deferred to the FCC's findings that edge provider innovation drives a virtuous cycle that incentivizes broadband deployment, broadband providers have the incentive and ability to discriminate against edge providers, and the benefits of the rules would outweigh their costs. The court found that these conclusions—all of which are economic in nature—were reasonable based on the evidence the FCC had offered.

Nevertheless, the court struck down the anti-blocking and anti-discrimination provisions as inconsistent with the Communications Act's express prohibition on treating non-common carrier services as common carriers. At the time of the Open Internet Order, broadband internet access service was not a common carrier service. And, as the court observed, the Communications Act of 1934 prohibits applying common carrier regulation to entities that are not common carriers. The court found that the language of the anti-discrimination rule "mirrors, almost precisely," the common carrier obligation not to engage in "any unjust or unreasonable discrimination." Furthermore, the anti-discrimination rule, like common carrier obligations, left little or no room for individualized bargaining. The court also struck down the anti-blocking rule because the FCC relied, in the Order and in its briefs, on the same justifications the court found insufficient for the anti-discrimination rule. The court upheld the disclosure requirement, however.

Having struck down the anti-discrimination rule and the anti-blocking rule, and upholding the disclosure rule, the court remanded the case to the FCC for further proceedings.

3.   The Aftermath of *Verizon*

In response to the *Verizon* decision, in May 2014 the FCC adopted a Notice of Proposed Rulemaking (NPRM) to establish a variation on the rules adopted in the Open Internet Order, in the hopes that these modified rules would pass court review. The NPRM first proposed to enhance the transparency requirements to gather more information about the service offered to consumers. Second, to address the D.C. Circuit's anti-blocking rule concerns, the NPRM proposed to amend the rule so that it does not preclude broadband providers from negotiating individual arrangements with similarly situated edge providers. Third, the NPRM proposed an anti-discrimination rule that prohibits "commercially unreasonable" practices, but still allows providers to serve customers and carry traffic on an individually negotiated basis.

As an alternative to tweaking the Open Internet Order rules, the NPRM includes several paragraphs asking if the FCC should reclassify broadband Internet service as a Title II service, echoing former Chairman Julius Genachowski's unpopular Third Way proposal. However, the general sense was that Chairman Wheeler was focused on adjusting the anti-discrimination and anti-blocking rules to meet the roadmap laid out by the D.C. Circuit.

The debate changed in early November 2014, when President Obama shared his views on how to achieve net neutrality. On November 10, 2014, President Obama issued a press release announcing a website and a YouTube video calling for the FCC to reclassify the Internet as a Title II service. Soon after, Commissioner Wheeler began to emphasize reclassification as his preferred approach.

. . .

———

As noted above, the Court of Appeals for the D.C. Circuit decision in Verizon v. Federal Communic. Comm'n, 740 F.3d 623 (D.C. Cir. 2014), held that the FCC had authority to "promulgate rules governing broadband providers' treatment of Internet traffic," but the anti-discrimination and anti-blocking provisions of the Open Internet Order were nonetheless invalid because the FCC had previously classified broadband providers as "information services," rather than common carriers subject to Title II of the Communications Act.

In response to the decision, the FCC began rulemaking proceedings and sought public comment "on how best to protect and promote an open Internet." These proceedings resulted in the 2015 Open Internet Order, 80 Fed. Reg. 19,738 (Apr. 13, 2015), which took effect on June 12, 2015. In a press release on its website, the FCC asserted that the Open Internet rules will "protect and maintain open, uninhibited access to legal online content without broadband Internet access providers being allowed to block, impair, or establish fast/slow lanes to lawful content." The FCC grounded its authority to promulgate the rules on Title II of the Communications Act and Section 706 of the Telecommunications Act of 1996; in other words, the FCC voted to treat broadband Internet like telecommunications services rather than information services but agreed to refrain or "forbear" from enforcing certain common carrier obligations on broadband providers, such as price-setting. The FCC asserted that broadband providers are "conduits, not speakers, with respect to broadband Internet access services." The FCC further asserted that the rules "are tailored to the important government interest in maintaining an open Internet as a platform for expression, among other things. In June 2015, the D.C. Circuit dismissed a request filed by a wireless industry trade group to stay the Open Internet Order. The court did, however, grant a request for an expedited hearing. U.S. Telecom Ass'n v. FCC, No. 15–1063, (D.C. Cir. June 11, 2015).

NOTES AND QUESTIONS

1.   In light of the dynamic nature of the Internet, do net neutrality regulations threaten to stifle innovation? Is self-regulation preferable?

2.   In many instances, broadband is delivered to the user via the facilities of a cable television company. In an early attempt to achieve something like net neutrality, the City of Portland, Oregon, attempted to use its franchise authority to prevent the local cable company from allowing its transmission facilities to be used by a broadband operator that discriminated in favor of its own proprietary services. The Ninth Circuit held that the federal Communications Act denied the city that power. See AT&T Corp. v. City of Portland, 216 F.3d 871 (9th Cir. 2000).

3.   The decisions in the AT&T and Comcast cases held only that the FCC and state and local governments lack statutory authority to require open access to the Internet. If Congress were to give such authority, would the legislation violate the First Amendment? What precedents might the providers invoke in support of a constitutional right to control access?

———

In this chapter we have seen a number of rationales for according some media speech less than full First Amendment protection, either because of the identity of the speaker or because of the nature of the speech. But some of those distinctions are becoming harder to maintain. Television is sometimes delivered via the Internet; the content of most print media is now also available online; cable companies and telephone companies sometimes provide Internet service. If the permissible level of regulation varies by medium, what is the appropriate level? Commercial speech is sometimes hard to separate from fully protected speech. Infomercials and advertorials are still generally identifiable in print and on television, but on the Internet it is often impossible to know whether the speaker has an undisclosed commercial interest. Product placement (paying to have a product used or depicted) is rampant in entertainment and sports. Should a message be treated as commercial speech anytime a commercial purpose can be shown?

The easiest answer to these questions might be to treat all speech and all speakers alike for First Amendment purposes. Would courts be willing to give maximum protection to advertising and pornography? If not, would reduced protection for the most important speech be an acceptable price to pay for ending the disparate treatment of certain speech and speakers?

PART II

LEGAL ISSUES ARISING FROM PUBLICATION

CHAPTER IV

DEFAMATION

In Part One we considered various forms of direct government regulation of media. Part Two considers the tort law's impact on media. Historically, defamation, which comprises the distinct but related torts of libel and slander, has affected media more dramatically than any other tort. Defamation is the oldest of the tort actions brought against media, and it is in defamation that the constitutional limitations on tort liability for speech are most fully developed.

Until 1964 defamation was purely a matter of state law, predominantly common law. Defamatory speech, like fighting words and obscenity, was deemed to be outside the scope of First Amendment protection. Beginning in 1964 however, the Supreme Court began superimposing constitutional requirements over the common law framework of defamation, which was already complex and confusing. As a result, the current law of defamation is an amalgam of state law (both statutory and common law) and constitutional law (mainly federal, but occasionally derived from state constitutions). This chapter synthesizes these different strands to the extent that the present state of the law permits without attempting to track every step in the transformation of the law to its present state. Nonetheless, as you read this chapter, you should pay close attention to the source of the legal rule being applied—whether statutory, common law, or constitutional—because this will often have important procedural, jurisdictional, and substantive consequences.

At common law a defamation plaintiff made out a prima facie case by showing that the defendant had published a defamatory statement concerning the plaintiff. (That formula is deceptively simple because, as we shall see, "published," "defamatory," and "concerning the plaintiff" are all terms of art.) Today, at least in cases that are brought against media, the plaintiff must prove that defendant published a *false* defamatory statement *of fact* concerning the plaintiff and was guilty of some level of *fault* with respect to the falsity of the statement. The plaintiff may also have to show that he or she has suffered demonstrable harm. We attempt in the following sections to treat each of these requirements separately. They are closely interrelated, however, and each can be fully appreciated only in connection with the others.

A. WHAT IS DEFAMATION?

The first question to be answered in every libel or slander case is whether the statement complained about is defamatory. Although the goal of defamation law is to protect reputation, whether a statement is actionable as defamation cannot be determined simply by asking whether it harmed the plaintiff's reputation. Many truthful statements that harm reputation are not defamatory, and a defamatory statement may be actionable without any proof that it actually harmed the plaintiff's reputation. But defamatory statements are not necessarily actionable; for example, they are not actionable unless they are also false. Whether a statement is "defamatory" depends upon the answers to several different inquiries.

MacElree v. Philadelphia Newspapers, Inc.
Supreme Court of Pennsylvania, 1996.
674 A.2d 1050.

■ FLAHERTY, J.

. . .

On September 28, 1991, two carloads of young men came from New York City to the campus of Lincoln University (Lincoln) in Chester County. The New Yorkers went to a university dormitory looking for girls, whereupon a fight ensued between the New Yorkers and Lincoln students. The visitors were taken into custody by Lincoln campus police officers. A group of fifty to one hundred Lincoln students gathered and stormed the campus security office where the New Yorkers were being held, and more violence erupted.

In the November 1, 1991 edition of the Philadelphia Inquirer (Inquirer) an article by B.J. Phillips described the incident at Lincoln. . . .

. . . [University President] Sudarkasa questioned remarks by the Chester County district attorney that one of the New Yorkers had been stabbed. When D.A. James MacElree replied with quotations from police reports, the university's lawyer, Richard Glanton, accused him of electioneering—"the David Duke of Chester County running for office by attacking Lincoln."

[David Duke is a former Grand Wizard of the Ku Klux Klan and a former Louisiana state representative. He was a candidate in the Republican presidential primaries in 1992 and in the general election for President in 1988, where he expressed racist and anti-Semitic views. For more, see generally Douglas D. Rose, ed., Emergence of David Duke and the Politics of Race (UNC Press 1992).]

[MacElree, filed suit against Philips and the Inquirer, alleging that the statement attributed to Glanton was defamatory and that Glanton never made it.] The court of common pleas granted appellees' preliminary objections in the nature of a demurrer. . . . The superior court affirmed, agreeing with the trial court that the statement in question was not actionable defamation. [ ] According to the superior court, the action had to be dismissed unless a reasonable reader would interpret the statement, taken in context, as defamatory. . . . The court classified the reference to David Duke as a bare metaphor which could only be defamatory if it had been supplemented with factual allegations.

. . .

In an action for defamation, it is the court's duty to determine if the publication is capable of the defamatory meaning ascribed to it by the party bringing suit. [ ] In order to sustain an allegation of libel, the burden is on the complaining party to establish that the publication being challenged is defamatory. [ ] If the court concludes that the publication is not capable of defamatory meaning, the case should be dismissed. [ ]

. . . Because we hold that the statement could be defamatory, we reverse the superior court's affirmance of the trial court's order dismissing appellant's complaint and remand this matter for further proceedings.

In assessing whether a publication is defamatory, we must determine if the communication "tends so to harm the reputation of [the complaining party] as to lower him in the estimation of the community or to deter third persons from associating or dealing with him." Birl v. Philadelphia Electric Co., 167 A.2d 472, 475 (1960) (quoting Restatement of Torts § 559 (1938)). In reading the charge that appellant was electioneering and was the David Duke of Chester County, a reasonable person could conclude that this was an accusation that appellant was abusing his power as the district attorney, an elected office, to further racism and his own political aspirations. Such an accusation amounts to a charge of misconduct in office, as appellant alleges in his complaint. See Sweeney v. Philadelphia Record Co., 126 F.2d 53, 54 (3d Cir. 1942) (charging a public officer with a crime or misdemeanor in office is libel per se). At this stage, we are bound to accept as true this allegation along with all others set forth in appellant's complaint. [ ] Therefore, we hold that the superior court mistakenly characterized the misquoted language attributed to Glanton as merely labeling appellant a racist.

The superior court also incorrectly implied that an allegedly defamatory remark which makes up only a small portion of an article is not defamatory. There is no legal basis for such an implication. . . . [S]pecific language may be defamatory even though the subject of the defamatory language is not the focus of the article. Moreover, a publication may be sympathetic towards its subject overall while particular portions have a defamatory meaning.

In reading the complained of language in context with the entire article, the superior court concluded that in light of the balance of the article, the mention of appellant was flattering when compared to the impression given of Lincoln officials. [ ] The fact that Lincoln officials may have been portrayed less favorably than appellant does not support a conclusion that the comment about appellant was not capable of being defamatory. As we stated in Corabi v. Curtis Publishing Co., 273 A.2d

899, 907 (1971), "the mere susceptibility of the publication to an interpretation which would render it innocuous [does not] conclusively defeat a right of action for libel."

Appellees cite several cases in support of their position that an accusation of racism is not actionable libel. *Sweeney,* supra (cause of action for defamation not found where "appellant is charged with being a bigoted person who, actuated by a prejudice of an unpleasant and undesirable kind, opposed a foreign born Jew for a judicial appointment"); Raible v. Newsweek, Inc., 341 F.Supp. 804, 807 (W.D. Pa. 1972) ("[T]o call a person a bigot or other appropriate name descriptive of his political, racial, religious, economic, or sociological philosophies gives no rise to an action for libel.") [ ].

The statement we are presented with here could be interpreted as more than a simple accusation of racism. As stated before, the statement could be construed to mean that appellant was acting in a racist manner in his official capacity as district attorney. Because there was doubt as to the defamatory nature of the complained of language, appellees' demurrer should have been overruled.

. . .

■ CAPPY, JUSTICE, concurring.

. . . I write separately to emphasize that the majority's holding today does not change the law of defamation with regard to an allegation of racism. The rule continues to be that a mere allegation of racism without more is, as a matter of law, not actionable in defamation. . . .

. . . Because, at this stage of the proceedings, it cannot be said with certainty that the statement published by the Appellees amounted to a mere allegation of racism, the preliminary objections in the nature of a demurrer should have been overruled. Indeed, because there is doubt as to the statement's precise import, and as to whether reasonable minds could understand the statement to constitute a charge of abuse of public office, i.e., that the District Attorney was persecuting Lincoln in order to curry favor with the voters by playing to the voters' supposed prejudice so as to advance his own political career, the demurrer should have been denied. Accordingly, I concur with the majority.

NOTES AND QUESTIONS

1. What makes this statement "more than a simple accusation of racism"? Would any accusation of racism made by a public official be actionable on the theory that it could be interpreted as official misconduct? In defamation cases it is the role of the judge to determine whether a statement is capable of a defamatory meaning. Only if the judge answers this question yes should the jury be allowed to determine whether the statement was defamatory in the actual circumstances of the case.

2.   MacElree contended that the university's lawyer, Glanton, never made the statements attributed to him by the Inquirer. Even if Glanton did make the statements, the traditional rule is that anyone who repeats a libel "adopts" it as his own and is responsible as if he were the originator of the statement. This principle is known as the "republication" rule. As you will see in this chapter, this rule has a number of exceptions and nuances.

3.   In a negligence case a plaintiff cannot establish a cause of action unless she can establish that she has been injured. In defamation cases, courts show little interest in that question. The initial question is not whether the statement caused injury, but whether it is defamatory. The Restatement (Second) of Torts § 559 defines a defamatory statement as whether the statement "tends so to harm the reputation of [the complaining party] as to lower him in the estimation of the community or to deter third persons from associating or dealing with him." Other definitions specify the feelings a defamatory statement must engender in its audience. For example, New York courts have defined a defamatory statement as one that "tends to expose a person to hatred, contempt or aversion, or to induce an evil or unsavory opinion of him in the minds of a substantial number in the community." See Nichols v. Item Publishers, Inc., 132 N.E.2d 860 (N.Y. 1956). Regardless of which definition a court adopts, the question is not whether the statement actually caused injury, but whether it had a "tendency" to do so. The explanation for the tort's lack of focus on harm may be that libel and slander were crimes before they were torts, or it may be that at the time they became torts, tort law focused more on wrongs than on injuries. Would it be better to begin the analysis of a defamation case by asking whether the statement caused any provable harm?

4.   Courts typically decided whether a statement is defamatory by asking how the statement "could" or "would" have been interpreted by a "reasonable reader." Why is it unnecessary to know how the statement was actually understood?

5.   Why is mere name-calling not actionable as defamation, even though it might harm the target's reputation? In Ward v. Zelikovsky, 643 A.2d 972 (N.J. 1994), the court held that it was not defamatory to call a woman a "bitch" or to say that she hated Jews. The rationale was not that such accusations are incapable of harming reputation, but that making them actionable would unduly inhibit speech. As the *Ward* court explained, "The most important reason [for denying a cause of action] is the chilling effect such a holding would cast over a person's freedom of expression." Does the same rationale apply in *MacElree*?

6.   Whether the statement complained of is defamatory often requires two quite different inquiries: What does the statement mean, and is the imputation (i.e., the meaning ascribed to the statement by the outcome of the first inquiry) one the law makes actionable? Courts usually collapse these into a single inquiry that asks whether the statement is capable of a defamatory meaning. The following discussion attempts to keep these two inquiries separate, but jury instructions and judicial opinions often collapse them into one.

1. WHAT DO THE WORDS MEAN?

Evaluating the Language. The *MacElree* court asked how a "reasonable reader" would interpret the allegedly defamatory statement. Other courts have fleshed out the reasonable reader standard by specifying that whether a statement is defamatory must be judged " 'according to the fair and natural meaning which will be given it by reasonable persons of ordinary intelligence.' " See Romaine v. Kallinger, 537 A.2d 284 (N.J. 1988). Why is the standard a "reasonable reader" as opposed to the "most impressionable" reader? Is the court employing a type of "reasonable person" test, or is this a test that allows the court to make its own substantive judgment about the meaning of the statement?

Implications. "Libel by implication" is sometimes discussed as if it is a special or unusual subspecies of defamation, but in fact it is quite common. Words rarely do their work without the assistance of inferences. As in the principal case, courts usually do not distinguish between the explicit and implicit messages that a statement conveys. Implications do require special consideration, however, when the defendant says it did not recognize or intend the implication that the plaintiff claims. That problem is addressed later in this chapter when we consider fault issues.

Extrinsic Information. Sometimes a statement innocent on its face takes on a defamatory meaning because of extrinsic information known to recipients of the statement. For example, suppose an article stated only that the plaintiff had often been seen at "123 Hay Road," but some (or all) of the readers knew that there was a brothel at that address. A plaintiff is allowed to show extrinsic facts that would explain why the statement would be understood in a defamatory sense by those who knew the unstated facts, e.g., that 123 Hay Road is known to be a brothel. Such extrinsic information is called the "inducement" and the inference that may be drawn by those who know the facts (in this example, the inference that plaintiff patronizes prostitutes) is called the "innuendo."

Ambiguity. Words often have more than one meaning, and one of those may be defamatory while other meanings of the same word are not. Most courts say that it is for the trier of fact to decide whether ambiguous statements would be understood in a defamatory or non-defamatory sense. A few states, however, embrace an "innocent construction rule," which holds that if the statement can reasonably be construed in an innocent sense when the words are given their natural and obvious meaning, it is not actionable. The Illinois Supreme Court embraces an innocent construction rule, but holds that plaintiffs can avoid the rule by proving actual damages. Tuite v. Corbitt, 866 N.E.2d 114 (Ill. 2006). Applying this rule, the Seventh Circuit subsequently held that the *Tuite* court's interpretation of the innocent construction rule required dismissal of an academic researcher's complaint about the best-selling book *Freakonomics*; the book had maintained that other researchers were unable to replicate the plaintiff's research findings. The plaintiff had alleged that this language implied that his research was faked or incompetent, but the court held that the statement could also mean only that the other researchers had used different assumptions, models, or methodologies. See Lott v. Levitt, 556 F.3d 564 (7th Cir. 2009). Note that the Pennsylvania Supreme Court rejected the innocent construction rule in Corabi v. Curtis Publishing Co., 273 A.2d 899 (Pa. 1971), which is cited in *MacElree* above.

Context. The *MacElree* court wrote that the allegedly defamatory statement must be "taken in context." If the recipients can be assumed to have read the entire publication, that makes obvious sense. A single passage should not be actionable if it is surrounded by material that removes the defamatory sting of the pinpointed passage. But often it cannot be assumed that every recipient received the exculpating information. Headlines, captions, and teasers, for example, cannot tell the full story, and sometimes the truncated message they convey is defamatory. In what is probably a concession to the practical needs of journalism, courts usually deny recovery to the plaintiff unless the juxtaposition of headline and text makes it difficult to indulge the fiction that recipients will ingest the publication whole. This is explored later in this chapter as well.

2. IS THE ASCRIBED MEANING DEFAMATORY?

Once the meaning of the statement has been determined, there remains the question whether the statement is of a sort that the law makes actionable as defamation? As a matter of policy, the law refuses to make actionable many statements that harm reputation. "Defamatory" is a term of art that encompasses social, practical, and jurisprudential considerations as well as free speech values.

Opprobrium. MacElree adopted the Restatement definition of a defamatory statement as one that would "deter third persons from associating or dealing with the [defamed] person." This definition must be viewed with some skepticism. Today a statement is not likely to be actionable as defamation unless it suggests some moral opprobrium. For example, epithets and insults are not defamatory. Apparently the *MacElree* court puts "simple accusations of racism" in the same category. Nor is it defamatory to state erroneously that a person is dead or that a professional person is battling cancer, even though such statements might well cause loss of good will or confidence and seem quite likely to deter third parties from dealing with the plaintiff. See Decker v. Princeton Packet, Inc., 561 A.2d 1122 (N.J. 1989) (death); Golub v. Enquirer/Star Group, Inc., 681 N.E.2d 1282 (N.Y. 1997) (cancer). Note, however, that such statements could place the plaintiff in a false light and, therefore, a cause of action founded in privacy is possible even when one in defamation is not. This is explored further in Chapter Five.

Divergent values and the "substantial and respectable minority" standard. In whose eyes must a statement be defamatory? Which members of the community must think less of the plaintiff in order for an allegedly defamatory statement to be actionable? Whether a statement is defamatory is a value-laden inquiry, and moral values are not universally shared. Assume a newspaper publishes an article stating that John Smith shared a glass of champagne with his wife to celebrate their anniversary. Is this statement defamatory? What if John Smith is a Baptist preacher whose moral beliefs (and those of his congregation) forbid the drinking of alcohol?

Traditionally courts said that whether a statement is defamatory must be viewed from the perspective of "right-thinking" people. See, e.g., Kimmerle v. New York Evening Journal, Inc., 186 N.E. 217 (N.Y. 1933). A more modern expression of the same idea is that a statement is not defamatory unless it would tend to prejudice the plaintiff "in the eyes of a substantial and respectable minority of the community." See Restatement (Second) of Torts § 559, comment *e*. This has allowed the courts to hold that it is not defamatory to call a prison inmate an informer, for example. See Sanguedolce v. Wolfe, 62 A.3d 810 (N.H. 2013) (statement that an inmate had testified against a criminal defendant was not defamatory among "law-abiding citizens"); Robert D. Sack, Sack on Defamation § 2:4.3 (4th ed. 2010). For an extended discussion of this subject, contending that courts camouflage policy choices through the construction of the "substantial and respectable community" in defamation cases, see Lyrissa Lidsky, Defamation, Reputation, and the Myth of Community, 71 Wash. L. Rev. 1, 30 (1996).

Humor. Can a person be defamed by a joke, satire, or parody? It is not enough to show that the statement was understood in a defamatory sense by some recipients. See New Times Inc. v. Isaacks, 146 S.W.3d 144 (Tex. 2004). A seventh-grader was arrested and held in a juvenile detention center for five days after he wrote an assigned Halloween story that the principal thought contained terroristic threats. An alternative newspaper spoofed the episode with a story called "Stop the Madness" which depicted the fictitious jailing of a six-year-old for writing a book report about cannibalism and fanaticism. It attributed made-up quotes to the juvenile judge who had jailed the seventh-grader and the district attorney who had defended the judge's action.

The judge and the district attorney sued, claiming some readers believed they had actually said and done the things attributed to them. Lower courts denied summary judgment on the ground that the story failed to provide adequate notice that it was satire or parody. The Texas Supreme Court reversed:

> The court of appeals has underestimated the "reasonable reader." As the relevant cases show, the hypothetical reasonable person—the mythic Cheshire cat who darts about the pages of

the tort law—is no dullard. He or she does not represent the lowest common denominator, but reasonable intelligence and learning. He or she can tell the difference between satire and sincerity. . . .

The appropriate inquiry is objective, not subjective. Thus, the question is not whether some actual readers were misled, as they inevitably will be, but whether the hypothetical reasonable reader could be. [ ] Thus, we focus on a single objective inquiry: whether the satire can be reasonably understood as stating actual fact. . . .

This is not the same as asking whether all readers actually understood the satire, or "got the joke." Intelligent, well-read people act unreasonably from time to time, while the hypothetical reasonable reader, for purposes of defamation law, does not. In a case of parody or satire, courts must analyze the words at issue with detachment and dispassion, considering them in context and as a whole, as a reasonable reader would consider them.

The court noted that although readers who read only the first few sentences of the spoof might think it recounted actual facts, those who read the entire story would realize it was satire.

Compare Peoples Bank and Trust v. Globe International Publishing Co., 773 F.Supp. 1235 (W.D. Ark. 1991). Under the headline "World's oldest newspaper carrier, 101, quits because she's pregnant!" the Sun, a supermarket tabloid, published a story saying that a woman who had been delivering papers in Australia for 94 years became pregnant by a man she met on her paper route. The story was accompanied by a photo of plaintiff Nellie Mitchell, a 96-year old newsstand operator in Mountain Home, Arkansas. The defendant argued that the story could not be understood in a defamatory sense because "everyone is well aware that it is physically impossible for a 101- or 96-year-old woman to be pregnant," but the judge held that the implication of sexual promiscuity could be. The case proceeded to trial and a jury returned a general verdict for the newspaper on the libel claim but awarded Mitchell substantial damages on the alternate theory of false light invasion of privacy, as recounted in Chapter Five.

Sometimes the question in these cases is merely one of meaning: could the statement be taken seriously or not? More often, as in the case involving Nellie Mitchell, the issue is how much of it could be taken seriously. Satire and parody work only if the recipients believe there is *some* truth in what's said. In such cases the question is not so much whether the meaning is defamatory as whether the law should subject these forms of expression to the same straight-faced analysis that it applies to news reporting and other more literal forms of expression.

Figurative Speech. A statement is not actionable if it cannot reasonably be interpreted as stating actual facts about a person. This rule immunizes several different types of statements. One is statements too fantastic or improbable to be believed. See, e.g., Pring v. Penthouse International Ltd., 695 F.2d 438 (10th Cir. 1982) (denying liability for implication that Miss America contestant was able to levitate men by oral sex). Another is words used in "a loose figurative sense." Thus, it was not actionable to use Jack London's famous definition of a scab—"a traitor to his God, his country, his family and his class"—to describe plaintiff. See Letter Carriers v. Austin, 418 U.S. 264 (1974). A third type of speech immunized by this rule is rhetorical hyperbole. A newspaper published a citizen's charge that plaintiff was "blackmailing" the city in connection with pending real estate negotiations. The Supreme Court held that the First Amendment precluded the state from treating this as actionable defamation because, in context, the word was "no more than rhetorical hyperbole, a vigorous epithet used by those who considered Bresler's vigorous negotiating position extremely unreasonable." Greenbelt Cooperative Publishing Ass'n v. Bresler, 398 U.S. 6 (1970). For further discussion of these cases and their significance, see Milkovich v. Lorain Journal Co., 497 U.S. 1 (1990), highlighted later in this chapter.

3. ROLES OF JUDGE AND JURY

Sometimes courts in defamation cases indicate that the court's role is only to determine whether the statement is "clearly defamatory" or "clearly not defamatory," and that all other questions are for the jury. The matter, however, is not quite that simple. Is it "clearly not defamatory" to say that a person is dead or has cancer or hates Jews? Reasonable people might well disagree as to whether those imputations are harmful to reputation or as to how "right-thinking people" feel about communism. Yet the courts typically make these decisions themselves instead of submitting them to a jury. The reasons for this judicial assertiveness are rarely articulated. Perhaps judges believe that they are at least as well equipped as jurors to determine the meaning of words and assess their effect; that is, after all, what judges spend most of their time doing. It may also reflect a belief that what is actionable as defamation is freighted with policy considerations. The law could treat epithets and insults as defamation, but judges may believe they have better things to do. It could make humor or hyperbole actionable when someone fails to get the joke or misunderstands the nonliteral use of language, but that would exact a price in terms of richness and diversity of expression. Whatever the reasons, the inquiry usually made in other settings to determine whether a question is for the jury—could reasonable minds differ?—is of limited help in determining the jury's role here.

It is clear that the judge and jury are answering different questions. The first question, always for the judge, is whether the statement is "capable of a defamatory meaning." If the judge believes the answer is "no" because no reasonable person could interpret the statement as the plaintiff urges, or for any of the more complex reasons suggested above, the case is dismissed. Only if the judge answers yes to the first question is the jury asked to decide the second, namely whether the defendant's statement was in fact defamatory under all the circumstances of the case. This determination may involve interpretation of ambiguous language or evaluation of context or community mores. Or it may simply reflect the jury's disagreement with the judge. Having already held that the statement is capable of a defamatory meaning, there is little room for the judge to overturn such a determination.

B. Special Damages, Libel Per Se, Libel Per Quod, Slander Per Se

1. Slander Per Se

In most cases, the principles outlined in the preceding section determine whether the statement is within the ambit of the law of defamation, and courts make that decision without inquiring into the nature or extent of the plaintiff's harm. In a few subsets of defamation cases, however, the courts hold that even if a plaintiff establishes that the statement is defamatory under these principles, recovery is barred unless the plaintiff shows "special harm." Up to this point it has been unnecessary to distinguish between libel and slander, but now we must do so, because whether a plaintiff must show special harm depends largely on whether the case is classified as libel or slander.

In slander, the general rule is that a plaintiff has no cause of action unless the statement is (1) defamatory, and (2) causes demonstrable pecuniary loss, or "special harm." An exception (which nearly swallows the rule) allows recovery without proof of special harm if the statement is "slanderous per se." The concepts of "special harm" and "per se" are generally relevant only in slander cases, but occasionally they creep into libel cases. How the distinction between libel and slander is drawn, and the effect of that distinction on the special harm requirement, are issues in the following case.

Matherson v. Marchello
New York Appellate Division, Second Department, 1984.
100 A.D.2d 233.

■ TITONE, J.P.

. . .

On October 28, 1980, radio station WBAB conducted an interview with the members of a singing group called "The Good Rats." Following a commercial which advertised a Halloween party at an establishment known as "OBI," a discussion ensued in which various members of the group explained that they are no longer permitted to play at OBI South because:

"Good Rat #1: Well, you know, we had that law suit with Mr. Matherson.

"A Good Rat: And we used to fool around with his wife.

"Good Rat #1: And we won.

"A Good Rat: One of us used to fool around with his wife. He wasn't into that too much.

"D. J.: Oh yea.

"Good Rat #1: (interrupted and joined by another Good Rat) We used to start off our gigs over there with the National Anthem, and he was very upset about that, now all of a sudden he's very patriotic and he's using it in his commercials.

"A Good Rat: I don't think it was his wife that he got so upset about, I think it was when somebody started messing around with his boyfriend that he really freaked out. Really.

(Laughter)

"That did it man."

Plaintiffs, who are husband and wife, subsequently commenced this action against "The Good Rats" (as individuals and against their record company), alleging that the words "we used to fool around with his wife" and "I don't think it was his wife that he got upset about, I think it was when somebody started messing around with his boyfriend that he really freaked out" were defamatory. They seek compensatory and punitive damages for humiliation, mental anguish, loss of reputation and injury to their marital relationship as well as for the loss of customers, business opportunities and good will allegedly suffered by Mr. Matherson. [The lower court] granted defendants' motion to dismiss. . . .

Preliminarily, we observe that if special damages are a necessary ingredient of plaintiffs' cause of action, Special Term properly found the allegations of the complaint to be deficient.

Special damages consist of "the loss of something having economic or pecuniary value" (Restatement, Torts 2d, § 575, comment *b*) which "must flow directly from the injury to reputation caused by the defamation; not from the [emotional] effects of defamation" (Sack, Libel, Slander, and Related Problems, § VII.2.2, 345–346; [ ]) and it is settled law that they must be fully and accurately identified "with sufficient particularity to identify actual losses." [ ] When loss of business is claimed, the persons who ceased to be customers must be named and the losses itemized. [ ] "Round figures" or a general allegation of a dollar amount as special damages do not suffice. [ ] Consequently, plaintiffs' non-specific conclusory allegations do not meet the stringent requirements imposed for pleading special damages. [ ]

We must, therefore, determine whether an allegation of special damages is necessary. In large measure, this turns on which branch of the law of defamation is involved. As a result of historical accident, which, though not sensibly defensible today, is so well settled as to be beyond our ability to uproot it [ ], there is a schism between the law governing slander and the law governing libel [ ].

A plaintiff suing in slander must plead special damages unless the defamation falls into any one of four per se categories [ ]. Those categories consist of allegations (1) that the plaintiff committed a crime [ ], (2) that tend to injure the plaintiff in his or her trade, business or profession [ ], (3) that plaintiff has contracted a loathsome disease [ ], and (4) that impute unchastity to a woman [ ].[2] The exceptions were established apparently for no other reason than a recognition that by their nature the accusations encompassed therein would be likely to cause material damage [ ].

On the other hand, a plaintiff suing in libel need not plead or prove special damages. . . .[3] Thus, unlike the law of slander, in the law of libel the existence of damage is conclusively presumed from the publication itself and a plaintiff may rely on general damages. . . .

. . .

Traditionally, the demarcation between libel and slander rested upon whether the words were written or spoken [ ]. Written defamations were considered far more serious because, at the time the distinction arose, few persons could read or write and, therefore, anything which was written would carry a louder ring of purported truth [ ]. In addition, a written defamation could be disseminated more widely and carried a degree of permanence.

With the advent of mass communication, the differential was blurred. Motion pictures were held to be libel [ ]. No set rule developed with respect to radio and television [ ]. In some cases, distinction was drawn between [extemporaneous] speech, which was classified as slander, and words read from a script, which were classified as libel [ ]. This distinction was the subject of considerable criticism. [ ]

---

[2]   The first three categories were established relatively early. The fourth is of more recent vintage, having first been put into effect in England by the Slander of Women Act of 1891. . . . We do not view these categories as fixed or rigid and, in appropriate circumstances, a new category may be judicially established [ ].

[3]   We have avoided the use of the terms libel per se and libel per quod because, as explained in this footnote, the cases and commentators are divided on the question of whether any meaningful distinction exists between the two. It is clear that when the defamatory import is apparent from the face of the publication itself without resort to any other source, the libel, often referred to as libel per se, is actionable without proof of special harm [ ]. Libel per quod, on the other hand, has been traditionally defined as an encompassing libel in which the defamatory import can only be ascertained by reference to facts not set forth in the publication [ ].

We today hold that defamation which is broadcast by means of radio or television should be classified as libel. As we have noted, one of the primary reasons assigned to justify the imposition of broader liability for libel than for slander has been the greater capacity for harm that a writing is assumed to have because of the wide range of dissemination consequent upon its permanence in form. Given the vast and far-flung audiences reached by the broadcasting media today, it is self-evident that the potential harm to a defamed person is far greater than that involved in a single writing. [ ] Section 568A of the Restatement of Torts, Second, and the more recent decisions in sister States [ ] opt for holding such defamation to be libel and we perceive no basis for perpetuating a meaningless, outmoded distinction.

On the question of whether the allegedly defamatory statements are actionable, our scope of review is limited. . . . Unless we can say, as a matter of law, that the statements could not have had a defamatory connotation, it is for the jury to decide whether or not they did. [ ]

Taken in the context of a rock and roll station's interview with musicians, and taking note of contemporary usage, we have no difficulty in concluding that the words "fooling around with his wife" could have been interpreted by listeners to mean that Mrs. Matherson was having an affair with one of the defendants. Such charges are clearly libelous. . . .

The second comment—"I don't think it was his wife that he got upset about, I think it was when somebody started messing around with his boyfriend that he really freaked out"—presents a far more subtle and difficult question. [ ] [Defendants] claim that many public officials have acknowledged their homosexuality and, therefore, no social stigma may be attached to such an allegation. We are constrained to reject defendants' position at this time.

It cannot be said that social opprobrium of homosexuality does not remain with us today. Rightly or wrongly, many individuals still view homosexuality as immoral (see Newsweek Aug. 8, 1983, p. 33, containing the results of a Gallup poll; [ ]). Legal sanctions imposed upon homosexuals in areas ranging from immigration [ ] to military service (Watkins v. United States Army, 721 F.2d 687) have recently been reaffirmed despite the concurring Judge's observation in *Watkins* [ ] that it "demonstrates a callous disregard for the progress American law and society have made toward acknowledging that an individual's choice of life style is not the concern of government, but a fundamental aspect of personal liberty." [ ]

In short, despite the fact that an increasing number of homosexuals are publicly expressing satisfaction and even pride in their status, the potential and probable harm of a false charge of homosexuality, in terms of social and economic impact, cannot be ignored. . . .

[Because both statements were treated as libel, plaintiff was not required to prove special damages, so the judgment of the trial court was reversed.]

NOTES AND QUESTIONS

1.   Which of the justifications offered for the differing treatment of written and oral defamation is strongest? In addition to those offered by the court, consider the possibility that a writing might be given more weight because it requires more thought and planning than a spontaneous oral utterance, which might simply be tossed off. In California, defamation by radio and television is slander. See Cal. Civil Code §§ 46, 48.5(4). Defamation on the Internet is generally assumed to be libel. Based on the above justifications, should a podcast be treated as libel or slander?

2.   Because the court decided to treat broadcast defamation as libel, it was unnecessary to decide whether the defamatory imputations would fit within one of the slander per se categories. The imputation that Mrs. Matherson had committed adultery with one of the Good Rats would seem to clearly fall within the "unchastity of a woman" category. (But note that the trial judge thought Mrs. Matherson had to prove special harm; the opinion contains no explanation of this.)

3.   What about the imputation of homosexuality regarding Mr. Matherson? The unspoken assumption of the common law seems to have been that accusing a man of unchastity was not sufficiently likely to cause material damage. But in this era of legal, if not actual, equality in sexual matters, such a distinction is untenable. A few states have responded by redefining the category to make it gender neutral. See, e.g., Nazeri v. Missouri Valley College, 860 S.W.2d 303 (Mo. 1993) (extending the fourth category to any "serious sexual misconduct," following § 569, comment f of the Restatement (Second) of Torts). Homosexuality, however, is not synonymous with either unchastity or sexual misconduct. Nevertheless, a number of older courts held that an allegation of homosexuality is slanderous per se. Those cases are cited in *Nazeri.*

The tide is turning if not turned on this issue. "[T]he prior cases categorizing statements that falsely impute homosexuality as defamatory per se," a New York court wrote in 2013, "are based upon the flawed premise that it is shameful and disgraceful to be described as lesbian, gay or bisexual." Yonaty v. Mincolla, 97 A.D.3d 141, 144 (N.Y. App. Div. 2012). Some years earlier, a district judge for the Southern District of New York had similarly rejected the claim that being called gay is defamatory. See Stern v. Cosby, 246 F.R.D. 453 (S.D.N.Y. 2007). A federal district judge in Massachusetts reached the same result in a ringing repudiation of the notion that homosexuality can be defamatory in the eyes of a "substantial and respectable community." Albright v. Morton, 321 F.Supp. 2d 130 (D. Mass. 2004).

2. LIBEL PER SE

"Libel per se" is an unfortunate term used to mean at least three entirely different things. One meaning is parallel to slander per se—a written statement is libel per se if it falls within one of the four categories recognized in slander per se. This use of libel per se is simply erroneous. Historically libel never employed the categories of slander per se, and the reasons for employing those in slander were to avoid the full range of liabilities that existed in libel.

Those states that use "libel per se" in a sense parallel to "slander per se" also employ the special damages requirement in a parallel way: Plaintiffs whose libel does not fall into one of the four categories must prove special damages.

A second meaning is that the statement is defamatory as a matter of law, i.e., incapable of a non-defamatory meaning. This usage is analytically confused. Whether a statement is libelous depends on a great many issues other than whether it is defamatory—e.g., whether it is false, whether it is privileged, etc. A statement therefore may be defamatory as a matter of law without being libelous as a matter of law.

A third usage is to signify that the defamatory meaning is apparent on the face of the statement. In this usage, the essential meaning of "libel per se" is simply that the plaintiff need not plead and prove extrinsic facts. Courts that employ this usage call written statements that are defamatory on their face "libel per se," and use the term "libel per quod" to describe statements that are not defamatory on their face but may be defamatory because of extrinsic facts. See, e.g., Holtzscheiter v. Thomson Newspapers Inc., 506 S.E.2d 497 (S.C. 1998), holding that the only consequence of treating a statement as "libel per quod" was to permit the plaintiff to show the defamatory meaning of the statement through extrinsic evidence.

Some courts, however, attach a further consequence when the statement is not defamatory on its face. They hold that some or all cases of "libel per quod" require proof of special damages. Sometimes they require such proof in all cases where the statement is not defamatory on its face. Sometimes they require proof of special damages if the statement is not defamatory on its face *and* its innuendo does not fit within the slander per se categories. See Robert D. Sack, Sack on Defamation 2–98 (3d ed. 1999).

Historically there was no special damages requirement in libel, and some states still do not impose one in libel cases of any kind. The courts that do so appear either to be confused about the relationship between libel and slander, or to have decided not to try to undo the results of previous confusion in their states. Extension of the special damage requirement beyond its historical role has little to commend it, particularly since the requirement functions only as a threshold, not a limit on recovery: even if special damages must be proven, a plaintiff who is able to do so is not limited to those damages but becomes eligible for all of the damages that any other plaintiff might receive. See, e.g., Schaffer v. Zekman, 554 N.E.2d 988 (Ill. App. Ct. 1990).

C. IDENTIFICATION OF PLAINTIFF

The plaintiff must show that he or she was the person defamed or was among a smaller group that was defamed. The early common law asked whether the statement was "of and concerning" plaintiff, and libel lawyers perpetuate this archaic expression by referring to "the of-and-concerning issue." The question is actually quite straightforward: was the statement understood to refer to the plaintiff? The question is not whether the defendant intended to refer to the plaintiff; that may be relevant on fault issues but not on the identification issue. In most cases, identification is not an issue at all, because the plaintiff is named or is identified visually or by reference to the position he or she holds. Identification of plaintiff becomes an issue principally in the three types of cases discussed below.

Identification by Implication. A plaintiff may be identified by implications that arise either from the face of the publication or from extrinsic facts that tell at least some recipients of the message that it refers to the plaintiff. An example of the former is the juxtaposition of words and visual images in such a way that the words are understood to refer to the person pictured. See, e.g., Clark v. American Broadcasting Cos., Inc., 684 F.2d 1208 (6th Cir. 1982). The defendant there used videotape of street scenes to illustrate a report about prostitution. The plaintiff, who had been photographed without her knowledge while walking on a city street, was shown on the screen while the narrator was describing the prevalence of prostitution in the neighborhood. The implication was that she was a prostitute.

The plaintiff may be identified by physical characteristics or circumstances that are known to viewers or readers. Proof of extrinsic facts necessary to identify the plaintiff is sometimes called "colloquium." In Doe v. Hagar, 765 F.3d 855 (8th Cir. 2015), for example, musician Sammy Hagar wrote an autobiography asserting that a woman had blackmailed him by falsely asserting she was pregnant with his child. The Eighth Circuit held, inter alia, that a jury could conclude that the book included sufficient identifying details to permit those who knew the plaintiff to recognize her.

Group Libel. Different problems arise when the statement is about a group of individuals. When will a statement about a group of which the plaintiff is a part be deemed to harm the personal reputation of a plaintiff?

There are at least two variables in these cases. One is the size of the group, and the other is the inclusiveness of the language. A statement that "all lawyers are crooks" does not defame all lawyers. However, a charge made against a small group may defame all members of that group. For example, a newspaper article may assert that "the officers" of a corporation have embezzled funds. If there are only four officers of the corporation, each of them may be defamed, even though the statement is that "one of the officers of the corporation" had embezzled funds. The group is small enough so that all four officials are put under a shadow, and most states would permit all four to sue.

As the group grows larger, the impact of the statement depends on the inclusiveness of the language as well as the size of the group. A book about Dallas published decades ago stated that "some" Neiman-Marcus department store models were "call girls. . . . The salesgirls are good, too—pretty and often much cheaper. . . ." And "most of the [male] sales staff are fairies, too." (As suggested above, implications of homosexuality through such derogatory words and otherwise were considered defamatory at the time.)

Suits were filed by all nine models, 30 of the 382 saleswomen, and 15 of the 25 salesmen. The defendants did not challenge the right of the nine models to sue. The other two groups were challenged as being too large.

The claim of "the salesgirls" was dismissed. The result would be the same even if the authors had explicitly referred to "all"—and even if all 382 had sued. The judge cited cases rejecting lawsuits when the statements attacked all officials of a statewide union or all the taxicab drivers in Washington, D.C.

On the other hand, the salesmen's case was allowed to proceed. Its facts were close to others involving members of a posse, or the 12 doctors on a hospital's residential staff. Neiman-Marcus v. Lait, 13 F.R.D. 311 (S.D.N.Y. 1952). Would the result have been the same if the authors had referred to "some" or "a few" of the men?

For a more recent example, see Diaz v. NBC Universal, 37 Media L. Rep. 1993 (2d Cir. 2009) ("In view of the large size of this group (consisting of 400 individuals [who are current and former DEA agents], or even potentially 233 . . .), and that [the film at issue] makes reference only to three-quarters of the group, i.e. 'some' of its members, appellants' claim is incapable of supporting a jury's finding that the allegedly libelous statements refer to them as individuals").

A few states have statutes purporting to make it a crime to defame a class of people because of their race or religion. The Supreme Court, 5–4, upheld the constitutionality of such a statute in Beauharnais v. Illinois, 343 U.S. 250 (1952), but the validity of such statutes seems questionable in light of the Supreme Court's decision in R.A.V. v. City of St. Paul, 505 U.S. 377 (1992), which struck down a "bias-motivated crime ordinance" as impermissibly content-based because it singled out only

" 'fighting words' that insult, or provoke violence, 'on the basis of race, color, creed, religion or gender.' "

Entities Other than Natural Persons. Corporations do not have reputations in the full sense that individuals do, but they may sue for the types of reputational harm that they are capable of suffering. Section 561 of the Restatement (Second) of Torts suggests that a for-profit corporation may sue if "the matter tends to prejudice it in the conduct of its business or to deter others from dealing with it." The same is true of partnerships and labor unions. A non-profit organization may sue if it "depends upon financial support from the public, and the matter tends to interfere with its activities by prejudicing it in public estimation."

Defamation of a corporation or other non-natural legal entity may defame the individuals who own or manage it, but only if the accusation implies that the individuals were personally involved in or responsible for the matter that is the subject of the defamation. Thus, defamation of a closely held corporation may defame the major stockholder, particularly if the individual and the corporation have the same name. See Schiavone Construction Co. v. Time Inc., 619 F.Supp. 684 (D.N.J. 1985), related appeal, 847 F.2d 1069 (3d Cir. 1988).

D. FAULT

At common law, libel and slander were strict liability torts in the sense that plaintiff was not required to show that the defendant had been negligent or guilty of some other form of fault. By the middle of the twentieth century the possibility that liability without fault might be imposed for defamatory speech seemed increasingly troublesome from a First Amendment perspective.

In what became one of the most famous and important cases in all of constitutional jurisprudence, the Supreme Court decided that the common law of libel violated the First Amendment, at least when public officials used it against the media. The Court's solution to this problem was to require as a matter of First Amendment law a showing of fault—indeed, a high level of fault—with respect to the truth or falsity of the defamatory statement. Although this solution obviously implicated the falsity issue as well as fault, the Court did not focus explicitly on falsity. As we shall see in a part of this chapter that follows, the impact on the falsity issue became apparent only later.

1. ACTUAL MALICE

a. APPLICATION TO PUBLIC OFFICIALS

New York Times Co. v. Sullivan (Together with Abernathy v. Sullivan)

Supreme Court of the United States, 1964.
376 U.S. 254.

[This action was based on a full-page advertisement in the New York Times on behalf of several individuals and groups protesting a "wave of terror" against blacks involved in non-violent demonstrations in the South. Plaintiff, one of three elected commissioners of Montgomery, the capital of Alabama, was in charge of the police department. When he demanded a retraction, the Times responded that it failed to see how he was defamed, even though it did subsequently publish a retraction at the request of the Alabama governor, whose complaint was similar to Sullivan's. Plaintiff then filed suit against the Times and four clergymen whose names appeared in the ad. Plaintiff alleged that the third and the sixth paragraphs of the advertisement libeled him]:

> "In Montgomery, Alabama, after students sang 'My Country, 'Tis of Thee' on the State Capitol steps, their leaders were expelled from school, and truckloads of police armed with shotguns and teargas ringed the Alabama State College Campus. When the entire student body protested to state authorities by refusing to re-register, their dining hall was padlocked in an attempt to starve them into submission."
>
> . . .
>
> "Again and again the Southern violators have answered Dr. King's peaceful protests with intimidation and violence. They have bombed his home almost killing his wife and child. They have assaulted his person. They have arrested him seven times—for 'speeding,' 'loitering' and similar 'offenses.' And now they have charged him with 'perjury'—a *felony* under which they could imprison him for *ten years*. . . ."

[Plaintiff claimed that the ad accused him, in his capacity as supervisor of the police, of overseeing a campaign of violence, and he brought witnesses who testified that they understood the ad to refer to him. Plaintiff established that he had not participated in the events attributed to the police, but he brought no evidence that he had suffered pecuniary loss as a result of the libel. The defendants conceded that the ad contained several inaccuracies: the students sang the national anthem, not My Country, 'Tis of Thee; nine students were expelled, not for leading the demonstration, but for demanding service at a lunch counter in the county courthouse; the dining hall was never padlocked; police never literally ringed the campus though they were deployed nearby in large numbers; they were not called to the campus in connection with the demonstration; Dr. King had been arrested only four times; and officers disputed his account of the alleged assault.]

[The trial judge instructed the jury that the statements were libel per se, that the jury should decide whether they were made "of and concerning" the plaintiff and, if so, that general damages were to be presumed. Although noting that punitive damages required more than carelessness, he refused to charge that they required a finding of actual intent to harm or "gross negligence and recklessness." He also refused to order the jury to separate its award of general and punitive damages. The jury returned a verdict for $500,000—the full amount demanded. The Alabama Supreme Court affirmed, holding that malice could be found in several aspects of the Times' conduct.]

■ MR. JUSTICE BRENNAN delivered the opinion of the Court.

    . . .

We may dispose at the outset of two grounds asserted to insulate the judgment of the Alabama courts from constitutional scrutiny. The first is the proposition relied on by the State Supreme Court—that "The Fourteenth Amendment is directed against State action and not private action." That proposition has no application to this case. Although this is a civil lawsuit between private parties, the Alabama courts have applied a state rule of law which petitioners claim to impose invalid restrictions on their constitutional freedoms of speech and press. It matters not that that law has been applied in a civil action and that it is common law only, though supplemented by statute. [ ] The test is not the form in which state power has been applied but, whatever the form, whether such power has in fact been exercised. [ ]

The second contention is that the constitutional guarantees of freedom of speech and of the press are inapplicable here, at least so far as the Times is concerned, because the allegedly libelous statements were published as part of a paid, "commercial" advertisement. [The argument was rejected.]

II.

Under Alabama law as applied in this case, a publication is "libelous per se" if the words "tend to injure a person . . . in his reputation" or to "bring [him] into public contempt"; the trial court stated that the standard was met if the words are such as to "injure him in his public office, or impute misconduct to him in his office, or want of official integrity, or want of fidelity to a public trust. . . ." The jury must find that the words were published "of and concerning" the plaintiff, but where the plaintiff is a public official his place in the governmental hierarchy is sufficient evidence to support a finding that his reputation has been affected by statements that reflect upon the agency of which he is in charge. Once "libel per se" has been established, the defendant has no defense as to stated facts unless he can persuade the jury that they were true in all their particulars. [ ] His privilege of "fair comment" for expressions of opinion depends on the truth of the facts upon which the comment is based. [ ] Unless he can discharge the burden of proving truth, general damages are presumed, and may be awarded without proof of pecuniary injury. A showing of actual malice is apparently a prerequisite to recovery of punitive damages, and the defendant may in any event forestall a punitive award by a retraction meeting the statutory requirements. Good motives and belief in truth do not negate an inference of malice, but are relevant only in mitigation of punitive damages if the jury chooses to accord them weight. [ ]

The question before us is whether this rule of liability, as applied to an action brought by a public official against critics of his official conduct, abridges the freedom of speech and of the press that is guaranteed by the First and Fourteenth Amendments.

Respondent relies heavily, as did the Alabama courts, on statements of this Court to the effect that the Constitution does not protect libelous publications. Those statements do not foreclose our inquiry here. None of the cases sustained the use of libel laws to impose sanctions upon expression critical of the official conduct of public officials. . . . In deciding the question now, we are compelled by neither precedent nor policy to give any more weight to the epithet "libel" than we have to other "mere labels" of state law. NAACP v. Button, 371 U.S. 415, 429 (1963). Like insurrection, contempt, advocacy of unlawful acts, breach of the peace, obscenity, solicitation of legal business, and the various other formulae for the repression of expression that have been challenged in this Court, libel can claim no talismanic immunity from constitutional limitations. It must be measured by standards that satisfy the First Amendment.

The general proposition that freedom of expression upon public questions is secured by the First Amendment has long been settled by our decisions. . . . Mr. Justice Brandeis, in his concurring opinion in Whitney v. California, 274 U.S. 357, 375–376 (1927), gave the principle its classic formulation:

> Those who won our independence believed . . . that public discussion is a political duty; and that this should be a fundamental principle of the American government. . . . Believing in the power of reason as applied through public discussion, they eschewed silence coerced by law—the argument of force in its worst form. Recognizing the occasional tyrannies of governing majorities, they amended the Constitution so that free speech and assembly should be guaranteed.

Thus we consider this case against the background of a profound national commitment to the principle that debate on public issues should be uninhibited, robust, and wide-open, and that it may well include vehement, caustic, and sometimes unpleasantly sharp attacks on government and public officials. [ ] The present advertisement, as an expression of grievance and protest on one of the major public issues of our time, would seem clearly to qualify for the constitutional protection. The question is whether it forfeits that protection by the falsity of some of its factual statements and by its alleged defamation of respondent.

Authoritative interpretations of the First Amendment guarantees have consistently refused to recognize an exception for any test of truth—whether administered by judges, juries, or administrative officials—and especially one that puts the burden of proving truth on the speaker. Cf. Speiser v. Randall, 357 U.S. 513, 525–526 (1958). The constitutional protection does not turn upon "the truth, popularity, or social utility of the ideas and beliefs which are offered." NAACP v. Button, 371 U.S. 415, 445 (1963). As Madison said, "Some degree of abuse is inseparable from the proper use of every thing; and in no instance is this more true than in that of the press." 4 Elliot's Debates on the Federal Constitution (1876), p. 571. . . .

That erroneous statement is inevitable in free debate, and that it must be protected if the freedoms of expression are to have the "breathing space" that they "need . . . to survive," NAACP v. Button, 371 U.S. 415, 433 (1963), was [ ] recognized by the Court of Appeals for the District of Columbia Circuit in Sweeney v. Patterson, 128 F.2d 457, 458 [ ]. Judge Edgerton spoke for a unanimous court which affirmed the dismissal of a Congressman's libel suit based upon a newspaper article charging him with anti-Semitism in opposing a judicial appointment. He said:

> Cases which impose liability for erroneous reports of the political conduct of officials reflect the obsolete doctrine that the governed must not criticize their governors. . . . The interest of the public here outweighs the interest of appellant or any other individual. The protection of the public requires not merely discussion, but information. Political conduct and views which some respectable people approve, and others condemn, are constantly imputed to Congressmen. Errors of fact, particularly in regard to a man's mental states and processes, are inevitable. . . . Whatever is added to the field of libel is taken from the field of free debate.[13]

Injury to official reputation affords no more warrant for repressing speech that would otherwise be free than does factual error. Where judicial officers are involved, this Court has held that concern for the

---

[13] See also Mill, On Liberty (Oxford: Blackwell, 1947), at 47: " . . . [T]o argue sophistically, to suppress facts or arguments, to misstate the elements of the case, or misrepresent the opposite opinion . . . all this, even to the most aggravated degree, is so continually done in perfect good faith, by persons who are not considered, and in many other respects may not deserve to be considered, ignorant or incompetent, that it is rarely possible, on adequate grounds, conscientiously to stamp the misrepresentation as morally culpable; and still less could law presume to interfere with this kind of controversial misconduct."

dignity and reputation of the courts does not justify the punishment as criminal contempt of criticism of the judge or his decision. Bridges v. California, 314 U.S. 252 (1941). This is true even though the utterance contains "half-truths" and "misinformation." [ ] .... If judges are to be treated as "men of fortitude, able to thrive in a hardy climate," sure the same must be true of other government officials, such as elected city commissioners. Criticism of their official conduct does not lose its constitutional protection merely because it is effective criticism and hence diminishes their official reputations.

If neither factual error nor defamatory content suffices to remove the constitutional shield from criticism of official conduct, the combination of the two elements is no less inadequate. This is the lesson to be drawn from the great controversy over the Sedition Act of 1798, 1 Stat. § 596, which first crystallized a national awareness of the central meaning of the First Amendment. . . .

Although the Sedition Act was never tested in this Court, the attack upon its validity has carried the day in the court of history. Fines levied in its prosecution were repaid by Act of Congress on the ground that it was unconstitutional. . . . The invalidity of the Act has also been assumed by Justices of this Court. [ ] These views reflect a broad consensus that the Act, because of the restraint it imposed upon criticism of government and public officials, was inconsistent with the First Amendment.

. . .

What a State may not constitutionally bring about by means of a criminal statute is likewise beyond the reach of its civil law of libel. The fear of damage awards under a rule such as that invoked by the Alabama courts here may be markedly more inhibiting than the fear of prosecution under a criminal statute. [ ] Alabama, for example, has a criminal libel law which subjects to prosecution "any person who speaks, writes, or prints of and concerning another any accusation falsely and maliciously importing the commission by such person of a felony, or any other indictable offense involving moral turpitude," and which allows as punishment upon conviction a fine not exceeding $500 and a prison sentence of six months. [ ] Presumably a person charged with violation of this statute enjoys ordinary criminal-law safeguards such as the requirements of an indictment and of proof beyond a reasonable doubt. These safeguards are not available to the defendant in a civil action. . . . And since there is no double-jeopardy limitation applicable to civil lawsuits, this is not the only judgment that may be awarded against petitioners for the same publication.[18] Whether or not a newspaper can survive a succession of such judgments, the pall of fear and timidity

---

[18] The Times states that four other libel suits based on the advertisement have been filed against it by others who have served as Montgomery City Commissioners and by the Governor of Alabama; that another $500,000 verdict has been awarded in the only one of these cases that has yet gone to trial; and that the damages sought in the other three total $2,000,000.

imposed upon those who would give voice to public criticism is an atmosphere in which the First Amendment freedoms cannot survive. . . .

The state rule of law is not saved by its allowance of the defense of truth. . . . Allowance of the defense of truth, with the burden of proving it on the defendant, does not mean that only false speech will be deterred.[19] Even courts accepting this defense as an adequate safeguard have recognized the difficulties of adducing legal proofs that the alleged libel was true in all its factual particulars. See, e.g., Post Publishing Co. v. Hallam, 59 F.530, 540 (6th Cir. 1893); see also Noel, Defamation of Public Officers and Candidates, 49 Col. L. Rev. 875, 892 (1949). Under such a rule, would-be critics of official conduct may be deterred from voicing their criticism, even though it is believed to be true and even though it is in fact true, because of doubt whether it can be proved in court or fear of the expense of having to do so. They tend to make only statements which "steer far wider of the unlawful zone." Speiser v. Randall, supra, 357 U.S., at 526. The rule thus dampens the vigor and limits the variety of public debate. It is inconsistent with the First and Fourteenth Amendments.

The constitutional guarantees require, we think, a federal rule that prohibits a public official from recovering damages for a defamatory falsehood relating to his official conduct unless he proves that the statement was made with "actual malice"—that is, with knowledge that it was false or with reckless disregard of whether it was false or not. An oft-cited statement of a like rule, which has been adopted by a number of state courts, is found in the Kansas case of Coleman v. MacLennan, 78 Kan. 711, 98 P.281 (1908). . . .

Such a privilege for criticism of official conduct is appropriately analogous to the protection accorded a public official when *he* is sued for libel by a private citizen. In Barr v. Matteo, 360 U.S. 564, 575 (1959), this Court held the utterance of a federal official to be absolutely privileged if made "within the outer perimeter" of his duties. The States accord the same immunity to statements of their highest officers, although some differentiate their lesser officials and qualify the privilege they enjoy. But all hold that all officials are protected unless actual malice can be proved. The reason for the official privilege is said to be that the threat of damage suits would otherwise "inhibit the fearless, vigorous, and effective administration of policies of government" and "dampen the ardor of all but the most resolute, or the most irresponsible, in the unflinching discharge of their duties." Barr v. Matteo, supra, 360 U.S., at 571. Analogous considerations support the privilege for the citizen-critic of government. It is as much his duty to criticize as it is the official's duty to administer. . . . As Madison said, [ ], "the censorial power is in the

---

[19] Even a false statement may be deemed to make a valuable contribution to public debate, since it brings about "the clearer perception and livelier impression of truth, produced by its collision with error." Mill, On Liberty (Oxford: Blackwell, 1947), at 15; see also Milton, Areopagitica, in Prose Works (Yale, 1959), Vol. II, at 561.

people over the Government, and not in the Government over the people."
It would give public servants an unjustified preference over the public
they serve, if critics of official conduct did not have a fair equivalent of
the immunity granted to the officials themselves.

We conclude that such a privilege is required by the First and
Fourteenth Amendments.

III.

We hold today that the Constitution delimits a State's power to
award damages for libel in actions brought by public officials against
critics of their official conduct. Since this is such an action, the rule
requiring proof of actual malice is applicable. While Alabama law
apparently requires proof of actual malice for an award of punitive
damages, where general damages are concerned malice is "presumed."
Such a presumption is inconsistent with the federal rule. . . . Since the
trial judge did not instruct the jury to differentiate between general and
punitive damages, it may be that the verdict was wholly an award of one
or the other. But it is impossible to know, in view of the general verdict
returned. Because of this uncertainty, the judgment must be reversed
and the case remanded.

Since respondent may seek a new trial, we deem that considerations
of effective judicial administration require us to review the evidence in
the present record to determine whether it could constitutionally support
a judgment for respondent. . . .

Applying these standards, we consider that the proof presented to
show actual malice lacks the convincing clarity which the constitutional
standard demands, and hence that it would not constitutionally sustain
the judgment for respondent under the proper rule of law. The case of the
individual petitioners requires little discussion. Even assuming that they
could constitutionally be found to have authorized the use of their names
on the advertisement, there was no evidence whatever that they were
aware of any erroneous statements or were in any way reckless in that
regard. The judgment against them is thus without constitutional
support.

As to the Times, we similarly conclude that the facts do not support
a finding of actual malice. [The testimony of the Secretary of the Times
that he believed the advertisement to be "substantially correct" was "at
least a reasonable one, and there was no evidence to impeach the witness'
good faith in holding it." Nor was the later retraction for the governor
evidence of actual malice toward plaintiff. Leaving open the question of
whether failure to retract "may ever constitute such evidence," it could
not suffice here because the letter showed reasonable doubt whether the
ad referred to plaintiff at all, and also because the letter was not a final
refusal. As to evidence that the Times published the ad without first
checking news stories in its own files, the Court stated that the "mere
presence" of such stories "does not, of course, establish that the Times

'knew' the advertisement was false, since the state of mind required for actual malice would have to be brought home to the persons in the Times' organization having responsibility for the publication of the advertisement." Those persons relied on the "good reputation of many of those whose names were listed as sponsors of the advertisement, and upon the letter from A. Philip Randolph, known to them as a responsible individual, certifying that the use of the names was authorized."]

We also think the evidence was constitutionally defective in another respect: it was incapable of supporting the jury's finding that the allegedly libelous statements were made "of and concerning" respondent. Respondent relies on the words of the advertisement and the testimony of six witnesses to establish a connection between it and himself. . . . There was no reference to respondent in the advertisement, either by name or official position. . . . [Moreover, the statements about the police] were false only in that the police had been "deployed near" the campus but had not actually "ringed" it and had not gone there in connection with the State Capitol demonstration, and in that Dr. King had been arrested only four times. The ruling that these discrepancies between what was true and what was asserted were sufficient to injure respondent's reputation may itself raise constitutional problems, but we need not consider them here. Although the statements may be taken as referring to the police, they did not on their face make even an oblique reference to respondent as an individual. Support for the asserted reference must, therefore, be sought in the testimony of respondent's witnesses. But none of them suggested any basis for the belief that respondent himself was attacked in the advertisement beyond the bare fact that he was in overall charge of the Police Department and thus bore official responsibility for police conduct; to the extent that some of the witnesses thought respondent to have been charged with ordering or approving the conduct or otherwise being personally involved in it, they based this notion not on any statements in the advertisement, and not on any evidence that he had in fact been so involved, but solely on the unsupported assumption that, because of his official position, he must have been. This reliance on the bare fact of respondent's official position was made explicit by the Supreme Court of Alabama. . . .

This proposition has disquieting implications for criticism of governmental conduct. For good reason, "no court of last resort in this country has ever held, or even suggested, that prosecutions for libel on government have any place in the American system of jurisprudence." [ ] The present proposition would sidestep this obstacle by transmuting criticism of government, however impersonal it may seem on its face, into personal criticism, and hence potential libel, of the officials of whom the government is composed. There is no legal alchemy by which a State may thus create the cause of action that would otherwise be denied for a publication which, as respondent himself said of the advertisement, "reflects not only on me but on the other Commissioners and the community." Raising as it does the possibility that a good-faith critic of government will be penalized for his criticism, the proposition relied on by the Alabama courts strikes at the very center of the constitutionally protected area of free expression. We hold that such a proposition may not constitutionally be utilized to establish that an otherwise impersonal attack on governmental operations was a libel of an official responsible for those operations. Since it was relied on exclusively here, and there was no other evidence to connect the statements with respondent, the evidence was constitutionally insufficient to support a finding that the statements referred to respondent.

The judgment of the Supreme Court of Alabama is reversed and the case is remanded to that court for further proceedings not inconsistent with this opinion.

Reversed and remanded.

■ MR. JUSTICE BLACK, with whom MR. JUSTICE DOUGLAS joins, concurring.

. . . "Malice," even as defined by the Court, is an elusive, abstract concept, hard to prove and hard to disprove. The requirement that malice be proved provides at best an evanescent protection for the right critically to discuss public affairs and certainly does not measure up to the sturdy safeguard embodied in the First Amendment. Unlike the Court, therefore, I vote to reverse exclusively on the ground that the Times and the individual defendants had an absolute unconditional constitutional right to publish in the Times advertisement their criticisms of the Montgomery agencies and officials. . . .

The half-million-dollar verdict does give dramatic proof, however, that state libel laws threaten the very existence of an American press virile enough to publish unpopular views on public affairs and bold enough to criticize the conduct of public officials. . . . In fact, briefs before us show that in Alabama there are now pending eleven libel suits by local and state officials against the Times seeking $5,600,000 and five such suits against the Columbia Broadcasting System seeking $1,700,000. Moreover, this technique for harassing and punishing a free press—now that it has been shown to be possible—is by no means limited to cases with racial overtones; it can be used in other fields where public feelings may make local as well as out-of-state newspapers easy prey for libel verdict seekers. . . .

■ MR. JUSTICE GOLDBERG, with whom MR. JUSTICE DOUGLAS joins, concurring in the result.

. . . In my view, the First and Fourteenth Amendments to the Constitution afford to the citizen and to the press an absolute, unconditional privilege to criticize official conduct despite the harm which may flow from excesses and abuses. . . .

NOTES AND QUESTIONS

1.   What is the problem with strict liability? Would a negligence standard raise the same problems? Would the absolute privilege suggested by the concurring opinions be preferable? In Garrison v. Louisiana, 379 U.S. 64 (1964), the Court explained why it rejected the absolute privilege proposed by the concurring opinions:

> Although honest utterance, even if inaccurate, may further the fruitful exercise of the right of free speech, it does not follow that the lie, knowingly and deliberately published about a public official, should enjoy a like immunity. At the time the First Amendment was adopted, as today, there were those unscrupulous enough and skillful enough to use the deliberate or reckless falsehood as an effective political tool to unseat the public servant or even topple an administration. [ ] That speech is used as a tool for political ends does not automatically bring it under the protective mantle of the Constitution. For the use of the known lie as a tool is at once at odds with the premises of democratic government and with the orderly manner in which economic, social, or political change is to be effected. Calculated falsehood falls into that class of utterances which "are no essential part of any exposition of ideas, and are of such slight social value as a step to truth that any benefit that may be derived from them is clearly outweighed by the social interest in order and morality. . . ." [Chaplinsky]. Hence the knowingly false statement and the false statement made with reckless disregard of the truth, do not enjoy constitutional protection.

2.   Why did the Court see the introduction of "actual malice" as the solution to the constitutional problem? The Court ascribed the "chilling effect" to the burdens and risks of proving truth. Might the problem have been solved by shifting to the plaintiff the burden of proving falsity? Does the Court's determination that "actual malice" requires proof that the statement was made with "knowledge that it was false or with reckless disregard of whether it was false or not" implicitly shift the burden on the issue of truth or falsity? We shall consider this further later in this chapter.

3.   Justice Brennan's concern, that speakers might be induced to "steer far wider of the unlawful zone" than legally necessary, has been articulated by others as the concern that fear of liability has the potential to "chill" speech. In the passage from Speiser v. Randall that is cited in the principal case, the Court wrote that where speech is close to the line between lawful and unlawful,

> the possibility of mistaken fact-finding—inherent in all litigation— will create the danger that the legitimate utterance will be penalized. The man who knows that he must bring forth proof and persuade another of the lawfulness of his conduct necessarily must steer far wider of the unlawful zone than if the state must bear these burdens.

How is this concern relevant to the problems raised by libel law?

4.   Toward the end, the opinion discusses whether the libel was of and concerning the plaintiff. Why isn't that a jury question?

b.   EXTENSION OF THE NEW YORK TIMES RULE TO PUBLIC FIGURES

Three years after *New York Times*, the Supreme Court extended the public official rule to public figure plaintiffs in the companion cases of Curtis Publishing Co. v. Butts and Associated Press v. Walker, 388 U.S. 130 (1967).

In *Butts*, the defendant magazine had accused the plaintiff athletic director of disclosing his team's game plan to an opposing coach before their game. Although he was on the staff of a state university, Butts was paid by a private alumni organization. In *Walker*, the defendant news service reported that the plaintiff, a former United States Army general who resigned to engage in political activity, had personally led students in an attack on federal marshals who were enforcing a desegregation order at the University of Mississippi.

In both cases, lower courts affirmed substantial jury awards against the defendants and refused to apply the *Times* doctrine on the ground that public officials were not involved. The Supreme Court divided several ways, affirming *Butts*, 5–4, and reversing *Walker*, 9–0. Chief Justice Warren wrote the pivotal opinion in which he concluded that both men were "public figures" and explained why the *New York Times* rule should apply to "public figures" as well.

> To me, differentiation between "public figures" and "public officials" and adoption of separate standards of proof for each has no basis in law, logic, or First Amendment policy. Increasingly in this country, the distinctions between governmental and private sectors are blurred. . . . Depression, war, international tensions, national and international markets, and the surging growth of science and technology have precipitated national and international problems that demand national and international solutions. While these trends and events have occasioned a consolidation of governmental power, power has also become much more organized in what we have commonly considered to be the private sector. In many situations, policy determinations which traditionally were channeled through formal political institutions are now originated and implemented through a complex array of boards, committees, commissions, corporations, and associations, some only loosely connected with the Government. This blending of positions and power has also occurred in the case of individuals so that many who do not hold public office at the moment are nevertheless intimately involved in the resolution of important public questions or, by reason of their fame, shape events in areas of concern to society at large.

Viewed in this context then, it is plain that although they are not subject to the restraints of the political process, "public figures," like "public officials," often play an influential role in ordering society. And surely as a class these "public figures" have as ready access as "public officials" to mass media of communication, both to influence policy and to counter criticism of their views and activities. Our citizenry has a legitimate and substantial interest in the conduct of such persons, and freedom of the press to engage in uninhibited debate about their involvement in public issues and events is as crucial as it is in the case of "public officials." The fact that they are not amenable to the restraints of the political process only underscores the legitimate and substantial nature of the interest, since it means that public opinion may be the only instrument by which society can attempt to influence their conduct.

He found that, on the merits, the actual malice standard had not been met in *Walker*. In *Butts* he found that defendant's counsel had deliberately waived the *Times* doctrine and he also found evidence establishing reckless disregard of the truth. He thus voted to reverse *Walker* and affirm *Butts*.

Justice Harlan, joined by three others, argued that something less than the *Times* standard should apply to public figures because criticism of government was not involved:

We consider and would hold that a "public figure" who is not a public official may also recover damages for a defamatory falsehood whose substance makes substantial danger to reputation apparent, on a showing of highly unreasonable conduct constituting an extreme departure from the standards of investigation and reporting ordinarily adhered to by responsible publishers.

Applying that standard, Justice Harlan concluded that Walker had failed to establish a case, but that Butts had shown that the Saturday Evening Post had ignored elementary precautions in preparing a potentially damaging story. Together with the Chief Justice's vote, there were five votes to affirm *Butts*. Justices Brennan, White, Black, and Douglas voted to reverse both cases.

Later in this chapter we will explore the methods courts use to distinguish "public figures" from "private figures." In the meantime, we turn to the consequences that flow from labeling a person "public" for defamation law purposes.

c.   APPLYING THE ACTUAL MALICE STANDARD

If the Court had left it to the jury to decide whether "actual malice" was present, New York Times v. Sullivan would have had a limited effect on the law of libel. But the Court did not stop there, and most of the impact of the decision resulted from the Court's subsequent refinements of the "actual malice" concept and its adoption of ancillary procedural rules that greatly restricted the jury's power. Together, these have made actual malice an obstacle that few plaintiffs can overcome.

i.   Substantive Issues

What must a plaintiff show to satisfy the "actual malice" standard? The Supreme Court has addressed that question several times since *New York Times*.

Garrison v. Louisiana. The Court extended *New York Times* to criminal libel, holding that "only those false statements made with the high degree of awareness of their probable falsity demanded by *New York Times* may be the subject of either civil or criminal sanctions." 379 U.S. 64 (1964). The decision signaled that the standard was to focus on subjective awareness of falsity and therefore bore little resemblance to the tort law concept of recklessness.

St. Amant v. Thompson. The defendant repeated false charges against plaintiff without checking the charges or investigating the source's reputation for veracity. The Supreme Court concluded that "reckless disregard" had not been shown. 390 U.S. 727 (1968). The Court explained that actual malice

> is not measured by whether a reasonably prudent man would have published, or would have investigated before publishing. There must be sufficient evidence to permit the conclusion that the defendant in fact entertained serious doubts as to the truth of his publication. . . .
>
> . . .
>
> The defendant in a defamation action brought by a public official cannot, however, automatically insure a favorable verdict by testifying that he published with a belief that the statements were true. The finder of fact must determine whether the publication was indeed made in good faith. Professions of good faith will be unlikely to prove persuasive, for example, where a story is fabricated by the defendant, is a product of his imagination, or is based wholly on an unverified anonymous telephone call. Nor will they be likely to prevail when the publisher's allegations are so inherently improbable that only a reckless man would have put them in circulation. Likewise, recklessness may be found where there are obvious reasons to doubt the veracity of the informant or the accuracy of his reports.

Harte-Hanks Communications, Inc. v. Connaughton. A newspaper accused a judicial candidate of having used "dirty tricks" to smear his opponent, the incumbent. A unanimous Court upheld an award of $5,000 compensatory and $195,000 punitive damages. 491 U.S. 657 (1989).

The evidence of "dirty tricks" relied heavily on a source whose credibility had been seriously impugned by other witnesses and whose version of the episode was unconfirmed. Reviewing the record extensively, the Court concluded that actual malice could be found from (1) the newspaper's failure to interview "the one witness that both [the plaintiff and the source] claimed would verify their conflicting accounts of the relevant events," a failure that the Court found "utterly bewildering"; (2) the paper's failure to listen to a tape that the paper had been told exonerated plaintiff, which plaintiff had delivered to the paper at the paper's request; (3) an earlier editorial on the election, which "could be taken to indicate that [the editor] had already decided to publish [the source's] allegations, regardless of how the evidence developed and regardless of whether or not [the source's] story was credible upon ultimate reflection"; (4) discrepancies in testimony of defendant's witnesses that would support a finding that "the failure to conduct a complete investigation involved a deliberate effort to avoid the truth."

Accepting the jury's implicit determination that the newspaper's explanations for not interviewing the crucial witness and for not listening to the tape were not credible, "it is likely that the newspaper's inaction was a product of a deliberate decision not to acquire knowledge of facts that might confirm the probable falsity of [the source's] charges. Although failure to investigate will not alone support a finding of actual malice [*St. Amant*], the purposeful avoidance of the truth is in a different category."

In a footnote at that point, the Court noted that it was not suggesting that a newspaper must accept or be shaken by vehement denials. These are "so commonplace in the world of polemical charge and countercharge that, in themselves, they hardly alert the conscientious reporter to the likelihood of error."

In passing, the Court observed that a "newspaper's motive in publishing the story—whether to promote an opponent's candidacy or to increase its circulation—cannot provide a sufficient basis for finding actual malice."

Masson v. New Yorker Magazine, Inc. Plaintiff alleged that a magazine article written by Janet Malcolm had attributed to plaintiff fabricated quotations that hurt his reputation. For example, Malcolm quoted Masson as calling himself an "intellectual gigolo" and "greatest analyst who ever lived." Masson learned of these quotations (and others) when he was contacted by a fact-checker for the New Yorker Magazine and immediately disputed them, but the magazine ran Malcolm's story anyway. The exact quotations could not be found in the defendant's extensive tape recordings of her interviews with Masson, though Masson clearly had made very inflammatory statements to much the same effect. Although lower courts upheld summary judgment for Malcolm and the New Yorker, the Supreme Court reversed and held that Masson was entitled to a jury finding on the issue of actual malice. 501 U.S. 496 (1991).

The plaintiff argued that "excepting corrections of grammar or syntax, publication of a quotation with knowledge that it does not contain the words the public figure used demonstrates actual malice." The Court was unwilling to go that far. Interviewers often must reconstruct interviews from notes. Use of language that the subject did not use does not amount to actual malice in that situation. Even if an interview is tape recorded, the "full and exact statement will be reported in only rare circumstances."

> We conclude that a deliberate alteration of the words uttered by a plaintiff does not equate with knowledge of falsity for purposes of [*Times*] unless the alteration results in a material change in the meaning conveyed by the statement. The use of quotation to attribute words not in fact spoken bears in a most important way on that inquiry, but it is not dispositive in every case.

On remand in *Masson*, the Ninth Circuit concluded that although a publisher who has no "obvious reasons to doubt" the accuracy of a story "is not required to initiate an investigation that might plant such doubt," once fact-checking raises doubts, "the publisher must act reasonably in dispelling it." Although this approach puts publishers who fact-check stories "at somewhat of a disadvantage compared to other publisher such as newspapers and supermarket tabloids that cannot or will not engage in thorough fact-checking," the different treatment "makes considerable sense:"

> Readers of reputable magazines such as the New Yorker are far more likely to trust the verbatim accuracy of the stories they read than are the readers of supermarket tabloids or even daily newspapers, where they understand the inherent limitations in the fact-finding process. The harm inflicted by a misstatement in a publication known for scrupulously investigating the accuracy of its stories can be far more serious than a similar misstatement in a publication known not to do so.

Masson v. New Yorker Magazine, Inc., 960 F.2d 896 (9th Cir. 1992).

The court did, however, dismiss the case against the publisher of the book into which the New Yorker articles were converted. The publisher was entitled to rely on the New Yorker's reputation for accuracy and on its rejection of the plaintiff's complaints about the series. The book publisher had no "obvious reasons to doubt" the story's accuracy and thus no obligation to investigate. A jury eventually ruled in favor of Malcolm and the New Yorker, finding that one of the quotations was not defamatory, one was not published with actual malice, and the rest were not false. The Ninth Circuit affirmed. See 85 F.3d 1394 (9th Cir. 1996).

NOTES AND QUESTIONS

1.   *St. Amant* holds that failure to investigate, without more, does not constitute actual malice. Yet in *Connaughton* the defendant's failure to conduct a thorough investigation helped persuade the Court that the newspaper had made a "deliberate decision not to acquire knowledge of facts that might confirm the probable falsity" of the statement. What, if anything, makes *Connaughton* something more than a failure-to-investigate case? Is *Connaughton* a reckless disregard case or a case of knowing falsity?

2.   If Malcolm knew Masson did not say the defamatory things she attributed to him, why does this constitute actual malice only if the alteration "results in a material change in the meaning conveyed by the statement"? Does this treatment of deliberate falsification imply anything about knowing but inadvertent falsehoods, e.g., a mental lapse that causes a writer to name Jones as the murderer when she intended to name Smith?

3.   *Actual Malice in the Lower Courts.* Many important questions about actual malice have been addressed only by lower courts. For example, proof that a reporter harbored ill will toward a plaintiff will support a finding of actual malice "only when combined with other, more substantial evidence of a defendant's bad faith." See Tavoulareas v. Piro, 817 F.2d 762 (D.C. Cir. 1987) (en banc). Likewise, proof that an article is unfair does not establish actual malice because it "has no tendency to prove that the publisher believed it to be false." See Westmoreland v. CBS, Inc., 601 F.Supp. 66 (S.D.N.Y. 1984).

Does failure to "take down" an attack advertisement once one has been notified of its falsity constitute actual malice? The answer to that question may depend on what form the notice takes. In Bertrand v. Mullin, 846 N.W.2d 884 (Iowa 2014), the Iowa Supreme Court addressed a libel action brought by a Republican candidate for elective office against his Democratic opponent who ran an "attack ad" during their campaign. The plaintiff alleged that he had notified the defendant of the ad's implied falsity by pointing it out during a public political forum, and that the defendant's failure to remove the ad afterwards established actual malice. The court, however, held that "[a] candidate does not purposely avoid the truth if the truth is buried in political grandstanding and rhetoric."

A full analysis of the myriad issues surrounding proof of actual malice is beyond the scope of this chapter. A good place to start further research is Sack on Defamation: Libel, Slander and Related Problems (PLI 4th ed. 2010).

4.   *Actual Malice and Implications.* As noted above, the defamatory sting of a statement can be implicit rather than explicit. Can actual malice be shown when the implication alleged by the plaintiff is one the defendant knew was false (or seriously doubted) but claims it did not intend to convey? Courts have offered a variety of answers to this question. Some have held that there can be no finding of actual malice unless the defendant intended

to convey the defamatory meaning, see Dodds v. American Broadcasting Co., 145 F.3d 1053 (9th Cir. 1998), or endorsed that meaning, see White v. Fraternal Order of Police, 909 F.2d 512 (D.C. Cir. 1990). Some say the plaintiff must prove "that the alleged implication is the principal inference a reasonable reader or viewer will draw from the publication as having been intended by the publisher." See Sassone v. Elder, 626 So.2d 345 (La. 1993). It has also been suggested that there can be no recovery for false implications as long as the explicit statements are true. See, e.g., Schaefer v. Lynch, 406 So.2d 185 (La. 1981).

5. *Vicarious Liability for Actual Malice.* Rarely will a plaintiff be able to show that the *corporation* as an entity that published or broadcast the defamation knew or had serious doubts about its falsity. It is generally enough to show that the employee who caused the statement to be published did. Freelance writers usually are treated as independent contractors, and their actual malice is not imputed to the publisher.

———

ii. *Procedural Issues*

Although the actual malice rule provides important substantive protections for media, the procedural protections adopted by the Supreme Court in New York Times v. Sullivan have played a very important role in defeating libel claims as well. Public official and public figure plaintiffs must prove actual malice with convincing clarity, rather than the usual preponderance of the evidence. Although the Supreme Court has never explained the justification for the convincing clarity standard, it is clear that this procedural protection tilts the scales in favor of defendants in libel actions, and can be outcome determinative. In Long v. Arcell, 618 F.2d 1145 (5th Cir. 1980), for example, the trial judge granted the defendant newspaper a judgment notwithstanding the verdict because plaintiff had presented sufficient evidence to establish actual malice by a preponderance but had failed to establish it by clear and convincing evidence. Moreover, in cases governed by the Federal Rules of Civil Procedure, the convincing clarity requirement gives judges a strong tool to dismiss libel cases prior to trial. The Supreme Court validated the use of this tool in Anderson v. Liberty Lobby, Inc., 477 U.S. 242 (1986). There, the Court held, 6–3, that the standard for considering summary judgment motions under Federal Rule 56 must take into account the burden plaintiff will have to meet at trial. For public plaintiffs, then, the judge hearing a summary judgment motion must decide "whether the evidence in the record could support a reasonable jury finding either that the plaintiff has shown actual malice by clear and convincing evidence or that the plaintiff has not." Note, however, that *Liberty Lobby* was decided on nonconstitutional grounds, leading several states to decline to follow it. See Dairy Stores, Inc. v. Sentinel Publishing Co., 516 A.2d 220 (N.J. 1986) (applying a "genuine issue of material fact" standard and observing that "[t]he clear-and-convincing test inevitably implicates a weighing of the evidence, an exercise that intrudes into the province of the jury"); Moffatt v. Brown, 751 P.2d 939 (Alaska 1988) (similar).

Finally, the requirement of clear and convincing evidence has been bolstered by the corollary requirement that appellate courts "independently review the record as a whole" to assure that actual malice has been shown with the required clarity. In Bose Corp. v. Consumers Union, 466 U.S. 485 (1984), the Supreme Court explained that the requirement that appellate courts independently review the record to support the findings of actual malice "reflects a deeply held conviction that judges—and particularly members of this Court—must exercise such review in order to preserve the precious liberties established and ordained by the Constitution. The question whether the evidence in the record in a defamation case is of the convincing clarity required to strip the utterance of First Amendment protection is not merely a question for the trier of fact. Judges, as expositors of the Constitution, must independently decide whether the evidence in the record is sufficient to cross the constitutional threshold that bars the entry of any judgment that is not supported by clear and convincing proof of "actual malice."

The independent-review requirement, which has been a tremendous boon to media defendants, is criticized in Henry P. Monaghan, Constitutional Fact Review, 85 Colum. L. Rev. 229 (1985).

iii. Defendants' Refusal to Disclose Evidence

Because actual malice is defined in terms of subjective awareness of falsity, it invites inquiry into the defendant's journalistic decision processes. Media defendants often resist disclosing these matters. In Herbert v. Lando, 441 U.S. 153 (1979), Colonel Anthony Herbert sued the producer and reporter of the television program "60 Minutes" and the CBS network for remarks on the program about his conduct while in military service in Vietnam. During his deposition, Lando, the producer, generally responded but refused to answer some questions about why he made certain investigations and not others, what he concluded about the honesty of certain people he interviewed for the program, and about conversations he had with Mike Wallace, the reporter, in the preparation of the program segment. Lando contended that these thought processes and internal editorial discussions were protected from disclosure by the First Amendment. The Supreme Court disagreed.

Justice White, for the Court, understood the defendants to be arguing that "the defendant's reckless disregard of truth, a critical element, could not be shown by direct evidence through inquiry into the thoughts, opinions, and conclusions of the publisher but could be proved only by objective evidence from which the ultimate fact could be inferred." This was a barrier of some substance, "particularly when defendants themselves are prone to assert their good-faith belief in the truth of their publications, and libel plaintiffs are required to prove knowing or reckless falsehood with 'convincing clarity.'"

Although pretrial discovery techniques had led to "mushrooming litigation costs," this was happening in all areas of litigation. Until major changes in pretrial procedures were developed for all cases, the Court would rely on "what in fact and in law are ample powers of the district judge to prevent abuse."

Confidential Sources. Media do enjoy more limited privileges to withhold information, however. As we shall discuss at length in Chapter Nine, most courts recognize a "reporter's privilege" under the First Amendment or a state shield statute. These permit a reporter or editor to refuse to disclose confidential sources under certain circumstances, and in some instances they also prevent forced disclosure of non-confidential information, such as notes and outtakes. If the libel defendant is held to be protected by such a privilege, disclosure cannot be compelled and the plaintiff must proceed without the information, as would be the case with any other privileged evidence.

This can be a serious, if not fatal, obstacle to a plaintiff who must prove actual malice. The plaintiff may suspect that the source is one that the defendant knew was unreliable (or that there was no independent source), but that will be difficult to prove if the defendant cannot be required to identify the source.

In most instances, the reporter's privilege is not absolute and can be overcome if the plaintiff meets certain tests of materiality and necessity. If no privilege is available in the jurisdiction, or if the court decides that the balance of interests requires disclosure despite the privilege, the libel defendant can be ordered to reveal the source. Refusal can lead to contempt proceedings or sanctions of the sort normally imposed on defendants who refuse to comply with valid discovery orders. One court, for example, decided to impose a "no-source presumption," meaning that the jury would be instructed to assume that the confidential source did not exist in making the finding of actual malice. Downing v. Monitor Pub. Co., 415 A.2d 683 (N.H. 1980). Another court entered a pre-trial default judgment against the Boston Globe and one of its reporters for failing to disclose its source for an allegedly defamatory article. The jury awarded $1.68 million in damages ($240,000 in economic damages and $1.44 million for emotional distress) against the newspaper and $420,000 against the reporter. Both awards were affirmed on appeal. See Ayash v. Dana-Farber Cancer Institute, 822 N.E.2d 667 (Mass. 2005).

Such extreme sanctions are unusual, however. Usually the courts hold that the sanction must be no more severe than necessary to offset the disadvantage placed on the plaintiff by the refusal to disclose. In Oak Beach Inn Corp. v. Babylon Beacon, Inc., 464 N.E.2d 967 (N.Y. 1984), striking the defendant's answer was held to be excessive where the defendant had agreed to defend against the allegation of actual malice by relying on proof of its own independent investigation rather than placing any reliance on its source. Confidential source problems in the libel area are reviewed in Robert G. Berger, The "No-Source" Presumption: The Harshest Remedy, 36 Am. U. L. Rev. 603 (1987).

2. NEGLIGENCE

a. PRIVATE PLAINTIFFS

The discussion of public officials, public figures, and actual malice implies that the constitutional limitations on defamation law might be different for private plaintiffs. Indeed they are, but perhaps not as different as they seem at first.

Gertz v. Robert Welch, Inc.

Supreme Court of the United States, 1974.
418 U.S. 323.

[Plaintiff, an attorney, was retained to represent the family of a youth killed by Nuccio, a Chicago policeman. In that capacity, plaintiff attended the coroner's inquest and filed an action for damages but played no part in a criminal proceeding in which Nuccio was convicted of second degree murder. Respondent published American Opinion, a monthly outlet for the views of the John Birch Society. As part of its efforts to alert the public to an alleged nationwide conspiracy to discredit local police, the magazine's editor engaged a regular contributor to write about the Nuccio episode. The article that appeared charged a frame-up against Nuccio and portrayed plaintiff as a "major architect" of the plot. It also falsely asserted that he had a long police record, was an official of the Marxist League for Industrial Democracy, and was a "Leninist" and a "Communist-fronter." The editor said he had no reason to doubt the charges and made no effort to verify them.]

[Gertz filed an action for libel in District Court because of diversity of citizenship. The trial judge first ruled that Gertz was not a public official or public figure and that under Illinois law there was no defense. The jury awarded $50,000. On further reflection, the judge granted the defendant judgment notwithstanding the jury's verdict on the theory that the *Times* rule should be extended to all defamation relating to matters of public concern. While the appeal was pending, a plurality of the Supreme Court embraced that theory in Rosenbloom v. Metromedia, Inc., 403 U.S. 29 (1971). The court of appeals, relying on the plurality opinion in *Rosenbloom,* affirmed because of the absence of clear and convincing evidence of actual malice. Gertz appealed, arguing that plaintiffs who were not public figures or public officials should not have to show actual malice.]

■ MR. JUSTICE POWELL delivered the opinion of the Court.

. . .

We begin with the common ground. Under the First Amendment there is no such thing as a false idea. However pernicious an opinion may seem, we depend for its correction not on the conscience of judges and juries but on the competition of other ideas. But there is no constitutional value in false statements of fact. Neither the intentional lie nor the careless error materially advances society's interest in "uninhibited, robust, and wide-open" debate on public issues. . . .

Although the erroneous statement of fact is not worthy of constitutional protection, it is nevertheless inevitable in free debate. . . . Our decisions recognize that a rule of strict liability that compels a publisher or broadcaster to guarantee the accuracy of his factual assertions may lead to intolerable self-censorship. Allowing the media to avoid liability only by proving the truth of all injurious statements does not accord adequate protection to First Amendment liberties. . . . The First Amendment requires that we protect some falsehood in order to protect speech that matters.

The need to avoid self-censorship by the news media is, however, not the only societal value at issue. If it were, this Court would have embraced long ago the view that publishers and broadcasters enjoy an unconditional and indefeasible immunity from liability for defamation. . . .

The legitimate state interest underlying the law of libel is the compensation of individuals for the harm inflicted on them by defamatory falsehood. We would not lightly require the State to abandon this purpose, for, as Mr. Justice Stewart has reminded us, the individual's right to the protection of his own good name "reflects no more than our basic concept of the essential dignity and worth of every human being—a concept at the root of any decent system of ordered liberty." . . . [ ]

. . .

The *New York Times* standard defines the level of constitutional protection appropriate to the context of defamation of a public person. Those who, by reason of the notoriety of their achievements or the vigor and success with which they seek the public's attention, are properly classed as public figures and those who hold governmental office may recover for injury to reputation only on clear and convincing proof that the defamatory falsehood was made with knowledge of its falsity or with reckless disregard for the truth. This standard administers an extremely powerful antidote to the inducement to media self-censorship of the common-law rule of strict liability for libel and slander. And it exacts a correspondingly high price from the victims of defamatory falsehood. Plainly many deserving plaintiffs, including some intentionally subjected to injury, will be unable to surmount the barrier of the *New York Times* test. Despite this substantial abridgment of the state law right to compensation for wrongful hurt to one's reputation, the Court has concluded that the protection of the *New York Times* privilege should be available to publishers and broadcasters of defamatory falsehood concerning public officials and public figures. [ ] We think that these decisions are correct, but we do not find their holdings justified solely by reference to the interest of the press and broadcast media in immunity from liability. Rather, we believe that the *New York Times* rule states an accommodation between this concern and the limited state interest present in the context of libel actions brought by public persons. For the reasons stated below, we conclude that the state interest in compensating injury to the reputation of private individuals requires that a different rule should obtain with respect to them.

. . .

[W]e have no difficulty in distinguishing among defamation plaintiffs. The first remedy of any victim of defamation is self-help— using available opportunities to contradict the lie or correct the error and thereby to minimize its adverse impact on reputation. Public officials and public figures usually enjoy significantly greater access to the channels of effective communication and hence have a more realistic opportunity to counteract false statements than private individuals normally enjoy.[9] Private individuals are therefore more vulnerable to injury, and the state interest in protecting them is correspondingly greater.

More important than the likelihood that private individuals will lack effective opportunities for rebuttal, there is a compelling normative consideration underlying the distinction between public and private defamation plaintiffs. An individual who decides to seek governmental office must accept certain necessary consequences of that involvement in public affairs. He runs the risk of closer public scrutiny than might otherwise be the case. And society's interest in the officers of government is not strictly limited to the formal discharge of official duties. As the Court pointed out in [Garrison v. Louisiana], the public's interest extends to "anything which might touch on an official's fitness for office. . . . Few personal attributes are more germane to fitness for office than dishonesty, malfeasance, or improper motivation, even though these characteristics may also affect the official's private character."

Those classed as public figures stand in a similar position. Hypothetically, it may be possible for someone to become a public figure through no purposeful action of his own, but the instances of truly involuntary public figures must be exceedingly rare. For the most part those who attain this status have assumed roles of especial prominence

---

[9] Of course, an opportunity for rebuttal seldom suffices to undo harm of defamatory falsehood. Indeed, the law of defamation is rooted in our experience that the truth rarely catches up with a lie. But the fact that the self-help remedy of rebuttal, standing alone, is inadequate to its task does not mean that it is irrelevant to our inquiry.

in the affairs of society. Some occupy positions of such persuasive power and influence that they are deemed public figures for all purposes. More commonly, those classed as public figures have thrust themselves to the forefront of particular public controversies in order to influence the resolution of the issues involved. In either event, they invite attention and comment.

Even if the foregoing generalities do not obtain in every instance, the communications media are entitled to act on the assumption that public officials and public figures have voluntarily exposed themselves to increased risk of injury from defamatory falsehood concerning them. No such assumption is justified with respect to a private individual. He has not accepted public office or assumed an "influential role in ordering society." Curtis Publishing Co. v. Butts [ ] (Warren, C. J., concurring in result). He has relinquished no part of his interest in the protection of his own good name, and consequently he has a more compelling call on the courts for redress of injury inflicted by defamatory falsehood. Thus, private individuals are not only more vulnerable to injury than public officials and public figures; they are also more deserving of recovery.

For these reasons we conclude that the States should retain substantial latitude in their efforts to enforce a legal remedy for defamatory falsehood injurious to the reputation of a private individual. . . .

We hold that, so long as they do not impose liability without fault, the States may define for themselves the appropriate standard of liability for a publisher or broadcaster of defamatory falsehood injurious to a private individual. This approach provides a more equitable boundary between the competing concerns involved here. It recognizes the strength of the legitimate state interest in compensating private individuals for wrongful injury to reputation, yet shields the press and broadcast media from the rigors of strict liability for defamation. At least this conclusion obtains where, as here, the substance of the defamatory statement "makes substantial danger to reputation apparent." [*Butts*] This phrase places in perspective the conclusion we announce today. Our inquiry would involve considerations somewhat different from those discussed above if a State purported to condition civil liability on a factual misstatement whose content did not warn a reasonably prudent editor or broadcaster of its defamatory potential. Cf. Time, Inc. v. Hill, 385 U.S. 374 (1967). Such a case is not now before us, and we intimate no view as to its proper resolution.

IV.

. . . [W]e endorse this approach in recognition of the strong and legitimate state interest in compensating private individuals for injury to reputation. But this countervailing state interest extends no further than compensation for actual injury. For the reasons stated below, we hold that the States may not permit recovery of presumed or punitive damages, at least when liability is not based on a showing of knowledge of falsity or reckless disregard for the truth.

The common law of defamation is an oddity of tort law, for it allows recovery of purportedly compensatory damages without evidence of actual loss. Under the traditional rules pertaining to actions for libel, the existence of injury is presumed from the fact of publication. Juries may award substantial sums as compensation for supposed damage to reputation without any proof that such harm actually occurred. The largely uncontrolled discretion of juries to award damages where there is no loss unnecessarily compounds the potential of any system of liability for defamatory falsehood to inhibit the vigorous exercise of First Amendment freedoms. Additionally, the doctrine of presumed damages invites juries to punish unpopular opinion rather than to compensate individuals for injury sustained by the publication of a false fact. More to the point, the States have no substantial interest in securing for plaintiffs such as this petitioner gratuitous awards of money damages far in excess of any actual injury.

We would not, of course, invalidate state law simply because we doubt its wisdom, but here we are attempting to reconcile state law with a competing interest grounded in the constitutional command of the First Amendment. It is therefore appropriate to require that state remedies for defamatory falsehood reach no farther than is necessary to protect the legitimate interest involved. It is necessary to restrict defamation plaintiffs who do not prove knowledge of falsity or reckless disregard for the truth to compensation for actual injury. We need not define "actual injury," as trial courts have wide experience in framing appropriate jury instructions in tort actions. Suffice it to say that actual injury is not limited to out-of-pocket loss. Indeed, the more customary types of actual harm inflicted by defamatory falsehood include impairment of reputation and standing in the community, personal humiliation, and mental anguish and suffering. Of course, juries must be limited by appropriate instructions, and all awards must be supported by competent evidence concerning the injury, although there need be no evidence which assigns an actual dollar value to the injury.

We also find no justification for allowing awards of punitive damages against publishers and broadcasters held liable under state-defined standards of liability for defamation. In most jurisdictions jury discretion over the amounts awarded is limited only by the gentle rule that they not be excessive. Consequently, juries assess punitive damages in wholly unpredictable amounts bearing no necessary relation to the actual harm caused. And they remain free to use their discretion selectively to punish expressions of unpopular views. Like the doctrine of presumed damages, jury discretion to award punitive damages unnecessarily exacerbates the danger of media self-censorship, but, unlike the former rule, punitive damages are wholly irrelevant to the state interest that justifies a negligence standard for private defamation actions. They are not compensation for injury. Instead, they are private fines levied by civil juries to punish reprehensible conduct and to deter its future occurrence. In short, the private defamation plaintiff who establishes liability under a less demanding standard than that stated by *New York Times* may recover only such damages as are sufficient to compensate him for actual injury.

V.

. . . [R]espondent contends that we should affirm the judgment below on the ground that petitioner is either a public official or a public figure. There is little basis for the former assertion. Several years prior to the present incident, petitioner had served briefly on housing committees appointed by the mayor of Chicago, but at the time of publication he had never held any remunerative governmental position. Respondent admits this but argues that petitioner's appearance at the coroner's inquest rendered him a "de facto public official." Our cases recognize no such concept. Respondent's suggestion would sweep all lawyers under the *New York Times* rule as officers of the court and distort the plain meaning of the "public official" category beyond all recognition. We decline to follow it.

Respondent's characterization of petitioner as a public figure raises a different question. That designation may rest on either of two alternative bases. In some instances an individual may achieve such pervasive fame or notoriety that he becomes a public figure for all purposes and in all contexts. More commonly, an individual voluntarily injects himself or is drawn into a particular public controversy and thereby becomes a public figure for a limited range of issues. In either case such persons assume special prominence in the resolution of public questions.

Petitioner has long been active in community and professional affairs. He has served as an officer of local civic groups and of various professional organizations, and he has published several books and articles on legal subjects. Although petitioner was consequently well known in some circles, he had achieved no general fame or notoriety in the community. None of the prospective jurors called at the trial had ever heard of petitioner prior to this litigation, and respondent offered no proof that this response was atypical of the local population. We would not lightly assume that a citizen's participation in community and professional affairs rendered him a public figure for all purposes. Absent clear evidence of general fame or notoriety in the community, and pervasive involvement in the affairs of society, an individual should not be deemed a public personality for all aspects of his life. It is preferable to reduce the public-figure question to a more meaningful context by looking to the nature and extent of an individual's participation in the particular controversy giving rise to the defamation.

In this context it is plain that petitioner was not a public figure. He played a minimal role at the coroner's inquest, and his participation related solely to his representation of a private client. He took no part in the criminal prosecution of Officer Nuccio. Moreover, he never discussed either the criminal or civil litigation with the press and was never quoted as having done so. He plainly did not thrust himself into the vortex of this public issue, nor did he engage the public's attention in an attempt to influence its outcome. We are persuaded that the trial court did not err in refusing to characterize petitioner as a public figure for the purpose of this litigation.

. . . Because the jury was allowed to impose liability without fault and was permitted to presume damages without proof of injury, a new trial is necessary. We reverse and remand for further proceedings in accord with this opinion.

[Justice Blackmun concurred and joined the Court's opinion, providing the deciding vote. He predicted *Gertz* would have "little, if any, practical effect on the functioning of responsible journalism." Chief Justice Burger dissented, stating that he "would prefer to allow this area of law to continue to evolve as it has up to now with respect to private citizens rather than embark on a new doctrinal theory which has no jurisprudential ancestry." Justice Brennan dissented on the grounds that a negligence standard would encourage press self-censorship in reporting on public affairs. Justice Douglas also dissented.]

■ MR. JUSTICE WHITE, dissenting.

. . .

[T]he law has heretofore put the risk of falsehood on the publisher where the victim is a private citizen and no grounds of special privilege are invoked. The Court would now shift this risk to the victim, even though he has done nothing to invite the calumny, is wholly innocent of fault, and is helpless to avoid his injury. . . . The press today is vigorous and robust. To me, it is quite incredible to suggest that threats of libel suits from private citizens are causing the press to refrain from publishing the truth. I know of no hard facts to support that proposition, and the Court furnishes none.

The communications industry has increasingly become concentrated in a few powerful hands operating very lucrative businesses reaching across the Nation and into almost every home. Neither the industry as a whole nor its individual components are easily intimidated, and we are fortunate that they are not. Requiring them to pay for the occasional damage they do to private reputation will play no substantial part in their future performance or their existence.

. . .

It is difficult for me to understand why the ordinary citizen should himself carry the risk of damage and suffer the injury in order to vindicate First Amendment values by protecting the press and others from liability for circulating false information. This is particularly true because such statements serve no purpose whatsoever in furthering the public interest or the search for truth but, on the contrary, may frustrate that search and at the same time inflict great injury on the defenseless individual. The owners of the press and the stockholders of the communications enterprises can much better bear the burden. And if they cannot, the public at large should somehow pay for what is essentially a public benefit derived at private expense.

NOTES AND QUESTIONS

1. Why did the majority in *Gertz* choose to base the constitutional standard on the status of the plaintiff (whether the plaintiff is a private or public figure) rather than the status of the speech (whether the speech was of public concern)?

2. After this decision, what could Gertz hope to recover if he were able to show negligence but not actual malice? Did he suffer "actual injury"? His strategy when his case was retried under the new rules may give some clues. He continued to claim presumed and punitive damages, and he offered evidence of actual malice. The jury awarded him $100,000 compensatory damages and $300,000 punitive damages. On appeal, the court affirmed. It concluded that the jury could find the magazine itself guilty of "actual malice" because the editor had solicited an author with a "known and unreasonable propensity to label persons or organizations as Communist to write the article; and after the article was submitted made virtually no effort to check the validity of statements that were defamatory *per se* of Gertz, and in fact added further defamatory material based on [the writer's] 'facts.'" Would this be so if he were an independent contractor? It also held that the actual malice of the writer could be imputed to the magazine. Gertz v. Robert Welch, Inc., 680 F.2d 527 (7th Cir. 1982).

3. Even if a plaintiff shows actual malice, state law may preclude or limit punitive damages. Some states require a showing of some further element, such as animosity toward plaintiff, in addition to actual malice. Some states do not permit punitive damages at all, and some do not permit them in libel cases. Many tort reform statutes limit the amount of punitive damages; although these statutes were written primarily with physical injury cases in mind, they may apply also to defamation actions.

4. Justice Powell said negligence-based liability is permissible "at least . . . where, as here, the substance of the defamatory statement 'makes substantial danger to reputation apparent.' . . . Our inquiry would involve considerations somewhat different from those discussed above if a State purported to condition civil liability on a factual misstatement whose content did not warn a reasonably prudent editor or broadcaster of its defamatory potential." Is he suggesting that actual malice might be required for statements that are defamatory only by virtue of extrinsic facts? That such statements are not actionable at all? These questions remain unresolved.

5.   *State Law Alternatives. Gertz* establishes only a federal constitutional minimum, leaving the states free to adopt other rules that are more protective of speech. Most of these require private plaintiffs to prove actual malice. New York requires private plaintiffs to prove "that the publisher acted in a grossly irresponsible manner without due consideration for the standards of information gathering and dissemination ordinarily followed by responsible parties." Chapadeau v. Utica Observer-Dispatch, Inc., 341 N.E.2d 569 (N.Y. 1975). This rule applies only to defamations that occur "within the sphere of legitimate public concern," but media decisions as to what are matters of public concern "will not be second-guessed as long as they are sustainable." Gaeta v. New York News, Inc., 465 N.E.2d 802 (N.Y. 1984).

6.   In his *Gertz* dissent, Justice White argued that strict liability for defamation was justified by the need to protect defamation victims, at least "where the publisher is no doubt aware from the nature of the material that it would be inherently damaging to reputation." Justice White saw little danger of chilling the press, which is "vigorous and robust." Was Justice White correct in predicting that the imposition of strict liability for defamation of private citizens poses little risk of chilling free speech? Is it the same today in troubling economic times for media? For an argument that strict liability is especially pernicious in defamation, see David A. Anderson, Libel and Press Self-Censorship, 53 Tex. L. Rev. 422 (1975).

7.   The Ninth Circuit, in line with other circuits, held that the requirements of *Gertz* apply to lawsuits against bloggers no less than lawsuits against traditional media. The defendant blogger in the case maintained the site obsidianfinancesucks.com, which was devoted to "one-sided" and hyperbolic criticism of the plaintiff. Nonetheless, the court concluded that "[t]he protections of the First Amendment do not turn on whether the journalist was a trained journalist, formally affiliated with traditional news entities, engaged in conflict-of-interest disclosure, went beyond just assembling others' writings, or tried to get both sides of the story." Obsidian Financial Group LLC v. Cox, 740 F.3d 1284 (9th Cir. 2014). The court noted that every other circuit to address the issue had held that First Amendment protections in libel cases apply equally to the institutional press and individual speakers. It cited cases from the Second, Third, Fourth, Eighth, Tenth, and D.C. Circuits.

b.   ADMINISTERING THE NEGLIGENCE STANDARD

Before we explore the many questions raised by the private plaintiff rules adopted in *Gertz*, it is important to note that most cases do not present these questions. Most reported cases against media (and, we would expect, unreported cases as well) are litigated as "actual malice" cases and not as negligence cases, for reasons that are fairly obvious. First, plaintiffs mentioned in the mainstream media at least are likely to be either admittedly public or found to be public. Second, unless a private plaintiff is willing to forgo presumed and punitive damages, he or she must prove actual malice anyway. If the plaintiff succeeds in doing so, there is no occasion to focus on the meaning of "actual injury." Conversely, a plaintiff who cannot establish "actual injury"—no matter what that is held to encompass—also must prove actual malice. As a result, negligence-based liability for defamation is of minor importance in media cases. It plays a larger role in business litigation, perhaps because pecuniary losses in those cases are likely to be large enough to be worth litigating over.

The Standard. Justice Powell phrased the permissible standard in private-plaintiff cases negatively: states may use whatever standard they wish "so long as they do not impose liability without fault." No state has adopted a fault standard lower than negligence.

If negligence is the standard, the first question is whether the standard is professional negligence or ordinary care. This may be significant both in formulating the standard and in determining whether expert testimony is required (or permitted) to show the standard and the deviation. The states that have addressed this question have split. Compare Troman v. Wood, 340 N.E.2d 292 (Ill. 1975) (rejecting the professional negligence approach because it would make prevailing newspaper practices controlling and might lead toward a progressive depreciation of the standard of care) with Gobin v. Globe Pub. Co., 531 P.2d 76 (Kan. 1975) (adopting a variation on the medical malpractice standard: "the conduct of the reasonably careful publisher or broadcaster in the community or in similar communities under the existing circumstances.")

Evidence of Negligence. The Restatement (Second) of Torts § 580B, comment h, suggests that the reasonableness of the investigation varies with the following factors: 1. "The time element"—investigations may be shorter for topical news than for a story that has no time pressure. 2. "The nature of the interest promoted by publication"—a story informing the public of matters important in a democracy may warrant quicker publication than a story involving "mere gossip." 3. "Potential damage to plaintiff if the communication proves to be false"—whether the statement is defamatory on its face; how many readers will understand the defamation; how harmful is the charge.

One court has stated two other factors: the nature and reliability of the source of the information and the "reasonableness in checking the veracity of the information, considering its cost in terms of money, time, personnel, urgency of the publication, nature of the news and any other pertinent element." Torres-Silva v. El Mundo, 1977 PR Sup. LEXIS 3097 (P.R. 1977). Why should courts give less protection to reputation when the media acts under self-imposed time constraints?

c.   ACTUAL INJURY

As we have already seen, the subject of damages was complicated enough at common law. Whether a plaintiff needed to show "special" damages and, if so, what constituted "special" damages produced much litigation. The Supreme Court's introduction, in *Gertz*, of "actual injury damages" did not purport to track any pre-existing concept of damages. Indeed the Court went out of its way to use examples that showed that the new term was not the equivalent of "special" damages. Aside from these few sentences in *Gertz*, the Court's only guidance as to what "actual injury" means comes from Time, Inc. v. Firestone, 424 U.S. 448 (1976). There, the plaintiff had withdrawn her claim for reputational harm on the eve of trial and the defendant argued that this barred her from recovering under *Gertz*. The Court disagreed. If Florida permitted recoveries in defamation actions that did not claim harm to reputation, *Gertz* did not forbid it:

> In [*Gertz*] we made it clear that States could base awards on elements other than injury to reputation, specifically listing "personal humiliation, and mental anguish and suffering" as examples of injuries which might be compensated consistently with the Constitution upon a showing of fault.

In *Firestone* the plaintiff had presented evidence from her minister, her attorney, and several friends and neighbors as to her emotional state. One was a physician who testified to "having to administer a sedative to respondent in an attempt to reduce discomfort wrought by her worrying about the article." Plaintiff also testified that she feared the effect that the false report of her adultery might have on her young son when he grew older. "The jury decided these injuries should be compensated by an award of $100,000," the Court wrote. "We have no warrant for re-examining this determination."

Note that states may choose to require proof of reputational injury even though, constitutionally, they need not do so. See, e.g., Schlegal v. Ottumwa Courier, 585 N.W.2d 217 (Iowa 1998) (refusing to allow recovery for defamation without proof of harm to reputation). Note also that some courts have embraced the actual injury concept as a replacement for the common law special harm requirement discussed earlier in this chapter. For example, in Nazeri v. Missouri Valley College, a defamation case noted earlier, the court held that plaintiffs in libel and slander cases alike "need not concern themselves with whether the defamation was per se or per quod, nor with whether special damages exist, but must prove actual damages in all cases."

The New Jersey Supreme Court further complicated the damages issue by holding that plaintiffs in private-figure/private-concern libel cases may obtain "vindicatory damages" without proving actual injury. As a matter of state law, a private-figure plaintiff defamed in a matter that is not of public concern will be able to survive a summary judgment motion by claiming presumed damages; however, the plaintiff will be permitted to recover only nominal damages if he or she fails to prove actual injury. The court was urged to ban presumed damages outright, but declined because "the doctrine of presumed damages continues to have vitality by permitting a plaintiff to survive summary judgment and to obtain nominal damages at trial." But the court also wrote: "To receive a compensatory award for reputational loss, a plaintiff will be required to prove actual harm, pecuniary or otherwise, to his reputation through the production of evidence." See W.J.A. v. D.A., 43 A.3d 1148 (N.J. 2012).

The Texas Supreme Court held that a plaintiff may recover only for actual injury to reputation even when actual malice is shown. Waste Management of Texas Inc. v. Texas Disposal Systems Landfill Inc., 219 S.W.3d 563 (Tex. App. 2014). The defendant there had argued that corporate defamation plaintiffs may only recover for lost profits, rehabilitative expenses, and diminished value of the corporation, but the decision drew no distinction between corporate and individual plaintiffs. The court acknowledged that *Gertz* would allow presumed damages when actual malice is shown, but said it was "extending the reasoning" of *Gertz*. The court allowed the plaintiff to recover $450,000 in "remediation damages," but reversed the jury's $5 million award for harm to reputation because that figure was not supported by evidence of actual injury.

Even when reputational damages are limited to actual injury, the court noted that these damages are noneconomic for purposes of a state statute that caps punitive damages. The statute allows punitive damages equal to twice the amount of economic damages awarded, but caps them at $750,000 if the compensatory damage award is for noneconomic damages. The court remanded for recalculation of the amount of punitive damages, but did not say whether the remediation damages should be considered economic or noneconomic.

3. LIABILITY WITHOUT FAULT

Have *Sullivan* and *Gertz* occupied the entire field of defamation? Are there any categories of cases left in which states are free to impose strict liability in libel cases? In which they may award presumed or punitive damages without a showing of "actual malice"?

Dun & Bradstreet v. Greenmoss Builders. Justice Powell's opinion in *Gertz* did not speak of all defendants, but of "publishers and broadcasters." Many thought this meant non-media defendants would not receive the benefit of the *Gertz* limitations. But in Dun & Bradstreet, Inc. v. Greenmoss Builders, Inc., 472 U.S. 749 (1985), a majority of the justices rejected any distinction between media and non-media defendants, although that was not the basis of decision. Justice White said it "makes no sense to give the most protection to those publishers who reach the most readers and therefore pollute the channels of communication with the most misinformation and do the most damage to private reputation."

Justice Brennan, joined by Justices Marshall, Blackmun, and Stevens, also rejected the distinction. First, in light of the growing power of mass media and their growing concentration, "protection for the speech of non-media defendants is essential to ensure a diversity of perspectives" that opinion noted. In addition, "transformations in the technological and economic structure of the communications industry [have produced] an increasing convergence of what might be labeled 'media' and 'nonmedia.' "

Since this case, non-media defendants have not been stripped of *Gertz* protection solely because they are not media.

The *Dun & Bradstreet* case was decided on a different rationale. A different majority held that states may award presumed and punitive damages without proof of actual malice to private plaintiffs who are defamed in "speech on matters of purely private concern."

> While such speech is not totally unprotected by the First Amendment, [ ] its protections are less stringent. In *Gertz,* we found that the state interest in awarding presumed and punitive damages was not "substantial" in view of their effect on speech at the core of First Amendment concern. [ ] This interest, however, *is* "substantial" relative to the incidental effect these remedies may have on speech of significantly less constitutional interest. The rationale of the common law rules has been the experience and judgment of history that "proof of actual damage will be impossible in a great many cases where, from the character of the defamatory words and the circumstances of publication, it is all but certain that serious harm has resulted in fact." [ ] As a result, courts for centuries have allowed juries to presume that some damage occurred from many defamatory utterances and publications. [ ] This rule furthers the state interest in providing remedies for defamation by ensuring that those remedies are effective. In light of the reduced constitutional value of speech involving no matters of public concern, we hold that the state interest adequately supports awards of presumed and punitive damages—even absent a showing of "actual malice." . . .

> In addition, the speech here, like advertising, is hardy and unlikely to be deterred by incidental state regulation. See [*Virginia Pharmacy*, discussed earlier]. It is solely motivated by the desire for profit, which, we have noted, is a force less likely to be deterred than others. [ ] Arguably, the reporting here was also more objectively verifiable than speech deserving of greater protection. [ ] In any case, the market provides a powerful incentive to a credit reporting agency to be accurate, since false credit reporting is of no use to creditors. Thus, any incremental "chilling" effect of libel suits would be of decreased significance.

Justices White and Chief Justice Burger concurred in the judgment. They agreed that *Gertz* should not protect Dun & Bradstreet from presumed and punitive damages, but they would have gone further and repudiated *Gertz* as to all private plaintiffs.

The dissenters believed the majority was cutting away the protective mantle of *Gertz*. "Without explaining what *is* a 'matter of public concern,' the plurality opinion proceeds to serve up a smorgasbord of reasons why the speech at issue here is not, [ ] and on this basis affirms" the award. Any standard that can be gleaned from the opinions is "impoverished" and "irreconcilable with First Amendment principles. The credit reporting at issue here surely involves a subject matter of sufficient public concern to require the comprehensive protections of *Gertz*."

The case involved a credit report that erroneously maintained that the plaintiff corporation had filed for bankruptcy. The dissenters argued that such a report would clearly be a matter of public concern if reported in the local newspaper, and they said it should make no difference that Dun & Bradstreet sent the report only to five subscribers.

Justice Brennan asserted in a footnote that, since the subject matter "would clearly receive the comprehensive protections of *Gertz* were the speech publicly disseminated, [the] factor of confidential circulation to a limited number of subscribers is perhaps properly understood as the linchpin" of Justice Powell's analysis.

Initially, media expressed concern that *Dun & Bradstreet* might lead courts to second-guess editorial judgments and deny the protection of *Gertz* for media defamation arising out of matters the courts decided were not of "public concern." But so far courts generally have not done so in defamation cases, and media defendants have not been held liable without at least the *Gertz* requirements being met.

Defamation in Commercial Speech. It is possible—though not authoritatively established—that the constitutional protections of *Times* and *Gertz* are not applicable when the defamation occurs in commercial speech. In Procter & Gamble Co. v. Amway Corp., 242 F.3d 539 (5th Cir. 2001), Procter & Gamble sued Amway Corporation under a variety of federal and state unfair competition and product disparagement laws for harm allegedly caused when an Amway employee distributed a voice mail message repeating a rumor linking P & G with Satanism. The trial court had dismissed the suit in part because P & G was unable to prove that the Amway employee acted with actual malice. The Fifth Circuit reversed on this point, finding that the voice mail could constitute commercial speech and that because commercial speech is not protected from government regulation when the speech is false, there is no reason to protect false commercial speech from civil liability:

> *Central Hudson* [a case described in Chapter Two, and other commercial speech decisions] combined with the Court's plain statements that false commercial speech receives no protection,

foreclose us from importing the actual-malice standard from defamation into the law of false commercial speech. Thus, if the trier of fact determines that the Amway distributor's motives in spreading the Satanism rumor were economic and that the speech therefore was commercial, this false commercial speech cannot qualify for the heightened protection of the First Amendment, so P & G is not required to show actual malice in proving its Lanham Act claim.

The court rejected a suggestion that a negligence standard be adopted for such cases, arguing that it would blur the line the Supreme Court has drawn between protected and unprotected speech.

E. THE PUBLIC-PRIVATE DISTINCTION

Although comparatively few media libel cases are actually tried as negligence-based private-plaintiff cases, there continue to be numerous opinions addressing the public-private distinction. Most involve summary judgment motions, either granted or denied, in which the defendant claims the plaintiff is public and cannot show actual malice. Plaintiffs who cannot show actual malice at that stage are doomed unless they can persuade the judge that they are private and therefore need not do so. If they can survive these motions, they can at least get to trial and they therefore have some chance of obtaining a settlement, even if their chances of ultimately succeeding under the *Gertz* rules are slim. This may help to explain why so many plaintiffs seek to be treated as "private" and so few actually go to trial under that scheme

Because the decision processes are different, we treat the issue of identifying public figures separately from the issue of public officials.

1. WHO IS A PUBLIC OFFICIAL?

In Rosenblatt v. Baer, 383 U.S. 75 (1966), plaintiff Baer had been hired by the three elected county commissioners to supervise a public recreation facility owned by the county. When Baer sued over a newspaper attack on the management of the facility, Justice Brennan's majority opinion held that Baer appeared to be a "public official" under criteria suggested by the rationale for the *Times* rule:

> There is, first, a strong interest in debate on public issues, and, second, a strong interest in debate about those persons who are in a position significantly to influence the resolution of those issues. Criticism of government is at the very center of the constitutionally protected area of free discussion. . . . It is clear, therefore, that the "public official" designation applies at the very least to those among the hierarchy of government employees who have, or appear to the public to have, substantial

responsibility for or control over the conduct of government affairs.

... Where a position in government has such apparent importance that the public has an independent interest in the qualifications and performance of the person who holds it, beyond the general public interest in the qualifications and performance of all government employees, both elements we identified in *New York Times* are present and the *New York Times* malice standards apply.[13]

Rosenblatt remains the Court's definitive articulation of the test for determining whether a person is a public official. A dictum in Hutchinson v. Proxmire, 443 U.S. 111 (1979), a case discussed in the next section, noted that the Court had not "provided precise boundaries for the category of 'public official'; it cannot be thought to include all public employees, however."

Candidates. Not surprisingly the Court quickly and unanimously extended the *Times* rationale to candidates on the ground that "it can hardly be doubted that the constitutional guarantee has its fullest and most urgent application precisely to the conduct of campaigns for political office." Monitor Patriot Co. v. Roy, 401 U.S. 265 (1971); see also Ocala Star-Banner Co. v. Damron, 401 U.S. 295 (1971).

Perhaps less inevitably the Court decided in *Roy* that the *Times* rule should include "anything which might touch on an official's fitness for office" when a candidate's behavior is being discussed:

A candidate who, for example, seeks to further his cause through the prominent display of his wife and children can hardly argue that his qualities as a husband or father remain of "purely private" concern. And the candidate who vaunts his spotless record and sterling integrity cannot convincingly cry "Foul!" when an opponent or an industrious reporter attempts to demonstrate the contrary. Any test adequate to safeguard First Amendment guarantees in this area must go far beyond the customary meaning of the phrase "official conduct."

Given the realities of our political life, it is by no means easy to see what statements about a candidate might be altogether without relevance to his fitness for the office he seeks. The clash of reputations is the staple of election campaigns, and damage to reputation is, of course, the essence of libel. But whether there remains some exiguous area of defamation against which

---

[13] It is suggested that this test might apply to a night watchman accused of stealing state secrets. But a conclusion that the *New York Times* malice standards apply could not be reached merely because a statement defamatory of some person in government employ catches the public's interest: that conclusion would virtually disregard society's interest in protecting reputation. The employee's position must be one which would invite public scrutiny and discussion of the person holding it, apart from the scrutiny and discussion occasioned by the particular charges in controversy.

a candidate may have full recourse is a question we need not decide in this case.

In *Roy* a newspaper column published three days before the election falsely accused a candidate for the U.S. Senate of criminal activity many years earlier. The Court concluded that a "charge of criminal conduct, no matter how remote in time or place, can never be irrelevant to an official's or a candidate's fitness for office" for purposes of applying the *Times* rule.

In *Damron* a newspaper reported two weeks before a local election that a candidate had been charged with perjury, when in fact his brother was the one charged. Again, the *Times* rule applied.

Public Employees. There is virtual unanimity that police officers are public officials for defamation purposes. See Britton v. Koep, 470 N.W.2d 518 (Minn. 1991), asserting that other states "unanimously have held that police officers, undercover agents, and deputy sheriffs are public officials. The rationale appears to be that, even for those who work undercover or anonymously, [ ] those officers possess significant powers granted by the government." But see Madsen v. United Television Inc., 797 P.2d 1083 (Utah 1990), in which the court refused to decide whether a "police officer is *ipso facto* a public official."

As to other categories of public employees, whether they are treated as public figures depends on the nature of their powers and duties. A firefighter who sued over a newscast about his termination for inability to pass the EMT examination was held not to be a public official. The court thought it "strain[ed] credibility to say that [plaintiff], as a low-ranking fire fighter, had substantial responsibility over the conduct of governmental affairs." Jones v. Palmer Communications Inc., 440 N.W.2d 884 (Iowa 1989).

2. WHO IS A PUBLIC FIGURE?

In *Gertz* the Court found "no difficulty distinguishing among defamation plaintiffs" on the basis of their public or private status. In fact, in subsequent cases members of the Supreme Court have not been able to agree among themselves as to who is a public figure. We briefly summarize the Supreme Court's public figure cases and then turn to the efforts of the lower courts.

The Firestone Case. In Time Inc. v. Firestone, 424 U.S. 448 (1976), Time Magazine incorrectly reported that a member of "one of America's wealthier industrial families" had received a divorce because of his wife's adultery. A five-member majority held plaintiff to be private: "Respondent did not assume any role of especial prominence in the affairs of society, other than perhaps Palm Beach society, and she did not thrust herself to the forefront of any particular public controversy in order to influence the resolution of the issues involved in it." The fact that the case may have been of great public interest, did not make plaintiff a public figure. Moreover, the Court observed, plaintiff was compelled to go to court to seek relief in a marital dispute and her involvement was not voluntary. The fact that she held "a few" press conferences during the case did not change her otherwise private status. She did not attempt to use them to influence the outcome of the trial or to thrust herself into an unrelated dispute.

The Wolston Case. In Wolston v. Reader's Digest Ass'n, 443 U.S. 157 (1979), defendant's 1974 book incorrectly listed plaintiff as one of a group "who were convicted of espionage or falsifying information or perjury and/or contempt charges following espionage indictments or who fled to the Soviet bloc to avoid prosecution." In fact, he had been indicted for and convicted of contempt of court but not indicted for espionage.

During the six weeks in 1958 between his failure to appear and his sentencing, plaintiff's case was the subject of 15 stories in Washington and New York newspapers. "This flurry of publicity subsided" following the sentencing, and plaintiff "succeeded for the most part in returning to the private life he had led" prior to the subpoena. A six-member majority held plaintiff private because he had neither "voluntarily thrust" nor "injected" himself into the forefront of the controversy surrounding the investigation of Soviet espionage in the United States. Wolston had not "engaged the attention of the public in an attempt to influence the resolution of the issues involved. . . . He did not in any way seek to arouse public sentiment in his favor and against the investigation. Thus, this is not a case where a defendant invites a citation for contempt in order to use the contempt citation as a fulcrum to create public discussion about the methods being used in connection with an investigation or prosecution."

The Hutchinson Case. In Hutchinson v. Proxmire, 443 U.S. 111 (1979), decided the same day as *Wolston,* defendant, a United States Senator, had criticized government grants to certain scientists, including plaintiff, on the grounds that the grants were examples of wasteful government spending on unjustifiable scientific research. (Absolute privilege, discussed later in this chapter did not apply because the claimed defamations were in press releases and newsletters.)

The eight-member majority held plaintiff to be private. Neither the fact that plaintiff had successfully applied for federal funds nor that he had access to media to respond to Senator Proxmire's charges "demonstrates that Hutchinson was a public figure prior to the controversy." Rather, his "activities and public profile are much like those of countless members of his profession. His published writings reach a relatively small category of professionals concerned with research in human behavior." Those charged with defamation "cannot, by their own conduct, create their own defense by making the claimant a public figure. See [*Wolston*]." Nor had plaintiff "assumed any role of public prominence in the broad question of concern about expenditures."

Although *Gertz, Firestone, Wolston*, and *Hutchinson* all reject the defendant's claim that the plaintiff is a public figure, in fact a great many plaintiffs are treated as public figures. Frequently they do not contest the issue, and when they do they often lose. *Gertz* suggested that some plaintiffs are public figures for all purposes and some for more limited purposes. We employ that distinction, but courts sometimes do not.

a.   GENERAL-PURPOSE PUBLIC FIGURES

According to one definition,

[A] general public figure is a well-known "celebrity," his name a "household word." The public recognizes him and follows his words and deeds, either because it regards his ideas, conduct, or judgment as worthy of the attention or because he actively pursues that consideration.

Waldbaum v. Fairchild Publications, Inc., 627 F.2d 1287 (D.C. Cir. 1980). Is that definition consistent with *Gertz*? Is it a useful way to approach the question? See also Buckley v. Littell, 539 F.2d 882 (2d Cir. 1976) (William F. Buckley, Jr.); Carson v. Allied News Co., 529 F.2d 206 (7th Cir. 1976) (Johnny Carson); Chuy v. Philadelphia Eagles Football Club, 595 F.2d 1265 (3d Cir. 1979) (a professional football player who was alleged to have a career-ending disease is a public figure). All except *Waldbaum* were decided before *Hutchinson* and *Wolston*. Which of the following might meet the quoted standard: Julian Assange? Mark Zuckerberg? Michael Jordan? Michael Moore? J.K. Rowling? David Mamet? Oprah Winfrey? To what segment of the public must the person be known? Is recognition by law students a fair gauge of "celebrity"?

Although there are few contested cases holding plaintiffs to be general-purpose public figures, many plaintiffs do not challenge the defendant's characterization of them as public figures. See, e.g., Kaelin v. Globe Communications Corp., 162 F.3d 1036 (9th Cir. 1998) (houseguest of O. J. Simpson); Church of Scientology International v. Time Warner Inc., 26 Med. L. Rptr. 2394 (S.D.N.Y. 1998) (religious group). In these it is of course impossible to know whether the plaintiffs considered themselves general or limited-purpose public figures, or whether they even took note of the distinction.

b.   LIMITED-PURPOSE PUBLIC FIGURES

WFAA-TV, Inc. v. McLemore
Supreme Court of Texas, 1998.
978 S.W.2d 568.

■ HANKINSON, JUSTICE, delivered the opinion for a unanimous Court.

In this defamation suit arising out of the 1993 Bureau of Alcohol, Tobacco and Firearms (ATF) raid on the Branch Davidian compound at

Mount Carmel, we decide whether a media plaintiff, one of only a few journalists to report live from the scene of the raid, whose reports were rebroadcast worldwide, and who willingly gave numerous interviews about his role in the failed raid, is a public figure. The plaintiff sued WFAA-TV Channel 8 in Dallas alleging that its news reports concerning his role in the failed raid damaged his reputation in the community. The trial court denied WFAA's motion for summary judgment, and the court of appeals affirmed. [ ] Because we conclude that the plaintiff in this case became a limited-purpose public figure after thrusting himself to the forefront of the controversy surrounding the failed ATF assault, we reverse the court of appeals' judgment and render judgment that the plaintiff take nothing.

On February 28, 1993, ATF agents approached the Mount Carmel compound occupied by the Branch Davidians, a small religious sect that had amassed an arsenal of illegal weaponry. Two local media outlets, KWTX-TV Channel 10 in Waco and the Waco Tribune-Herald, learned from various sources that a major law enforcement operation would proceed at Mount Carmel that morning. KWTX-TV dispatched reporter John McLemore and cameraman Dan Mullony to report on the event.

When the ATF agents attempted to enter one of the buildings on the compound, they became involved in a gunfight with the Davidians. During the battle, four ATF agents and three Davidians were killed, and twenty ATF agents were wounded. McLemore and Mullony, the only media representatives to follow the agents onto the compound, reported live from the midst of the firefight.

[Two days after the gunfight, media reports began to focus on why the ATF raid had failed. A Houston newspaper reporter interviewed on ABC's "Nightline" said ATF agents believed they were set up by reporters for the local newspaper and television station, "who were already at the compound" and "hiding in the trees" when they arrived. WFAA in Dallas picked up the story and repeated the report that ATF agents saw local media hiding in trees at the compound before the attack began. During these broadcasts, WFAA showed video footage of McLemore on the compound grounds and named him as one of three or four local news personnel whose presence had tipped off the Davidians. In fact, no news people were on the premises before the agents arrived, no one was hiding in the trees, and the Davidians been alerted to the impending raid earlier when a different television reporter asked directions on a nearby road from a motorist who happened to be a member of the sect. Soon after the reports aired, McLemore sued WFAA-TV and other media defendants. The trial court granted summary judgment to the other defendants on various grounds. WFAA-TV moved for summary judgment on the ground that McLemore was a public figure and could not show actual malice.]

Because a defamation plaintiff's status dictates the degree of fault he or she must prove to render the defendant liable, the principal issue in this case is whether McLemore is a public figure. The question of public-figure status is one of constitutional law for courts to decide. [ ] ...

To determine whether an individual is a limited-purpose public figure, the Fifth Circuit has adopted a three-part test:

(1) the controversy at issue must be public both in the sense that people are discussing it and people other than the immediate participants in the controversy are likely to feel the impact of its resolution;

(2) the plaintiff must have more than a trivial or tangential role in the controversy; and

(3) the alleged defamation must be germane to the plaintiff's participation in the controversy.

Trotter, 818 F.2d at 433 (citing Tavoulareas v. Piro, 817 F.2d 762, 772–73 (D.C. Cir. 1987) (en banc)); see also Waldbaum v. Fairchild Pub., Inc. 627 F.2d 1287, 1296–98 (D.C. Cir. 1980). Although the *Trotter/Waldbaum* test does not distinguish between plaintiffs who have voluntarily injected themselves into a controversy and those who are involuntarily drawn into a controversy, some courts have held that plaintiffs who are drawn into a controversy cannot be categorized as limited-purpose public figures.[1] Because, as we explain below, McLemore clearly voluntarily injected himself into the controversy at issue, we need not decide in this case whether "voluntariness" is a requirement under the limited-purpose public-figure test we apply. . . .

Applying the *Trotter/Waldbaum* limited-purpose public-figure elements to this case, we must first determine the controversy at issue. [ ] In *Waldbaum*, the D.C. Circuit elaborated on how to determine the existence and scope of a public controversy:

To determine whether a controversy indeed existed and, if so, to define its contours, the judge must examine whether persons actually were discussing some specific question. A general concern or interest will not suffice. The court can see if the press was covering the debate, reporting what people were saying and uncovering facts and theories to help the public formulate some judgment.

[ ] In this case, numerous commentators, analysts, journalists, and public officials were discussing the raid and the reasons why the ATF raid failed. . . . [T]he press was actively covering the debate over why the ATF raid failed. Many such discussions focused on the role of the local media in the ATF's failure to capture the Davidian compound. The controversy

---

[1] See, e.g., Lerman v. Flynt Distrib. Co., Inc., 745 F.2d 123, 136–37 (2d Cir. 1984) (adopting four-part limited public-figure test, requiring defendant to prove plaintiff: (1) "successfully invited public attention to his views in an effort to influence others prior to the incident that is the subject of litigation (2) voluntarily injected himself into a public controversy related to the subject of the litigation; (3) assumed a position of prominence in the public controversy; and (4) maintained regular and continuing access to the media"). . . .

surrounding the Branch Davidian raid was public, both in the sense that people were discussing it and people other than the immediate participants in the controversy were likely to feel the impact of its resolution. [ ] While the court of appeals defined the controversy as limited to "McLemore's personal ethical standards as a journalist," we do not view it so narrowly. Based on the facts outlined above, we conclude that the public controversy at issue is the broader question of why the ATF agents failed to accomplish their mission.

To determine that an individual is a public figure for purposes of the public controversy at issue, the second *Trotter/Waldbaum* element requires the plaintiff to have had more than a trivial or tangential role in the controversy. [ ] In considering a libel plaintiff's role in a public controversy, several inquiries are relevant and instructive: (1) whether the plaintiff actually sought publicity surrounding the controversy, [ ]; (2) whether the plaintiff had access to the media, see, e.g., *Gertz*, [ ] [Curtis Publishing v. Butz] and (3) whether the plaintiff "voluntarily engag[ed] in activities that necessarily involve[d] the risk of increased exposure and injury to reputation," [ ]. "By publishing your views you invite public criticism and rebuttal; you enter voluntarily into one of the submarkets of ideas and opinions and consent therefore to the rough competition in the marketplace." Dilworth v. Dudley, 75 F.3d 307, 309 (7th Cir. 1996).

The record reflects that McLemore acted voluntarily to invite public attention and scrutiny on several occasions and in several different ways during the course of the public debate on the failed ATF raid. For example, McLemore was the only journalist to go onto the grounds of the compound, while other reporters assigned to cover the raid did not. By reporting live from the heart of the controversial raid, McLemore assumed a risk that his involvement in the event would be subject to public debate. Following the battle, McLemore spoke to other members of the press about the attempted raid, conveying his pride in his coverage from the midst of the gunfight, and portraying himself as a hero in assisting wounded ATF agents when he remarked that his role in the raid was "at considerable personal risk" and in contrast to other journalists who "were pinned down in a ditch" outside the compound. As a journalist, McLemore had ready, continual access to the various media sources. To one group of reporters, he explained that "as a journalist, I was . . . pleased to see that my coverage of this story was being broadcast to a wide audience." Thus, by choosing to engage in activities that necessarily involved increased public exposure and media scrutiny, McLemore played more than a trivial or tangential role in the controversy and, therefore, bore the risk of injury to his reputation. [ ]

The third and final element we consider—that the alleged defamation is germane to the plaintiff's participation in the controversy—is also satisfied in this case. [ ] McLemore alleges that

WFAA defamed him by displaying footage of his coverage from the scene of the compound during the raid, while reporting that federal officials believed a member of the local media informed the Branch Davidians about the ATF raid. Therefore, the alleged defamation directly relates to McLemore's participation in the controversy. He was on the scene in his role as a journalist, as conveyed by the footage WFAA broadcast, and WFAA's alleged defamatory comments are indeed germane to McLemore's participation in the controversy over the media's role in the failed attack. [ ] Accordingly, McLemore reached limited-purpose public-figure status through his employment-related activities when he voluntarily injected himself into the Branch Davidian raid.

[The summary judgment motion was supported by an affidavit in which the WFAA-TV reporter stated that her reporting was based on "public allegations by responsible, respected, and well-informed journalists and news organizations" which she believed to be accurate. The court said this, in the absence of controverting evidence from McLemore, negated actual malice.]

NOTES AND QUESTIONS

1.   If McLemore had not spoken to other media about his role in the raid, would his coverage of it have been enough to make him a public figure? Note that the court says "he voluntarily injected himself into the Branch Davidian raid" even though he was assigned to cover it by his employer. Did he voluntarily inject himself into it by covering it better (or at least more aggressively) than others?

2.   Could McLemore have been found a public figure under the test set out by the Second Circuit in footnote 1? The court says the public controversy is "why the ATF agents failed to accomplish their mission." How did McLemore participate in that controversy?

3.   Although it is not mentioned in the opinion, McLemore was in fact something of a hero. When the shooting began, he ran to his news vehicle under fire and called for ambulances. When a cease-fire was negotiated, he used the vehicle to carry several wounded agents out of range of the Davidians' guns. Against orders from his newsroom, he did not go on air with his dramatic eyewitness account of the raid until he had delivered the wounded agents to the medical triage area. The next day, the director of the ATF called to thank him for his bravery and assistance. See Ann Zimmerman, Caught in the crossfire, Dallas Observer Oct. 29, 1998, at 19. Do these additional facts strengthen the claim that he became a public figure?

4.   Most courts share this court's view that the public-private issue is a question for the judge to decide. Why is this so? The issue may involve classic factual questions: how widely known was the plaintiff? Did the plaintiff have media access? Was there a pre-existing public controversy? Was the plaintiff's participation voluntary? If the issue were submitted to the jury, how would the jury be instructed on other issues, such as fault and damages?

Is avoidance of complicated, conditional instructions a sufficient reason for treating the question as one of law?

5. Are universities general public figures or limited public figures? In Makaeff v. Trump University, 715 F.3d 254 (9th Cir. 2013), the Ninth Circuit determined that though real estate developer (and, later, presidential hopeful) Donald Trump may have been a public figure for all purposes, Trump University, L.L.C., a for-profit university he founded, was only a limited public figure. Trump University brought suit against a "[d]isgruntled former customer" who accused it of fraudulent business practices in letters and online. The court wrote:

> To be clear: Trump University is not a public figure because Donald Trump is famous and controversial. Nor is Trump University a public figure because it utilized Donald Trump as a celebrity pitchman. Trump University is a limited public figure because a public debate existed regarding its aggressively advertised educational practices. Did Trump's famous moniker draw public attention when Trump University's business practices proved worthy of debate? Perhaps. However, having traded heavily on the name and fame of its founder and chairman, Trump University was in no position to complain if the public's interest in Trump fueled the flames of the legitimate controversy that its business practices engendered.

Another controversial educational institution was labelled a limited-purpose public figure by the U.S. Court of Appeals for the Sixth Circuit in Thomas M. Cooley Law School v. Kurzon Strauss, LLP, 759 F.3d 522, 525 (6th Cir. 2014). The law school sued for defamation after an attorney at the defendant law firm posted allegedly defamatory statements on a website titled JD Underground. The statements asserted that the law school had "grossly inflate[d] its post-graduate employment data and salary information."

On appeal, the Sixth Circuit upheld the trial court's dismissal, concluding that plaintiff had been unable to "demonstrate that a reasonable jury could find by clear and convincing evidence that defendants published [the statements about Cooley] with actual malice."

In determining Cooley's status as a limited-purpose public figure, the Sixth Circuit relied heavily on the Supreme Court's ruling in *Gertz*. First, it ruled that a public controversy existed "regarding whether law schools were reporting accurate post-graduate employment data and whether law school graduates can afford to pay back their loans." The court further held that Cooley had "voluntarily injected itself into the public debate" regarding the difficult employment landscape and financial burden faced by law school graduates. Finally, the court pointed out that Cooley had "access to channels of effective communication to express its position, including its website, advertisements, recruiting materials, written publications, and career services presentations."

The Sixth Circuit then rejected the claim that the Kurzon Strauss attorney had made the allegedly defamatory statements with actual malice. It reasoned that there was no foundation for a conclusion that defendants entertained any "serious doubts" about the truth of the statements.

Do these two decisions indicate that all universities will be at least limited public figures when criticism is based on how well they educate students?

c.   INVOLUNTARY PUBLIC FIGURES

Some of the tests for public figure status seem to require that the plaintiff's participation be voluntary; others do not. Involuntary public figures have been rare. Among the few that have been found so far are Meeropol v. Nizer, 560 F.2d 1061, (2d Cir. 1977) (children of convicted spies Julius and Ethel Rosenberg); Carson v. Allied News Co., 529 F.2d 206 (7th Cir. 1976) (Johnny Carson's wife—unless she was "voluntary" because she married a famous person); Street v. National Broadcasting Co., 645 F.2d 1227 (6th Cir. 1981) (main prosecution witness in famous Scottsboro case of 1931, in which nine black youths in Alabama were accused of raping plaintiff and another white woman; alleged defamation occurred 40 years after trial). Are these cases consistent with *Gertz* and *Wolston?*

In Dameron v. Washington Magazine, Inc., 779 F.2d 736 (D.C. Cir. 1985), plaintiff had been the only air traffic controller on duty in 1974 when a plane approaching Dulles Airport crashed into Mt. Weather. Plaintiff testified in the administrative and judicial proceedings that followed. In that case, claims based on controller negligence were dismissed. In 1982, a plane crashed into the Potomac River. The story on the 1982 crash in defendant's city magazine included a sidebar on earlier local plane crashes and their causes. In that list the 1974 crash was attributed to "controller" failure. Plaintiff sued for libel. The district judge granted summary judgment in favor of the magazine.

The court of appeals held that persons "can become involved in public controversies and affairs without their consent or will. Air-controller Dameron, who had the misfortune to have a tragedy occur on his watch, is such a person" and became an involuntary public figure for the limited purpose of discussions of the Mt. Weather crash. The court acknowledged that the test set out in *Waldbaum* [cited in the principal case], which was controlling in the District of Columbia, required an "inquiry into the plaintiff's voluntary actions that have caused him to become embroiled in a public controversy." But the court said:

> This analysis clearly must be modified somewhat to accommodate the possibility of a potentially involuntary limited-purpose public figure that is presented here. We think, however, that the facts here satisfy the Supreme Court's definition of a public figure and an appropriately modified

Waldbaum inquiry. There was indisputably a public controversy here. Nor can it be doubted that the alleged defamation was germane to the question of controller responsibility for air safety in general and the Mt. Weather crash in particular. There is no question that Dameron played a central, albeit involuntary, role in this controversy.

The case was distinguishable from *Wolston* because Dameron was "a central figure, however involuntarily, in the discrete and specific public controversy with respect to which he was allegedly defamed—the controversy over the cause of the Mt. Weather crash." Wolston was tangential to the investigation of Soviet espionage in general. If Dameron can prove that he was not a cause of the Mt. Weather crash, might he still be a central figure in the "controversy" over the cause of that crash? Would this amount to permitting the defendant to make Dameron a public figure by falsely accusing him?

In the principal case, the court said it need not decide whether persons can become public figures involuntarily because McLemore was a voluntary public figure. Might the case have been more appropriately analyzed as an involuntary plaintiff case, along the lines of *Dameron*?

Plaintiffs who are involved with organized crime figures may be found to be involuntary public figures. See, e.g., Marcone v. Penthouse International, Ltd., 754 F.2d 1072 (3d Cir. 1985). So too a person whose job brought him into constant contact, socially and officially, with a group of high ranking public officials, some of whom were involved in drugs. When one of them died of a drug overdose, plaintiff became a limited-purpose public figure. Clyburn v. News World Communications, Inc., 903 F.2d 29 (D.C. Cir. 1990). But see Wells v. Liddy, 186 F.3d 505, 539 (4th Cir. 1999) (holding that the involuntary public figure category should be limited to the "exceedingly rare" case in which the plaintiff becomes a "central figure in a significant public controversy" and "assume[s] the risk of publicity") and Alharbi v. Beck, 62 F.Supp.3d 202 (D. Mass. 2014) (injured bystander at Boston Marathon bombing later cleared as a suspect had not assumed the risk of publicity; moreover, "even if a private person meets the definition of an involuntary public figure as a matter of bad luck during a public controversy, the status is of limited duration" and evaporates once that person is no longer a suspect).

F. FALSITY

1. BURDEN OF PROOF

During the period when the English government rigorously used the law of criminal libel, truth was not a defense on the theory that unfavorable truths about government or officials were even more likely to stir up anti-government attitudes and actions than were falsehoods. But in civil libel, the common law long ago recognized truth as a defense provided the defendant published with good motives and for justifiable ends, and eventually the proviso was dropped, making truth a complete defense. New York Times v. Sullivan implied that treating truth as a defense might not be enough, but the Supreme Court did not address the matter explicitly until it decided the following case.

Philadelphia Newspapers, Inc. v. Hepps

Supreme Court of the United States, 1986.
475 U.S. 767.

[The Philadelphia Inquirer published a series of five investigative articles the thrust of which was that a chain of "Thrifty" stores, whose principal owner was Hepps, was "connected with underworld figures and organized crime." Hepps and his corporation and franchisees brought a libel suit against the corporate parent of the newspaper and the individual staffers who wrote the series. A state statute gave the defendants the burden of proving truth, but the trial judge believed that was unconstitutional and instructed the jury that the plaintiff bore the burden of proving falsity. The jury found for defendants. The Pennsylvania Supreme Court reversed, holding that the statute controlled the burden of proof issue and was not unconstitutional.]

■ JUSTICE O'CONNOR delivered the opinion of the Court. . . .

. . . We believe that the common law's rule on falsity—that the defendant must bear the burden of proving truth—must . . . fall here to a constitutional requirement that the plaintiff bear the burden of proving falsity, as well as fault, before recovering damages.

There will always be instances when the fact-finding process will be unable to resolve conclusively whether the speech is true or false; it is in those cases that the burden of proof is dispositive. Under a rule forcing the plaintiff to bear the burden of showing falsity, there will be some cases in which plaintiffs cannot meet their burden despite the fact that the speech is in fact false. The plaintiff's suit will fail despite the fact that, in some abstract sense, the suit is meritorious. Similarly, under an alternative rule placing the burden of showing truth on defendants, there would be some cases in which defendants could not bear their burden despite the fact that the speech is in fact true. Those suits would succeed despite the fact that, in some abstract sense, those suits are unmeritorious. Under either rule, then, the outcome of the suit will sometimes be at variance with the outcome that we would desire if all speech were either demonstrably true or demonstrably false.

This dilemma stems from the fact that the allocation of the burden of proof will determine liability for some speech that is true and some that is false, but all of such speech [as] is unknowably true or false. Because the burden of proof is the deciding factor only when the evidence is ambiguous, we cannot know how much of the speech affected by the allocation of the burden of proof is true and how much is false. In a case presenting a configuration of speech and plaintiff like the one we face here, and where the scales are in such an uncertain balance, we believe that the Constitution requires us to tip them in favor of protecting true speech. To ensure that true speech on matters of public concern is not deterred, we hold that the common-law presumption that defamatory speech is false cannot stand when a plaintiff seeks damages against a media defendant for speech of public concern.[4]

In the context of governmental restriction of speech, it has long been established that the government cannot limit speech protected by the First Amendment without bearing the burden of showing that its restriction is justified. [ ] It is not immediately apparent from the text of the First Amendment, which by its terms applies only to governmental action, that a similar result should obtain here: a suit by a private party is obviously quite different from the government's direct enforcement of its own laws. Nonetheless, the need to encourage debate on public issues that concerned the Court in the governmental-restriction cases is of concern in a similar manner in this case involving a private suit for damages: placement by state law of the burden of proving truth upon media defendants who publish speech of public concern deters such speech because of the fear that liability will unjustifiably result. [ ] Because such a "chilling" effect would be antithetical to the First Amendment's protection of true speech on matters of public concern, we believe that a private-figure plaintiff must bear the burden of showing that the speech at issue is false before recovering damages for defamation from a media defendant. To do otherwise could "only result in a deterrence of speech which the Constitution makes free." [ ]

We recognize that requiring the plaintiff to show falsity will insulate from liability some speech that is false, but unprovably so. Nonetheless, the Court's previous decisions on the restrictions that the First Amendment places upon the common law of defamation firmly support our conclusion here with respect to the allocation of the burden of proof. In attempting to resolve related issues in the defamation context, the Court has affirmed that "[t]he First Amendment requires that we protect some falsehood in order to protect speech that matters." . . .

We note that our decision adds only marginally to the burdens that the plaintiff must already bear as a result of our earlier decisions in the law of defamation. The plaintiff must show fault. A jury is obviously more likely to accept a plaintiff's contention that the defendant was at fault in publishing the statements at issue if convinced that the relevant

---

4   We . . . have no occasion to consider the quantity of proof of falsity that a private-figure plaintiff must present to recover damages. Nor need we consider what standards would apply if the plaintiff sues a non-media defendant, see Hutchinson v. Proxmire, 443 U.S. 111, 133, n.16 (1979), or if a State were to provide a plaintiff with the opportunity to obtain a judgment that declared the speech at issue to be false but did not give rise to liability for damages. [Footnote relocated].

statements were false. As a practical matter, then, evidence offered by plaintiffs on the publisher's fault in adequately investigating the truth of the published statements will generally encompass evidence of the falsity of the matters asserted. See Keeton, Defamation and Freedom of the Press, 54 Texas L. Rev. 1221, 1236 (1976). See also Franklin & Bussel, The Plaintiff's Burden in Defamation: Awareness and Falsity, 25 Wm. & Mary L. Rev. 825, 856–857 (1984).

For the reasons stated above, the judgment of the Pennsylvania Supreme Court is reversed, and the case is remanded for further proceedings not inconsistent with this opinion.

■ JUSTICE BRENNAN, with whom JUSTICE BLACKMUN joins, concurring.

. . . I write separately only to note that, while the Court reserves the question whether the rule it announces applies to non-media defendants, [ ] I adhere to my view that such a distinction is "irreconcilable with the fundamental First Amendment principle that '[t]he inherent worth of . . . speech in terms of its capacity for informing the public does not depend upon the identity of the source, whether corporation, association, union, or individual.' " [ ]

. . .

■ JUSTICE STEVENS, with whom THE CHIEF JUSTICE, JUSTICE WHITE, and JUSTICE REHNQUIST join, dissenting.

. . .

In my opinion deliberate, malicious character assassination is not protected by the First Amendment to the United States Constitution. That Amendment does require the target of a defamatory statement to prove that his assailant was at fault, and I agree that it provides a constitutional shield for truthful statements. I simply do not understand, however, why a character assassin should be given an absolute license to defame by means of statements that can be neither verified nor disproved. The danger of deliberate defamation by reference to unprovable facts is not a merely speculative or hypothetical concern. Lack of knowledge about third parties, the loss of critical records, an uncertain recollection about events that occurred long ago, perhaps during a period of special stress, the absence of eyewitnesses—a host of factors may make it impossible for an honorable person to disprove malicious gossip about his past conduct, his relatives, his friends, or his business associates.

The danger of which I speak can be illustrated within the confines of this very case. Appellants published a series of five articles proclaiming [repeatedly that federal authorities had found a criminal tie between plaintiffs and "underworld figures."] The defamatory character of these statements is undisputed. Yet the factual basis for the one specific allegation contained in them is based on an admitted relationship between [plaintiffs] and a third party. The truth or falsity of that statement depends on the character and conduct of that third party—a matter which the jury may well have resolved against the plaintiffs on the ground that they could not disprove the allegation on which they bore the burden of proof.[8]

. . .

[In a footnote, the dissenters said they would hold that public plaintiffs also need not prove falsity, if that issue were before the Court.]

NOTES AND QUESTIONS

1. How might Hepps disprove the allegation that he or his business interests had underworld connections? Would his own testimony denying such connections be sufficient if the jury believed him?

2. The plaintiffs' proof problems were complicated by the fact that the newspaper refused to disclose the sources of its information. A state statute protected the newspaper's right to keep sources confidential. The trial judge refused the plaintiffs' request to instruct the jury that it could draw inferences adverse to the defendants from their failure to present affirmative evidence as to the truthfulness of their sources. Plaintiffs did not appeal that decision, and the Court rejected plaintiffs' suggestion that these circumstances should affect the decision on burden of proof.

3. Note that the decision leaves the states free to treat truth as a defensive matter when the defamatory matter is not of public concern and perhaps when the defendant is not media. However, the Supreme Court has not treated nonmedia defendants differently, and lower courts generally apply *Hepps* to non-media cases. See, e.g., Burroughs v. FFP Operating Partners, 28 F.3d 543 (5th Cir. 1994). Virtually all of the statements media are sued over are treated as matters of public concern, as are many of the statements at issue in non-media litigation. Some states require all plaintiffs to prove falsity. See, e.g., Savage v. Pacific Gas & Electric Co., 21 Cal.App.4th 434 (Cal. App. 1993).

The Iowa Supreme Court observed that U.S. Supreme Court jurisprudence does not compel the "media/nonmedia dichotomy," but the Iowa court nonetheless maintained the distinction in libel cases involving private-figure plaintiffs and matters of private concern. Bierman v. Weier, 826 N.W.2d 436 (Iowa 2013). In such cases, "[a] media defendant benefits from the bar on presumed damages and the requirement to prove fault and falsity, whereas a nonmedia defendant is subject to the presumptions of damages, falsity, and malice if a traditional case of defamation per se has been established." The court justified giving media defendants preferential treatment in private-figure libel cases on the grounds that non-media defendants "have fewer incentives to self-police the truth of what they are saying. . . . Also, because they are not in the communications business, they may care less about their reputation for veracity." The court worried that the

---

[8]   At trial, the individual plaintiff simply denied knowledge of Joseph Scalleat's employment with Beer Sales Consultants and of BSC's employment by three Thrifty Stores. [ ]

Internet and social media give nonmedia speakers "a greater capacity for harm without corresponding reasons to be accurate in what they are saying."

4.   Some courts have concluded that falsity must be shown with convincing clarity. Compare Steaks Unlimited, Inc. v. Deaner, 623 F.2d 264 (3d Cir. 1980), and Buckley v. Littell, 539 F.2d 882 (2d Cir. 1976) (requiring convincing clarity on falsity element), with Liberty Lobby, Inc. v. Dow Jones & Co., 838 F.2d 1287 (D.C. Cir. 1988) and In re Standard Jury Instructions, 575 So.2d 194 (Fla. 1991) (use "fair preponderance of the evidence").

5.   Lower courts also disagree as to whether the First Amendment requires independent appellate review of the falsity element. Compare Liberty Lobby, Inc. v. Dow Jones & Co., 838 F.2d 1287 (D.C. Cir. 1988) and Rouch v. Enquirer & News of Battle Creek, 487 N.W.2d 205 (Mich. 1992) (independent review on falsity) with Hinerman v. The Daily Gazette Co., 423 S.E.2d 560 (W. Va. 1992) (no independent review on falsity).

6.   At common law, defendants were not required to prove literal truth of the charge but only to show that it was "substantially" true. Thus, if the defendant charged the plaintiff with stealing $25,000 from a bank, truth was established even if the actual amount was only $12,000. This idea has survived the switch in burden of proof. In Masson v. New Yorker Magazine, discussed earlier, the Court captured the common law's spirit in observing that the law of libel "overlooks minor inaccuracies and concentrates upon substantial truth." Thus, the test was whether what was published "would have had a different effect upon the mind of the reader from that which the pleaded truth would have produced." After Hepps, the "substantial truth" doctrine has become one of "material falsity": the statement must be not merely technically false but materially so.

Material Falsity. Air Wisconsin Airlines Corp. v. Hoeper, 134 S.Ct. 852 (2014), was the first libel case decided by the Supreme Court during the tenure of Chief Justice John Roberts. Indeed, it was the first libel case decided by the Supreme Court in almost a quarter of a century. Although *Hoeper* dealt with a narrow issue concerning the interpretation of a federal statutory immunity under the Aviation and Transportation Security Act (ATSA), 49 U.S.C. § 44901 et. seq. (2001), dicta in the case gave some insight into the application of the concept of material falsity. The statute immunizes from civil liability airlines and airline employees who report suspicious behavior to the Transportation Security Administration. The immunity does not apply to "any disclosure made with actual knowledge that the disclosure was false, inaccurate, or misleading" or "any disclosure made with reckless disregard as to the truth or falsity of that disclosure." §44941 (b). The issue before the Court was whether courts may deny immunity to an air carrier under the ATSA without determining that the air carrier's disclosures to the TSA were materially false. The court unanimously held that courts must determine that a defendant's disclosures were materially false before imposing liability for defamation. The court split, 6–3, however, on the application of the "material falsity" standard to the facts of *Hoeper*.

In *Hoeper* an employee of Air Wisconsin reported to the Transportation Safety Administration that an Air Wisconsin pilot was a possible threat and might be unstable. Earlier in the day, the pilot had failed a flight simulation test and lost his temper, shouting and cursing at Air Wisconsin employees conducting the test. Air Wisconsin previously had stated it would fire the pilot if he failed the test. After the pilot's outburst, employees of Air Wisconsin discussed his behavior and the fact that a TSA program allowed him to carry a weapon on an aircraft. An employee then reported the pilot as mentally unstable, potentially armed, and disgruntled over having been fired. The pilot sued for defamation.

Air Wisconsin moved for summary judgment based on the ATSA immunity provisions, but the trial judge denied the motion on the grounds that "the jury was entitled to resolve disputed issues of fact that controlled the determination of immunity." After rejecting the airline's claim of immunity, the jury found its statements to TSA were defamatory and made with actual malice. However, the trial judge did not instruct the jury that Air Wisconsin was immune from liability if its statements were materially true. The trial judge entered the jury's verdict of $1.2 million, and the airline appealed.

The Supreme Court of Colorado affirmed, holding that Air Wisconsin's statements were not entitled to immunity because clear and convincing evidence supported the jury's finding that Air Wisconsin had recklessly accused the pilot of suffering from mental instability.

The U.S. Supreme Court held that Air Wisconsin was entitled to statutory immunity under the ATSA and reversed the Colorado Supreme Court. In an opinion by Justice Sotomayor, the Court held that the airline could not be denied immunity under the ATSA absent a determination that its statements were materially false. Further, the Court held that the ATSA did not permit states to impose liability for statements made to the TSA that are materially true but recklessly made. Rather than sending the case back to Colorado state courts for a determination of material falsity, a majority of the Justices concluded that Air Wisconsin's statements about the instability of the pilot were materially true.

The Court reached this conclusion by looking to the legislative history, text and purpose of the immunity provision. Congress borrowed the language of the immunity provision from the Supreme Court's defamation jurisprudence defining "actual malice," which requires plaintiffs to prove material falsity. Because the Court had settled this understanding of actual malice already when Congress enacted the ATSA, the Court presumed that Congress meant to incorporate this understanding into the immunity provision. This understanding was consistent with textual language in the statute and with Congress's purpose of "encouraging airline employees to report suspicious activities" without fear of liability for doing so. "It would defeat this purpose to deny immunity for substantially true reports, on the theory that the person making the report had not yet gathered enough information to be certain of its truth."

The Court provided guidance to lower courts as to how to determine material falsity for purposes of applying the statutory immunity. The Court insisted that the material falsity standard applies differently in deciding whether a statement is defamatory than it does in deciding whether ATSA immunity applies. Although in both instances the defamatory statement must produce a different effect on the reader than the truth would, "the identity of the relevant reader or listener varies according to the context." The relevant "hypothetical reader or listener" for immunity purposes is a security officer, and the relevant inquiry is whether that reader or listener would have responded to the truth differently than they would respond to the defendant's false statement. In other words, if the defendant's true statements would make the TSA official perceive and respond to a threat to the same extent that the defendant's false statements would, then the defendant qualifies for ATSA immunity. To defeat this immunity, a plaintiff must establish "a substantial likelihood that a reasonable security officer would consider [the false information, whether omitted or misrepresented] important in determining a response to the supposed threat."

Applying this standard, a majority of the Court concluded that "even if a jury were to find the historical facts in the manner most favorable to [the plaintiff pilot], Air Wisconsin is entitled to ATSA immunity as a matter of law." The truthful statements Air Wisconsin made concerning the possibility that the plaintiff-pilot was armed and upset about losing his job were enough to trigger a reasonable security officer to investigate the situation. Finally, the gist of the statement that the pilot was unstable was consistent with the truthful facts that he had "blown up" in anger after his failed test, and the Air Wisconsin employees who witnessed it were worried about what he might do later.

Justice Scalia, joined by Justices Thomas and Kagan, dissented from Court's holding that Air Wisconsin's statements were not materially false, on the grounds that the application of the standard is a "fact bound question better left to the lower courts." He wrote that, under a "reasonable-jury standard, I do not see how we can possibly hold as a matter of law that Air Wisconsin's report was not materially false."

2. FALSITY AND OPINION

If the Constitution requires plaintiffs to prove falsity, it would seem to follow that it does not permit liability for statements that by their nature are *incapable* of being proved false. This implication of *Hepps* was not immediately appreciated, but it has turned out to be as important as the explicit holding of the case. Before *Hepps*, lower courts wrestled with the problem of defamation by statements couched as opinion. Many of them recognized a constitutional defense for "opinion." A good example is Ollman v. Evans, 750 F.2d 970 (D.C. Cir. 1984) (en banc). There, syndicated columnists Evans and Novak had argued against the proposed appointment of a Marxist political science professor to head the Department of Government and Politics at the University of Maryland. Among other statements, the column quoted a political scientist who, refusing to be identified, was said to have asserted that "Ollman has no status within the profession, but is a pure and simple activist." The president of the University of Maryland rejected the appointment.

The trial judge's dismissal was affirmed by a split court that produced seven opinions. The lead opinion emphasized four factors for analysis: (1) "the common usage or meaning of the specific language of the challenged statements itself"; (2) "the statement's verifiability—is the statement capable of being objectively characterized as true or false?"; (3) "the full context of the statement—the entire article or column"; and (4) "the broader context or setting in which the statement appears. Different types of writing have ... widely varying social conventions which signal to the reader the likelihood of a statement's being either fact or opinion." This quickly became the most popular method of analyzing opinion cases.

After lower courts spent some years arguing over the *Ollman* approach, and four years after *Hepps*, the Supreme Court addressed the issue.

Milkovich v. Lorain Journal Co.

Supreme Court of the United States, 1990.
497 U.S. 1.

[Milkovich was coach of Maple Heights High School's wrestling team, which was involved in a brawl with a competing team. After a hearing, the Ohio High School Athletic Association (OHSAA) censured Milkovich and placed his team on probation. Parents of some of the team members sued to enjoin OHSAA from enforcing the probation, contending OHSAA's investigation and hearing violated due process. Milkovich and Scott, the superintendent, testifying at a judicial hearing on the suit, both denied that Milkovich had incited the brawl through his behavior toward the crowd and a meet official. The judge granted the restraining order sought by the parents. A sports columnist who had attended the meet, but not the judicial hearing, wrote about the hearing in a column published the next day in the defendant newspaper. The headline was "Maple beat the law with the 'big lie.'" The theme of the column was that at the judicial hearing, Milkovich and Scott misrepresented Milkovich's role in the altercation and thereby prevented the team from receiving the punishment it deserved. The concluding paragraphs of the column were as follows:

> "Anyone who attended the meet, whether he be from Maple Heights, Mentor [the opposing school] or impartial observer, knows in his heart that Milkovich and Scott lied at the hearing after each having given his solemn oath to tell the truth."

> "But they got away with it."

> "Is that the kind of lesson we want our young people learning from their high school administrators and coaches?"

> "I think not."

Milkovich and Scott both sued the newspaper, alleging that the column accused them of perjury. After 15 years of litigation and several appeals, the Ohio Court of Appeals held in Milkovich's case that the column was constitutionally protected opinion and granted the newspaper's motion for summary judgment. The Supreme Court reversed.]

■ CHIEF JUSTICE REHNQUIST delivered the opinion of the Court.

... Respondents would have us recognize, in addition to the established safeguards [established in our prior cases], still another First Amendment-based protection for defamatory statements which are categorized as "opinion" as opposed to "fact." For this proposition they rely principally on the following dictum from our opinion in *Gertz*:

> Under the First Amendment there is no such thing as a false idea. However pernicious an opinion may seem, we depend for its correction not on the conscience of judges and juries but on the competition of other ideas. But there is no constitutional value in false statements of fact. [ ]

Judge Friendly appropriately observed that this passage "has become the opening salvo in all arguments for protection from defamation actions on the ground of opinion, even though the case did not remotely concern the question." [Cianci v. New Times Publishing Co., 639 F.2d 54 (2d Cir. 1980).] Read in context, though, the fair meaning of the passage is to equate the word "opinion" in the second sentence with the word "idea" in the first sentence. Under this view, the language was merely a reiteration of Justice Holmes' classic "marketplace of ideas" concept. [ ]

Thus we do not think this passage from *Gertz* was intended to create a wholesale defamation exemption for anything that might be labeled "opinion." ... Not only would such an interpretation be contrary to the tenor and the context of the passage, but it would also ignore the fact that expressions of "opinion" may often imply an assertion of objective fact.

If a speaker says, "In my opinion John Jones is a liar," he implies a knowledge of facts which lead to the conclusion that Jones told an untruth. Even if the speaker states the facts upon which he bases his opinion, if those facts are either incorrect or incomplete, or if his assessment of them is erroneous, the statement may still imply a false assertion of fact. Simply couching such statements in terms of opinion does not dispel these implications; and the statement, "In my opinion Jones is a liar," can cause as much damage to reputation as the statement, "Jones is a liar." As Judge Friendly aptly stated: "[It] would be destructive of the law of libel if a writer could escape liability for accusations of [defamatory conduct] simply by using, explicitly or implicitly, the words 'I think,' " See *Cianci* [ ] ...

Apart from their reliance on the *Gertz* dictum, respondents do not really contend that a statement such as, "In my opinion John Jones is a liar," should be protected by a separate privilege for "opinion" under the First Amendment. But they do contend that in every defamation case the First Amendment mandates an inquiry into whether a statement is "opinion" or "fact," and that only the latter statements may be actionable. They propose that a number of factors developed by the lower courts (in what we hold was a mistaken reliance on the *Gertz* dictum) be considered in deciding which is which. But we think the " 'breathing space' ", which " 'freedoms of expression require to survive' " [ ] is adequately secured by existing constitutional doctrine without the creation of an artificial dichotomy between "opinion" and fact.

Foremost, we think *Hepps* stands for the proposition that a statement on matters of public concern must be provable as false before there can be liability under state defamation law, at least in situations, like the present, where a media defendant is involved.[6] Thus, unlike the statement, "In my opinion Mayor Jones is a liar," the statement, "In my opinion Mayor Jones shows his abysmal ignorance by accepting the teachings of Marx and Lenin," would not be actionable. *Hepps* ensures that a statement of opinion relating to matters of public concern which does not contain a provably false factual connotation will receive full constitutional protection.

Next, the *Bresler-Letter Carriers-Falwell* line of cases provide protection for statements that cannot "reasonably [be] interpreted as stating actual facts" about an individual. [ ] This provides assurance that public debate will not suffer for lack of "imaginative expression" or the "rhetorical hyperbole" which has traditionally added much to the discourse of our Nation. [ ]

The [constitutional fault] requirements further ensure that debate on public issues remains "uninhibited, robust, and wide-open." . . .

We are not persuaded that, in addition to these protections, an additional separate constitutional privilege for "opinion" is required to ensure the freedom of expression guaranteed by the First Amendment. The dispositive question in the present case then becomes whether or not a reasonable fact-finder could conclude that the statements [in the column] imply an assertion that petitioner Milkovich perjured himself in a judicial proceeding. We think this question must be answered in the affirmative. . . . This is not the sort of loose, figurative or hyperbolic language which would negate the impression that the writer was seriously maintaining petitioner committed the crime of perjury. Nor does the general tenor of the article negate this impression.

---

[6]   In *Hepps* the Court reserved judgment on cases involving non-media defendants, [ ] and accordingly we do the same. Prior to *Hepps*, of course, where public-official or public-figure plaintiffs were involved, the *New York Times* rule already required a showing of falsity before liability could result. [ ]

We also think the connotation that petitioner committed perjury is sufficiently factual to be susceptible of being proved true or false. A determination of whether petitioner lied in this instance can be made on a core of objective evidence by comparing, inter alia, petitioner's testimony before the trial court. As the [Ohio Supreme Court noted in the case of the superintendent,] "[w]hether or not H. Don Scott did indeed perjure himself is certainly verifiable by a perjury action with evidence adduced from the transcripts and witnesses present at the hearing. Unlike a subjective assertion the averred defamatory language is an articulation of an objectively verifiable event." [ ] So too with petitioner Milkovich.

The numerous decisions discussed above establishing First Amendment protection for defendants in defamation actions surely demonstrate the Court's recognition of the Amendment's vital guarantee of free and uninhibited discussion of public issues. But there is also another side to the equation; we have regularly acknowledged the "important social values which underlie the law of defamation." . . .

We believe our decision in the present case holds the balance true. The judgment of the Ohio Court of Appeals is reversed and the case remanded for further proceedings not inconsistent with this opinion.

[Justice Brennan, joined by Justice Marshall, dissented. He said the Court addressed the opinion issue "cogently and almost entirely correctly," and agreed that the lower courts had been under a "misimpression that there is a so-called opinion privilege wholly in addition to the protections we have already found to be guaranteed by the First Amendment." But he disagreed with the application of agreed principles to the facts. He characterized the columnist's assumption that Milkovich lied as "patently conjecture" and asserted that conjecture is as important to the free flow of ideas and opinions as "imaginative expression" and "rhetorical hyperbole," which the majority agreed are protected. He offered several examples:

> Did NASA officials ignore sound warnings that the Challenger Space Shuttle would explode? Did Cuban-American leaders arrange for John Fitzgerald Kennedy's assassination? Was Kurt Waldheim a Nazi officer? Such questions are matters of public concern long before all the facts are unearthed, if they ever are. Conjecture is a means of fueling a national discourse on such questions and stimulating public pressure for answers from those who know more.

The dissent argued that the language of the column itself made clear to readers that the columnist was engaging in speculation, personal judgment, emotional rhetoric, and moral outrage. "No reasonable reader could understand [the columnist] to be impliedly asserting—as fact—that Milkovich had perjured himself."]

NOTES AND QUESTIONS

1.   Is it for the judge or jury to decide whether a statement "is sufficiently factual to be susceptible of being proved true or false?" In the principal case, did the Court decide as a matter of law that the statement was sufficiently factual, or did it merely hold that a jury should be allowed to decide that question? Lower courts are sharply divided as to whether there is any jury role in connection with this issue. Compare Piersall v. SportsVision of Chicago, 595 N.E.2d 103 (Ill. App. Ct. 1992) (judge decides) with Yetman v. English, 811 P.2d 323 (Ariz. 1991) (jury decides).

2.   The majority writes that "the statement, 'In my opinion Mayor Jones shows his abysmal ignorance by accepting the teachings of Marx and Lenin,' would not be actionable." If the mayor does not accept the teachings of Marx and Lenin, might the statement be actionable? Does the Court mean only that the statement that the mayor is abysmally ignorant is not actionable if the rest of the statement is true?

3.   The procedural history of the *Milkovich* case, described at length in omitted portions of the majority opinion, illustrates the persistence and endurance that libel litigation sometimes demands of its participants. The column was published in 1974. The case settled shortly after the 1990 opinion.

4.   Is this approach to the opinion problem likely to produce different results than the *Ollman* approach? Does the context in which the defamatory statement is used play any role in the Milkovich analysis? That question has generated much discussion since *Milkovich*.

5.   By interpreting state constitutions to be more protective of speech than the federal constitution, some state courts give opinion more protection than *Milkovich* requires. New York has gone furthest in this regard. In Immuno AG. v. Moor-Jankowski, 567 N.E.2d 1270 (N.Y. 1991), the New York Court of Appeals held that the state constitution requires that more attention be paid to the context of the defamatory statement than does the federal constitution after *Milkovich*. It said its own pre-*Milkovich* decisions continue to provide the appropriate means of determining whether a statement is actionable under the state constitution. "[W]e believe an analysis that begins by looking at the content of the whole communication, its tone and apparent purpose [ ] better balances the values at stake than an analysis that first examines the challenged statements for express and implied factual assertions, and finds them actionable unless couched in loose, figurative or hyperbolic language in charged circumstances."

6.   Does evaluating scientific opinion pose problems for courts that are different than evaluating other types of constitutionality protected opinion? In ONY, Inc., v. Cornerstone Therapeutics, 720 F.3d 490 (2d Cir. 2013), a producer of lung surfactants administered to premature infants brought claims of false advertising, deceptive trade practices, injurious falsehood, and interference with prospective economic advantage against the authors and publishers of a peer-reviewed scientific journal for publishing a study criticizing the surfactant. The study found that plaintiff's lung surfactant

was less effective than that of a competitor who had funded and provided the data for the study. The published article disclosed the authors' potential conflict of interest. A district court dismissed the plaintiff's complaint. The appeals court affirmed the dismissal, holding that the defendants' published statements were "protected scientific opinion."

The court discussed the problems posed by applying the opinion privilege to "scientific academic discourse." Although scientific conclusions are in principle verifiable, "courts are ill-equipped to undertake to referee such controversies. Instead, the trial of ideas plays out in the pages of peer-reviewed journals, and the scientific public sits as the jury."

The court declined the plaintiff's invitation to wade into the dispute over the effectiveness of its surfactant. The court noted that the plaintiff was not contending "that the data presented in the article were fabricated or fraudulently created," merely "that the inferences drawn from those data were the wrong ones." Thus, the defendants' "non-actionable scientific conclusions" could not form the basis for any of the plaintiff's statutory or common law claims.

––––––––

Online Review Sites. Yelp is a social media site that allows customers to describe their experiences with local businesses and rate them on a five-star scale. By 2015 Yelp users had written more than 61 million reviews of businesses ranging from hair salons to burger joints. A 2012 Harvard study revealed that a one-star drop in ratings on Yelp reduced a business's revenue by five to nine percent. Michael Luca & Georgios Zervas, Fake It Till You Make It: Reputation, Competition, and Yelp Review Fraud; see also Dina Mayzlin, Yaniv Dover, and Judith A Chevalier, Promotional Reviews: An Empirical Investigation of Online Review Manipulation, The National Bureau of Economic Research (2012).

Yelp reviews, however, remain an imperfect guide to customer sentiment. Although Yelp filters user ratings to weed out untrustworthy reviews, up to 20 percent of all Yelp reviews were fake, according to the same 2012 Harvard study cited above. By that date Yelp had even begun to sue those who falsified reviews, recognizing them as a threat to its business model.

Yelp has also been sued by businesses harmed by negative reviews. In Levitt v. Yelp, 765 F.3d 1123 (9th Cir. 2014), for example, small business owners sued the review service for allegedly extorting advertising payments from them by creating fake negative reviews and otherwise manipulating the reviews of their businesses. They filed a class action asserting violations of California's Unfair Competition Law and Business and Professions Code, civil extortion, and attempted civil extortion. The trial court held that the claims based on Yelp's failure to remove negative reviews were barred by Section 230 of the Communications Decency Act of 1996, a statute discussed in full later in this chapter, and that plaintiffs had pled "insufficient facts from which to infer that Yelp authored or manipulated the negative reviews and ratings." The trial court also found insufficient plaintiffs' pleadings regarding extortionate threats by Yelp. After the plaintiffs amended their complaint, the trial court again dismissed, based largely on the same reasoning.

A Ninth Circuit panel affirmed on the grounds that the plaintiffs had failed to state any claim on which relief could be granted without addressing the CDA immunity issue. The court held that Yelp had not engaged in unfair competition, economic extortion, or attempted extortion. Even if Yelp manipulated user reviews, the plaintiffs had not alleged sufficiently that Yelp "*wrongfully* threatened economic loss by manipulating user reviews." Manipulating reviews (if it happened) does not constitute "wrongful use of economic fear" and is thus not extortion because, as the court noted, business owners have "no pre-existing right to have positive reviews appear on Yelp's website." Thus, even if Yelp acted to withhold positive reviews, it would merely be "withholding a benefit that Yelp makes possible and maintains." The court suggested that the business owners might have had a claim for trade libel based on this conduct, but they did not plead trade libel.

The court similarly rejected the argument that Yelp's marketing of its advertising coupled with manipulation of negative reviews to make them more prominent was extortionate:

> The business owners may deem the posting or order of user reviews as a threat of economic harm, but it is not unlawful for Yelp to post and sequence the reviews. As Yelp has the right to charge for legitimate advertising services, the threat of economic harm that Yelp leveraged is, at most, hard bargaining.

The court also found that the plaintiffs had not alleged sufficient facts to support their claim that it was Yelp that had authored negative reviews. It concluded:

> We emphasize that we are not holding that *no* cause of action exists that would cover conduct such as that alleged, if adequately pled. But for all the reasons noted, extortion is an exceedingly narrow concept as applied to fundamentally economic behavior. The business owners have not alleged a legal theory or plausible facts to support the theories they do argue.

In other words, the court determined that the plaintiffs had not chosen the right causes of action to address Yelp's alleged wrongdoing, which means that Yelp is likely to face yet more lawsuits over its reviews.

Another case involving online reviews addressed more squarely the nature of opinion on review sites. In Seaton v. TripAdvisor, 728 F.3d 592 (6th Cir. 2013), plaintiff Kenneth Seaton, the sole owner of Grand Resort Hotel and Convention Center ("Grand Resort"), sued TripAdvisor for defamation, false light, and invasion of privacy for placing his hotel on its "2011 Dirtiest Hotels List." After removing the case to federal court, TripAdvisor filed a motion to dismiss, asserting that its placement of the Grand Resort on the list constituted non-actionable opinion. Seaton then moved to amend his complaint to add additional claims for trade libel or injurious falsehood and tortious interference with prospective business relationships. The district court granted TripAdvisor's motion to dismiss and denied Seaton's motion to amend as futile.

The Sixth Circuit affirmed, holding that TripAdvisor's placement of Seaton's hotel on its dirtiest hotels list was "not capable of being understood as defamatory." The court based this conclusion, first, on the fact that the "superlative" adjective "dirtiest" was "loose, hyperbolic language." Second, the court looked at the "general tenor" of the list, which billed itself as a product of user reviews rather than "scientific study," with the user reviews being full of hyperbole and subjective accounts of travelers' experiences. Finally, the court placed the TripAdvisor list in the "broader context" of online rankings. TripAdvisor's compilation of user comments was part of broader online trend: "[T]op ten" lists and the like appear with growing frequency on the web." Thus, "a reasonable observer understands that placement on and ranking within the bulk of such lists constitutes opinion, not a provable fact." Although the plaintiff contended that TripAdvisor employed a flawed methodology for ranking user comments, the court found that "the subjective weighing of factors cannot be proven false and therefore cannot be the basis of a defamation claim." Indeed, the court's opinion repeatedly stressed the subjectivity of such rankings as a basis for affirming dismissal of plaintiff's claim.

Remedies for Online Defamation. Can a court issue a post-trial injunction requiring a defendant to remove from his website statements he made that a civil jury has found to be defamatory? The Texas Supreme Court answered that question in the affirmative in Kinney v. Barnes, 443 S.W.3d 87 (Tex. 2014), though it rejected the plaintiff's argument that the defendant should be permanently enjoined from making future statements similar to those that had been adjudicated defamatory. The court reasoned that speech that has been adjudicated defamatory by a jury falls into a category of speech unprotected by the First Amendment, and therefore an injunction requiring removal is not an unconstitutional prior restraint. An injunction against future speech, by contrast, runs the risk of chilling constitutionally protected expression:

> Given the inherently contextual nature of defamatory speech, even the most narrowly crafted of injunctions risks enjoining protected speech because the same statement made at a different time and in a different context may no longer be

actionable. Untrue statements may later become true; unprivileged statements may later become privileged.

Noting that the U.S. Supreme Court had never "definitively addressed" the issue, the Texas Supreme Court cited the Texas Constitution as the basis for its holding regarding injunctions against future speech.

What are the implications of this decision? Can a court issue a post-trial injunction requiring a defendant to remove information that has been found to invade privacy? What about a criminal record that has been expunged? [Editor's Note: One of the authors of the casebook, Lyrissa Lidsky, submitted an amicus brief and was cited in the case.]

G. PUBLICATION AND REPUBLICATION

Publication is a term of art in the law of defamation. It is the communication of the allegedly defamatory material to a third person. Generally, that means anyone other than the defamer and the person defamed. It can be accomplished by any means—written, oral, broadcast, printed, photographic, etc. A defamatory accusation made only to the person defamed normally is not actionable because it is not "published." But if it is foreseeable that the person defamed will be required to pass it along to a third person (e.g. an employer or supervisor), the original defamer may be liable even though the person defamed is the only true "publisher" of the defamation. See, e.g., Purcell v. Seguin State Bank, 999 F.2d 950 (5th Cir. 1993).

Republication, strictly speaking, is not a term of art. It simply refers to the repetition of defamatory material originated by someone else. Such repetition is actually a new "publication" and the repeater is a "publisher," liable as if he or she originated the defamatory statement. Thus, a broadcaster who merely reports as news someone else's defamatory accusation is as fully liable, at least potentially, as the accuser. A newspaper that publishes a defamatory letter to the editor, or a radio station that broadcasts the defamatory comments of a call-in guest on a talk show, is similarly liable. The rationale for this rule is that without it media and others could defame at will merely by finding someone to whom they can attribute the defamatory statements. It is sometimes called the "republication rule," but it means only that republication is treated the same as publication.

The "republication rule" is seriously at odds with the expectations and practices of some new communications technologies. A culture of more or less uninhibited repetition developed on the Internet, apparently oblivious to the effects of the republication rule. Most courts have held that republication through a hyperlink, for example, is not republication for the purposes of defamation. "[T]hough a link and reference may bring readers' attention to the existence of an article," the Third Circuit explained, "they do not republish the article." In re Philadelphia

Newspapers, 690 F.3d 161 (3d Cir. 2012). Should the single publication rule not protect Internet posts, New York's highest court had held a decade earlier, "there would be a serious inhibitory effect on the open, pervasive dissemination of information and ideas over the Internet, which is, of course, its greatest beneficial promise." Firth v. State, 775 N.E.2d 463 (N.Y. 2002).

An additional protection is provided to Internet-based publishers through statutory means. When the expectations of the Internet republication culture clashed with the traditional assumptions embodied in the republication rule, Congress intervened.

1. PUBLISHERS AND DISTRIBUTORS

Zeran v. America Online, Inc.
United States Court of Appeals, Fourth Circuit, 1997.
129 F.3d 327.

Before WILKINSON, CHIEF JUDGE, RUSSELL, CIRCUIT JUDGE, and BOYLE, Chief United States District Judge for the Eastern District of North Carolina, sitting by designation.

■ WILKINSON, CHIEF JUDGE:

Kenneth Zeran brought this action against America Online, Inc. ("AOL"), arguing that AOL unreasonably delayed in removing defamatory messages posted by an unidentified third party, refused to post retractions of those messages, and failed to screen for similar postings thereafter. The district court granted judgment for AOL on the grounds that the Communications Decency Act of 1996 ("CDA")—47 U.S.C. § 230—bars Zeran's claims. Zeran appeals, arguing that § 230 leaves intact liability for interactive computer service providers who possess notice of defamatory material posted through their services. . . . Section 230, however, plainly immunizes computer service providers like AOL from liability for information that originates with third parties. Accordingly, we affirm the judgment of the district court.

"The Internet is an international network of interconnected computers," currently used by approximately 40 million people worldwide. [ ] One of the many means by which individuals access the Internet is through an interactive computer service. These services offer not only a connection to the Internet as a whole, but also allow their subscribers to access information communicated and stored only on each computer service's individual proprietary network. [ ] AOL is just such an interactive computer service. Much of the information transmitted over its network originates with the company's millions of subscribers. They may transmit information privately via electronic mail, or they may communicate publicly by posting messages on AOL bulletin boards, where the messages may be read by any AOL subscriber.

[Zeran alleged that a few days after the 1995 bombing of the federal building in Oklahoma City, which killed more than 160 people, someone posted a message on an AOL bulletin board advertising "Naughty Oklahoma T-Shirts" featuring offensive and tasteless slogans related to the bombing of the Alfred P. Murrah Federal Building in Oklahoma City. Those interested in purchasing the shirts were instructed to call "Ken" at Zeran's home phone number in Seattle. Zeran received many angry and derogatory messages, including death threats. He could not change his phone number because he relied on its availability to the public in running his business out of his home. Later that day, Zeran called AOL and informed a company representative of his predicament. The representative assured Zeran that the posting would be removed.

Over the next few days, additional messages were posted advertising additional shirts, bumper stickers, and key chains with new tasteless slogans, asking interested buyers to call Zeran's phone number and advising them to "please call back if busy." The angry, threatening phone calls intensified. Zeran called AOL repeatedly and was told by company representatives that the individual account from which the messages were posted would soon be closed. Zeran was receiving an abusive phone call approximately every two minutes. An Oklahoma City radio station, KRXO, received a copy of the first AOL posting, related the message's contents on the air, attributed them to "Ken" at Zeran's phone number, and urged the listening audience to call the number. After this radio broadcast, Zeran was inundated with death threats and other violent calls from Oklahoma City residents. The number of calls to Zeran's residence finally subsided to fifteen per day after an Oklahoma City newspaper exposed the AOL posting as a hoax.

Suits against KRXO and AOL were transferred to Eastern District of Virginia. The district court granted AOL judgment on the pleadings under Federal Rule 12(c), based on the claim that Section 230 was a complete defense. This appeal followed.]

Zeran did not bring any action against the party who posted the offensive messages.[1]

. . . Zeran seeks to hold AOL liable for defamatory speech initiated by a third party. He argued to the district court that once he notified AOL of the unidentified third party's hoax, AOL had a duty to remove the defamatory posting promptly, to notify its subscribers of the message's false nature, and to effectively screen future defamatory material. . . .

The relevant portion of § 230 states: "No provider or user of an interactive computer service shall be treated as the publisher or speaker of any information provided by another information content provider." 47 U.S.C. § 230(c)(1). By its plain language, § 230 creates a federal

---

[1] Zeran maintains that AOL made it impossible to identify the original party by failing to maintain adequate records of its users. The issue of AOL's record keeping practices, however, is not presented by this appeal.

immunity to any cause of action that would make service providers liable for information originating with a third-party user of the service. Specifically, § 230 precludes courts from entertaining claims that would place a computer service provider in a publisher's role. Thus, lawsuits seeking to hold a service provider liable for its exercise of a publisher's traditional editorial functions—such as deciding whether to publish, withdraw, postpone or alter content—are barred.

The purpose of this statutory immunity is not difficult to discern. Congress recognized the threat that tort-based lawsuits pose to freedom of speech in the new and burgeoning Internet medium. The imposition of tort liability on service providers for the communications of others represented, for Congress, simply another form of intrusive government regulation of speech. Section 230 was enacted, in part, to maintain the robust nature of Internet communication and, accordingly, to keep government interference in the medium to a minimum. In specific statutory findings, Congress recognized the Internet and interactive computer services as offering "a forum for a true diversity of political discourse, unique opportunities for cultural development, and myriad avenues for intellectual activity." Id. § 230(a)(3). . . .

None of this means, of course, that the original culpable party who posts defamatory messages would escape accountability. While Congress acted to keep government regulation of the Internet to a minimum, it also found it to be the policy of the United States "to ensure vigorous enforcement of Federal criminal laws to deter and punish trafficking in obscenity, stalking, and harassment by means of computer." Id. § 230(b)(5). Congress made a policy choice, however, not to deter harmful online speech through the separate route of imposing tort liability on companies that serve as intermediaries for other parties' potentially injurious messages.

Another important purpose of § 230 was to encourage service providers to self-regulate the dissemination of offensive material over their services. In this respect, § 230 responded to a New York state court decision, Stratton Oakmont, Inc. v. Prodigy Servs. Co., 1995 WL 323710 (N.Y. Sup. May 24, 1995). There, the plaintiffs sued Prodigy—an interactive computer service like AOL—for defamatory comments made by an unidentified party on one of Prodigy's bulletin boards. The court held Prodigy to the strict liability standard normally applied to original publishers of defamatory statements, rejecting Prodigy's claims that it should be held only to the lower "knowledge" standard usually reserved for distributors. The court reasoned that Prodigy acted more like an original publisher than a distributor both because it advertised its practice of controlling content on its service and because it actively screened and edited messages posted on its bulletin boards.

Congress enacted § 230 to remove the disincentives to self regulation created by the *Stratton Oakmont* decision. Under that court's holding, computer service providers who regulated the dissemination of offensive material on their services risked subjecting themselves to liability, because such regulation cast the service provider in the role of a publisher. Fearing that the specter of liability would therefore deter service providers from blocking and screening offensive material, Congress enacted § 230's broad immunity "to remove disincentives for the development and utilization of blocking and filtering technologies that empower parents to restrict their children's access to objectionable or inappropriate online material." 47 U.S.C. § 230(b)(4). In line with this purpose, § 230 forbids the imposition of publisher liability on a service provider for the exercise of its editorial and self-regulatory functions.

Zeran argues, however, that the § 230 immunity eliminates only publisher liability, leaving distributor liability intact. Publishers can be held liable for defamatory statements contained in their works even absent proof that they had specific knowledge of the statement's inclusion. W. Page Keeton et al., Prosser and Keeton on the Law of Torts § 113, at 810 (5th ed. 1984). According to Zeran, interactive computer service providers like AOL are normally considered instead to be distributors, like traditional news vendors or book sellers. Distributors cannot be held liable for defamatory statements contained in the materials they distribute unless it is proven at a minimum that they have actual knowledge of the defamatory statements upon which liability is predicated. [ ] Zeran contends that he provided AOL with sufficient notice of the defamatory statements appearing on the company's bulletin board. This notice is significant, says Zeran, because AOL could be held liable as a distributor only if it acquired knowledge of the defamatory statements' existence.

[Zeran] asserts that Congress' use of only the term "publisher" in § 230 indicates a purpose to immunize service providers only from publisher liability. He argues that distributors are left unprotected by § 230 and, therefore, his suit should be permitted to proceed against AOL. We disagree. Assuming arguendo that Zeran has satisfied the requirements for imposition of distributor liability, this theory of liability is merely a subset, or a species, of publisher liability, and is therefore also foreclosed by § 230.

The terms "publisher" and "distributor" derive their legal significance from the context of defamation law. Although Zeran attempts to artfully plead his claims as ones of negligence, they are indistinguishable from a garden variety defamation action. Because the publication of a statement is a necessary element in a defamation action, only one who publishes can be subject to this form of tort liability. Restatement (Second) of Torts § 558(b) (1977). [ ] Publication does not only describe the choice by an author to include certain information. In addition, both the negligent communication of a defamatory statement and the failure to remove such a statement when first communicated by another party—each alleged by Zeran here under a negligence label—constitute publication. Restatement (Second) of Torts § 577. [ ] In fact, every repetition of a defamatory statement is considered a publication. [ ]

In this case, AOL is legally considered to be a publisher. "[E]veryone who takes part in the publication . . . is charged with publication." [ ] Even distributors are considered to be publishers for purposes of defamation law:

> Those who are in the business of making their facilities available to disseminate the writings composed, the speeches made, and the information gathered by others may also be regarded as participating to such an extent in making the books, newspapers, magazines, and information available to others as to be regarded as publishers. They are intentionally making the contents available to others, sometimes without knowing all of the contents—including the defamatory content—and sometimes without any opportunity to ascertain, in advance, that any defamatory matter was to be included in the matter published.

[Prosser & Keeton] at 803. AOL falls squarely within this traditional definition of a publisher and, therefore, is clearly protected by § 230's immunity.

Zeran contends that decisions like *Stratton Oakmont* and Cubby, Inc. v. CompuServe Inc., 776 F.Supp. 135 (S.D.N.Y. 1991), recognize a legal distinction between publishers and distributors. He misapprehends, however, the significance of that distinction for the legal issue we consider here. It is undoubtedly true that mere conduits, or distributors, are subject to a different standard of liability. As explained above, distributors must at a minimum have knowledge of the existence of a defamatory statement as a prerequisite to liability. But this distinction signifies only that different standards of liability may be applied within the larger publisher category, depending on the specific type of publisher concerned. See Keeton et al., [ ] at 799–800 (explaining that every party involved is charged with publication, although degrees of legal responsibility differ). To the extent that decisions like *Stratton* and *Cubby* utilize the terms "publisher" and "distributor" separately, the decisions correctly describe two different standards of liability. *Stratton* and *Cubby* do not, however, suggest that distributors are not also a type of publisher for purposes of defamation law.

Zeran simply attaches too much importance to the presence of the distinct notice element in distributor liability. The simple fact of notice surely cannot transform one from an original publisher to a distributor in the eyes of the law. To the contrary, once a computer service provider receives notice of a potentially defamatory posting, it is thrust into the role of a traditional publisher. The computer service provider must decide whether to publish, edit, or withdraw the posting. In this respect, Zeran seeks to impose liability on AOL for assuming the role for which § 230 specifically proscribes liability—the publisher role.

. . .

Zeran next contends that interpreting § 230 to impose liability on service providers with knowledge of defamatory content on their services is consistent with the statutory purposes outlined in Part IIA. Zeran fails, however, to understand the practical implications of notice liability in the interactive computer service context. Liability upon notice would defeat the dual purposes advanced by § 230 of the CDA. Like the strict liability imposed by the *Stratton Oakmont* court, liability upon notice reinforces service providers' incentives to restrict speech and abstain from self-regulation.

If computer service providers were subject to distributor liability, they would face potential liability each time they receive notice of a potentially defamatory statement—from any party, concerning any message. Each notification would require a careful yet rapid investigation of the circumstances surrounding the posted information, a legal judgment concerning the information's defamatory character, and an on-the-spot editorial decision whether to risk liability by allowing the continued publication of that information. Although this might be feasible for the traditional print publisher, the sheer number of postings on interactive computer services would create an impossible burden in the Internet context. [ ] Because service providers would be subject to liability only for the publication of information, and not for its removal, they would have a natural incentive simply to remove messages upon notification, whether the contents were defamatory or not. [ ] Thus, like strict liability, liability upon notice has a chilling effect on the freedom of Internet speech.

. . .

[The court rejected Zeran's argument that his suit was not covered by the statute because it was enacted after the postings in question. His suit had been filed after the effective date of the act, and the statute said "No cause of action may be brought and no liability may be imposed under any State or local law that is inconsistent with this section."]

NOTES AND QUESTIONS

1. Is this decision based on the relationship between "publisher" and "distributor" at common law or on the court's reading of the statute?

2. If Internet service providers like AOL need immunity from liability for republishing defamation, why not radio stations that use live call-in formats? Newspapers that publish letters to the editor?

3.   What arguments justify the court's analysis of AOL's situation after it received notice from Zeran? Was there reason to doubt Zeran's complaint when it came in? Should that be relevant?

4.   Might Zeran have a cause of action based on either (1) AOL's refusal to help him identify the person who posted the statements (if that person is identifiable) or (2) AOL's claim that its operating structure does not permit it to identify such posters? See Barnes v. Yahoo!, 570 F.3d 1096 (9th Cir. 2009), in which the Ninth Circuit allowed a plaintiff to pursue a promissory estoppel claim based on her allegation that she relied on Yahoo! promise to remove the offending material. The court held that Section 230's immunity didn't apply because enforcement of Yahoo!'s promise to remove the offending material would not treat it as a publisher or speaker for liability purposes. Should ISPs change their "take-down" policies in light of *Barnes*?

5.   If the potential liability of the originator offers sufficient protection for reputation in this context (where the practices of the medium make it especially difficult to identify that person), is there any reason to retain the republication rule in any context?

6.   The *Zeran* court notes that Section 230 was a response to the *Stratton Oakmont* decision. The latter was a trial court decision that was not appealed. If the statute was an overreaction to one lower court case, should that affect the courts' interpretation of it?

––––––––

Could the judge have forced AOL to identify the person who posted the false information about Zeran if it had the ability to do so? The Supreme Court has recognized that individuals have a qualified right to speak anonymously. See McIntyre v. Ohio Elections Comm'n, 514 U.S. 334 (1995). If Internet service providers like AOL must turn over information about a subscriber anytime someone complains about that subscriber's speech, clearly the right to speak anonymously will be compromised. The difficulty for courts, however, is that it is not always easy to discern at the outset whether a case involves defamation. For example, calling a company a "scam" might be defamatory or it might be mere hyperbole, depending on the context. If a mere allegation of libel, without more, is enough to force the unmasking of the alleged defamer, the First Amendment right to speak anonymously has little meaning. How, then, should courts balance the right to speak anonymously against a plaintiff's right to pursue a defamation action?

Courts have developed legal doctrines to deal with this problem. For example, in Independent Newspapers Inc. v. Brodie, 966 A.2d 432 (Md. 2009), a local newspaper operated an Internet forum for which it required participants to register. Several people posted comments accusing the plaintiff of deliberately burning down a historic building, polluting a waterway, and other transgressions. The trial court dismissed the plaintiff's libel case against the newspaper under Section 230 of the

Communications Decency Act, but ordered the newspaper to comply with the plaintiff's subpoenas for names of the pseudonymous posters.

The appellate court reviewed at length the historical and policy arguments for protecting anonymous speech and surveyed approaches various courts have taken to protect it on the Internet. It held that before compelling disclosure of the identity of a poster, the court must be satisfied that the plaintiff has attempted to alert the poster that a subpoena is being sought and has allowed time for the poster to oppose the application, must require the plaintiff to specify precisely what is claimed to be defamatory, and must determine that the complaint sets forth a prima facie case of defamation. Even if all those steps are taken, the court should not compel disclosure unless it determines that the strength of the defamation case and the need for disclosure outweigh the poster's interests in anonymity. Three concurring justices agreed with all but the final requirement, objecting that the balancing test "invites the lower courts to apply, on an *ad hoc* basis, a 'superlaw' of Internet defamation that can trump the well-established defamation law."

Most courts use one of four tests in determining whether to reveal an anonymous poster's identity, all of which consider the strength of the underlying lawsuit, which can involve defamation, invasion of privacy, or another related tort claim. The first and easiest for the plaintiff to meet is the good faith test, one that will allow the commenter to be unmasked if the plaintiff in the underlying case has shown sufficient facts to support the defamation claim. The second, a higher standard, considers the strength of the plaintiffs claim, albeit in a general sense, allowing the anonymous poster's identity to be revealed if the underlying claim would survive a motion to dismiss. The third, the prima facie test, as in *Brodie*, requires some proof for each element of the plaintiff's underlying claim. The highest standard of the four, the summary judgment standard, forces the plaintiff to prove to the satisfaction of the court that the underlying claim would survive a motion for summary judgment. Thomson v. Jane Doe, 356 P.3d 727 (Wash. Ct. App. 2015).

In *Thomson*, an anonymous commenter had posted a critical review of an attorney and the way the attorney had allegedly handled a divorce case. The court held that the test that best applied would vary depending upon the type of speech at issue, suggesting that commercial speech was deserving of the least protection (the good faith standard) while political speech the highest (the summary judgment standard). It ultimately applied the prima facie standard in the case at bar and refused to unmask the commenter, finding that the plaintiff had not supported her claim with sufficient facts. Compare that outcome with the one in Hadley v. Doe, 34 N.E.3d 549 (Ill. 2015), in which the court ordered an internet service provider to unmask an anonymous commenter who had suggested that the plaintiff, a politician, was a child molester who had attempted suicide. Using the motion to dismiss standard, the court found that the commenter's allegations of criminal conduct (child sexual abuse) were defamatory per se and therefore not worthy of protection. It also rejected the commenter's argument that such Internet communication was hyperbolic and therefore not believable.

———

Applicability of Section 230. Though there are some notable exceptions, Section 230 has been interpreted very broadly. Renting computers with Internet access to customers was found to constitute the provision of an "interactive computer service" and therefore qualify for immunity under Section 230 of the CDA. See PatentWizard, Inc. v. Kinko's, Inc., 163 F.Supp. 2d 1069 (D.S.D. 2001). Operating a Web-based chat room has also been found to fit within Section 230. Schneider v. Amazon.com, Inc., 31 P.3d 37 (Wash. Ct. App. 2001). One case even applied the immunity when the ISP had contracted with and paid the author of the allegedly defamatory material or his online "reports" and reserved the right to edit his reports. See Blumenthal v. Drudge, 992 F.Supp. 44 (D.D.C. 1998). In Klayman v. Zuckerberg, 753 F.3d 1354 (D.C. Cir. 2014), the D.C. Circuit also interpreted Section 230 broadly. There, the court rejected a claim by an activist that an injunction should issue and that Facebook should forgo immunity for the tort of assault because Facebook failed to take down a page calling for the killing of Jews.

A few courts have attempted, however, to limit the broad scope of Section 230 immunity, most notably, in Fair Housing Council of San Fernando Valley v. Roommates.com, 521 F.3d 1157 (9th Cir. 2008) (en banc). The court, 8–3, held that a website's active involvement in soliciting the content supplied by its users deprived the website's operators of CDA immunity in a housing discrimination action. The website offered a "roommate-matching" service, and required users of the service to answer questionnaires with information about gender, sexual orientation, and whether children would be living in the user's household. The Ninth Circuit held that three aspects of the Roommates.com website deprived it of CDA immunity. First, requiring users to answer questions about their sex, family status, and sexual orientation made the website an "information content provider" rather than a conduit for information supplied by third parties. Second, the creation of user profiles based on answers to the required questionnaire made Roommates.com an information "developer" rather than a "passive transmitter of information provided by others." Third, the creation of a search engine that allowed "discriminatory filtering" by users—that is, filtering based on gender and other illegal criteria—made Roommates.com "forfeit any immunity to which it was otherwise entitled." The court distinguished Roommates.com's search function from search engines like Google, which "provide[d] neutral tools to carry out what may be unlawful or illicit searches." The court also stressed that "an editor's minor changes to the spelling, grammar and length of third-party content do not strip him of Section 230 immunity." What are the implications of this case for defamation law? What about the now-defunct juicycampus.com, which solicited gossip from university students and promised to organize its site so that the anonymity of those who supplied information would be absolutely protected?

In Jones v. Dirty World Entertainment, 755 F.3d 398 (6th Cir. 2014), a different court answered those questions at least in part. It held that a website operator's seeming encouragement of defamatory posts, including naming the website "The Dirty," calling posters "The Dirty Army," and highlighting certain scandalous or provocative posts and commenting on them, did not deprive the operator of immunity under Section 230. The court held that immunity would be lost only when the website operator had "materially contributed" to the defamatory statements made by third parties.

The next year, Washington State's highest court rejected blanket Section 230 immunity for the website known as Backpage.com. In J.S. v. Village Voice Media Holdings, 359 P.3d 714 (Wash. 2015), plaintiffs' claims were that "children [were] bought and sold for sexual services online on Backpage.com in advertisements" that "the defendants [had] help[ed to] develop" and that CDA immunity should, therefore, not foreclose a trial. The court agreed in principle. "It is important to ascertain whether in fact Backpage designed its posting rules to induce sex trafficking to determine whether Backpage is subject to suit under the CDA," the court wrote. If the plaintiff were able to offer such evidence, the court reasoned, the website could be found to have materially contributed to the illegal conduct that the plaintiffs alleged and CDA immunity would not apply. Six months later, a federal appeals court applied CDA immunity to protect the same website from similar claims in a different case. Doe v. Backpage.com, 2016 U.S. App. Lexis 4671 (1st Cir. Mar. 14, 2016). "This is a hard case," the court wrote, "hard in the sense that the law requires that we . . . deny relief to plaintiffs whose circumstances evoke outrage."

For additional cases expressing dissatisfaction with the broad scope of Section 230 immunity, see Doe v. GTE Corp., 347 F.3d 655 (7th Cir. 2003); Chicago Lawyers' Committee for Civil Rights Under the Law, Inc. v. Craigslist, Inc., 519 F.3d 666 (7th Cir. 2008).

2. NEUTRAL REPORTAGE

Much of the law of defamation operates to soften the impact of the republication rule. The statute applied in *Zeran* is a legislative abrogation of the rule. As a matter of common law, media and other defendants often avoid liability by claiming a privilege to defame, and most of these are privileges to republish someone else's defamation. The republication rule is also mitigated by a constitutional privilege recognized by some courts.

In Edwards v. National Audubon Society, Inc., 556 F.2d 113 (2d Cir. 1977), the court wrote, "[W]hen a responsible, prominent organization . . . makes serious charges against a public figure, the First Amendment protects the accurate and disinterested reporting of those charges, regardless of the reporter's private views regarding their validity." [ ] That principle has come to be called the neutral report privilege. *Edwards* held that The New York Times could not be held liable for having reported the Audubon Society's defamatory accusations against a group of prominent scientists. The court said the evidence did not support a jury finding the reporter acted with actual malice because he had serious doubts about the truth of the charges, but said that even if he did, the publication was protected by the neutral report principle. Another court explained the rationale as follows:

> The theory underlying the privilege is that the reporting of defamatory allegations relating to an existing public controversy has significant informational value for the public regardless of the truth of the allegations: If the allegations are true, their reporting provides valuable information about the target of the accusation; if the allegations are false, their reporting reflects in a significant way on the character of the accuser. In either event, according to the theory, the very making of the defamatory allegations sheds valuable light on the character of the controversy (its intensity and perhaps viciousness). As we understand it, the theory also rests on a distinction between publication and republication. Applying this distinction, proponents of the neutral reportage privilege urge that the reporting of a false and defamatory accusation should be deemed neither defamatory nor false if the report accurately relates the accusation, makes it clear that the republisher does not espouse or concur in the accusation, and provides enough additional information (including, where practical, the response of the defamed person) to allow the readers to draw their own conclusions about the truth of the accusation.

Khawar v. Globe International, Inc., 965 P.2d 696 (Cal. 1998).

The neutral report privilege is by no means universal; some state and federal appellate courts have rejected it entirely. See Dickey v. CBS, Inc., 583 F.2d 1221 (3d Cir. 1978); McCall v. Courier-Journal & Louisville Times, 623 S.W.2d 882 (Ky. 1981); Postill v. Booth Newspapers, Inc., 325 N.W.2d 511 (Mich. Ct. App. 1982); Hogan v. Herald Co., 84 A.D.2d 470 (N.Y. App. Div. 1982), while some that have adopted it have disagreed as to its elements. Compare, e.g., Martin v. Wilson Pub. Co., 497 A.2d 322 (R.I. 1985) (holding that the privilege applies "only in the extremely limited situation in which the publication accurately attributes such statements to an identified and responsible source") with Barry v. Time,

Inc., 584 F.Supp. 1110 (N.D. Cal. 1984) (applying privilege to report of accusations made by other than a "responsible" person or organization). The Supreme Court has never held that the First Amendment mandates a neutral report privilege; in Harte-Hanks Communications v. Connaughton, the Court declined to decide the issue. See 491 U.S. at 660 n.1 (1989). After reviewing this history, the Pennsylvania Supreme Court predicted that the Supreme Court would not adopt the neutral report privilege, and on that basis refused to recognize it. See Norton v. Glenn, 860 A.2d 48 (Pa. 2004), cert. denied, 544 U.S. 956 (2005).

Despite the lack of consensus about the existence or scope of the privilege, there may be situations that cry out for some such protection. Suppose the President of the United States told an interviewer that the Vice President was plotting to kill him; should a media defendant that reported the President's statement without endorsing its truth be potentially liable? Note that if the defendant believed the President's statement was false, New York Times v. Sullivan would offer no protection.

In view of the extent to which the republication rule is vitiated by exceptions such as Section 230 and the neutral report privilege, would it be wise to abandon the rule? Would abandonment of the rule release a flood of republished defamation? Considering the success of Internet service providers in getting Congress to solve *their* problem with the republication rule, should the media seek a statutory solution? If so, what should they ask for? A statute adopting the neutral report privilege? Some broader immunity from republication liability?

H. COMMON LAW PRIVILEGES

1. THE NATURE OF PRIVILEGES

Over the centuries the law of defamation has developed numerous privileges to protect those who make defamatory statements. Privileges are defenses; it is up to the defendant to plead privilege and prove facts necessary to establish the applicability of the privilege. Some privileges are "absolute" in the sense that if the occasion gives rise to an absolute privilege, there will be no liability even if the speaker deliberately lied about the plaintiff. High executive officials, judges, and participants in judicial proceedings have an absolute privilege to speak freely on matters relevant to their obligations. No matter how such a speaker abuses the privilege by lying, no tort liability will flow. See Barr v. Matteo, 360 U.S. 564 (1959). The federal constitution and most state constitutions create a similar privilege for legislators, immunizing them from liability for defamatory statements made during debate.

Few absolute privileges are available to media. One protects broadcasters who are required by federal statute to grant equal opportunity on the air to all candidates for the same office. If a candidate allowed to broadcast under this statute commits defamation, the broadcaster is not liable. See Farmers Educational & Cooperative Union of America v. WDAY, Inc., 360 U.S. 525 (1959). Cable operators are immune from liability for defamation presented by others on access channels. See 47 U.S.C. § 558.

Most privileges are "conditional" or "qualified" (the terms mean the same). The defendant who can establish the applicability of such a privilege will prevail unless the plaintiff can show that the speaker "abused" the privilege. The plaintiff shows abuse by proving that the defendant did not honestly believe what he said or that defendant published more information or published it more widely than was justified by the occasion that provided the privilege. Most courts have defined abuse in terms of the defendant's using the occasion for purposes other than what was intended by the creation of the privilege. For example, under the common law conditional privilege for communications between persons having a mutual interest, one may malign a third party to one's partner if one honestly believes the statement and if it relates to the affairs of the partnership. But one may not lie or gratuitously discuss the third party's personal affairs with that partner, or discuss even appropriate matters with the partner if others are present. Efforts to extend this type of privilege to reports by mass media have failed.

Most common law privileges primarily benefit non-media speakers. For example, privileges similar to the mutual interest privilege discussed above protect employers who talk to other employers about prospective employees, businesses that exchange credit information, and discussions among family members. Another protects a person who defames someone to protect his or her own interests (e.g., by erroneously accusing someone of stealing the speaker's property), and another protects defamatory statements made to law enforcement officers.

2. FAIR COMMENT

The fair comment privilege protects literary, artistic, and similar kinds of criticism, regardless of its merit, as long as it is made honestly, with honesty being measured by the accuracy of the critic's descriptive observations. If the critic describing the work gives the "facts" accurately and fairly, the critic's honest conclusions are privileged as "fair comment." Classic cases discussing the privilege are Triggs v. Sun Printing & Pub. Ass'n, 71 N.E. 739 (N.Y. 1904), Adolf Philipp Co. v. New Yorker Staats-Zeitung, 165 A.D. 377 (N.Y. App. Div. 1914), and Cherry v. Des Moines Leader, 86 N.W. 323 (Iowa 1901).

Originally this privilege was confined to literary and artistic criticism, but eventually defendants began claiming the privilege of fair comment with regard to other matters of public interest, including the conduct of politicians. The privilege claimed would permit citizens—and media—to criticize and argue about the conduct of their officials. Most courts greatly restricted this use of the privilege by holding that criticism of officials was not privileged unless it was based upon true underlying facts. The leading case was Post Publishing Co. v. Hallam, 59 F.530 (6th Cir. 1893), in which Judge Taft wrote:

> The existence and extent of privilege in communications are determined by balancing the needs and good of society against the right of an individual to enjoy a good reputation when he has done nothing which ought to injure it. The privilege should always cease where the sacrifice of the individual right becomes so great that the public good to be derived from it is outweighed. . . . But, if the privilege is to extend to cases like that at bar, then a man who offers himself as a candidate must submit uncomplainingly to the loss of his reputation, not with a single person or a small class of persons, but with every member of the public, whenever an untrue charge of disgraceful conduct is made against him, if only his accuser honestly believes the charge upon reasonable ground. . . . [T]he danger that honorable and worthy men may be driven from politics and public service by allowing too great latitude in attacks upon their characters outweighs any benefit that might occasionally accrue to the public from charges of corruption that are true in fact, but are incapable of legal proof. . . .

A few courts interpreted the fair comment privilege more broadly. They held that false assertions of facts relating to matters of public interest were themselves privileged if they were honestly believed to be true, and that comments based on those facts were also privileged if honestly believed. See Coleman v. MacLennan, 78 Kan. 711, 98 P.281 (1908), in which the court rejected *Hallam*'s fears with the observation that "men of unimpeachable character from all political parties continually present themselves as candidates in sufficient numbers to fill the public offices and manage the public institutions" in Kansas despite the broader interpretation of the fair report privilege.

In New York Times v. Sullivan, the Supreme Court eventually embraced the Coleman v. MacLennon view as a matter of constitutional law. That development, together with the controversy over the neutral report privilege discussed in the preceding section, have largely mooted the argument over extending the privilege to public affairs.

3. FAIR AND ACCURATE REPORT

Of all the state law privileges, the one most important to media is the privilege to publish a fair and accurate report of official proceedings. Much of the day-to-day content of media consists of reporting on the activities of government, and this privilege covers most of that coverage. In its classic application, the privilege protects journalists when they report someone else's defamatory statement in a court proceeding, a city council meeting, or a legislative hearing. While the applications of the privilege are well established, disputes over its contours continue to arise.

Salzano v. North Jersey Media Group
Supreme Court of New Jersey, 2010.
993 A.2d 778.

■ LONG, J. . . .

In June 2004, NorVergence, Inc., a telecommunications company, abruptly laid off approximately 1,300 employees and disconnected the services it provided to thousands of small businesses. . . . [Bankruptcy and related proceedings began, including one that led to a default judgment of more than $1.72 million dollars].

Plaintiff Thomas John Salzano is the son of the former chief managing officer/consultant of NorVergence [but] was never an employee of NorVergence. [Nevertheless, a complaint filed by a bankruptcy trustee against Salzano alleged that he had misappropriated a significant amount of company funds for his own use.]

On March 2, 2006, defendant, The Record, published a report with the headline, "Man accused of stealing $ 500,000 for high living," and the subheading "NorVergence funds were taken." [The article read:]

> The son of the mastermind behind NorVergence, a bankrupt Newark telecommunications firm, allegedly stole close to $500,000 from the company, using the money to pay for drinks, trips to area clubs and for a five-bedroom Glen Ridge house, according to court papers filed Wednesday in U.S. Bankruptcy Court in Newark.

> Thomas John Salzano, son of Thomas N. Salzano, the chief managing officer of bankrupt NorVergence, was accused of using two company checks—one in the amount of $ 61,200 dated July 1, 2003, and another for $140,000 dated July 29, 2003—to help pay for "the purchase of his personal residence located at 20 Argyle St., Glen Ridge," the papers said.

> The complaint, filed by U.S. Trustee Charles Forman, also alleges that Thomas John Salzano used a NorVergence corporate American Express card to charge "personal expenses, such as outings to bars and clubs, clothing and other personal expenses" unrelated to NorVergence business.

> The charges totaling $ 268,795 were made between November 25, 2002, and March 24, 2004.

> Neither Forman nor Salzano could be reached for comment.

NorVergence's abrupt bankruptcy in July 2004[ ] threw 1,300 people out of work and left thousands of small-business customers without phone and Internet service.

Legal battles raged when customers tried to get out of equipment leases that NorVergence had sold to more than 40 banks and leasing companies. In many cases, settlements have been reached, brokered by state attorneys general, providing some relief to deeply angry NorVergence customers.

Last year, a U.S[.] District Court ordered a $ 181.7 million default judgment against NorVergence in a case brought by the Federal Trade Commission.

Creditors assert the company owes $ 550 million.

Thomas John Salzano was never an employee of NorVergence, according to court papers. His father, Thomas N. Salzano, was paid hundreds of thousands of dollars as a consultant. His uncle, Peter J. Salzano, served as CEO.

Thomas John Salzano and his father started a Kenilworth business last year called Charity Snack, which also went belly-up.

The complaint filed Wednesday asks that Salzano repay what he allegedly took, plus punitive damages. In addition, the papers claim that because of his "unlawful misappropriation of [NorVergence's] funds, and fraudulent transfer[s] and unjust enrichment[,]" the house at 20 Argyle St. belongs to the trustee, whose job it is to recover any and all company assets.

The five-bedroom, three-bath home at 20 Argyle St. is listed for sale at $699,000, just reduced, according to a real estate Web site.

On the same date, the report was posted on the website of defendant NorthJersey.com, with the same headline but without the subheading. On March 9, 2006, the report was republished by defendant, Glen Ridge Voice, under the headline, "Argyle residence allegedly bought with stolen funds." It was also posted on the website of LeasingNews.org under the headline, "NorVergence BK charges Salzano son stealing $ 1/2 MM."

[P]laintiff filed a pro se complaint alleging defamation and associated torts against [the publisher] defendants [whose attorneys] argued, among other things, that [the defendants'] reporting was covered by the fair-report privilege, and that, in the alternative, the reports were not defamatory because they were accurate and not made maliciously. . . .

At issue here is the fair-report privilege [one "recognized by common law or statute in at least forty-seven states and the District of Columbia"], which protects the publication of defamatory matters that appear in a report of an official action or proceeding, or of a meeting open to the public that deals with a matter of public concern. The fair-report privilege reflects the judgment that the need, in a self-governing society, for free-flowing information about matters of public interest outweighs concerns over the uncompensated injury to a person's reputation. . . .

In all, the majority of jurisdictions that have considered the issue extend the fair-report privilege to encompass initial pleadings and filings.

The rationale for [this] modern approach is four-pronged according to [Solaia Tech. v. Specialty Publ'g Co., 852 N.E.2d 825, 842 (2006)]:

> First, the filing of a complaint is itself a public act. Second, the privilege serves the public's interest in the judicial system, and this interest begins with the filing of a complaint. Third, a judicial-action limitation on the privilege would purportedly decrease the risk of publishing scurrilous pleadings, but this limitation is ineffective: Simply because a suit has proceeded to the point where judicial action of some kind has taken place does not necessarily mean that the suit is less likely to be groundless and brought in bad faith. Fourth, the public has a sophisticated understanding of the court system and is capable of evaluating information gleaned from a complaint. . . .

We now align ourselves with the weight of modern authority and hold that the fair-report privilege extends to defamatory statements contained in filed pleadings that have not yet come before a judicial officer. Indeed, the initial pleadings exception is at odds with the reality that the complaint is open to public view. . . . Members of the public simply cannot attend every single court case and cannot oversee every single paper filing, although clearly entitled to do so. Thus, it is critical for the press to be able to report fairly and accurately on every aspect of the administration of justice, including the complaint and answer, without fear of having to defend a defamation case and without the inhibitory effect of such fear. . . . Indeed, if a citizen presents himself at the local courthouse, there is no question but that he can see filed pleadings for himself. They are not sanitized nor are they filtered through a veracity lens. . . .

We turn then to this case. At issue here is a report regarding a bankruptcy complaint. That a bankruptcy court is a part of the apparatus of the administration of justice is indisputable. . . . As such, the [bankruptcy] complaint is as much a part of the judicial process as anything that takes place after "judicial action" occurs. Thus, for the reasons that we have expressed, defendants' report of the contents of the bankruptcy complaint is subject to the application of the fair-report privilege. To the extent that the Appellate Division ruled otherwise based on the initial pleadings exception, we reverse. . . .

Because the application of the privilege is dependent on the fairness and accuracy of the report, we next turn to that analysis. . . . Although a reporter is allowed to make factual errors and omissions, the fair-report privilege will not protect a story if the errors and omissions mislead readers.

Here, although the headline "NorVergence funds were taken," without any other detail, is imprecise insofar as the fact of the "taking" had not been adjudicated, the headline is not to be considered in a vacuum but must be viewed on the backdrop of the entire report. . . . Indeed, we presume that the public reads the entire article when we assess its fairness and accuracy. Here, the article stated that it was reporting the "allegations" in the trustee's complaint and that it was the trustee who charged that plaintiff had fraudulently received NorVergence assets. . . .

To be sure, the report and headline used the words "stolen" and "stealing," which were not used in the complaint; however, plaintiff's contention that that made the report inaccurate is wide of the mark. . . . Put another way, to an ordinary citizen, the "sting" of the reports was essentially the same as that of the complaint insofar as the trustee alleged that plaintiff "unlawfully diverted, converted and misappropriated" NorVergence funds "for his own personal benefit." The use of the word "steal" was simply not the kind of distortion that we have recognized as stripping a report of a public proceeding of its protections. . . .

As the Appellate Division correctly observed, "a finer point can be put" on the trustee's allegations. However, although the publication is not a verbatim regurgitation of the complaint, it does not need to be. It is substantially correct and that is all that is required. . . .

We have thus far focused solely on the statements based on the bankruptcy complaint to the effect that plaintiff "stole money" from NorVergence. However, that is not the only claim advanced by plaintiff, who also contends that he was defamed by the reports asserting that he and his father "started a Kenilworth business last year called Charity Snack which also went belly-up." Because that statement, which at least impliedly suggests a lack of business skill, was not derived from the bankruptcy complaint, it is not insulated by the fair-report privilege.

Thus, plaintiff may proceed with his suit based on that issue. . . .

■ JUSTICE HOENS, concurring in part and dissenting in part.

I concur in the majority's conclusion that the time has come for us to reject the initial pleadings exception to the fair reporting privilege and I concur in the majority's persuasive and thorough explanation of why that exception has no place in our jurisprudence. . . .

I dissent, however, from the majority's analysis of the application of the fair reporting privilege in this case because I cannot agree with the majority's conclusion that the news articles that are the focus of this litigation meet the test of "full, fair and accurate." Instead, in my view, those news reports fall short of the standard that we have traditionally applied, with the result that they should not be cloaked in the protection that the privilege affords. . . .

[T]he majority has overlooked the significant shortcomings of these news reports [and] this Court has been careful to make it clear that the privilege is not a license for sensationalizing and does not authorize or protect false or misleading reports. . . .

[T]he real inaccuracy, and one that in my view takes the news accounts outside of the privilege, lies in the use of variations of the verb "steal" both in the headlines and in the body of the reports. . . . [A] long common law history demonstrates that some false accusations, including false accusations of a crime, are so obviously damaging to one's reputation that no proof of special damages is required in order for an award to be appropriate. Words of that type carry unique and plainly pejorative connotations entitling their target to relief simply because they have been uttered. By implication, therefore, words like that convey a special sting, making them worthy of our careful scrutiny if we are to agree that they nonetheless will be cloaked in privilege.

Because in common understanding the word "steal" describes a criminal act, the headline and the opening sentence conveyed, unmistakably, the message that the subject of the story was being prosecuted for a crime. That, in turn, surely conjured up in the mind of any objective and reasonable reader the mental image of the now all-too-familiar "perp walk" on the evening news that is sure to follow.

For me . . . part and parcel of the privilege must be that the news entity acts as a neutral filter of the information, reporting it as blandly or as harshly as it would appear to us had we read, heard, or seen it ourselves. . . . This news story [instead] has all of the elements that cry out for this Court to pull aside the cloak of privilege, for it misleads by innuendo, insinuates criminal prosecutions are afoot, and implies by distortion. It does not qualify as a news report that is full, fair and accurate and I therefore cannot agree that it is worthy of the protection that follows the invocation of an absolute privilege.

NOTES AND QUESTIONS

1.   The court discusses a number of reasons that have been asserted to support the fair report privilege. Which is most persuasive? Are the purposes of the privilege served by applying it to proceedings that are not open to the public? Should all publishers, including all Internet websites, be protected in this way? Or does the dissenting opinion's suggestion that such protection should disappear when the information is sensationalized have even greater resonance at a time when ethics restrictions are not in place for many publishers?

2.   *Actual Reliance.* In order to qualify for the fair and accurate report privilege, must the journalist actually rely on an official report? A leading

case on actual reliance is Bufalino v. Associated Press, 692 F.2d 266 (2d Cir. 1982), in which the Second Circuit held that actual reliance was required because encouraging a defendant to engage in a "frantic search of official records" once litigation begins does nothing to support the policies underlying the privilege, namely promoting the reporting of government actions and meetings. See also Grant v. Commercial Appeal, 2015 Tenn. App. LEXIS 750 (Tenn. Ct. App. Sept. 18, 2015) ("Here, the inclusion of certain investigatory interviews and descriptions clearly falls outside of the scope of the fair report privilege because their ties to any official proceedings are tenuous at best"). The Third Circuit, applying Pennsylvania law, reached a contrary decision in Medico v. Time, Inc., 643 F.2d 134 (3d Cir. 1981). In *Medico*, the court held that it was immaterial where a reporter gets his information as long as the published story fairly and accurately "reflects the contents of the official materials."

3.   *Source Attribution.* Must the journalist attribute information to an official source in order to qualify for the privilege? In most cases, the answer appears to be yes. In Dameron v. Washington Magazine, 779 F.2d 736 (D.C. Cir. 1985), the D.C. Circuit held that the purpose of the fair and accurate report privilege is not furthered when "the average reader would be unlikely to understand the article (or the pertinent section thereof) to be a report on or summary of an official document or proceeding." Therefore, the court stated that the privilege would not apply unless either "specific attribution" or "overall context" notify the reader that the defendant is "quoting, paraphrasing, or otherwise drawing upon" official sources (whether reports or proceedings). Compare *Medico*, in which the court found the privilege applicable even though Time Magazine did not "explicitly credit" a leaked FBI report because the magazine article, "taken in context" could "reasonably be understood to inform the reader" that the author was relying on FBI sources.

4.   As the *Salzano* court noted, some states have adopted legislation to codify the fair and accurate report privilege. These may vary from the common law in the scope of coverage and other limitations.

5.   In most states the fair report privilege is not "qualified" in the usual sense; the defendant need not believe the truth of the defamation and does not lose the privilege by publishing too widely. See, e.g., Rosenberg v. Helinski, 616 A.2d 866 (Md. 1992). Instead, the privilege is lost simply if the report is not "fair and accurate."

6.   Fairness and accuracy are necessarily terms of art, since few media reports, especially of complex proceedings, are entirely fair or accurate. As courts have noted, journalists "must be accorded some degree of liberality" in condensing what goes on in a legislative or other official proceeding. When a report is "not misleading" and is "composed and phrased in good faith under the exigencies of a publication deadline, [it should not] be thereafter parsed and dissected on the basis of precise denotative meanings which may literally, although not contextually, be ascribed to the words used." See, e.g., Holy Spirit Ass'n for the Unification of World Christianity v. New York Times Co., 399 N.E.2d 1185 (N.Y. 1979); see also Lee v. TMZ Prods., 2015

U.S. Dist. LEXIS 104387 (D.N.J. Aug. 10, 2015) (finding that the privilege applied even though the media did not use words like "alleged" and "accused" in describing a police report). The test for accuracy is similar to the test for "material falsity." Thus, in Koniak v. Heritage Newspapers, Inc., 499 N.W.2d 346 (Mich. Ct. App. 1993), the defendant reported that plaintiff had been charged with assaulting someone 30 to 55 times when in fact he had been charged with eight assaults. The court observed that "whether plaintiff assaulted his stepdaughter once, eight times or thirty times would have little effect on the reader."

A Texas appeals court, however, refused to apply the privilege when media reported that a "pediatrician" had been sanctioned for inappropriate sexual conduct with a "patient." The original press release authored by the Texas Medical Board had not identified the plaintiff's specialty and no child was involved. "The broadcasts, therefore, were potentially more damaging to [the plaintiff's] reputation than an account consistent with the press release would have been," the court wrote. "As a result, the broadcasts were not a fair, true, and impartial account of the [Board's] press release." KBMT Operating Co., LLC v. Toledo, 434 S.W.3d 276 (Tex. App. 2014).

———

Truth, Privilege, and Republication. Most courts insist that a distinction must be made between accuracy in repeating an allegation contained in an official government publication and the truth of the underlying matter asserted. Thus, a media defendant cannot assert a *truth* defense simply because it is true that a government official said something about the plaintiff. To take advantage of a truth defense, instead, the defendant would have to show that the statement was, in fact, truthful. The republication rule makes repeating a defamatory statement made by a third party equivalent to originating the defamatory statement; the person who republishes the defamatory statement stands in the shoes of the originator for liability purposes. The fair and accurate report rule modifies the republication rule by immunizing fair and accurate republication of official government reports or proceedings. The republisher gets the benefit of the fair and accurate report privilege whether or not the underlying matter reported is true.

Under the republication rule, however, even an accurate report that plaintiff was arrested and charged with a crime may be treated as republication of the accusation that he or she committed the crime. In Rouch v. Enquirer & News of Battle Creek, Mich., 398 N.W.2d 245 (Mich. 1986), a case mentioned earlier in this chapter, the newspaper reported the plaintiff's arrest for rape. After plaintiff, who was never charged, was exonerated, he sued the newspaper. The court treated the issue as one of privilege rather than truth, and rejected the paper's reliance on the state's privilege for fair reporting on the ground that an "arrest that amounts to no more than an apprehension" was not a "proceeding." The statute, the court noted, was not intended to create a "government action," "arrest record," or "public records" privilege.

The legislature reacted by amending the privilege statute, Mich. Comp. Laws § 600.2911, to extend protection to "a fair and true report of matters of public record, a public and official proceeding, or of a governmental notice, announcement, written or recorded report or record generally available to the public, or act or action of a public body."

Not all courts, however, are careful to distinguish between a truth defense and a fair and accurate report privilege. For example, a series of Texas decisions held that the law "only requires proof that allegations were in fact made and under investigation in order to prove substantial truth." KTRK Television v. Felder, 950 S.W.2d 100 (Tex. App. 1997), citing McIlvain v. Jacobs, 794 S.W.2d 14 (Tex. 1990). The Texas Supreme Court eventually made clear that it did not intend to treat accurate reports of third-party allegations as substantial truth. A 5–3 majority endorsed the view of the Restatement (Second) of Torts Sec. 581A, cmt. e (1977): "When one person repeats a defamatory statement that he attributes to some other person, it is not enough for the person who repeats it to show that the statement was made by the other person. The truth of the defamatory charges that he has thus repeated is what is to be established."

The court wrote that lower Texas courts and the Fifth Circuit had misinterpreted *McIlvain* when they held that it created a substantial truth defense for accurate reports about official investigations; *McIlvain* held only that "a government investigation that finds allegations to be true is one method of proving substantial truth." The dissenters said this was an unduly restrictive reading of *McIlvain*. See Neely v. Wilson, 418 S.W.3d 52 (Tex. 2013).

Likewise, in Global Relief Foundation, Inc. v. New York Times Co., 390 F.3d 973 (7th Cir. 2004), The New York Times and others reported truthfully that the Global Relief Foundation, an Islamic charity, was being investigated for funding terrorism and that the government was considering freezing its assets. The charity sued for libel. A district judge granted summary judgment for the defendants on the ground that the allegations were substantially true, and the Second Circuit affirmed. The charity argued that the defendants could not rely on that defense unless it was actually guilty of funding terrorism. The Second Circuit rejected this argument. Although the court found that plaintiff's evidence "demonstrates a genuine issue on whether [the charity] has ever funded terrorist activity," the evidence did not create a genuine issue with regard to the "true gist or sting of the publications"—the allegation that the government was investigating the charity. The court therefore concluded: "Whether the government was justified in its probe is irrelevant to the defamation claims when these media defendants accurately reported on the investigation itself."

The "Wire Service Defense." The common law recognizes a variation of the fair report privilege that protects republication of stories provided by reputable wire services—at least in the absence of some information that casts doubt on the accuracy of the wire service's story. For a decision citing the earlier history of the doctrine, see Howe v. Detroit Free Press, Inc., 555 N.W.2d 738 (Mich. Ct. App. 1996), aff'd 586 N.W.2d 85 (Mich. 1998). There, a newspaper published a wire service story that said a major league baseball pitcher was a member of a family that was a "prisoner of his father's drinking problems." In the father's libel suit, the court concluded that the newspaper had a privilege to publish the wire service story unless it "knows the story is false or . . . the release itself contains unexplained inconsistencies." To require the newspaper to "independently verify the accuracy of every wire-service release it desires to reproduce would force smaller publishers to confine themselves to stories about purely local events, and would make it difficult for smaller, local news organizations to compete with publishers who could afford to either verify every story or assume the risk of litigation."

Should this privilege be extended to material obtained from other media generally? This matter becomes especially relevant as news aggregation becomes more commonplace on news websites and otherwise. New York law recognizes a qualified privilege that protects a media entity when it republishes defamatory material obtained from any other news outlet unless the republisher "had, or should have had, substantial reason to question the accuracy of the articles or the bona fides of (the) reporter." The New York Post invoked this privilege when it was sued by Richard Jewell over its coverage of the Olympic Bombing in Atlanta. Based on the reporting of other news organizations, the Post published a column and several articles depicting Jewell, the person who found the bomb at the Olympics, as a "Rambo," "fat, failed," "disaster," "desperate to stand out as a hero," "disgraced former deputy," and "home-grown failure." The Post moved for summary judgment, claiming it had relied on reports from the Associated Press and CNN that named Jewell as a suspect in the bombing. A federal district court denied the motion. The Post's writers could not remember which reports they had used, and the judge said this made it impossible to determine as a matter of law whether they had reason to doubt the accuracy of those reports. See Jewell v. NYP Holdings Inc., 23 F.Supp. 2d 348 (S.D.N.Y. 1998). This case was eventually settled, along with suits by Jewell against NBC, CNN, and WABC, for a total of more than $2 million.

I. OTHER ISSUES

1. RETRACTION

At common law a defendant who retracts the defamatory statement may offer the evidence of retraction in mitigation of damages. The promptness, prominence, and forthrightness of the retraction will affect the extent to which it is effective in undoing or minimizing the harm, and therefore are factors (usually for the jury to weigh) in determining the extent to which the retraction reduces the damages.

Most of the states have retraction statutes, which may or may not abrogate the common law rule. Some of these seem to do no more than the common law, but most go further. Some apply even if the defamation is intentional. Most limit the type or amount of damages a plaintiff may recover unless the plaintiff gives the defendant an opportunity to retract and the defendant fails to do so. Many are available only to media defendants.

One of the most elaborate retraction statutes is that of California, Cal. Civ. Code § 48a. It provides that in any action for libel against a newspaper or slander in a broadcast, the plaintiff may recover only special damages unless a correction is demanded and not published or broadcast. The prospective plaintiff's demand must be written, must specify the statements claimed to be defamatory, and must be served on the defendant within 20 days after the plaintiff learns of the publication or broadcast. If the defendant fails to publish or broadcast a retraction "in substantially as conspicuous a manner in said newspaper or on said broadcasting station as were the statements claimed to be libelous, in a regular issue thereof published or broadcast within three weeks after such service, plaintiff . . . may recover general, special, and exemplary damages."

Statutes of this type put considerable pressure on both the plaintiff and the defendant. A defendant may have to decide whether to retract before it has had a full opportunity to determine whether the statement in question is false. A plaintiff who is unaware of the need to request a retraction or the deadline for doing so may inadvertently forfeit a good cause of action. And since many plaintiffs are unable to prove substantial amounts of economic loss, they may be effectively barred from recovery even if the retraction fails to undo all the harm. Courts sometimes strain to construe the statutes in a way that will avoid these results.

It is interesting to consider retraction statutes in the context of Internet publication, where defamatory statements are easily republished by increasing numbers of non-affiliates who may never learn of any retraction.

2. JURISDICTION AND LIBEL TOURISM

The Supreme Court has held that the First Amendment does not exempt libel defendants from general rules regarding jurisdiction in distant places. See Keeton v. Hustler Magazine, Inc., 465 U.S. 770 (1984) (allowing a state to assert jurisdiction based on defendant's minimal circulation there even though neither plaintiff nor defendant was domiciled there and most of the damage to reputation occurred elsewhere). Since people (and media) who communicate via Internet have little power to prevent access to their material, they are potentially subject to suit in any jurisdiction.

U.S. courts have used several different approaches to limit defendants' exposure to suit in distant jurisdictions for content published on the Internet. One influential approach focuses on the "nature and quality of the commercial activity that an entity conducts over the Internet" and particularly the degree of interactivity of the Internet forum. See Zippo Mfg. Co. v. Zippo Dot Com, Inc., 952 F.Supp. 1119 (W.D. Pa. 1997); Toys R Us v. Step Two S.A., 318 F.3d 446 (3d Cir. 2003). Under this approach, Internet users who actively do business with customers in the forum state are subject to jurisdiction there. Those who only passively make information available there are not. Those who engage in some interactivity with their readers, as by providing an open forum, are subject to jurisdiction in a state only if they "manifest an intent to target and focus on" readers in that state, Young v. New Haven Advocate, 315 F.3d 256 (4th Cir. 2002), or if the publication "is directed at" the state, Revell v. Lidov, 317 F.3d 467 (5th Cir. 2002).

Another approach used, particularly in defamation cases, focuses on where the effects of the defamation are felt and whether the defendants "expressly aimed" their conduct at the forum state. In Calder v. Jones, 465 U.S. 783 (1984), the Supreme Court held that the National Enquirer magazine was subject to specific jurisdiction in California even though the reporter and editor worked at the magazine's headquarters in Florida. The Court held that jurisdiction was proper because the effects of an allegedly defamatory article in the magazine were felt in California. The article was about an actor who lived in California and dealt with her activities in that state; moreover, 600,000 copies of the magazine were sold in California, and the intentional acts of the publishers "were expressly aimed at California" because they "knew that the brunt of [reputational] injury would be felt" there.

The Supreme Court again addressed the personal jurisdiction analysis in intentional torts cases in Walden v. Fiore, 134 S.Ct. 1115 (2014). There, the Court clarified that "[t]he crux of Calder was that the reputation-based 'effects' of the alleged libel connected the defendants to California, not just to the plaintiff. The strength of that connection was largely a function of the libel tort. However scandalous a newspaper might be, it can lead to a loss of reputation only if communicated to (and read and understood by) third persons." It was this effect on the California audience, coupled with the California focus of the article, that "connected the defendants' conduct to California, not just to a plaintiff who lived there."

Under this test, would a person who posts a defamatory statement about a California resident on Facebook be subject to personal jurisdiction in California if there are no other contacts with the forum?

See Burdick v. Superior Court, 233 Cal.App.4th (Cal.App. 2015) (holding that Illinois resident who posted an allegedly defamatory statement about California residents on Facebook was not subject to personal jurisdiction in California because the post was not "expressly aimed" at California even though it could "be inferred from the posting itself that [defendant] knew Plaintiffs resided in California and understood they would suffer injury [there]").

Many countries have jurisdictional rules that allow foreign defendants to be sued in their courts and under their law. Because material posted on the Internet by conventional media as well as others can be accessed in any country, it is therefore arguably "published" there and thus arguably subject to jurisdiction. In Dow Jones & Co. v. Gutnick (2002) 210 C.L.R. 575, for example, the Australian High Court held that the New York publisher of Barron's magazine could be sued in Australia under Australian law for statements made on Barron's website about an Australian businessman, even though the publisher had no physical presence in Australia and only a small number of Australian subscribers.

Since other countries' defamation laws are considerably less protective of defendants than those of the United States, the prospect of having to defend abroad is generally an unwelcome one for American media. The term "libel tourism" is sometimes used to describe plaintiffs' attempt to forum shop for a jurisdiction with the most favorable libel laws.

After several U.S. states, including New York, Florida, and Illinois, adopted legislation to protect U.S. citizens from the threat of "libel tourism," Congress passed a federal "libel tourism" law in 2010. The federal law is called the Securing the Protection of our Enduring and Established Constitutional Heritage Act, Pub. L. No. 111–223, 28 U.S.C. §§ 4101 et seq. (2010). The Act provides that domestic courts "shall not recognize or enforce a foreign judgment for defamation" unless the party seeking enforcement establishes either (1) that "the defamation law applied in the foreign courts' adjudication produced at least as much protection for freedom of speech and press . . . as would be provided by the first amendment to the Constitution of the United States and by the constitution and law of the State in which the domestic court is located;" or (2) that "the party opposing recognition or enforcement of that foreign judgment would have been found liable for defamation by a domestic court applying the first amendment to the Constitution of the United States and the constitution and law of the State in which the domestic court is located." 28 U.S.C. § 4102. The Act also provides that domestic courts cannot recognize or enforce judgments for defamation against interactive computer service providers that would be inconsistent with the immunity provisions of 47 U.S.C. § 230 (the Section 230 CDA immunity discussed earlier in the chapter). The U.S. citizen against whom a foreign judgment is entered has a right to seek a declaratory judgment in the U.S. court establishing that the foreign judgment is "repugnant to the Constitution or laws of the United States." 28 U.S.C. § 4104.

The disparity between U.S. and U.K. libel law diminished somewhat with the decision of the House of Lords in Jameel v. Wall Street Journal Europe, [2006] UKHL 44. The decision recognized a defense for false and defamatory statements if they are the product of responsible journalism and are in the public interest. The case arose when the Journal's European edition named Jameel's London-based company as one of several prominent Saudi businesses and individuals whose bank accounts were being monitored to determine whether they were being used to divert money to terrorist groups. The newspaper invoked Reynolds v. Times Newspapers Ltd., (2001) 2 A.C. 127, the most speech-protective previous English decision, but that case was held inapplicable because the jury found that the newspaper had not given Jameel sufficient opportunity to respond to the allegation before publishing it. The Court of Appeal affirmed a £40,000 judgment. (The amount may seem low by earlier English standards, but in recent years the courts of the U.K. have severely restricted libel awards. The stakes remain high, however, because in England the loser must pay the lion's share of the winner's attorneys' fees, which in a case like *Jameel* likely would exceed £1 million.)

The House of Lords held that this and other lower court interpretations of *Reynolds* were too restrictive. Lord Hoffman wrote that courts should focus on two clusters of questions. The first is whether the article as a whole is on a subject of public interest and the defamatory statement is sufficiently related to that subject, making allowances for differences of editorial judgment. The second inquiry is "whether the steps taken to gather and publish the information were responsible and fair." The newspaper had made extensive efforts to verify, and its inability to secure Jameel's comment in time to meet its deadline was not fatal to its defense.

Jameel's invitation to courts to decide whether the journalist is responsible and whether the material is in the public interest might sound unwelcome to most American libel lawyers, but in England the decision was viewed by both the judiciary and editors as a major advance in freeing the press from oppressive libel laws. If it does so, it might alleviate the risks of being sued in England.

3. SLAPP MOTIONS

Multiple states have enacted anti-SLAPP statutes, which originally were designed to protect citizens (e.g., environmentalists) against groundless libel suits filed by their adversaries (e.g., polluting industries) to discourage them from exercising their right to protest. SLAPP is an acronym for "Strategic Lawsuit Against Public Participation." Typically the statutes permit a defendant to file an early motion to strike the complaint. Claims that anti-SLAPP statutes violate a plaintiff's right to a jury trial generally have been unsuccessful. See, e.g., Lee v. Pennington, 830 So.2d 1037 (La. App. 2002).

In a number of states, most notably California, SLAPP motions have been an important line of defense for media for years. See Lafayette Morehouse, Inc. v. Chronicle Pub. Co., 37 Cal.App.4th 855 (Cal. App. 1995) (holding that a newspaper was entitled to invoke the SLAPP procedure).

California's statute was enacted in the 1990s to quell "a disturbing increase in lawsuits brought primarily to chill the valid exercise of the constitutional rights of freedom of speech." Cal Code Civ Proc § 425.16. The statute is similar to other states' laws in that it creates a "special motion to strike" any cause of action springing from speech "in connection with a public issue." In California and elsewhere, much of news reporting is recognized as speech in connection with a public issue. In Association for Los Angeles Deputy Sheriffs v. Los Angeles Times, 239 Cal.App.4th 808 (Cal. App. 2015), for example, a newspaper's anti-SLAPP motion successfully protected against a lawsuit springing from privacy concerns in a news story about police hiring practices.

A number of the anti-SLAPP statutes require that courts first determine the viability of the underlying claim. California's statute suggests that the motion should be granted "unless the court determines that the plaintiff has established that there is a probability that the plaintiff will prevail on the claim." Therefore, an anti-SLAPP claim must explore the merits of an underlying action and may not be as protective of media as it may seem. Consider, for example, Gates v. Discovery Communications, 101 P.3d 552 (Cal. 2004), in which a media defendant ultimately succeeded in striking an invasion of privacy complaint, but only after protracted litigation and the court's decision to overturn existing California law.

Under the California statute, the grant or denial of a SLAPP motion is immediately appealable, with the result that many questions of defamation law are now resolved in SLAPP proceedings in that state. The law also provides for the award of attorneys' fees to the prevailing party. See, e.g., Braun v. Chronicle Publishing Co., 52 Cal.App.4th 1036 (Cal. App. 1997) (awarding the San Francisco Chronicle $17,000 in attorneys' fees against a medical director who had alleged that the newspaper libeled her in an investigative series about the training center she managed).

At least one district court has questioned whether the protections of anti-SLAPP statutes are available to defendants in diversity actions. See 3M Co. v. Boulter, 842 F.Supp. 2d 85 (D.D.C. 2012) (holding that the SLAPP statute at issue conflicts with Rules 12 and 56 of the Federal Rules of Civil Procedure and therefore is not applicable in federal courts).

Other courts, however, have held that the statutes are "substantive" and although they may overlap with the federal rules, the statutes are not inconsistent and therefore may be applied by federal courts. See, e.g., Makaeff v. Trump University, 715 F.3d 254 (9th Cir. 2013) (applying California's anti-SLAPP statute as a substantive rather than procedural law, despite concurrences by Chief Judge Alex Kozinski and Judge Richard Paez asserting that Ninth Circuit precedent had erred in reaching this result and should be overturned); Godin v. Schencks, 629 F.3d 79 (1st Cir. 2010); Henry v. Lake Charles Am. Press, LLC, 566 F.3d 164 (5th Cir. 2009).

There is some movement toward enacting a federal anti-SLAPP statute. A bill called the SPEAK FREE Act of 2015 was introduced in the House of Representatives in Spring 2015. H.R. 2304, 114th Cong., 1st Sess., May 13, 2015.

If the special rules created by SLAPP statutes are not to swallow the entire field of defamation, courts must find a way to limit them to meritless or oppressive lawsuits. The Illinois Supreme Court refused to apply that state's SLAPP statute where "it [was] apparent that the true goal of plaintiff's claims [was] not to interfere with and burden defendants' free speech and petition rights, but to seek damages for the personal harm to his reputation from defendants' alleged defamatory and tortious acts." The court construed the statute to apply only where the suit is "solely based on defendant's rights of petition, speech, association, or participation in government." Sandholm v. Kuecker, 962 N.E.2d 418 (Ill. 2012). Here too, is it possible to determine the plaintiff's "true goal" without deciding the merits of the case?

4. REFORM

A generation or more ago there was much agitation to reform libel law. Reformers argued that its complexity imposed significant restraints on free speech without doing much to protect reputation. Some proposed dramatic changes, such as overruling *Sullivan* or substituting declaratory relief for awards of damages. See Richard A. Epstein, Was *New York Times v. Sullivan* Wrong? 53 U. Chi. L. Rev. 782 (1986); Marc A. Franklin, A Declaratory Judgment Alternative to Current Libel Law, 74 Cal. L. Rev. 809 (1986); Pierre N. Leval, The No-Money, No-Fault Libel Suit: Keeping *Sullivan* in its Proper Place, 101 Harv. L. Rev. 1287 (1988); Randall P. Bezanson, The Libel Tort Today, 45 Wash. & Lee L. Rev. 535 (1988); David A. Anderson, Is Libel Law Worth Reforming, 140 U. Pa. L. Rev. 487 (1991). Others suggested modest changes, such as limiting damages or assessing legal fees against parties who are not proceeding in good faith. See Paul A. LeBel, Reforming the Tort of Defamation: An Accommodation of the Competing Interests Within the Current Constitutional Framework, 66 Neb. L. Rev. 249 (1987).

The reform movement lost some steam because, it appeared, legal protections had helped media defendants survive many lawsuits. From 1983 to 2003, for example, 73 percent of the libel, privacy, and other content-related cases against media were decided in media's favor on a motion to dismiss. As late as 2014, the Media Law Resource Center reported that there had been only twelve trials in the United States in the preceding two-year period involving libel, privacy, or related claims against media defendants.

Note, however, that such a number does not include cases that reached some form of settlement before trial and that such statistics do not consider the cost of litigation from the filing of a complaint onward: those costs averaged $180,000 per lawsuit according to a 2015 insurance industry release. Moreover, more recently, media defendants won fewer than 40 percent of the cases that made it to trial and jury awards were said to average $2.6 million dollars, with a median award of $300,000. See News Notes, Quantity of Media Trials Continues Downward Trend, MLRC Reports, 37 Med. L. Rep. No. 12, March 24, 2009; MLRC's Study of Media Trials (2012 & 2014).

In 2010, the executive director of the Media Law Resource Center suggested that the Internet had inevitably increased these financial and law-based concerns; online publications had led to "a steady growth in litigation over content on the Internet." David Savage, Online Rants Can Turn Costly, Los Angeles Times, Aug. 23, 2010. Such lawsuits, the article explained, were difficult to track and therefore may not be included in any overall report on media's wins and losses in court.

Older calls for reform, therefore, may have increasing relevance. Today, many media organizations are smaller with significant economic concerns. The most timid or the most financially insecure media are of course subject to the same rules of libel law as the richest and most aggressive of media. Is it possible for the law to achieve the right level of deterrence for all types of media? If we must choose between overprotection of the most powerful media or underprotection of the weakest, which should we choose?

CHAPTER V

PROTECTING PRIVACY

The law first began recognizing a distinct cause of action for invasion of privacy over a century ago. Although the legal idea of privacy had existed for decades, as suggested by the 1804 case involving Thomas Jefferson referenced in the first chapter, its firm foundation came from perhaps the most famous of all law review articles, The Right to Privacy, written by future Supreme Court Justice Louis D. Brandeis and his law partner Samuel Warren, published in the Harvard Law Review in 1890. Journalism for the masses had started to flourish, and conflicted sharply with Victorian notions of propriety, modesty, and morality. Warren and Brandeis, likely appalled by the potential for the growth of photojournalism and the practices of the Boston newspapers (though such practices were decidedly tame by today's publishing standards), wrote:

> The press is overstepping in every direction the obvious bounds of propriety and of decency. Gossip is no longer the resource of the idle and of the vicious, but has become a trade, which is pursued with industry as well as effrontery. To satisfy a prurient taste the details of sexual relations are spread broadcast in the columns of the daily papers. To occupy the indolent, column upon column is filled with idle gossip, which can only be procured by intrusion upon the domestic circle. . . . When personal gossip attains the dignity of print, and crowds the space available for matters of real interest to the community, what wonder that the ignorant and thoughtless mistake its relative importance. Easy of comprehension, appealing to that weak side of human nature which is never wholly cast down by the misfortunes and frailties of our neighbors, no one can be surprised that it usurps the place of interest in brains capable of other things. Triviality destroys at once robustness of thought and delicacy of feelings. No enthusiasm can flourish, no generous impulse can survive under its blighting influence.

Working with a variety of rather remote precedents from other areas of law, the authors developed an argument that courts should recognize an action for invasion of privacy by media publication. See Samuel D. Warren and Louis D. Brandeis, The Right to Privacy, 4 Harv. L. Rev. 193 (1890).

The courts were initially unreceptive to the creation of a tort for invasion of privacy by the press, but they gradually accepted the arguments of Warren and Brandeis and broadened the common law right of privacy to include several different interests. By 1960 Professor

Prosser was able to identify four distinct privacy torts. One is a remedy for publicly disclosing private facts. Another is for depicting a person in a false light. A third is for commercial exploitation of a person's name or likeness. A fourth is for intruding—physically or through the use of technology—into a person's solitude. See William L. Prosser, Privacy, 48 Cal. L. Rev. 383 (1960).

Although the various privacy actions are primarily common law creations, they are quite different from most other common law torts. Unlike libel and slander, which were well developed long before the First Amendment was ratified, privacy law developed at the same time that expansive doctrines protecting freedom of expression were taking root in American law. As a result, the tort of privacy is heavily infused with First Amendment thinking, to the point that it is not always clear whether a particular piece of privacy doctrine is tort law or constitutional law.

Privacy law has been influenced to an unusual extent by extrajudicial thinking as well. As noted above, the remedy originated mainly from a law review article. Privacy law was given its modern form by Prosser. The Restatement (Second) of Torts, for which Prosser was Reporter, adopted not only his four-branch division of the subject, but also, to a large extent, his description of each branch of the tort. Since the privacy torts were not yet solidified in most states, the Restatement had great influence on the development of privacy law and that influence continues to today. Given modern courts' reliance upon the Restatement in privacy cases, judicial decisions reflect the views of Prosser and the Restatement at least as much as the Restatement reflects judicial thinking.

Outside of the torts arena, many of the major developments in U.S. privacy law in the past 40 years have come about as a result of new statutes enacted to address specific privacy issues. The 1970s witnessed considerable activity on the federal level—prompted largely by the growing use of computers within the federal government—including enactment of the Privacy Act of 1974.[1] The 1970s also saw the appointment of a Privacy Protection Study Commission to examine the government's use of personal data.

The next period of intense legislative activity on the privacy front began in the late 1990s. In 1998, for example, 2,367 privacy bills were introduced or carried over in state legislatures; 42 states enacted a total of 786 bills. This surge in activity was a response to the dramatic growth of Internet usage at that time with related privacy concerns for online privacy, as well as the adoption of significant privacy laws by European and other countries.

---

[1]   In 2012, the Supreme Court in F.A.A. v. Cooper, 132 S.Ct. 1441 (2012), decided that the Act gave an individual a cause of action for damages against a federal agency that improperly disclosed private information, but that the "actual damages" authorized by the statute did not include damages for mental and emotional harm.

Courts have been asked to interpret these privacy statutes in lawsuits springing from publication of the protected material. In 2015 the U.S. Court of Appeals for the Seventh Circuit, for example, was asked to decide the constitutionality of the federal Drivers Privacy Protection Act, 18 U.S.C. § 2721, after a newspaper published information it had gathered from a drivers' license database. The news article at issue described a lineup in which police officers stood with the more distinctive suspect; to contrast the differences between the officers and the suspect, the article reported the officers' height, weight, eye color, and more. The plaintiff officers argued that reporters had violated the DPPA's provision against knowing disclosure of "personal information" accessed through a license database. The court agreed. "Although [the newspaper] claims that, in acquiring and disclosing truthful information, it engaged only in 'perfectly routine, traditional journalism,' " the court wrote, "it cannot escape the fact that it acquired that truthful information unlawfully." The court's holding looked to the statute's privacy protections, weighed what it considered personal information unnecessary to the story, and held that "where members of the press unlawfully obtain sensitive information that, in context, is of marginal public value, the First Amendment does not guarantee them the right to publish that information." Under this interpretation, the statute protected certain personal information in a way that made later publication by news media punishable. Dahlstrom v. Sun-Times Media, LLC, 777 F.3d 937 (7th Cir. 2015). This case is discussed more fully in Chapter Ten.

The Federal Trade Commission also continued to play an important and growing role in privacy regulation by enforcing online data protection and improving online data security. As one commentator noted, the FTC had "initiated far more enforcement actions, levied greater fines and set forth a more comprehensive enforcement agenda than any other data protection authority." Omer Tene, Introducing the Casebook of FTC Privacy Law, Feb. 27, 2014, available at https://www.privacyassociation.org/publications/introducing_the_casebook_of_ftc_privacy_law.

The FTC's authority to enforce privacy arguably derives from Section 5 of the Federal Trade Commission Act, 15 U.S.C. §45. Section 5 authorizes the FTC to prevent "unfair or deceptive acts or practices in or affecting commerce." Other privacy statutes also give the FTC authority, such as the Gramm-Leach-Bliley Act, which requires financial institutions to protect customer privacy, and the Children's Online Privacy Protection Act. The FTC's authority to sanction companies whose faulty data security practices expose customers' personal information was upheld in FTC v. Wyndham Worldwide Corp., 10 F. Supp. 3d 602 (D.N.J. 2014).

We consider in this book only the tort law of privacy and recent statutory developments that concern the mass media. There are many other types of privacy law, such as the constitutional right of privacy that protects certain personal rights involving contraception and abortion, and statutory rights of privacy that are designed to limit acquisition and use of personal information by government agencies or regulated commercial entities, such as banks or utilities. Those privacy laws are beyond the scope of this book, but they nevertheless form an important part of the context in which courts evaluate privacy claims and interpret privacy statutes affecting the media.

Even when limited only to those issues that concern the mass media, however, privacy issues are too diverse to be confined to a single chapter. This chapter examines the three torts and statutory developments applicable to the *publication* of information by the mass media. Chapter Eight addresses the fourth privacy tort—intrusion—together with other torts arising from newsgathering. Privacy concerns also arise in the context of laws giving the press and public a right of access to information. These matters are dealt with in Chapters Ten and Eleven.

A. PUBLIC DISCLOSURE OF PRIVATE FACTS

1. THE TORT

This branch of privacy, one that creates liability for truthful revelations under certain circumstances, protects far less privacy than its name might suggest. As a matter of tort law, there is no cause of action unless (1) the defendant publicly discloses (or "gives publicity to") (2) a private fact and (3) the disclosure is highly offensive to a person of reasonable sensibilities and (4) is of no legitimate public concern. Restatement (Second) of Torts, § 652D. With regard to the last element, some courts substitute the term "newsworthiness" for "legitimate public concern," but the latter is probably more accurate, because it suggests that the issue has a normative as well as a descriptive aspect. What is highly offensive is of course a matter of contemporary mores, which are themselves influenced by media practices in disclosing personal facts. In a society that values media and expression, courts may find it difficult to suggest that people have no legitimate concern in receiving information. In addition to these tort limitations, constitutional law imposes further restrictions on the cause of action, as we shall see shortly.

As the effect of these limitations becomes clear, you may wish to consider whether the tort protects enough privacy to justify its continued existence in its present form.

Haynes v. Alfred A. Knopf, Inc.

United States Court of Appeals, Seventh Circuit, 1993.
8 F.3d 1222.

[The book, "The Promised Land: The Great Black Migration and How it Changed America," by Nicholas Lemann, used the life of Ruby Lee Daniels to illustrate its themes about the social, political, and economic effects of the movement of blacks from the rural South to the cities of the North between 1940 and 1970. The author switched back and forth between discussion of that migration in general, and its personal dimensions as reflected in Ms. Daniels's descriptions of her life and experiences, beginning when she was a sharecropper in Mississippi and progressing through her move to Chicago and her life there over the next 40 years. Among the things she discussed was her relationship with her ex-husband, Luther Haynes. She depicted him as a heavy-drinking ne'er-do-well who neglected their children, could not keep a job, was unfaithful, and eventually left her for another woman. The court quoted one excerpt:

> Luther began to drink too much. When he drank he got mean, and he and Ruby would get into ferocious quarrels. He was still working but he wasn't always bringing his paycheck home. . . .
> It got to the point where [Luther] would go out on Friday evenings after picking up his paycheck and Ruby would hope he wouldn't come home, because she knew he would be drunk. On the Friday evenings when he did come home—over the years Ruby developed a devastating imitation of Luther, and could recreate the scene quite vividly—he would walk into the apartment, put on a record and turn up the volume, and saunter into their bedroom, a bottle in one hand and a cigarette in the other, in the mood for love. On one such night, Ruby's last child, Kevin, was conceived. Kevin always had something wrong with him—he was very moody, he was scrawny, and he had a severe speech impediment. Ruby was never able to find out exactly what the problem was, but she blamed it on Luther; all that alcohol must have gotten into his sperm, she said.

Haynes admitted many of the incidents in the book, but they had all occurred 25 years earlier, and since then he had reformed, remarried, and lived an exemplary life. He and his present wife, Dorothy, sued the author and publisher for libel and invasion of privacy. The trial court granted summary judgment for the defendants, and the Court of Appeals affirmed. The court held that the Hayneses had no cause of action for libel because the defamatory statements about them were substantially true.]

Before POSNER, CHIEF JUDGE, and MANION and WOOD, CIRCUIT JUDGES.

■ POSNER, CHIEF JUDGE:

. . .

Even people who have nothing rationally to be ashamed of can be mortified by the publication of intimate details of their life. Most people in no way deformed or disfigured would nevertheless be deeply upset if nude photographs of themselves were published in a newspaper or a book. They feel the same way about photographs of their sexual activities, however "normal," or about a narrative of those activities, or about having their medical records publicized. Although it is well known that every human being defecates, no adult human being in our society wants a newspaper to show a picture of him defecating. The desire for privacy illustrated by these examples is a mysterious but deep fact about human personality. It deserves and in our society receives legal protection. The nature of the injury shows, by the way, that the defendants are wrong to argue that this branch of the right of privacy requires proof of special damages. [ ]

But this is not the character of the depictions of the Hayneses in The Promised Land. Although the plaintiffs claim that the book depicts their "sex life" and "ridicules" Luther Haynes's lovemaking (the reference is to the passage we quoted in which the author refers to Ruby's "devastating imitation" of Luther's manner when he would come home Friday nights in an amorous mood), these characterizations are misleading. No sexual act is described in the book. No intimate details are revealed. Entering one's bedroom with a bottle in one hand and a cigarette in the other is not foreplay. Ruby's speculation that Kevin's problems may have been due to Luther's having been a heavy drinker is not the narration of a sexual act.

. . .

. . . The revelations in the book are not about the intimate details of the Hayneses' life. They are about misconduct, in particular Luther's. (There is very little about Dorothy in the book, apart from the fact that she had an affair with Luther while he was still married to Ruby and that they eventually became and have remained lawfully married.) The revelations are about his heavy drinking, his unstable employment, his adultery, his irresponsible and neglectful behavior toward his wife and children. So we must consider cases in which the right of privacy has been invoked as a shield against the revelation of previous misconduct.

Two early cases illustrate the range of judicial thinking. In Melvin v. Reid, 297 P. 91 (Cal. App. 1931), the plaintiff was a former prostitute, who had been prosecuted but acquitted of murder. She later had married and (she alleged) for seven years had lived a blameless respectable life in a community in which her lurid past was unknown—when all was revealed in a movie about the murder case which used her maiden name. The court held that these allegations stated a claim for invasion of privacy. The Hayneses' claim is similar although less dramatic. They have been a respectable married couple for two decades. Luther's alcohol problem is behind him. He has steady employment as a doorman. His wife is a nurse, and in 1990 he told Lemann that the couple's combined income was $60,000 a year. He is not in trouble with the domestic relations court. He is a deacon of his church. He has come a long way from sharecropping in Mississippi and public housing in Chicago and he and his wife want to bury their past just as Mrs. Melvin wanted to do and in Melvin v. Reid was held entitled to do. [ ] In Luther Haynes's own words, from his deposition, "I know I haven't been no angel, but since almost 30 years ago I have turned my life completely around. I stopped the drinking and all this bad habits and stuff like that, which I deny, some of [it] I didn't deny, because I have changed my life. It take me almost 30 years to change it and I am deeply in my church. I look good in the eyes of my church members and my community. Now, what is going to happen now when this public reads this garbage which I didn't tell Mr. Lemann to write? Then all this is going to go down the drain. And I worked like a son of a gun to build myself up in a good reputation and he has torn it down."

But with Melvin v. Reid compare Sidis v. F-R Publishing Corp., 113 F.2d 806 (2d Cir. 1940), another old case but one more consonant with modern thinking about the proper balance between the right of privacy and the freedom of the press. A child prodigy had flamed out; he was now an eccentric recluse. The New Yorker ran a "where is he now" article about him. The article, entitled "April Fool," did not reveal any misconduct by Sidis but it depicted him in mocking tones as a comical failure, in much the same way that the report of Ruby's "devastating imitation" of the amorous Luther Haynes could be thought to have depicted him as a comical failure, albeit with sinister consequences absent from Sidis's case. The invasion of Sidis's privacy was palpable. But the publisher won. No intimate physical details of Sidis's life had been revealed; and on the other side was the undoubted newsworthiness of a child prodigy, as of a woman prosecuted for murder. Sidis, unlike Mrs. Melvin, was not permitted to bury his past.

. . .

. . . People who do not desire the limelight and do not deliberately choose a way of life or course of conduct calculated to thrust them into it nevertheless have no legal right to extinguish it if the experiences that have befallen them are newsworthy, even if they would prefer that those experiences be kept private. The possibility of an involuntary loss of privacy is recognized in the modern formulations of this branch of the privacy tort, which require not only that the private facts publicized be such as would make a reasonable person deeply offended by such publicity but also that they be facts in which the public has no legitimate interest. [ ]

The two criteria, offensiveness and newsworthiness, are related. An individual, and more pertinently perhaps the community, is most offended by the publication of intimate personal facts when the community has no interest in them beyond the voyeuristic thrill of penetrating the wall of privacy that surrounds a stranger. The reader of a book about the black migration to the North would have no legitimate interest in the details of Luther Haynes's sex life; but no such details are disclosed. Such a reader does have a legitimate interest in the aspects of Luther's conduct that the book reveals. For one of Lemann's major themes is the transposition virtually intact of a sharecropper morality characterized by a family structure "matriarchal and elastic" and by an "extremely unstable" marriage bond to the slums of the northern cities, and the interaction, largely random and sometimes perverse, of that morality with governmental programs to alleviate poverty. Public aid policies discouraged Ruby and Luther from living together, public housing policies precipitated a marriage doomed to fail. No detail in the book claimed to invade the Hayneses' privacy is not germane to the story that the author wanted to tell, a story not only of legitimate but of transcendent public interest.

The Hayneses question whether the linkage between the author's theme and their private life really is organic. They point out that many social histories do not mention individuals at all, let alone by name. That is true. Much of social science, including social history, proceeds by abstraction, aggregation, and quantification rather than by case studies. . . . But it would be absurd to suggest that cliometric or other aggregative, impersonal methods of doing social history are the only proper way to go about it and presumptuous to claim even that they are the best way. Lemann's book has been praised to the skies by distinguished scholars, among them black scholars covering a large portion of the ideological spectrum—Henry Louis Gates, Jr., William Junius Wilson, and Patricia Williams. Lemann's methodology places the individual case history at center stage. If he cannot tell the story of Ruby Daniels without waivers from every person who she thinks did her wrong, he cannot write this book.

Well, argue the Hayneses, at least Lemann could have changed their names. But the use of pseudonyms would not have gotten Lemann and Knopf off the legal hook. The details of the Hayneses' lives recounted in the book would identify them unmistakably to anyone who has known the Hayneses well for a long time (members of their families, for example), or who knew them before they got married; and no more is required. . . . Lemann would have had to change some, perhaps many, of the details. But then he would no longer have been writing history. He would have been writing fiction. . . . Reporting the true facts about real people is necessary to "obviate any impression that the problems raised in the [book] are remote or hypothetical." [ ] And surely a composite portrait of ghetto residents would be attacked as racial stereotyping.

The Promised Land does not afford the reader a titillating glimpse of tabooed activities. The tone is decorous and restrained. Painful though it is for the Hayneses to see a past they would rather forget brought into the public view, the public needs the information conveyed by the book, including the information about Luther and Dorothy Haynes, in order to evaluate the profound social and political questions that the book raises. . . . [A]ll the discreditable facts about the Hayneses that are contained in judicial records are beyond the power of tort law to conceal; and the disclosure of those facts alone would strip away the Hayneses' privacy as effectively as The Promised Land has done. (This case, it could be argued, has stripped them of their privacy, since their story is now part of a judicial record—the record of this case.) We do not think it is an answer that Lemann got his facts from Ruby Daniels rather than from judicial records. The courts got the facts from Ruby. We cannot see what difference it makes that Lemann went to the source.

Ordinarily the evaluation and comparison of offensiveness and newsworthiness would be, like other questions of the application of a legal standard to the facts of a particular case, matters for a jury, not for a judge on a motion for summary judgment. But summary judgment is properly granted to a defendant when on the basis of the evidence obtained in pretrial discovery no reasonable jury could render a verdict for the plaintiff, [ ], and that is the situation here. . . .

. . .

Does it follow, as the Hayneses' lawyer asked us rhetorically at oral argument, that a journalist who wanted to write a book about contemporary sexual practices could include the intimate details of named living persons' sexual acts without the persons' consent? Not necessarily, although the revelation of such details in the memoirs of former spouses and lovers is common enough and rarely provokes a lawsuit even when the former spouse or lover is still alive. The core of the branch of privacy law with which we deal in this case is the protection of those intimate physical details the publicizing of which would be not merely embarrassing and painful but deeply shocking to the average person subjected to such exposure. The public has a legitimate interest in sexuality, but that interest may be outweighed in such a case by the injury to the sensibilities of the person made use of by the author in such a way. [ ] At least the balance would be sufficiently close to preclude summary judgment for the author and publisher. [ ]

The judgment for the defendants is AFFIRMED.

NOTES AND QUESTIONS

1.   Before he became a judge, the author of the *Haynes* opinion suggested that a person who seeks to withhold some part of his or her past is trying to present a misrepresentation to the public. Although the individual is free to try to hide this information, Professor Posner argued that the law should not

impose sanctions on those who tell the public the truth about such a person. Richard Posner, The Right of Privacy, 12 Ga. L. Rev. 393 (1978). Is that consistent with the view of privacy he took in *Haynes*?

2.   Judge Posner's assertion that offensiveness and newsworthiness are related criteria is unusual. Courts usually analyze them as independent variables. Is it true that disclosures are more offensive if they are of no legitimate public concern?

3.   Would it make a difference in determining whether the disclosures were offensive or newsworthy if Ms. Daniels had discussed her life with her ex-husband on a tabloid TV show? Would it matter whether the tone of the discussion was salacious instead of decorous?

4.   The court emphasizes that its decision does not necessarily mean that authors are free to reveal intimate details of people's sex lives. If the author had been writing a book on race and sexuality, why wouldn't he be free to quote Ms. Daniels's detailed descriptions of Haynes's sex life on the same theory that enables him to quote her descriptions of Haynes's job history and drinking habits? Is the court suggesting that some disclosures would be actionable no matter how legitimate the public concern?

5.   In an unreported case, a later federal court decided that a CNN producer had a valid disclosure of private facts complaint when a newspaper reported that she had dated or "hooked up" with certain men. Benz v. Wash. Newspaper Publ'g Co., 2006 U.S. Dist. LEXIS 71827 (D.D.C. Sept. 29, 2006). Holding that the plaintiff's "personal, romantic life [was] not a matter of public concern," the court wrote that it was "persuaded that it is unlikely that an unmarried, professional woman in her 30s would want her private life about whom she had dated and had sexual relations revealed in the gossip column of a widely distributed newspaper." Should the focus be on what the plaintiff wishes kept from the public, what the public is interested in, or something else?

6.   Passage of time between the occurrence of an event and publication might be relevant to the offensiveness of the disclosure, the legitimacy of the public concern, or to whether the information is truly private. What role did it play in *Haynes*? In the *Melvin* and *Sidis* cases (both described in the principal case)? Does the issue have a constitutional dimension? Surprisingly, hints at the protection of such older information, similar to a right to be forgotten or right to erasure, appear in the Restatement. There, authors suggest that a once-robber turned obscure and repentant citizen whose past life of crime is revealed by a newspaper quite possibly has a publication of private facts claim. Restatement (Second) of Torts, § 652D, illustration 26. The constitutional problems with such an example are noted later in this chapter.

7.   Professor Sonja R. West argues that truthful autobiographical speech deserves First Amendment protection from privacy actions because it "adds vital knowledge to the public debate while also preserving the essence of human autonomy." Sonja R. West, The Story of Me: The Underprotection of Autobiographical Speech, 84 Wash. U. L. Rev. 905 (2006). Would this put an

individual's privacy at the mercy of every former spouse or lover who wishes to engage in autobiographical speech? Is all autobiographical speech inherently newsworthy?

8.   An important issue in public disclosure of private facts cases often is whether the disclosures of intimate details were germane to the matter of public concern. How did the court decide that the facts about Luther Haynes were "germane" to the broader themes of the book? Was "naming names" necessary? An argument frequently offered to justify naming a person about whom embarrassing private facts are disclosed is that identifying the person strengthens the credibility and impact of the article. In Gilbert v. Medical Economics Co., 665 F.2d 305 (10th Cir. 1981), the plaintiff was an anesthesiologist who had been involved in two alleged instances of malpractice. The magazine Medical Economics used her photograph and facts about her personal and professional life to illustrate a story headlined "Who Let This Doctor in the O.R.? The Story of a Fatal Breakdown in Medical Policing." The article discussed the plaintiff's psychiatric history and marital problems. She contended there was no evidence that these matters had any connection with the alleged malpractice. Upholding summary judgment for the magazine, the court held that the disclosures were "substantially relevant to the newsworthy topic of policing the medical profession" and that identifying her by name "obviate[d] any impression that the problems raised in the article are remote or hypothetical, thus providing an aura of immediacy and even urgency. . . ." The court also wrote that editors should be free to draw an inference that the personal matters had a causal relationship with the malpractice, even if no court or other tribunal had so found. "Because the inferences of causation drawn in this case are not, as a matter of law, so purely conjectural that no reasonable editor could draw them other than through guesswork and speculation, we hold that defendants did not abuse their editorial discretion in this case. . . . Although application of the newsworthiness standard to undisputed facts may well present a jury question in some cases, here objective and reasonable minds could not differ in finding the article in question to be privileged in its entirety. . . ." Is there any circumstance in which identifying the person *would not* enhance the credibility and impact of the story?

9.   Should newsworthiness be judged according to a reasonable editor standard or simply a reasonable person standard? Although the court in *Gilbert* applied a reasonable editor standard to determine newsworthiness, a California court appeared to reject that standard in Diaz v. Oakland Tribune, Inc., 139 Cal. App. 3d 118 (Cal. App. 1983). There, a newspaper columnist wrote: "The students at the College of Alameda will be surprised to learn that their student body president, Toni Diaz, is no lady, but is in fact a man whose real name is Antonio. Now, I realize, that in these times, such a matter is no big deal, but I suspect his classmates in P.E. 97 may wish to make other showering arrangements." Diaz, who had had a sex change operation, won a verdict of $250,000 compensatory and $525,000 punitive damages. The court of appeals reversed because of errors in the jury instructions, but rejected the defendants' argument that the newsworthiness issue should not have been submitted to the jury. The court then went on to

analyze the newsworthiness of the article without reference to editorial judgment:

> [W]e find little if any connection between the information disclosed and Diaz's fitness for office. The fact that she is a transsexual does not adversely reflect on her honesty or judgment. . . . Nor does the fact that she was the first woman student body president, in itself, warrant that her entire private life be open to public inspection. . . . Nor is there merit to defendants' claim that the changing roles of women in society make this story newsworthy. . . . Therefore we conclude that the jury was the proper body to answer the question whether the article was newsworthy or whether it extended beyond the bounds of decency.

The court held that the evidence was sufficient to support an award of punitive damages, although it cautioned the trial judge to scrutinize any such award on retrial to be sure it was not excessive. It held that the award of $250,000 compensatory damages, almost all for emotional distress, was not excessive as a matter of law. After this decision the parties settled for a sum reported to be substantial.

10.   What role, if any, should journalism ethics codes play in determinations of newsworthiness? The Society of Professional Journalists, an organization to which many news reporters and editors belong, has a well-respected ethics code that suggests that ethical publishers consider "potential harm or discomfort" created by a story, "[a]void pandering to lurid curiosity," "[s]how compassion for those who may be affected by news," and "[r]ealize that private people have a greater right to control information about themselves than public figures." Should such provisions provide any guidance in a newsworthiness determination? The organization suggests not, but a small number of courts have used them in this way. See, e.g., Conradt v. NBC, 536 F. Supp. 2d 380 (S.D.N.Y. 2008), in which the court used the SPJ Code of Ethics to find potential tort liability on the part of NBC reporters who had recorded the attempted arrest of a former prosecutor who then committed suicide.

11.   Consider the following definition for newsworthiness:

> Because the Supreme Court has warned courts to be "chary of deciding what is and is not news," the publication of any truthful information is presumptively newsworthy and of public interest and, therefore, is protected from tort-based and related claims. This presumption of newsworthiness may be overcome only in truly exceptional cases, when the degradation of human dignity caused by the disclosure clearly outweighs the public's interest in the disclosure.

Amy Gajda, The First Amendment Bubble (Harvard Univ. Press 2015).

Is such a definition, including its presumption of newsworthiness, too protective of media? Or is its focus on the dignity of the individual likely to cause judges to focus too strongly on emotional harm over newsworthiness?

Would any of the cases in this chapter likely have a different outcome if such a test had been used?

12. Professor Erwin Chemerinsky contends that it is "inherently at odds with the freedom of speech protected by the First Amendment" to have courts determine whether speech deals with a matter of "legitimate public interest." He would therefore restrict the tort to cases involving disclosures that create a "substantial threat to safety." Erwin Chemerinsky, Protecting Truthful Speech: Narrowing the Tort of Public Disclosure of Private Facts, 11 Chapman L. Rev. 423, 425 (2008).

Public Figures. In *Haynes*, the court was concerned with a generalized description of a private figure's romantic life. Twenty years later the gossip website Gawker published a surreptitiously recorded and graphic sex tape featuring celebrity wrestler Hulk Hogan. In response to Hogan's invasion of privacy claim, Gawker argued that it had the right to decide for itself and for its readers what was newsworthy. Gawker Media v. Bollea, 129 So. 3d 1196 (Fla. Dist. Ct. App. 2014).

Deciding a preliminary injunction motion filed by Hogan, the court seemed to agree with Gawker's assessment of its rights. "[I]t was within Gawker Media's editorial discretion to publish the written report and video excerpts," the court held, noting that, under Florida law, it was the "primary function of the publisher to determine what is newsworthy and that the court should generally not substitute its judgment for that of the publisher."

The court dismissed the authority of an earlier case offered as persuasive precedent by Hogan. That case involved a videotape made by the actor Pamela Anderson Lee and musician Brett Michaels of their sexual activities. An Internet company had obtained the sex tape, and Michaels and Lee sought an injunction against distribution on various grounds, including violation of their rights to privacy and copyright infringement. In considering the privacy claim, the judge noted that Lee had appeared nude in "magazines, movies and publicly distributed videotapes." He also noted that she had appeared in a widely distributed videotape "depicting sexual relations between Lee and her husband Tommy Lee." The judge wrote, however, that he was "not prepared to conclude that public exposure of one sexual encounter forever removes a person's privacy interest in all subsequent and previous sexual encounters." Moreover, Michaels also had a "privacy interest in his sex life," and the "visual and aural details" of sexual relations "are ordinarily considered private even for celebrities." With regard to newsworthiness, the judge wrote that "[i]t is difficult if not impossible to articulate a social value that will be advanced by dissemination of the [sex] Tape." There, the judge granted a preliminary injunction barring display of the tape on the grounds that Lee and Michaels had showed a likelihood of success on the merits of their claims that distribution would violate their rights of publicity and privacy and infringe their copyrights. See Michaels v. Internet Entertainment Group, Inc., 5 F. Supp. 2d 823 (C.D. Cal. 1998).

The *Gawker* court dismissed the *Michaels* case as one focused narrowly on commercial interests in a sex tape, not on the tape's newsworthiness. In contrast, it noted the more journalistic tones in the Hogan-Gawker dispute: "Gawker Media has not attempted to sell the Sex Tape or any of the material creating the instant controversy, for that matter [but rather] reported on [the wrestler's] extramarital affair and complementary thereto posted excerpts from the video."

Even though Gawker won the preliminary injunction motions, Hulk Hogan's underlying privacy claims continued in Florida state court. In 2016, a Florida jury awarded Hogan $150 million in damages. Gawker promised an appeal. Nick Madigan, Jury Tacks On $25 Million to Gawker's Bill in Hulk Hogan Case, N.Y. Times, Mar. 21, 2016.

Of some relevance here, the Restatement suggests in part that even public figures have privacy rights in sexual information: while "the home life and daily habits of a motion picture actress may be of legitimate and reasonable interest to the public that sees her on the screen," the Restatement reads, this is not unlimited and "some intimate details of her life, such as sexual relations," she is entitled to keep private. Generally, the Restatement suggests that "[s]exual relations, for example, are normally entirely private matters." Restatement (Second) of Torts, § 652D (1977), comments b and h. Is a line appropriately drawn at sexual information? The Restatement embraces a broad definition for newsworthiness—including news items "of more or less deplorable popular appeal"—but draws a "common decency" line at "morbid and sensational prying for its own sake with which a reasonable member of the public, with decent standards, would say that he had no concern." Is the Hulk Hogan sex tape sensational prying or did its many viewers prove its appeal and legitimate interest? Does the jury verdict in the Hogan case suggest that the Restatement's description of community standards concerning publication of graphic sexual information remains accurate? Relevant to the question of community standards, a California statute that became effective in 2015 gives a plaintiff the right to bring a civil action against anyone who "intentionally distributes by any means a photograph, film, videotape, recording, or any other reproduction" of the plaintiff without consent if the material "exposes an intimate body part" or shows the plaintiff in a sexual act. The statute exempts material that "constitutes a matter of public concern" without defining that phrase further. Cal. Civ. Code § 1708.85 (2015). If Hogan had sued Gawker pursuant to this statute, would Gawker likely have avoided liability? Or is this statute one very much in line with the balancing test in the Restatement's provision against the publication of private facts?

Involuntary Public Figures. One of the first significant publication of private fact cases to raise directly the issue of privacy in sexual information involved an involuntary public figure. During an assassination attempt on President Ford in San Francisco, Oliver Sipple struck the arm of the assailant, Sara Jane Moore, as she sought to aim a second shot at the President. Sipple was the object of extensive media attention, including stories that disclosed his homosexuality and that suggested that because of it Ford had not expressed appropriate gratitude to Sipple. Sipple, asserting that some relatives did not know of his sexual orientation, sued the San Francisco Chronicle. The newspaper defended in part on the argument that privacy was not involved because Sipple had marched in gay parades and had acknowledged that multiple people in San Francisco knew he was gay.

Summary judgment for the paper was affirmed on appeal. First, the facts were not private. Second, they were newsworthy. The article was prompted by "legitimate political considerations, i.e., to dispel the false public opinion that gays were timid, weak and unheroic figures," the court wrote, "and to raise the equally important political question whether the President of the United States entertained a discriminatory attitude or bias against a minority group such as homosexuals." Sipple v. Chronicle Publishing Co., 154 Cal. App. 3d 1040 (Cal. App. 1984). Was the court correct in deciding that it was acceptable to reveal one individual's private life for reasons of better public understanding? To journalists, the use of an individual's story to tell a broader tale as the court suggested was appropriate in *Sipple* is known as "personalization," and helps to make a news story more interesting. Note how often the personalization of a story sparks a publication of private fact lawsuit in the case descriptions in this chapter.

Privacy Rights of Survivors. The cause of action for invasion of privacy, like that for defamation, is usually considered personal. That means it usually does not survive the death of the victim and does not give rise to any cause of action by survivors. Occasionally, however, courts permit survivors to recover for what appears to be an invasion of a decedent's privacy. In Reid v. Pierce County, 961 P.2d 333 (Wash. 1998), employees of the county medical examiner displayed autopsy photos at cocktail parties and in scrapbooks compiled for their own amusement. The Washington Supreme Court held that surviving relatives had a cause of action for invasion of their common law right of privacy. Citing a long line of cases recognizing a cause of action for mutilating or mishandling corpses, the court suggested that misuse of photos differed only in degree. The existence of a statute making autopsy records confidential and a county policy forbidding employees from taking autopsy photos for personal purposes reinforced the court's conclusion that "the immediate relatives of a decedent have a protectable privacy interest in the autopsy records of the decedent." The court therefore reversed the trial court's dismissal of the relatives' invasion of privacy claim.

In a similar case a decade later, a California appeals court found that surviving family members had a valid publication of private facts claim after two police officers sent friends Halloween emails featuring gruesome images of a teenager who had died in a car accident. Catsouras v. Department of California Highway Patrol, 181 Cal. App. 4th 856 (Cal. App. 2010). "As cases from other jurisdictions make plain," the court wrote, "family members have a common law privacy right in the death images of a decedent." The court pointedly noted that the case did not involve press freedoms, however. Should the type of defendant in such a lawsuit matter? What if a website that specifically publishes death images had published the gruesome images? Should such a publication be protected by press freedoms when publication by a police officer is not?

In a case involving mainstream media's publication of a death image, Green v. Chicago Tribune Co., 675 N.E.2d 249 (Ill. App. Ct. 1996), the court suggested that a valid privacy right may exist in surviving relatives even when the underlying case involves the press. "In the present case," the court wrote in finding a valid publication of private facts claim, "the complaint alleges the Tribune did substantially publicize plaintiff . . . by publishing a photograph of her dead son . . . and by identifying her as [his] mother" in addition to publishing words she said to her son's body. The case quickly settled thereafter.

A Ninth Circuit decision also seemingly recognized a right of privacy in survivors under somewhat similar facts. See Marsh v. County of San Diego, 680 F.3d 1148 (9th Cir. 2012) (holding that a child's mother "has a constitutionally protected right to privacy over her child's death images" and that prosecutors who give them to media can be liable for their actions). And in the context of exempting private matters from disclosure under the federal Freedom of Information Act, the Supreme Court has held that survivors have cognizable privacy interests. See National Archives and Records Administration v. Favish. Both *Marsh* and *Favish* are discussed more fully in Chapter Ten. .

The Publicity Requirement. Recall that the Restatement requires that the plaintiff prove "publicity" for a valid claim; publicity "means that the matter is made public," the Restatement reads, "by communicating it to the public at large, or to so many persons that the matter must be regarded as substantially certain to become one of public knowledge." Restatement (Second) of Torts, § 652D, comment a. Traditionally, the publicity requirement is met if a defendant communicates to approximately ten people, though the precise number varies by jurisdiction. What if the defendant shares scandalous information with the sole publisher of a scandal-focused website? Should sharing with one person likely to publish more widely suffice for publicity today? Some recent courts have suggested as much. See Judge v. Saltz Plastic Surgery, 44 Media L. Rep. 1326, n.6 (Utah 2016) (holding that a jury could "very reasonably and sensibly conclude" that giving information to one reporter who was doing a story on the topic would satisfy the publicity requirement).

Rejecting the Privacy Action. All but a handful of states recognize the "private facts" tort. The most notable of the states that refuse the action is New York, where the Court of Appeals rejected the idea of common law remedies for invasion of privacy in 1902 and has not retreated from that position. See Roberson v. Rochester Folding Box Co., 64 N.E. 442 (N.Y. 1902). In New York the only remedy for any of the four types of tortious invasion of privacy is a statute that permits actions for damages and injunctions for unauthorized use of a person's name or likeness, but only if the use is "for advertising purposes, or for the purposes of trade." N.Y. Civ. Rts. Law §§ 50–51.

That New York statute was found to be an insufficient legal safeguard for a group of people including children who were photographed in their homes by a neighbor professional photographer with a telephoto camera lens. The neighbor later published the photos on the Internet and sold them as art photography in a series he titled The Neighbors. The plaintiffs lived in a New York City apartment building with a largely glass façade. "Defendant photographed the building's residents surreptitiously," the court explained, "hiding himself in the shadows of his darkened apartment." While refusing to find the neighbors' claims valid under the statute because of the statute's advertising-heavy focus, the court wrote that the case "highlight[ed] the limitations of New York's statutory privacy tort as a means of redressing harm that may be caused by this type of technological home invasion and exposure of private life." The court also rejected the plaintiffs' intentional infliction of emotional distress claims on the grounds that the photographers' conduct was not "atrocious, indecent and utterly despicable," even though it was "invasive" and he had targeted plaintiffs and their children in their homes. The opinion concluded with a call to the legislature to act: "Needless to say, as illustrated by the troubling facts here, in these times of heightened threats to privacy posed by new and ever more invasive technologies," the court wrote, "we call upon the Legislature to revisit this important issue." Foster v. Svenson, 128 A.D.3d 150 (N.Y. App. Div. 2015).

Other state courts have also rejected the tort, albeit on different grounds. In Anderson v. Fisher Broadcasting Companies, Inc., 712 P.2d 803 (Or. 1986), the court rejected the privacy action brought by an accident victim against a television station that had used film of him bleeding and in pain in promotional spots for a forthcoming special news report on emergency medical treatment. In so doing, the court observed:

What is "private" so as to make its publication offensive likely differs among communities, between generations, and among ethnic, religious, or other social groups, as well as among individuals. Likewise, one reader's or viewer's "news" is

another's tedium or trivia. The editorial judgment of what is
"newsworthy" is not so readily submitted to the ad hoc review of
a jury as [the lower court] believed. It is not properly a
community standard. Even when some editors themselves vie to
tailor "news" to satisfy popular tastes, others may believe that
the community should see or hear facts or ideas that the
majority finds uninteresting or offensive.

The court said Oregon does not recognize a cause of action for public
disclosure "unless the manner or purpose of defendant's conduct is
wrongful in some respect apart from causing the plaintiff's hurt feelings."
See also Hall v. Post, 372 S.E.2d 711 (N.C. 1988), rejecting the action
largely because it will generally duplicate the action for intentional
infliction of emotional distress.

2.   CONSTITUTIONAL LIMITATIONS

We turn now to cases in which the issue is not the tort law of privacy,
but constitutional limitations on that law. In fact, that distinction is hard
to maintain. In many of the cases we considered above, discussions of tort
law were intermingled with discussions about constitutional
ramifications. In the *Haynes* case, for example, omitted portions of the
opinion discuss the constitutional cases in this section for guidance in
interpreting the offensiveness and newsworthiness elements of the tort.
Although we separate the tort and constitutional aspects for the sake of
analytical clarity, it is important to recognize that courts often
intermingle them.

In 1975 the Supreme Court decided its first "private facts" case. Cox
Broadcasting Corp. v. Cohn, 420 U.S. 469 (1975). A 17-year-old had been
raped in Georgia and did not survive. A Georgia criminal statute made it
a misdemeanor for "any news media or any other person to print and
publish, broadcast, televise or disseminate through any other medium of
public discussion . . . the name or identity of any female who may have
been raped." During a recess in a criminal hearing in the case, a
television reporter was allowed to inspect the indictment, which named
the victim. Cox Broadcasting used the victim's name in reporting on the
case that night.

The victim's father brought a tort action for disclosure of his
daughter's name. The state supreme court held that the complaint stated
a common law action for damages. A First Amendment defense was
rejected on the ground that the statute was an authoritative declaration
that Georgia considered a rape victim's name not to be a matter of public
concern. The court could discern "no public interest or general concern
about the identity of the victim of such a crime as will make the right to
disclose the identity of the victim rise to the level of First Amendment
protection."

The Supreme Court reversed. Cox Broadcasting argued for a "broad holding that the press may not be made criminally or civilly liable for publishing information that is neither false nor misleading but absolutely accurate, however damaging it may be to reputation or individual sensibilities." Justice White's majority opinion avoided the broad question by addressing the decidedly narrower question of "whether the State may impose sanctions on the accurate publication of the name of a rape victim obtained from public records—more specifically, from judicial records which are maintained in connection with a public prosecution and which themselves are open to public inspection. We are convinced that the State may not do so."

Justice White noted that members of the public rely on the press to bring them facts about the operation of government in a convenient form. Without such information, "most of us and many of our representatives would be unable to vote intelligently or to register opinions on the administration of government generally." The "commission of crime, prosecutions resulting from it, and judicial proceedings arising from the prosecutions . . . are without question events of legitimate concern to the public and consequently fall within the responsibility of the press to report the operations of government."

Justice White noted that the developing law of privacy afforded the press a privilege to report the events of judicial proceedings. "By placing the information in the public domain on official court records, the State must be presumed to have concluded that the public interest was thereby being served. Public records by nature are of interest to those concerned with the administration of government, and a public benefit is performed by the reporting of the true contents of the records by the media." Freedom to publish material released by government is of "critical importance to our type of government in which the citizenry is the final judge of the proper conduct of public business." In such situations, "the States may not impose sanctions on the publication of truthful information contained in official court records open to public inspection."

The Court was "reluctant to embark on a course that would make public records generally available to the media but forbid their publication if offensive to the sensibilities of the supposed reasonable man. Such a rule would make it very difficult for the media to inform citizens about the public business and yet stay within the law. The rule would invite timidity and self-censorship and very likely lead to the suppression of many items that would otherwise be published and that should be made available to the public. . . . If there are privacy interests to be protected in judicial proceedings, the States must respond by means which avoid public documentation or other exposure of private information. Once true information is disclosed in public court documents open to public inspection, the press cannot be sanctioned for publishing it." The Court noted that it was implying nothing about any constitutional questions that might arise from a state policy of closing judicial proceedings or records to public access.

Chief Justice Burger concurred only in the judgment. Justice Rehnquist dissented on the ground that the state courts had not rendered a final judgment.

Old Court Records. Does *Cox Broadcasting* protect the disclosure of privacy-invading information from court records indefinitely? Before that decision, some courts had held that matters of public record could become private with the passage of time. In Briscoe v. Reader's Digest Association, 483 P.2d 34 (Cal. 1971), an article reported that 11 years earlier plaintiff had hijacked a truck in Kentucky, for which he had served time. The subject sued for invasion of privacy, alleging that he had been rehabilitated and was living in California with family and friends who did not know of his past. Although the conviction was a matter of public record, the court held that the complaint stated a cause of action. "Ideally, his neighbors should recognize his present worth and forget his past life of shame. But men are not so divine as to forgive the past trespasses of others, and plaintiff therefore endeavored to reveal as little as possible of his past life."

The California Supreme Court eventually overruled *Briscoe*, holding that *Cox Broadcasting* and subsequent Supreme Court cases had established an absolute right of the press to publish information from open court records regardless of the passage of time. A state interest in the rehabilitation of offenders falls short of the "state interest of the highest order" that would be necessary to permit liability. Gates v. Discovery Communications, Inc., 101 P.3d 552 (Cal. 2004). The plaintiff in *Gates* was a man who had served a three-year prison term as an accessory to murder but had led a lawful, productive, and obscure life after his release. Thirteen years after the murder, the defendants broadcast a television documentary about the crime, including the name and photo of the plaintiff. The court held that "[n]either that the defendants' documentary was of an historical nature nor that it involved 'reenactments,' rather than first-hand coverage, of the events reported diminishes any constitutional protection it enjoys."

———————

After *Cox Broadcasting* the Court decided three cases which, though not themselves tort actions for invasion of privacy, were destined to affect the Court's response to the public disclosure tort. Two of these cases are detailed in Chapter Two: *Landmark Communications,* in which the Court held that a state could not fine a newspaper for reporting that a judge was under investigation, and *Daily Mail,* which held that the state could not prosecute a newspaper for identifying a juvenile suspect in a homicide case. The third case was Oklahoma Publishing Co. v. District Court, 430 U.S. 308 (1977), in which a judge admitted the press and public to a juvenile hearing but subsequently ordered the press not to publish the offender's name or photograph. The Court held that because the information had been publicly revealed at the hearing, the judge could not prohibit the media from publishing it. Then came the following case to solidify the strength of the protection for media in such cases.

Florida Star v. B.J.F.

Supreme Court of the United States, 1989.
491 U.S. 524.

■ JUSTICE MARSHALL delivered the opinion of the Court.

Florida Stat. section 794.03 (1987) makes it unlawful to "print, publish, or broadcast . . . in any instrument of mass communication" the name of the victim of a sexual offense. Pursuant to this statute, appellant The Florida Star was found civilly liable for publishing the name of a rape victim which it had obtained from a publicly released police report. The issue presented here is whether this result comports with the First Amendment. We hold that it does not.

I

The Florida Star is a weekly newspaper which serves the community of Jacksonville, Florida, and which has an average circulation of approximately 18,000 copies. A regular feature of the newspaper is its "Police Reports" section. The section, typically two to three pages in length, contains brief articles describing local criminal incidents under police investigation. On October 20, 1983, appellee B.J.F. reported to the Duval County, Florida, Sheriff's Department (the Department) that she had been robbed and sexually assaulted by an unknown assailant. The Department prepared a report on the incident which identified B.J.F., by her full name. The Department then placed the report in its press room. The Department does not restrict access either to the press room or to the reports made available therein.

A Florida Star reporter-trainee sent to the press room copied the police report verbatim, including B.J.F.'s full name, on a blank duplicate of the Department's forms. A Florida Star reporter then prepared a one-paragraph article about the crime, derived entirely from the trainee's copy of the police report. The article included B.J.F.'s full name. It appeared in the "Robberies" subsection of the "Police Reports" section on October 29, 1983, one of fifty-four police blotter stories in that day's edition. . . .

In printing B.J.F.'s full name, The Florida Star violated its internal policy of not publishing the names of sexual offense victims.

[B.J.F. sued the newspaper on the theory that the newspaper violated the portion of the statute quoted above and the Sheriff's Department on the theory that it violated another provision making it a crime "to cause or allow" information identifying a victim of a sexual offense to be published or broadcast. The Sheriff's Department settled for $2,500. The Star's motion to dismiss was denied.]

At the ensuing day-long trial, B.J.F. testified that she had suffered emotional distress from the publication of her name. She stated that she had heard about the article from fellow workers and acquaintances; that her mother had received several threatening phone calls from a man who stated that he would rape B.J.F. again; and that these events had forced B.J.F. to change her phone number and residence, to seek police protection, and to obtain mental health counseling. In defense, The Florida Star put forth evidence indicating that the newspaper had learned B.J.F.'s name from the incident report released by the Department, and that the newspaper's violation of its internal rule against publishing the names of sexual offense victims was inadvertent.

At the close of B.J.F.'s case, and again at the close of its defense, The Florida Star moved for a directed verdict. On both occasions, the trial judge denied these motions. He ruled from the bench that section 794.03 was constitutional because it reflected a proper balance between the First Amendment and privacy rights, as it applied only to a narrow set of "rather sensitive . . . criminal offenses." [ ] At the close of the newspaper's defense, the judge granted B.J.F.'s motion for a directed verdict on the issue of negligence, finding the newspaper per se negligent based upon its violation of section 794.03. [ ] This ruling left the jury to consider only the questions of causation and damages. The judge instructed the jury that it could award B.J.F. punitive damages if it found that the newspaper had "acted with reckless indifference to the rights of others." [ ] The jury awarded B.J.F. $75,000 in compensatory damages and $25,000 in punitive damages. Against the actual damage award, the judge set off B.J.F.'s settlement with the Department.

The First District Court of Appeal affirmed in a three-paragraph per curiam opinion. . . . The Supreme Court of Florida denied discretionary review.

The Florida Star appealed to this Court. We noted probable jurisdiction, [ ], and now reverse.

II

The tension between the right which the First Amendment accords to a free press, on the one hand, and the protections which various statutes and common-law doctrines accord to personal privacy against the publication of truthful information, on the other, is a subject we have addressed several times in recent years. Our decisions in cases involving government attempts to sanction the accurate dissemination of information as invasive of privacy, have not, however, exhaustively considered this conflict. On the contrary, although our decisions have without exception upheld the press' right to publish, we have emphasized each time that we were resolving this conflict only as it arose in a discrete factual context.

The parties to this case frame their contentions in light of a trilogy of cases which have presented, in different contexts, the conflict between truthful reporting and state-protected privacy interests. [The Court briefly reviewed *Cox Broadcasting, Oklahoma Publishing,* and *Daily Mail.*]

Appellant takes the position that this case is indistinguishable from *Cox Broadcasting.* [ ] Alternatively, it urges that our decisions in the above trilogy, and in other cases in which we have held that the right of the press to publish truth overcame asserted interests other than personal privacy, can be distilled to yield a broader First Amendment principle that the press may never be punished, civilly or criminally, for publishing the truth. [ ] Appellee counters that the privacy trilogy is inapposite, because in each case the private information already appeared on a "public record," [ ] and because the privacy interests at stake were far less profound than in the present case. [ ] In the alternative, appellee urges that *Cox Broadcasting* be overruled and replaced with a categorical rule that publication of the name of a rape victim never enjoys constitutional protection. [ ]

We conclude that imposing damages on appellant for publishing B.J.F.'s name violates the First Amendment, although not for either of the reasons appellant urges. Despite the strong resemblance this case bears to *Cox Broadcasting,* that case cannot fairly be read as controlling here. The name of the rape victim in that case was obtained from courthouse records that were open to public inspection, a fact which Justice White's opinion for the Court repeatedly noted, [ ] (noting "special protected nature of accurate reports of *judicial* proceedings") (emphasis added). Significantly, one of the reasons we gave in *Cox Broadcasting* for invalidating the challenged damages award was the important role the press plays in subjecting trials to public scrutiny and thereby helping guarantee their fairness. [ ] That role is not directly compromised where, as here, the information in question comes from a police report prepared and disseminated at a time at which not only had no adversarial criminal proceedings begun, but no suspect had been identified.

Nor need we accept appellant's invitation to hold broadly that truthful publication may never be punished consistent with the First Amendment. Our cases have carefully eschewed reaching this ultimate question, mindful that the future may bring scenarios which prudence counsels our not resolving anticipatorily. [ ] Indeed, in *Cox Broadcasting,* we pointedly refused to answer even the less sweeping question "whether truthful publications may ever be subjected to civil or criminal liability" for invading "an area of privacy" defined by the State. [ ] Respecting the fact that press freedom and privacy rights are both "plainly rooted in the traditions and significant concerns of our society," we instead focused on the less sweeping issue of "whether the State may impose sanctions on the accurate publication of the name of a rape victim obtained from public records—more specifically, from judicial records which are maintained in connection with a public prosecution and which themselves are open to public inspection." [ ] We continue to believe that the sensitivity and significance of the interests presented in clashes between First Amendment and privacy rights counsel relying on limited principles that sweep no more broadly than the appropriate context of the instant case.

In our view, this case is appropriately analyzed with reference to such a limited First Amendment principle. It is the one, in fact, which we articulated in *Daily Mail* in our synthesis of prior cases involving attempts to punish truthful publication: "[I]f a newspaper lawfully obtains truthful information about a matter of public significance then state officials may not constitutionally punish publication of the information, absent a need to further a state interest of the highest order." [ ] According the press the ample protection provided by that principle is supported by at least three separate considerations, in addition to, of course, the overarching "public interest, secured by the Constitution, in the dissemination of truth." [ ] The cases on which the *Daily Mail* synthesis relied demonstrate these considerations.

First, because the *Daily Mail* formulation only protects the publication of information which a newspaper has "lawfully obtain[ed]," [ ], the government retains ample means of safeguarding significant interests upon which publication may impinge, including protecting a rape victim's anonymity. To the extent sensitive information rests in private hands, the government may under some circumstances forbid its non-consensual acquisition, thereby bringing outside of the *Daily Mail* principle the publication of any information so acquired. To the extent sensitive information is in the government's custody, it has even greater power to forestall or mitigate the injury caused by its release. The government may classify certain information, establish and enforce procedures ensuring its redacted release, and extend a damages remedy against the government or its officials where the government's mishandling of sensitive information leads to its dissemination. Where information is entrusted to the government, a less drastic means than punishing truthful publication almost always exists for guarding against the dissemination of private facts. [ ][8]

A second consideration undergirding the *Daily Mail* principle is the fact that punishing the press for its dissemination of information which is already publicly available is relatively unlikely to advance the interests in the service of which the State seeks to act. It is not, of course, always the case that information lawfully acquired by the press is known, or accessible, to others. But where the government has made certain

---

[8] The *Daily Mail* principle does not settle the issue of whether, in cases where information has been acquired *unlawfully* by a newspaper or by a source, government may ever punish not only the unlawful acquisition, but the ensuing publication as well. This issue was raised but not definitively resolved in New York Times Co. v. United States, 403 U.S. 713 (1971), and reserved in [*Landmark Communications*]. We have no occasion to address it here.

information publicly available, it is highly anomalous to sanction persons other than the source of its release. . . .

A third and final consideration is the "timidity and self-censorship" which may result from allowing the media to be punished for publishing certain truthful information. [ ] *Cox Broadcasting* noted this concern with overdeterrence in the context of information made public through official court records, but the fear of excessive media self-suppression is applicable as well to other information released without qualification, by the government. A contrary rule, [denying] protection to those who rely on the government's implied representations of the lawfulness of dissemination, would force upon the media the onerous obligation of sifting through government press releases, reports, and pronouncements to prune out material arguably unlawful for publication. This situation could inhere even where the newspaper's sole object was to reproduce, with no substantial change, the government's rendition of the event in question.

Applied to the instant case, the *Daily Mail* principle clearly commands reversal. The first inquiry is whether the newspaper "lawfully obtain[ed] truthful information about a matter of public significance." [ ] It is undisputed that the news article describing the assault on B.J.F. was accurate. In addition, appellant lawfully obtained B.J.F.'s name. Appellee's argument to the contrary is based on the fact that under Florida law, police reports which reveal the identity of the victim of a sexual offense are not among the matters of "public record" which the public, by law, is entitled to inspect. [ ] But the fact that the state officials are not required to disclose such reports does not make it unlawful for a newspaper to receive them when furnished by the government. Nor does the fact that the Department apparently failed to fulfill its obligation under section 794.03 not to "cause or allow to be . . . published" the name of a sexual offense victim make the newspaper's ensuing receipt of this information unlawful. Even assuming the Constitution permitted a State to proscribe *receipt* of information, Florida has not taken this step. It is clear, furthermore, that the news article concerned "a matter of public significance," [ ] in the sense in which the *Daily Mail* synthesis of prior cases used that term. That is, the article generally, as opposed to the specific identity contained within it, involved a matter of paramount public import: the commission, and investigation, of a violent crime which had been reported to authorities. [ ]

The second inquiry is whether imposing liability on appellant pursuant to section 794.03 serves "a need to further a state interest of the highest order." [*Daily Mail*] Appellee argues that a rule punishing publication furthers three closely related interests: the privacy of victims of sexual offenses; the physical safety of such victims, who may be targeted for retaliation if their names become known to their assailants;

and the goal of encouraging victims of such crimes to report these offenses without fear of exposure. [ ]

At a time in which we are daily reminded of the tragic reality of rape, it is undeniable that these are highly significant interests, a fact underscored by the Florida Legislature's explicit attempt to protect these interests by enacting a criminal statute prohibiting much dissemination of victim identities. We accordingly do not rule out the possibility that, in a proper case, imposing civil sanctions for publication of the name of a rape victim might be so overwhelmingly necessary to advance these interests as to satisfy the *Daily Mail* standard. For three independent reasons, however, imposing liability for publication under the circumstances of this case is too precipitous a means of advancing these interests to convince us that there is a "need" within the meaning of the *Daily Mail* formulation for Florida to take this extreme step. [ ]

First is the manner in which appellant obtained the identifying information in question. As we have noted, where the government itself provides information to the media, it is most appropriate to assume that the government had, but failed to utilize, far more limited means of guarding against dissemination than the extreme step of punishing truthful speech. That assumption is richly borne out in this case. B.J.F.'s identity would never have come to light were it not for the erroneous, if inadvertent, inclusion by the Department of her full name in an accident report made available in a press room open to the public. Florida's policy against disclosure of rape victims' identities, reflected in section 794.03, was undercut by the Department's failure to abide by this policy. Where, as here, the government has failed to police itself in disseminating information, it is clear under *Cox Broadcasting, Oklahoma Publishing*, and *Landmark Communications* that the imposition of damages against the press for its subsequent publication can hardly be said to be a narrowly tailored means of safeguarding anonymity. [ ] Once the government has placed such information in the public domain, "reliance must rest upon the judgment of those who decide what to publish or broadcast," [*Cox Broadcasting*] and hopes for restitution must rest upon the willingness of the government to compensate victims for their loss of privacy, and to protect them from the other consequences of its mishandling of the information which these victims provided in confidence.

That appellant gained access to the information in question through a government news release makes it especially likely that, if liability were to be imposed, self-censorship would result. Reliance on a news release is a paradigmatically "routine newspaper reporting techniqu[e]." [*Daily Mail*] The government's issuance of such a release, without qualification, can only convey to recipients that the government considered dissemination lawful, and indeed expected the recipients to disseminate the information further. Had appellant merely reproduced the news release prepared and released by the Department, imposing civil damages would surely violate the First Amendment. The fact that appellant converted the police report into a news story by adding the linguistic connecting tissue necessary to transform the report's facts into full sentences cannot change this result.

A second problem with Florida's imposition of liability for publication is the broad sweep of the negligence per se standard applied under the civil cause of action implied from section 794.03. Unlike claims based on the common law tort of invasion of privacy, [ ] civil actions based on section 794.03 require no case-by-case findings that the disclosure of a fact about a person's private life was one that a reasonable person would find highly offensive. On the contrary, under the per se theory of negligence adopted by the courts below, liability follows automatically from publication. This is so regardless of whether the identity of the victim is already known throughout the community; whether the victim has voluntarily called public attention to the offense; or whether the identity of the victim has otherwise become a reasonable subject of public concern—because, perhaps, questions have arisen whether the victim fabricated an assault by a particular person. Nor is there a scienter requirement of any kind under section 794.03, engendering the perverse result that truthful publications challenged pursuant to this cause of action are less protected by the First Amendment than even the least protected defamatory falsehoods: those involving purely private figures, where liability is evaluated under a standard, usually applied by a jury, of ordinary negligence. See *Gertz v. Robert Welch, Inc.*, [ ]. We have previously noted the impermissibility of categorical prohibitions upon media access where important First Amendment interests are at stake. See Globe Newspaper Co. v. Superior Court, 457 U.S. 596, 608 (1982) (invalidating state statute providing for the categorical exclusion of the public from trials of sexual offenses involving juvenile victims.) More individualized adjudication is no less indispensable where the State, seeking to safeguard the anonymity of crime victims, sets its face against publication of their names.

Third, and finally, the facial underinclusiveness of section 794.03 raises serious doubts about whether Florida is, in fact, serving, with this statute, the significant interests which appellee invokes in support of affirmance. Section 794.03 prohibits the publication of identifying information only if this information appears in an "instrument of mass communication," a term the statute does not define. Section 794.03 does not prohibit the spread by other means of the identities of victims of sexual offenses. An individual who maliciously spreads word of the identity of a rape victim is thus not covered, despite the fact that the communication of such information to persons who live near, or work with, the victim may have consequences equally devastating as the exposure of her name to large numbers of strangers. [ ]

When a State attempts the extraordinary measure of punishing truthful publication in the name of privacy, it must demonstrate its commitment to advancing this interest by applying its prohibition evenhandedly, to the smalltime disseminator as well as the media giant. Where important First Amendment interests are at stake, the mass scope of disclosure is not an acceptable surrogate for injury. A ban on disclosures effected by "instrument[s] of mass communication" simply cannot be defended on the ground that partial prohibitions may effect partial relief. [ ] Without more careful and inclusive precautions against alternative forms of dissemination, we cannot conclude that Florida's selective ban on publication by the mass media satisfactorily accomplishes its stated purpose.

III

Our holding today is limited. We do not hold that truthful publication is automatically constitutionally protected, or that there is no zone of personal privacy within which the State may protect the individual from intrusion by the press, or even that a State may never punish publication of the name of a victim of a sexual offense. We hold only that where a newspaper publishes truthful information which it has lawfully obtained, punishment may lawfully be imposed, if at all, only when narrowly tailored to a state interest of the highest order, and that no such interest is satisfactorily served by imposing liability . . . under the facts of this case. The decision below is therefore reversed.

■ JUSTICE SCALIA, concurring in part and concurring in the judgment.

I think it sufficient to decide this case to rely upon the third ground set forth in the Court's opinion [ ]: that a law cannot be regarded as protecting an interest "of the highest order" [ ], and thus as justifying a restriction upon truthful speech, when it leaves appreciable damage to that supposedly vital interest unprohibited. I would anticipate that the rape victim's discomfort at the dissemination of news of her misfortune among friends and acquaintances would be at least as great as her discomfort at its publication by the media to people to whom she is only a name. Yet the law in question does not prohibit the former in either oral or written form. Nor is it clear, as I think it must be to validate this statute, that Florida's general privacy law would prohibit such gossip. Nor, finally, is it credible that the interest meant to be served by the statute is the protection of the victim against a rapist still at large—an interest that arguably would extend only to mass publication. There would be little reason to limit a statute with that objective to rape alone; or to extend it to all rapes, whether or not the felon has been apprehended and confined. In any case, the instructions here did not require the jury to find that the rapist was at large.

This law has every appearance of a prohibition that society is prepared to impose upon the press but not upon itself. Such a prohibition does not protect an interest "of the highest order." For that reason, I agree that the judgment of the court below must be reversed.

[Justice White, joined by Chief Justice Rehnquist and Justice O'Connor, dissented. He argued that *Daily Mail* was distinguishable because it involved disclosure of the name of the perpetrator of a murder. "Surely the rights of those accused of crimes and those who are their victims must differ with respect to privacy concerns. That is, whatever rights alleged criminals have to maintain their anonymity pending an adjudication of guilt—the rights of crime victims must be infinitely more substantial."

Justice White then turned to the Court's "independent" reasons for its result. First, the government's release of the information was "inadvertent." When the state makes a mistake in its efforts to protect privacy "it is not too much to ask the press, in instances such as this, to respect simple standards of decency and refrain from publishing a victim's name, address, and/or phone number." In a footnote at this point, Justice White noted that the Court's proper concern for a free press should "be balanced against rival interests in a civilized and humane society. An absolutist view of the former leads to insensitivity as to the latter."

As to the Court's second reason—that Florida was judging the Star by too strict a liability standard—Justice White thought the point unavailable on this record because the jury found the Star reckless. In any event, it was permissible for the standard of care to be set by the legislature rather than the courts.

As to the third point—underinclusiveness—Justice White read the earlier cases to be concerned about singling out "one segment of the news media or press for adverse treatment"—print media as opposed to broadcast media or large newspapers as opposed to small newspapers. He was willing to accept the apparent legislative conclusion that "neighborhood gossips do not pose the danger and intrusion to rape victims that 'instrument[s] of mass communication' do. Simply put: Florida wanted to prevent the widespread distribution of rape victims' names, and therefore enacted a statute tailored almost as precisely as possible to achieving that end." Finally, it was entirely possible that Florida's common law of privacy would apply against neighborhood gossips in an appropriate case.

Justice White then turned to "more general principles at issue here to see if they recommend the Court's result." Justice White feared that the result would "obliterate one of the most noteworthy legal inventions of the 20th-century: the tort of the publication of private facts." If the plaintiff here could not prevail it was hard to imagine who could win such a case. The problem with the majority opinion was not that it tried to strike a balance but that it accorded too little weight to B.J.F.'s interests. There was no public interest in identifying the plaintiff here and "no public interest in immunizing the press from liability in the rare cases where a State's efforts to protect a victim's privacy have failed."]

NOTES AND QUESTIONS

1.   The Court seems to agree that the state interests advanced by the plaintiff in support of liability "are highly significant." When the state interest is sufficient but the remedy suppresses more speech than is necessary, the Court usually condemns it on the ground that it is "not narrowly tailored." But notice that in this case the Court does not separate the two inquiries; instead, it suggests that the statute is "too precipitous a means of advancing these interests to convince us that there is a 'need' within the meaning of the *Daily Mail* formulation. . . ." Elsewhere the court writes that the state's interests are not "satisfactorily served" by imposing liability. If this is something different from "not narrowly tailored," the Court has not explained how it differs.

2.   Do the views of rape victims (or the public at large) count in assessing the importance of the state interests? Justice Marshall asserted that word-of-mouth discussion of the rape "may have consequences equally devastating" to the victim as media dissemination. Justice Scalia speculated that dissemination among the victim's friends and acquaintances causes discomfort "at least as great." Suppose victims complained to the legislature only about media dissemination, and the legislature decided to address that problem without taking on the enforcement difficulties that would be encountered in trying to deal with gossip. In deciding whether the remedy is underinclusive, is a court free to define for itself the problem being addressed by the legislature?

3.   Suppose B.J.F. had sued for the common law tort of public disclosure of private facts instead of negligence per se. Would a judgment in her favor still have been unconstitutional because of the state's failure to prevent the sheriff's office from disclosing her name? Note that the Court's opinion describes each of the three objections to liability as "independent."

4.   In *Haynes*, discussed in the first part of this chapter, the court concluded that the plaintiffs' claim failed as a matter of tort law. If it had met the tort law requirements, would it have been barred by *Florida Star*? Is preventing disclosure of the type of information at issue in *Haynes* a state interest of the highest order? Would tort liability on those facts be a narrowly tailored remedy? The *Haynes* opinion suggested that *Florida Star* "was careful not to hold that states can never provide a tort remedy to a person about whom truthful, but intensely private, information of some interest to the public is published." The Court has indeed repeatedly emphasized in its privacy cases involving the media that its decisions are purposefully narrow.

5.   Recall that in *Philadelphia Newspapers, Inc. v. Hepps*, the Supreme Court held that "a private-figure [defamation] plaintiff cannot recover damages without also showing that the statements at issue are false" and wrote that punishing true speech was "antithetical to the First Amendment's protection. . . ." Professor Susan Gilles has argued that "[i]f the

constitutional requirement of proof of falsity articulated in libel cases is extended to privacy cases, then the private-facts tort is unconstitutional." Does it make sense to extend that requirement to this tort action? See Susan M. Gilles, Promises Betrayed: Breach of Confidence as a Remedy for Invasions of Privacy, 43 Buff. L. Rev. 1, 8 (1995).

6.   *Florida Star* was the Court's first application of a balancing methodology to a tort case. The "*Daily Mail* principle" arose from a criminal proceeding where the party defending the restriction on speech was the state. When that methodology is applied to a tort action, it is a private litigant who must identify the state's interests and defend the means that the state has chosen, whether through a statute or the courts' development of its common law, to protect those interests. B.J.F. lost because she was unable to defend the state's choice of means: its failure to prevent the police from releasing her name, its failure to impose liability on individuals as well as media, and its failure to require her to make out a common-law case for invasion of privacy. The burden this places on the private litigants like B.J.F. who are forced to defend the state's choice of statutory or common-law remedy are significant:

> When the challenged restraint is a tort judgment, . . . [t]he threat [to free speech] exists not within the corners of a document, but in the operation of the common law, the articulation of which is scattered, incomplete, possibly changing, and sometimes contradictory. Often the content and effect of the common law is itself being contested in the very proceeding in which its constitutionality is to be decided. The instigator of the particular threat to speech is a private litigant and the governmental actor is the court that is asked to provide a remedy. No other agent of the state is present, so the job of speaking for it is left to the plaintiff and the court. To the extent the court takes on this responsibility, it is both advocate and judge. As the voice of the common law, the court identifies, articulates, and defends the state interest served by the challenged rule, and as guardian of the Constitution the court judges the rule's validity.

David A. Anderson, First Amendment Limitations on Tort Law, 69 Brook. L. Rev. 755, 755 (2004).

7.   In Bloch v. Ribar, 156 F.3d 673 (6th Cir. 1998), the court held that a sheriff's disclosure at a news conference of details about the plaintiff's rape violated her constitutional right of privacy. Because that constitutional right had not been previously established, the court said the sheriff was immune from liability under 42 U.S.C. § 1983. "In light of our ruling in the present case, however, public officials in this circuit will now be on notice that such a privacy right exists" and therefore will not be able in the future to claim the defense of qualified immunity. The court said the constitutional right does not extend to all privacy interests, but only those that implicate "a fundamental right or one implicit in the concept of ordered liberty." It added "a rape victim has a fundamental right of privacy in preventing government officials from gratuitously and unnecessarily releasing the intimate details

of the rape where no penological purpose is being served." Is this civil rights action an adequate remedy for the privacy violation?

Lawfully Obtained. Note that the sheriff's department settled B.J.F.'s claim that releasing her name to the newspaper was unlawful, yet the Court says the information was "lawfully obtained" because there was no statute forbidding the newspaper from receiving it. Does "lawfully obtained" refer only to the publisher? In Bartnicki v. Vopper, 532 U.S. 514 (2001), discussed more fully in Chapter Eight, the Supreme Court wrote that the First Amendment does not necessarily protect publication of information lawfully obtained by the publisher from sources who obtained it unlawfully, but the Court protected the publication in that case on the ground that the privacy interests were weak and the public interest in disclosure was strong. The case involved the surreptitious recording of a phone call suggesting criminal activity that was sent to and aired by a radio station.

Enjoining Invasions of Privacy. Although injunctions in defamation cases have long been impermissible for non-constitutional reasons, the situation in privacy is not so clear. In a defamation case, a verdict for the plaintiff can at least undo some of the damage in theory. An award of damages cannot recapture lost privacy; indeed, as the *Haynes* opinion noted, the litigation is likely to cause a further loss of privacy. The traditional equity requirement of "no adequate remedy at law" therefore seems to be met.

Twice the Supreme Court has been prepared to address the issue. The first case involved an unauthorized biography of a sports star. The Supreme Court asked the parties specifically to address the propriety of injunctive relief. Julian Messner, Inc. v. Spahn, 393 U.S. 818 (1968). Then the parties settled the case. 393 U.S. 1046 (1969). The second time, the Court heard argument in a case in which a patient was trying to prevent her analyst from publishing a book about the therapy. Plaintiff claimed that the disguises used in the book were too thin to protect her privacy and that an implied covenant barred such a book. The state courts had enjoined publication of the book pending the outcome of the litigation. The Supreme Court granted certiorari, Roe v. Doe, 417 U.S. 907 (1974), heard arguments, and then dismissed the writ as having been "improvidently granted." 420 U.S. 307 (1975). On remand, the state court found liability and ordered all of the books, except for 220 that had been distributed early, destroyed. Doe v. Roe, 93 Misc. 2d 201 (N.Y. Sup. Ct. 1977).

In a case involving the documentary film "Titticut Follies," the state courts had enjoined the general distribution of the movie because it invaded the privacy of inmates of a state institution for the criminally insane. The Supreme Court denied certiorari over a long dissent by Justice Harlan, joined by Justice Brennan. Justice Douglas also dissented. Wiseman v. Massachusetts, 398 U.S. 960 (1970). A petition for rehearing was denied over the dissents of Justices Harlan, Brennan, and Blackmun. Justice Douglas did not participate. 400 U.S. 860 (1970).

Injunctions to protect privacy are rare, however. For example, a court rejected an actress's attempt to enjoin her former husband from revealing—and the National Enquirer from publishing—aspects of her personal life, such as her alleged use of drugs and alcohol and her sexual relationships. Instead, the court noted, the plaintiff's remedy was a possible damages action for defamation or privacy. Gilbert v. National Enquirer, 43 Cal. App.4th 1135 (Cal. App. 1996).

B. FALSE LIGHT PRIVACY

The conventional idea of invasion of privacy as conceived by Warren and Brandeis involved true statements about aspects of plaintiff's life that others had no business knowing. But along the way, a few cases involved falsehoods that placed the plaintiff in an offensively false light but did not harm his or her "reputation" so as to permit an action for defamation. As one example, a group used the plaintiff's name without authorization on a petition to the governor to veto a bill. Although falsely stating that plaintiff had signed the petition would not have been defamatory, the court found the situation actionable because it cast plaintiff in a false light. See Hinish v. Meier & Frank Co., 113 P.2d 438 (Or. 1941).

Time, Inc. v. Hill. The false light action was significantly limited by Time, Inc. v. Hill, 385 U.S. 374 (1967). In September 1952 James Hill and his family were held hostage in their home for nineteen hours by three escaped convicts who apparently treated them decently. The incident received extensive nationwide coverage. Thereafter the Hills moved to another state, sought seclusion and refused to make public appearances. A novel modeled on the event was published the following year. In 1955, Life magazine in a short article and photo spread announced that a play and a motion picture were being made from the novel, which they said was "inspired" by the Hill episode. The play, "a heart-stopping account of how a family rose to heroism in a crisis," would enable the public to see the Hill story "reenacted." Photographs in the magazine showed actors performing scenes from the play at the house at which the original events had occurred.

Suit was brought in New York under that state's peculiar privacy statute, noted earlier, which provides a remedy only for uses "for advertising purposes or for the purposes of trade." Case law in New York had held that falsification could be evidence that the use was for trade purposes rather than for public information. The Hills alleged that the story was false because the novel and the play included fictitious incidents of the convicts committing violence on the father and uttering a "verbal sexual insult" at the daughter. The state courts allowed recovery after lengthy litigation.

The Supreme Court, by a very fragile majority, decided that the magazine had a constitutional privilege to comment on matters of public interest. The Court used the defamation analogy that was then being developed in the wake of the *New York Times* case and applied it to this false light privacy case, holding that there could be no liability unless the falsity was either deliberate or reckless. (The Court had not yet decided what fault standard governed defamation actions by private citizens.)

The opinions in the *Hill* case give little clue as to whether the falsity of the magazine's account made it more objectionable to the Hills than a truthful account would have been. Leonard Garment, the lawyer who originally represented the Hills, later wrote that two psychiatrists testified that Mrs. Hill "had come through the original hostage incident fairly well but had fallen apart when the Life article brought back her memories transformed into her worst nightmares and presented them to the world as reality." Garment eventually turned the case over to his law partner, Richard Nixon, who argued the case in the Supreme Court. See Leonard Garment, Annals of Law: The Hill Case, The New Yorker, Apr. 17, 1989. Garment also asserted that the "blood and gore" and "leering sexuality" depicted by the magazine caused Mrs. Hill distress above that caused by the truthful parts of the article. See Gary T. Schwartz, Explaining and Justifying a Limited Tort of False Light Invasion of Privacy, 41 Case W. Res. L. Rev. 885 (1991).

The preliminary vote of the Court in Time, Inc. v. Hill favored the Hills. For the story and the draft opinions at that first stage, see Bernard Schwartz, The Unpublished Opinions of the Warren Court 240–303 (1985). See also Harry Kalven, Jr., The Reasonable Man and the First Amendment: *Hill, Butts,* and *Walker,* 1967 Sup. Ct. Rev. 267.

Cantrell v. Forest City Publishing Co.

Supreme Court of the United States, 1974.
419 U.S. 245.

■ MR. JUSTICE STEWART delivered the opinion of the Court.

Margaret Cantrell and four of her minor children brought this diversity action in a Federal District Court for invasion of privacy against the Forest City Publishing Co., publisher of a Cleveland newspaper, the Plain Dealer, and against Joseph Eszterhas, a reporter formerly employed by the Plain Dealer, and Richard Conway, a Plain Dealer photographer. The Cantrells alleged that an article published in the Plain Dealer Sunday Magazine unreasonably placed their family in a false light before the public through its many inaccuracies and untruths. The District Judge struck the claims relating to punitive damages as to all the plaintiffs and dismissed the actions of three of the Cantrell children in their entirety, but allowed the case to go to the jury as to Mrs. Cantrell and her oldest son, William. The jury returned a verdict [for $60,000] against all three of the respondents for compensatory money damages in favor of these two plaintiffs.

The Court of Appeals for the Sixth Circuit reversed, holding that, in the light of the First and Fourteenth Amendments, the District Judge should have granted the respondents' motion for a directed verdict as to all the Cantrells' claims. . . .

I.

In December 1967, Margaret Cantrell's husband Melvin was killed along with 43 other people when the Silver Bridge across the Ohio River at Point Pleasant, West Virginia, collapsed. The respondent Eszterhas was assigned by the Plain Dealer to cover the story of the disaster. He wrote a "news feature" story focusing on the funeral of Melvin Cantrell and the impact of his death on the Cantrell family.

Five months later, after conferring with the Sunday Magazine editor of the Plain Dealer, Eszterhas and photographer Conway returned to the Point Pleasant area to write a follow-up feature. The two men went to the Cantrell residence, where Eszterhas talked with the children and Conway took 50 pictures. Mrs. Cantrell was not at home at any time during the 60 to 90 minutes that the men were at the Cantrell residence.

Eszterhas' story appeared as the lead feature in the August 4, 1968, edition of the Plain Dealer Sunday Magazine. The article stressed the family's abject poverty; the children's old, ill-fitting clothes and the deteriorating condition of their home were detailed in both the text and accompanying photographs. As he had done in his original prize-winning article on the Silver Bridge disaster, Eszterhas used the Cantrell family to illustrate the impact of the bridge collapse on the lives of the people in the Point Pleasant area.

It is conceded that the story contained a number of inaccuracies and false statements. Most conspicuously, although Mrs. Cantrell was not present at any time during the reporter's visit to her home, Eszterhas wrote, "Margaret Cantrell will talk neither about what happened nor about how they are doing. She wears the same mask of non-expression she wore at the funeral. She is a proud woman. Her world has changed. She says that after it happened, the people in town offered to help them out with money and they refused to take it." Other significant misrepresentations were contained in details of Eszterhas' descriptions of the poverty in which the Cantrells were living and the dirty and dilapidated conditions of the Cantrell home.

The case went to the jury on a so-called "false light" theory of invasion of privacy. In essence, the theory of the case was that by publishing the false feature story about the Cantrells and thereby making them the objects of pity and ridicule, the respondents damaged Mrs. Cantrell and her son William by causing them to suffer outrage, mental distress, shame, and humiliation.

II.

. . .

The District Judge in the case before us, in contrast to the trial judge in Time, Inc. v. Hill, did instruct the jury that liability could be imposed only if it concluded that the false statements in the Sunday Magazine feature article on the Cantrells had been made with knowledge of their falsity or in reckless disregard of the truth. No objection was made by any of the parties to this knowing-or-reckless-falsehood instruction. Consequently, this case presents no occasion to consider whether a State may constitutionally apply a more relaxed standard of liability for a publisher or broadcaster of false statements injurious to a private individual under a false-light theory of invasion of privacy, or whether the constitutional standard announced in Time, Inc. v. Hill applies to all false-light cases. Cf. [Gertz]. Rather, the sole question that we need decide is whether the Court of Appeals erred in setting aside the jury's verdict.

III.

At the close of the petitioners' case-in-chief, the District Judge struck the demand for punitive damages. He found that Mrs. Cantrell had failed to present any evidence to support the charges that the invasion of privacy "was done maliciously within the legal definition of that term." The Court of Appeals interpreted this finding to be a determination by the District Judge that there was no evidence of knowing falsity or reckless disregard of the truth introduced at the trial. Having made such a determination, the Court of Appeals held that the District Judge should have granted the motion for a directed verdict for respondents as to all the Cantrells' claims. [ ]

. . .

Although the verbal record of the District Court proceedings is not entirely unambiguous, the conclusion is inescapable that the District Judge was referring to the common-law standard of malice rather than to the New York Times "actual malice" standard when he dismissed the punitive damages claims. . . .

Moreover, the District Judge was clearly correct in believing that the evidence introduced at trial was sufficient to support a jury finding that the respondents Joseph Eszterhas and Forest City Publishing Co. had published knowing or reckless falsehoods about the Cantrells.[5] There was no dispute during the trial that Eszterhas, who did not testify, must

---

[5]   Although we conclude that the jury verdicts should have been sustained as to Eszterhas and Forest City Publishing Co., we agree with the Court of Appeals' conclusion that there was insufficient evidence to support the jury's verdict against the photographer Conway. . . .

have known that a number of the statements in the feature story were untrue. In particular, his article plainly implied that Mrs. Cantrell had been present during his visit to her home and that Eszterhas had observed her "wear[ing] the same mask of non-expression she wore [at her husband's] funeral." These were "calculated falsehoods," and the jury was plainly justified in finding that Eszterhas had portrayed the Cantrells in a false light through knowing or reckless untruth.

The Court of Appeals concluded that there was no evidence that Forest City Publishing Co. had knowledge of any of the inaccuracies contained in Eszterhas' article. However, there was sufficient evidence for the jury to find that Eszterhas' writing of the feature was within the scope of his employment at the Plain Dealer and that Forest City Publishing Co. was therefore liable under traditional doctrines of *respondeat superior*. . . .

For the foregoing reasons, the judgment of the Court of Appeals is reversed and the case is remanded to that court with directions to enter a judgment affirming the judgment of the District Court as to the respondents Forest City Publishing Co. and Joseph Eszterhas.

It is so ordered.

■ MR. JUSTICE DOUGLAS, dissenting.

. . .

A bridge accident catapulted the Cantrells into the public eye and their disaster became newsworthy. To make the First Amendment freedom to report the news turn on subtle differences between common-law malice and actual malice is to stand the Amendment on its head. Those who write the current news seldom have the objective, dispassionate point of view—or the time—of scientific analysts. They deal in fast-moving events and the need for "spot" reporting. The jury under today's formula sits as a censor with broad powers—not to impose a prior restraint, but to lay heavy damages on the press. The press is "free" only if the jury is sufficiently disenchanted with the Cantrells to let the press be free of this damages claim. That regime is thought by some to be a way of supervising the press which is better than not supervising it at all. But the installation of the Court's regime would require a constitutional amendment. Whatever might be the ultimate reach of the doctrine Mr. Justice Black and I have embraced, it seems clear that in matters of public import such as the present news reporting, there must be freedom from damages lest the press be frightened into playing a more ignoble role than the Framers visualized.

I would affirm the judgment of the Court of Appeals.

NOTES AND QUESTIONS

1. How would the courts analyze a defamation action brought by the Cantrells? A public disclosure privacy action?

2.   What is the nature of the respondeat superior problem in *Cantrell?* Might the decision on this point be significant in future defamation cases in determining whose behavior to evaluate in considering liability?

3.   Justice Stewart analyzes this case as involving the "false light" category of privacy. Might it also be analyzed as a public disclosure privacy case in which the media claimed the defense of newsworthiness but lost because the defense is not available when the material reported is deliberately or recklessly false? What are the differences between the two analyses?

4.   How are compensatory damages to be measured in this case? Is the falsity relevant in that calculation?

5.   One of the elements of the false light tort at common law is that the depiction must be one that would be highly offensive to a person of reasonable sensibilities. Might this requirement, rigorously applied, preclude recovery in cases like *Hill* and *Cantrell?*

The logic of the Supreme Court's libel decision in *Gertz* suggests that private figure plaintiffs in false light cases might be able to recover without proof of actual malice. However, the Court has never addressed the issue directly, and lower courts have struggled with the question of whether actual malice or negligence is required. One argument is that actual malice should still be required in false light cases involving matters of private concern because the injury involved in such cases is not as serious as the injury in defamation cases. See Restatement (Second) of Torts § 652E, cmt. d ("Pending further enlightenment from the Supreme Court, therefore, this Section provides that liability for invasion of privacy for placing the plaintiff in a false light may exist if the defendant acted with knowledge of the falsity of the statement or in reckless disregard as to truth or falsity. The Caveat leaves open the question of whether there may be liability based on a showing of negligence as to truth or falsity."). In Lovgren v. Citizens First Nat. Bank of Princeton, 534 N.E.2d 987 (Ill. 1989), the court held that all plaintiffs must prove actual malice as an element of a false light claim based on "the nature of the tort." To illustrate this point, the court quoted Prosser & Keeton on Torts (5th ed. 1984): "Recovery for an invasion of privacy on the ground that the plaintiff was depicted in a false light makes sense only when the account, if true, would not have been actionable as an invasion of privacy. In other words, the outrageous character of the publicity comes about in part by virtue of the fact that some part of the matter reported was false and deliberately so."

False Light and Defamation. A few years after *Cantrell,* in Zacchini v. Scripps-Howard Broadcasting Co., an appropriation case noted later in this chapter, the Court approvingly quoted Dean Prosser's statement that the interest protected in false light actions "is clearly that of reputation, with the same overtones of mental distress as in defamation." Under this view, why might a state permit liability for errors that do not harm reputation? Might the *Masson* case, discussed in Chapter Four, be better analyzed as a false light case?

Some courts explain the false light action as a remedy for cases in which the falsehood causes emotional distress without causing harm to reputation. In Flowers v. Carville, 310 F.3d 1118 (9th Cir. 2002), the court held that Gennifer Flowers could maintain separate false light and defamation claims against the publisher of James Carville's book accusing her of lying about her relationship with President Clinton. It held that the false light action could compensate for emotional injuries not covered by the defamation claim.

Should all the common law and statutory limitations on defamation, such as retraction statutes, special damage requirements, and statutes of limitations, apply as well to false light privacy?

In Fellows v. National Enquirer, Inc., 721 P.2d 97 (Cal. 1986), defendant's article asserted that "Gorgeous Angie Dickinson's all smiles about the new man in her life—TV producer Arthur Fellows. Angie's steady-dating Fellows all over TinselTown, and happily posed for photographers with him as they exited the swanky Spago restaurant in Beverly Hills." Accompanying the article was a photograph of Dickinson and Fellows over the caption stating that Dickinson was "Dating a Producer."

Fellows demanded a retraction under Cal. Civil Code § 48a, asserting that plaintiff "has never dated Miss Dickinson, is not 'the new man in her life,' and has been married to Phyllis Fellows for the last 18 years." Defendant refused retraction and plaintiff sued for libel and false light privacy. Plaintiff withdrew his libel claim and proceeded solely on a false light claim with no allegation of special damages.

Under California law, libel that relied on extrinsic facts had to be supported by special damages. Cal. Civil Code § 45a. Plaintiff's privacy claim asserted that he had been falsely portrayed as the "new man" in Dickinson's life and as "steady-dating" her. The trial judge dismissed the privacy claim for lack of special damages and the decision was affirmed on appeal.

The clear purpose of Section 45a was to provide additional protection to libel defendants. Since "virtually every published defamation would support an action for false light invasion of privacy, exempting such actions from the requirement of proving special damages would render the statute a nullity." Under this rationale is there any state requirement that protects libel defendants that would not also be applied to plaintiffs who sue on a false light theory? What should happen if a false light claim is based on language that does not rise to the level of being defamatory? The court went out of its way to announce that its ruling did not apply to false light claims "that would be actionable as a public disclosure of private facts had the representation made in the publication been true."

Plaintiffs' lawyers often plead false light in the alternative with a libel claim, and it often fails for the same reason that the defamation claim fails. If the latter survives, the false light claim may be dropped. One of the examples of a case in which a false light claim succeeded when a libel action failed is Peoples Bank and Trust v. Globe International Pub., Inc., 978 F.2d 1065 (8th Cir. 1992), noted earlier in Chapter Four. There, plaintiff was the estate of a 96-year-old woman whose photo was used in a supermarket tabloid, the Sun, to illustrate a story about a 101-year-old Australian newspaper carrier whom the Sun reported had become pregnant by one of her customers. The woman sued for both libel and false light but died before final judgment. The jury found for the newspaper on the libel claim but for the plaintiff on the false light claim. Since both verdicts were general, they provided no explanation of the jury's reasoning.

The newspaper suggested that the story was intended as fiction and could not have been understood otherwise. But the court of appeals decided that the Sun had comingled factual and fictional stories so thoroughly that "[a]t trial even its own writers could not tell which stories were true and which were completely fabricated." The jury could find that readers could reasonably have believed that the story portrayed actual facts, and that the newspaper "recklessly failed to anticipate that result." The court upheld an award of $850,000 in punitive damages, but held that an award of $650,000 compensatory damages was excessive because there was no evidence of lost earning capacity, permanent injury, medical expenses, or future pain and suffering. On remand the district judge reduced the compensatory award to $150,000. 817 F. Supp. 72 (W.D. Ark. 1993).

False Light by Association. A few cases have recognized a false light cause of action by persons whose photographs have appeared in certain magazines or websites without their consent. One involved a model whose nude photographs appeared in Hustler magazine. Douglass v. Hustler Magazine, Inc., 769 F.2d 1128 (7th Cir. 1985). After the court described the magazine's contents, it concluded that a jury could reasonably find that the magazine was offensive and that "to be depicted as voluntarily associated with [Hustler] . . . is unquestionably degrading to a normal person, especially if the depiction is erotic." The court agreed that a cause of action was stated, but for other reasons, plaintiff's judgment was reversed and a new trial ordered. See also Braun v. Flynt, 726 F.2d 245 (5th Cir. 1984).

In Dempsey v. National Enquirer, 702 F. Supp. 927 (D. Me. 1988), the court refused to apply these cases to an article that appeared in the National Enquirer. Plaintiff, a pilot, had fallen out of a light plane in flight but had clung to the open boarding ladder on the side and survived his co-pilot's emergency landing with only a few scratches. He sued the Enquirer on the theory that its story implied that he had willingly told his story to the Enquirer. The court doubted that the article implied this, but said "even if the article could imply that the plaintiff consented to the publication," the complaint failed to show that "association per se with the [National Enquirer] would be highly objectionable to a reasonable person." *Douglass* and *Braun* did not apply because there was no allegation here that the Enquirer was a magazine like the ones involved in those cases.

The same plaintiff had more success in a separate suit against the Enquirer's sibling, the Star. The Star presented the pilot's story under his byline, with an introduction saying "Here, Dempsey . . . tells in his own words how he found himself suddenly thrust into the ultimate daredevil stunt." The article was a dramatic first-person account, even though Dempsey said he had never been interviewed by the Star, had not given them information, and had not written the story. The court refused to dismiss his false light claim. The judge said the article "unequivocally attributed authorship to the plaintiff," thereby portraying him falsely in a way that could be found to be highly offensive to a reasonable person.

In a more recent example, a federal trial court in Pennsylvania found a potentially valid false light claim in a case brought by a man whose mugshot appeared on two mugshot-only websites in a way that the plaintiff claimed gave others a false impression that he had a criminal history. Finding a potential false light claim because of the websites' focus on criminality and because the man's arrest and all charges had been expunged, the court noted that the website design—including the use of the word "busted"—plausibly created the impression that the plaintiff was a criminal and was guilty and that he should be monitored for criminal activity in the future. Taha v. Bucks County, 9 F. Supp. 3d 490 (E.D. Pa. 2014). The plaintiff in the case was not as successful in his claim that his image had been appropriated by the website.

Rejecting and Embracing the Tort. Though two-thirds of the states have accepted false light, a few states have doubted the utility of the tort and have rejected it.

For example, the Texas Supreme Court, 5–4, rejected the false light action even though lower courts and federal district courts applying Texas law had recognized it for a decade. See Cain v. Hearst Corp., 878 S.W.2d 577 (Tex. 1994). The case was brought by a prisoner serving a life sentence for murder. He did not challenge portions of a newspaper story that said he murdered his lawyer to marry the lawyer's widow and murdered another man for his money, but he objected to passages saying he was a member of the "Dixie mafia" and was believed to have killed as many as eight people. He filed his false light suit six months after the statute of limitations for libel had run.

The majority worried that false light often overlaps with defamation or intentional infliction of emotional distress, and its potential to chill speech was too great to justify retaining the tort for the few instances where it would offer the only remedy. The dissenters noted that many tort remedies overlap. They argued that the chilling effect could be controlled by limiting the tort to serious and harmful falsehoods and applying fault and procedural limitations similar to those applied to defamation.

The Florida and North Carolina Supreme Courts rejected false light based on similar reasoning. Jews for Jesus, Inc. v. Rapp. 997 So.2d 1098 (Fla. 2008) (rejecting false light because it "is largely duplicative of existing torts, but without the attendant protections of the First Amendment"); Renwick v. The News and Observer Publishing Co., 312 S.E.2d 405 (N.C. 1984) (observing that false light and defamation often overlap, and the limited benefits that would flow from an independent tort of false light do not justify recognition given its potential for chilling speech).

The Ohio Supreme Court, in contrast, changed its mind and adopted the false light tort in 2007, suggesting that such a shift was necessary in order to protect citizens from newer Internet-based harms. Welling v. Weinfeld, 866 N.E.2d 1051 (Ohio 2007). Even though the underlying case did not involve media, the court complained that an increase in Internet publishing meant that "barriers to generating publicity [were] slight" and that "the ethical standards regarding the acceptability of certain discourse [had] been lowered." False light, therefore, became a viable tort in Ohio, even though the court had rejected the tort two decades before. "As the ability to do harm has grown," the court wrote, "so must the law's ability to protect the innocent."

In 2014 the Nevada Supreme Court cited the *Welling* case in a decision adopting the false light tort in the state. The Supreme Court later granted certiorari in Franchise Tax Bd. v. Hyatt, 335 P.3d 125 (Nev. 2014), on unrelated matters.

C. APPROPRIATION

1. NATURE OF THE TORT

"Appropriation" claims involve attempts by people to control the exploitation of their names, likenesses, and fame and any pecuniary value attached to them. Depending upon the state and the facts at issue, these claims can be called appropriation, misappropriation, right of publicity, or right to publicity. The New York statute that protects against the use of unauthorized photographs in advertising sprang from a 1902 lawsuit in which a court held that a young plaintiff whose image had been used on a bag of flour without permission had no privacy right. Roberson v. Rochester Folding Box Co., 64 N.E. 442 (N.Y. 1902). Outraged, the New York legislature enacted the statute in response. In 1905, the Georgia Supreme Court found in favor of the plaintiff in a similar lawsuit based upon unauthorized use of a man's photograph in an advertisement for insurance. Pavesich v. New England Life Ins. Co., 50 S.E. 68 (Ga. 1905). In this way, appropriation is the first of the privacy torts to have been routinely accepted.

A slightly different claim, though often used interchangeably with misappropriation, is called the right of publicity; it gives even public figures who might otherwise embrace publicity a right to control their images. The concept was initially discussed in Haelan Laboratories v. Topps Chewing Gum, Inc., 202 F.2d 866 (2d Cir. 1953), in which the court wrote of the need to protect the proprietary interest of celebrities in their names and likenesses. *Haelan* involved a famous baseball player who had assigned the right to the use of his name and likeness to a bubblegum manufacturer for the promotion of its products. A competing manufacturer subsequently induced the ballplayer to enter into a similar contract with full knowledge of the pre-existing agreement. The court recognized the ballplayer's right to control commercial use of his name and likeness as a method through which such misappropriation could be prevented.

Generally speaking the tort is described as a remedy for unauthorized use of a person's name or likeness. For example, the Restatement (Second) of Torts § 652C provides: "One who appropriates to his own use or benefit the name or likeness of another is subject to liability to the other for invasion of privacy." A Texas statute, known colloquially as "The Buddy Holly Act" because it was passed to prevent unauthorized exploitation of the late singer's memory, similarly prohibits unconsented use of "a deceased individual's name, voice, signature, photograph, or likeness in any manner. . . ." Tex. Prop. Code Ch. 4 (Actions & Remedies) § 26.011.

If the tort were really this broad, it would indeed be a major problem for media, given media's routine use of names and photographs in news stories and magazine covers. In fact, the remedy is mostly confined to commercial exploitation, such as unauthorized use of a person's likeness in an advertisement or endorsement of a product or service. The Texas statute quoted above exempts any use of a name or likeness in a play, book, film, radio or television program, magazine or newspaper article, political material, or work of art, or even in an advertisement for any of the foregoing. The common law tort also usually provides no remedy when a person's name or likeness is appropriated for purposes of journalism, entertainment, or satire.

As a result, this branch of privacy law is usually of little concern to media outside of their advertising departments. We briefly consider it here to round out our discussion of privacy and to touch on the few areas where it may affect media more directly. Students should keep in mind that remedies available under this tort may sometimes overlap with those available through federal unfair competition law, such as the Lanham Act.

A majority of states recognize a tort for appropriation of name or likeness. At least nineteen states have right of publicity statutes, and many states have adopted a right of publicity by common law. California recognizes both a statutory and common law right of publicity. The California statute is below.

Unauthorized Commercial Use of Name, Voice, Signature, Photograph or Likeness

Cal. Civil Code § 3344 (2007).

(a) Any person who knowingly uses another's name, voice, signature, photograph, or likeness, in any manner, on or in products, merchandise, or goods, or for purposes of advertising or selling, or soliciting purchases of, products, merchandise, goods or services, without such person's prior consent . . . shall be liable for any damages sustained by the person or persons injured as a result thereof. In addition, in any action brought under this section, the person who violated the section shall be liable to the injured party or parties in an amount equal to the greater of seven hundred fifty dollars ($750) or the actual damages suffered by him or her as a result of the unauthorized use, and any profits from the unauthorized use that are attributable to the use and are not taken into account in computing the actual damages.

. . .

(c) Where a photograph or likeness of an employee of the person using the photograph or likeness appearing in the advertisement or other publication prepared by or in behalf of the user is only incidental, and not essential, to the purpose of the publication in which it appears, there shall arise a rebuttable presumption affecting the burden of producing evidence that the failure to obtain the consent of the employee was not a knowing use of the employee's photograph or likeness.

(d) For purposes of this section, a use of a name, voice, signature, photograph, or likeness in connection with any news, public affairs, or sports broadcast or account, or any political campaign, shall not constitute a use for which consent is required under subdivision (a).

(e) The use of a name, voice, signature, photograph, or likeness in a commercial medium shall not constitute a use for which consent is required under subdivision (a) solely because the material containing such use is commercially sponsored or contains paid advertising. Rather it shall be a question of fact whether or not the use of the person's name, voice, signature, photograph, or likeness was so directly connected with the commercial sponsorship or with the paid advertising as to constitute a use for which consent is required under subdivision (a).

Does subsection (d) of the California statute eliminate the possibility that this statute will be applied to the media? Would the statute likely be unconstitutional without this subsection? Does this subsection eliminate whatever constitutional concerns the statute might otherwise raise?

There are several important limitations on actions under this statute. One limitation is the statute's application to purely "commercial speech or at least to speech that does not contribute significantly to a matter of public interest." In Hoffman v. Capital Cities/ABC, 255 F.3d 1180 (9th Cir. 2001), Los Angeles Magazine had combined the face and head of actor Dustin Hoffman with a photo of the body of a male model wearing a silk gown and high heels designed by contemporary fashion designers. The illustration was part of a fashion spread called "Grand Illusions," and the copy read: "By using state-of-the-art digital magic, we clothed some of cinema's most enduring icons in fashions by the hottest designers." The Hoffman composite was an allusion to his title role in the movie "Tootsie," in which he dressed as a woman.

The court reversed an award to Hoffman of over $3 million. It found that the use of Hoffman's photo was not "pure commercial speech," noting that the magazine "did not use Hoffman's image in a traditional advertisement printed merely for the purpose of selling a particular product" nor "did the article simply advance a commercial message."

> "Grand Illusions" appears as a feature article on the cover of the magazine and in the table of contents. It is a complement to and a part of the issue's focus on Hollywood past and present. Viewed in context, the article as a whole is a combination of fashion photography, humor, and visual and verbal editorial comment on classic films and famous actors. Any commercial aspects are "inextricably entwined" with expressive elements, and so they cannot be separated out "from the fully protected whole." . . . [C]ommon sense tells us this is not a simple advertisement.

As a result, the Ninth Circuit concluded that the article was entitled to "full First Amendment protection" unless the altered photograph was defamatory and published with *New York Times* actual malice, and it said the record would not support such a claim.

Another limitation is that there may be a First Amendment defense if the use of the name or likeness is "transformative." See Comedy III Productions, Inc. v. Gary Saderup, Inc., 21 P.3d 797 (Cal. 2001). Borrowing a concept from intellectual property law, the court wrote that "when an artist is faced with a right of publicity challenge to his or her work, he or she may raise as affirmative defense that the work is protected by the First Amendment inasmuch as it contains significant transformative elements or that the value of the work does not derive primarily from the celebrity's fame." The court pointed to celebrity images of Andy Warhol, which it said were "able to convey a message that went beyond the commercial exploitation of celebrity images and became a form of ironic social comment on the dehumanization of celebrity itself." But the court held that the sale of lithographs and t-shirts bearing images of the Three Stooges were not protected by the First Amendment because they made "no significant transformative or creative contribution" to those images.

———

Another limitation on appropriation or right of publicity claims involving news media more directly is a doctrine called the real relationship or incidental use test. There, if a publisher uses an image of an individual to entice the reader into buying a magazine or to illustrate a news story, that image must have a real relationship to the text within the publication. If it does, the use of the image is likely to be protected as "incidental" to the publication's commercial status. This test is usually met, especially with regard to mainstream news publishers. "The fact that the defendant is engaged in the business of publication, for example of a newspaper, out of which he makes or seeks to make a profit," the Restatement reads, "is not enough to make the incidental publication a commercial use of the name or likeness." Restatement (Second) of Torts, § 652C, comment d.

The following court decision finds no real relationship between the use of a plaintiff's images and nearby newsworthy text and, therefore, a greater than incidental use by a publisher.

Toffoloni v. LFP Publishing Group, LLC

United States Court of Appeals, Eleventh Circuit, 2009.
572 F.3d 1201.

■ WILSON, CIRCUIT JUDGE:

. . .

Maureen Toffoloni is the mother and the administrator of the estate of Nancy Benoit. Benoit and her son, both Georgia residents, were murdered by her husband, Christopher Benoit, in June 2007. Christopher Benoit then committed suicide. Prior to her death, Benoit was a model and professional woman wrestler. Christopher Benoit was a well-known professional wrestler. Their deaths garnered a great deal of domestic and international media attention.

Approximately twenty years before her death, Benoit posed nude for photographer Mark Samansky, who took both photographs and a video of her. Toffoloni alleges that, immediately after the shoot, her daughter asked Samansky to destroy the photographs and video and believed that

Samansky had destroyed them. However, Samansky kept the video, from which he extracted nude and partially nude photographic stills of Benoit. Samansky conveyed the photographic stills to LFP, which published them in the March 2008 issue of *Hustler* magazine.

[Toffoloni sought an injunction against LFP and damages for violation of the right of publicity in Georgia state court, and LFP removed the case to federal district court. The district court dismissed Toffoloni's suit on the ground that "Ms. Benoit's death was a 'legitimate matter of public interest and concern.' " Toffoloni appealed.]

Georgia recognizes a right of publicity to protect against "the appropriation of another's name and likeness . . . without consent and for the financial gain of the appropriator . . . whether the person whose name and likeness is used is a private citizen, entertainer, or . . . a public figure who is not a public official." Martin Luther King, Jr. Ctr. for Soc. Change, Inc. v. Am. Heritage Prods., Inc., 296 S.E.2d 697, 703 (1982). "The right of publicity may be defined as [an individual's] right to the exclusive use of his or her name and likeness." [ ] . . .

. . .

Georgia first recognized the right of publicity in Cabaniss v. Hipsley, 151 S.E.2d 496 (1966). The court held that the plaintiff, who was an exotic dancer, could recover from the Atlanta Playboy Club for its unauthorized use of her photograph in an entertainment magazine advertising the club. The court explained that "[u]nlike intrusion, disclosure, or false light, appropriation does not require the invasion of something secret, secluded or private pertaining to plaintiff, nor does it involve falsity. . . . The interest protected . . . is not so much a mental as a proprietary one, in the exclusive use of the plaintiff's name and likeness as an aspect of his identity." [ ] Since the right of publicity is a "proprietary" right, "the measure of damages is the value of the use of the appropriated publicity." [ ]

Subsequent to *Cabaniss,* the Georgia courts have expanded the right of publicity to "recognize[ ] the rights of private citizens, as well as entertainers, not to have their names and photographs used for the financial gain of the user without their consent, where such use is not authorized as an exercise of freedom of the press." [ ] Additionally, the Supreme Court of Georgia held "that the right of publicity survives the death of its owner and is inheritable and devisable."

The Restatement (Second) of Torts, however, tempers the right of publicity, providing that:

> No one has the right to object merely because his name or his appearance is brought before the public, *since neither is in any way a private matter, and both are open to public observation.* It is only when the publicity is given for the purpose of appropriating to the defendant's benefit the commercial or other

values associated with the name or the likeness that the right to privacy is invaded.

. . .

Analysis of LFP's Publication of the Nude Photographs

This case requires us to consider the nature and extent of the newsworthiness exception to the right of publicity. . . . Toffoloni argues that she should be allowed to sue for damages incident to the publication of nude pictures of her deceased daughter because those photographs were published against her express direction and were violative of her daughter's right of publicity. LFP responds that it published an article on the life, career, and tragic death of Benoit, which "includes comment on the modest beginnings of Ms. Benoit's career, and is accompanied by images of Ms. Benoit from that time." LFP argues that the article and related images are of substantial public interest and are therefore newsworthy.

. . . We review the district court's grant of LFP's motion to dismiss for failure to state a claim upon which relief can be granted [ ] *de novo.* [ ]

I.   The Incidental Relationship Between the Article and Photographs

First, it seems clear that had LFP published the nude photographs of Benoit by themselves—i.e., without a corresponding news article—the publication would not qualify within the newsworthiness exception. The fact of Benoit's nudity is not in and of itself newsworthy. [ ] The nude photographs "impart [ ] no information to the reading public."[ ] The photographs, by themselves, serve no "legitimate purpose of disseminating news . . . and needlessly expose[ ] aspects of the plaintiff's private life to the public." [ ] Indeed, people are nude every day, and the news media does not typically find the occurrence worth reporting.

Here, however, LFP published the photographs alongside a biographical piece on Benoit's career. The biographical piece, in and of itself, certainly falls within the newsworthiness exception. [ ] The question before us is whether a brief biographical piece can ratchet otherwise protected, personal photographs into the newsworthiness exception.

As the Second Circuit has held, "it is appropriate for a court to consider whether the public interest aspect of the publication is merely incidental to its commercial purpose." Titan Sports, Inc. v. Comics World Corp., 870 F.2d 85, 87–88 (2d Cir. 1989). [ ] Although LFP argues that the photographs were illustrative of the substantive, biographical article included in *Hustler,* our review of the publication demonstrates that such is not the case. These photographs were not incidental to the article. Rather, the article was incidental to the photographs.

The magazine cover advertises "WRESTLER CHRIS BENOIT'S MURDERED WIFE NUDE." The table of contents lists "NANCY BENOIT Exclusive Nude Pics of Wrestler's Doomed Wife." Neither the cover nor the table of contents makes any reference to the accompanying article. The article is entitled "NANCY BENOIT Au Naturel: The long-lost images of wrestler Chris Benoit's doomed wife." The title and page frame, which reads "EXCLUSIVE PICS! EXCLUSIVE PICS!," comprise about one-third of the first page. A second third of the page is devoted to two nude photographs of Benoit. The final third of the page discusses Benoit's murder and her nude photo shoot, twice referencing her brief desire to be a model. The second page of the article is entirely devoted to photographs, displaying eight additional photographs of Benoit. The heart of this article was the publication of nude photographs—not the corresponding biography.

. . . LFP's brief biography of Benoit's life, even with its reference to her youthful pursuit of modeling, is merely incidental to its publication of her nude photographs. Therefore, the biographical piece cannot suffice to render the nude photographs newsworthy.

II. *Relationship of the Photographs to the Incident of Public Concern*

Furthermore, we are convinced that the nude photographs are not connected to the incident of public concern. LFP would have us rule that someone's notorious death constitutes a carte blanche for the publication of any and all images of that person during his or her life, regardless of whether those images were intentionally kept private and regardless of whether those images are of any relation to the incident currently of public concern. We disagree.

The Georgia courts have never held, nor do we believe that they would hold, that if one is the victim of an infamous murder, one's entire life is rendered the legitimate subject of public scrutiny. Such a ruling would eviscerate the Georgia right of publicity, allowing the exception to swallow the rule. Rather, the Georgia courts have consistently indicated that there are timeliness or relatedness boundaries that circumscribe the breadth of public scrutiny to the incident of public interest.

. . .

The photographs published by LFP neither relate to the incident of public concern conceptually nor correspond with the time period during which Benoit was rendered, against her will, the subject of public scrutiny. The photographs bear no relevance—let alone "substantial relevance"—to the "matter of legitimate public interest." [ ] On these facts, were we to hold otherwise, LFP would be free to publish any nude photographs of almost anyone without their permission, simply because the fact that they were caught nude on camera strikes someone as "newsworthy." Surely that debases the very concept of a right to privacy.

III. *Economic Ramifications of LFP's Publication of the Photographs*

Finally, we are guided by the Seventh Circuit's opinion in Douglass v. Hustler Magazine, Inc., 769 F.2d 1128 (7th Cir. 1985), to conclude that LFP may be held liable in damages for violation of the right of publicity when it published images of Benoit that had economic value without her permission let alone without compensating her estate.

. . . Benoit does not seem to have ever sought to have nude photographs of herself published. As stated by the Supreme Court of Georgia, "a person who avoids exploitation during life is entitled to have his image protected against exploitation after death just as much *if not more than* a person who exploited his image during life." Martin Luther King, 296 S.E.2d at 706 (emphasis added).

. . . Crude though the concept may seem in this context, Toffoloni is entitled to control when and whether images of her daughter are made public in order to maximize the economic benefit to be derived from her daughter's posthumous fame.

    . . .

NOTES AND QUESTIONS

1.   What implications does this case have for entertainment journalism? If a celebrity dies, for example, may a publication run childhood photos of the celebrity in connection with stories about the death without fear of a right of publicity claim? Or does the case turn on the fact that it involved nude photos?

2.   What of the court's strong language suggesting that the images have "no relevance" to anything newsworthy? If you were arguing the case on behalf of the publisher, how might you try to link the photos with some journalistic relevance?

3.   Does the misappropriation tort protect privacy interests or property interests? As applied in many states, it and related torts seem to protect both. A person may wish to prevent exploitation of his or her personality altogether; such a person seems to be asserting a privacy interest. But a person might also be perfectly willing to have his or personality exploited if the price is right. In this setting the interest looks more like a property right. All professional models and many athletes, actors, and musicians make a business of selling rights to exploit their names or likenesses. The term "right of publicity" (effectively the opposite of a "right of privacy") describes this interest in preserving the pecuniary value of one's personality and has important implications for its judicial development. With regard to the right of publicity, does the right survive the death of the celebrity in whom the right is based? That is, can a celebrity's heirs or assigns prevent unauthorized exploitation after the famous person has died? Courts that have found the right to be descendible have analogized it to an ordinary property right or a copyright, both of which are inheritable. In contrast, courts that have found no descendible right have analogized it to privacy rights, which are personal in nature, and have stressed the line-drawing difficulties inherent in any development of a right that survives the death of the celebrity. The Restatement suggests that appropriation claims are inheritable. Restatement (Second) of Torts, § 652I, comment b ("[s]ince appropriation of name or likeness is similar to impairment of a property right

and involves an aspect of unjust enrichment of the defendants or his estate, survival rights may be held to exist following . . . death").

4.   At least twelve states have statutes that protect the right of publicity after the death of the person involved. In California, for example, the right of "deceased personality" is provided for in Cal. Civil Code § 990, which protects the commercial value of the "personality" of someone even if he or she never sought to exploit that value during his or her lifetime. The California law makes clear that the rights of "deceased personality" are "property rights, freely transferable, in whole or in part, by contract or by means of trust or testamentary documents, whether the transfer occurs before the death of the deceased personality, by the deceased personality or his or her transferees, or, after the death of the deceased personality, by the person or persons in whom the rights vest under this section or the transferees of that person or persons." Other states restrict the law only to people whose "personality" had commercial value during their lifetime. As noted above, the Restatement specifically suggests that the appropriation privacy tort can be brought after death by surviving relatives or others who have been given licensing rights to the decedent's image.

5.   What about digital technology that makes it possible to create "virtual actors" who look, sound, and move on the screen like the real people they recreate? Consider that in 1992 the U.S. Court of Appeals for the Ninth Circuit allowed a suit by Vanna White, who appeared on the television game show "Wheel of Fortune," to proceed against Samsung Electronics for an advertisement for Samsung VCRs featuring a "robot, dressed in a wig, gown, and jewelry . . . consciously selected to resemble White's hair and dress. The robot was posed next to a game board which is instantly recognizable as the Wheel of Fortune game show set, in a stance for which White is famous." White claimed a violation of California's right of publicity statute, Cal. Civil Code § 3344, and federal trademark law, 15 U.S.C. § 1125(a). The appellate court found that White's suit presented sufficient questions of fact to overturn the trial's court grant of summary judgment against her. See White v. Samsung Electronics America, Inc., 971 F.2d 1395, 1397 (9th Cir. 1992), rehearing en banc denied, 989 F.2d 1512 (9th Cir. 1993).

6.   Professor Mark McKenna contends that the right of publicity tort would be more coherent if courts would conceptualize it as protecting "the right of autonomous self-definition" rather than economic interests. This conception of the tort would focus on commercial uses of an individual's identity that "suggest sponsorship or endorsement or attempt to rework the meaning of her identity." Under this conception, uses of an individual's identity that are "merely referential" and do not "redefine" that identity or "suggest endorsement" would not be tortious. Mark P. McKenna, The Right of Publicity and Autonomous Self-Definition, 67 U. Pitt. L. Rev. 225, 291 (2005).

———

Athletes and Appropriation. As explained earlier, athletes have had significant impact on appropriation-related jurisprudence, especially the right of publicity, a concept that initially sprang from a case involving a professional baseball player.

Recall that in 2014, the U.S. Court of Appeals for the Seventh Circuit found that professional basketball player Michael Jordan had valid right of publicity and misappropriation-like claims under Illinois law against a grocery store that published an ad congratulating him on his induction into the Basketball Hall of Fame. "[A]n ad congratulating a famous athlete can only be understood as a promotional device for the advertiser," the court held, finding the ad to be commercial speech and allowing Jordan's right of publicity and other claims to go to trial. Jordan v. Jewel Food Stores, Inc., 743 F.3d 509 (7th Cir. 2014). A jury later awarded Jordan nearly $9 million dollars for the misuse of his identity in a case involving a separate but similar ad that promoted a different grocery store. Both cases settled soon after, but the terms of the settlements are confidential. Michael Jordan Reaches Settlement with Jewel, Dominick's, Chicago Tribune, Nov. 23, 2015.

College athletes have also sued for publicity rights. In Hart v. Electronic Arts, Inc., 717 F.3d 141 (3d Cir. 2013), a former college football player sued Electronic Arts for a violation of his right of publicity for using his likeness in its videogame, NCAA Football. NCAA Football depicts college teams and their players, using "life-like" player avatars and short factually-accurate player biographies. As part of the videogame, gamers can choose a college team, control it for a number of seasons, and make minimal alterations to the players' virtual likenesses. EA licensed the right to use team information from the NCAA, but not the rights to use the likenesses or biographical information of the individual players. Plaintiff could not have licensed the rights to use his name or likeness, because NCAA rules prohibited it.

Plaintiff challenged EA's creation of a character and avatar that resembled him. The character had the same team, position, number, height, weight, and throwing distance as Hart and shared significant aspects of his biographical information. Additionally, the avatar's physical likeness resembled Hart's, and the avatar even wore Hart's signature armband and visor. The district court granted a motion for summary judgment against Hart, but the Third Circuit reversed.

In "a case of first impression," the Third Circuit analyzed the right of publicity claim under a "Transformative Use Test" adapted from copyright law's fair use test. The transformative use test relied especially on the first fair use factor: the purpose and character of the use. The court's opinion surveyed cases from other jurisdictions applying the transformative use test and drew guidance from them regarding transformative uses. Quoting the California Supreme Court, for example, the opinion focused on the need for a work to have "transformative elements or creative contributions," though it noted that these "can take many forms." The court further explained that "[a] work is transformative if it adds 'new expression.' That expression alone is sufficient; it need not convey any 'meaning or message.' "

In applying its new test, the court first looked to whether EA's use of Hart's "identity" was transformative, noting that both Hart's likeness and biographical information comprised his "identity." The court observed that the physical appearance of the avatar closely resembled Hart, down to his notable accessories. Further, Hart's biographical information was also accurate. Next, the court looked to the context in which EA used Hart's identity. Context encompasses both location and activity, neither of which the court found to be transformative, noting that Hart's avatar played college football in a college football stadium as opposed to some "fanciful" location such as outer space. After identity and context, the court looked to whether gamers could transform the avatar. Although gamers could alter Hart's likeness to some extent, the court cautioned that "[i]nteractivity cannot be an end unto itself," and that "the mere presence of [the ability to modify the avatar], without more, cannot satisfy the Transformative Use Test." Finally, the court looked to the goal of EA in its creation of the game, and whether use of Hart's identifying features was critical to the "sum and substance" of that goal. EA's motivation in using the identities of college teams and their players was to create a realistic gaming experience, which "seeks to capitalize on the respective fan bases for the various teams and players." EA's use of actual players and teams not only appealed to fans, but also rivals' need for "some cathartic readjustment of history" for bitter losses. The court found Hart's unaltered likeness was central to the game in this aspect, enticing fans to play "as, or alongside," known players.

In 2014 Electronic Arts and the NCAA settled similar cases brought by former college football and basketball players. Tom Farrey, Players, Game Makers Settle for $40M, ESPN Online, May 31, 2014. Subsequently, the U.S. Court of Appeals for the Ninth Circuit held in 2015 that EA would likely not prevail in a lawsuit that "balance[d] the right of publicity of former professional football players against [a] First Amendment right to use their likenesses in [the] Madden NFL series of video games." The video game company had tried again to argue its "incidental use" of the players' identities, but the court held that the "use of the former players' likenesses . . . [was] central to [the game's] main commercial purpose—to create a realistic virtual simulation of football games involving current and former NFL teams." Davis v. Electronic Arts, 775 F.3d 1172 (9th Cir. 2015). The Supreme Court later denied certiorari.

In 2016 the Eighth Circuit ruled that there was a difference between that use and use of players' images in NFL-produced films. There, players had sued for right of publicity because they had appeared in NFL films "describing significant games, seasons, and players in the NFL's history." The appeals court held in part that the films were expressive speech, not commercial speech, and that the news value and public interest in the film footage trumped plaintiffs' right of publicity claims. Dryer v. National Football League, 814 F.3d 938 (8th Cir. 2016).

2.   UNAUTHORIZED COVERAGE OF ENTERTAINMENT ACTS

The Zacchini Case. Hugo Zacchini performed a human cannonball act at a county fair. Persons attending the fair were not charged a separate admission to see Zacchini's act. A television reporter covering the fair with the permission of fair officials filmed Zacchini's act over Zacchini's objection, and the 15-second segment was shown on the local news that night with favorable commentary.

Zacchini sued the station for, among other things, "unlawful appropriation of plaintiff's professional property." The trial court granted the station's motion for summary judgment. The Ohio Supreme Court held that one may not use the name or likeness of another for the taker's own benefit even if the use was not commercial. That court nevertheless granted judgment for the station, on the ground that the film was about a matter of legitimate public interest and its use in a newscast was privileged.

The Supreme Court reversed 5–4, holding that the Ohio Supreme Court mistakenly believed such a privilege was required by the First Amendment:

> It is evident, and there is no claim here to the contrary, that petitioner's state-law right of publicity would not serve to prevent respondent from reporting the newsworthy facts about petitioner's act. Wherever the line in particular situations is to be drawn between media reports that are protected and those that are not, we are quite sure that the First and Fourteenth Amendments do not immunize the media when they broadcast a performer's entire act without his consent. The Constitution no more prevents a State from requiring respondent to compensate petitioner for broadcasting his act on television than it would privilege respondent to film and broadcast a copyrighted dramatic work without liability to the copyright owner. . . .

The Court said that by protecting Zacchini's performance from unauthorized broadcast, "Ohio has recognized what may be the strongest case for a 'right of publicity'—involving not the appropriation of an entertainer's reputation to enhance the attractiveness of a commercial product, but the appropriation of the very activity by which the entertainer acquired the reputation in the first place."

Justice Powell, joined by Justices Brennan and Marshall, dissented, arguing that use of the film was part of routine news coverage protected by the First Amendment "absent a strong showing by the plaintiff that the news broadcast was a subterfuge or cover for private or commercial exploitation." Justice Powell said the majority's "repeated incantation of a single formula: 'a performer's entire act' " was not a sufficiently clear standard to resolve even the case at hand. "One may assume that the actual firing was preceded by some fanfare, possibly stretching over several minutes, to heighten the audience's anticipation. . . . If this is found to have been the case on remand, then respondent could not be said to have appropriated the 'entire act' in its 15-second newsclip—and the Court's opinion then would afford no guidance for the resolution of the case."

Justice Stevens dissented on the ground that the case should have been remanded to the Ohio Supreme Court to clarify whether its decision rested on state law or First Amendment principles. Zacchini v. Scripps-Howard Broadcasting Co., 433 U.S. 562 (1977).

Although the decision clearly indicates that a state need not confine its remedies for misappropriation to instances where the use is commercial, the states have not been eager to abandon that limitation. Moreover, the Court's use of the "entire act" rubric does not encourage reliance on *Zacchini* because media rarely make unauthorized use of a performer's entire act.

Promoters of entertainment and sports events normally protect their rights by controlling access to the event. Terms of admission often prohibit use of cameras or tape recorders entirely, or specify portions of performances that may be recorded or photographed. Broadcasting rights are protected by allowing only those who have contracted with the promoters to set up their broadcasting equipment. Performers, in turn, protect their interests through their contracts with the promoters; whether the promoter has a right to authorize live broadcast of a concert, for example, is determined by the terms of the contract between the performer and the promoter.

If Zacchini did not protect his rights contractually, why should the courts provide him a remedy through tort law? The television station was permitted—probably even encouraged—by the fair officials to broadcast film of various events at the fair. Should they be entitled to rely on that invitation without inquiring into the officials' authority to extend it?

Plaintiffs generally have been unsuccessful when they have tried to invoke *Zacchini* to create a cause of action not otherwise provided by the law of copyright or the tort of commercial exploitation of name or likeness. Actress Ginger Rogers relied on *Zacchini* in an attempt to prevent Federico Fellini from using the title "Ginger and Fred" for his 1986 movie about an Italian dancing couple. The district court characterized *Zacchini* as a "narrowly drawn opinion effectively limited to its facts," and distinguished it on the ground that "Ginger and Fred" did not threaten Rogers' economic viability. Rogers v. Grimaldi, 695 F. Supp. 112 (S.D.N.Y. 1988), affirmed 875 F.2d 994 (2d Cir. 1989).

3. SELF-PROMOTION

Media sometimes encounter this branch of the law when they use photos or film of people to promote their publications or programs.

A publication's use of an earlier story to advertise its own product does not come within "advertising purposes" under the New York privacy statute, for example. In Booth v. Curtis Publishing Co., 15 A.D.2d 343 (N.Y. App. Div. 1962), aff'd without opinion, 182 N.E.2d 812 (N.Y. 1962), Holiday magazine published a photograph of actress Shirley Booth in a story about a prominent resort. The color photograph was "a very striking one, show[ing] Miss Booth in the water up to her neck, but wearing a brimmed, high-crowned street hat of straw." Several months after the story appeared, Holiday took out full-page advertisements in the New Yorker and Advertising Age magazines. Both reprinted the Booth photograph as a sample of the content of Holiday magazine. "Because of the photograph's striking qualities it would be quite effective in drawing attention to the advertisements; but it was also a sample of magazine content."

The court found the use of the photograph to be an incidental mentioning of plaintiff in the course of advertising itself. "It stands to reason that a publication can best prove its worth and illustrate its content by submission of complete copies of or extraction from past editions. . . . And, of course, it is true that the publisher must advertise in other public media, just as it must by poster, circular, cover, or soliciting letter. This is a practical necessity which the law may not ignore in giving effect to the purposes of the statute."

Although the court recognized that "realistically" the use of the photograph attracted the attention of the reader, that use was outweighed by the magazine's need to demonstrate its content. Finally, nothing in the advertisement suggested that plaintiff endorsed defendant's magazine.

4. FALSE OR MISLEADING PROMOTIONAL MATERIAL

Celebrities have had considerable success with appropriation claims over false or misleading promotional material. The line between the false light and appropriation branches of privacy law is often blurred in these cases. And the publishers are often not mainstream news organizations.

The actor José Solano, Jr., for example, brought suit against Playgirl magazine for its use without his consent of his picture on its front cover. He made claims for both false light and appropriation under the California statute. The district court granted the magazine summary judgment, finding that the picture showing Solano bare-chested and the headline "TV Guys. Primetime's Sexy Young Stars Exposed" did not create a false impression and that, in any event, Solano could not prove actual malice. But the Ninth Circuit ruled that the use of a photograph in which Solano was only partially clothed and the word "exposed" in the headline could have given readers the false impression that Solano appeared nude within the magazine. The court pointed to evidence from depositions of Playgirl staff indicating that they were aware that some people might be misled by the cover and held that that was sufficient to allow a jury to conclude that Playgirl acted with actual malice. The court distinguished the case involving actor Dustin Hoffman referred to earlier, on the basis that the text of that article made clear that digital techniques had been used to alter the actor's photograph. See Solano v. Playgirl, Inc., 292 F.3d 1078 (9th Cir. 2002).

———

Given all these nuances in appropriation-related law, consider this series of hypotheticals from Steven Shiffrin, The First Amendment and Economic Regulation: Away from a General Theory of the First Amendment, 78 Nw. U. L. Rev. 1212, 1257 n. 275 (1983):

> A magazine may have a profit motive in taking a particular position on a particular subject, but the courts will ordinarily not count that motivation as significant. In thinking about profit motive and the dissemination of truth consider these examples: (1) Without his consent, Mercedes Benz *truthfully* advertises that Frank Sinatra drives a Mercedes. Sinatra sues for misappropriation. Does it make a difference if Mercedes in its ad says, "We didn't ask Sinatra's permission to tell you this" or "Sinatra doesn't want us to tell you this but . . . "? (2) Suppose *Time* magazine writes a story on Mercedes Benz and puts Sinatra on the cover with a picture of his Mercedes. Suppose they put Sinatra on the cover purely for reasons of profit. (3) Suppose Time Inc. advertises: "Get the recent issue of *Time* with Frank Sinatra on the cover with his Mercedes." (4) Suppose *Time* truthfully advertises: "Sinatra doesn't want us to tell you this, but he is one of our regular readers."

Which of these uses might be actionable?

———

On the development of the tort law of privacy generally, see Ken Gormley, One Hundred Years of Privacy, 1992 Wis. L. Rev. 1335 (1992). Randall P. Bezanson, The Right to Privacy Revisited: Privacy, News, and Social Change, 1890–1990, 80 Cal. L. Rev. 1133 (1992). Robert C. Post, The Social Foundations of Privacy: Community and Self in the Common Law Tort, 77 Cal. L. Rev. 957 (1989). Daniel Solove, Understanding Privacy (2008); Samantha Barbas, The Social Origins of the Personality Torts, 67 Rutgers U.L. Rev. 393 (2015); Danielle Keats Citron, Mainstreaming Privacy Torts, 98 Cal. L. Rev. 1805 (2010): Neil Richards and Daniel Solove, Prosser's Privacy Law: A Mixed Legacy, 98 Cal. L. Rev. 1887 (2010).

D. PROTECTIVE PRIVACY IN EUROPE AND ITS EFFECT IN THE UNITED STATES

Much of the recent debate about privacy in the United States and elsewhere has focused on the collection and use of personal information in government and commercial electronic databases. Concern has intensified with the development of technologies that allow the automatic collection of such information from Internet users by means of "cookies," "spyware," and other unnoticed data collection methods. For the most part, this affects only the business aspects of media and so far has only marginally affected journalism.

The collection and use of personal information in the United States is regulated by a growing array of statutes beyond those we have already noted here. Although these statutes rarely act on the media directly, they may limit the availability of information on which the press may draw, as did the federal Driver Privacy Protection Act.

In 1995 the European Union adopted a Data Protection Directive that caused considerable consternation among American media. The Directive required members of the EU to adopt legislation protecting individuals' privacy from various uses of information in databases and specified what such legislation must do. It required businesses that compile databases to notify individuals as to the uses to which the information might be put, allow them to forbid some uses, and give them rights to see and correct the information relating to them. See Directive 95/46 of the European Parliament and of the Council, Oct. 24, 1995.

The Directive did not apply to the United States, but contained a provision prohibiting the transfer of personally identifiable information from EU countries into or out of non-EU countries that did not have similar data protection policies. Data-protection policies in the U.S. are much less protective of personal information.

American companies in general feared that the restrictions on transfer of data into and out of EU countries would interfere with the internationalization of banking, credit, and marketing, and media organizations feared that it might inhibit the use of information for journalistic purposes.

With regard to media, the directive contained an exception for "journalistic purposes." Moreover, under intense lobbying by American companies, the U.S. and the EU negotiated an agreement that allowed transfer of information to or from U.S. businesses if they voluntarily adopted one of several alternative methods of protecting individuals' privacy. As a result, the impact on U.S. journalism was minimal, but many Europeans remained dissatisfied with the U.S. response, and many in the U.S. remained wary of future attempts to strengthen international restraints on use of personal information.

In October 2015, the European Court of Justice (ECJ) declared the safe harbor agreement invalid because it did not provide adequate protections for the personal data of Europeans. An Austrian privacy advocate had claimed that Facebook did not adequately protect his privacy, and the court agreed. Schrems v. Data Protection Commissioner, Oct. 6, 2015.

In addition, a 2014 decision by the European Court of Justice recognized a privacy right commonly referred to as the right to be forgotten or the right to erasure. The court held that search engines like Google must remove certain privacy-invading links from their search results. The case arose in Spain, where a man complained that a Google search of his name turned up a 12-year-old newspaper story about proceedings against him for debt. He contended that the story, although accurate, was no longer relevant because the matter had been fully resolved. He demanded that Google remove the link that pulled up the story when users entered his name in a Google search. The Court held that the 1995 Data Protection Directive of the European Parliament gave individuals a right to insist on removal of information that is "inadequate, irrelevant, or no longer relevant, or excessive in relation to the purposes for which they were processed and in the light of the time that has elapsed Case C–131/12, Google Spain SL, Google Inc. v. Agencia Española de Protetión de Datos (AEPD), Mario Costeja Gonzáles, Court of Justice (Grand Chamber), 13 May 2014.

The court held that operators of search engines are engaged in "processing of personal data" within the meaning of the Directive and are subject to the Directive when they set up a branch or subsidiary to promote and sell advertising space on a site in an EU country. The decision states a principle of law binding on all members of the EU, but enforcement is left to the courts of each country. Those courts should determine:

> whether the data subject has a right that the information in question relating to him personally should, at this point in time, no longer be linked to his name by a list of results displayed following a search made on the basis of his name, without it being necessary in order to find such a right that the inclusion of the information in question in that list causes prejudice to the subject.

The individual's privacy rights "override, as a rule, not only the economic interest of the operator of the search engine but also the interest of the general public in having access to that information," the court wrote, unless "the role played by the data subject in public life" justifies the interference with the individual's privacy rights.

Search engines are not required to remove a link until the subject makes a request.

Despite the Restatement example noted earlier that suggests that an individual might have privacy rights with regard to a long-ago crime, and some rare cases that the passage of time could indeed create a right to privacy in once-public information, there is no jurisprudential or legislative shift toward a similar right in the United States. Indeed, as explored earlier, there are serious questions regarding the constitutionality of the right to be forgotten or right to erasure. The vast majority of courts that have considered the question focus on the underlying truth of the information and how it was once public. In January 2015 the United States Court of Appeals for the Second Circuit, for example, ruled that a woman who had been arrested in 2010 and whose arrest had later been nullified could not order a record of the arrest removed from websites. She had argued that the nullification made the arrest information false and defamatory and that it therefore should be erased under Connecticut's Erasure Statute, one that mandates that government records be erased after a nullifying prosecutorial decision. But the court found that no "amount of wishing can undo [the] historical truth" of the arrest and of the information about it that might exist elsewhere. The government's legal concept of nullification, therefore, could not undo the fact that the arrest itself was already publically known outside of government records. Martin v. Hearst Corp., 777 F.3d 546 (2d Cir. 2015).

CHAPTER VI

LIABILITY FOR EMOTIONAL, ECONOMIC, AND PHYSICAL HARM

Both the common law and First Amendment doctrines governing defamation and invasion of privacy are well defined. This chapter considers the types of civil liability that may arise when the mass communication of information causes harms to interests other than reputation or privacy. Because First Amendment doctrine in these areas is still developing, it may be helpful to think of these materials as a study in the formulation of a First Amendment response to problems that had not previously been thought to raise free speech issues. The Supreme Court's contributions to this process, represented by Hustler Magazine, Inc. v. Falwell, Snyder v. Phelps, and Cohen v. Cowles Media Co., seem to point in very different directions.

A. EMOTIONAL DISTRESS

1. INTENTIONAL INFLICTION

Most states recognize a tort action of intentional infliction of emotional distress. Like the privacy torts, this tort developed in the last century. Most states have adopted some version of the elements of the tort as set forth in the Restatement (Second) of Torts § 46. This section requires a successful litigant to establish that (1) the defendant engaged in outrageous conduct and acted (2) intentionally or recklessly in (3) causing (4) severe emotional distress. Actionable conduct sometimes has no purpose other than to inflict emotional distress, such as maliciously telling a woman that her husband was murdered, or has another purpose but goes beyond the pale of tolerable conduct, such as harassment by a debt collector.

First Amendment concerns are at issue in many intentional infliction cases, as the following opinion shows.

Hustler Magazine, Inc. v. Falwell
Supreme Court of the United States, 1988.
485 U.S. 46.

■ CHIEF JUSTICE REHNQUIST delivered the opinion of the Court.

Petitioner Hustler Magazine, Inc., is a magazine of nationwide circulation. Respondent Jerry Falwell, a nationally known minister who has been active as a commentator on politics and public affairs, sued petitioner and its publisher, petitioner Larry Flynt. . . .

The inside front cover of the November 1983 issue of Hustler Magazine featured a "parody" of an advertisement for Campari Liqueur that contained the name and picture of respondent and was entitled "Jerry Falwell talks about his first time." This parody was modeled after actual Campari ads that included interviews with various celebrities about their "first times." Although it was apparent by the end of each interview that this meant the first time they sampled Campari, the ads clearly played on the sexual double entendre of the general subject of "first times." Copying the form and layout of these Campari ads, Hustler's editors chose respondent as the featured celebrity and drafted an alleged "interview" with him in which he states that his "first time" was during a drunken incestuous rendezvous with his mother in an outhouse. The Hustler parody portrays respondent and his mother as drunk and immoral, and suggests that respondent is a hypocrite who preaches only when he is drunk. In small print at the bottom of the page, the ad contains the disclaimer, "ad parody—not to be taken seriously." The magazine's table of contents also lists the ad as "Fiction; Ad and Personality Parody."

Soon after the November issue of Hustler became available to the public, respondent brought this diversity action in the United States District Court for the Western District of Virginia against Hustler Magazine, Inc., Larry C. Flynt, and Flynt Distributing Co. Respondent stated in his complaint that publication of the ad parody in Hustler entitled him to recover damages for libel, invasion of privacy, and intentional infliction of emotional distress. The case proceeded to trial. At the close of the evidence, the District Court granted a directed verdict for petitioners on the invasion of privacy claim. The jury then found against respondent on the libel claim, specifically finding that the ad parody could not "reasonably be understood as describing actual facts about [respondent] or actual events in which [he] participated." [ ] The jury ruled for respondent on the intentional infliction of emotional distress claim, however, and stated that he should be awarded $100,000 in compensatory damages, as well as $50,000 each in punitive damages from petitioners [Hustler Magazine and Flynt]. Petitioners' motion for judgment notwithstanding the verdict was denied.

On appeal, the [Fourth Circuit] affirmed the judgment against petitioners. [ ] The court rejected petitioners' argument that the "actual malice" standard of *New York Times Co. v. Sullivan*, [ ], must be met before respondent can recover for emotional distress. The court agreed that because respondent is concededly a public figure, petitioners are "entitled to the same level of first amendment protection in the claim for intentional infliction of emotional distress that they received in [respondent's] claim for libel." [ ] But this does not mean that a literal application of the actual malice rule is appropriate in the context of an emotional distress claim. In the court's view, the *New York Times* decision emphasized the constitutional importance not of the falsity of the statement or the defendant's disregard for the truth, but of the heightened level of culpability embodied in the requirement of "knowing . . . or reckless" conduct. Here, [in the view of the Fourth Circuit] the *New York Times* standard is satisfied by the state-law requirement, and the jury's finding, that the defendants have acted intentionally or recklessly.[3] The Court of Appeals then went on to reject the contention that because the jury found that the ad parody did not describe actual facts about respondent, the ad was an opinion that is protected by the First Amendment. As the court put it, this was "irrelevant," as the issue is "whether [the ad's] publication was sufficiently outrageous to constitute intentional infliction of emotional distress." [ ] Petitioners then filed a petition for rehearing en banc, but this was denied by a divided court. Given the importance of the constitutional issues involved, we granted certiorari.

This case presents us with a novel question involving First Amendment limitations upon a State's authority to protect its citizens from the intentional infliction of emotional distress. We must decide whether a public figure may recover damages for emotional harm caused by the publication of an ad parody offensive to him, and doubtless gross and repugnant in the eyes of most. Respondent would have us find that a State's interest in protecting public figures from emotional distress is sufficient to deny First Amendment protection to speech that is patently offensive and is intended to inflict emotional injury, even when that speech could not reasonably have been interpreted as stating actual facts about the public figure involved. This we decline to do.

At the heart of the First Amendment is the recognition of the fundamental importance of the free flow of ideas and opinions on matters of public interest and concern. "[T]he freedom to speak one's mind is not only an aspect of individual liberty—and thus a good unto itself—but also is essential to the common quest for truth and the vitality of society as a whole." [*Bose*] We have therefore been particularly vigilant to ensure that individual expressions of ideas remain free from governmentally imposed sanctions. The First Amendment recognizes no such thing as a "false" idea. [*Gertz*] As Justice Holmes wrote, "[W]hen men have realized that time has upset many fighting faiths, they may come to believe even more than they believe the very foundations of their own conduct that the ultimate good desired is better reached by free trade in ideas—that the best test of truth is the power of the thought to get itself accepted in the competition of the market. . . ." [*Abrams*]

---

[3] Under Virginia law, in an action for intentional infliction of emotional distress a plaintiff must show that the defendant's conduct (1) is intentional or reckless; (2) offends generally accepted standards of decency or morality; (3) is causally connected with the plaintiff's emotional distress; and (4) caused emotional distress that was severe. [ ]

The sort of robust political debate encouraged by the First Amendment is bound to produce speech that is critical of those who hold public office or those public figures who are "intimately involved in the resolution of important public questions or, by reason of their fame, shape events in areas of concern to society at large." [*Walker* and *Butts*] (Warren, C.J., concurring in result). Justice Frankfurter put it succinctly in Baumgartner v. United States, 322 U.S. 665, 673–674 (1944), when he said that "[o]ne of the prerogatives of American citizenship is the right to criticize public men and measures." Such criticism, inevitably, will not always be reasoned or moderate; public figures as well as public officials will be subject to "vehement, caustic, and sometimes unpleasantly sharp attacks," [*New York Times*]. "[T]he candidate who vaunts his spotless record and sterling integrity cannot convincingly cry 'Foul!' when an opponent or an industrious reporter attempts to demonstrate the contrary." [*Monitor Patriot Co.*]

Of course, this does not mean that any speech about a public figure is immune from sanction in the form of damages. Since [*New York Times*] we have consistently ruled that a public figure may hold a speaker liable for the damage to reputation caused by publication of a defamatory falsehood, but only if the statement was made "with knowledge that it was false or with reckless disregard of whether it was false or not." [ ] False statements of fact are particularly valueless; they interfere with the truth-seeking function of the marketplace of ideas, and they cause damage to an individual's reputation that cannot easily be repaired by counterspeech, however persuasive or effective. See [*Gertz*] n.9. But even though falsehoods have little value in and of themselves, they are "nevertheless inevitable in free debate," [*Gertz*], and a rule that would impose strict liability on a publisher for false factual assertions would have an undoubted "chilling" effect on speech relating to public figures that does have constitutional value. "Freedoms of expression require 'breathing space.'" [*Hepps*, quoting *New York Times*] This breathing space is provided by a constitutional rule that allows public figures to recover for libel or defamation only when they can prove both that the statement was false and that the statement was made with the requisite level of culpability.

Respondent argues, however, that a different standard should apply in this case because here the State seeks to prevent not reputational damage, but the severe emotional distress suffered by the person who is the subject of an offensive publication. Cf. Zacchini v. Scripps-Howard Broadcasting Co., 433 U.S. 562 (1977) (ruling that the "actual malice" standard does not apply to the tort of appropriation of a right of publicity). In respondent's view, and in the view of the Court of Appeals, so long as the utterance was intended to inflict emotional distress, was outrageous, and did in fact inflict serious emotional distress, it is of no constitutional import whether the statement was a fact or an opinion, or whether it was true or false. It is the intent to cause injury that is the gravamen of the tort, and the State's interest in preventing emotional harm simply outweighs whatever interest a speaker may have in speech of this type.

Generally speaking the law does not regard the intent to inflict emotional distress as one which should receive much solicitude, and it is quite understandable that most if not all jurisdictions have chosen to make it civilly culpable where the conduct in question is sufficiently "outrageous." But in the world of debate about public affairs, many things done with motives that are less than admirable are protected by the First Amendment. In Garrison v. Louisiana, [ ], we held that even when a speaker or writer is motivated by hatred or ill-will his expression was protected by the First Amendment:

> "Debate on public issues will not be uninhibited if the speaker must run the risk that it will be proved in court that he spoke out of hatred; even if he did speak out of hatred, utterances honestly believed contribute to the free interchange of ideas and the ascertainment of truth." [ ]

Thus while such a bad motive may be deemed controlling for purposes of tort liability in other areas of the law, we think the First Amendment prohibits such a result in the area of public debate about public figures.

Were we to hold otherwise, there can be little doubt that political cartoonists and satirists would be subjected to damages awards without any showing that their work falsely defamed its subject. Webster's defines a caricature as "the deliberately distorted picturing or imitating of a person, literary style, etc. by exaggerating features or mannerisms for satirical effect." [ ] The appeal of the political cartoon or caricature is often based on exploration of unfortunate physical traits or politically embarrassing events—an exploration often calculated to injure the feelings of the subject of the portrayal. The art of the cartoonist is often not reasoned or evenhanded, but slashing and one-sided. One cartoonist expressed the nature of the art in these words:

> "The political cartoon is a weapon of attack, of scorn and ridicule and satire; it is least effective when it tries to pat some politician on the back. It is usually as welcome as a bee sting and is always controversial in some quarters." Long, The Political Cartoon: Journalism's Strongest Weapon, The Quill, 56, 57 (Nov. 1962).

Several famous examples of this type of intentionally injurious speech were drawn by Thomas Nast, probably the greatest American cartoonist to date, who was associated for many years during the post-Civil War era with Harper's Weekly. In the pages of that publication Nast conducted a graphic vendetta against William M. "Boss" Tweed and his corrupt associates in New York City's "Tweed Ring." It has been described by one historian of the subject as "a sustained attack which in its passion and effectiveness stands alone in the history of American graphic art." M. Keller, The Art and Politics of Thomas Nast 177 (1968). Another writer explains that the success of the Nast cartoon was achieved "because of the emotional impact of its presentation. It continuously goes beyond the bounds of good taste and conventional manners." C. Press, The Political Cartoon 251 (1981).

Despite their sometimes caustic nature, from the early cartoon portraying George Washington as an ass down to the present day, graphic depictions and satirical cartoons have played a prominent role in public and political debate. Nast's castigation of the Tweed Ring, Walt McDougall's characterization of presidential candidate James G. Blaine's banquet with the millionaires at Delmonico's as "The Royal Feast of Belshazzar," and numerous other efforts have undoubtedly had an effect on the course and outcome of contemporaneous debate. Lincoln's tall, gangling posture, Teddy Roosevelt's glasses and teeth, and Franklin D. Roosevelt's jutting jaw and cigarette holder have been memorialized by political cartoons with an effect that could not have been obtained by the photographer or the portrait artist. From the viewpoint of history it is clear that our political discourse would have been considerably poorer without them.

Respondent contends, however, that the caricature in question here was so "outrageous" as to distinguish it from more traditional political cartoons. There is no doubt that the caricature of respondent and his mother published in Hustler is at best a distant cousin of the political cartoons described above, and a rather poor relation at that. If it were possible by laying down a principled standard to separate the one from the other, public discourse would probably suffer little or no harm. But we doubt that there is any such standard, and we are quite sure that the pejorative description "outrageous" does not supply one. "Outrageousness" in the area of political and social discourse has an inherent subjectiveness about it which would allow a jury to impose liability on the basis of the jurors' tastes or views, or perhaps on the basis of their dislike of a particular expression. An "outrageousness" standard thus runs afoul of our longstanding refusal to allow damages to be awarded because the speech in question may have an adverse emotional impact on the audience. See NAACP v. Claiborne Hardware Co., 458 U.S. 886, 910 (1982) ("Speech does not lose its protected character . . . simply because it may embarrass others or coerce them into action"). And, as we stated in FCC v. Pacifica Foundation, 438 U.S. 726 (1978):

> "[T]he fact that society may find speech offensive is not a sufficient reason for suppressing it. Indeed, if it is the speaker's opinion that gives offense, that consequence is a reason for according it constitutional protection. For it is a central tenet of the First Amendment that the government must remain neutral in the marketplace of ideas." [ ]

See also Street v. New York, 394 U.S. 576, 592 (1969) ("It is firmly settled that . . . the public expression of ideas may not be prohibited merely because the ideas are themselves offensive to some of their hearers").

Admittedly, these oft-repeated First Amendment principles, like other principles, are subject to limitations. We recognized in *Pacifica Foundation*, that speech that is " 'vulgar,' 'offensive,' and 'shocking' " is "not entitled to absolute constitutional protection under all circumstances." [ ] In Chaplinsky v. New Hampshire, 315 U.S. 568 (1942), we held that a state could lawfully punish an individual for the use of insulting " 'fighting' words—those which by their very utterance inflict injury or tend to incite an immediate breach of the peace." [ ] These limitations are but recognition of the observation in [*Dun & Bradstreet*] that this Court has "long recognized that not all speech is of equal First Amendment importance." But the sort of expression involved in this case does not seem to us to be governed by any exception to the general First Amendment principles stated above.

We conclude that public figures and public officials may not recover for the tort of intentional infliction of emotional distress by reason of publications such as the one here at issue without showing in addition that the publication contains a false statement of fact which was made with "actual malice," i.e., with knowledge that the statement was false or with reckless disregard as to whether or not it was true. This is not merely a "blind application" of the *New York Times* standard, [ ], it reflects our considered judgment that such a standard is necessary to give adequate "breathing space" to the freedoms protected by the First Amendment.

Here it is clear that respondent Falwell is a "public figure" for purposes of First Amendment law.[5] The jury found against respondent on his libel claim when it decided that the Hustler ad parody could not "reasonably be understood as describing actual facts about [respondent] or actual events in which [he] participated." [ ] The Court of Appeals interpreted the jury's finding to be that the ad parody "was not reasonably believable," [ ], and in accordance with our custom we accept this finding. Respondent is thus relegated to his claim for damages awarded by the jury for the intentional infliction of emotional distress by "outrageous" conduct. But for reasons heretofore stated this claim cannot, consistently with the First Amendment, form a basis for the award of damages when the conduct in question is the publication of a caricature such as the ad parody involved here. The judgment of the Court of Appeals is accordingly

---

[5]   Neither party disputes this conclusion. Respondent is the host of a nationally syndicated television show and was the founder and president of a political organization formerly known as the Moral Majority. He is also the founder of Liberty University in Lynchburg, Virginia, and is the author of several books and publications. [ ]

Reversed.

■ JUSTICE KENNEDY took no part in the consideration or decision of this case.

■ JUSTICE WHITE, concurring in the judgment.

As I see it, the decision in [*New York Times*] has little to do with this case, for here the jury found that the ad contained no assertion of fact. But I agree with the Court that the judgment below, which penalized the publication of the parody, cannot be squared with the First Amendment.

NOTES AND QUESTIONS

1.   Why are the limitations imposed by tort law insufficient to protect free speech in this case? Is the First Amendment implicated any time state law imposes liability for speech? Speech on matters of public concern? Or is it implicated in this case only because the tort employs the test of "outrageousness"? Is the tort's "focus on outrageousness . . . inherently malleable in ways that are intolerable to First Amendment values?" See Benjamin C. Zipursky, Snyder v. Phelps, Outrageousness, and the Open Texture of Tort Law, 60 DePaul L. Rev. 473 (2011) (contending that "the tort's elements, properly applied, are sufficient to prevent its use to punish unpopular speakers"). Snyder is excerpted later in this chapter.

2.   In a deposition Flynt testified that his objective in publishing the parody was to "assassinate" Falwell's integrity. See 797 F.2d 1270, 1273 (4th Cir. 1986). Is that relevant to whether the publication was tortious? To whether it was protected by the First Amendment?

3.   Falsity is not an element of the tort of intentional infliction of emotional distress. Yet this decision permits recovery only if the plaintiff can prove that the distress-inflicting statement contains a false statement of fact. Is this added requirement designed to prevent truthful statements from being held tortious, or is it merely to make the actual malice test available in a tort where it otherwise would not work?

4.   What is the appropriate analytical framework for claims by crime victims or witnesses or undercover police officers who say that their identification by media has subjected them to threats, or at least a risk, of physical harm? Some of these are brought as invasion of privacy claims, some as intentional infliction of emotional distress, and some as negligence cases. For example, in Times Mirror Co. v. Superior Court (Doe), 198 Cal.App.3d 1420 (Cal. App. 1988), the complaint alleged that plaintiff Doe returned home at midnight to find her roommate dead on the floor. She looked up to confront a man. She then fled the apartment and called the police. The newspaper published a story that identified the plaintiff by name as having discovered the body. Plaintiff's suit for invasion of privacy centered on the claim that the story had told the murderer the identity of the only witness in the case and had thus subjected her to an increased risk of harm. The trial court's denial of summary judgment was affirmed, 2–1. The majority rejected an "absolute" First Amendment defense for printing the name of a witness. (There was a dispute whether the name had come from an official source or

from the work.) The newspaper relied on cases like Smith v. Daily Mail, for the proposition that absent an interest of the highest order the state may not punish a defendant for publishing lawfully obtained truthful information. The court rejected the claim: "The state must investigate violent crimes and protect witnesses. Already reluctant witnesses will be more hesitant to provide information if their names will appear in the morning paper. The state's interest is particularly strong when the criminal is still at large. The state's interest is reflected in the regular police policy not to release the identity of witnesses. . . . The interest of the state to protect witnesses and to conduct criminal investigations is sufficient to overcome the Times' First Amendment right to publish Doe's name." The dissenter contended that plaintiff "unhappily . . . became an involuntary public figure [and that, therefore, as] a matter of law, the publication of Doe's name was newsworthy." After summary judgment was denied, the parties settled. Editor & Publisher, Mar. 18, 1989. See also Hyde v. City of Columbia, 637 S.W.2d 251 (Mo. Ct. App. 1982) (relying on *Gertz* to uphold a negligence action based on an article identifying a woman who escaped from an abductor who was still at large); Sanchez Duran v. Detroit News, Inc., 504 N.W.2d 715 (Mich. Ct. App. 1993) (denying action to Colombian judge who fled to the United States after death threats and whose local residence was reported by defendant papers). The *Sanchez Duran* plaintiff sought to live a low-profile but not secret life. What if the papers assert that they published the story to warn plaintiff's neighbors of the danger? Does it matter whether pleadings are designated as public record? Might a privilege apply?

———

The determination of whether speech is of public concern is an important and often outcome-determinative issue in cases brought against the media for defamation, invasion of privacy, and intentional infliction of emotional distress. In the case below, the Supreme Court seemingly takes a broad view of what types of speech involve "matters of public concern."

Snyder v. Phelps

Supreme Court of the United States
562 U.S. 443 (2011).

■ CHIEF JUSTICE ROBERTS delivered the opinion of the Court.

. . .

Fred Phelps founded the Westboro Baptist Church in Topeka, Kansas, in 1955. The church's congregation believes that God hates and punishes the United States for its tolerance of homosexuality, particularly in America's military. . . . [T]hey have picketed nearly 600 funerals [to spread their message, including the funeral of Marine Lance Coporal Matthew Snyder, who was killed in the line of duty in Iraq.]

Phelps became aware of Matthew Snyder's funeral and decided to travel to Maryland with six other Westboro Baptist parishioners (two of his daughters and four of his grandchildren) to picket. On the day of the memorial service, the Westboro congregation members picketed on public land adjacent to public streets near the Maryland State House, the United States Naval Academy, and Matthew Snyder's funeral. The Westboro picketers carried signs [stating:] "God Hates the USA/Thank God for 9/11," "America is Doomed," "Don't Pray for the USA," "Thank God for IEDs," "Thank God for Dead Soldiers," "Pope in Hell," "Priests Rape Boys," "God Hates Fags," "You're Going to Hell," and "God Hates You."

[The picketing took place 1,000 feet from the church. Snyder's father, the plaintiff in this tort action against Westboro, could not see what was written on the picket signs on his way to the funeral, but he saw them while watching a news broadcast of the protest later that night. He sued Phelps, his daughters, and Westboro for defamation, publicity given to private life, intentional infliction of emotional distress, intrusion upon seclusion, and civil conspiracy. A federal district court granted summary judgment for Westboro on the defamation and publicity claims. A jury found for Snyder on the intentional infliction, intrusion, and civil conspiracy claims and awarded him $2.9 million in compensatory and $8 million in punitive damages. The punitive award was remitted to $2.1 million. The Court of Appeals reversed on First Amendment grounds, and the Supreme Court granted certiorari.]

Whether the First Amendment prohibits holding Westboro liable for its speech in this case turns largely on whether that speech is of public or private concern, as determined by all the circumstances of the case. "[S]peech on 'matters of public concern' . . . is 'at the heart of the First Amendment's protection.'" Dun & Bradstreet, Inc. v. Greenmoss Builders, Inc., 472 U.S. 749, 758–759 (1985) (opinion of Powell, J.). . . .

. . . [W]here matters of purely private significance are at issue, First Amendment protections are often less rigorous. *Hustler*. That is because restricting speech on purely private matters does not implicate the same constitutional concerns as limiting speech on matters of public interest: "[T]here is no threat to the free and robust debate of public issues; there is no potential interference with a meaningful dialogue of ideas"; and the "threat of liability" does not pose the risk of "a reaction of self-censorship" on matters of public import. *Dun & Bradstreet*.

We noted a short time ago, in considering whether public employee speech addressed a matter of public concern, that "the boundaries of the public concern test are not well defined." San Diego v. Roe, 543 U.S. 77 (2004) (per curiam). Although that remains true today, we have articulated some guiding principles, principles that accord broad protection to speech to ensure that courts themselves do not become inadvertent censors.

Speech deals with matters of public concern when it can "be fairly considered as relating to any matter of political, social, or other concern to the community," *Connick,* or when it "is a subject of legitimate news interest; that is, a subject of general interest and of value and concern to the public," *San Diego.* The arguably "inappropriate or controversial character of a statement is irrelevant to the question whether it deals with a matter of public concern." [ ].

[W]e concluded in San Diego v. Roe that, in the context of a government employer regulating the speech of its employees, videos of an employee engaging in sexually explicit acts did not address a public concern; the videos "did nothing to inform the public about any aspect of the [employing agency's] functioning or operation." 543 U.S., at 84.

Deciding whether speech is of public or private concern requires us to examine the " 'content, form, and context' " of that speech, " 'as revealed by the whole record.' " *Dun & Bradstreet* (quoting *Connick*). As in other First Amendment cases, the court is obligated "to 'make an independent examination of the whole record' in order to make sure that 'the judgment does not constitute a forbidden intrusion on the field of free expression.' " In considering content, form, and context, no factor is dispositive, and it is necessary to evaluate all the circumstances of the speech, including what was said, where it was said, and how it was said.

The "content" of Westboro's signs plainly relates to broad issues of interest to society at large, rather than matters of "purely private concern." . . . While the[ ] messages [on Westboro's signs] may fall short of refined social or political commentary, the issues they highlight—the political and moral conduct of the United States and its citizens, the fate of our Nation, homosexuality in the military, and scandals involving the Catholic clergy—are matters of public import. The signs certainly convey Westboro's position on those issues, in a manner designed. . . to reach as broad a public audience as possible. And even if a few of the signs—such as "You're Going to Hell" and "God Hates You"—were viewed as containing messages related to Matthew Snyder or the Snyders specifically, that would not change the fact that the overall thrust and dominant theme of Westboro's demonstration spoke to broader public issues.

Apart from the content of Westboro's signs, Snyder contends that the "context" of the speech—its connection with his son's funeral—makes the speech a matter of private rather than public concern. The fact that Westboro spoke in connection with a funeral, however, cannot by itself transform the nature of Westboro's speech. . . .

. . . Westboro had been actively engaged in speaking on the subjects addressed in its picketing long before it became aware of Matthew Snyder, and there can be no serious claim that Westboro's picketing did not represent its "honestly believed" views on public issues. There was no pre-existing relationship or conflict between Westboro and Snyder that might suggest Westboro's speech on public matters was intended to mask an attack on Snyder over a private matter. [ ]

. . .

Westboro's choice to convey its views in conjunction with Matthew Snyder's funeral made the expression of those views particularly hurtful to many, especially to Matthew's father. . . . But Westboro conducted its picketing peacefully on matters of public concern at a public place adjacent to a public street. Such space occupies a "special position in terms of First Amendment protection." [ ] "[W]e have repeatedly referred to public streets as the archetype of a traditional public forum," noting that " '[t]ime out of mind' public streets and sidewalks have been used for public assembly and debate." Frisby v. Schultz, 487 U.S. 474, 480 (1988).

. . . Maryland now has a law imposing restrictions on funeral picketing, Md.Crim. Law Code Ann. § 10–205 (Lexis Supp. 2010), as do 43 other States and the Federal Government. To the extent these laws are content neutral, they raise very different questions from the tort verdict at issue in this case. Maryland's law, however, was not in effect at the time of the events at issue here. . . .

Simply put, the church members had the right to be where they were. Westboro alerted local authorities to its funeral protest and fully complied with police guidance on where the picketing could be staged. The picketing was conducted under police supervision some 1,000 feet from the church, out of the sight of those at the church. The protest was not unruly; there was no shouting, profanity, or violence.

The record confirms that any distress occasioned by Westboro's picketing turned on the content and viewpoint of the message conveyed, rather than any interference with the funeral itself. A group of parishioners standing at the very spot where Westboro stood, holding signs that said "God Bless America" and "God Loves You," would not have been subjected to liability. It was what Westboro said that exposed it to tort damages.

. . .

The jury here was instructed that it could hold Westboro liable for intentional infliction of emotional distress based on a finding that Westboro's picketing was "outrageous." "Outrageousness," however, is a highly malleable standard with "an inherent subjectiveness about it which would allow a jury to impose liability on the basis of the jurors' tastes or views, or perhaps on the basis of their dislike of a particular expression." *Hustler.* [ ] What Westboro said, in the whole context of how and where it chose to say it, is entitled to "special protection" under the First Amendment, and that protection cannot be overcome by a jury finding that the picketing was outrageous.

. . .

Westboro believes that America is morally flawed; many Americans might feel the same about Westboro. Westboro's funeral picketing is certainly hurtful and its contribution to public discourse may be negligible. But Westboro addressed matters of public import on public property, in a peaceful manner, in full compliance with the guidance of local officials. The speech was indeed planned to coincide with Matthew Snyder's funeral, but did not itself disrupt that funeral, and Westboro's choice to conduct its picketing at that time and place did not alter the nature of its speech.

Speech is powerful. It can stir people to action, move them to tears of both joy and sorrow, and—as it did here—inflict great pain. On the facts before us, we cannot react to that pain by punishing the speaker. As a Nation we have chosen a different course—to protect even hurtful speech on public issues to ensure that we do not stifle public debate. That choice requires that we shield Westboro from tort liability for its picketing in this case. [Affirmed.]

NOTES AND QUESTIONS

1.   What was "outrageous" about the defendants' conduct: the content on the picket signs, the location of the signs and protesters, or both? Neither the appellate court nor the Supreme Court ever decided whether the picketers had committed any tort, because Phelps waived any tort law defenses in order to obtain a First Amendment decision that would insulate him from liability in all states. In the Fourth Circuit, a concurring judge believed it unnecessary to reach the First Amendment issues because in his view the evidence would not support recovery under Maryland tort law. He said there was no intrusion because the picketers did not disrupt the funeral, did not confront Snyder, and were in a public place. As to intentional infliction of emotional distress, he thought Maryland case law required more egregious conduct than the WBC members had engaged in. The Fourth Circuit majority said Phelps's waiver precluded the court from deciding whether any tort had been committed.

2.   In dissent, Justice Samuel Alito labeled Westboro's speech a "vicious verbal assault" and a "brutal[ ] attack," and he implicitly criticized the media for allowing themselves to be exploited by WBC to gain publicity for its views. Did the majority determine the WBC protest was of public concern in part because the media covered it? Should the majority have given more weight to the argument that the Westboro protestors were exploiting the funeral of a private citizen to attract public and news media attention to their views? Does it matter whether the target audience of the speech was the family of Matthew Snyder or the general public?

3.   Justice Alito indicated that the First Amendment did not give the WBC speakers the right to protest in this case because they had "almost limitless opportunities" to voice their opinions on "moral, religious, and political issues" in other contexts. In light of the widespread availability of access to the internet and social media, should the First Amendment continue to protect a right to engage in protest on government property? Most public protests are peaceful, but even peaceful protests disrupt businesses. Is there

a First Amendment right to convey a message in the format or context where it is most likely to be heard or seen or covered by the news media?

4.   Might the means by which information is obtained be so outrageous as to support a claim for intentional infliction of emotional distress? Would applying the tort to intrusive newsgathering constitute only an incidental burden on speech? In a much-publicized New York case, Hedda Nussbaum and her lover were charged in connection with the death of her adopted daughter. Nussbaum was committed to a private psychiatric hospital. A photographer for the New York Post trespassed onto the grounds and used a telephoto lens to get a photo of Nussbaum with another patient, which the newspaper published. The other patient, whose psychiatric treatment had been unknown to all but her immediate family, sued for, among other things, intentional infliction of emotional distress. The court disposed of the claim on tort law grounds, concluding that the photographer's conduct was not "such atrocious, indecent, and utterly despicable conduct as to meet the rigorous requirements of an intentional infliction of emotional distress claim." Howell v. New York Post Co., 612 N.E.2d 699 (N.Y. 1993). In 2016, the New York Court of Appeals similarly found in favor of television reporters who had recorded and broadcast a man's unsuccessful medical treatment in a hospital emergency room without permission from his surviving family. There too the court suggested that the conduct, "the broadcasting of a patient's last moment of life without consent," though "reprehensible," did not rise to the level of outrageousness necessary to sustain the tort. Chanko v. American Broadcasting Companies, 2016 WL 1247664 (N.Y. Mar. 31, 2016). The court did find potential liability against the hospital and treating physician, however, for breach of patient confidentiality.

5.   Can groups sue for intentional infliction of emotional distress? The Arizona Supreme Court refused to permit a claim for intentional infliction against a newspaper for printing a letter to the editor advocating violence against Muslims. Citizen Publishing Co. v. Miller, 115 P.3d 107 (Ariz. 2005). The Tucson Citizen published a letter arguing that "we" are engaged in "Holy War" in Iraq and should respond to further violence in Iraq by "proceed[ing] to the nearest mosque and execut[ing] five of the first Muslims we encounter." Plaintiffs sued the author of the letter and the Tucson Citizen for intentional infliction and assault, on behalf of "all Islamic-Americans who live in the area covered by the circulation of the Tucson Citizen." The trial court dismissed the assault claim but refused to dismiss the intentional infliction claim because the letter might constitute incitement. The intermediate appellate court declined review of the case, but the Arizona Supreme Court granted the Citizen's petition under "an unusual exercise of [its] discretionary review" based on the serious First Amendment concerns raised by the case. The court concluded that the letter to the editor involved a matter of public concern, and the publisher could be held liable in tort only if the letter constituted incitement, fighting words, or a "true threat." The court held that the letter did not advocate "imminent lawless action," but was instead cast as a possible response to future atrocities. In addition, the court noted that it was published in a newspaper rather than spoken to "an

angry mob." The letter generated vigorous responses from other citizens, which "is precisely what the First Amendment contemplates in matters of public concern—vigorous public debate, even when the impetus for such discourse is an outrageous statement." The court held that the letter did not constitute fighting words because the statements were not made in a "face-to-face confrontation with the target of the remarks." The court also held that the letter did not constitute a "true threat" and could not be understood as an expression of intent to commit an act of unlawful violence to a particular individual or group.

6.   In a New York case, the Appellate Division held that a bride singled out by a radio station's "Ugliest Bride" contest stated a cause of action for intentional infliction of emotional distress. See Esposito-Hilder v. SFX Broadcasting, Inc., 236 A.D.2d 186 (N.Y. App. Div. 1997). The complaint alleged that on the day the plaintiff's bridal photograph was published in a local newspaper, the station's disc jockeys engaged in a routine in which they made derogatory and disparaging comments about plaintiff's appearance and invited their listening audience to do the same. She alleged that because she worked for a rival station, defendants deviated from the ordinary routine of this "contest" by disclosing her full name, place of employment, and job supervisors. She also alleged she suffered severe emotional distress as a result of the broadcast. The court held that plaintiff could maintain a claim for emotional distress even though a defamation claim on the same facts would be barred by the special protection that the New York constitution provides for opinion. The court "attached[ed] particular significance" to the fact that the plaintiff was "a private individual" and that the defendants' statements about her were "a matter of virtually no 'public interest.' " The court also noted "that defendants' conduct represented a deliberate intent to inflict injury upon plaintiff based upon the claimed unprecedented expansion of its standard "routine" of the "Ugliest Bride" contest to include particulars concerning plaintiff's name, employer, supervisors and the like, and the fact that the parties are business competitors in the radio broadcast industry." Why is it significant that the plaintiff worked for the defendant's competitor? Is animosity toward a competitor different in any legally relevant way from Hustler's admitted animosity for Falwell? Is the court's determination that the "Ugliest Bride" contest was of limited public concern consistent with Snyder?

7.   Although the language in Snyder regarding matters of public concern seems broad, some courts have interpreted the decision more narrowly. In Holloway v. American Media, for example, a federal judge decided that the mother of a missing teenager named Natalee Holloway potentially had a valid action for intentional infliction of emotional distress after stories about the supposed location of the teenager's body appeared in the National Enquirer tabloid. Defense attorneys relied on Snyder unsuccessfully: "[I]t can be asserted fairly that the First Amendment protection described in Snyder," the court wrote, "does not extend to speech that is not 'honestly' believed or that is used as a weapon simply to mount a personal attack against someone over a private matter." 947 F. Supp. 2d 1252 (N.D. Ala. 2013). The case settled shortly thereafter. See also Gleason v. Smolinski, 125

A.3d 920 (Conn. 2015) (citing Greene v. Tinker, 332 P.3d 21 (Alaska 2014): "We agree with the Alaska Supreme Court's recent rejection of the 'sweeping' argument that all 'speech involving a matter of public concern is inactionable' under *Snyder*, and emphasize that the first amendment is 'not an all-purpose tort shield' ").

8.   A person who actually threatens another with physical harm cannot claim the protection of the First Amendment. See NAACP v. Claiborne Hardware Co., 458 U.S. 886 (1982). What about those who transmit others' threats or make it easier for others to carry out their threats? An anti-abortion group that distributed "Wanted" posters of doctors who performed abortions and facilitated their publication on a website was held liable for subjecting the doctors to a risk that they would be killed by third parties. See Planned Parenthood v. American Coalition of Life Activists, 290 F.3d 1058 (9th Cir. 2002) (en banc). The 6–5 majority held that because doctors who had been identified in prior posters had in fact been killed, under the circumstances the posters and Web postings amounted to "true threats" not protected by the First Amendment. The dissenters said because the defendants had not made threats themselves, their speech was fully protected.

2. NEGLIGENT INFLICTION

Liability for negligent infliction of emotional distress is still very limited and uncertain. Some courts allow recovery in certain special cases, such as negligent delivery of death messages or negligent handling of corpses. Some states permit recovery for the emotional injuries of those physically "impacted" or injured by a defendant's negligent conduct; others permit recovery of those in the zone of danger to be physically injured by a defendant's conduct. Some states permit recovery by persons who are present when close family members suffer physical injury or death from defendant's negligent conduct. Some courts have flirted with the possibility of broader recovery for negligently inflicted emotional distress, limited only by foreseeability and causation. This possibility seems to have faded, however, with decisions in several states backing away from such a broad cause of action. See, e.g., Thing v. La Chusa, 771 P.2d 814 (Cal. 1989). See also Restatement (Third) of Torts: Physical and Emotional Harm §47 (2012).

Nonetheless, in a few cases media have been held potentially liable for negligently inflicting emotional distress. See Doe v. American Broadcasting Cos., 152 A.D.2d 482 (N.Y. App. Div. 1989), holding that ABC could be liable for negligently inflicting emotional distress when its attempts to disguise the identity of a rape victim were incomplete and left her identifiable to her friends, contrary to the assurances the network had given her when she agreed to be interviewed.

B. ECONOMIC HARM

1. BREACH OF PROMISE

Cohen v. Cowles Media Co.
Supreme Court of the United States, 1991.
501 U.S. 663.

[Cohen was a public relations consultant employed in a Republican gubernatorial campaign. On condition that he not be identified as the source, he offered reporters documents (public court records) showing that the Democratic candidate for lieutenant governor had been convicted 12 years earlier of shoplifting. Reporters for two newspapers accepted the information on Cohen's terms, but their editors decided the source of the leak was part of the story and included Cohen's name over the protests of the reporters. Cohen lost his job and sued the newspapers. The Minnesota Supreme Court held that (1) the reporters' arrangement with Cohen did not amount to a contract, (2) he might have a cause of action for breach of the promise of confidentiality on a theory of promissory estoppel, but (3) permitting such a judgment would violate the First Amendment. Cohen appealed.]

■ JUSTICE WHITE delivered the opinion of the Court.

. . .

Respondents rely on the proposition that "if a newspaper lawfully obtains truthful information about a matter of public significance then state officials may not constitutionally punish publication of the information, absent a need to further a state interest of the highest order." Smith v. Daily Mail. That proposition is unexceptionable, and it has been applied in various cases that have found insufficient the asserted state interests in preventing publication of truthful, lawfully obtained information. See, e.g., Florida Star v. B.J.F.; Smith v. Daily Mail; *Landmark Communications*.

This case, however, is not controlled by this line of cases but, rather, by the equally well-established line of decisions holding that generally applicable laws do not offend the First Amendment simply because their enforcement against the press has incidental effects on its ability to gather and report the news. As the cases relied on by respondents recognize, the truthful information sought to be published must have been lawfully acquired. The press may not with impunity break and enter an office or dwelling to gather news. Neither does the First Amendment relieve a newspaper reporter of the obligation shared by all citizens to respond to a grand jury subpoena and answer questions relevant to a criminal investigation, even though the reporter might be required to reveal a confidential source. Branzburg v. Hayes. The press, like others interested in publishing, may not publish copyrighted material without obeying the copyright laws [ ]. Similarly, the media must obey the National Labor Relations Act [ ] and the Fair Labor Standards Act [ ]; may not restrain trade in violation of the antitrust laws [ ]; and must pay non-discriminatory taxes [ ]. It is, therefore, beyond dispute that "[t]he publisher of a newspaper has no special immunity from the application of general laws. He has no special privilege to invade the rights and liberties of others." [ ] Accordingly, enforcement of such general laws against the press is not subject to stricter scrutiny than would be applied to enforcement against other persons or organizations.

There can be little doubt that the Minnesota doctrine of promissory estoppel is a law of general applicability. It does not target or single out the press. Rather, insofar as we are advised, the doctrine is generally applicable to the daily transactions of all the citizens of Minnesota. The First Amendment does not forbid its application to the press.

Justice Blackmun suggests that applying Minnesota promissory estoppel doctrine in this case will "punish" respondents for publishing truthful information that was lawfully obtained. [ ] This is not strictly accurate because compensatory damages are not a form of punishment, as were the criminal sanctions at issue in Smith v. Daily Mail, supra. If the contract between the parties in this case had contained a liquidated damages provision, it would be perfectly clear that the payment to petitioner would represent a cost of acquiring newsworthy material to be published at a profit, rather than a punishment imposed by the State. The payment of compensatory damages in this case is constitutionally indistinguishable from a generous bonus paid to a confidential news source. In any event, as indicated above, the characterization of the payment makes no difference for First Amendment purposes when the law being applied is a general law and does not single out the press. Moreover, Justice Blackmun's reliance on cases like Florida Star v. B.J.F., supra, and Smith v. Daily Mail is misplaced. In those cases, the State itself defined the content of publications that would trigger liability. Here, by contrast, Minnesota law simply requires those making promises to keep them. The parties themselves, as in this case, determine the scope of their legal obligations, and any restrictions that may be placed on the publication of truthful information are self-imposed.

Also, it is not at all clear that respondents obtained Cohen's name "lawfully" in this case, at least for purposes of publishing it. Unlike the situation in *Florida Star*, where the rape victim's name was obtained through lawful access to a police report, respondents obtained Cohen's name only by making a promise that they did not honor. The dissenting opinions suggest that the press should not be subject to any law, including copyright law for example, which in any fashion or to any degree limits or restricts the press' right to report truthful information. The First Amendment does not grant the press such limitless protection.

Nor is Cohen attempting to use a promissory estoppel cause of action to avoid the strict requirements for establishing a libel or defamation claim. As the Minnesota Supreme Court observed here, "Cohen could not sue for defamation because the information disclosed [his name] was true." [ ] Cohen is not seeking damages for injury to his reputation or his state of mind. He sought damages in excess of $50,000 for breach of a promise that caused him to lose his job and lowered his earning capacity. Thus, this is not a case like Hustler Magazine, Inc. v. Falwell, where we held that the constitutional libel standards apply to a claim alleging that the publication of a parody was a state-law tort of intentional infliction of emotional distress.

Respondents and amici argue that permitting Cohen to maintain a cause of action for promissory estoppel will inhibit truthful reporting because news organizations will have legal incentives not to disclose a confidential source's identity even when that person's identity is itself newsworthy. Justice Souter makes a similar argument. But if this is the case, it is no more than the incidental, and constitutionally insignificant, consequence of applying to the press a generally applicable law that requires those who make certain kinds of promises to keep them. . . .

[The Court remanded to the Minnesota Supreme Court, which decided that Cohen had a valid claim for promissory estoppel and affirmed an award of $200,000.]

■ JUSTICE BLACKMUN, with whom JUSTICE MARSHALL and JUSTICE SOUTER join, dissenting.

    . . .

Contrary to the majority, I regard our decision in Hustler Magazine, Inc. v. Falwell, [ ] to be precisely on point. There, we found that the use of a claim of intentional infliction of emotional distress to impose liability for the publication of a satirical critique violated the First Amendment. There was no doubt that Virginia's tort of intentional infliction of emotional distress was "a law of general applicability" unrelated to the suppression of speech. Nonetheless, a unanimous Court found that, when used to penalize the expression of opinion, the law was subject to the strictures of the First Amendment. In applying that principle, we concluded, [ ] that "public figures and public officials may not recover for the tort of intentional infliction of emotional distress by reason of publications such as the one here at issue without showing in addition that the publication contains a false statement of fact which was made with 'actual malice,' " as defined by New York Times Co. v. Sullivan [ ]. In so doing, we rejected the argument that Virginia's interest in protecting its citizens from emotional distress was sufficient to remove from First Amendment protection a "patently offensive" expression of opinion. [ ][3]

As in *Hustler*, the operation of Minnesota's doctrine of promissory estoppel in this case cannot be said to have a merely "incidental" burden on speech; the publication of important political speech is the claimed violation. Thus, as in *Hustler*, the law may not be enforced to punish the expression of truthful information or opinion.[4] In the instant case, it is undisputed that the publication at issue was true.

To the extent that truthful speech may ever be sanctioned consistent with the First Amendment, it must be in furtherance of a state interest "of the highest order." *Smith*,[ ]. Because the Minnesota Supreme Court's opinion makes clear that the State's interest in enforcing its promissory estoppel doctrine in this case was far from compelling [ ], I would affirm that court's decision.

I respectfully dissent.

[Justice Souter also dissented, in an opinion in which Justice Marshall, Justice Blackmun, and Justice O'Connor joined. He argued that "the State's interest in enforcing a newspaper's promise of confidentiality [is] insufficient to outweigh the interest in unfettered publication of the information revealed in this case. . . ."]

Notes and Questions

1.   The Court's assertion that "generally applicable laws do not offend the First Amendment simply because their enforcement against the press has incidental effects on its ability to gather and report the news" could be a major retreat from the practice of looking carefully at the actual effects of innocuous-sounding restrictions on freedom of the press. But the result in *Cohen* could be explained by a much narrower principle: that the First Amendment does not protect the press from enforcement of self-imposed restrictions. Which is the more appropriate reading of the case?

---

[3] The majority attempts to distinguish *Hustler* on the ground that there the plaintiff sought damages for injury to his state of mind whereas the petitioner here sought damages "for a breach of a promise that caused him to lose his job and lowered his earning capacity." [ ] I perceive no meaningful distinction between a statute that penalizes published speech in order to protect the individual's psychological well being or reputational interest and one that exacts the same penalty in order to compensate the loss of employment or earning potential. Certainly, our decision in *Hustler* recognized no such distinction.

[4] The majority argues that, unlike the criminal sanctions we considered in Smith v. Daily Mail [ ], the liability at issue here will not "punish" respondents in the strict sense of that word. [ ] While this may be true, we have long held that the imposition of civil liability based on protected expression constitutes "punishment" of speech for First Amendment purposes. See, e.g., Pittsburgh Press Co. v. Pittsburgh Comm'n on Human Relations, 413 U.S. 376, 386, 93 S. Ct. 2553, 2559, 37 L. Ed. 2d 669 (1973) ("In the context of a libelous advertisement . . . this Court has held that the First Amendment does not shield a newspaper from *punishment* for libel when with actual malice it publishes a falsely defamatory advertisement") (emphasis added), citing New York Times Co. v. Sullivan, [ ]; Gertz v. Robert Welch, Inc., [ ]. . . . Though they be civil, the sanctions we review in this case are no more justifiable as "a cost of acquiring newsworthy material," [ ] than were the libel damages at issue in *New York Times Co.*, a permissible cost of disseminating newsworthy material.

2.   Is the majority in *Cohen* interpreting *Falwell* as a case aimed only at preventing litigants from sidestepping the constitutional law of defamation? Does the fact that Cohen was seeking damages for economic harm, namely the loss of his job, provide a basis for distinguishing his case from *Falwell*?

3.   If Cohen lost his job because of a false statement, he would have a cause of action for defamation only if he could overcome some serious constitutional obstacles. Why should he face no constitutional obstacles when he loses his job because of a true statement? Is it accurate to say that it was a broken promise, not just publication of a true statement, that cost him his job?

4.   If the state's application of its law of promissory estoppel raises no First Amendment problem because it does not "target or single out the press," how far does that principle extend? Are the media targeted or singled out by the law of defamation? Invasion of privacy? Intentional infliction of emotional distress? Negligent misrepresentation?

2.   NEGLIGENCE

Cohen is atypical in two respects. Most cases against media for economic harm involve loss suffered by a reader or viewer who relied on the content of a report to his or her detriment. Cohen, in contrast, was harmed by what was printed about him, and the harm was intentionally inflicted, while in most economic harm cases the media defendant is at most negligent.

The general tort rule that one owes no duty to avoid negligently causing purely economic harm protects media along with other potential defendants. For example, when an error in the Wall Street Journal caused financial loss to a reader who traded in bonds in reliance on the Journal's information, the court held that the reader's complaint against the newspaper failed to state a cause of action. The court relied on the general tort rule that one who negligently supplies false information for use by others in business transactions is liable only to members of a limited group whose transactions the speaker intends to influence. The opinion added: "[T]he competing public policy and constitutional concerns tilt decidedly in favor of the press when mere negligence is alleged." Gutter v. Dow Jones, Inc., 490 N.E.2d 898 (Ohio 1986).

3.   DISPARAGEMENT

Injurious falsehood, disparagement, and trade libel are different names for very similar torts. In each, the harm is not to the reputation of a person, but to the commercial value of a product or other property. The owner of the disparaged property has a cause of action for pecuniary loss caused by a falsehood that the defendant (1) should recognize is likely to harm the value of the property, and (2) makes with reckless disregard (or knowledge) of its falsity. See Restatement (Second) of Torts § 623A. These principles typically are invoked by the manufacturer of a product against a competitor (or other person) who uses falsehoods to interfere with the sale of the product, but they may also be invoked against media. See, e.g., *Bose v. Consumers Union*, noted in Chapter Four.

Blatty v. New York Times. Plaintiff, author of a novel, sued the newspaper for omitting his book from its best seller list. He alleged that his book had sold more copies than several of the books listed, and that the Times either knew this or negligently failed to ascertain it. He contended this amounted to disparagement of his book. The court unanimously affirmed dismissal of his suit. Blatty v. New York Times Co., 728 P.2d 1177 (Cal. 1986).

The majority relied on an analogy to the "of and concerning" requirement of defamation law. Since the plaintiff had not been named at all, the publication was not "of and concerning" him or his book. The majority thought this requirement should be applied by analogy to other torts such as injurious falsehood or disparagement. The majority suggested that without such a limit, cases barred under group libel principles might be brought on injurious falsehood grounds or disparagement instead. The "of and concerning" requirement, though it might immunize some statements that can harm an individual, is "too important to the vigor and openness of public discourse in a free society to be discouraged." The majority thought the state constitution required this result.

Three concurring justices rejected the emphasis on "of and concerning" because of the ease with which harm could be done by fraudulent omission. Nonetheless, they concluded that the allegations at most claimed negligence on the newspaper's part—and that this was insufficient for liability.

Was the alleged disparagement "of and concerning" Blatty's book? Should that be sufficient in a disparagement action? Is it significant that there might have been other books also "disparaged" by the Times's method of compiling its best seller lists? Should that preclude Blatty from recovering?

Auvil v. CBS. A trial judge rejected an argument based on the *Blatty* rationale in a case resulting from a health scare over apples. In 1989 the CBS television program "60 Minutes" presented a segment on the dangers of Washington State apples that had been treated with the chemical Alar. CBS quoted a report that described Alar as the "most potent" carcinogen in the nation's food supply and said children faced the greatest risk. The program aired at the height of the apple season in Washington, and consumer reaction made it impossible for many growers to sell their crops. A number of the growers sued CBS for disparagement.

In Auvil v. CBS "60 Minutes," 836 F.Supp. 740 (E.D. Wash. 1993), the district court decided that the plaintiffs' apples were sufficiently identified as a dangerous commodity, even if the growers were not named. But the judge granted CBS summary judgment on the ground that even if the statements were false, "they were about an issue that

LIABILITY FOR EMOTIONAL, ECONOMIC, AND PHYSICAL HARM

mattered, cannot be proven as false and therefore must be protected. . . . A news reporting service is not a scientific testing lab and these services should be able to rely on a scientific government report when they are relaying the report's results." The Ninth Circuit affirmed on this ground without considering the validity of the *Blatty* argument. See 67 F.3d 816 (9th Cir. 1995).

Veggie Libel Statutes. The Alar episode caused great concern among producers of perishable agricultural products, who saw it as confirmation that a panic touched off by a false health scare could cause them to lose their year's revenue before the fears could be alleviated. As a result of their lobbying, at least 13 states adopted statutes to make clear that such product disparagement suits are permitted. The Florida version, for example, permits producers of perishable products to sue anyone who damages the producer by "willful[ly] or malicious[ly]" disseminating "false information" that a food product is not safe for human consumption. "False information" is defined as "not based on reliable, scientific facts and reliable, scientific data which the disseminator knows or should have known to be false." Fla. Stat. Ann. § 865.065 (1995).

When the so-called "veggie libel statutes" were enacted, many in the media were concerned that they would threaten aggressive reporting about health risks from food. But the statutes have generally been construed narrowly and have not become important sources of media liability. See, e.g., Texas Beef Group v. Winfrey, 201 F.3d 680 (5th Cir. 2000). The Texas "False Disparagement of Perishable Food Products Act" allows producers of perishable food products to recover damages against a person who knowingly disseminates false information stating or implying that the product is unsafe. The Oprah Winfrey show broadcast a segment on "mad cow disease," which is believed to have killed a number of humans in Great Britain. A guest on the show asserted that there was a risk of a similar outbreak in the United States that would be worse than the AIDS syndrome. Winfrey responded by saying "I'll never eat another hamburger."

A group of cattle producers in the business of fattening cattle for slaughter filed suit, alleging that the broadcast caused a crash in the market for cattle ready for slaughter. The district judge granted Winfrey's motion for directed verdict on the ground that cattle on the hoof were not a "perishable" food product within the meaning of the statute, and also on the ground that there was no evidence that any of the defendants knew the falsity of the statements made about mad cow disease. The Fifth Circuit affirmed on the latter ground: "Stripped to its essentials, the cattlemen's complaint is that the [Winfrey] show did not present the Mad Cow issue in the light most favorable to United States beef. . . . So long as the factual underpinnings remained accurate, as they did here, the editing did not give rise to an inference that knowingly false information was being disseminated."

Most of the statutes require a showing of knowing falsity or reckless disregard of falsity. Is that constitutionally required? Most states define falsity in terms of "reasonable and reliable scientific data." Does that give insufficient protection to reporting on health concerns that are rejected by mainstream scientific thought?

Ag-Gag Laws. A loosely related statutory cause of action is created by "ag-gag" laws. Ag-gag laws attempt to protect agricultural producers by forbidding undercover filming and photography of agricultural operations. In other words, ag-gag laws tend to focus on newsgathering methods rather than publication. On what grounds might one challenge the constitutionality of such laws? Does it matter whether the purpose of such statutes is to deter animal rights groups from criticizing beef or other agricultural producers, or at least from obtaining videos or photos to accompany such criticisms? You may want to return to this question after you study the materials in Chapter Ten.

C. PHYSICAL HARM

The cases in which media cause physical harm seem virtually irreconcilable. There are many variables in these cases. Sometimes a reader or viewer causes harm by a "copycat" act emulating some action portrayed by the media. Sometimes the harm is caused by children, who may or may not appreciate the danger. Sometimes the media defendant has not merely provided an example, but has directed or suggested or advocated the harmful act. These are sometimes referred to loosely as "how-to" cases. In any of these types of cases, the injury is sometimes self-inflicted and sometimes inflicted on a third person. The nature of the speech that causes the injury varies widely: it may be news, an advertisement, pornography, a movie or a television show. It may be true or false. The defendant may have advocated or even incited the harmful act, or it may have been merely negligent, or even innocent. See, e.g., Saloomey v. Jeppesen & Co., 707 F.2d 671 (2d Cir. 1983), affirming recovery in both negligence and strict liability for erroneous aeronautical flight charts.

The courts have not developed any consistent scheme for evaluating these variables. Each of these variables seems to influence the result in one case or another, but a variable that seems important in one case may recede into the background in the next. That means that any method of organizing this section will bear scant resemblance to the approaches taken in some of the cases. We have organized it according to the theory of liability employed, and that approach tends to focus on the defendant's purpose, state of mind, or degree of fault. Because the courts have not consistently employed this focus, the lines between different bases of liability are often fuzzy. And as the following cases indicate, there is considerable substantive disagreement as to the amount of protection speech requires in physical harm cases.

1. INCITEMENT

Herceg v. Hustler Magazine, Inc.

United States Court of Appeals, Fifth Circuit, 1987.
814 F.2d 1017.

Before RUBIN, JOHNSON and JONES, CIRCUIT JUDGES.

■ ALVIN B. RUBIN, CIRCUIT JUDGE:

An adolescent read a magazine article that prompted him to commit an act that proved fatal. The issue is whether the publisher of the magazine may be held liable for civil damages.

I.

In its August 1981 issue, as part of a series about the pleasures—and dangers—of unusual and taboo sexual practices, Hustler Magazine printed "Orgasm of Death," an article discussing the practice of autoerotic asphyxia. This practice entails masturbation while "hanging" oneself in order to temporarily cut off the blood supply to the brain at the moment of orgasm. The article included details about how the act is performed and the kind of physical pleasure those who engage in it seek to achieve. The heading identified "Orgasm of Death" as part of a series on "Sexplay," . . . presented "to increase [readers'] sexual knowledge, to lessen [their] inhibitions and—ultimately—to make [them] much better lover[s]."

An editor's note, positioned on the page so that it is likely to be the first text the reader will read, states: "Hustler emphasizes the often-fatal dangers of the practice of 'autoerotic asphyxia,' and recommends that readers seeking unique forms of sexual release DO NOT ATTEMPT this method. The facts are presented here solely for an educational purpose."

The article begins by presenting a vivid description of the tragic results the practice may create. It describes the death of one victim and discusses research indicating that such deaths are alarmingly common: as many as 1,000 United States teenagers die in this manner each year. Although it describes the sexual "high" and "thrill" those who engage in the practice seek to achieve, the article repeatedly warns that the procedure is "neither healthy nor harmless," "it is a serious—and often fatal—mistake to believe that asphyxia can be controlled" and "beyond a doubt—. . . auto-asphyxiation is one form of sex play you try only if you're anxious to wind up in cold storage, with a coroner's tag on your big toe." The two-page article warns readers at least ten different times that the practice is dangerous, self-destructive and deadly. It states that persons who successfully perform the technique can achieve intense physical pleasure, but the attendant risk is that the person may lose consciousness and die of strangulation.

Tragically, a copy of this issue of Hustler came into the possession of Troy D., a fourteen-year-old adolescent, who read the article and attempted the practice. The next morning, Troy's nude body was found, hanging by its neck in his closet, by one of Troy's closest friends, Andy V. A copy of Hustler Magazine, opened to the article about the "Orgasm of Death," was found near his feet.

[Troy's mother and Andy V. brought this diversity case alleging incitement, negligence, products liability, dangerous instrumentality, and attractive nuisance. The trial judge dismissed all but incitement, which was the sole theory at trial. The jury found incitement and awarded each plaintiff compensatory and punitive damages. Hustler appealed from the denial of judgment non obstante verdicto and motion for a new trial. Plaintiffs did not cross-appeal from dismissal of their other claims.]

II.

The constitutional protection accorded to the freedom of speech and of the press is not based on the naive belief that speech can do no harm but on the confidence that the benefits society reaps from the free flow and exchange of ideas outweigh the costs society endures by receiving reprehensible or dangerous ideas. Under our Constitution, as the Supreme Court has reminded us, "there is no such thing as a false idea. However pernicious an opinion may seem we depend for its correction not on the conscience of judges and juries but on the competition of other ideas." [*Gertz*] We rely on a reverse Gresham's law, trusting to good ideas to drive out bad ones and forbidding governmental intervention into the free market of ideas. One of our basic constitutional tenets, therefore, forbids the state to punish protected speech, directly or indirectly, whether by criminal penalty or civil liability.

The Supreme Court has recognized that some types of speech are excluded from, or entitled only to narrowed constitutional protection. Freedom of speech does not protect obscene materials, child pornography, fighting words, incitement to imminent lawless activity, and purposefully-made or recklessly-made false statements of fact such as libel, defamation, or fraud. Whatever the problems created in attempting to categorize speech in such fashion, the Hustler article fits none of them.

Even types of speech protected generally by the first amendment may be subject to government regulation. Freedom of speech is not an absolute. If the state interest is compelling and the means of regulation narrowly tailored to accomplish a proper state purpose, regulation of expression is not forbidden by the first amendment. The extent of the danger created by a publication therefore is not immaterial in determining the state's power to penalize that publication for harm that ensues, but first amendment protection is not eliminated simply because publication of an idea creates a potential hazard. Whether the Hustler article, therefore, placed a dangerous idea into Troy's head is but one factor in determining whether the state may impose damages for that consequence. Against the important social goal of protecting the lives of adolescents like Troy, the Constitution requires us to balance more than Hustler's right to publish the particular article, subject to the possibility of civil liability should harm ensue, but also the danger that unclear or diminished standards of first amendment protection may both inhibit the expression of protected ideas by other speakers and constrict the right of the public to receive those ideas.

[The court emphasized that the only question before the court was the applicability of the incitement theory on these facts.]

III.

Appellate review of jury findings in cases implicating first amendment rights must remain faithful both to the substantial evidence standard set forth in Rule 52(a) and the constitutional obligation of appellate courts "to 'make an independent examination of the whole record' in order to make sure 'that the judgment does not constitute a forbidden intrusion on the field of free expression.' " [*Bose*] Although we must accept the jury's fact findings if they are fairly supported by the record, that requirement "does not inhibit an appellate court's power to correct errors of law, including those that may infect a so-called mixed finding of law and fact, or a finding of fact that is predicated on a misunderstanding of the governing rule of law."

The text of the Hustler article provides the best basis for deciding whether the article may be held to have incited Troy's behavior. The jury was also entitled to consider evidence concerning whether Troy read the article immediately prior to attempting the autoerotic asphyxiation procedure, the psychiatric testimony about the likely effect such an article would have on normal adolescent readers, and the evidence about the probable state of his mind at the time he entered upon the experiment that resulted in his death. . . . [I]t is apparent from the verdict that the jurors believed the testimony leading to the conclusion that Troy had read the article immediately before he entered in the acts that proved fatal and that his reaction to the article was not the result of any clinical psychological abnormality. Because these conclusions are adequately supported by evidence in the record, we accept them as true.

[The court stated that *Bose* also applied to the "jury's mixed finding of fact and law that the article culpably incited Troy's behavior."]

Although we are doubtful that a magazine article that is no more direct than "Orgasm of Death" can ever constitute an incitement in the sense in which the Supreme Court—in cases we discuss below—has employed that term to identify unprotected speech the states may punish without violating the first amendment, we first analyze the evidence on the theory that it might satisfy doctrinal tests relating to incitement, for that was the theory under which the case was tried and submitted. Substituting our judgment for the jury's, as we must, we hold that liability cannot be imposed on Hustler on the basis that the article was an incitement to attempt a potentially fatal act without impermissibly infringing upon freedom of speech.

[The court reviewed the *Brandenburg* discussion of incitement, concluding that plaintiff would have to prove: (1) Autoerotic asphyxiation is a lawless act; (2) Hustler advocated this act; (3) Hustler's publication went beyond "mere advocacy" and amounted to incitement; and (4) The incitement was directed to imminent action. The court also noted that in Hess v. Indiana, 414 U.S. 105 (1973), the Supreme Court emphasized that the "lawless action" had to be "imminent."]

We need not decide whether Texas law made autoerotic asphyxiation illegal or whether *Brandenburg* is restricted to the advocacy of criminal conduct. Even if the article paints in glowing terms the pleasures supposedly achieved by the practice it describes, as the plaintiffs contend, no fair reading of it can make its content advocacy, let alone incitement to engage in the practice.

Herceg and Andy V. complain that the article provides unnecessary detail about how autoerotic asphyxiation is accomplished. The detail is adapted from an article published by a psychiatrist in the Journal of Child Psychiatry. Although it is conceivable that, in some instances, the amount of detail contained in challenged speech may be relevant in determining whether incitement exists, the detail in "Orgasm of Death" is not enough to permit breach of the first amendment. The manner of engaging in autoerotic asphyxiation apparently is not complicated. To understand what the term means is to know roughly how to accomplish it. Furthermore, the article is laden with detail about all facets of the practice, including the physiology of how it produces a threat to life and the seriousness of the danger of harm.

Under *Brandenburg*, therefore, the article was entitled to first amendment protection. But the parties' and, apparently, the district court's effort to apply the *Brandenburg* analysis to the type of "incitement" with which Hustler was charged appears inappropriate. Incitement cases usually concern a state effort to punish the arousal of a crowd to commit a criminal action. The root of incitement theory appears to have been grounded in concern over crowd behavior. As John Stuart Mill stated in his dissertation, On Liberty, "An opinion that corn-dealers are starvers of the poor, or that private property is robbery ought to be unmolested when simply circulated through the press, but may justly incur punishment when delivered orally to an excited mob assembled before the house of a corn-dealer." In Noto v. United States [367 U.S. 290 (1961)], the Supreme Court expressed similar views about incitement: "the mere abstract teaching . . . of the moral propriety or even moral necessity for a resort to force and violence, is not the same as preparing a group for violent action and steering it to such action." Whether written material might ever be found to create culpable incitement unprotected by the first amendment is, however, a question that we do not now reach.

IV.

[The court, relying on the language from *New York Times Co. v. Sullivan* about the potential impact of civil damages, rejected a purported distinction between civil and criminal liability. If the state could not punish Hustler criminally, it could not permit the award of damages against the magazine.]

V.

In the alternative, Herceg and Andy suggest that a less stringent standard than the *Brandenburg* test be applied in cases involving non-political speech that has actually produced harm. Although political speech is at "the core of the First Amendment," [N.A.A.C.P. v. Claiborne Hardware Co., 458 U.S. 886, 926–27 (1982)], the Supreme Court generally has not attempted to differentiate between different categories of protected speech for the purposes of deciding how much constitutional protection is required. Such an endeavor would not only be hopelessly complicated but would raise substantial concern that the worthiness of speech might be judged by majoritarian notions of political and social propriety and morality. If the shield of the first amendment can be eliminated by proving after publication that an article discussing a dangerous idea negligently helped bring about a real injury simply because the idea can be identified as "bad," all free speech becomes threatened. An article discussing the nature and danger of "crack" usage—or of hang-gliding—might lead to liability just as easily. As is made clear in the Supreme Court's decision in *Hess*, the "tendency to lead to violence" is not enough. Mere negligence, therefore, cannot form the basis of liability under the incitement doctrine any more than it can under libel doctrine.

VI.

Finally, even if this court were to determine that the plaintiffs may establish a cause of action under a theory of negligence, that theory could not form the basis of affirming the decision below [because the plaintiffs tried the case solely on an incitement theory after defendant won summary judgment on the various other claims].

. . .

For the reasons stated above, the judgment of the district court is reversed.

■ EDITH H. JONES, CIRCUIT JUDGE, concurring and dissenting:

I concur in the result in this case only because I am persuaded that plaintiffs had an obligation to cross-appeal the court's dismissal of their claims based on negligence, attractive nuisance, and strict liability or dangerous instrumentality. . . .

What disturbs me to the point of despair is the majority's broad reasoning which appears to foreclose the possibility that any state might choose to temper the excesses of the pornography business by imposing civil liability for harms it directly causes. Consonant with the first amendment, the state can protect its citizens against the moral evil of obscenity, the threat of civil disorder or injury posed by lawless mobs and fighting words, and the damage to reputation from libel or defamation, to say nothing of the myriad dangers lurking in "commercial speech." Why cannot the state then fashion a remedy to protect its children's lives when they are endangered by suicidal pornography? To deny this possibility, I believe, is to degrade the free market of ideas to a level with the black market for heroin. Despite the grand flourishes of rhetoric in many first amendment decisions concerning the sanctity of "dangerous" ideas, no federal court has held that death is a legitimate price to pay for freedom of speech.

In less emotional terms, I believe the majority has critically erred in its analysis of this case under existing first amendment law. . . . I agree that "Orgasm of Death" does not conveniently match the current categories of speech defined for first amendment purposes. Limiting its constitutional protection does not, however, disserve any of these categories and is more appropriate to furthering the "majoritarian" notion of protecting the sanctity of human life. Finally, the "slippery slope" argument that if Hustler is held liable here, Ladies Home Journal or the publisher of an article on hang-gliding will next be a casualty of philistine justice simply proves too much: This case is not a difficult one in which to vindicate Troy's loss of life.

I.

Proper analysis must begin with an examination of Hustler generally and this article in particular. Hustler is not a bona fide competitor in the "marketplace of ideas." It is largely pornographic, whether or not technically obscene. One need not be male to recognize that the principal function of this magazine is to create sexual arousal. Consumers of this material so partake for its known physical effects much as they would use tobacco, alcohol or drugs for their effects. By definition, pornography's appeal is therefore non-cognitive and unrelated to, in fact exactly the opposite of, the transmission of ideas.

Not only is Hustler's appeal non-cognitive, but the magazine derives its profit from that fact. If Hustler stopped being pornographic, its readership would vanish.

According to the trial court record, pornography appeals to pubescent males. Moreover, although sold in the "adults only" section of newsstands, a significant portion of its readers are adolescent. Hustler knows this. Such readers are particularly vulnerable to thrill-seeking, recklessness, and mimicry. Hustler should know this. Hustler should understand that to such a mentality the warnings "no" or "caution" may be treated as invitations rather than taboos.

"Orgasm of Death" provides a detailed description how to accomplish autoerotic asphyxiation. The article appears in the "Sexplay" section of the magazine which, among other things, purports to advise its readers on "how to make you a much better lover." The warnings and cautionary comments in the article could be seen by a jury to conflict with both the explicit and subliminal message of Hustler, which is to tear down custom, explode myths and banish taboos about sexual matters. The article trades on the symbiotic connection between sex and violence. In sum, as Hustler knew, the article is dangerously explicit, lethal, and likely to be distributed to those members of society who are most vulnerable to its message. "Orgasm of Death," in the circumstances of its publication and dissemination, is not unlike a dangerous nuisance or a stick of dynamite in the hands of a child. Hustler's publication of this particular article bears the seeds of tort liability although, as I shall explain, the theory on which the case was tried is incorrect.

II.

First Amendment analysis is an exercise in line-drawing between the legitimate interests of society to regulate itself and the paramount necessity of encouraging the robust and uninhibited flow of debate which is the life-blood of government by the people. That some of the lines are blurred or irregular does not, however, prove the majority's proposition that it would be hopelessly complicated to delineate between protected and unprotected speech in this case. . . .

. . . Because of the solely commercial and pandering nature of the magazine neither Hustler nor any other pornographic publication is likely to be deterred by incidental state regulation. No sensitive first amendment genius is required to see that, as the Court concluded in *Dun & Bradstreet*, "[t]here is simply no credible argument that this type of [speech] requires special protection to insure that 'debate on public issues [will] be uninhibited, robust, and wide-open.'" [ ]

To place Hustler effectively on a par with *Dun & Bradstreet*'s "private speech" or with commercial speech, for purposes of permitting tort lawsuits against it hardly portends the end of participatory democracy, as some might contend. First, any given issue of Hustler may be found legally obscene and therefore entitled to no first amendment protection. Second, tort liability would result after-the-fact, not as a prior restraint, and would be based on harm directly caused by the publication in issue. [ ] Third, to the extent any chilling effect existed from the exposure to tort liability this would, in my view, protect society from loss of life and limb, a legitimate, indeed compelling, state interest. Fourth, obscenity has been widely regulated by prior restraints for over a century. Before Roth v. United States, 354 U.S. 476 (1957), there was no Hustler magazine and it would probably have been banned. Despite such regulation, it does not appear that the pre-*Roth* era was a political dark age. Conversely, increasing leniency on pornography in the past three decades has allowed pornography to flourish, but it does not seem to have corresponded with an increased quality of debate on "public" issues. These observations imply that pornography bears little connection to the core values of the first amendment and that political democracy has endured previously in the face of "majoritarian notions of social propriety."

. . .

The foregoing analysis immediately differentiates this case from Brandenburg v. Ohio, which addressed prior restraints on public advocacy of controversial political ideas. Placing Hustler on the same analytical plane with *Brandenburg* represents an unwarranted extension of that holding, which, unlike *Dun & Bradstreet* and the commercial speech cases, rests in the core values protected by the first amendment. Even *Brandenburg*, however, recognized that the state's regulatory interest legitimately extends to protecting the lives of its citizens from violence induced by speech. . . .

NOTES AND QUESTIONS

1.   What does the majority find wrong with the plaintiffs' reliance on an incitement theory? In dissent, Judge Jones suggested the plaintiff would have had a greater chance of success had she sued for negligence and the creation of an "attractive nuisance." Is she correct? Would the First Amendment bar the imposition of negligence liability on the publisher of true yet pornographic speech that causes harm to a minor?

2.   Is there a difference between (a) a pure news story about someone being killed by attempting autoerotic asphyxia, (b) a story that tells about the practice and suggests that it is erotically satisfying though very dangerous, and (c) an article that explicitly discusses the benefits and accurately conveys the dangers of the practice, and then instructs readers step-by-step on how to do it if they should wish to try it?

3.   Might the idea of "unnecessary detail" apply to a news article that detailed how a terrorist avoided airport security? What if the article had appeared in Hustler? Recall Judge Jones's statement that Hustler "is not a bona fide competitor in the 'marketplace of ideas.' "

4.   Is the nature of the publication relevant or only the nature of the article? What if Hustler had reproduced an article from the Journal of Child Psychiatry and added warnings against emulation? What if the issue of the Journal with the article (with no admonitions against emulation) had found its way into the hands of a psychiatrist's child who died as did Troy?

A Successful Incitement Case. A Los Angeles rock radio station with a predominantly teenage audience ran a contest involving a roaming disc jockey. The station announced the disc jockey's location on air and gave money to the listener who was the first to arrive at that location. In an effort to be first, a listener forced another car off the road, killing the elderly driver. The court noted that the jury could have found that the station was trying to "generate a competitive pursuit on public streets, accelerated by repeated importuning by radio to be the very first to arrive at a particular destination" and win the money. A wrongful death judgment against the station was upheld on appeal. Weirum v. RKO, 539 P.2d 36 (Cal. 1975).

The majority in *Herceg* distinguished *Weirum* by noting that the speech there "was merely a promotional device to encourage listeners to continue listening to the radio station," entitled to only limited protection as commercial speech. Moreover, the station had "included light-hearted warnings to listeners 'to get your kids out of the street' because of the reckless driving that the announcement might incite, and no warning of any kind was given to urge listeners who sought to win the prizes to use discretion in driving."

See David A. Anderson, Tortious Speech, 47 Wash. & Lee L. Rev. 71 (1990), arguing that "[i]f the incitement standard can ever permit liability for tortious speech causing physical injury, it should be satisfied by defendants' exhorting a teenage audience to engage in reckless driving that the station knew would be dangerous to others." The article argues that courts should not require, as the *Herceg* majority did, that the act causing injury be a "lawless" one. Showing that "the act was foreseeably dangerous should be enough; if the incitement test, which was developed to deal with criminal speech, is to be applied to tortious speech, it should at least be adapted to the new setting."

Copycat Cases. In some cases the media are alleged to have urged, instructed, or stimulated someone to cause physical harm. In others the allegation is merely that the media depicted something that the actor emulated. The latter are sometimes called "copycat" cases. Was *Herceg* such a case? Even if it was not, does its reasoning preclude liability in copycat cases generally?

An influential copycat case was Olivia N. v. National Broadcasting Co., 126 Cal.App.3d 488 (Cal. App. 1981), involving a made-for-television film presented nationally by the network at 8 p.m. The subject "was the harmful effect of a state-run home upon an adolescent girl who had become a ward of the state." In one scene the girl is attacked in the shower by a group of girls, one of whom is waving a plumber's helper "suggestively by her side." The film strongly suggests, though does not explicitly show, that the implement was used to rape the girl. A few days later, some juveniles who had seen the movie raped plaintiff with a soda bottle.

The court upheld a non-suit entered after plaintiff's opening statement when it became clear that plaintiff would rely on a negligence theory and not try to prove "incitement." This standard was necessary because the speech did not fall into any unprotected category and did not "advocate or encourage violent acts." Plaintiff's efforts to distinguish fiction from (implicitly more valuable or protected) "news programs and documentaries" failed because the distinction "was too blurred to protect adequately First Amendment values." The court quoted Winters v. New York, 333 U.S. 507 (1948): "Everyone is familiar with instances of propaganda through fiction. What is one man's amusement, teaches another's doctrine." If news and fiction could not be separated, and if a negligence theory were used, "a television network or local station could be liable when a child imitates activities portrayed in a news program or documentary."

The *Olivia N.* court distinguished *Weirum* case on the grounds that the defendant there had "actively and repeatedly encouraged listeners to speed to announced locations." No such urging was found in *Olivia N.*

It is often difficult to tell whether a program merely inspires emulation or does something more. Consider DeFilippo v. National Broadcasting Co., Inc., 446 A.2d 1036 (R.I. 1982), in which plaintiff's 13-year-old son was watching the Tonight Show with Johnny Carson and his guest, a professional stuntman named Robinson. Carson announced that after the commercial break he would attempt a stunt that involved dropping through a trapdoor with a noose around his neck. Robinson then said "Believe me, it's not something that you want to go and try. This is a stunt. . . ." The audience began to laugh, producing the following dialogue:

Robinson: I've got to laugh—you know, you're all laughing. . . .

Carson: Explain that to me.

Robinson: I've seen people try things like this. I really have. I happen to know somebody who did something similar to it, just fooling around, and almost broke his neck. . . .

The commercial break followed. After the break, Carson did the stunt accompanied by comic dialogue. Carson came through unscathed. Several hours after the broadcast, plaintiffs' son was found hanging from a noose in front of the television set which was still on and tuned to the station that had presented the Tonight Show.

The plaintiffs asserted a variety of theories, all of which were rejected. The only theory that would permit liability was incitement, and it failed because the son was apparently the only person alleged to have "emulated the action portrayed" on the show. Moreover, the quoted dialogue indicated that those on the show tried to prevent emulation—and certainly did not invite it. To permit recovery here "on the basis of one minor's action would invariably lead to self-censorship by broadcasters in order to remove any matter that may be emulated and lead to a law suit."

Which case is stronger on its facts for the plaintiff—*Herceg* or *DeFilippo*? In her opinion in *Herceg*, Judge Jones observed that *DeFilippo* and *Olivia N.* used "first amendment analysis with which I differ." Was *Herceg* a how-to-do-it case?

Alternatives to Negligence. In Walt Disney Productions, Inc. v. Shannon, 276 S.E.2d 580 (Ga. 1981), the court applied a "clear and present danger" standard. Defendant's "Mickey Mouse Club" television program announced that a "special feature on today's show is all about the magic you can create with sound effects." A participant showed the audience how to reproduce the sound of a tire coming off an automobile by "putting a BB pellet inside a 'large, round balloon,' filling the balloon with air, and rotating the BB inside the balloon. Craig, who was 11 years old, undertook to repeat what he had seen on television. He put a piece of lead almost twice the size of a BB into a 'large, skinny balloon.' He blew up the balloon and the balloon burst, impelling the lead into Craig's eye and partially blinding him."

Although the court could "envision situations in which an adult could be held liable in tort solely on the ground that statements uttered by him constituted an invitation to a child to do something causing the child injury," no such liability should flow unless "what the adult invited the child to do presented a clear and present danger that injury would in fact result. Although it can be said that what the defendants allegedly invited the child to do in this case posed a foreseeable risk of injury, it cannot be said that it posed a clear and present danger of injury." In a footnote, the court noted that "of an estimated 16 million children watching this program, only the plaintiff in this case reported an injury."

Why apply "clear and present danger" here? How might the judges in *Herceg* analyze this case? Would a negligence standard be appropriate? Can *Herceg* be analyzed as speech aimed at children? If children should have actions in any of these cases, should any defense be available to reduce damages?

Postscript. Even if one agrees that the social values protected by the First Amendment should cause courts in all or most of these cases to protect publishers or broadcasters from liability for what might otherwise be actionable under tort law, some have asked why the injured plaintiff should be left bearing the loss. The argument is vigorously made in Frederick Schauer, Uncoupling Free Speech, 92 Colum. L. Rev. 1321 (1992). Although most of the article is addressed to compensating victims of defamation, even those who are skeptical that many plaintiffs suffer severe damages in defamation will be hard pressed to deny the reality of the harm suffered in cases like *Olivia N.* and *Herceg*. In these situations he suggests that a victim compensation scheme is "worth contemplating."

Schauer's core hypothetical is a combination of two cases in which a group of boys injure a girl as detailed in a magazine that the boys have in their possession when apprehended. Schauer asks: "If it is 'our' First

Amendment, then why don't we and not Olivia N. pay for it?" The plaintiff's award under state tort law could be paid by a special fund. Even if "full" tort compensation were not forthcoming, the payment of medical and other out-of-pocket expenses "can be viewed as improving the existing model rather than as falling short of an ideal." How should such a fund be financed?

One advantage Schauer sees is that if the plaintiff recovered only, say, one fourth of what tort law would provide, society "would then understand, as it probably does not now, both the costs of a free speech system, and that the [smaller award] is the result not of necessity but of a conscious choice about where society wishes the immediate burden of its rights to fall." Even if the final decision should be against setting up such a fund, "going through the steps focuses us much more sharply on the costs of the First Amendment, and on the identity of those who are paying for them."

2.   AIDING AND ABETTING

Rice v. Paladin Enterprises, Inc.
United States Court of Appeals, Fourth Circuit, 1997.
128 F.3d 233.

Before WILKINS, LUTTIG, and WILLIAMS, CIRCUIT JUDGES.

■ LUTTIG, CIRCUIT JUDGE:

[Plaintiffs brought wrongful death and survival actions claiming that James Perry bought two books by mail order from defendant publisher: "Hit Man: A Technical Manual for Independent Contractors" and "How to Make a Disposable Silencer"; that Perry read both books and, one year later, followed them in many respects when he killed three people. Perry was hired by a man to kill the man's ex-wife, his eight-year-old quadriplegic son, and the son's nurse so the man could collect $2 million that the son had received as a settlement for his injuries. The case was in federal court on diversity grounds. Defendant moved for summary judgment, which the district court granted. The court of appeals began its opinion with some four pages of quotations from the book. In those, the author argues that "the professional hit man fills a need in society" and assures readers that "if my advice and the proven methods in this book are followed, certainly no one will ever know." The book gives detailed instructions about how to obtain assignments and arrange payments, and how to prepare for, execute, and cover up a murder. It assures readers that they will not be troubled by what they have done: "By the time you collect the balance of your contract fee, the doubts and fears of discovery have faded. Those feelings have been replaced by cockiness, a feeling of superiority, a new independence and self-assurance."]

[After reviewing the stipulated facts in detail, the court concluded that "In soliciting, preparing for, and committing these murders, Perry meticulously followed countless of Hit Man's 130 pages of detailed factual instructions on how to murder and to become a professional killer." The opinion is severely truncated here; only a reading of the full 34-page opinion can convey the depth of the court's antipathy toward Paladin's position.]

For reasons that are here of no concern to the court, Paladin has stipulated to a set of facts which establish as a matter of law that the publisher is civilly liable for aiding and abetting James Perry in his triple murder, unless the First Amendment absolutely bars the imposition of liability upon a publisher for assisting in the commission of criminal acts. As the parties stipulate: "The parties agree that the sole issue to be decided by the Court . . . is whether the First Amendment is a complete defense, as a matter of law, to the civil action set forth in the plaintiffs' Complaint. . . ."

Paladin, for example, has stipulated for purposes of summary judgment that Perry followed the above-enumerated instructions from Hit Man, as well as instructions from another Paladin publication, "How to Make a Disposable Silencer, Vol. II" in planning [,] executing, and covering up the murders. . . . Paladin has stipulated not only that, in marketing Hit Man, Paladin "intended to attract and assist criminals and would-be criminals who desire information and instructions on how to commit crimes," [ ], but also that it "intended and had knowledge" that Hit Man actually "would be used, upon receipt, by criminals and would-be criminals to plan and execute the crime of murder for hire." [ ] Indeed, the publisher has even stipulated that, through publishing and selling Hit Man, it assisted Perry in particular in the perpetration of the very murders for which the victims' families now attempt to hold Paladin civilly liable. [ ]

[These stipulations were made for purposes of the summary judgment motion only, and Paladin reserved the right to contest at trial all of the facts stipulated to here. Apparently the defendant's objective was to obtain an early decision that the First Amendment protected the book without submitting to extensive discovery as to the publisher's intentions or knowledge.]

Because long-established caselaw provides that speech—even speech by the press—that constitutes criminal aiding and abetting does not enjoy the protection of the First Amendment, and because we are convinced that such caselaw is both correct and equally applicable to speech that constitutes civil aiding and abetting of criminal conduct (at least where, as here, the defendant has the specific purpose of assisting and encouraging commission of such conduct and the alleged assistance and encouragement takes a form other than abstract advocacy), we hold, as urged by the Attorney General and the Department of Justice, that the First Amendment does not pose a bar to a finding that Paladin is civilly liable as an aider and abetter of Perry's triple contract murder. We also hold that the plaintiffs have stated against Paladin a civil aiding and abetting claim under Maryland law sufficient to withstand Paladin's motion for summary judgment. For these reasons, which we fully explain below, the district court's grant of summary judgment in Paladin's favor is reversed and the case is remanded for trial.

II.   [A.]

. . .

[E]very court that has addressed the issue, including this court, has held that the First Amendment does not necessarily pose a bar to liability for aiding and abetting a crime, even when such aiding and abetting takes the form of the spoken or written word.

[The court reviewed a line of cases sustaining convictions of tax protesters for aiding and abetting tax evasion even though the defendants were motivated by a political belief that the federal income tax is unconstitutional.]

Indeed, as the Department of Justice recently advised Congress, the law is now well established that the First Amendment, and *Brandenburg*'s "imminence" requirement in particular, generally poses little obstacle to the punishment of speech that constitutes criminal aiding and abetting, because "culpability in such cases is premised, not on defendants' 'advocacy' of criminal conduct, but on defendants' successful efforts to assist others by detailing to them the means of accomplishing the crimes." [ ] And, while there is considerably less authority on the subject, we assume that those speech acts which the government may criminally prosecute with little or no concern for the First Amendment, the government may likewise subject to civil penalty or make subject to private causes of action. Compare Garrison v. Louisiana (applying the same "actual malice" standard to both criminal libel prosecutions and private defamation actions) with New York Times v. Sullivan. . . .

[The court acknowledged that the Constitution might limit the state's power to impose liability for aiding and abetting in two ways. First, speech that in itself does not deserve protection is sometimes protected to prevent chilling valuable speech (citing New York Times v. Sullivan). But the court said this "poses no bar to the imposition of civil (or criminal) liability for speech acts which the plaintiff (or prosecution) can establish with specific, if not criminal, intent." Second, the states' power to impose liability for aiding and abetting might be limited to protect speech that amounted to "mere advocacy," but the court said Hit Man was far more.]

Here, it is alleged, and a jury could reasonably find [ ], that Paladin aided and abetted the murders at issue through the quintessential speech act of providing step-by-step instructions for murder (replete with photographs, diagrams, and narration) so comprehensive and detailed that it is as if the instructor were literally present with the would-be murderer not only in the preparation and planning, but in the actual commission of, and follow-up to, the murder; there is not even a hint that the aid was provided in the form of speech that might constitute abstract advocacy. . . . Moreover, although we do not believe such would be necessary, we are satisfied a jury could readily find that the provided instructions not only have no, or virtually no, non-instructional communicative value, but also that their only instructional communicative "value" is the indisputably illegitimate one of training persons how to murder and to engage in the business of murder for hire. . . .

Aid and assistance in the form of this kind of speech bears no resemblance to the "theoretical advocacy," [ ] the advocacy of "principles divorced from action," [ ] the "doctrinal justification," [ ] "the mere abstract teaching [of] the moral propriety or even moral necessity for a resort to force and violence," [ ] or any of the other forms of discourse critical of government, its policies, and its leaders, which have always animated, and to this day continue to animate, the First Amendment. Indeed, this detailed, focused instructional assistance to those contemplating or in the throes of planning murder is the antithesis of speech protected under *Brandenburg*. It is the teaching of the "techniques" of violence, [ ] the "advocacy and teaching of concrete action," [ ] the "prepar[ation] . . . for violent action and [the] steeling . . . to such action," [ ] It is the instruction in the methods of terror of which Justice Douglas spoke in Dennis v. United States, when he said, "If this were a case where those who claimed protection under the First Amendment were teaching the techniques of sabotage . . . I would have no doubts. The freedom to speak is not absolute; the teaching of methods of terror . . . should be beyond the pale. . . ." 341 U.S. 494, 581 (1951) (Douglas, J., dissenting). As such, the murder instructions in Hit Man are, collectively, a textbook example of the type of speech that the Supreme Court has quite purposely left unprotected, and the prosecution of which, criminally or civilly, has historically been thought subject to few, if any, First Amendment constraints. Accordingly, we hold that the First Amendment does not pose a bar to the plaintiffs' civil aiding and abetting cause of action against Paladin Press. If, as precedent uniformly confirms, the states have the power to regulate speech that aids and abets crime, then certainly they have the power to regulate the speech at issue here.

III. [A.]

[After reviewing Maryland cases, the court concluded that the state recognizes a civil action for aiding and abetting and stated:] [W]e are satisfied not only that the Maryland courts would conclude that an aiding and abetting cause of action would lie in the circumstances of this case, but also that plaintiffs have, by way of stipulation and otherwise, established a genuine issue of material fact as to each element of that cause of action ... even assuming that the First Amendment erects a heightened standard from that required under Maryland state law.

Even without these express stipulations of assistance, however, a reasonable jury could conclude that Paladin assisted Perry in those murders, from the facts that Perry purchased and possessed Hit Man and that the methods and tactics he employed in his murders ... so closely paralleled those prescribed in the book.... Without repeating these in detail here, Perry faithfully followed the book's instructions in making a home-made silencer, using a rental car with stolen out-of-state tags, murdering the victims in their own home, using an AR–7 rifle to shoot the victims in the eyes from point blank range, and concealing his involvement in the murders. The number and extent of these parallels to the instructions in Hit Man cannot be consigned, as a matter of law, to mere coincidence; the correspondence of techniques at least creates a jury issue as to whether the book provided substantial assistance, if it does not conclusively establish such assistance.

A jury likewise could reasonably find that Perry was encouraged in his murderous acts by Paladin's book. Hit Man does not merely detail how to commit murder and murder for hire; through powerful prose in the second person and imperative voice, it encourages its readers in their specific acts of murder....

Furthermore, even if the stipulation only established knowledge, summary judgment was yet inappropriate because a trier of fact could still conclude that Paladin acted with the requisite intent to support civil liability. Wholly apart from Paladin's stipulations, there are four bases upon which, collectively, if perhaps not individually, a reasonable jury could find that Paladin possessed the intent required under Maryland law, as well as the intent required under any heightened First Amendment standard. [ ]

[The four bases were as follows: (1) the jury could conclude from statements in the book itself that the publisher intended to assist in the achievement of criminal purposes; (2) the book's overt promotion of murder "is more than sufficient to create a triable issue of fact as to Paladin's intent in publishing and selling the manual." (3) the publisher's promotional material would permit a jury to conclude that "Paladin marketed Hit Man directly and even primarily to murderers and would-be criminals"; and (4) intent to aid and abet murder could be inferred because "Hit Man's only genuine use is the unlawful one of facilitating such murders." The court said a jury would not be unreasonable in dismissing, and might be unreasonable in accepting, Paladin's suggestions that Hit Man had value as entertainment or as information for law enforcement personnel.]

. . .

B.

Any argument that Hit Man is abstract advocacy entitling the book, and therefore Paladin, to heightened First Amendment protection under *Brandenburg* is, on its face, untenable. . . . Indeed, Paladin's protests notwithstanding, this book constitutes the archetypal example of speech which, because it methodically and comprehensively prepares and steels its audience to specific criminal conduct through exhaustively detailed instructions on the planning, commission, and concealment of criminal conduct, finds no preserve in the First Amendment. To the extent that confirmation of this is even needed, given the book's content and declared purpose to be "an instruction book on murder," [ ] that confirmation is found in the stark contrast between this assassination manual and the speech heretofore held to be deserving of constitutional protection.

. . .

. . . Hit Man is, pure and simple, a step-by-step murder manual, a training book for assassins. There is nothing even arguably tentative or recondite in the book's promotion of, and instruction in, murder.[10] To the contrary, the book directly and unmistakably urges concrete violations of the laws against murder and murder for hire and coldly instructs on the commission of these crimes. The Supreme Court has never protected as abstract advocacy speech so explicit in its palpable entreaties to violent crime.

. . .

IV.

. . .

Paladin and amici insist that recognizing the existence of a cause of action against Paladin predicated on aiding and abetting will subject broadcasters and publishers to liability whenever someone imitates or "copies" conduct that is either described or depicted in their broadcasts, publications, or movies. This is simply not true. In the "copycat" context, it will presumably never be the case that the broadcaster or publisher actually intends, through its description or depiction, to assist another or others in the commission of violent crime; rather, the information for the dissemination of which liability is sought to be imposed will actually have been misused *vis-a-vis* the use intended, not, as here, used precisely as intended. It would be difficult to overstate the significance of this

---

[10] The several brief "disclaimers" and "warnings" in Hit Man's advertisement description and on its cover, that the book's instructions are "for informational purposes only!" and "for academic study only!," and that "[n]either the author nor the publisher assumes responsibility for the use or misuse of the information contained in this book," are plainly insufficient in themselves to alter the objective understanding of the hundreds of thousands of words that follow, which, in purely factual and technical terms, tutor the book's readers in the methods and techniques of killing. These "disclaimers" and "warnings" obviously were affixed in order to titillate, rather than "to dissuade readers from engaging in the activity [the book] describes," as the district court suggested they might be understood, [ ].

difference insofar as the potential liability to which the media might be exposed by our decision herein is concerned.

And, perhaps most importantly, there will almost never be evidence proffered from which a jury even could reasonably conclude that the producer or publisher possessed the actual intent to assist criminal activity. In only the rarest case, as here where the publisher has stipulated in almost taunting defiance that it intended to assist murderers and other criminals, will there be evidence extraneous to the speech itself which would support a finding of the requisite intent; surely few will, as Paladin has, "stand up and proclaim to the world that because they are publishers they have a unique constitutional right to aid and abet murder." [ ] Moreover, in contrast to the case before us, in virtually every "copycat" case, there will be lacking in the speech itself any basis for a permissible inference that the "speaker" intended to assist and facilitate the criminal conduct described or depicted. Of course, with few, if any, exceptions, the speech which gives rise to the copycat crime will not directly and affirmatively promote the criminal conduct, even if, in some circumstances, it incidentally glamorizes and thereby indirectly promotes such conduct.

Additionally, not only will a political, informational, educational, entertainment, or other wholly legitimate purpose for the description or depiction be demonstrably apparent; but the description or depiction of the criminality will be of such a character that an inference of impermissible intent on the part of the producer or publisher would be unwarranted as a matter of law. So, for example, for almost any broadcast, book, movie, or song that one can imagine, an inference of unlawful motive from the description or depiction of particular criminal conduct therein would almost never be reasonable, for not only will there be (and demonstrably so) a legitimate and lawful purpose for these communications, but the contexts in which the descriptions or depictions appear will themselves negate a purpose on the part of the producer or publisher to assist others in their undertaking of the described or depicted conduct. [ ]

. . . News reporting, we can assume, no matter how explicit it is in its description or depiction of criminal activity, could never serve as a basis for aiding and abetting liability consistent with the First Amendment. It will be self-evident in the context of news reporting, if nowhere else, that neither the intent of the reporter nor the purpose of the report is to facilitate repetition of the crime or other conduct reported upon, but, rather, merely to report on the particular event, and thereby to inform the public.

A decision that Paladin may be liable under the circumstances of this case is not even tantamount to a holding that all publishers of instructional manuals may be liable for the misconduct that ensues when one follows the instructions which appear in those manuals. Admittedly, a holding that Paladin is not entitled to an absolute defense to the plaintiffs' claims here may not bode well for those publishers, if any, of factually detailed instructional books, similar to Hit Man, which are devoted exclusively to teaching the techniques of violent activities that are criminal per se. But, in holding that a defense to liability may not inure to publishers for their dissemination of such manuals of criminal conduct, we do not address ourselves to the potential liability of a publisher for the criminal use of published instructions on activity that is either entirely lawful, or lawful or not depending upon the circumstances of its occurrence. Assuming, as we do, that liability could not be imposed in these circumstances on a finding of mere foreseeability or knowledge that the instructions might be misused for a criminal purpose, the chances that claims arising from the publication of instructional manuals like these can withstand motions for summary judgment directed to the issue of intent seem to us remote indeed, at least absent some substantial confirmation of specific intent like that that exists in this case.

. . .

The judgment of the district court is hereby reversed, and the case remanded for trial.

NOTES AND QUESTIONS

1. On the eve of trial, Paladin agreed to a "multimillion-dollar" settlement with the plaintiffs and agreed to stop distributing the book. See David G. Savage, Publisher of "Hit Man" Manual Agrees to Settle Suit Over Triple Slaying, L.A. Times, May 22, 1999.

2. If a jury in this case could infer intent from the publisher's stated purposes, the book's promotion of murder, the publisher's marketing strategy, and the absence of legitimate uses for the book, is it clear that liability in the Hit Man case would be no precedent for "copycat" cases?

3. Why did the court find the defendant's stipulations "astonishing"? Was the court unduly influenced by them, given their tentative and tactical nature? Did the defendant's strategy backfire when the court decided that the facts would support liability even without the stipulations?

4. *Rice* reportedly marked the first time a U.S. publisher had been held subject to liability for a crime committed by a reader. Is the decision precedent for: (1) liability only on facts that satisfy *Brandenburg*? (2) reinterpretation of *Brandenburg* to eliminate its "imminence" requirement? (3) liability for aiding and abetting the commission of a crime even if the speech does not amount to incitement? (4) liability under any generally applicable theory for speech that is "tantamount to legitimately proscribable non-expressive conduct"?

5. If the information contained in the book had been written in a letter from one person to another, is there any doubt that it would constitute aiding

and abetting? Why is it more difficult to characterize the behavior as aiding and abetting when published to a mass audience?

———————

Natural Born Killers. A closely watched case after *Rice* was Byers v. Edmondson, 826 So.2d 551 (La. Ct. App. 2002). Two teenagers who said they were emulating the 1994 Oliver Stone movie Natural Born Killers, about two serial killers who become celebrities, went on a crime spree during which they shot and seriously wounded a store clerk. In a suit alleging that the movie incited imminent lawless activity, a state court initially denied the defendants' motion for summary judgment. Relying heavily on *Rice*, an intermediate appellate court affirmed. The court held that the First Amendment would not bar recovery if the makers of the movie intended to incite people to commit crimes. As evidence of such an intent, the plaintiffs noted that Stone had said in a 1996 interview, "The most pacifistic people in the world said they came out of this movie and wanted to kill somebody."

On remand, however, the trial judge granted the media defendants summary judgment on the ground that the plaintiffs would not be able to prove that the movie makers intended to stimulate violence. The Court of Appeal affirmed on the ground that the First Amendment barred recovery unless the plaintiffs proved incitement, and as a matter of law that could not be found. The court suggested that whether Stone intended for viewers to commit violent acts was irrelevant so long as the movie did not amount to incitement.

Does this case vindicate the *Rice* opinion's assurances that the decision there would not support recovery in copycat cases? Could evidence that a movie-maker knew the movie might inspire copycat crimes support an inference that she or he had the kind of "specific intent" that the court found in *Rice*?

Other courts have held that the First Amendment precludes liability even when the defendant was aware of the risk of copycat crimes. See, e.g., Yakubowicz v. Paramount Pictures Corp., 536 N.E.2d 1067 (Mass. 1989). That case involved a movie that depicted teen-age gang violence and was released during a school break to maximize attendance by high school students. After learning of several killings that were allegedly inspired by the movie, Paramount released theaters from their contractual obligations to show the film, but did not withdraw it. Plaintiff's decedent was killed by a youth who saw the film after these events. Despite the defendant's awareness of the risk, the court held that the First Amendment precluded liability in the absence of incitement.

3. NEGLIGENCE

As we have seen, tort law itself severely restricts liability for negligently causing emotional distress or economic harm. When the harm is physical, however, negligence law is generally applicable. The First Amendment therefore is likely to be the only protection for media who negligently cause physical harm. The use of incitement theory, at least when it is applied as rigorously as in *Herceg*, would seem to imply that the First Amendment permits no recovery under lesser standards of liability. The *Rice* court assumed that liability could not be imposed "on a finding of mere foreseeability or knowledge." But in fact there are a few cases imposing liability (or entertaining the possibility) on the basis of negligence, some enhanced version of negligence, or recklessness. Identifying the variables that persuade courts that they need not insist on proof of incitement (or some close relative such as aiding and abetting) is the challenge in these cases.

Braun v. Soldier of Fortune Magazine, Inc.

United States Court of Appeals, Eleventh Circuit, 1992.
968 F.2d 1110.

[Michael Savage placed the following personal service advertisement in Soldier of Fortune magazine:

GUN FOR HIRE: 37 year old professional mercenary desires jobs. Vietnam veteran. Discrete [sic] and very private. Body guard, courier, and other special skills. All jobs considered. [Telephone number and address].

The ad ran for ten months, and Savage said he received thirty to forty responses a week, most of them seeking his help in perpetrating criminal acts such as murder, kidnapping, and assault. One call was from an Atlanta man seeking to murder his business partner, Richard Braun. Savage and two other men went to Braun's home where one of the other men shot Braun to death and wounded his son Michael.

Michael Braun and his brother brought a wrongful death action in Alabama under Georgia law against the magazine for the death of their father. Michael also sued for his own personal injuries.

The publisher, managing editor, and advertising manager of Soldier of Fortune testified that they did not understand Savage's ad as referring to illegal activity and that they were unaware of criminal activity associated with any Soldier of Fortune ads prior to Braun's murder. The plaintiffs introduced evidence showing that a number of newspapers and magazines had carried stories describing links between other Soldier of Fortune ads and convictions for murder, kidnapping, extortion, and other crimes.

A jury awarded the sons $2,375,000 in compensatory and $10 million in punitive damages. The district court ordered remittitur reducing the punitive award to $2 million. The magazine and its parent corporation, collectively referred to as "SOF" in the opinion, appealed.]

Before ANDERSON and DUBINA, CIRCUIT JUDGES, and ESCHBACH, SENIOR CIRCUIT JUDGE.

■ ANDERSON, CIRCUIT JUDGE:

. . .

Georgia courts recognize a "general duty one owes to all the world not to subject them to an unreasonable risk of harm." [ ] Accordingly, the district court properly found that SOF had a legal duty to refrain from publishing advertisements that subjected the public, including appellees, to a clearly identifiable unreasonable risk of harm from violent criminal activity. . . .

1.   Risk-Utility Balancing

To determine whether the risk to others that an individual's actions pose is "unreasonable," Georgia courts generally apply a risk-utility balancing test. [ ] A risk is unreasonable if it is "of such magnitude as to outweigh what the law regards as the utility of the defendant's alleged negligent conduct." [ ] Simply put, liability depends upon whether the burden on the defendant of adopting adequate precautions is less than the probability of harm from the defendant's unmodified conduct multiplied by the gravity of the injury that might result from the defendant's unmodified conduct. [ ]

For the reasons stated below, we find that the district court properly struck the risk-utility balance when it instructed that the jury could hold SOF liable for printing Savage's advertisement only if the advertisement on its face would have alerted a reasonably prudent publisher to the clearly identifiable unreasonable risk of harm to the public that the advertisement posed. . . .

SOF relies heavily on Eimann v. Soldier of Fortune Magazine, Inc., 880 F.2d 830, (5th Cir. 1989), to support its contention that the district court erred in its application of risk-utility balancing to this case. In *Eimann,* the son and mother of a murder victim brought a wrongful death action under Texas law against SOF, seeking to hold SOF liable for publishing a personal service ad through which the victim's husband hired an assassin to kill her. The advertisement in question read:

EX-MARINES—67–69 'Nam Vets, Ex-DI, weapons specialist-jungle warfare, pilot, M.E., high risk assignments, U.S. or overseas. . . .

The district court instructed the jury that it could find SOF liable if "(1) the relation to illegal activity appears on the ad's face; or (2) 'the advertisement, embroidered by its context, would lead a reasonable publisher of ordinary prudence under the same or similar circumstances to conclude that the advertisement could reasonably be interpreted' as an offer to commit crimes." [ ] The jury found for plaintiffs and awarded them $1.9 million in compensatory damages and $7.5 million in punitive damages. [ ]

The Fifth Circuit reversed the jury's verdict. After applying Texas risk-utility balancing principles similar to Georgia's, the court concluded that "[t]he standard of conduct imposed by the district court against SOF is too high. . . .". . . .

SOF's reliance on *Eimann* is misplaced. We distinguish *Eimann* from this case based on the instructions to the respective juries. In *Eimann*, the district court violated risk-utility balancing principles when it allowed the jury to impose liability on SOF if a reasonable publisher would conclude "that the advertisement could reasonably be interpreted" as an offer to commit crimes. [ ] (emphasis added). The Fifth Circuit correctly observed that virtually anything might involve illegal activity, [ ], and that applying the district court's standard would mean that a publisher "must reject all [ambiguous] advertisements," [ ] (emphasis in original), or risk liability for any "untoward consequences that flow from his decision to publish" them. [ ]

In this case, the district court stressed in its instructions that the jury could hold SOF liable only if the ad on its face contained a "clearly identifiable unreasonable risk" of harm to the public. We are convinced that the district court's use of phrases like "clear and present danger" and "clearly identifiable unreasonable risk" properly conveyed to the jury that it could not impose liability on SOF if Savage's ad posed only an unclear or insubstantial risk of harm to the public and if SOF would bear a disproportionately heavy burden in avoiding this risk. The jury instructions in *Eimann*, in contrast, did not preclude the jury from imposing liability on the basis of an ambiguous advertisement that presented only an unclear risk of harm to the public.

. . .

2.   First Amendment Limitations

SOF further argues that the district court erred in instructing the jury to apply a negligence standard because the First Amendment forbids imposing liability on publishers for publishing an advertisement unless the ad openly solicits criminal activity. . . .

. . .

Imposing tort liability for publishing advertisements that result in injury directly implicates the First Amendment interest in commercial speech. It is well-settled that the First Amendment does not protect commercial speech "related to illegal activity," *Central Hudson*, and, thus, there is no constitutional interest in publishing personal service ads that solicit criminal activity [ ]. However, if state tort law places too heavy a burden on publishers with respect to the advertisements they print, the fear of liability might impermissibly impose a form of self-censorship on publishers. [ ] Such a chilling effect would compromise the First Amendment interest in commercial speech by depriving protected speech "of a legitimate and recognized avenue of access to the public." [ ]

This case poses a greater risk than one finds in ordinary commercial speech cases that a state's regulatory regime or tort law will impermissibly chill publishers from printing commercial speech that enjoys First Amendment protection. Most cases involving regulation of commercial speech present only a minor risk that overly broad speech regulation will chill protected commercial speech because, generally speaking, "advertising is linked to [the] commercial well-being" of the speaker. [ ] The advertiser's strong economic interest helps ensure that its particular message reaches the public, even in the face of restrictive regulations. However, "in the advertising context, a publisher only provides a forum for the actual speaker as a means of communicating with the listener." [ ] Accordingly, since "[p]ublishers do not tout their own products or services," they "have a far smaller financial interest than advertisers in the advancement of any one particular product or service." [ ]

SOF further argues that imposing liability on publishers for the advertisements they print indirectly threatens core, non-commercial speech to which the Constitution accords its full protection. Cf., *Central Hudson*. In *Eimann* [ ] the Fifth Circuit agreed that "the publication's editorial content would surely feel the economic crunch from loss of revenue that would result if publishers were required to reject all ambiguous advertisements." [ ] SOF also alleges that payment of the jury's verdict would force the magazine to close and, consequently, would deprive public debate of SOF's protected, non-commercial speech. [ ]

The district court was sensitive to the need to reconcile Georgia's interest in imposing liability on publishers for printing advertisements related to criminal activity with the First Amendment's concern that state law not chill protected expression. Accordingly, the court instructed the jury to apply a "modified" negligence standard under which SOF had no legal duty to investigate the ads it printed. . . . For the reasons set out below, we conclude that the district court's "modified" negligence standard satisfied the First Amendment's interests in protecting the commercial and core speech at issue in this case.

Supreme Court cases discussing the limitations the First Amendment places on state defamation law indicate that there is no constitutional infirmity in Georgia law holding publishers liable under a negligence standard with respect to the commercial advertisements they print. . . . In Gertz v. Robert Welch, Inc., the Court held that, as long as a state does not impose liability without fault, it may constitutionally hold a publisher liable for "defamatory falsehood injurious to the reputation of a private individual." In light of the fact that the Court has found that a negligence standard satisfies the First Amendment's concern for the non-commercial, core speech at issue in *Gertz*, we see no constitutional infirmity in Georgia tort law holding publishers liable under a negligence standard with respect to the commercial advertisements they print. [ ]

Past Supreme Court decisions indicate, however, that the negligence standard that the First Amendment permits is a "modified" negligence standard. The Court's decisions suggest that Georgia law may impose tort liability on publishers for injury caused by the advertisements they print only if the ad on its face, without the need to investigate, makes it apparent that there is a substantial danger of harm to the public. In *Gertz*, for example, the Court held that a state could impose liability on a publisher who negligently printed a defamatory statement whose substance made "substantial danger to reputation apparent." [ ] Significantly, the Court noted that its inquiry would be different "if a State purported to condition civil liability on a factual misstatement whose content did not warn a reasonably prudent editor or broadcaster of its defamatory potential." [ ]

Based upon the foregoing authorities, we conclude that the First Amendment permits a state to impose upon a publisher liability for compensatory damages for negligently publishing a commercial advertisement where the ad on its face, and without the need for investigation, makes it apparent that there is a substantial danger of harm to the public. . . . Furthermore, these limitations on tort liability ensure that the burden imposed on publishers will have a minimal impact on their advertising revenue, and, consequently, on their ability to publish non-commercial speech. [ ][8]

. . .

3.   Independent First Amendment Review

. . . In order to guarantee that the jury imposed no greater burden on SOF than the Constitution permits, we subject to independent examination the jury's finding that Savage's ad, on the face, would convey to a reasonably prudent publisher that it created a clearly identifiable unreasonable risk that the advertiser was available to commit serious violent crimes.

Our review of the language of Savage's ad persuades us that SOF had a legal duty to refrain from publishing it. Savage's advertisement (1) emphasized the term "Gun for Hire," (2) described Savage as a "professional mercenary," (3) stressed Savage's willingness to keep his assignments confidential and "very private," (4) listed legitimate jobs involving the use of a gun—bodyguard and courier—followed by a reference to Savage's "other special skills," and (5) concluded by stating that Savage would consider "[a]ll jobs." The ad's combination of sinister terms makes it apparent that there was a substantial danger of harm to the public. The ad expressly solicits all jobs requiring the use of a gun.

---

8   As for SOF's argument that the district court's judgment would force the magazine out of business and, thus, silence its protected speech, we observe that the Supreme Court has squarely rejected the notion that the First Amendment interest in protected speech requires that "publishers and broadcasters enjoy an unconditional and indefeasible immunity from [tort] liability." *Gertz*. [ ]

When the list of legitimate jobs—i.e., body guard and courier—is followed by "other special skills" and "all jobs considered," the implication is clear that the advertiser would consider illegal jobs. We agree with the district court that "the language of this advertisement is such that, even though couched in terms not explicitly offering criminal services, the publisher could recognize the offer of criminal activity as readily as its readers obviously did." [ ]

We emphasize that we are not adopting a per se rule that all advertisements using terms such as "Gun for Hire" present a clearly identifiable unreasonable risk of harm to the public from violent criminal activity. An advertiser certainly could use such terms in a metaphoric or humorous manner that would not indicate a clear risk of substantial danger to the public. However, viewing the advertisement that Savage submitted to SOF in its entirety, we conclude that the ad on its face makes it apparent that there was a substantial danger that Savage was soliciting illegal jobs involving the use of a gun. Thus, the First Amendment standard articulated above was satisfied.

. . .

For the foregoing reasons, we AFFIRM the district court's judgment.

■ ESCHBACH, SENIOR CIRCUIT JUDGE, dissenting . . .

I differ with the majority's application of the law to the facts of this case. Specifically, in discharging our duty of independent First Amendment review of the language of Savage's ad, [ ] I remain convinced that the language of the advertisement is ambiguous, rather than patently criminal as the majority believes. And although the majority has carefully culled the legal standards it applies from the jury instructions, I remain concerned over whether the instructions were clear enough that the jury could have done so as well. Because of the confluence of these two concerns—the ambiguity of both the advertisement and the jury instructions—I am not confident that the jury actually found that this advertisement was a clear solicitation for criminal activity. Under these circumstances, I am unable to uphold the crushing third-party liability the jury has imposed on Soldier of Fortune Magazine. I respectfully dissent.

NOTES AND QUESTIONS

1.   If the jury in the *Eimann* case had been given the same instructions as the jury in *Braun*, could it properly have imposed liability?

2.   In *Central Hudson*, the Supreme Court wrote: "For commercial speech to come within [the First Amendment] it must at least concern lawful activity. . . ." Why isn't that a sufficient answer to Soldier of Fortune's First Amendment argument?

3.   Is the basis of liability in *Braun* applicable only in commercial speech cases? Is an ad commercial speech when the advertiser is sued, but "core"

speech when the publisher is sued? Should the speech be analyzed as something in between when the publisher is sued? Recall that the defamation in New York Times v. Sullivan occurred in an advertisement.

4.   The court analogizes to *Gertz*, to hold that a "modified" negligence standard is sufficient to overcome First Amendment protections. In *Gertz*, however, the speech at issue was false; here it was not false (the advertiser apparently had whatever skills, capabilities, and willingness he advertised). Is the requirement of "defamatory, false and negligently so" more protective of the press than the negligence approach developed in *Braun*? Might the difference between harm to reputation and physical harm justify the difference?

5.   The plaintiffs in *Braun* apparently accepted a $200,000 settlement in satisfaction of the $4.375 million judgment. See James Brooke, For Soldier of Fortune, Bosnia Is Latest Front, N.Y. Times, Dec. 11, 1995.

6.   Recall that the plaintiff in *Florida Star* also alleged that the publication of her name resulted in threats of physical harm. If she had actually been physically harmed as a result of the publication of her name and had sued for that injury rather than invasion of privacy, would the result have been the same? See Orozco v. Dallas Morning News Inc., 975 S.W.2d 392 (Tex. App. 1998) (affirming summary judgment in favor of newspaper that published the name and residence of a criminal defendant who was shot as a result of the publication).

7.   In several highly publicized mass murder sprees, there have been claims that the perpetrators were influenced by repeated exposure to violent video games. Wrongful death claims against the manufacturers or distributors of the games sometimes fail on tort law grounds. In James v. Meow Media, Inc., 300 F.3d 683 (6th Cir. 2002), the court held that state law imposed no duty on video game makers to guard against the possibility that their products might cause minors who play them to commit crimes. The case arose from the 1997 shooting spree in Paducah, Kentucky, in which a high school student killed three schoolmates and injured many others. Subsequent investigation revealed that the perpetrator regularly played a number of interactive computer games that involved shooting virtual opponents. The court said if the shooting was triggered by the games, that result "was simply too idiosyncratic to expect the defendants to have anticipated it." The court found it unnecessary to decide First Amendment questions, but said liability under state law would raise significant First Amendment problems, which it said provided "yet another policy reason not to impose a duty of care." Recall that the Supreme Court held that video games receive full First Amendment protection in Brown v. Entertainment Merchants Assn., 564 U.S. 786 (2011).

8.   Are physical harm cases against Internet service providers restricted by the Communications Decency Act? Recall that the *Zeran* case held that the CDA gives ISPs absolute immunity for publishing defamatory statements of third parties, even if the ISP has notice of the defamatory content. Although *Zeran* was brought as a negligence claim, the court treated it as if it were a defamation claim. A sharply divided Florida Supreme Court held that the same logic applies to state law claims that cannot be considered defamation.

See Doe v. America Online, Inc., 783 So.2d 1010 (Fla. 2001). The complaint alleged that an anonymous AOL subscriber induced an 11-year-old boy to engage in sex acts which the subscriber videotaped and marketed through an AOL chat room. Answering certified questions in a negligence suit brought against AOL on behalf of the boy, the court relied heavily on *Zeran* to hold, 4–3, that the CDA applied to tort actions generally, thereby preempting all state common law remedies against ISPs for injuries resulting from material not originated by the ISP. The dissenters said *Zeran's* interpretation of the CDA, and the majority's extension of it to other torts, "frustrates the core concepts explicitly furthered by the Act and contravenes its express purposes." On the other hand, the U.S. Court of Appeals for the Ninth Circuit held in 2014 that Section 230 did not immunize a website from liability for failing to warn its users that criminals were using its website to lure users to a "fake audition" in order to assault them and record the assault for a pornographic video. In 2015, the court withdrew the 2014 opinion and set the case for reargument. Jane Doe v. Internet Brands, Inc. DBA Modelmayhem.com, 767 F.3d 894 (9th Cir. 2014), reargument ordered, No 12–56638 (9th Cir. Feb. 24, 2015).

CHAPTER VII

COPYRIGHT

Copyright law protects original creative works, such as photos, texts, movies, and songs, and gives those who create and own such works rights to control reproduction (copying) of the work as well as adaptation, distribution, public performance, and public display of the work. The media, old and new, are both plaintiffs and defendants in copyright lawsuits because they are both creators of content and users of content created by others. As new technologies make the copying and redistribution of content easier, copyright law becomes ever more important to media.

Authors and other copyright owners sometimes file claims against media for infringement. This aspect of copyright bears some resemblance to the torts considered in the preceding chapters: Media are sued for economic harm they allegedly cause by their publications or broadcasts, and the risk of such liability may raise First Amendment questions similar to those raised by other publication torts.

But media also are among the principal beneficiaries of copyright law. It prevents competitors from appropriating articles, photos, features, newscasts, and other expression. It gives media some control over ancillary uses of their products in electronic databases, online services, anthologies, and retrospectives, although, as the aggregation controversy described later indicates, the extent of that control is contested. Copyright law also gives media control over the work produced by their employees and enables them to gain control over the work of freelancers. Media therefore may find themselves at times trying to use copyright law to suppress someone else's speech.

Copyright law reflects assumptions about the system of freedom of expression that are quite at odds with those seen elsewhere in media law. The underlying premise of copyright law is that speech interests in the long run are best served by a system of regulation, even though that system may operate to suppress speech in the short run. Within its limited sphere, copyright is a system by which the government grants and protects exclusive rights to speak in the belief that this will ultimately produce more (or better) speech than a laissez faire approach. In other areas of this book we see such arguments rejected. Advocates of a right of access to media, for example, have argued that "[t]he government can lay down rules of the game that will promote rather than restrict free speech," but the Supreme Court in *Tornillo* wrote that editorial choices as to what to publish in a newspaper cannot be regulated consistently with the First Amendment. Copyright law does exactly that: it tells editors what they may or may not print, but the courts do not see that as raising similar First Amendment problems.

Copyright law also provides remedies that are rarely permitted elsewhere in law when the matter at issue is speech. Under some circumstances copyright infringement is punishable as a felony. Seizure and destruction of infringing works are remedies that, though not routine, are not uncommon. Statutory damages of up to $100,000 may be awarded without proof of harm. (Compare *Gertz v. Robert Welch*, limiting the states' power to award defamation damages in excess of actual injury.) Prior restraints are not disfavored in copyright law; a plaintiff who establishes "a reasonable likelihood of success" in an infringement case is presumed to be entitled to at least a preliminary injunction. (Compare New York Times Co. v. United States: "Any system of prior restraints of expression comes to this Court bearing a heavy presumption against its constitutional validity.")

This raises important questions about the nature of free speech. Does the operation of copyright law undermine the pervasive First Amendment argument that government regulation (or tort liability) is inimical to freedom of speech? Does copyright law call into question the traditional hostility to prior restraints on speech? Are copyright questions so different from the other issues considered in this course that both approaches can be correct?

A. A BRIEF SURVEY OF COPYRIGHT LAW

Article I, Section 8, of the Constitution gives Congress the power "to promote the progress of science and useful arts by securing for limited times to authors and inventors the exclusive right to their respective writings and discoveries. . . ." The first Congress used that authority to adopt copyright legislation, and it has been with us in some form ever since.

In 1976 Congress concluded more than a decade of hearings and debate by passing a new Copyright Act that substantially rewrote U.S. copyright law (codified as amended at 17 U.S.C. §§ 101 et seq.). Copyright law today applies to all works of authorship—including literature, music, drama, pantomime, choreography, photography, graphic art, sculpture, film, computer software, sound recordings, and architecture—provided that they are "fixed" and "original," regardless of whether they were published. 17 U.S.C. § 102. A work is "fixed" when it is embodied, by or with the permission of its creator, in "any tangible medium of expression," such as paper, computer disk, or video tape. A work is "original" if it "was independently created by the author" as opposed to being copied. 17 U.S.C. § 101. These requirements are deliberately broad and easy to satisfy. As a result, copyright law now protects almost every letter, memo, note, home video, photograph, text message, and e-mail, sometimes for as long as 120 years.

Copyright law does not protect facts, ideas, or concepts; however, copyright law does protect the *expression* of facts, ideas, or concepts. 17

U.S.C. § 102(b). In Feist Publications, Inc. v. Rural Telephone Service Company, a unanimous Supreme Court wrote: "The most fundamental axiom of copyright law is that '[n]o author may copyright his ideas or the facts he narrates. . . .' [C]opyright assures authors the right to their original expression, but encourages others to build freely upon the ideas and information conveyed by a work." 499 U.S. 340, 344–45 (1991). Expression includes not only the words, code, sounds, or visual elements that are used to depict a work, but also certain elements of plot, structure, character, and other elements that "lie beneath the work's surface." See Paul Goldstein, Copyright (2d ed.) § 2.3 (1996). The distinction between unprotected ideas and protected expression (often referred to as the "idea-expression dichotomy") is central to copyright law.

Copyright law no longer requires compliance with statutory formalities or application to the government as a condition for protection. Protection begins as soon as the work is "fixed" and lasts for 70 years past the life of the author. If the author is an organization, protection lasts for 120 years after creation or 95 years after publication, whichever expires first. However, there are still good reasons relating primarily to litigation strategy to register works with the Library of Congress and to put a copyright notice on them. The copyright notice also lets those who wish to use the work know who to contact for permission.

The law gives a creator, or, in some circumstances, a creator's employer (see below), five exclusive rights:

(1) the right to reproduce the copyrighted work, including, for example, the right to control photocopying a book, or cutting and pasting a news article or photo onto a new website;

(2) the right to adapt and prepare derivative works, such as translations or sequels;

(3) the right to distribute the work to the public, such as by selling, leasing, lending or renting;[1]

(4) the right to publicly perform the work; and

(5) the right to publicly display a copyrighted work.

For the period covered by the copyright, the law permits only the copyright holder to engage in, or to authorize someone else to engage in, any activity covered by the five exclusive rights. These exclusive rights may be transferred or licensed, individually or collectively, for use by others. 17 U.S.C. § 106. A licensing agreement often gives the licensee a right to use the copyrighted work for limited purposes and a limited time.

---

[1] The first sale doctrine provides that after the first distribution of a copy, the copyright owner cannot control what happens to the copy. The work can be resold without the owner's permission. Sound recordings, however, cannot be rented, except by libraries.

Courts have interpreted copyright law's infringement provisions very broadly. Individuals and institutions are liable not only for their own conduct, but also for the conduct of employees (under the doctrine of respondeat superior); the conduct of anyone whom they supervise and in whose work they have a financial interest (vicarious infringement); and the conduct of anybody whose infringing activity they knowingly induce, cause, or to which they materially contribute (contributory infringement). The law does not require that the defendant intend to infringe or have knowledge of the infringing conduct, except in the case of contributory infringement. Innocent intent or lack of knowledge may affect damages, but it does not affect liability.

Copyright law provides significant penalties for violating the exclusive rights, including injunctions, impoundment and destruction of infringing copies, actual damages and lost profits, statutory damages up to $100,000 per infringement, court costs, and attorneys' fees. The Act also provides criminal penalties for "[a]ny person who infringes a copyright willfully and for purposes of commercial advantage or private financial gain." 17 U.S.C. §§ 502–506.

B. COPYRIGHT LAW AND THE MASS MEDIA

Copyright law affects the activities of the media in many ways. This section addresses three of the most important.

1. COPYRIGHT OWNERSHIP

For media, the most important ownership question is the status of work created by their agents, including employees and freelancers. As noted above, copyright ownership initially vests in the creator of the work. There is one exception, however: when the work is "made for hire," the copyright owner is not the actual creator, but rather the employer or other person for whom the work was prepared. A work "made for hire" is either:

(1) a work prepared by an employee within the scope of his or her employment; or

(2) a work specially ordered or commissioned for use as a contribution to a collective work, as a part of a motion picture or other audiovisual work, as a translation, as a supplementary work, as a compilation, as an instructional text, as a test, as answer material for a test, or as an atlas, if the parties expressly agree in a written instrument signed by them that the work shall be considered a work made for hire.

17 U.S.C. § 101. Thus, a media organization normally is the initial owner of copyright in publications or broadcasts created by its employees. (Ownership may be transferred, of course, and specific rights may be

granted by license without actual transfer of ownership.) Whether a person is an employee is determined according to the common law of agency, which takes into account whether the worker was engaged in a skilled occupation, supplied the tools and the workplace, was retained for a brief time for the project in question and no others, had control over working hours and compensation of assistants, and was treated as an employee for purposes of benefits, social security and payroll taxes, worker's compensation, or unemployment taxes. See Community for Creative Non-Violence v. Reid, 490 U.S. 730 (1989), holding that a sculptor who created a sculpture for CCNV was not an employee even though he was engaged specifically to create the work and did so in conformance with CCNV's concept and general design ideas.

Copyright in a freelancer's work belongs to a publishing or broadcasting organization only if the work meets all three requirements of Section 101(2): it was specially ordered or commissioned (e.g., not received unsolicited); it was created as a contribution to one of the types of work described in the statute; and the parties agreed in writing that it was to be considered a work for hire.

Publishers or broadcasters who use the work of freelancers without meeting these conditions hold only rights they have contractually obtained, explicitly or implicitly, from the circumstances of the freelancer's submission of the work. Often this amounts to no more than a license to make first publication of the work. The freelancer retains all other rights, making the publisher or broadcaster liable for infringement should it make any further use of the work, as by publishing in an anthology, a year-end recapitulation, or a database.

If a contribution is neither the work of an employee nor a work for hire, its author retains the copyright. In the absence of an agreement to the contrary, the publisher of a collective work gets only "the privilege of reproducing and distributing the contribution as part of that particular collective work, any revision of that collective work, and any later collective work in the same series." 17 U.S.C. § 201(c). Moreover, the authors or their survivors may terminate such licenses after 35 years. 17 U.S.C. § 203. As a consequence, publishers may be unable to reuse those articles or illustrations in future works such as books, calendars, or special anniversary editions, and may lose their rights altogether after 35 years.

The same rules apply to freelance work when the publisher attempts to make it available on electronic databases. In 2001 The New York Times and other newspaper and magazine publishers attempted to place their periodicals in publicly available databases without securing copyright permissions from freelance writers whose work was included. When the authors sued for copyright infringement, the publishers claimed that the inclusion of the works in databases were "revisions" within the meaning of § 201(c). The district court accepted the publishers' theory, but the Second Circuit reversed and the Supreme Court affirmed. New York Times Co. v. Tasini, 533 U.S. 483 (2001).

The Court emphasized that the databases in question (NEXIS, New York Times OnDisc, and General Periodicals on Disc) permitted retrieval on an article-by-article basis. They did not merely convert intact periodicals from one medium to another, but were functionally equivalent to a vast file room in which "an inhumanly speedy librarian would search the room and provide copies of the articles matching patron-specified criteria. . . . Such a storage and retrieval system effectively overrides the Authors' exclusive right to control the individual reproduction and distribution of each article. . . ." Justice Stevens, joined by Justice Breyer, dissented, arguing that "the decision to convert the single collective work newspaper into a collection of individual ASCII files can be explained as little more than a decision that reflects the different nature of the electronic medium," and the conversion therefore should be considered a revision within the meaning of the statute.

By the time *Tasini* was decided, most publishers had adopted a practice of acquiring permission from all freelance contributors to place works in electronic databases. However, the decision exposed publishers to liability for infringing the copyrights of all earlier freelance contributors from whom they had not obtained permissions. The Times approached this problem by announcing that it would remove such articles from the Times's database unless the authors agreed to give up their rights with respect to electronic publication, and would not accept future contributions from them unless they agreed to give up their rights to compensation for electronic use of previous contributions. Tasini attempted to challenge those policies, but his complaint was dismissed on standing grounds. See 184 F. Supp. 2d 350 (S.D.N.Y. 2002).

2. FAIR USE

The grant of rights to the owner of the copyright is conditioned on a series of defenses set forth in 17 U.S.C. § 107–118. The most important affirmative defense to infringement claims is fair use. Section 107 of the Copyright Act defines fair use as follows:

> Notwithstanding the provisions of section 106, the fair use of a copyrighted work, including such use by reproduction in copies or phonorecords or by any other means specified by that section, *for purposes such as criticism, comment, news reporting, teaching* (including multiple copies for classroom use), *scholarship, or research,* is not an infringement of copyright. In determining whether the use made of a work in any particular case is a fair use the factors to be considered shall include—
>
> > (1) the purpose and character of the use, including whether such use is of a commercial nature or is for non-profit educational purposes;

(2)   the nature of the copyrighted work;

(3)   the amount and substantiality of the portion used in relation to the copyrighted work as a whole; and

(4)   the effect of the use upon the potential market for or value of the copyrighted work.

Both traditional media, such as newspapers, and newer types of content providers, such as Google, gather and republish content created by others and disseminate their own content to mass audiences. Thus, both routinely must determine what types of information gathering and dissemination constitute fair use, as you will see in the remainder of this chapter.

a.   FAIR USE AND THE NEWS

Copyright law is a double-edged sword: although media use it to protect their own publications and broadcasts, they sometimes find it an obstacle to their own journalistic objectives. In the following case, the publication of former President Gerald Ford's book was itself the news event being covered. Nonetheless, the Supreme Court held that a magazine violated copyright by quoting excerpts from the forthcoming book.

Harper & Row Publishers, Inc. v. Nation Enterprises

Supreme Court of the United States, 1985.
471 U.S. 539.

■ JUSTICE O'CONNOR delivered the opinion of the Court.

This case requires us to consider to what extent the "fair use" provision of the Copyright Revision Act of 1976, 17 U.S.C. § 107 (hereinafter the Copyright Act), sanctions the unauthorized use of quotations from a public figure's unpublished manuscript. In March 1979, an undisclosed source provided The Nation magazine with the unpublished manuscript of "A Time to Heal: The Autobiography of Gerald R. Ford." Working directly from the purloined manuscript, an editor of The Nation produced a short piece entitled "The Ford Memoirs—Behind the Nixon Pardon." The piece was timed to "scoop" an article scheduled shortly to appear in Time magazine. Time had agreed to purchase the exclusive right to print prepublication excerpts from the copyright holders, Harper & Row Publishers, Inc. (hereinafter Harper & Row) and Reader's Digest Association, Inc. (hereinafter Reader's Digest). As a result of The Nation article, Time canceled its agreement. Petitioners brought a successful copyright action [for $12,500] against The Nation. On appeal, the Second Circuit reversed the lower court's finding of infringement, holding that The Nation's act was sanctioned as a "fair use" of the copyrighted material. We granted certiorari, [ ], and we now reverse.

. . .

II

We agree with the Court of Appeals that copyright is intended to increase and not to impede the harvest of knowledge. But we believe the Second Circuit gave insufficient deference to the scheme established by the Copyright Act for fostering the original works that provide the seed and substance of this harvest. The rights conferred by copyright are designed to assure contributors to the store of knowledge a fair return for their labors. [ ]

. . .

As we noted last Term, "[the Constitution's] limited grant is a means by which an important public purpose may be achieved. It is intended to motivate the creative activity of authors and inventors by the provision of a special reward, and to allow the public access to the products of their genius after the limited period of exclusive control has expired." Sony Corp. of America v. Universal City Studios, 464 U.S. 417 (1984). "The monopoly created by copyright thus rewards the individual author in order to benefit the public." Id. at 477 (dissenting opinion). This principle applies equally to works of fiction and non-fiction. . . .

Section 106 of the Copyright Act confers a bundle of exclusive rights to the owner of the copyright. Under the Copyright Act, these rights—to publish, copy, and distribute the author's work—vest in the author of an original work from the time of its creation. In practice, the author commonly sells his rights to publishers who offer royalties in exchange for their services in producing and marketing the author's work. The copyright owner's rights, however, are subject to certain statutory exceptions. Among these is § 107 which codifies the traditional privilege of other authors to make "fair use" of an earlier writer's work. In addition, no author may copyright facts or ideas. The copyright is limited to those aspects of the work—termed "expression"—that display the stamp of the author's originality.

Creation of a non-fiction work, even a compilation of pure fact, entails originality. . . . The copyright holders of "A Time to Heal" complied with the relevant statutory notice and registration procedures. [ ] Thus there is no dispute that the unpublished manuscript of "A Time to Heal," as a whole, was protected by [§] 106 from unauthorized reproduction. Nor do respondents dispute that verbatim copying of excerpts of the manuscript's original form of expression would constitute infringement unless excused as fair use. [ ] Yet copyright does not prevent subsequent users from copying from a prior author's work those constituent elements that are not original—for example, quotations borrowed under the rubric of fair use from other copyrighted works, facts, or materials in the public domain—as long as such use does not unfairly appropriate the author's original contributions. [ ] Perhaps the controversy between the lower courts in this case over copyrightability is more aptly styled a dispute over whether The Nation's appropriation of unoriginal and uncopyrightable elements encroached on the originality embodied in the work as a whole. Especially in the realm of factual narrative, the law is currently unsettled regarding the ways in which uncopyrightable elements combine with the author's original contributions to form protected expression. . . .

We need not reach these issues, however, as The Nation has admitted to lifting verbatim quotes of the author's original language totaling between 300 and 400 words and constituting some 13% of [the 2,250 words in] The Nation article. In using generous verbatim excerpts of Mr. Ford's unpublished manuscript to lend authenticity to its account of the forthcoming memoirs, The Nation effectively arrogated to itself the right of first publication, an important marketable subsidiary right. For the reasons set forth below, we find that this use of the copyrighted manuscript, even stripped to the verbatim quotes conceded by the Nation to be copyrightable expression, was not a fair use within the meaning of the Copyright Act.

III [A.]

Fair use was traditionally defined as "a privilege in others than the owner of the copyright to use the copyrighted material in a reasonable manner without his consent." [ ] The statutory formulation of the defense of fair use in the Copyright Act of 1976 reflects the intent of Congress to codify the common-law doctrine. Section 107 requires a case-by-case determination whether a particular use is fair, and the statute notes four non-exclusive factors to be considered. This approach was "intended to restate the [pre-existing] judicial doctrine of fair use, not to change, narrow, or enlarge it in any way." H.R.Rep. No. 94–1476, p. 66 (1976) (hereinafter House Report). [ ]

"[T]he author's consent to a reasonable use of his copyrighted works ha[d] always been implied by the courts as a necessary incident of the constitutional policy of promoting the progress of science and the useful arts, since a prohibition of such use would inhibit subsequent writers from attempting to improve upon prior works and thus . . . frustrate the very ends sought to be attained." . . .

    . . .

Perhaps because the fair use doctrine was predicated on the author's implied consent to "reasonable and customary" use when he released his work for public consumption, fair use traditionally was not recognized as a defense to charges of copying from an author's as yet unpublished works. Under common-law copyright, "the property of the author . . . in his intellectual creation [was] absolute until he voluntarily part[ed] with the same." [ ] This absolute rule, however, was tempered in practice by the equitable nature of the fair use doctrine. In a given case, factors such as implied consent through *de facto* publication or performance or dissemination of a work may tip the balance of equities in favor of prepublication use. [ ] But it has never been seriously disputed that "the fact that the plaintiff's work is unpublished . . . is a factor tending to negate the defense of fair use." . . .

The [1976 revision of the] Copyright Act represents the culmination of a major legislative re-examination of copyright doctrine. [ ] Among its other innovations, it eliminated publication "as a dividing line between common law and statutory protection," [ ], extending statutory protection to all works from the time of their creation. It also recognized for the first time a distinct statutory right of first publication, which had previously been an element of the common-law protections afforded unpublished works. . . .

. . . [F]air use analysis must always be tailored to the individual case. [ ] The nature of the interest at stake is highly relevant to whether a given use is fair. . . . The right of first publication implicates a threshold decision by the author whether and in what form to release his work. First publication is inherently different from other § 106 rights in that only one person can be the first publisher; as the contract with Time illustrates, the commercial value of the right lies primarily in exclusivity. Because the potential damage to the author from judicially enforced "sharing" of the first publication right with unauthorized users of his manuscript is substantial, the balance of equities in evaluating such a claim of fair use inevitably shifts.

. . .

. . . The author's control of first public distribution implicates not only his personal interest in creative control but his property interest in exploitation of prepublication rights, which are valuable in themselves and serve as a valuable adjunct to publicity and marketing. See Belushi v. Woodward, 598 F. Supp. 36 (D.D.C. 1984) (successful marketing depends on coordination of serialization and release to public); Marks, Subsidiary Rights and Permissions, in What Happens in Book Publishing, 230 (C. Grannis ed. 1967) (exploitation of subsidiary rights is necessary to financial success of new books). Under ordinary circumstances, the author's right to control the first public appearance of his undisseminated expression will outweigh a claim of fair use.

B

Respondents, however, contend that First Amendment values require a different rule under the circumstances of this case. The thrust of the decision below is that "[t]he scope of [fair use] is undoubtedly wider when the information conveyed relates to matters of high public concern." . . . Respondents explain their copying of Mr. Ford's expression as essential to reporting the news story it claims the book itself represents. [ ] Respondents argue that the public's interest in learning this news as fast as possible outweighs the right of the author to control its first publication.

The Second Circuit noted, correctly, that copyright's idea/expression dichotomy "strike[s] a definitional balance between the First Amendment and the Copyright Act by permitting free communication of facts while still protecting an author's expression." 723 F.2d, at 203. No author may copyright his ideas or the facts he narrates. . . . As this Court long ago observed: "[T]he news element—the information respecting current events contained in the literary production—is not the creation of the writer, but is a report of matters that ordinarily are *publici juris;* it is the history of the day." International News Service v. Associated Press, 248 U.S. 215, 234 (1918). But copyright assures those who write and publish factual narratives such as "A Time to Heal" that they may at least enjoy the right to market the original expression contained therein as just compensation for their investment. [ ]

. . . The promise of copyright would be an empty one if it could be avoided merely by dubbing the infringement a fair use "news report" of the book. [ ]

. . .

It is fundamentally at odds with the scheme of copyright to accord lesser rights in those works that are of greatest importance to the public. Such a notion ignores the major premise of copyright and injures author and public alike.

. . .

IV

Fair use is a mixed question of law and fact [that an appellate court may address where the trial court "has found facts sufficient to evaluate each of the statutory factors"]. The four factors identified by Congress as especially relevant in determining whether the use was fair are: (1) the purpose and character of the use; (2) the nature of the copyrighted work; (3) the substantiality of the portion used in relation to the copyrighted work as a whole; (4) the effect on the potential market for or value of the copyrighted work. We address each one separately.

Purpose of the Use. . . . News reporting is one of the examples enumerated in § 107 to "give some idea of the sort of activities the courts might regard as fair use under the circumstances." . . . The fact that an article arguably is "news" and therefore a productive use is simply one factor in a fair use analysis.

. . . The Nation has every right to seek to be the first to publish information. But The Nation went beyond simply reporting uncopyrightable information and actively sought to exploit the headline value of its infringement, making a "news event" out of its unauthorized first publication of a noted figure's copyrighted expression.

The fact that a publication was commercial as opposed to non-profit is a separate factor that tends to weigh against a finding of fair use. "[E]very commercial use of copyrighted material is presumptively an unfair exploitation of the monopoly privilege that belongs to the owner of the copyright." [*Sony*] In arguing that the purpose of news reporting is not purely commercial, The Nation misses the point entirely. The crux of the profit/nonprofit distinction is not whether the sole motive of the use is monetary gain but whether the user stands to profit from exploitation of the copyrighted material without paying the customary price. [ ]

In evaluating character and purpose we cannot ignore The Nation's stated purpose of scooping the forthcoming hardcover and Time abstracts. [ ] The Nation's use had not merely the incidental effect but the *intended purpose* of supplanting the copyright holder's commercially valuable right of first publication. Also relevant to the "character" of the use is "the propriety of the defendant's conduct." [ ] Unlike the typical claim of fair use, The Nation cannot offer up even the fiction of consent as justification. Like its competitor newsweekly, it was free to bid for the right of abstracting excerpts from "A Time to Heal." . . .

Nature of the Copyrighted Work. . . . "A Time to Heal" may be characterized as an unpublished historical narrative or autobiography.[ ] The law generally recognizes a greater need to disseminate factual works than works of fiction or fantasy. . . . The Nation did not stop at [quoting] isolated phrases and instead excerpted subjective descriptions and portraits of public figures whose power lies in the author's individualized expression. Such use, focusing on the most expressive elements of the work, exceeds that necessary to disseminate the facts.

The fact that a work is unpublished is a critical element of its "nature." [ ] Our prior discussion establishes that the scope of fair use is narrower with respect to unpublished works. . . .

In the case of Mr. Ford's manuscript, the copyright holders' interest in confidentiality is irrefutable; the copyright holders had entered into a contractual undertaking to "keep the manuscript confidential" and required that all those to whom the manuscript was shown also "sign an agreement to keep the manuscript confidential." . . . The Nation's clandestine publication afforded no such opportunity for creative or quality control. [ ] A use that so clearly infringes the copyright holder's interests in confidentiality and creative control is difficult to characterize as "fair."

Amount and Substantiality of the Portion Used. Next, the Act directs us to examine the amount and substantiality of the portion used in relation to the copyrighted work as a whole. In absolute terms, the words actually quoted were an insubstantial portion of "A Time to Heal." The district court, however, found that "[T]he Nation took what was essentially the heart of the book." [ ] . . . A Time editor described the chapters on the pardon as "the most interesting and moving parts of the entire manuscript." ...

As the statutory language indicates, a taking may not be excused merely because it is insubstantial with respect to the *infringing* work. As Judge Learned Hand cogently remarked, "[N]o plagiarist can excuse the wrong by showing how much of his work he did not pirate." Sheldon v. Metro-Goldwyn Pictures Corp., 81 F.2d 49, 56 ([2d Cir. 1936]), []. Conversely, the fact that a substantial portion of the infringing work was copied verbatim is evidence of the qualitative value of the copied material, both to the originator and to the plagiarist who seeks to profit from marketing someone else's copyrighted expression.

Stripped to the verbatim quotes, the direct takings from the unpublished manuscript constitute at least 13% of the infringing article. [] The Nation article is structured around the quoted excerpts which serve as its dramatic focal points. [] In view of the expressive value of the excerpts and their key role in the infringing work, we cannot agree with the Second Circuit that the "magazine took a meager, indeed an infinitesimal amount of Ford's original language." []

Effect on the Market. ... This last factor is undoubtedly the single most important element of fair use. ... [O]nce a copyright holder establishes with reasonable probability the existence of a causal connection between the infringement and a loss of revenue, the burden properly shifts to the infringer to show that this damage would have occurred had there been no taking of copyrighted expression. [] Petitioners established a prima facie case of actual damage that respondent failed to rebut. [] The trial court properly awarded actual damages and accounting of profits. []

    ...

It is undisputed that the factual material in the balance of The Nation's article, besides the verbatim quotes at issue here, was drawn exclusively from the chapters on the pardon. The excerpts were employed as featured episodes in a story about the Nixon pardon—precisely the use petitioners had licensed to Time. The borrowing of these verbatim quotes from the unpublished manuscript lent The Nation's piece a special air of authenticity—as Navasky [The Nation's editor] expressed it, the reader would know it was Ford speaking and not The Nation. Thus it directly competed for a share of the market for prepublication excerpts. ...

V

... In sum, the traditional doctrine of fair use, as embodied in the Copyright Act, does not sanction the use made by The Nation of these copyrighted materials. Any copyright infringer may claim to benefit the public by increasing public access to the copyrighted work. [] But Congress has not designed, and we see no warrant for judicially imposing, a "compulsory license" permitting unfettered access to the unpublished copyrighted expression of public figures. . . .

[Justice Brennan, joined by Justices Marshall and White, dissented. They viewed the purpose of the copying as news reporting rather than commercial use and rejected the majority's "categorical presumption against prepublication fair use." The amount of material copied would not have been considered excessive if used in a book review and could not be considered less favorably because it appeared in a news report instead. Finally, Time's cancellation of its contract could not be accepted as proof of the negative effect of the copying on the serialization market, because that cancellation might have been the result of The Nation's protected publication of information and ideas from the manuscript, rather than the few quoted passages. . . . "The Court imposes liability on The Nation for no other reason than that The Nation succeeding in being first to provide certain information to the public."

The dissenters also rejected Harper & Row's claim that even if copying of the quotations was protected, the article as a whole was an infringement. The article did not track the structure and language of the original closely enough to support that theory, they argued.]

NOTES AND QUESTIONS

1.   Would the analysis change if The Nation's article had appeared a week after the book was published? A week after the Time publication?

2.   The Court makes much of the "right of first publication." Where is this right found? Given its importance in the Court's view, can any use of an unpublished work constitute fair use?

3.   The Court refers several times to how much of The Nation's article was taken from President Ford's memoir. Why is this relevant? Recall that Section 107 of the Copyright Act requires the reviewing court to consider "the amount and substantiality of the portion used in relation to the copyrighted work as a whole."

———

In a 2012 case, the Ninth Circuit affirmed that "[w]aving the news reporting flag is not a get out of jail free card in the copyright arena." Monge v. Maya Magazines, Inc., 688 F.3d 1164 (9th Cir. 2012). Two Latin-American celebrities—Noelia Lorenzo Monge and Jorge Reynoso—sued the publisher of a Spanish-language tabloid magazine for copyright infringement and misappropriation of likeness for publishing photos of their "clandestine" Las Vegas wedding two years before. A driver-bodyguard for the couple obtained the photos after the husband left a memory chip containing them in his car. The driver later sold the photos to the tabloid for $1,500. Only after publication did family members learn that the couple was married.

A federal district court dismissed the misappropriation claim and granted summary judgment on the copyright claim on the ground that publication of the newsworthy images was fair use. The celebrity couple appealed and the Ninth Circuit reversed.

As regarding the purpose and character of the use, the court found that although the previously unpublished photos were newsworthy, "fair use has bounds even in news reporting, and no per se public interest exception exists." Moreover, the tabloid's use was "minimally transformative" and "undisputedly commercial in nature." The court found the second fair use factor, the "nature of the copyrighted work," to be in "counter-balance." The photos were "marginally creative," the court suggested, but were unpublished. With regard to the third factor, the court found that the "amount and substantiality of the portion [of the copyrighted work] used" by the tabloid "weigh[ed] decisively against fair use." "Quantitatively," the court wrote, "every single photo of the wedding and almost every photo of the wedding night were published." Qualitatively, the tabloid did minimal cropping and published the "heart" of each photo. Finally, the court found that the tabloid's publication harmed both the "actual and potential market for the pictures." After the publication of the photos in the magazine, the couple could no longer sell photographs of their wedding themselves. The court therefore concluded that not a single fair use factor tipped in the tabloid's favor and wrote that the district court judge should have granted summary judgment for the celebrities instead.

The Second Circuit, in contrast, held that Bloomberg news service did not infringe Swatch Group's copyright by disseminating a sound recording of an earnings report conference call between Swatch and 333 invited investment analysts. Swatch did not invite the press to the conference call, but Bloomberg nonetheless obtained and disseminated a recording (presumably made by one of the invitees) to Bloomberg's paid subscribers. A district court granted summary judgment for Bloomberg on fair use grounds, and the Second Circuit affirmed. Swatch Group Mgmt. Services v. Bloomberg L.P., 756 F.3d 73 (2d Cir. 2014).

First, the court found that "whether one describes Bloomberg's activities as 'news reporting,' 'data delivery,' or any other turn of phrase, there can be no doubt that Bloomberg's purpose in obtaining and disseminating the recording at issue was to make important financial information about Swatch Group available" to investors and others. That Bloomberg profited from the dissemination of the recording did not alter the court's analysis, because almost all news services obtain profits by publishing factual information. The court further observed that the nature of Bloomberg's use of the recording supported a finding of fair use even though Bloomberg reproduced the original verbatim: "[T]he need to convey information to the public accurately may in some instances make it desirable and consonant with copyright law for a defendant *to faithfully reproduce an original work without alteration.*" (emphasis added) This use could even be considered "transformative" because, the court suggested, Bloomberg was publishing "factual information to an audience from which Swatch Group's purpose was to withhold it."

Analyzing the second fair use factor (i.e., the nature of the copyrighted work), the court found that Bloomberg's use of the recording did not threaten Swatch's copyright interests because the information disseminated was entirely factual and Swatch had already "publicly disseminated the spoken performance embodied in the recording." Third, the court assessed "the amount and substantiality of the portion used in relation to the copyrighted work as a whole." Although Bloomberg used the entire work, the use "was reasonable in light of its purpose of disseminating important financial information to investors and analysts." Fourth, Bloomberg's use of the sound recording had no market effect on the value of Swatch's unpublished recording, and Swatch created the recording for other advantages unrelated to "the possibility of receiving royalties." Finally, the "balance of factors" favored Bloomberg's dissemination being treated as a fair use, particularly given the importance of the public interest in financial information.

---

b.   FAIR USE AND NEWS AGGREGATION

News aggregators claim that what they do with news reports constitutes fair use. Section 107 lists news reporting as one of the types of expression most likely to be protected against infringement claims by the fair use defense, but courts have never interpreted that section to give carte blanche to copiers of news.

There are precedents that reject fair use defenses by pre-digital forerunners of the online aggregators. In Wainwright Securities, Inc. v. Wall Street Transcript Corp., 558 F.2d 91 (2d Cir. 1977), the court rejected a fair use defense by The Transcript, which published abstracts of corporate financial analyses prepared by Wainwright for sale to its clients. The court affirmed a finding that The Transcript's copying was substantial and diminished Wainwright's market for its reports. In another case, a fair use defense was rejected when the infringer translated articles from Japanese-language newspapers into English and sold the abstracts of the articles to customers. The court found that the infringer added no value to the reports, copied not merely facts but also substantial amounts of the expressive elements of the news stories, and supplanted the newspapers' product in the marketplace. See Nihon Keizai Shimbun, Inc. v. Comline Business Data, Inc., 166 F.3d 65 (2d Cir. 1999).

Cases like these are not likely to resolve categorically whether news aggregation is copyright infringement because fair use analysis is fact intensive. Aggregations may take less of the originator's product or fewer of its expressive elements, and may have different effects on the market for the product.

The common law may provide an alternative claim against news aggregators independent of copyright law: a long disused theory called "hot-news misappropriation," not to be confused with privacy-based misappropriation. The theory stems from International News Service v. Associated Press, 248 U.S. 215 (1918) (*INS*), a case that held that a newsgatherer has a protectable "quasi-property interest" in its news product, even though the news itself is not copyrightable. The case involved a claim by the Associated Press against a competing news service that obtained and redistributed the Associated Press's battlefront news releases during World War I. The Court reasoned that newsgathering requires "the expenditure of labor, skill, and money," and that allowing one news agency to appropriate another's product would destroy the incentive to gather news. The Court's decision protected the "labor value" that the AP invested in newsgathering, at least for a limited time.

That precedent has lain dormant most of the last 80 years, and some believe it has been preempted by federal copyright law. But a few modern day courts have applied it to Internet news aggregators. In Associated Press v. All Headline News Corp., 608 F. Supp. 2d 454 (S.D.N.Y. 2009), the district court held that the Associated Press stated a claim at common law for misappropriation against AHN, an Internet-based service that located breaking news stories and sold them to other web sites to which AHN marketed itself as a news provider. The AP alleged that AHN removed the AP's copyright notices, sometimes rewrote the AP reports, and sometimes copied them verbatim. The district court reasoned that New York law still recognized the cause of action approved in International News Service v. Associated Press, and the theory was not preempted by federal law as long as it was limited to cases involving "hot news."

The Second Circuit had previously held that a "narrow" hot news misappropriation claim is not preempted by the federal Copyright Act if "(i) a plaintiff generates or gathers information at a cost; (ii) the information is time-sensitive; (iii) a defendant's use of the information constitutes free riding on plaintiff's efforts; (iv) the defendant is in direct competition with a product or service offered by the plaintiffs; and (v) the ability of other parties to free-ride on the efforts of the plaintiff or others would so reduce the incentive to produce the product or service that its existence or quality would be substantially threatened." National Basketball Ass'n v. Motorola, Inc., 105 F.3d 841 (2d Cir. 1997) (holding that the maker of a hand-held pager that provided real-time information about basketball games could be liable for the common law tort of misappropriation).

In a 2011 news aggregation case, however, the Second Circuit held that an aggregation claim was preempted by copyright law. The decision in Barclays Capital Inc. v. Theflyonthewall.com, Inc., 650 F.3d 876 (2d Cir. 2011), rested on narrow grounds, and does not appear to preclude successful suits against news aggregators altogether. The case pitted the interests of newsgatherers against those of news aggregators; three large financial services firms sued Theflyonthewall.com for copyright infringement for redistributing their stock analysts' investment recommendations "through unauthorized channels of electronic distribution." The Internet subscription service website often obtained forthcoming research reports and recommendations via leaks from plaintiffs' employees or clients. The website would then quickly distribute the recommendations before the New York Stock Exchange opened, undercutting plaintiffs' ability to profit from their reports.

A district judge entered judgment against the website for copyright infringement and awarded statutory damages, a permanent injunction against direct copying and republication of the reports, and attorneys' fees for the portion of the litigation expenses associated with pursuing the copyright infringement claim. She also held that the website had engaged in "hot-news misappropriation" when it redistributed the recommendations from the plaintiffs firms' investment reports before the opening of the New York Stock Exchange.

The Second Circuit reversed. The court reasoned that the website was "reporting financial news—factual information on the Firms' Recommendations—through a substantial organizational effort. Therefore, [the] service—which collects, summarizes, and disseminates the news of the Firms' Recommendations—is not the '*INS*-like' product that could support a non-preempted cause of action for misappropriation."

The court further explained:

[W]e are mindful that the *INS* Court's concern was tightly focused on the practices of the parties to the suit before it: news, data, and the like, gathered and disseminated by one organization as a significant part of its business, taken by another entity and published as the latter's own in competition with the former. The language chosen by the *INS* Court seems to us to make clear the substantial distance between that case and this one.

. . .

By way of comparison, we might . . . speculate about a product a Firm might produce which might indeed give rise to a non-preempted "hot-news" misappropriation claim. If a Firm were to collect and disseminate to some portion of the public facts about securities recommendations in the brokerage industry (including, perhaps, such facts it generated itself—its own

Recommendations), and were [a website] to copy the facts contained in the Firm's hypothetical service, it might be liable to the Firm on a "hot-news" misappropriation theory. That would appear to be an *INS*-type claim and might survive preemption.

c.   FAIR USE, SEARCH ENGINES, AND TRANSFORMATIVE USES

Authors Guild v. Google, Inc.
United States Court of Appeals, Second Circuit.
804 F.3d 202 (2015).

■ LEVAL, CIRCUIT JUDGE:

. . .

Since 2004, Google has scanned, rendered machine-readable, and indexed more than 20 million books, including both copyrighted works and works in the public domain. [Google obtained access to these books through bilateral agreements with libraries around the world.] . . .

[Google's] search tool permits a researcher to identify those books, out of millions, that do, as well as those that do not, use the terms selected by the researcher. Google notes that this identifying information instantaneously supplied would otherwise not be obtainable in lifetimes of searching.

. . .

The search engine also makes possible new forms of research, known as "text mining" and "data mining." [Users may use the Google's search tools to analyze "the frequency of word and phrase usage over centuries" and "fluctuations of interest in a particular subject over time and space by showing increases and decreases in the frequency of reference and usage in different periods and different linguistic regions." Users can "also comb over the tens of millions of books Google has scanned in order to examine "word frequencies, syntactic patterns, and thematic markers" and to derive information on how nomenclature, linguistic usage, and literary style have changed over time"]

The Google Books search function also allows the user a limited viewing of text. In addition to telling the number of times the word or term selected by the searcher appears in the book, the search function will display a maximum of three "snippets" containing it. A snippet is a horizontal segment comprising ordinarily an eighth of a page. . . . Google makes permanently unavailable for snippet view one snippet on each page and one complete page out of every ten—a process Google calls "blacklisting."

Google also disables snippet view entirely for types of books for which a single snippet is likely to satisfy the searcher's present need for the book, such as dictionaries, cookbooks, and books of short poems.

Finally, since 2005, Google will exclude any book altogether from snippet view at the request of the rights holder by the submission of an online form.

Under its contracts with the participating libraries, Google allows each library to download copies—of both the digital image and machine-readable versions—of the books that library submitted to Google for scanning (but not of books submitted by other libraries). This is done by giving each participating library access to the Google Return Interface ("GRIN"). The agreements between Google and the libraries, although not in all respects uniform, require the libraries to abide by copyright law in utilizing the digital copies they download and to take precautions to prevent dissemination of their digital copies to the public at large. Through the GRIN facility, participant libraries have downloaded at least 2.7 million digital copies of their own volumes.

. . .

DISCUSSION

The ultimate goal of copyright is to expand public knowledge and understanding, which copyright seeks to achieve by giving potential creators exclusive control over copying of their works, thus giving them a financial incentive to create informative, intellectually enriching works for public consumption. This objective is clearly reflected in the Constitution's empowerment of Congress *"To promote the Progress of Science . . . by securing for limited Times to Authors . . . the exclusive Right to their respective Writings."* U.S. Const., Art. I, § 8, cl. 8 (emphasis added). Thus, while authors are undoubtedly important intended beneficiaries of copyright, the ultimate, primary intended beneficiary is the public, whose access to knowledge copyright seeks to advance by providing rewards for authorship.

. . . Although well established in the common law development of copyright, fair use was not recognized in the terms of our statute until the adoption of § 107 in the Copyright Act of 1976. 17 U.S.C. §§ 101 *et seq.*

[The court then highlighted the statute's language, including the four fair use factors, noting that Supreme Court precedent urged that the first, "the purpose and character of the secondary use," and the fourth, "the effect of the use upon the potential market for or value of the copyrighted work," were most critical, though each was important in a collective sense. It cited Campbell v. Acuff-Rose Music, Inc., 510 U.S. 569 (U.S. 1994), a fair use case, throughout.]

A. *Factor One*

(1) Transformative purpose. Campbell's explanation of the first factor's inquiry into the "purpose and character" of the secondary use focuses on whether the new work . . . adds something new, with a further purpose. . . . [I]t asks, in other words, whether and to what extent the

new work is 'transformative.' " [ ] [T]ransformative uses tend to favor a fair use finding because a transformative use is one that communicates something new and different from the original or expands its utility, thus serving copyright's overall objective of contributing to public knowledge.

. . . The Supreme Court's discussion in *Campbell* gave important guidance on assessing when a transformative use tends to support a conclusion of fair use. . . . Explaining why parody makes a stronger, or in any event more obvious, claim of fair use than satire, the Court stated,

> [T]he heart of any parodist's claim to quote from existing material . . . is the use of . . . a prior author's composition to . . . *comment [ ] on that author's works.* . . . If, on the contrary, the commentary has no critical bearing on the substance or style of the original composition, which the alleged infringer merely uses to get attention or to avoid the drudgery in working up something fresh, the claim to fairness in borrowing from another's work diminishes accordingly (if it does not vanish). . . . Parody needs to mimic an original to make its point, and so has some claim to use the creation of its victim's . . . imagination, whereas satire can stand on its own two feet and so requires justification for the very act of borrowing.

[ ] This part of the Supreme Court's discussion is significant in assessing Google's claim of fair use because . . . Google's claim of transformative purpose for copying from the works of others is to provide otherwise unavailable information about the originals.

. . .

[W]e first consider whether Google's search and snippet views functions satisfy the first fair use factor with respect to Plaintiffs' rights in their books. . . .

(2)   Search Function. We have no difficulty concluding that Google's making of a digital copy of Plaintiffs' books for the purpose of enabling a search for identification of books containing a term of interest to the searcher involves a highly transformative purpose, in the sense intended by *Campbell.* . . .

[T]he purpose of Google's copying of the original copyrighted books is to make available significant information *about those books,* permitting a searcher to identify those that contain a word or term of interest, as well as those that do not include reference to it. In addition . . . Google allows readers to learn the frequency of usage of selected words in the aggregate corpus of published books in different historical periods. We have no doubt that the purpose of this copying is the sort of transformative purpose described in *Campbell* as strongly favoring satisfaction of the first factor.

. . .

(3) Snippet View. Plaintiffs correctly point out . . . that the Google Books search function allows searchers to read snippets from the book searched, [which] adds important value to the basic transformative search function, which tells only whether and how often the searched term appears in the book. . . . For example, a searcher seeking books that explore Einstein's theories, who finds that a particular book includes 39 usages of "Einstein," will nonetheless conclude she can skip that book if the snippets reveal that the book speaks of "Einstein" because that is the name of the author's cat. In contrast, the snippet will tell the searcher that this is a book she needs to obtain if the snippet shows that the author is engaging with Einstein's theories.

Google's division of the page into tiny snippets is designed to show the searcher just enough context surrounding the searched term to help her evaluate whether the book falls within the scope of her interest (without revealing so much as to threaten the author's copyright interests). Snippet view thus adds importantly to the highly transformative purpose of identifying books of interest to the searcher. With respect to the first factor test, it favors a finding of fair use (unless the value of its transformative purpose is overcome by its providing text in a manner that offers a competing substitute for Plaintiffs' books, which we discuss under factors three and four below).

(4) Google's Commercial Motivation. Plaintiffs also contend that Google's commercial motivation weighs in their favor under the first factor. . . . Although Google has no revenues flowing directly from its operation of the Google Books functions, Plaintiffs stress that Google is profit-motivated and seeks to use its dominance of book search to fortify its overall dominance of the Internet search market, and that thereby Google indirectly reaps profits from the Google Books functions.

. . .

Our court has [ ] repeatedly rejected the contention that commercial motivation should outweigh a convincing transformative purpose and absence of significant substitutive competition with the original. See Cariou v. Prince, 714 F.3d 694, 708 (2d Cir. 2013), cert. denied [ ] ("The commercial/nonprofit dichotomy concerns the unfairness that arises when a secondary user makes unauthorized use of copyrighted material to capture significant revenues as a direct consequence of copying the original work. This factor must be applied with caution because, as the Supreme Court has recognized, Congress could not have intended a rule that commercial uses are presumptively unfair. Instead, the more transformative the new work, the less will be the significance of other factors, like commercialism, that may weigh against a finding of fair use.") [ ]

While we recognize that in some circumstances, a commercial motivation on the part of the secondary user will weigh against her, especially, as the Supreme Court suggested, when a persuasive transformative purpose is lacking, Campbell, 510 U.S. at 579, [ ] we see no reason in this case why Google's overall profit motivation should prevail as a reason for denying fair use over its highly convincing transformative purpose, together with the absence of significant substitutive competition, as reasons for granting fair use. Many of the most universally accepted forms of fair use, such as news reporting and commentary, quotation in historical or analytic books, reviews of books, and performances, as well as parody, are all normally done commercially for profit.

B. Factor Two

The second fair use factor directs consideration of the "nature of the copyrighted work." While the "transformative purpose" inquiry discussed above is conventionally treated as a part of first factor analysis, it inevitably involves the second factor as well. One cannot assess whether the copying work has an objective that differs from the original without considering both works, and their respective objectives.

[ ] While each of the three Plaintiffs' books in this case is factual, we do not consider that as a boost to Google's claim of fair use. If one (or all) of the plaintiff works were fiction, we do not think that would change in any way our appraisal. Nothing in this case influences us one way or the other with respect to the second factor considered in isolation. To the extent that the "nature" of the original copyrighted work necessarily combines with the "purpose and character" of the secondary work to permit assessment of whether the secondary work uses the original in a "transformative" manner, as the term is used in *Campbell,* the second factor favors fair use not because Plaintiffs' works are factual, but because the secondary use transformatively provides valuable information about the original, rather than replicating protected expression in a manner that provides a meaningful substitute for the original.

C. Factor Three

The third statutory factor instructs us to consider "the amount and substantiality of the portion used in relation to the copyrighted work as a whole." . . . The larger the amount, or the more important the part, of the original that is copied, the greater the likelihood that the secondary work might serve as an effectively competing substitute for the original, and might therefore diminish the original rights holder's sales and profits.

(1) Search Function. The Google Books program has made a digital copy of the entirety of each of Plaintiffs' books. Notwithstanding the reasonable implication of Factor Three that fair use is more likely to be favored by the copying of smaller, rather than larger, portions of the original, courts have rejected any categorical rule that a copying of the entirety cannot be a fair use. Complete unchanged copying has repeatedly been found justified as fair use when the copying was

reasonably appropriate to achieve the copier's transformative purpose and was done in such a manner that it did not offer a competing substitute for the original. . . .

[In this case,] not only is the copying of the totality of the original reasonably appropriate to Google's transformative purpose, it is literally necessary to achieve that purpose. If Google copied less than the totality of the originals, its search function could not advise searchers reliably whether their searched term appears in a book (or how many times).

While Google *makes* an unauthorized digital copy of the entire book, it does not reveal that digital copy to the public. The copy is made to enable the search functions to reveal limited, important information about the books. With respect to the search function, Google satisfies the third factor test. . . .

(2) Snippet View. . . . What matters [in assessing Google's provision of snippet view] is not so much "the amount and substantiality of the portion used" *in making a copy,* but rather the amount and substantiality of *what is thereby made accessible* to a public for which it may serve as a competing substitute. . . .

Without doubt, enabling searchers to see portions of the copied texts could have determinative effect on the fair use analysis. The larger the quantity of the copyrighted text the searcher can see and the more control the searcher can exercise over what part of the text she sees, the greater the likelihood that those revelations could serve her as an effective, free substitute for the purchase of the plaintiff's book. We nonetheless conclude that, at least as presently structured by Google, the snippet view does not reveal matter that offers the marketplace a significantly competing substitute for the copyrighted work.

Google has constructed the snippet feature in a manner that substantially protects against its serving as an effectively competing substitute for Plaintiffs' books. [Bolstering this conclusion are] the small size of the snippets (normally one eighth of a page), the blacklisting of one snippet per page and of one page in every ten, the fact that no more than three snippets are shown—and no more than one per page—for each term searched, and the fact that the same snippets are shown for a searched term no matter how many times, or from how many different computers, the term is searched. In addition, Google does not provide snippet view for types of books, such as dictionaries and cookbooks, for which viewing a small segment is likely to satisfy the searcher's need. The result of these restrictions is, so far as the record demonstrates, that a searcher cannot succeed, even after long extended effort to multiply what can be revealed, in revealing through a snippet search what could usefully serve as a competing substitute for the original.

[O]ther restrictions built into the program work together to ensure that, even after protracted effort over a substantial period of time, only small and randomly scattered portions of a book will be accessible. In an effort to show what large portions of text searchers can read through persistently augmented snippet searches, Plaintiffs' counsel employed researchers over a period of weeks to do multiple word searches on Plaintiffs' books. In no case were they able to access as much as 16% of the text, and the snippets collected were usually not sequential but scattered randomly throughout the book. . . .

The fact that Plaintiffs' searchers managed to reveal nearly 16% of the text of Plaintiffs' books overstates the degree to which snippet view can provide a meaningful substitute. At least as important as the percentage of words of a book that are revealed is the manner and order in which they are revealed. Even if the search function revealed 100% of the words of the copyrighted book, this would be of little substitutive value if the words were revealed in alphabetical order, or any order other than the order they follow in the original book. It cannot be said that a revelation is "substantial" in the sense intended by the statute's third factor if the revelation is in a form that communicates little of the sense of the original. The fragmentary and scattered nature of the snippets revealed, even after a determined, assiduous, time-consuming search, results in a revelation that is not "substantial," even if it includes an aggregate 16% of the text of the book. If snippet view could be used to reveal a coherent block amounting to 16% of a book, that would raise a very different question beyond the scope of our inquiry.

D. Factor Four

The fourth fair use factor, "the effect of the [copying] use upon the potential market for or value of the copyrighted work," focuses on whether the copy brings to the marketplace a competing substitute for the original, or its derivative, so as to deprive the rights holder of significant revenues because of the likelihood that potential purchasers may opt to acquire the copy in preference to the original. Because copyright is a commercial doctrine whose objective is to stimulate creativity among potential authors by enabling them to earn money from their creations, the fourth factor is of great importance in making a fair use assessment. See Harper & Row, 471 U.S. at 566 (describing the fourth factor as "undoubtedly the single most important element of fair use").

Campbell stressed the close linkage between the first and fourth factors, in that the more the copying is done to achieve a purpose that differs from the purpose of the original, the less likely it is that the copy will serve as a satisfactory substitute for the original. [] . . . However, *Campbell*'s observation as to the likelihood of a secondary use serving as an effective substitute goes only so far. Even if the *purpose* of the copying is for a valuably transformative purpose, such copying might nonetheless harm the value of the copyrighted original if done in a manner that results in widespread revelation of sufficiently significant portions of the original as to make available a significantly competing substitute. The question for us is whether snippet view, notwithstanding its transformative purpose, does that. We conclude that, at least as snippet view is presently constructed, it does not.

Especially in view of the fact that the normal purchase price of a book is relatively low in relation to the cost of manpower needed to secure an arbitrary assortment of randomly scattered snippets, we conclude that the snippet function does not give searchers access to effectively competing substitutes. Snippet view, at best and after a large commitment of manpower, produces discontinuous, tiny fragments, amounting in the aggregate to no more than 16% of a book. This does not threaten the rights holders with any significant harm to the value of their copyrights or diminish their harvest of copyright revenue.

We recognize that the snippet function can cause *some* loss of sales. There are surely instances in which a searcher's need for access to a text will be satisfied by the snippet view, resulting in either the loss of a sale to that searcher, or reduction of demand on libraries for that title, which might have resulted in libraries purchasing additional copies. But the possibility, or even the probability or certainty, of some loss of sales does not suffice to make the copy an effectively competing substitute that would tilt the weighty fourth factor in favor of the rights holder in the original. There must be a meaningful or significant effect "upon the potential market for or value of the copyrighted work." 17 U.S.C. § 107(4).

Furthermore, the type of loss of sale envisioned above will generally occur in relation to interests that are not protected by the copyright. A snippet's capacity to satisfy a searcher's need for access to a copyrighted book will at times be because the snippet conveys a historical fact that the searcher needs to ascertain. For example, a student writing a paper on Franklin D. Roosevelt might need to learn the year Roosevelt was stricken with polio. By entering "Roosevelt polio" in a Google Books search, the student would be taken to (among numerous sites) a snippet from page 31 of Richard Thayer Goldberg's *The Making of Franklin D. Roosevelt* (1981), telling that the polio attack occurred in 1921. This would satisfy the searcher's need for the book, eliminating any need to purchase it or acquire it from a library. But what the searcher derived from the snippet was a historical fact. Author Goldberg's copyright does not extend to the facts communicated by his book. It protects only the author's manner of expression. . . .

Even if the snippet reveals some authorial expression, because of the brevity of a single snippet and the cumbersome, disjointed, and incomplete nature of the aggregation of snippets made available through snippet view, we think it would be a rare case in which the searcher's interest *in the protected aspect* of the author's work would be satisfied by what is available from snippet view, and rarer still—because of the cumbersome, disjointed, and incomplete nature of the aggregation of snippets made available through snippet view—that snippet view could provide a significant substitute for the purchase of the author's book.

Accordingly, considering the four fair use factors in light of the goals of copyright, we conclude that Google's making of a complete digital copy of Plaintiffs' works for the purpose of providing the public with its search and snippet view functions (at least as snippet view is presently designed) is a fair use and does not infringe Plaintiffs' copyrights in their books.

. . .

NOTES AND QUESTIONS

1.   Judge Leval noted in a footnote to the *Authors Guild* decision that nonprofit educational uses of copyrighted materials are not automatically presumed to be fair use because otherwise "[a]uthors who write for educational purposes, and publishers who invest substantial funds to publish educational materials, would lose the ability to earn revenues if users were permitted to copy the materials freely merely because such copying was in the service of a nonprofit educational mission." What are the implications of this statement for non-profit media organizations?

2.   Is Judge Leval's comparison between the Google search functions and parody convincing?

3.   In 2015 the Authors Guild unsuccessfully petitioned the Supreme Court for certiorari. On its website, it explained that it did so in order to defend authors' rights to their works in a digital age and it likened Google's use to thievery:

> Google copied 20 million books to create a massive and uniquely valuable database, all without asking for copyright permission or paying their authors a cent. It mines this vast natural language storehouse for various purposes, not least among them to improve the performance of its search and translation services. The problem is that before Google created Book Search, it digitized and made many digital copies of millions of copyrighted books, which the company never paid for. It never even bought a single book. That, in itself, was an act of theft. If you did it with a single book, you'd be infringing. . . .
>
> A truism of the digital age is: whoever controls the data owns the future. Google's exclusive access to such an enormous slice of the world's linguistic output cemented its market dominance and continues to this day to further its corporate profits.

Authors Guild v. Google: Questions and Answers, www.authorsguild.org, Dec. 31, 2015.

Is the Authors Guild's concern about Google's dominance hyperbole or does it have some merit, especially in the context of news media?

d. UNPUBLISHED MATERIAL

Copyright exists not only in material prepared for publication, but also (ever since the 1976 Copyright Act) in communications never intended to be published, such as letters, memoranda, and tape recordings of a person's conversations or ruminations. This creates a potential problem for media: Do they violate copyright when they quote such material in news reports? Copyright owners typically object to unauthorized use for commercial reasons: the owner wants to be paid, or wants to prevent the use in question in order to preserve the future commercial value of the work. Sometimes, however, an owner objects to unauthorized use because he wishes to avoid publicity or prevent embarrassment or exposure of wrongdoing. If the copyright owner is successful, copyright law may lead to the suppression of information of significant public concern.

The Salinger Case. The Second Circuit held that J.D. Salinger, author of "Catcher in the Rye," and other novels and short stories, could prevent a biographer from quoting his unpublished letters even though Salinger had no intention of publishing them himself. In fact, he had objected to their use primarily because he did not want a biography of him to be written at all. See Salinger v. Random House, Inc., 811 F.2d 90 (2d Cir. 1987).

The court thought *The Nation* case required it to place "special emphasis on the unpublished nature of Salinger's letters." Analyzing the fair use issue in that light, it found that only one of the factors favored the biographer, Hamilton. "Hamilton's purpose in using the Salinger letters to enrich his scholarly biography weighs the first fair use factor in Hamilton's favor. . . ."

The other factors all favored Salinger. Because the copyrighted letters were unpublished, the second factor (the nature of the copyrighted work) weighed "heavily" in favor of Salinger. So did the third factor (amount copied). The court said close paraphrases, as well as direct quotes, should be counted in making this determination. Counting paraphrases, the court concluded that Hamilton had used at least 10 percent of 42 letters, and at least one-third of 17 letters. "The taking is significant not only from a quantitative standpoint but from a qualitative one as well. The copied passages, if not the 'heart of the book,' [ ] are at least an important ingredient of the book as it now stands. To a large extent, they make the book worth reading. The letters are quoted or paraphrased on at least 40 percent of the book's 192 pages." [Note that the statute suggests that the issue is the portion used in relation to the *copyrighted* work, not in relation to the infringing use.]

The fourth factor, effect on the market, weighed "slightly" in Salinger's favor, even though the court conceded that the book would not displace the market for the letters. "[T]he need to assess the effect on the market for Salinger's letters is not lessened by the fact that their author has disavowed any intention to publish them during his lifetime. First, the proper inquiry concerns the 'potential market' for the copyrighted work [ ]. Second, Salinger has the right to change his mind. He is entitled to protect his *opportunity* to sell his letters, an opportunity estimated by his literary agent to have a current value in excess of $500,000."

Is protection of an author's privacy within the purposes of the copyright system? Which elements of the fair use analysis are affected if an author's objective in invoking copyright law is not to protect his or her own right to profit from the work, but to prevent anyone from publishing it? How might such an outcome affect news reporting? The author of the *Salinger* opinion endorses the use of copyright law to protect privacy in Jon O. Newman, Copyright Law and the Protection of Privacy, 12 Colum.-VLA J.L. & Arts 459 (1988).

The New Era Cases. The Second Circuit also addressed the use of copyright law to suppress information in two cases involving unflattering biographies of L. Ron Hubbard, the founder of the Church of Scientology. The first case was New Era Publications International v. Henry Holt & Co., 873 F.2d 576 (2d Cir. 1989). It involved a biography that contended Hubbard and the Church of Scientology had glorified his image over a period of 30 years through various embellished and distorted accounts of Hubbard's life. In many instances the evidence of alleged discrepancies and distortions came from Hubbard's own unpublished works, such as letters and diaries, in which New Era held copyright.

New Era sought to enjoin publication of the biography in the United States. The case was decided at the trial level by Judge Pierre Leval, who had tried the *Salinger* case (and later was promoted to the bench of the Second Circuit and authored the *Authors Guild* decision). He concluded that the book contained 44 passages that would not qualify as fair use under *Salinger,* but he nevertheless exercised his equitable discretion to deny the injunction. He conceded that injunctive relief is common in copyright cases, but said those typically involve "piracy of artistic creations motivated exclusively by greed." This case was different:

> [A]n injunction would ... suppress an interesting, well-researched, provocative study of a figure who, claiming both scientific and religious credentials, has wielded enormous influence over millions of people. . . . The abhorrence of the First Amendment to prior restraint is so powerful a force in shaping so many areas of our law, it would be anomalous to presume casually its appropriateness for all cases of copyright infringement. . . .

> In the past, efforts to suppress critical biography through the copyright injunction have generally not succeeded because courts (sometimes straining) have found fair use. [ ] The conflict between freedom of speech and the injunctive remedy was thus avoided. Since *Salinger,* however, the issue is inescapable.

He concluded that New Era's damages remedy was adequate to protect its copyright interests with far less harm to First Amendment interests. 695 F. Supp. 1493 (S.D.N.Y. 1988).

The Second Circuit disagreed with Judge Leval's appraisal. But the court affirmed the denial of the injunction on the ground of laches, because New Era had taken no steps to protect its rights until the book was in print even though it had known for several years that it was being prepared.

As for Judge Leval's First Amendment concerns, the court was not persuaded "that any . . . not accommodated by the Copyright Act are implicated in this action. Our observation that the fair use doctrine encompasses all claims of First Amendment in the copyright field [ ] has never been repudiated. See, e.g., [*Harper & Row*.] An author's expression of an idea, as distinguished from the idea itself, is not considered subject to the public's 'right to know.' [ ]."

The importance of the distinction between published and unpublished material is illustrated by a second *New Era* case, which involved a different biography that used only Hubbard's published writings. The district court found 103 infringing passages in the biography and enjoined its publication. The Second Circuit (a different panel from the one that decided *New Era I*) reversed, finding that all the passages were protected as fair use. The four factors all favored the biographer, the court said. The author's purpose was not to appropriate Hubbard's work, but "for the entirely legitimate purpose of making his point that Hubbard was a charlatan and the Church a dangerous cult." None of the works copied were unpublished, and most were viewed as being factual rather than creative. Thus, the nature of the copyrighted work favored the biographer. The book used only a small percentage of any of Hubbard's works, and the court did not view the quoted passages as containing the "heart" of the copyrighted material. The biography might dissuade the public from buying Hubbard's works, but only because it depicted him unfavorably, and the court said copyright law does not protect against that sort of injury. See New Era Publications v. Carol Publishing Group, 904 F.2d 152 (2d Cir. 1990).

Congress responded to these cases in 1992 by adding the following to Section 107: "The fact that a work is unpublished shall not itself bar a finding of fair use if such finding is made upon consideration of all of the above factors."

e.   LETTERS TO THE EDITOR

Because the writer of a letter owns the copyright in it, he or she may impose conditions on the right to publish it, just as any other copyright holder may grant a conditional license to use of the copyrighted work, but fair use analysis may permit the publisher to ignore the conditions under some circumstances. In Diamond v. Am-Law Publishing Corp., 745 F.2d

142 (2d Cir. 1984), defendant American Lawyer published a story reporting that a formal grievance had been filed against the plaintiff, a lawyer. The plaintiff wrote defendant demanding an apology and a retraction. The editor invited the plaintiff to write a letter stating that no grievance had been filed. Plaintiff then sent a long letter making that point and also attacking the reporting practices of the defendant. The letter stated that "You are authorized to publish this letter but only in its entirety." Defendant published excerpts from the letter that made the point about the grievance but omitted, without showing any deletions, the parts attacking the defendant.

The lawyer sued for infringement but lost because although the newspaper had no license to print the letter as edited, it could do so as a matter of fair use. The non-use or editing of the letter did not put the copyrighted work in an unfair or distorted light. The omissions involved an unrelated matter and did not mislead the public about the contents of the entire letter. (Even if it did, it was not clear that this made it a copyright violation.) In any event, the use was for comment or news reporting, uses protected under Section 107. Finally, plaintiff could show no present or future use of the letter that had been adversely affected by defendant's use.

C. FIRST AMENDMENT IMPLICATIONS OF COPYRIGHT ENFORCEMENT

First Amendment challenges to copyright restrictions traditionally have been rejected on the ground that copyright law itself contains sufficient protections for free speech. The Supreme Court gave this answer to the First Amendment argument in the *Nation* case, supra. Many commentators vigorously dispute this proposition, however. See, e.g., Lawrence Lessig, Free Culture (2004), arguing that copyright has become a means by which a few large media companies, holding thousands of copyrights, monopolize culture, stifle creativity, and thwart development of new technologies.

Professor Neil Netanel argues that judicial immunization of copyright law from First Amendment scrutiny is anomalous because the dramatic expansion of copyright law in the past half-century has taken place at the same time that the Supreme Court interpreted the First Amendment broadly to protect speech in other areas. He contends that courts should subject copyright restrictions to the kind of intermediate scrutiny employed in *Turner Broadcasting*, should require copyright holders to bear the burden of disproving fair use, and should award damages rather than injunctive relief when a user invokes a colorable but unsuccessful fair use defense. See Neil Netanel, Locating Copyright Within the First Amendment Skein, 54 Stan. L. Rev. 1, 85–86 (2001).

Professor Edwin Baker argued that under a proper understanding of the First Amendment, existing copyright doctrines such as fair use and non-protection of facts and ideas make copyright restrictions on commercial copying constitutionally acceptable, but such restrictions generally should not be applied to non-commercial copying. "Copyright legislation that restricts an individual's expressive choices and copyright rules that limit the media's capacity to perform the democratic roles of a free press should be found unconstitutional under the First Amendment." C. Edwin Baker, First Amendment Limits on Copyright, 55 Vand. L. Rev. 891, 951 (2002).

Eldred v. Ashcroft. The Supreme Court has not been sympathetic to the argument that copyright law is insufficiently protective of free speech interests. In Eldred v. Ashcroft, 537 U.S. 186 (2003), the Court rejected claims that the Copyright Term Extension Act of 1998, which extended the term of copyright from 50 to 70 years beyond the death of the author, violated both the Commerce Clause and the First Amendment. As for the claim that the term was now so long that it exceeded the Copyright Clause's authorization to protect copyright for "limited times," the Court said it was within Congress's power to fix the limit. As for the First Amendment claim:

> [T]he Copyright Clause and the First Amendment were adopted close in time. This proximity indicates that, in the Framers' view, copyright's limited monopolies are compatible with free speech principles. . . . [C]opyright law contains built-in First Amendment accommodations. [ ] First, it distinguishes between ideas and expression and makes only the latter eligible for copyright protection. . . . Second, the "fair use" defense allows the public to use not only facts and ideas contained in a copyrighted work, but also expression itself in certain circumstances.

The Court wrote that copyrights are not "categorically immune from challenges under the First Amendment. . . . But when, as in this case, Congress has not altered the traditional contours of copyright protection, further First Amendment scrutiny is unnecessary."

Justice Stevens dissented on Copyright Clause grounds, and Justice Breyer on First Amendment grounds. Justice Breyer said the statute required closer constitutional analysis, though not necessarily intermediate scrutiny:

> This statute will cause serious expression-related harm. It will likely restrict traditional dissemination of copyrighted works. It will likely inhibit new forms of dissemination through the use of new technology. It threatens to interfere with efforts to preserve our Nation's historical and cultural heritage and efforts to use that heritage, say, to educate our Nation's children. It is easy to understand how the statute might benefit the private financial interests of corporations or heirs who own existing copyrights. But I cannot find any constitutionally legitimate, copyright-

related way in which the statute will benefit the public. Indeed, in respect to existing works, the serious public harm and the virtually nonexistent public benefit could not be more clear.

[T]he statute cannot be understood rationally to advance a constitutionally legitimate interest. The statute falls outside the scope of legislative power that the Copyright Clause, read in light of the First Amendment, grants to Congress. I would hold the statute unconstitutional.

In what circumstances might enforcement of the Copyright Act violate the First Amendment? Time Inc. v. Bernard Geis Associates, 293 F. Supp. 130 (S.D.N.Y. 1968), involved the Zapruder film of the assassination of President Kennedy. Plaintiff bought and copyrighted Zapruder's film. Defendant wanted to produce a study of the assassination but could not come to terms with plaintiff on getting a license to use the photographs. Instead, defendant prepared sketches that were admittedly copied very closely from published copies of the Zapruder film. The court found the need for copying the expression very strong because of the difficulty of paraphrasing photographs and the central importance of the film. After concluding that the defendant's book would not be likely to hurt the sales of plaintiff's possible future books or motion pictures incorporating the film, it found fair use.

If it were shown that the book had indeed seriously hurt plaintiff's sales of the copyrighted material, then fair use might not have been available. In such a case the copyright statute would permit Time Inc. to seek compensatory damages or the defendant's profits attributable to the infringement, and perhaps an injunction and punitive damages. Would the First Amendment permit these remedies?

Enjoining Infringement. If copyright is "not categorically immune" from First Amendment scrutiny, one might expect that prior restraints, at least, would be difficult to sustain. But, as the *Salinger* case makes clear, injunctions are not disfavored in copyright law. Media attempts to bring the "heavy presumption of unconstitutionality" to bear on injunctions in this area have met with little success. See, e.g., In re Capital Cities/ABC, Inc., 918 F.2d 140 (11th Cir. 1990). There, a plaintiff claiming to own exclusive rights to the story sought to enjoin ABC from broadcasting a movie about a Vietnam POW who collaborated with the enemy. The court said the trial judge could view the film, decide which portions violated the plaintiff's copyright, and enjoin the broadcast of those portions of the movie. ABC argued that this would be a classic exercise of judicial censorship in violation of the First Amendment. But the court said it was a proper way of balancing ABC's First Amendment rights against the plaintiff's copyright interests. "Such a 'surgical' restraint does not 'give directives as to the content of expression,' only the manner of expression." See also Elvis Presley Enterprises, Inc. v. Passport Video, 349 F.3d 622 (9th Cir. 2003), asserting that "if the use of the alleged infringer is not fair use, there are no First Amendment prohibitions against granting a preliminary injunction."

The availability of preliminary injunctions poses one of the most significant conflicts between copyright law and traditional First Amendment law, and has become increasingly controversial. The Supreme Court has written that the goals of copyright law are "not always best served by automatically granting injunctive relief." Campbell v. Acuff-Rose Music, Inc., 510 U.S. 569, 578 n. 10 (1994) (the case referred to in the *Authors Guild* opinion). In the *Tasini* case, the Court noted that its holding that the publishers were infringing the copyrights of freelancers did not necessarily mean that an injunction should issue.

As we saw in Chapter Two, prior restraints against publication are rarely permissible. For an extended argument that this hostility to content-based prior restraints should extend to copyright injunctions too, see Mark A. Lemley and Eugene Volokh, Freedom of Speech and Injunctions in Intellectual Property Cases, 48 Duke L.J. 147, 147–198 (1998). The authors conclude that there are no persuasive distinctions between preliminary injunctions in copyright infringement cases and other prior restraints. If that is true, does it suggest that the traditional disfavor with which courts view prior restraints should be applied to copyright injunctions, or that preliminary injunctions should be more widely permitted in other contexts?

PART III

LEGAL ISSUES ARISING FROM NEWSGATHERING

CHAPTER VIII

NEWSGATHERING TORTS

Once members of the media obtain information, their right to publish it is generally protected by the First Amendment. Newsgathering activities, however, do not receive the same level of First Amendment protection as publication. Courts generally take the view that the First Amendment provides little or no protection for torts (or crimes) committed in the course of gathering news.

As a general proposition, that surely is sensible: few would expect the First Amendment to protect a reporter's right to commit burglary or a photographer's right to trespass into a person's home to gather news. But is it clear that liability for torts committed in the course of newsgathering is of no First Amendment concern? Suppose a state made it a tort to engage in uninvited telephone solicitation and subjected news media to liability for telephoning people at their homes to solicit their comments about newsworthy matters: would courts dismiss a constitutional challenge merely by branding the conduct as tortious? In Branzburg v. Hayes, the seminal reporter's privilege case excerpted and discussed in Chapter Nine, the Supreme Court recognized that "without some protection for seeking out the news, freedom of the press could be eviscerated." Nevertheless, the level of protection the media receives diminishes sharply when the tort occurs in the process of gathering information: despite the *Branzburg* language acknowledging the importance of newsgathering, many lower court decisions emphasize that the Supreme Court "has repeatedly declined to confer on the media an expansive right to gather information." Dahlstrom v. Sun-Times Media, 777 F.3d 937 (7th Cir. 2015).

Although the cases considered in this chapter all begin with a complaint about something the media did in the course of gathering information, they often also include claims for harm caused by publication of the information that was obtained. Such claims at times cloud the distinction between publishing torts and newsgathering torts. For a time a disproportionate number of these cases originated in California, but today courts throughout the country are addressing lawsuits springing in some part from newsgathering.

A. INTRUSION

Intrusion is a branch of the law of privacy, which we considered in Chapter Five. Section 652B of the Restatement (Second) of Torts sets forth the elements of intrusion: "One who intentionally intrudes, physically or otherwise, upon the solitude or seclusion of another or his private affairs or concerns, is subject to liability to the other for invasion of his privacy, if the intrusion would be highly offensive to a reasonable person." Notice that while the other privacy torts deal with harm caused by publication, intrusion deals with the harm caused by conduct, including newsgathering activities.

The tort, therefore, does not require publication, but the fact that the defendant's conduct was done for the purposes of publication may influence outcomes, as the following case suggests.

Shulman v. Group W Productions, Inc.

Supreme Court of California, 1998.
955 P.2d 469.

As Modified on Denial of Rehearing.

■ WERDEGAR, JUSTICE.

. . .

In the present case, we address the balance between privacy and press freedom in the commonplace context of an automobile accident. Plaintiffs, two members of a family whose activities and position did not otherwise make them public figures, were injured when their car went off the highway, overturning and trapping them inside. A medical transport and rescue helicopter crew came to plaintiffs' assistance, accompanied on this occasion by a video camera operator employed by a television producer. The cameraman filmed plaintiffs' extrication from the car, the flight nurse and medic's efforts to give them medical care during the extrication, and their transport to the hospital in the helicopter. The flight nurse wore a small microphone that picked up her conversations with other rescue workers and with one of the plaintiffs. This videotape and sound track were edited into a segment that was broadcast, months later, on a documentary television show, *On Scene: Emergency Response*. Plaintiffs, who consented neither to the filming and recording nor to the broadcasting, allege the television producers thereby intruded into a realm of personal privacy and gave unwanted publicity to private events of their lives.

The trial court granted summary judgment for the producers on the ground that the events depicted in the broadcast were newsworthy and the producers' activities were therefore protected under the First Amendment to the United States Constitution. The Court of Appeal reversed, finding triable issues of fact exist as to one plaintiff's claim for publication of private facts and legal error on the trial court's part as to both plaintiffs' intrusion claims. Agreeing with some, but not all, of the Court of Appeal's analysis, we conclude summary judgment was proper as to plaintiffs' cause of action for publication of private facts, but not as to their cause of action for intrusion.[2]

---

[2] Five justices (Chief Justice George, Justice Mosk, Justice Kennard, Justice Chin and myself) conclude summary judgment was proper on the cause of action for publication of private facts. Five justices (Chief Justice George, Justice Kennard, Justice Baxter, Justice Brown and

I.   Publication of Private Facts

[The majority held that the broadcast of plaintiffs' words and images was newsworthy as a matter of law and therefore could not be the basis for a public disclosure of private facts claim. The dissenting justices would have left this issue to the jury.]

II.   Intrusion

Of the four privacy torts identified by Prosser, the tort of intrusion into private places, conversations or matters is perhaps the one that best captures the common understanding of an "invasion of privacy." It encompasses unconsented-to physical intrusion into the home, hospital room or other place the privacy of which is legally recognized, as well as unwarranted sensory intrusions such as eavesdropping, wiretapping, and visual or photographic spying. (See Rest.2d Torts, § 652B, com. b., [ ], and illustrations.) It is in the intrusion cases that invasion of privacy is most clearly seen as an affront to individual dignity. . . .

. . . [T]he action for intrusion has two elements: (1) intrusion into a private place, conversation or matter, (2) in a manner highly offensive to a reasonable person. We consider the elements in that order.

We ask first whether defendants "intentionally intrude[d], physically or otherwise, upon the solitude or seclusion of another," that is, into a place or conversation private to Wayne or Ruth. (Rest.2d Torts, § 652B; [ ]) "[T]here is no liability for the examination of a public record concerning the plaintiff. . . . [or] for observing him or even taking his photograph while he is walking on the public highway." [ ]. To prove actionable intrusion, the plaintiff must show the defendant penetrated some zone of physical or sensory privacy surrounding, or obtained unwanted access to data about, the plaintiff. The tort is proven only if the plaintiff had an objectively reasonable expectation of seclusion or solitude in the place, conversation or data source. [ ]

Cameraman Cooke's mere presence at the accident scene and filming of the events occurring there cannot be deemed either a physical or sensory intrusion on plaintiffs' seclusion. Plaintiffs had no right of ownership or possession of the property where the rescue took place, nor any actual control of the premises. Nor could they have had a reasonable expectation that members of the media would be excluded or prevented from photographing the scene; for journalists to attend and record the scenes of accidents and rescues is in no way unusual or unexpected. [ ]

Two aspects of defendants' conduct, however, raise triable issues of intrusion on seclusion. First, a triable issue exists as to whether both plaintiffs had an objectively reasonable expectation of privacy in the interior of the rescue helicopter, which served as an ambulance. Although

---

myself) conclude summary judgment was improper on the cause of action for intrusion. Part I of this opinion's discussion expresses the views of a majority of the court's members. [ ] Part II expresses a majority's views except for the reservations stated by Justice Brown. [ ]

the attendance of reporters and photographers at the scene of an accident is to be expected, we are aware of no law or custom permitting the press to ride in ambulances or enter hospital rooms during treatment without the patient's consent. [ ] Other than the two patients and Cooke, only three people were present in the helicopter, all Mercy Air staff. As the Court of Appeal observed, "[i]t is neither the custom nor the habit of our society that any member of the public at large or its media representatives may hitch a ride in an ambulance and ogle as paramedics care for an injured stranger." [ ]

Second, Ruth was entitled to a degree of privacy in her conversations with Carnahan and other medical rescuers at the accident scene, and in Carnahan's conversations conveying medical information regarding Ruth to the hospital base. Cooke, perhaps, did not intrude into that zone of privacy merely by being present at a place where he could hear such conversations with unaided ears. But by placing a microphone on Carnahan's person, amplifying and recording what she said and heard, defendants may have listened in on conversations the parties could reasonably have expected to be private.

The Court of Appeal held plaintiffs had no reasonable expectation of privacy at the accident scene itself because the scene was within the sight and hearing of members of the public. The summary judgment record, however, does not support the Court of Appeal's conclusion; instead, it reflects, at the least, the existence of triable issues as to the privacy of certain conversations at the accident scene, as in the helicopter. The videotapes (broadcast and raw footage) show the rescue did not take place "on a heavily traveled highway," as the Court of Appeal stated, but in a ditch many yards from and below the rural superhighway, which is raised somewhat at that point to bridge a nearby crossroad. From the tapes it appears unlikely the plaintiffs' extrication from their car and medical treatment at the scene could have been observed by any persons who, in the lower court's words, "passed by" on the roadway. Even more unlikely is that any passersby on the road could have heard Ruth's conversation with Nurse Carnahan or the other rescuers.

Whether Ruth expected her conversations with Nurse Carnahan or the other rescuers to remain private and whether any such expectation was reasonable are, on the state of the record before us, questions for the jury. We note, however, that several existing legal protections for communications could support the conclusion that Ruth possessed a reasonable expectation of privacy in her conversations with Nurse Carnahan and the other rescuers. A patient's conversation with a provider of medical care in the course of treatment including emergency treatment, carries a traditional and legally well-established expectation of privacy. [ ]

. . .

We turn to the second element of the intrusion tort, offensiveness. . . .

[A]ll the circumstances of an intrusion, including the motives or justification of the intruder, are pertinent to the offensiveness element. Motivation or justification becomes particularly important when the intrusion is by a member of the print or broadcast press in the pursuit of news material. Although, as will be discussed more fully later, the First Amendment does not immunize the press from liability for torts or crimes committed in an effort to gather news [ ], the constitutional protection of the press does reflect the strong societal interest in effective and complete reporting of events, an interest that may—as a matter of tort law—justify an intrusion that would otherwise be considered offensive. While refusing to recognize a broad privilege in newsgathering against application of generally applicable laws, the United States Supreme Court has also observed that "without some protection for seeking out the news, freedom of the press could be eviscerated." (Branzburg v. Hayes (1972) [ ]).

In deciding, therefore, whether a reporter's alleged intrusion into private matters (i.e., physical space, conversation or data) is "offensive" and hence actionable as an invasion of privacy, courts must consider the extent to which the intrusion was, under the circumstances, justified by the legitimate motive of gathering the news. Information collecting techniques that may be highly offensive when done for socially unprotected reasons—for purposes of harassment, blackmail or prurient curiosity, for example—may not be offensive to a reasonable person when employed by journalists in pursuit of a socially or politically important story. Thus, for example, "a continuous surveillance which is tortious when practiced by a creditor upon a debtor may not be tortious when practiced by media representatives in a situation where there is significant public interest [in discovery of the information sought]." (Hill, Defamation and Privacy Under the First Amendment (1976) 76 Colum. L.Rev. 1205, 1284.)

The mere fact the intruder was in pursuit of a "story" does not, however, generally justify an otherwise offensive intrusion; offensiveness depends as well on the particular method of investigation used. At one extreme, " 'routine . . . reporting techniques,' " such as asking questions of people with information ("including those with confidential or restricted information") could rarely, if ever, be deemed an actionable intrusion. [ ] At the other extreme, violation of well-established legal areas of physical or sensory privacy—trespass into a home or tapping a personal telephone line, for example—could rarely, if ever, be justified by a reporter's need to get the story. Such acts would be deemed highly offensive even if the information sought was of weighty public concern; they would also be outside any protection the Constitution provides to newsgathering. (Cohen v. Cowles Media Co., [ ]; *Dietemann*, [ ].)

Between these extremes lie difficult cases, many involving the use of photographic and electronic recording equipment. Equipment such as hidden cameras and miniature cordless and directional microphones are powerful investigative tools for newsgathering, but may also be used in ways that severely threaten personal privacy. California tort law provides no bright line on this question; each case must be taken on its facts.

On this summary judgment record, we believe a jury could find defendants' recording of Ruth's communications to Carnahan and other rescuers, and filming in the air ambulance, to be " 'highly offensive to a reasonable person.' " [ ] With regard to the depth of the intrusion [ ], a reasonable jury could find highly offensive the placement of a microphone on a medical rescuer in order to intercept what would otherwise be private conversations with an injured patient. In that setting, as defendants could and should have foreseen, the patient would not know her words were being recorded and would not have occasion to ask about, and object or consent to, recording. Defendants, it could reasonably be said, took calculated advantage of the patient's "vulnerability and confusion." [ ] Arguably, the last thing an injured accident victim should have to worry about while being pried from her wrecked car is that a television producer may be recording everything she says to medical personnel for the possible edification and entertainment of casual television viewers.

For much the same reason, a jury could reasonably regard entering and riding in an ambulance—whether on the ground or in the air—with two seriously injured patients to be an egregious intrusion on a place of expected seclusion. . . .

Nor can we say as a matter of law that defendants' motive—to gather usable material for a potentially newsworthy story—necessarily privileged their intrusive conduct as a matter of common law tort liability. A reasonable jury could conclude the producers' desire to get footage that would convey the "feel" of the event—the real sights and sounds of a difficult rescue—did not justify either placing a microphone on Nurse Carnahan or filming inside the rescue helicopter. . . . A reasonable jury could find that defendants, in placing a microphone on an emergency treatment nurse and recording her conversation with a distressed, disoriented and severely injured patient, without the patient's knowledge or consent, acted with highly offensive disrespect for the patient's personal privacy . . .

Turning to the question of constitutional protection for newsgathering, one finds the decisional law reflects a general rule of *nonprotection*: the press in its newsgathering activities enjoys no immunity or exemption from generally applicable laws. [ ]

"It is clear that the First Amendment does not invalidate every incidental burdening of the press that may result from the enforcement of civil and criminal laws of general applicability. Under prior cases, otherwise valid laws serving substantial public interests may be enforced against the press as against others, despite the possible burden that may be imposed." (Branzburg v. Hayes, [ ]) California's intrusion tort and section 632 [the California eavesdropping statute] are both laws of general applicability. They apply to all private investigative activity, whatever its purpose and whoever the investigator, and impose no greater restrictions on the media than on anyone else. . . .

. . . The conduct of journalism does not depend, as a general matter, on the use of secret devices to record private conversations. *Dietemann*, [ ] More specifically, nothing in the record or briefing here suggests that reporting on automobile accidents and medical rescue activities depends on secretly recording accident victims' conversations with rescue personnel or on filming inside an occupied ambulance. Thus, if any exception exists to the general rule that "the First Amendment does not guarantee the press a constitutional right of special access to information not available to the public generally" *Branzburg* [ ], such exception is inapplicable here.

. . .

[The court reversed the grant of summary judgment for the defense on the intrusion claim and remanded for trial.]

■ CHIN, JUSTICE, concurring and dissenting.

[After discussing the private facts claims, Justice Chin explained why he dissented from the holding that the intrusion claims should be remanded.]

Ruth's expectations notwithstanding, I do not believe that a reasonable trier of fact could find that defendants' conduct in this case was "highly offensive to a reasonable person," the test adopted by the plurality. Plaintiffs do not allege that defendants, though present at the accident rescue scene and in the helicopter, interfered with either the rescue or medical efforts, elicited embarrassing or offensive information from plaintiffs, or even tried to interrogate or interview them. Defendants' news team evidently merely recorded newsworthy events "of legitimate public concern" [ ] as they transpired. Defendants' apparent motive in undertaking the supposed privacy invasion was a reasonable and nonmalicious one: to obtain an accurate depiction of the rescue efforts from start to finish. The event was newsworthy, and the ultimate broadcast was both dramatic and educational, rather than tawdry or embarrassing.

. . .

In short, to turn a jury loose on the defendants in this case is itself "highly offensive" to me. I would reverse the judgment of the Court of Appeal with directions to affirm the summary judgment for defendants on all causes of action.

■ BROWN, JUSTICE, concurring and dissenting.

I concur in the plurality's conclusion that summary judgment should not have been granted as to the cause of action for intrusion, and I generally concur in its analysis of that cause of action.[1] I respectfully dissent, however, from the conclusion that summary judgment was proper as to plaintiff Ruth Shulman's cause of action for publication of private facts. [Justice Brown's extensive discussion of the private facts claim is omitted.]

NOTES AND QUESTIONS

1.   After this decision the parties reached a settlement that included an agreement not to disclose its terms. The plaintiffs' lawyer asserted that it was hypocritical of the defendants to insist on confidentiality. "For eight years these defendants maintained that what happened to Ruth was in the public domain, and now they insist the settlement be top secret. Don't you think the resolution of this case is of greater public interest than her ordeal ever was?" See National Law Journal, Sept. 14, 1999. Is there merit in this complaint about confidential settlements? Do you agree with the lawyer's assessment of newsworthiness?

2.   Assume a bystander at the accident scene had purposely placed himself close enough so that he could overhear conversations between Ruth and Nurse Carnahan. Would Ruth have a cause of action against the bystander for intrusion? Would the fact that a bystander was able to overhear these conversations defeat Ruth's claim against the producers of On Scene: Emergency Response? Would it at least defeat that portion of the claim based on the filming and audiotaping at the accident scene? Or is there some suggestion in the opinion that privacy exists in a public space even when some are able to overhear?

3.   The court notes that an intrusion is actionable only if it is "highly offensive to a reasonable person." Here, the court suggests that when news media is alleged to have intruded in pursuit of news, "motivation or justification becomes particularly important." If an intrusion produces highly newsworthy information, should that preclude any finding of offensiveness?

4.   Has the ubiquitous use of accident scenes in reality television today lessened the offensiveness of what occurred in Shulman? Note that the dissent suggests as much even as early as 1998.

---

[1] I decline to join the plurality opinion's discussion of the intrusion cause of action in its entirety. As the plurality notes, "[t]he conduct of journalism does not depend, as a general matter, on the use of secret devices to record private conversations." [ ] Therefore, I do not share the view that "[e]quipment such as hidden cameras and miniature cordless and directional microphones are powerful investigative tools for newsgathering." [ ] On a more fundamental level, I disagree with the artificial barrier the plurality erects between the publication of private facts and the intrusion causes of action. Unlike the plurality, for instance, I would hold that the depth of the intrusion into private affairs and the lawfulness of the news media's conduct are relevant to *both* causes of action.

As the *Shulman* case indicates, newsgathering intrusions today are likely to involve recording and/or photography in addition to or in lieu of personal intrusion by the reporter. The California Invasion of Privacy Act, Cal. Pen. Code § 632, prohibits recording of "any communication carried on in circumstances as may reasonably indicate that any party to the communication desires it to be confined to the parties thereto, but exclud[ing] a communication made in a public gathering ... or in any other circumstance in which the parties to the communication may reasonably expect that the communication may be overheard or recorded." The Shulmans belatedly tried to amend their pleadings to include a claim under this statute, but the trial court barred it as untimely. The court alluded to the statute only as an indication that the defendants' filming and recording could be considered highly offensive. Often, however, plaintiffs make claims under such statutes in addition to their common law intrusion claims. We consider wiretapping and eavesdropping statutes in more detail later in this chapter, but as the following case illustrates, courts often have to consider the interplay of the statutes and the common law tort.

Sanders v. American Broadcasting Companies, Inc.

Supreme Court of California, 1999.
978 P.2d 67.

■ WERDEGAR, J.

Defendant Stacy Lescht, a reporter employed by defendant American Broadcasting Companies, Inc. (ABC), obtained employment as a "telepsychic" with the Psychic Marketing Group (PMG), which also employed plaintiff Mark Sanders in that same capacity. While she worked in PMG's Los Angeles office, Lescht, who wore a small video camera hidden in her hat, covertly videotaped her conversations with several coworkers, including Sanders.

Sanders sued Lescht and ABC for, among other causes of action, the tort of invasion of privacy by intrusion. Although a jury found for Sanders on the intrusion cause of action, the Court of Appeal reversed the resulting judgment in his favor on the ground that the jury finding for the defense on another cause of action, violation of Penal Code section 632, established Sanders could have had no reasonable expectation of privacy in his workplace conversations because such conversations could be overheard by others in the shared office space. We granted review to determine whether the fact a workplace interaction might be witnessed by others on the premises necessarily defeats, for purposes of tort law, any reasonable expectation of privacy the participants have against covert videotaping by a journalist. We conclude it does not: In an office or other workplace to which the general public does not have unfettered access, employees may enjoy a limited, but legitimate, expectation that their conversations and other interactions will not be secretly videotaped by undercover television reporters, even though those conversations may not have been completely private from the participants' coworkers. For this reason, contrary to the Court of Appeal's holding, the jury's finding as to Penal Code section 632 did not require the trial court to enter nonsuit on, or otherwise dispose of, Sanders' cause of action for tortious intrusion. Nor, we also conclude, were the jury instructions on the intrusion cause of action prejudicially erroneous.

Although we reverse, for these reasons, the Court of Appeals' judgment for defendants, we do not hold or imply that investigative journalists necessarily commit a tort by secretly recording events and conversations in offices, stores or other workplaces. Whether a reasonable expectation of privacy is violated by such recording depends on the exact nature of the conduct and all the surrounding circumstances. In addition, liability under the intrusion tort requires that the invasion be highly offensive to a reasonable person, considering, among other factors, the motive of the alleged intruder. (Shulman v. Group W Productions, Inc. [discussed earlier in this chapter]; Miller v. National Broadcasting Co., 187 Cal.App.3d 1463 (Cal. App. 1986).) The scope of our review in this case does not include any question regarding the offensiveness element of the tort, and we therefore express no view on the offensiveness or inoffensiveness of defendants' conduct. We hold only that, where the other elements of the intrusion tort are proven, the cause of action is not defeated as a matter of law simply because the events or conversations upon which the defendant allegedly intruded were not completely private from all other eyes and ears.

. . .

In 1992, plaintiff Mark Sanders was working as a telepsychic in PMG's Los Angeles office, giving "readings" to customers who telephoned PMG's 900 number (for which they were charged a per-minute fee). The psychics' work area consisted of a large room with rows of cubicles, about 100 total, in which the psychics took their calls. Each cubicle was enclosed on three sides by five-foot-high partitions. The facility also included a separate lunch room and enclosed offices for managers and supervisors. During the period of the claimed intrusion, the door to the PMG facility was unlocked during business hours, but PMG, by internal policy, prohibited access to the office by nonemployees without specific permission. An employee testified the front door was visible from the administration desk and a supervisor greeted any nonemployees who entered.

[Defendant Lescht obtained employment as a telepsychic in PMG's Los Angeles office. While on the job, Lescht secretly videotaped and audiotaped conversations she had with her co-workers, including two conversations with Sanders. The first conversation took place in an aisle outside Lescht's cubicle. It was conducted in moderate tones, and other co-workers passing by joined in. The second conversation took place in Sanders's cubicle, with Sanders and Lescht speaking "in relatively soft voices. . . . During this second, longer conversation, Sanders discussed his personal aspirations and beliefs and gave Lescht a psychic reading."]

Sanders pled two causes of action against Lescht and ABC based on the videotaping itself: violation of Penal Code section 632 (hereafter section 632) and the common law tort of invasion of privacy by intrusion. The court ordered trial on these counts bifurcated, with the section 632 count tried first. In a special verdict form, the jury was asked whether the conversation upon which defendants allegedly intruded was conducted "in circumstances in which the parties to the communication may reasonably have expected that the communications may have been overheard." Based on the jury's affirmative answer to this question, the trial court ordered judgment entered for defendants on the section 632 cause of action.

Defendants then moved to dismiss the remaining cause of action for intrusion, for an order of nonsuit, and to reopen their earlier motion for summary judgment on this cause of action. After receiving written submissions and hearing argument, the court denied these motions, allowing trial to go forward on the issue of liability for photographic intrusion. In reliance on Dietemann v. Time, Inc., 449 F.2d 245 ([9th Cir.] 1971), which the trial court viewed as articulating a "subtort with regard to invasion of privacy by photographing," the trial court ruled plaintiff could proceed on the theory he had a limited right of privacy against being covertly videotaped by a journalist in his workplace, even though his interaction with that journalist may have been witnessed, and his conversations overheard, by coworkers. At the conclusion of the second phase of trial, the jury found defendants liable on the cause of action for invasion of privacy by intrusion. In subsequent trial phases, the jury fixed compensatory damages at $335,000; found defendants had acted with malice, fraud or oppression; and awarded exemplary damages of about $300,000.

[The Court of Appeals reversed and ordered judgment for the defendants, holding that] the jury finding on the section 632 action barred any recovery for intrusion.

. . .

While *Shulman* reiterated the requirement that an intrusion plaintiff have a reasonable expectation of privacy, neither in *Shulman* nor in any other case have we stated that an expectation of privacy, in order to be reasonable for purposes of the intrusion tort, must be of absolute or complete privacy. . . .

. . .

This case squarely raises the question of an expectation of limited privacy. On further consideration, we adhere to the view suggested in *Shulman*: privacy, for purposes of the intrusion tort, is not a binary, all-or-nothing characteristic. There are degrees and nuances to societal recognition of our expectations of privacy: the fact the privacy one expects in a given setting is not complete or absolute does not render the expectation unreasonable as a matter of law. Although the intrusion tort is often defined in terms of "seclusion" [ ] the seclusion referred to need not be absolute. "Like 'privacy,' the concept of 'seclusion' is relative. The mere fact that a person can be seen by someone does not automatically mean that he or she can legally be forced to be subject to being seen by everyone." [ ]

Dietemann v. Time, Inc., upon which the trial court relied, does, indeed, exemplify the idea of a legitimate expectation of limited privacy. Reporters for a news magazine deceitfully gained access to a quack doctor's home office, where they secretly photographed and recorded his examination of one of them. [ ] The court held the plaintiff could, under California law, reasonably expect privacy from press photography and recording, even though he had invited the reporters—unaware of their true identity—into his home office: "Plaintiff's den was a sphere from which he could reasonably expect to exclude eavesdropping newsmen. He invited two of defendant's employees to the den. One who invites another to his home or office takes a risk that the visitor may not be what he seems, and that the visitor may repeat all he hears and observes when he leaves. But he does not and should not be required to take the risk that what is heard and seen will be transmitted by photograph or recording, or in our modern world, in full living color and hi-fi to the public at large. . . ." Id. at p. 249; see also Boddie v. American Broadcasting Cos., 694 F.Supp. 1304 (N.D. Ohio 1988) (Journalists' covert recording of interview may violate federal anti-wiretapping statute even though plaintiff knew her interlocutors were journalists: "it remains an issue of fact for the jury whether [plaintiff] had an expectation that the interview was not being recorded and whether that expectation was justified under the circumstances.")

. . .

Defendants' claim, that a "complete expectation of privacy" is necessary to recover for intrusion, thus fails as inconsistent with case law as well as with the common understanding of privacy. Privacy for purposes of the intrusion tort must be evaluated with respect to the identity of the alleged intruder and the nature of the intrusion. As seen below, moreover, decisions on the common law and statutory protection of workplace privacy show that the same analysis applies in the workplace as in other settings; consequently, an employee may, under some circumstances, have a reasonable expectation of visual or aural privacy against electronic intrusion by a stranger to the workplace, despite the possibility the conversations and interactions at issue could be witnessed by coworkers or the employer.

. . .

Finally, defendants rely on . . . Desnick v. American Broadcasting Companies, Inc., 44 F.3d 1345 (7th Cir. 1995) [which held that there was no actionable invasion of privacy when agents of ABC, posing as patients, covertly recorded or videotaped doctors' conversations with the "patients" in the doctors' offices.]

In *Desnick*, the question was whether the covert videotaping by "testers" posing as patients was a tortious invasion of privacy. The appellate court held it was not, partly because "the only conversations that were recorded were conversations with the testers themselves." [ ] "The test patients entered offices that were open to anyone expressing a desire for ophthalmic services and videotaped physicians engaged in professional, not personal, communications with strangers (the testers themselves)." [ ]

The *Desnick* court characterized the doctor-patient relationship as one between a service provider and a customer and therefore viewed these parties' conversations in the medical office as essentially public conversations between strangers. We need not agree or disagree with this characterization in order to see that it renders the decision's reasoning inapplicable to the question before us. We are concerned here with interactions between coworkers rather than between a proprietor and customer. As the briefed question is framed, the interactions at issue here could not have been witnessed by the general public, although they could have been overheard or observed by other employees in the shared workplace.

. . .

To summarize, we conclude that in the workplace, as elsewhere, the reasonableness of a person's expectation of visual and aural privacy depends not only on who might have been able to observe the subject interaction, but on the identity of the claimed intruder and the means of intrusion. [*Shulman*; *Dietemann*; . . .] For this reason, we answer the briefed question affirmatively: a person who lacks a reasonable expectation of complete privacy in a conversation, because it could be seen and overheard by coworkers (but not the general public), may nevertheless have a claim for invasion of privacy by intrusion based on a television reporter's covert videotaping of that conversation.

Defendants warn that "the adoption of a doctrine of per se workplace privacy would place a dangerous chill on the press' investigation of abusive activities in open work areas, implicating substantial First Amendment concerns." We adopt no such per se doctrine of privacy. We hold only that the possibility of being overheard by coworkers does not, as a matter of law, render unreasonable an employee's expectation that his or her interactions within a nonpublic workplace will not be videotaped in secret by a journalist. In other circumstances, where, for example, the workplace is regularly open to entry or observation by the public or press, or the interaction that was the subject of the alleged intrusion was between proprietor (or employee) and customer, any expectation of privacy against press recording is less likely to be deemed reasonable. Nothing we say here prevents a media defendant from attempting to show, in order to negate the offensiveness element of the intrusion tort, that the claimed intrusion, even if it infringed on a reasonable expectation of privacy, was "justified by the legitimate motive of gathering the news." [ ] As for possible First Amendment defenses, any discussion must await a later case, as no constitutional issue was decided by the lower courts or presented for our review here.

. . .

. . . [T]he fact that coworkers may have observed a workplace interaction does not as a matter of law eliminate all expectations of privacy the participants may reasonably have had vis-à-vis covert videotaping by a stranger to the workplace. For this reason, the jury's finding as to an expectation of being overheard by coworkers did not as a matter of law preclude imposition of liability for common law intrusion. The trial court correctly denied defendants' midtrial motions for dismissal, nonsuit, and summary judgment.

[The court rejected defendants' claims that the jury had been erroneously instructed, and remanded for consideration of other procedural and evidentiary questions, issues involving the types and amounts of damages awarded, and "any of defendants' appellate claims other than those we have expressly addressed."]

NOTES AND QUESTIONS

1.   What exactly were Sanders's reasonable expectations of privacy? That his conversations would not become known to anyone other than coworkers? That they would not be secretly recorded? That they would not be broadcast to the general public?

2.   Suppose the employer had covertly (in the interest of candor or verisimilitude) videotaped him in order to use the scenes in a training video for newly hired telepsychics. Might Sanders still have a cause of action for intrusion? Would such a recording potentially be less offensive?

3.   If the concept of privacy is relative, in the sense that reasonable expectations may vary depending on "the identity of the claimed intruder and the means of intrusion," what implications does that have for the other tort branches of privacy law? In private facts cases, like *Haynes* and *Florida Star*, both discussed in Chapter Five, does whether the matter disclosed is "private" depend on the identity of the discloser and/or the means by which it is disclosed?

4.   The opinion notes that no First Amendment issues were involved in the decision. How should those issues be framed? In Dietemann v. Time, Inc., which is cited several times in *Sanders*, the Court of Appeals for the Ninth Circuit emphatically rejected the claim that investigative reporting requires special First Amendment protection:

> The defendant claims that the First Amendment immunizes it from liability for invading plaintiff's den with a hidden camera and its concealed electronic instruments because its employees were gathering news and its instrumentalities "are indispensable tools of investigative reporting." We agree that newsgathering is an integral part of news dissemination. We strongly disagree, however, that the hidden mechanical contrivances are "indispensable tools" of newsgathering. Investigative reporting is an ancient art; its successful practice long antecedes the invention of miniature cameras and electronic devices. The First Amendment has never been construed to accord newsmen immunity from torts or crimes committed during the course of newsgathering. The First Amendment is not a license to trespass, to steal, or to intrude by electronic means into the precincts of another's home or office. . . .

5.   The opinion suggests that ABC could still win on the ground that the intrusion was not highly offensive because its purpose was newsgathering. Might the fact that Sanders's expectations of privacy were incomplete also be relevant on the offensiveness issue?

6.   After remand of the *Sanders* case, a California appeals court rejected ABC's claim that the damage award could not include damages resulting from the broadcast. "The argument assumes that it is only the wrongful intrusion, not the broadcast, that causes damage. Here, however, the damages from the intrusion were increased by the fact that the intrusion was broadcast." The court held that ABC had failed to preserve its claim that the intrusion did not meet the offensiveness requirement of California law. It denied Sanders's claim for over $500,000 in attorneys fees on the ground that Sanders had not "demonstrated why the interests of justice demand that his fees be paid out of something other than his substantial [$635,000] judgment." The court added a footnote saying, "The large size of the award adequately compensates Sanders for being secretly taped twice, despite being a self-professed psychic who nonetheless was unable to divine that Lescht secreted a camera in her hat and a microphone in her brassiere." See Sanders v. American Broadcasting Cos., 1999 WL 1458129 (Cal. App. 1999) (unpublished opinion).

———

   Galella v. Onassis. One of the most famous complaints about intrusive newsgathering involved photographer Ron Galella and the widow of President John F. Kennedy. Galella was the first prominent "paparazzo" in the United States. He won fame largely by photographing Jacqueline Kennedy Onassis and her children. Eventually Onassis caused Galella to be arrested; he sued her for violation of his civil rights, and she counterclaimed for injunctive relief against Galella's continuous efforts to photograph her and her children. At trial she showed that Galella jumped in the path of John F. Kennedy, Jr., as he was riding his bicycle in Central Park across the way from his home, interrupted Caroline Kennedy at tennis, invaded the children's private schools, and came uncomfortably close in a power boat to Onassis swimming. He bribed doormen and romanced a family servant to keep him advised of the movements of the family. The government intervened on Onassis's side in its capacity as protector of the children's safety.

The district court found that the photographer had engaged in harassment, intentional infliction of emotional distress, assault and battery, commercial exploitation of defendant's personality, and invasion of privacy. It found that Galella had on occasion intentionally physically touched Onassis and her daughter, caused fear of physical contact in his frenzied attempts to get their pictures, followed Onassis and her children too closely in an automobile, and endangered the safety of the children while they were swimming, water skiing, and horseback riding.

The court of appeals noted that it was unclear whether New York law recognized the common law torts of invasion of privacy, but affirmed the injunction under New York's statute prohibiting harassment:

> Of course legitimate countervailing social needs may warrant some intrusion despite an individual's reasonable expectation of privacy and freedom from harassment. However the interference allowed may be no greater than that necessary to protect the overriding public interest. Mrs. Onassis was properly found to be a public figure and thus subject to news coverage. [ ] Nonetheless, Galella's action went far beyond the reasonable bounds of news gathering. When weighed against the *de minimis* public importance of the daily activities of [Onassis], Galella's constant surveillance, his obtrusive and intruding presence, was unwarranted and unreasonable. If there were any doubt in our minds, Galella's inexcusable conduct toward [the] children would resolve it.

As for Galella's claim that his activity was protected by the First Amendment, the court wrote: "There is no such scope to the First Amendment right. Crimes and torts committed in news gathering are not protected. Branzburg v. Hayes, 408 U.S. 665 (1972); [ ]; Dietemann v. Time Inc., 449 F.2d 245 (9th Cir. 1971)[ ]. There is no threat to a free press in requiring its agents to act within the law."

The trial court had enjoined Gallela from approaching within 50 yards of Jacqueline Onassis or 75 yards of her children, but the court of appeals found that those limits "unnecessarily infringe[d] on reasonable efforts to 'cover' defendant." It modified the lower court's order to prevent the defendant from coming within 25 feet of Mrs. Onassis or 30 feet of the children. A dissenting judge thought the district court's injunction should have been affirmed without modification. Galella v. Onassis, 487 F.2d 986 (2d Cir. 1973).

Nine years later, Galella was found guilty of 12 violations of the injunction by taking photographs within 25 feet of Mrs. Onassis. The judge suspended a fine of $120,000 when Galella agreed to pay the $10,000 in legal fees incurred by Onassis and agreed never again to photograph her. Galella v. Onassis, 533 F.Supp. 1076 (S.D.N.Y. 1982).

Anti-Paparazzi Legislation. Accusations that photographers pursuing her car contributed to the death of Princess Diana in Paris in 1997 created a wave of public concern about press treatment of celebrities, particularly by freelance photographers who sell their photos to tabloids. California enacted a statute making it a tort to use visual or auditory enhancing devices to obtain photos or recordings of a person "engaging in a personal or familial activity under circumstances in which the plaintiff had a reasonable expectation of privacy," whether or not there is a physical trespass. Violators are liable for up to three times the amount of compensatory damages, and also for punitive damages and disgorgement of profits. The statute also attempts to reach the media who use paparazzi by exposing them to liability for causing a violation of the statute, "regardless of whether there is an employer-employee relationship." Cal. Civ. Code. § 1708.8. It suggests that "private, personal, and familial" activities include:

> Intimate details of the plaintiff's personal life under circumstances in which the plaintiff has a reasonable expectation of privacy.

> Interaction with the plaintiff's family or significant others under circumstances in which the plaintiff has a reasonable expectation of privacy.

> . . .

> Any activity that occurs on a residential property under circumstances in which the plaintiff has a reasonable expectation of privacy.

> Other aspects of the plaintiff's private affairs or concerns under circumstances in which the plaintiff has a reasonable expectation of privacy.

Does this statute cover anything that is not already covered by the common law tort of intrusion? What are its implications for news media more generally?

Another California statute that potentially affects paparazzi is a vehicle code provision that prohibits reckless driving "with the intent to capture any type of visual image, sound recording, or other physical impression of another person for a commercial purpose." Cal. Vehicle Code § 40008.

Paparazzi and the tabloids that are the main buyers of their images argue that they are trying to break through the carefully crafted images that celebrities cultivate to expose the truth about them. Should that justification be taken into account in deciding whether paparazzi and other push-the-envelope media deserve First Amendment protection?

B. TRESPASS

A person commits a trespass when he enters property in the possession of another without authorization or consent. Generally a cause of action for trespass is available only to the possessor of the land. In the preceding cases, the Shulmans had no power to exclude others from the roadside or the helicopter, and Sanders had no property interests in his workplace, which probably explains why these plaintiffs sued for intrusion rather than trespass. But Sanders' employer might have had a trespass action; when media enter private property to gather information about newsworthy events and are sued by the possessor of the land, they enjoy no immunity from the ordinary law of trespass. Courts sometimes adapt tort law to accommodate unique issues presented when reporters trespass to gather news, but there is no reliable First Amendment defense to an action for trespass.

In what has become a classic media trespass case, WCBS-TV in New York City directed a reporter and camera crew to visit restaurants that had been cited for health code violations. Plaintiff's restaurant was one of those filmed. The jury found CBS liable for trespass and awarded plaintiff $1,200 in compensatory damages and $250,000 in punitive damages. After the verdict (in a passage approved on appeal), the trial judge stated:

> The instructions given to the crew, whether specific to this event or as standing operating procedure, were to avoid seeking an appointment or permission to enter any of the premises where a story was sought, but to enter unannounced catching the occupants by surprise; "with cameras rolling" in the words of CBS' principal witness, [the reporter Rich]. From the evidence the jury was entitled to conclude that following this procedure the defendant's employees burst into plaintiff's restaurant in noisy and obtrusive fashion and following the loud commands of the reporter, Rich, to photograph the patrons dining, turned their lights and camera upon the dining room. Consternation, the jury was informed, followed. Patrons waiting to be seated left the restaurant. Others who had finished eating, left without waiting for their checks. Still others hid their faces behind napkins or table cloths or hid themselves beneath tables. (The reluctance of the plaintiff's clientele to be video taped was never explained, and need not be. Patronizing a restaurant does not

carry with it an obligation to appear on television). [The] president of the plaintiff and manager of its operations, refused to be interviewed, and as the camera continued to "roll" he pushed the protesting Miss Rich and her crew from the premises. All told, the CBS personnel were in the restaurant not more than ten minutes, perhaps as little as one minute, depending on the testimony the jury chose to credit. The jury by its verdict clearly found the defendant guilty of trespass and from the admissions of CBS' own employees they were guilty of trespass. The witness Rich sought to justify her crew's entry into the restaurant by calling it, on a number of occasions, a "place of public accommodation," but, as she acknowledges, they did not seek to avail themselves of the plaintiff's "accommodation"; they had no intention of purchasing food or drink.

On appeal, the court held that the compensatory damage award was justified, but that there should be a new trial on the amount of punitive damages because the trial judge erroneously excluded testimony from a defense witness as to CBS's motive and purpose in entering the restaurant. Le Mistral, Inc. v. Columbia Broad. Sys., 61 A.D.2d 491 (N.Y. App. Div. 1978).

The Fletcher Case. An attempt to create a newsgathering defense to a trespass action succeeded in an early Florida case, Florida Publishing Co. v. Fletcher, 340 So.2d 914 (Fla. 1976). A 17-year-old girl perished in a fire at her home. News media representatives, including a photographer for the local newspaper, were invited into the badly damaged home by the fire marshal. The fire marshal ran out of film for his own camera and asked the newspaper photographer to take a picture of a "silhouette" left on the floor after the victim's body was removed, to demonstrate that the body was already on the floor before the heat from the fire damaged the floor. The photographer complied and gave a copy of the photo to police and fire officials. This photo and others were published in the newspaper the next day. The victim's mother, who had been out of town at the time of the fire, first learned of the facts surrounding her daughter's death from the newspaper story and accompanying photos.

The mother sued the newspaper for trespass, invasion of privacy, and intentional infliction of emotional distress. The trial court and the court of appeal granted judgment for defendant on the last two counts, but the court of appeal held that Mrs. Fletcher had a cause of action for trespass. The Florida Supreme Court reversed this determination, holding that the landowner impliedly consented to entry by news personnel under these circumstances, by virtue of longstanding custom and practice. The newspaper had presented affidavits of news editors and law enforcement officials stating that it was a longstanding practice in Florida for news media representatives to enter private premises where a disaster of great public interest occurred, as long as they entered at the invitation of law enforcement officials and caused no physical damage to the premises. The case therefore came within the rule that there is no trespass where the entry is under circumstances from which the consent of the owner may be implied.

Whether because it turned on peculiar facts, or because courts have little enthusiasm for its result, *Fletcher* has not been widely followed. Even in Florida, it has not been interpreted expansively. In Green Valley School Inc. v. Cowles Florida Broadcasting, Inc., 327 So.2d 810 (Fla. Dist. Ct. App. 1976), television reporters had been invited to accompany officers on a midnight raid in search of evidence of sexual misbehavior and drug use at a controversial boarding school. The station's "custom and practice" defense to the school's trespass suit was rejected by the court of appeals. "In this jurisdiction, a law enforcement officer is not as a *matter of law* endowed with the right or authority to invite people of his choosing to invade private property and participate in a midnight raid of the premises." The Florida Supreme Court dismissed the station's appeal on the ground that the court of appeals decision was not in conflict with the principle endorsed in *Fletcher*. 340 So. 2d 1154 (Fla. 1976).

Other Trespass Matters. Beginning in 2015 New York City banned all reality television program filming within its hospital emergency rooms. The ban was sparked by incidents involving patients whose medical emergencies had been taped in the city's hospitals and were later broadcast on television. Though the ban may not affect individual patients' trespass claims based on being filmed in waiting areas, it may help solidify the seclusion and offensiveness prongs of any intrusion lawsuit springing from filming in hospitals more generally, a suggestion made by the *Shulman* court years earlier.

Trespass is a crime as well as a tort, and newsgatherers are occasionally prosecuted. As in tort actions, the First Amendment usually provides no defense. See, e.g., Stahl v. State, 665 P.2d 839 (Okla. Crim. 1983) (upholding trespass conviction of reporters who followed demonstrators onto site of proposed nuclear power plant); City of Oak Creek v. Ah King, 436 N.W.2d 285 (Wis. 1989) (upholding disorderly conduct conviction of television cameraman who ignored "no trespassing" signs to get to site of airliner crash).

———

Drones, small unmanned aircraft that can be equipped with cameras, have created newer and interesting trespass-related civil and criminal issues. Some journalists have embraced the idea of drone-assisted news coverage, suggesting that it gives newsgatherers the ability to capture images in locations that would be unreachable without the technology. Privacy advocates argue in response that drone use will lead to further privacy invasions because the aircraft have the ability to travel onto private property and view otherwise unviewable private situations.

Drone-related legislation passed in the mid-2010s often limited the government's use of drones in criminal searches. Some states, however, suggested additional limitations that could well affect newsgathering activities. In 2016 Wisconsin's statute, for example, read:

> Whoever uses a drone . . . with the intent to photograph, record, or otherwise observe another individual in a place or location where the individual has a reasonable expectation of privacy is guilty of Class A misdemeanor.

Wis. Stat. § 942.10.

That same year an Oregon statute gave property owners and occupiers the ability to bring an action against a drone operator for what amounts to a trespass as long as the defendant had flown the drone over the property at least once before and had been asked by the plaintiff not to do so. ORS § 837.380. There is no mention of any special exception for newsgathering activities within the body of either statute.

In December 2015 the FAA announced new drone registration rules applicable to all drone operators, suggesting that "new aviators" who owned drones would be welcomed into the FAA's culture of "safety and responsibility." Press Release, FAA Announces Small UAS Registration Rule, www.faa.gov (Dec. 14, 2015). The registration rules do not exempt media and specifically cover those drones with cameras on board.

C. CONSTITUTIONAL VIOLATIONS

Berger v. Hanlon

U.S. Court of Appeals, Ninth Circuit, 1997.
129 F.3d 505.

Before: SCHROEDER and KLEINFELD, CIRCUIT JUDGES, and BREWSTER, DISTRICT JUDGE.

■ SCHROEDER, CIRCUIT JUDGE:

When federal agents searched the ranch of Paul and Erma Berger in March of 1993, they acted not only pursuant to a search warrant, but also pursuant to a written contract with appellees Cable News Network and Turner Broadcasting System, authorizing the filming and recording of the search for broadcast on their environmental television shows "Earth Matters" and "Network Earth." The media wanted footage of the discovery of evidence showing that Paul Berger was poisoning eagles, and the government wanted the publicity.

After Mr. Berger was convicted of one misdemeanor count for using a pesticide in a manner inconsistent with its labeling, [ ] and acquitted of three felony counts of the killing of at least one eagle, the Bergers sued both the media and the federal agents under Bivens v. Six Unknown Named Agents of Fed. Bureau of Narcotics, 403 U.S. 388 (1971), for the violation of their constitutional rights.... The Bergers' principal contentions under federal law are that (1) the federal agents violated their Fourth Amendment rights by permitting commercial television cameras to film the search and by assisting the media in their search for dramatic material, and (2) the media acted sufficiently in concert with the federal agents to be held accountable for that violation as government actors.

. . .

[A] magistrate judge issued a search warrant for the Bergers' ranch, authorizing the search of the ranch and appurtenant structures, excluding the residence, for evidence indicating the taking of wildlife. According to the Bergers, the magistrate judge had no knowledge of the planned media participation during the search, and there is no contention by the appellees that when the magistrate judge issued the warrant, he approved the videotaping of the search for broadcast purposes.

According to the Bergers, the media participated in a pre-search briefing the day before the search, at which the federal appellees shared with the media details of the material included in the warrant and supporting materials that were supposed to remain under seal until after the search.

On the morning of the search, the government team, accompanied by a media crew, gathered on a county road leading to the ranch, to discuss the execution of the warrant. The cameras videotaped that gathering. The broadcast team then proceeded with [agents of the U.S. Fish and Wildlife Service and an assistant U.S. attorney] in a caravan of approximately ten vehicles to a point near the Bergers' ranch. Media cameras mounted on the outside of government vehicles, or placed in their interior, documented every move made by the federal appellees. At all times during and immediately prior to the search, USFWS Special Agent Joel Scrafford was wired with a hidden CNN microphone which was continuously transmitting live audio to the CNN technical crew.

Mr. Berger approached and met the caravan in a pickup truck on the road leading up to the ranch. Agent Scrafford proceeded to inform Mr. Berger of the search warrant, and asked him whether he could ride to the house in Mr. Berger's truck so that he could explain to Mrs. Berger what they were going to do. Mr. Berger allowed Agent Scrafford to ride with him in the pickup truck. Upon arriving at the Bergers' residence, the two men entered the house together. Audio recorded at the site indicates that Mr. Berger consented to Agent Scrafford's entry into the home at this time. The parties disagree on whether the agents who entered the residence with Agent Scrafford searched the residence for incriminating evidence, and whether Agent Scrafford's subsequent entries into the home were consented to. However, it is undisputed that Agent Scrafford recorded all his conversations with the Bergers inside the house.

The Bergers were not informed that Agent Scrafford was wearing a microphone or that the cameras that were visible during the search belonged to the media. The media recorded more than eight hours of tape and it broadcast both the video footage and the sound recordings made in the house.

[The district court ruled that the federal agents were entitled to qualified immunity on the ground that the illegality of their actions was not clearly established at the time of the search. The court of appeals reversed that determination, but was in turn reversed by the U.S. Supreme Court, which held that the federal officers were immune. See Hanlon v. Berger, 526 U.S. 808 (1999). The district court rejected the Bergers' claim that the media had become government actors for purposes of *Bivens* liability.]

. . .

The Media as Government Actors

The final issue we must consider in the Bergers' *Bivens* action is whether the media appellees may be held liable even though they were not agents or employees of the federal government. Ordinarily, *Bivens* liability and the corresponding liability of state actors under 42 U.S.C. § 1983, attaches only to the acts of government officials. [ ]. Private parties may be held liable, however, if they are deemed to have acted "under color of law." [ ]

In deciding whether conduct of private parties amounts to government action we engage in a highly factual inquiry. . . .

The appropriate test in this case is the joint action test. The Supreme Court has said it is satisfied when the plaintiff is able to establish an agreement, or conspiracy between a government actor and a private party. [ ]

In this case we have not only a verbal agreement, but a written contractual commitment between the government and the media to engage jointly in an enterprise that only the government could lawfully institute—the execution of a search warrant—for the mutual benefit of both the private interests of the media and the government officials' interest in publicity. It is also alleged that the federal entities shared confidential information with the media. Indeed, the record in this case suggests that the government officers planned and executed the search in a manner designed to enhance its entertainment, rather than its law enforcement value, by engaging in, for example, conversations with Mr. Berger for the purpose of providing interesting soundbites, and to portray themselves as tough, yet caring investigators, rather than to further their investigation. This satisfies the joint action test.

. . .

[The court remanded the case to the district court for further consideration of the *Bivens* claim and also of state law claims for trespass and intentional infliction of emotional distress.]

NOTES AND QUESTIONS

1.   The Supreme Court denied CNN's petition for certiorari, 575 U.S. 961 (1998), and the district court rejected a renewed motion to dismiss. CNN then settled with the Bergers, in an agreement that included a confidentiality clause preventing the parties from revealing the amount of the settlement.

2.   The *Bivens* case, noted in *Berger*, governs liability of federal officials for civil rights violations. The corresponding liability of state agents is based on 42 U.S.C. § 1983. Both causes of action require plaintiffs to show a violation of the Constitution. In Wilson v. Layne, 526 U.S. 603 (1999), the Supreme Court established that "it is a violation of the Fourth Amendment for police to bring members of the media or other third parties into a home during the execution of a warrant when the presence of the third parties in the home was not in aid of the execution of the warrant." However, just because police may be liabile under Wilson v. Layne by bringing the media into a home does not necessarily mean the media who accompany them are liable for violations of the occupants' civil rights. In Parker v. Boyer, 93 F.3d 445 (8th Cir. 1996), a federal appellate court held that a television crew that acted without the assistance of the police in deciding to enter the house to videotape the events there was not acting under color of law. A dissenting judge asserted that proof that the news crew "came to the location with the police and could not have entered if the police had not done so first" was enough to establish that the crew was acting under color of law.

3.   Since the decisions in *Berger, Wilson,* and *Parker,* there have been few civil rights claims against media arising out of their participation in searches, probably because once it was established that officials could be liable for inviting media to accompany them, they ceased doing so.

Newsgatherers as Plaintiffs. Sometimes journalists who are trying to cover a story are roughed up by law enforcement officers. In addition to the ordinary criminal law remedies for assault or official oppression, and tort law actions for battery or false imprisonment, they may have claims for civil rights violations. In Asociación de Periodistas de Puerto Rico v. Mueller, 529 F.3d 52 (1st Cir. 2008), Puerto Rican television and radio journalists alleged that they were attacked by FBI agents while trying to cover an FBI raid at the home of an activist in the Puerto Rican independence movement. The journalists said they were attempting to obey orders to leave the area when agents attacked them with batons and pepper spray.

The journalists alleged that the agents violated their rights under the First and Fourth Amendments. The district court granted summary judgment for the agents, but the court of appeals reversed. It held that the journalists had no First Amendment right to cover the raid, but noted they might prevail on the Fourth Amendment claim by showing that the agents used force that was unreasonable under the circumstances.

Negative police behaviors in response to newsgathering activities also appear in cases involving citizen journalists or ordinary individuals who decide to record something they believe is newsworthy. This is explored later in this chapter.

D. WIRETAPPING AND EAVESDROPPING

The federal government and all the states have criminal statutes forbidding wiretapping (intercepting telephone conversations or other electronic communications by accessing the signal) and eavesdropping (unconsented or unauthorized recording or transmitting of communications). The federal Electronic Communications Privacy Act, 18 U.S.C. § 2510 et seq. and many state statutes permit a person to eavesdrop on or wiretap a conversation to which he or she is a party. These are called "one-party consent" statutes, although of course they do not really involve consent in the usual sense; a tortfeasor cannot consent on behalf of the victim. Because journalists usually are parties to the conversations they record, one-party consent statutes usually do not give rise to liability in newsgathering situations.

Statutes that require the consent of all parties are of far greater concern to the media. The statutes also vary in other ways. For example, the Maryland statute makes it a felony to intercept any wire, oral, or electronic communication, even if the communication is not private or confidential, see Md. Cts. & Jud. Proc. § 10–401, while the California statute (as we saw in *Sanders*) applies only if the parties could reasonably expect that they would not be overheard or recorded. These state to state variations create many pitfalls. For example, it is not clear whether a journalist in a one-party consent state may legally tape a phone call to a person in a state that requires consent of all parties.

Under the federal act, even a taping by a participant may be illegal if it is done "for the purpose of committing any criminal or tortious act." 18 U.S.C. § 2511(2)(d). The illegality of the taping does not itself satisfy this requirement. In Sussman v. American Broadcasting Cos., 186 F.3d 1200 (9th Cir. 1999), which arose out of undercover newsgathering similar to that in *Sanders*, the plaintiffs argued that since the taping was tortious (as determined in *Sanders*), this purpose requirement was met. But the court wrote "the focus is not upon whether the interception itself violated another law; it is upon whether the *purpose* for the interception—its intended use—was criminal or tortious." Since the intended use was to broadcast a newsworthy story, the taping was not for an illegal or tortious purpose even if the means of obtaining it was tortious.

Sussman rejected a suggestion that the federal statute was intended to exempt newsgathering altogether. "Congress could have drafted the statute so as to exempt all journalists from its coverage, but did not. Instead, it treated journalists just like any other party who tapes conversations surreptitiously." The court suggested that a news organization that secretly videotaped bedroom activities for a legitimate newsgathering purpose (e.g., listening for "pillow talk" about some newsworthy event) could be liable under the federal statute if the use of the tape also had an unlawful purpose such as tortious disclosure of private facts. "The existence of the lawful purpose would not sanitize a tape that was also made for an illegitimate purpose; the taping would violate 2511."

Constitutionality of "All-Party Consent" Statutes. Reporters and others challenged a Florida statute that forbade taping without the consent of all parties. They claimed the use of concealed recording equipment was essential to investigative reporting for three reasons: it aided accuracy of reporting; persons being interviewed would not be candid if they knew they were being recorded; and the recording provided corroboration in case of suits for defamation.

The Florida Supreme Court rejected the challenge. The statute allows "each party to a conversation to have an expectation of privacy from interception by another party to the conversation. It does not exclude any source from the press, intrude upon the activities of the news media in contacting sources, prevent the parties to the communication from consenting to the recording, or restrict the publication of any information gained from the communication. First Amendment rights do not include a constitutional right to corroborate news gathering activities when the legislature has statutorily recognized the private rights of individuals." In response to the argument that secret recording may be the only way to get credible information about crime, the court stated that protection against intrusion might extend even to a person "reasonably suspected of committing a crime." Shevin v. Sunbeam Television Corp., 351 So.2d 723 (Fla. 1977).

Expectations of Privacy. Many of the statutes, whether they require the consent of all parties or only one, make wiretapping or eavesdropping actionable only if it violates the plaintiff's reasonable expectation of privacy. In view of the widespread availability of technology that makes spying relatively easy, when do people have reasonable expectations that their conversations are private?

The California Supreme Court decided that a party to a telephone conversation can have a reasonable expectation that no one is listening on an extension line. See Ribas v. Clark, 696 P.2d 637 (Cal. 1985). A wife asked the defendant to listen in on an extension phone as she talked to her estranged husband. The defendant then testified in an arbitration hearing about matters she overheard. The husband sued for violation of the California wiretapping statute. The court read the statute broadly to bar "far more than illicit wiretapping," including the recording of a conversation without the other's consent:

> While one who imparts private information risks the betrayal of his confidence by the other party, a substantial distinction has been recognized between the secondhand repetition of the contents of a conversation and its simultaneous dissemination to an unannounced second auditor, whether that auditor be a person or mechanical device. [ ]

> As one commentator has noted, such secret monitoring denies the speaker an important aspect of privacy of communication— the right to control the nature and extent of the firsthand dissemination of his statement. [ ] Partly because of this factor, the Privacy Act has been read to require the assent of all parties to a communication before another may listen.

Are statutes that forbid eavesdropping and wiretapping without regard to expectations of privacy preferable?

———

The federal statute, and many of the state laws as well, forbid not only the actual wiretapping or eavesdropping, but also the use of the intercepted communication by third parties who know that it was recorded illegally. Even if a news organization had nothing to do with the taping, the nature of the material or the circumstances under which it came to the news organization often suggest that it must have been obtained illegally. Whether the First Amendment permits such statutes to be enforced against news media that use material illegally obtained by others came before the Supreme Court in the following case.

Bartnicki v. Vopper

Supreme Court of the United States, 2001.
532 U.S. 514.

■ JUSTICE STEVENS delivered the opinion of the Court.

[During contentious negotiations between a Pennsylvania school board and a teachers' union, Bartnicki, the union's chief negotiator, used the cellular phone in her car to call Kane, the president of the local union. The two discussed the timing of a proposed strike, difficulties created by public comment on the negotiations, and the need for a dramatic response to the board's intransigence. At one point, Kane said: " 'If they're not gonna move for three percent, we're gonna have to go to their, their homes. . . . To blow off their front porches, we'll have to do some work on some of those guys. (PAUSES). Really, uh, really and truthfully because this is, you know, this is bad news. (UNDECIPHERABLE).' "]

[Someone who was never identified intercepted and recorded this conversation. Jack Yocum, the head of a local taxpayers' organization that opposed the union's demands, testified that he found a tape of the conversation in his mailbox and recognized the voices of Bartnicki and Kane. He gave the tape to Vopper, host of a local radio talk show. Vopper, who had been critical of the union, played the tape on his talk show. Another station also broadcast the tape, and local newspapers published its contents.]

[Bartnicki and Kane filed suit in federal court against Vopper, his radio station, Yocum, and other representatives of the media, alleging that each of the defendants "knew or had reason to know" that the recording of the private telephone conversation was illegal under both federal and Pennsylvania wiretapping statutes. The federal act, 18 U.S.C. § 2511(1)(a), forbids interception by a person not a party to the conversation, and subsection (c) provides that any person who "intentionally discloses, or endeavors to disclose, to any other person the contents of any wire, oral, or electronic communication, knowing or having reason to know that the information was obtained through the interception of a wire, oral, or electronic communication in violation of this subsection; . . . shall be punished. . . ." The Pennsylvania Act contains a similar provision. Both statutes also authorize suits for damages.]

[In answer to certified questions from the District Court, the Court of Appeals held that the federal and Pennsylvania wiretapping statutes were content-neutral and therefore subject to intermediate scrutiny. Applying that standard, the majority in the Court of Appeals concluded that the statutes were invalid because they deterred significantly more speech than necessary to protect the privacy interests at stake.]

. . .

IV

The constitutional question before us concerns the validity of the statutes as applied to the specific facts of these cases. Because of the procedural posture of these cases, it is appropriate to make certain important assumptions about those facts. We accept petitioners' submission that the interception was intentional, and therefore unlawful, and that, at a minimum, respondents "had reason to know" that it was unlawful. Accordingly, the disclosure of the contents of the intercepted conversation by Yocum to school board members and to representatives of the media, as well as the subsequent disclosures by the media defendants to the public, violated the federal and state statutes. Under the provisions of the federal statute, as well as its Pennsylvania analog, petitioners are thus entitled to recover damages from each of the respondents. The only question is whether the application of these statutes in such circumstances violates the First Amendment.[8]

In answering that question, we accept respondents' submission on three factual matters that serve to distinguish most of the cases that have arisen under § 2511. First, respondents played no part in the illegal interception. Rather, they found out about the interception only after it occurred, and in fact never learned the identity of the person or persons who made the interception. Second, their access to the information on the tapes was obtained lawfully, even though the information itself was intercepted unlawfully by someone else. [ ] Third, the subject matter of the conversation was a matter of public concern. If the statements about the labor negotiations had been made in a public arena—during a bargaining session, for example—they would have been newsworthy. This would also be true if a third party had inadvertently overheard Bartnicki making the same statements to Kane when the two thought they were alone.

V

We agree with petitioners that § 2511(1)(c), as well as its Pennsylvania analog, is in fact a content-neutral law of general applicability. . . .

On the other hand, the naked prohibition against disclosures is fairly characterized as a regulation of pure speech. [S]ubsection (c) is not a regulation of conduct. It is true that the delivery of a tape recording might be regarded as conduct, but given that the purpose of such a delivery is to provide the recipient with the text of recorded statements, it is like the delivery of a handbill or a pamphlet, and as such, it is the kind of "speech" that the First Amendment protects.[11] . . .

VI

As a general matter, "state action to punish the publication of truthful information seldom can satisfy constitutional standards." [*Daily Mail*] More specifically, this Court has repeatedly held that "if a newspaper lawfully obtains truthful information about a matter of public significance then state officials may not constitutionally punish publication of the information, absent a need . . . of the highest order." *Id.;* see also *Florida Star*; *Landmark Communications*.

Accordingly, in *New York Times Co. v. United States*, the Court upheld the right of the press to publish information of great public concern obtained from documents stolen by a third party. In so doing,

---

[8]   In answering this question, we draw no distinction between the media respondents and Yocum. See, e.g., New York Times Co. v. Sullivan, 376 U.S. 254 (1964); First Nat. Bank of Boston v. Bellotti, 435 U.S. 765 (1978).

[11]   Put another way, what gave rise to statutory liability in this suit was the information communicated on the tapes. See Boehner v. McDermott, 191 F.3d 463, 484 (D.C. Cir. 1999) (Sentelle, J., dissenting) ("What . . . is being punished . . . here is not conduct dependent upon the nature or origin of the tapes; it is speech dependent upon the nature of the contents").

that decision resolved a conflict between the basic rule against prior restraints on publication and the interest in preserving the secrecy of information that, if disclosed, might seriously impair the security of the Nation. In resolving that conflict, the attention of every Member of this Court was focused on the character of the stolen documents' contents and the consequences of public disclosure. Although the undisputed fact that the newspaper intended to publish information obtained from stolen documents was noted in Justice Harlan's dissent, [ ] neither the majority nor the dissenters placed any weight on that fact.

However, *New York Times v. United States* raised, but did not resolve, the question "whether, in cases where information has been acquired *unlawfully* by a newspaper or by a source, government may ever punish not only the unlawful acquisition, but the ensuing publication as well." [ ] The question here, however, is a narrower version of that still-open question. Simply put, the issue here is this: "Where the punished publisher of information has obtained the information in question in a manner lawful in itself but from a source who has obtained it unlawfully, may the government punish the ensuing publication of that information based on the defect in a chain?" [ ]

. . .

The Government identifies two interests served by the statute—first, the interest in removing an incentive for parties to intercept private conversations, and second, the interest in minimizing the harm to persons whose conversations have been illegally intercepted. We assume that those interests adequately justify the prohibition in § 2511(1)(d) against the interceptor's own use of information that he or she acquired by violating § 2511(1)(a), but it by no means follows that punishing disclosures of lawfully obtained information of public interest by one not involved in the initial illegality is an acceptable means of serving those ends.

The normal method of deterring unlawful conduct is to impose an appropriate punishment on the person who engages in it. If the sanctions that presently attach to a violation of § 2511(1)(a) do not provide sufficient deterrence, perhaps those sanctions should be made more severe. But it would be quite remarkable to hold that speech by a law-abiding possessor of information can be suppressed in order to deter conduct by a non-law-abiding third party. . . .

[P]etitioners cite no evidence that Congress viewed the prohibition against disclosures as a response to the difficulty of identifying persons making improper use of scanners and other surveillance devices and accordingly of deterring such conduct, and there is no empirical evidence to support the assumption that the prohibition against disclosures reduces the number of illegal interceptions.

Although this suit demonstrates that there may be an occasional situation in which an anonymous scanner will risk criminal prosecution by passing on information without any expectation of financial reward or public praise, surely this is the exceptional case. Moreover, there is no basis for assuming that imposing sanctions upon respondents will deter the unidentified scanner from continuing to engage in surreptitious interceptions. Unusual cases fall far short of a showing that there is a "need . . . of the highest order" for a rule supplementing the traditional means of deterring antisocial conduct. The justification for any such novel burden on expression must be "far stronger than mere speculation about serious harms." [ ] Accordingly, the Government's first suggested justification for applying § 2511(1)(c) to an otherwise innocent disclosure of public information is plainly insufficient.

The Government's second argument, however, is considerably stronger. Privacy of communication is an important interest. . . .

"In a democratic society privacy of communication is essential if citizens are to think and act creatively and constructively. Fear or suspicion that one's speech is being monitored by a stranger, even without the reality of such activity, can have a seriously inhibiting effect upon the willingness to voice critical and constructive ideas." President's Commission on Law Enforcement and Administration of Justice, The Challenge of Crime in a Free Society 202 (1967).

Accordingly, it seems to us that there are important interests to be considered on *both* sides of the constitutional calculus. In considering that balance, we acknowledge that some intrusions on privacy are more offensive than others, and that the disclosure of the contents of a private conversation can be an even greater intrusion on privacy than the interception itself. As a result, there is a valid independent justification for prohibiting such disclosures by persons who lawfully obtained access to the contents of an illegally intercepted message, even if that prohibition does not play a significant role in preventing such interceptions from occurring in the first place.

We need not decide whether that interest is strong enough to justify the application of § 2511(c) to disclosures of trade secrets or domestic gossip or other information of purely private concern. [ ] In other words, the outcome of these cases does not turn on whether § 2511(1)(c) may be enforced with respect to most violations of the statute without offending the First Amendment. The enforcement of that provision in these cases, however, implicates the core purposes of the First Amendment because it imposes sanctions on the publication of truthful information of public concern.

In these cases, privacy concerns give way when balanced against the interest in publishing matters of public importance. As Warren and Brandeis stated in their classic law review article: "The right of privacy does not prohibit any publication of matter which is of public or general interest." The Right to Privacy, 4 Harv. L.Rev. 193, 214 (1890). One of the costs associated with participation in public affairs is an attendant loss of privacy. . . .

Our opinion in New York Times Co. v. Sullivan, 376 U.S. 254 (1964), reviewed many of the decisions that settled the "general proposition that freedom of expression upon public questions is secured by the First Amendment." [ ]

We think it clear that parallel reasoning requires the conclusion that a stranger's illegal conduct does not suffice to remove the First Amendment shield from speech about a matter of public concern. The months of negotiations over the proper level of compensation for teachers at the Wyoming Valley West High School were unquestionably a matter of public concern, and respondents were clearly engaged in debate about that concern. That debate may be more mundane than the Communist rhetoric that inspired Justice Brandeis' classic opinion in *Whitney v. California*, but it is no less worthy of constitutional protection.

The judgment is affirmed.

■ JUSTICE BREYER, with whom JUSTICE O'CONNOR joins, concurring.

I join the Court's opinion. I agree with its narrow holding limited to the special circumstances present here: (1) the radio broadcasters acted lawfully (up to the time of final public disclosure); and (2) the information publicized involved a matter of unusual public concern, namely, a threat of potential physical harm to others. I write separately to explain why, in my view, the Court's holding does not imply a significantly broader constitutional immunity for the media.

. . .

As a general matter, despite the statutes' direct restrictions on speech, the Federal Constitution must tolerate laws of this kind because of the importance of these privacy and speech-related objectives. [ ] Rather than broadly forbid this kind of legislative enactment, the Constitution demands legislative efforts to tailor the laws in order reasonably to reconcile media freedom with personal, speech-related privacy.

Nonetheless, looked at more specifically, the statutes, as applied in these circumstances, do not reasonably reconcile the competing constitutional objectives. Rather, they disproportionately interfere with media freedom. For one thing, the broadcasters here engaged in no unlawful activity other than the ultimate publication of the information another had previously obtained. They "neither encouraged nor participated directly or indirectly in the interception." [ ] No one claims that they ordered, counseled, encouraged, or otherwise aided or abetted the interception, the later delivery of the tape by the interceptor to an intermediary, or the tape's still later delivery by the intermediary to the media. . . .

For another thing, the speakers had little or no *legitimate* interest in maintaining the privacy of the particular conversation. That conversation involved a suggestion about "blow[ing] off . . . front porches" and "do[ing] some work on some of those guys," [ ], thereby raising a significant concern for the safety of others. Where publication of private information constitutes a wrongful act, the law recognizes a privilege allowing the reporting of threats to public safety. [ ] Even where the danger may have passed by the time of publication, that fact cannot legitimize the speaker's earlier privacy expectation. Nor should editors, who must make a publication decision quickly, have to determine present or continued danger before publishing this kind of threat.

Further, the speakers themselves, the president of a teacher's union and the union's chief negotiator, were "limited public figures," for they voluntarily engaged in a public controversy. They thereby subjected themselves to somewhat greater public scrutiny and had a lesser interest in privacy than an individual engaged in purely private affairs. [ ]

This is not to say that the Constitution requires anyone, including public figures, to give up entirely the right to private communication, *i.e.,* communication free from telephone taps or interceptions. But the subject matter of the conversation at issue here is far removed from that in situations where the media publicizes truly private matters. [ ]

Thus, in finding a constitutional privilege to publish unlawfully intercepted conversations of the kind here at issue, the Court does not create a "public interest" exception that swallows up the statutes' privacy-protecting general rule. Rather, it finds constitutional protection for publication of intercepted information of a special kind. Here, the speakers' legitimate privacy expectations are unusually low, and the public interest in defeating those expectations is unusually high. Given these circumstances, along with the lawful nature of respondents' behavior, the statutes' enforcement would disproportionately harm media freedom.

. . .

■ CHIEF JUSTICE REHNQUIST, with whom JUSTICE SCALIA and JUSTICE THOMAS join, dissenting.

. . .

These laws are content neutral; they only regulate information that was illegally obtained; they do not restrict republication of what is already in the public domain; they impose no special burdens upon the media; they have a scienter requirement to provide fair warning; and they promote the privacy and free speech of those using cellular telephones. It is hard to imagine a more narrowly tailored prohibition of the disclosure of illegally intercepted communications, and it distorts our precedents to review these statutes under the often fatal standard of strict scrutiny. These laws therefore should be upheld if they further a substantial governmental interest unrelated to the suppression of free speech, and they do.

Congress and the overwhelming majority of States reasonably have concluded that sanctioning the knowing disclosure of illegally intercepted communications will deter the initial interception itself, a crime which is extremely difficult to detect. It is estimated that over 20 million scanners capable of intercepting cellular transmissions currently are in operation, [ ] notwithstanding the fact that Congress prohibited the marketing of such devices eight years ago [ ]. As Congress recognized, "[a]ll too often the invasion of privacy itself will go unknown. Only by striking at all aspects of the problem can privacy be adequately protected." [ ]

. . .

[T]he incidental restriction on alleged First Amendment freedoms is no greater than essential to further the interest of protecting the privacy of individual communications. Were there no prohibition on disclosure, an unlawful eavesdropper who wanted to disclose the conversation could anonymously launder the interception through a third party and thereby avoid detection. Indeed, demand for illegally obtained private information would only increase if it could be disclosed without repercussion. The law against interceptions, which the Court agrees is valid, would be utterly ineffectual without these antidisclosure provisions.

. . .

. . . The Court concludes that the private conversation between Gloria Bartnicki and Anthony Kane is somehow a "debate . . . worthy of constitutional protection." [ ] Perhaps the Court is correct that "[i]f the statements about the labor negotiations had been made in a public arena—during a bargaining session, for example—they would have been newsworthy."[ ] The point, however, is that Bartnicki and Kane had no intention of contributing to a public "debate" at all, and it is perverse to hold that another's unlawful interception and knowing disclosure of their conversation is speech "worthy of constitutional protection." [ ] The Constitution should not protect the involuntary broadcast of personal conversations. Even where the communications involve public figures or concern public matters, the conversations are nonetheless private and worthy of protection. Although public persons may have forgone the right to live their lives screened from public scrutiny in some areas, it does not and should not follow that they also have abandoned their right to have a private conversation without fear of it being intentionally intercepted and knowingly disclosed.

. . .

NOTES AND QUESTIONS

1.　Although the Court concedes that the wiretapping statutes are content neutral, it applies a form of strict scrutiny, apparently on the ground that the statutes regulate "pure speech." Do they? If so, does this case announce a new First Amendment principle—that content-neutral regulation of pure speech triggers strict scrutiny? In footnote 11, the Court suggests that the statutes punish speech because of "the nature of its contents." Does the fact that the statutes impose liability for broadcasting the tape only if the contents of the tape were illegally recorded make them content-based?

2.　What exactly is the matter of public concern at issue in the case? To Justices Breyer and O'Connor, it was the "threat of potential physical harm to others" that made the tape "a matter of unusual public concern." This, together with the facts that the plaintiffs were public figures and the defendants did not participate in the eavesdropping, seem to be the "special circumstances" that convinced them that the decision is a narrow one that does not broadly immunize media from liability for using illegally obtained information.

3.　If the other members of the majority do not view the holding that narrowly, what do they view as the matter of public concern? Is it the teachers' dispute? If so, does Justice Stevens's opinion indicate that a person's (or at least a public figure's) *views* about a matter of public concern are themselves a matter of public concern? Or is he saying that the views themselves may be private, but because they relate to a matter of public concern, the interest in protecting privacy isn't strong enough to overcome the First Amendment interest in publication of truthful information?

4.　The Court in *Bartnicki* suggested that its opinion was narrow and that such a limited focus was in line with its "repeated refusal to answer categorically whether truthful publication may ever be punished consistent with the First Amendment." The two concurring Justices in *Bartnicki* pointed to a celebrity sex tape as one place where they would draw the line and would find the publisher liable: Such a tape would be a "truly private matter," they wrote, crediting the Pamela Anderson Lee case as one that rightly held that the "broadcast of [a] videotape recording of sexual relations between [a] famous actress and [a] rock star [was] not a matter of legitimate public concern." The Lee case, Michaels v. Internet Entertainment Group, 5 F. Supp. 2d 823 (C.D. Cal. 1998), was one rejected by an early court hearing Hulk Hogan's request for a preliminary injunction that would have ordered Gawker to remove Hogan's sex tape; the court decided that the Lee case was not relevant to a determination of newsworthiness. Considering the language of the dissent, might this signal at least a 5–4 majority at the Supreme Court in 2001 in favor of drawing a press freedom-privacy line at intimate sexual relations?

5.　After *Bartnicki*, what should media conclude about the risks of using information that they know was unlawfully obtained by someone else? That they can safely use such information as long as they were not involved in the illegal acquisition? That they may be liable for such use unless there are special circumstances sufficient to convince a court that liability would "disproportionately interfere with media freedom"? In this connection, note that the vote of at least one of the two concurring justices was necessary to make a majority.

Interpreting Bartnicki. Would the result in *Bartnicki* have been different if Yocum had known who had taped the conversation? If he had known that the tape was illegally recorded before he listened to it? If Vopper had asked Yocum to give him the tape instead of receiving it passively? The First Circuit thought that none of those circumstances would call for a different result. See Jean v. Massachusetts State Police, 492 F.3d 24 (1st Cir. 2007). There, a man whose nanny-cam recorded the state police conducting a warrantless search of his home contacted the plaintiff, a woman named Mary T. Jean, who operated a website critical of the local district attorney, and told her about the raid and his audio and video recording of it. She posted the recording on her website. The state police threatened to prosecute Jean under the state eavesdropping statute unless she removed the recording. She obtained an injunction preventing the prosecution on the ground that it was barred by *Bartnicki.*

The First Circuit affirmed, rejecting the state's attempts to distinguish *Bartnicki.* As for the argument that *Bartnicki* did not control because Jean, the plaintiff in the Massachusetts case, unlike Yocum in *Barnicki,* knew who made the illegal recording, the court decided that that fact made the state's interest in prosecuting a subsequent publisher of the recording even weaker, because if the interceptor is known the state can protect its interests by prosecuting that person. *Bartnicki* could not be limited to persons who learned of the illegal taping only after listening because the decision protected Vopper, who knew of the illegality before listening, as well as Yocum, who did not. The court said the fact that Yocum was the passive recipient of a tape given to him anonymously, while Jean, the plaintiff in the Massachusetts case, encouraged the man who taped the raid to give it to her, made no difference because both Yocum and Jean had the same opportunity to refuse to disclose the tape.

Encouraging the illegal taping itself may be a different matter, however. In Peavy v. WFAA-TV, Inc., 221 F.3d 158 (5th Cir. 2000), the court held that state and federal wiretap acts are subject only to intermediate scrutiny where there is evidence that the media defendant encouraged and gave instructions regarding the illegal taping. The Fifth Circuit reversed a summary judgment for the defendants because of evidence that the media defendant might have participated in the interceptions. The governmental interests that *Bartnicki* later found insufficient to overcome strict scrutiny—eliminating incentives to wiretap and protecting the privacy of electronic communications—were sufficient in the Fifth Circuit's view to survive intermediate scrutiny. When the Supreme Court decided *Bartnicki,* it took note of the *Peavy* decision, and noted that it was distinguishable because of the possibility that the television station had been involved in the illegal taping.

In *Peavy,* the television station did not broadcast the tapes in question, but the court held that, unless it had also acquired the information by other, nonprohibited means, it could be liable for disclosing the substance of the tapes under language in the federal statute prohibiting "use" of illegally taped conversations. The station eventually settled the case on terms it refused to disclose.

More recently, the Seventh Circuit found that a newspaper could be liable for publishing personal information about police officers that it had acquired from a drivers' license database, in violation of a federal statute. Dahlstrom v. Sun-Times Media, 777 F.3d 937 (7th Cir. 2015). In Dahlstrom, the court explained that the Sun-Times "knowingly obtained [from government sources] this additional identifying information from motor vehicle records maintained by the Secretary of State." *Bartnicki*'s holding did not compel a different result because the court decided that the balance between the newsworthiness of the published information and the privacy interests was different. In *Dahlstrom* media had reported the physical characteristics of police officers who participated in a police lineup; the information had been accessed through a drivers' license database by unnamed others in violation of federal law. "Because the Officers' privacy expectations in their personal information [including physical descriptions and additional information taken from drivers licenses] are significantly greater—and the public value of that information is significantly lesser—than in *Bartnicki*," the court wrote, "a ruling in [the newspaper's] favor would represent a substantial extension of *Bartnicki*"'s "narrow holding." *Dahlstrom* is given additional consideration in Chapters Five and Ten.

Liability of Middlemen. A congressman was held liable for serving as a conduit between the people who illegally taped a conversation and newspapers that published the contents. See Boehner v. McDermott, 484 F.3d 573 (D.C. Cir. 2007). Congressman John Boehner, who was then chairman of the House Republican Conference, while driving his car in Florida participated in a telephone conference call with then-Speaker Newt Gingrich and other Republican leaders to discuss Gingrich's agreement to accept a reprimand from the House Ethics Committee if the committee would agree not to hold a hearing on his alleged ethics violation. John and Alice Martin, Florida residents listening on a radio scanner, recorded the conversation and discussed it with their Democratic congresswoman. She suggested that they give the tape to Congressman McDermott, a Democrat and co-chair of the House Ethics Committee. McDermott gave copies of the tape to The New York Times and two other newspapers. The papers all published reports based on the contents of the tape, which they said showed Gingrich violated his agreement with the ethics committee. The papers honored their promise not to identify McDermott as the source, but when the stories came out the Martins revealed that they had given the tape to McDermott.

The Martins were fined $500 each for eavesdropping, McDermott resigned from the ethics committee, and Gingrich eventually resigned from the House. McDermott was not prosecuted, but Boehner sued him for damages under the section of the statute prohibiting intentional disclosure of a communication that the discloser knows was recorded in violation of the statute. The district court dismissed the complaint on the ground that imposing liability for "disclosure of truthful and lawfully obtained information on a matter of substantial public concern" would violate the First Amendment. The Court of Appeals, en banc, reversed 5–4. The majority said *Bartnicki* did not protect McDermott because under rules of the House of Representatives he was forbidden to disclose evidence relating to a committee investigation. "*Bartnicki* does not stand for the proposition that anyone who has lawfully obtained truthful information of public importance has a First Amendment right to disclose that information. . . . There are many federal provisions that forbid individuals from disclosing information they have lawfully obtained. The validity of these provisions has long been assumed. Grand jurors, court reporters, and prosecutors, for instance, may 'not disclose a matter occurring before the grand jury.' "

Four dissenting judges thought *Bartnicki* established McDermott's constitutional right to disclose the tape just as surely as it established the right of the press to do so. "We do not believe the First Amendment permits this interdiction of public information either at the stage of the newspaper-reading public, of the newspaper-publishing communicators, or at the stage of Representative McDermott's disclosure to the news media." The deciding vote was cast by Judge Griffith, who believed McDermott could be held liable despite *Bartnicki* because he voluntarily relinquished his First Amendment rights as a member of the ethics committee

Citizen Journalism and Police Encounters. Recording technology has enabled citizens to film unexpected encounters with police; the resulting cases often consider whether such citizens violate eavesdropping or wiretapping laws, and whether the First Amendment trumps such laws that would otherwise prohibit such recording. The Seventh Circuit addressed citizens' "right to record police" in ACLU v. Alvarez, 679 F.3d 583 (7th Cir. 2012). There, the American Civil Liberties Union sued to enjoin enforcement of Illinois' all-party consent eavesdropping statute, which forbids recording oral communications, whether private or not. The ACLU had planned to initiate a "police accountability program" to make audio and visual recordings of police officers performing their duties in public places. The district court held that the ACLU had not alleged a cognizable injury because there was no First Amendment "right to audio record." The Seventh Circuit reversed and ordered a preliminary injunction, finding that the ACLU had shown a strong likelihood of success on the merits. The eavesdropping statute triggered First Amendment scrutiny, the court wrote, because it "restrict[ed] a medium of expression commonly used for the preservation and communication of information and ideas." The court described the First Amendment interest more specifically:

> [T]he eavesdropping statute restricts a medium of expression—the use of a common instrument of communication—and thus an integral step in the speech process. As applied here, it interferes with the gathering and dissemination of information about government officials performing their duties in public. Any way you

look at it, the eavesdropping statute burdens speech and press rights and is subject to heightened First Amendment scrutiny.

The court held that whether strict or intermediate scrutiny applied, the state's important interest in protecting conversational privacy was insufficient to support the application of the eavesdropping statute to recording of police officers "performing their duties in public places and engaging in public communications audible to persons who witness the events." In these instances, the police officers simply had no reasonable expectation of privacy with regard to their communications, and thus the eavesdropping statute did not serve its asserted ends.

The court further suggested that that its decision would not necessarily affect the constitutionality of electronic privacy statutes in other states because "[a]s best we can tell, the Illinois statute is the broadest of its kind; no other wiretapping or eavesdropping statute prohibits the open recording of police officers lacking any expectation of privacy." [The court presumably referred here to both audio and visual recording; the statute targets "record[ing]" of conversations.]

Judge Richard Posner dissented:

> The constitutional right that the majority creates is likely to impair the ability of police both to extract information relevant to police duties and to communicate effectively with persons whom they speak with in the line of duty. An officer may freeze if he sees a journalist recording a conversation between the officer and a crime suspect, crime victim, or dissatisfied member of the public. He may be concerned when any stranger moves into earshot, or when he sees a recording device (even a cell phone, for modern cell phones are digital audio recorders) in the stranger's hand. To distract police during tense encounters with citizens endangers public safety and undermines effective law enforcement.

See also Glik v. Cunniffe, 655 F.3d 78 (1st Cir. 2011) (holding that a bystander to an arrest has an unambiguous and clearly established First Amendment "right to videotape police carrying out their duties in public" and rejecting police officers' defense of qualified immunity for arresting the bystander); Gericke v. Weare Police Dep't, 753 F.3d 1 (1st Cir. 2014) (upholding trial courts' denial of summary judgment, and holding that police officers were not entitled to qualified immunity from a retaliatory prosecution claim based on the arrest of the plaintiff for filming the police during a traffic stop). But see Crawford v. Geiger, 2015 U.S. Dist. LEXIS 126538 (N.D. Ohio Sept. 22, 2015) (citing cases from the Third and Fourth Circuits that suggest the uncertainty of law in the area and upholding qualified immunity because of the "unsettled constitutional status of the ability, without fear of arrest, to record what one can otherwise lawfully see and hear").

The Definition for Journalist. Courts deciding cases that involve the videotaping of police activities and other events have at times focused at least in part on the meaning of the word "journalist," worried that there may be additional First Amendment considerations in cases involving traditional newsgatherers. Some courts have defined the word broadly enough to include most everyone. Consider the following language from *Glik*, the First Circuit opinion noted above:

> The First Amendment right to gather news is, as the Court has often noted, not one that inures solely to the benefit of the news media; rather, the public's right of access to information is coextensive with that of the press. . . . Moreover, changes in technology and society have made the lines between private citizen and journalist exceedingly difficult to draw. The proliferation of electronic devices with video-recording capability means that many of our images of current events come from bystanders with a ready cell phone or digital camera rather than a traditional film crew, and news stories are now just as likely to be broken by a blogger at her computer as a reporter at a major newspaper. Such developments make clear why the news-gathering protections of the First Amendment cannot turn on professional credentials or status.

Such broad notions of newsgathering have led courts to suggest implicitly or explicitly that many different parties are, in fact, acting in a journalistic capacity. A federal district court suggested that a protester who had attempted to record his own Transportation Security Administration exchange was gathering news. Mocek v. City of Albuquerque, 3 F.Supp. 3d 1002 (D.N.M. 2014). Similarly, a federal trial court suggested that an arrestee who had attempted to record his arrest was newsgathering and implied that the general public has the right to cover news. *Crawford*, 2015 U.S. Dist. LEXIS 126538. And in Foster v. Svenson, 128 A.D.3d 150 (N.Y. App. Div. 2015), an appellate court in New York applied a newsworthiness exemption to find no liability on the part of the art photographer who photographed his "neighbors" through the windows of their apartments.

One of the best examples of the growing definitional issue is a New Jersey case involving the university student-creator of a "web gripe site" that focused on his very strong personal complaints about a dean. The student argued that police seized his computer in violation of a statute enacted to protect news media from newsroom searches and seizures, one that had not required interpretation in three decades. J.O. v. Township of Bedminster, 77 A.3d 1242 (N.J. Super. Ct. App. Div. 2013). The state appellate court rejected the website creator's claim that he should be protected under the statute, differentiating between more traditional newsgatherers and disseminators and those who simply post their videos on the Internet:

> Today, a cellphone can be used by a pedestrian to take a video of an incident of police brutality that will be played on the evening news broadcast. The same phone can be used to record a kitten who refuses to leave a warm bath, producing a video seen by close to four million people on YouTube. In each case, it could be argued that the person who took the video engaged in an activity described in the [statute that protects news media]. Nonetheless, we are confident that the Legislature did not intend to provide protection

above and beyond that provided by the Fourth Amendment to someone based upon the posting of a video of a wet kitten on the Internet.

On the precise facts of the case, the court decided that the webpage creator had never claimed that he was a journalist when police arrived at his home, that he had tried to distance himself from the website so that his identity would not be immediately apparent, and that he had described his website as one "where kindred spirits can come together to heal and to learn how to enjoy life after escaping" the dean. He was, therefore, not protected under the newsroom-protective statute.

Compare that holding with that of a Florida appellate court that held that a graduate student who blogged under a pseudonym should have received presuit notice of a lawsuit as would a traditional media defendant. Comins v. VanVoorhis, 135 So.3d 545 (Fla. Dist. Ct. App. 2014). The Florida court wrote:

> In employing the word "blog," we consider a site operated by a single individual or a small group that has primarily an informational purpose, most commonly in an area of special interest, knowledge or expertise of the blogger, and which usually provides for public impact or feedback. In that sense, it appears clear that many blogs and bloggers will fall within the broad reach of "media," and, if accused of defamatory statements, will qualify as a "media defendant" for purposes of Florida's defamation law. . . ."

Does the Florida court's suggestion that "many" bloggers would qualify as news media, signaling that some would not, mean that it would have decided the New Jersey case as did the New Jersey court? Should it be worrisome that courts parse websites in order to decide whether they qualify as journalism or not?

Consider the following attempt at a definition for the word journalist:

> A journalist is one who publishes reliable and substantiated news and information in context meant for multiple others so that those others may learn things of interest about the community in which they live or about the persons who comprise the community. A journalist is not one who simply publishes self-interested musings or the papers or the documents of another; he or she focuses on information of interest to the public, analyzes the information contained within those papers or documents, and publishes that analysis. A publisher who follows a well-accepted ethics code or an ethics code based upon well-accepted principles is presumptively a journalist. Not everyone is a journalist, however, and most random publishers—even publishers of truth—are not.

Amy Gajda, The First Amendment Bubble (Harvard University Press 2015).

Is such a definition too restrictive? Would it change the outcome of any of the decisions above in which courts found it necessary to describe journalists and journalistic activities?

This definitional question is considered additionally in Chapter Nine.

E. MISREPRESENTATION

Journalists sometimes engage in subterfuge, or what is sometimes called pretexting, to get information or documentation that would not otherwise be available. In these cases journalists engage in misrepresentation, at least implicitly, passing themselves off as employees or customers rather than newsgatherers. Sometimes the plaintiff alleges that the misrepresentation itself constitutes a tort or negates a defense that would otherwise be available; sometimes the misrepresentation is asserted as an element in some other tort. Consider the implications for journalism in the following case.

<h3 style="text-align:center">Taus v. Loftus</h3>

Supreme Court of California, 2007.
151 P.3d 1185.

■ GEORGE, C.J.

[Nicole Taus was a woman who believed she had recovered repressed memories of childhood sexual abuse with the help of a psychiatrist, David Corwin. Elizabeth Loftus was a psychologist who wrote articles debunking the use of recovered memory techniques in such cases, one for a scientific journal and one for a magazine aimed at lay readers. To gain material for her articles, Loftus interviewed Margie Cantrell, a woman who had been Taus's foster mother during Taus's adolescence. Cantrell alleged that Loftus represented herself as a person working with Corwin to help her recover her memories when in fact she was seeking to discredit the psychiatrist's work.

Taus sued Loftus and others for defamation, negligent infliction of emotional distress, invasion of privacy, and fraud. The defendants moved under the California anti-SLAPP statute [discussed in Chapter Four] to strike the complaint on the ground that the plaintiff could not demonstrate a probability of prevailing. The court of appeals held that the plaintiff could proceed on claims of defamation, disclosure of private facts, and intrusion. The California Supreme Court struck all but the intrusion claim, which it held survived the SLAPP motion unless "the plaintiff is unable to demonstrate both that the claim is legally sufficient and that there is sufficient evidence to establish a prima facie case with respect to the claim."]

Cantrell indicates in her declaration [as a witness supporting Taus's claim] that when she arrived for the interview with Loftus, Loftus was seated in a room with a man. When Cantrell entered and introduced herself, "Dr. Loftus smiled and welcomed me, saying again that she was working with Dr. Corwin and was actually his supervisor in connection with the study of Nicole." According to Cantrell's declaration: "Dr. Loftus asked if she could record the interview on audiotape," and "relying entirely on [Loftus's] representations that she worked with Dr. Corwin," Cantrell agreed. The declaration continues: "The questioning lasted several hours I believe. During the course of the interview the questioning about Nicole seemed to become increasingly hostile. I became concerned and asked Dr. Loftus if she really worked with Dr. Corwin or something to that effect. . . . I recall that my confrontation caused a reaction on the part of both the man and the woman. I told them that I felt that they had not been honest with me and asked them what they were really doing. They did not respond. I became frightened. . . . I demanded that they turn the recording machine off. I believe that they did so. . . . I demanded that they give me the tape. They refused. . . . I left immediately, extremely upset."

Cantrell further states in her declaration that after subsequently learning from Corwin that Loftus was not associated with him, "I felt humiliated because I had been talking about Nicole's confidential matters with someone I was led to believe was bound to respect her confidentiality." Cantrell states that "[s]ince this incident, Nicole and I have become estranged," and that "I am informed that, because of the interview, Nicole believes that I am no longer trustworthy. This saddens me deeply." Cantrell further indicates that "I would never have consented to be interviewed by [Loftus] if she had disclosed her true identity and focus and would have said nothing about Nicole without Nicole's full knowing and voluntary consent."

After the Cantrell declaration was filed, Loftus filed a supplemental declaration that stated in relevant part: "I unequivocally deny that I ever represented myself to Ms. Cantrell—or anyone else—as 'working with David Corwin, M.D.' or that I in any way implied or suggested that I was his 'supervisor' or words to this effect. Ms. Cantrell may possibly have misunderstood me when I undoubtedly mentioned Dr. Corwin's interviews with Plaintiff. However, again, I in no way represented myself as associated with Dr. Corwin nor would I." [Loftus denied that the interview was tape recorded.]

. . .

As a general matter, of course, a person's relatives and close friends frequently are privy to a great deal of the person's most private personal and family secrets-including, for example, potentially embarrassing and harmful information concerning the person's medical condition, the person's sexual activities and orientation, whether the person has been subjected to sexual or physical abuse either within his or her family or otherwise, and the person's youthful indiscretions or misbehavior. Unlike a person's appearance or activities that occur in a public place [ ], and unlike personal information about a person that is contained in a public record open to inspection by the general public as a matter of law [ ], personal information about a person that happens to be known by the person's relatives or close friends is not information that has entered the public domain. A person's interest in preserving the privacy of such information—the very interest the intrusion tort was designed to protect—would be substantially undermined if a would-be investigator could employ any means whatsoever to extract or obtain such private information from a relative or close friend.

To put forth a few extreme examples, it is clear that a person's reasonable expectation of privacy would be violated if a private investigator—who was determined to obtain private information about the person that was otherwise unavailable to the investigator—broke into the home of a relative or close friend of the target of the investigation and copied a diary or other private papers that the target had left with the relative or friend for safekeeping, or, alternatively, physically threatened, blackmailed, wiretapped, hypnotized, or administered a drug to such a relative or friend to obtain private information about the target that the relative or friend would not have voluntarily disclosed. (See, e.g., Sheets v. Salt Lake County (10th Cir. 1995) 45 F.3d 1383 [holding that the plaintiff husband had a reasonable expectation of privacy in entries in his wife's diary that related to him: "The fact that Mr. Sheets did not author the information does not prohibit him from having a distinct privacy interest in the dissemination of information written about the personal aspects of his life. . . . We find that information conveyed to one's spouse or that one's spouse has observed about one's character, marriage, finances, and business to be personal in nature and subject to a reasonable expectation of privacy"].) Although in each of those instances the relative or friend would be able to pursue his or her own distinct tort cause of action against the private investigator, in many cases the most serious harm or damage will have been incurred by the person whose private information was the target of and the impetus for the intrusive misconduct, and the intrusion-into-private-matters tort is specifically intended to provide a remedy to the person who has sustained an invasion of his or her privacy by virtue of the misconduct. [ ]

In the present case, Loftus was seeking to obtain from Cantrell, plaintiff's former foster mother, personal information about plaintiff relating both to plaintiff's memory of ostensible sexual abuse to which plaintiff had been subjected as a child by her mother, and to the effect of plaintiff's asserted recovery of that memory on plaintiff's subsequent behavior and emotional well-being—certainly the type of information as to which a person ordinarily would possess a reasonable expectation of privacy. (In this regard, it is relevant to recall that at the time Cantrell agreed to speak to Loftus about these matters . . . the circumstance that plaintiff assertedly had been sexually abused as a child was not a matter of general or public knowledge.) Furthermore, as revealed by Loftus's declaration, through her questioning of Cantrell, Loftus was able to obtain access to previously undisclosed information concerning plaintiff's alleged promiscuity and drug use following her 1995 session with

Corwin—again, the kind of very personal and potentially embarrassing or detrimental information as to which a person ordinarily would possess a reasonable expectation of privacy.

Of course, unlike some of the hypothetical scenarios described above, in the present case Loftus did not obtain access to this very personal information about plaintiff by breaking into Cantrell's home or by wiretapping her telephone, but instead obtained the information by questioning Cantrell. Because plaintiff had agreed to permit Corwin to use her case study at educational seminars and in an article published in a scientific journal—albeit without identifying plaintiff by name—it may well be that plaintiff could not have had an objectively reasonable expectation that an investigator or academic researcher, like Loftus, would not discover her identity and pose probing questions to Cantrell relating to such personal matters. In any event, because, as explained below, as a matter of law Loftus's simple engagement in such questioning would not constitute "highly offensive" conduct [ ], it is clear that plaintiff would have no cause of action under the intrusion tort if, in response to such questioning by Loftus, Cantrell freely and voluntarily revealed this personal information about plaintiff to Loftus.

According to Cantrell's declaration, however, Loftus did not simply approach Cantrell with questions about plaintiff, but instead misrepresented her (Loftus's) relationship with Corwin (a psychiatrist with whom plaintiff had a friendly and trusting professional relationship)—stating that she (Loftus) was Corwin's associate or supervisor—in order to persuade Cantrell to disclose personal information about plaintiff to Loftus. If Loftus engaged in such behavior, we cannot say, as a matter of law, that such questionable and unorthodox action constitutes conduct that plaintiff reasonably should have foreseen or anticipated. Instead, we believe a jury could find that plaintiff reasonably expected that an investigator would not seek and obtain access to such personal information about her from a relative or friend *by falsely posing as an associate or supervisor of a mental health professional in whom plaintiff had confided.*

. . .

An amicus curiae brief filed in this court on behalf of a number of news media entities and organizations cautions against permitting a cause of action for intrusion to be based solely on uncorroborated allegations made—by a "source" interviewed by a reporter or other investigator—that assert the reporter or investigator obtained information from the source through misrepresentation. The amicus curiae brief argues that in many instances in which a reporter utilizes information obtained from a source to write an article that the source ultimately is unhappy with, the source may claim, after the fact, that the reporter—to obtain the information disclosed in the article—failed to be forthright in disclosing his or her motives, position or point of view to the source. The brief maintains that permitting a subject about whom unflattering information has been obtained from a third party source to sue the reporter or investigator for offensive intrusion into the subject's privacy on the basis of such a claim of misrepresentation would have an undesirable chilling effect on the gathering and publication of newsworthy material. The amicus curiae brief points to a number of cases that have rejected a cause of action for intrusion based on information revealed by a third party, even in circumstances in which the plaintiff alleged that a reporter or investigator employed some sort of fraud or subterfuge to obtain the information. (See, e.g., Desnick v. American Broadcasting Co. [44 F.3d 1345 (7th Cir. 1995)].

The concerns raised by the amicus curiae brief appear quite reasonable and clearly demonstrate the danger and inadvisability of adopting a broad rule under which any type of misrepresentation by a reporter, investigator, or scholar to obtain information would be considered sufficient to support a cause of action for intrusion into private matters.

At the same time, however, we believe it is important to recognize that there are at least some types of misrepresentations that are of such an especially egregious and offensive nature—and are quite distinguishable from the types of ruses that ordinarily may be employed in gathering news—that they properly may be considered "beyond the pale" for purposes of the intrusion tort, even when the misrepresentation is made to friends or relatives of the subject of an inquiry who are under no legal obligation not to reveal private information about the subject of the inquiry. For example, consider an instance in which an unscrupulous or overly ambitious investigative reporter or private investigator, interested in discovering whether a public official (or any other person) has a particular medical condition or is taking a specific medication, makes a telephone call to a spouse, adult child, or close friend of the official, pretends to be an emergency room physician or paramedic, and asks the relative or friend to disclose the medical information ostensibly to assist in the treatment of the official. Even though (1) a public official's right of privacy is limited in many respects, (2) the information in question, because of the official's position, might well be considered "newsworthy" for publication purposes, and (3) the relative or friend might be under no legal obligation to keep the information confidential, we believe a jury reasonably could find that this type of misrepresentation is "highly offensive" to a reasonable person and that the subject of the inquiry had an "objectively reasonable expectation of seclusion or solitude in the . . . data source" [ ] that was violated by the investigator's use of such a tactic to obtain private information from a relative or friend who would not have divulged the information but for the flagrant nature of the misrepresentation.

The alleged misrepresentation at issue in the present case, of course, is not as egregious as that described in the foregoing hypothetical example, but the asserted misrepresentation in question nonetheless is of a particularly serious and potentially offensive nature that does share a number of the troubling aspects of that hypothetical. . . . As noted, Cantrell's declaration states that Loftus misrepresented herself as associated with—indeed even the supervisor of—Corwin, a psychiatrist in whom Cantrell knew plaintiff had confided and with whom plaintiff had an on-going, friendly professional relationship. Cantrell states in her declaration that Loftus's asserted misrepresentation led Cantrell to believe that Loftus "was bound to respect [plaintiff's] confidentiality" and that she (Cantrell) "never would have consented to be interviewed by [Loftus] if [Loftus] had disclosed her true identity and focus and [that she (Cantrell)] would have said nothing about [plaintiff] without [plaintiff's] full knowing and voluntary consent." And Loftus's declaration discloses that in the course of her interview with Cantrell, Cantrell revealed a number of highly private matters regarding plaintiff that a parental figure who cared about her foster child's welfare ordinarily would not be expected to disclose to a stranger—for example, that in 1995, shortly after apparently recovering her memories of her childhood sexual abuse, plaintiff "started sleeping with boys and doing drugs."

In our view, intentionally misrepresenting oneself as an associate or colleague of a mental health professional who has a close personal relationship with the person about whom one is seeking information would be a particularly serious type of misrepresentation, and one significantly different from the more familiar practice of a news reporter or investigator in shading or withholding information regarding his or her motives when interviewing a potential news source. Special legal protection is provided to information communicated in the course of a physician-patient or psychotherapist-patient relationship [ ], and even if plaintiff's relationship with Corwin was not of a nature that would bring information revealed to Corwin within an evidentiary privilege, the relationship bore a close similarity to such a relationship. Misrepresentations of this nature by either a reporter or an academic investigator could undermine legitimate professional relationships and would be especially troublesome, because they would take advantage of the desire and willingness of relatives and friends to provide assistance to professionals who they believe will use any personal information that is revealed to help the subject of the inquiry.

Because of these special and unusual considerations, we believe that if a trier of fact were to find that Loftus engaged in the particular type of misrepresentations alleged by Cantrell, the conduct properly could be found "highly offensive" for purposes of the intrusion-into-private-matters tort and liability could be imposed upon Loftus.[22]

In the present case, of course, Loftus has denied engaging in any misrepresentation to obtain information from Cantrell (or anyone else), but defendants assert that even if Loftus made a misrepresentation to Cantrell, Loftus's actions should be considered, as a matter of law, *not* highly offensive, in light of plaintiff's consent to Corwin's use of her case study in educational seminars and a published article. Even if plaintiff's consent to the public use of her case study rendered her a limited public figure, however, that status would not in itself justify the use of the particular type of misrepresentation here at issue. . . .

Furthermore, although it is conceivable that there may be some circumstances in which the need for information is so vital that resort to even the type of very questionable investigative tactic here at issue could not properly be found to be highly offensive to a reasonable person, we believe it is clear that this case does not fall within that narrow category. Here, although the additional information concerning plaintiff that Loftus sought to obtain from Cantrell was newsworthy, there was no profound or overriding public need that, as a matter of law, justified resort to the particular type of potentially insidious stratagem that, according to Cantrell, was utilized by Loftus in this case. [ ]

Thus, we conclude that in light of the particular nature of the misrepresentation attributed to Loftus by the Cantrell declaration, the Court of Appeal properly determined that the evidence presented by plaintiff is sufficient to establish a prima facie case under the intrusion-into-private-matters tort.

    . . .

---

[22] In *Shulman*, in discussing the application of the offensiveness element in the context of activities engaged in by the news media, we stated that "[i]n deciding . . . whether a reporter's alleged intrusion into private matters . . . is 'offensive' and hence actionable as an invasion of privacy, courts must consider the extent to which the intrusion was, under the circumstances, justified by the legitimate motive of gathering the news. Information-collecting techniques that may be highly offensive when done for socially unprotected reasons—for purposes of harassment, blackmail or prurient curiosity, for example—may not be offensive to a reasonable person when employed by journalists in pursuit of a socially or politically important story."

A number of journalistic codes of ethics caution that "surreptitious methods of gathering information" should be avoided "except when traditional open methods will not yield information vital to the public." Society of Prof. Journalists, Code of Ethics (1996) . . . ; see also Radio–Television News Directors Assn., Code of Ethics of Prof. Conduct ["Professional electronic journalists should [¶] . . . [¶][u]se surreptitious newsgathering techniques . . . only if there is no other way to obtain stories of significant public importance and only if the technique is explained to the audience"] . . . ; Steele, *When Might It Be Appropriate to Use Deception/Misrepresentation/Hidden Cameras in Newsgathering?* (Feb. 1, 1995) for Poynter Institute Ethics Series [listing, as one of the necessary prerequisites to the use of deception or misrepresentation in newsgathering, "[w]hen the information obtained is of profound importance. It must be of vital public interest, such as revealing great 'system failure' at the top levels, or it must prevent profound harm to individuals"].

■ Concurring and Dissenting Opinion by MORENO, J. (in which BAXTER, J., joins).

I agree with the majority in every respect except one: I respectfully disagree that Taus has an action against Loftus for the tort of intrusion into private matters (hereafter sometimes the intrusion tort), based on Loftus's alleged misrepresentations to Taus's foster mother, Margie Cantrell, in order to obtain supposedly private information about Taus. As explained below, Taus had no reasonable expectation that Cantrell would keep information she had observed about Taus's behavior private. Therefore, Taus should not be able to sue Loftus for unlawful intrusion. As also explained below, to the extent Taus preferred that Cantrell only speak to an investigator who held certain agreeable views, that preference could not be called an expectation of privacy, and the enforcement of that preference through tort law is antithetical to free academic inquiry.

. . .

III.

At the outset, we must be clear that the question is not whether Cantrell had a reasonable expectation that her privacy would be breached by an investigator who got her to reveal private information under false pretenses. The question rather is whether Taus has a reasonable expectation that Cantrell's observations of Taus's behavior while acting as her foster mother would remain private. The majority cites no case for the proposition that person A has a reasonable, legally protectable, expectation that person B will not reveal to person C observations person B has about person A's life. As we stated in *Shulman*, " '[O]ne who imparts private information risks the betrayal of his confidence by the other party. . . .' " An expectation of privacy is even less reasonable when what is at issue is not private information that has been communicated, in which some implication of confidentiality may sometimes arise, but rather disclosure of observations of a person's behavior. As one court observed, the intrusion tort "was not created to protect against . . . the garnering of information from third parties. . . . Gathering information about appellant from third parties, 'even if pursued using subterfuge and fraud, cannot constitute. . . . an intrusion upon [appellant's] solitude or seclusion. The Court has found no authority, nor has [appellant] cited any, which suggests the contrary.' "

. . .

[Justice Moreno argued that "under the particular circumstances of this case," Taus had no reasonable expectation that Cantrell would keep the information revealed to Loftus about her private, for several reasons. First, because Taus had agreed to allow Loftus to use her case study in seminars and scientific articles, and the case had become central to the recovered memory controversy, it was likely that some researcher would discover her identity and start asking questions. Second, Cantrell had no legal obligation to refrain from revealing information about Taus and no well-established custom or habit forbade her from doing so. Third, Taus's behavior might have already been generally known in the community.]

It may be that Taus would have preferred that Cantrell not reveal the further intimate details of her life to Loftus because, unlike Corwin, and unlike the friends or neighbors that Cantrell might have spoken to, Taus perceived Loftus as threatening because she was contesting claims that Taus had been sexually abused. In fact, it is fairly apparent that the impetus for this litigation is not Loftus's investigative techniques but her perceived adversarial stance toward Corwin and, derivatively, toward Taus. But by any ordinary sense, the desire to deny an investigator information based on the investigator's viewpoint cannot be called an expectation of privacy or seclusion, and the enforcement of Taus's preference through tort law is contrary to free academic inquiry and the First Amendment.

. . .

. . . The majority's desire to protect society from the kind of misrepresentations alleged in the present case is understandable, and it may be argued that a person could avoid intrusion suits of this kind by simply telling the truth. But of course Loftus vigorously denies having made any misrepresentations. The real question is whether we should subject academics and other investigators to right to privacy suits based on allegations that the means of obtaining information from a third party was unscrupulous, when the information obtained is itself not something an individual can reasonably expect to be kept private.

To insist that the reasonable expectation of privacy requirement be rigorously adhered to is not simply a matter of formal doctrinal correctness, but serves to enforce an important constitutional and policy principle. Permitting suits that do not meet this requirement will likely chill vigorous journalistic investigation because of the inherently problematic nature of the relationship between journalists and their news sources. . . . While the media organizations may not be correct that journalists should enjoy a blanket immunity from all such suits based on alleged misrepresentations to third party news sources, at the very least, no suit should be allowed when the plaintiff has not demonstrated a reasonable expectation that the information in question would be kept private but for the misrepresentations.

. . .

————

NOTES AND QUESTIONS

1.   What is the alleged misrepresentation that makes Taus's claim actionable? Suppose Loftus had merely claimed to be a believer in the recovered memory phenomenon? Suppose she had given Taus that

impression, without making any explicit statement to that effect? If such conduct would not support a claim for intrusion, why not? Is anything less than an outright lie insufficient to meet the "highly offensive" requirement?

2.   The journalists' codes of ethics cited in footnote 22 all condoned misrepresentation under some circumstances. The majority suggested that "there may be some circumstances in which the need for information is so vital that resort to even the type of very questionable investigative tactic here at issue" would not be actionable. None of these statements attempts to define those circumstances. Is it impossible to do so in advance? If so, which is the better solution: leave the matter to case-by-case adjudication, or adopt a rule that makes misrepresentation at least presumptively actionable (or nonactionable)?

3.   Note that even the dissenting justices rejected the argument of the media amici for blanket immunity from all intrusion suits based on alleged misrepresentations to third-party news sources. Would anything less alleviate the journalists' concern that sources who are unhappy with the uses made of their information will sue on the ground they gave the information based on misrepresentations?

Violating Agreements. Journalists often gain access or information by agreeing to conditions: for example, agreeing not to photograph certain scenes or not to report certain facts. Recall the outcome in Cohen v. Cowles Media Co., 501 U.S. 663 (U.S. 1991), when such a promise is broken; there, the Court found a newspaper liable for breach of contract for revealing certain information it had promised to keep confidential.

Breach of such a promise may be actionable as misrepresentation if the promise was made with no intention of keeping it. That theory was the basis of a fraud claim against a magazine whose photographer took photos of an open casket at a funeral after allegedly promising not to do so. See Showler v. Harper's Magazine Foundation, 222 Fed. Appx. 755 (10th Cir. 2007). The decedent was killed in action in Iraq, the first member of the Oklahoma National Guard to be killed in action since the Korean War. Harper's commissioned the photographer to do a photo essay on grieving families of war casualties and published a photo of the dead soldier in his casket. The suit, by the soldier's father and grandfather, claimed intentional infliction of emotional distress and invasion of privacy as well as fraud (misrepresentation). The district court granted summary judgment for the defendants on all the claims, and the Tenth Circuit affirmed. The trial court said the fraud claim failed because if the photographer made any promise, it was to the funeral director and not to the family. The Tenth Circuit affirmed not on that ground, but for want of evidence that the photographer made the alleged promise intending to break it. The plaintiffs argued that his intent was a question of credibility to be resolved by the jury, but the court said the plaintiffs were required to produce some evidence to refute the photographer's declaration as to his intention. The Court of Appeals also said there was no evidence that the plaintiffs relied on any misrepresentation, because the funeral was open to the public and the family did not exclude media.

Does the availability of this theory of recovery raise a concern similar to that voiced by the media amici in *Taus*—that people who are unhappy with coverage will sue for misrepresentation? Should the law attempt to spare journalists the risk of an adverse jury finding that they accepted a condition not intending to comply with it?

Food Lion, Inc. v. Capital Cities/ABC, Inc.

United States Court of Appeals for the Fourth Circuit, 1999.
194 F.3d 505.

Before NIEMEYER, MICHAEL, and MOTZ, CIRCUIT JUDGES

■ MICHAEL, CIRCUIT JUDGE:

[Producers of ABC's PrimeTime Live decided to conduct an undercover investigation of allegations of unsanitary meat handling practices at Food Lion stores. They authorized ABC reporters Lynne Dale (Lynne Litt at the time) and Susan Barnett to apply for jobs with the grocery chain, submitting applications with false identities and references and fictitious local addresses. The applications failed to mention the reporters' concurrent employment with ABC and otherwise misrepresented their educational and employment experiences. Based on these applications, a South Carolina Food Lion store hired Barnett as a deli clerk, and a North Carolina Food Lion store hired Dale as a meat wrapper trainee. Barnett worked for Food Lion for two weeks, and Dale for one week. They used tiny cameras ("lipstick" cameras, for example) and microphones concealed on their bodies to secretly record 45 hours of footage of Food Lion employees treating, wrapping and labeling meat, cleaning machinery, and discussing the practices of the meat department.

PrimeTime Live eventually broadcast a program including videotape that appeared to show Food Lion employees repackaging and redating fish that had passed the expiration date, grinding expired beef with fresh beef, and applying barbeque sauce to chicken past its expiration date in order to mask the smell and sell it as fresh in the gourmet food section. The program included statements by former Food Lion employees alleging even more serious mishandling of meat at Food Lion stores in several states. The truth of the PrimeTime Live broadcast was not an issue in the litigation.

Food Lion sued ABC and the PrimeTime Live producers and reporters (the "ABC defendants") for fraud, breach of the duty of loyalty, trespass, and unfair trade practices. It sought to recover (1) administrative costs and wages paid in connection with the employment of Dale and Barnett, (2) broadcast (publication) damages for matters such as loss of good will, lost sales and profits, and diminished stock value, and (3) punitive damages. The jury found all of the ABC defendants liable to Food Lion for fraud and violation of the North Carolina Unfair and Deceptive Trade Practices Act (UTPA). It found Dale and Barnett liable for trespass and breach of the duty of loyalty. The district court ruled that damages allegedly incurred by Food Lion as a result of ABC's broadcast of PrimeTime Live—"lost profits, lost sales, diminished stock value or anything of that nature"—could not be recovered because these damages were not proximately caused by the tortious acts of the defendants. The jury awarded Food Lion $1,400 in compensatory damages on its fraud claim, $1.00 each on its duty of loyalty and trespass claims, and $1,500 on its UTPA claim. The jury awarded $5,545,750 in punitive damages on the fraud claim against ABC and its two producers, Kaplan and Rosen, but did not award punitive damages against the reporters. In post-trial proceedings the district court ruled that the punitive damages award was excessive, and Food Lion accepted a remittitur to a total of $315,000. After trial the ABC defendants moved for judgment as a matter of law on all claims, the motion was denied, and the defendants appealed. Food Lion cross-appealed, contesting the district court's ruling that the damages the grocery chain sought as a result of the PrimeTime Live broadcast were not recoverable in this action.]

. . .

II.   [A.]

1.

[The court held 2–1 that Food Lion could not recover for fraud. Food Lion alleged that it spent money hiring and training the ABC employees in reliance on implied representations that they were bona fide applicants who would work more than a week or two. The majority said Food Lion could not have expected Litt and Barnett to work for any particular length of time because they were at-will employees, and Food Lion therefore could not claim to have reasonably relied on their misrepresentations when it incurred these costs. Food Lion also alleged that it was fraudulently induced to pay them wages by their implied representations that they were loyal employees working in Food Lion's interests. But the majority said Food Lion paid the employees because they did the work, not because of statements on their applications, and the misrepresentations therefore were not the proximate cause of the wages paid.]

2.

ABC argues that Dale and Barnett cannot be held liable for a breach of duty of loyalty to Food Lion under existing tort law in North and South Carolina. . . .

. . . Up to now, disloyal conduct by an employee has been considered tortious in North and South Carolina in three circumstances. First, the tort of breach of duty of loyalty applies when an employee competes directly with her employer, either on her own or as an agent of a rival company. [ ] Second, the tort applies when the employee misappropriates her employer's profits, property, or business opportunities. [ ] Third, the tort applies when the employee breaches her employer's confidences. [ ]

Because Dale and Barnett did not compete with Food Lion, misappropriate any of its profits or opportunities, or breach its confidences, ABC argues that the reporters did not engage in any disloyal conduct that is tortious under existing law. Indeed, the district court acknowledged that it was the first court to hold that the conduct in question "would be recognized by the Supreme Courts of North Carolina and South Carolina" as tortiously violating the duty of loyalty. [ ] We believe the district court was correct to conclude that those courts would decide today that the reporters' conduct was sufficient to breach the duty of loyalty and trigger tort liability.

What Dale and Barnett did verges on the kind of employee activity that has already been determined to be tortious. The interests of the employer (ABC) to whom Dale and Barnett gave complete loyalty were adverse to the interests of Food Lion, the employer to whom they were unfaithful. ABC and Food Lion were not business competitors but they were adverse in a fundamental way. ABC's interest was to expose Food Lion to the public as a food chain that engaged in unsanitary and deceptive practices. Dale and Barnett served ABC's interest, at the expense of Food Lion, by engaging in the taping for ABC while they were on Food Lion's payroll. In doing this, Dale and Barnett did not serve Food Lion faithfully, and their interest (which was the same as ABC's) was diametrically opposed to Food Lion's. In these circumstances, we believe that the highest courts of North and South Carolina would hold that the reporters—in promoting the interests of one master, ABC, to the detriment of a second, Food Lion—committed the tort of disloyalty against Food Lion.

. . .

3.

. . .

In North and South Carolina, as elsewhere, it is a trespass to enter upon another's land without consent. [ ] Accordingly, consent is a defense to a claim of trespass. [ ] Even consent gained by misrepresentation is sometimes sufficient. See *Desnick* [ ]. The consent to enter is canceled out, however, "if a wrongful act is done in excess of and in abuse of authorized entry." [ ]

We turn first to whether Dale and Barnett's consent to be in nonpublic areas of Food Lion property was void from the outset because of the resume misrepresentations. "Consent to an entry is often given legal effect" even though it was obtained by misrepresentation or concealed intentions. [*Desnick*]. Without this result, a restaurant critic could not conceal his identity when he ordered a meal, or a browser pretend to be interested in merchandise that he could not afford to buy. Dinner guests would be trespassers if they were false friends who never would have been invited had the host known their true character, and a consumer who in an effort to bargain down an automobile dealer falsely claimed to be able to buy the same car elsewhere at a lower price would be a trespasser in a dealer's showroom. [Id.]

We like *Desnick*'s thoughtful analysis about when a consent to enter that is based on misrepresentation may be given effect. In *Desnick* ABC sent persons posing as patients needing eye care to the plaintiffs' eye clinics, and the test patients secretly recorded their examinations. Some of the recordings were used in a PrimeTime Live segment that alleged intentional misdiagnosis and unnecessary cataract surgery. *Desnick* held that although the test patients misrepresented their purpose, their consent to enter was still valid because they did not invade "any of the specific interests[relating to peaceable possession of land] the tort of trespass seeks to protect:" the test patients entered offices "open to anyone expressing a desire for ophthalmic services" and videotaped doctors engaged in professional discussions with strangers, the testers; the testers did not disrupt the offices or invade anyone's private space; and the testers did not reveal the "intimate details of anybody's life." [ ] *Desnick* supported its conclusion with the following comparison:

"Testers" who pose as prospective home buyers in order to gather evidence of housing discrimination are not trespassers even if they are private persons not acting under color of law. The situation of [ABC's] "testers" is analogous. Like testers seeking evidence of violation of anti-discrimination laws, [ABC's] test patients gained entry into the plaintiffs' premises by misrepresenting their purposes (more precisely by a misleading omission to disclose those purposes). But the entry was not invasive in the sense of infringing the kind of interest of the plaintiffs that the law of trespass protects; it was not an interference with the ownership or possession of land. [ ]

We return to the jury's first trespass finding in this case, which rested on a narrow ground. The jury found that Dale and Barnett were trespassers because they entered Food Lion's premises as employees with consent given because of the misrepresentations in their job applications. Although the consent cases as a class are inconsistent, we have not found any case suggesting that consent based on a resume misrepresentation turns a successful job applicant into a trespasser the moment she enters the employer's premises to begin work. Moreover, if we turned successful resume fraud into trespass, we would not be protecting the interest underlying the tort of trespass—the ownership and peaceable possession

of land. See [*Desnick*]. Accordingly, we cannot say that North and South
Carolina's highest courts would hold that misrepresentation on a job
application alone nullifies the consent given to an employee to enter the
employer's property, thereby turning the employee into a trespasser. The
jury's finding of trespass therefore cannot be sustained on the grounds of
resume misrepresentation.

There is a problem, however, with what Dale and Barnett did after
they entered Food Lion's property. The jury also found that the reporters
committed trespass by breaching their duty of loyalty to Food Lion "as a
result of pursuing [their] investigation for ABC." We affirm the finding
of trespass on this ground because the breach of duty of loyalty—
triggered by the filming in non-public areas, which was adverse to Food
Lion—was a wrongful act in excess of Dale and Barnett's authority to
enter Food Lion's premises as employees. [ ]

. . .

. . . [T]he South Carolina courts make clear that the law of trespass
protects the peaceable enjoyment of property. [ ] It is consistent with that
principle to hold that consent to enter is vitiated by a wrongful act that
exceeds and abuses the privilege of entry.

Here, both Dale and Barnett became employees of Food Lion with
the certain consequence that they would breach their implied promises
to serve Food Lion faithfully. They went into areas of the stores that were
not open to the public and secretly videotaped, an act that was directly
adverse to the interests of their second employer, Food Lion. Thus, they
breached the duty of loyalty, thereby committing a wrongful act in abuse
of their authority to be on Food Lion's property.

. . .

4.

[The court reversed the finding of liability under the North Carolina
Unfair and Deceptive Trade Practices Act on the ground that the statute,
the primary purpose of which was to protect consumers, was available to
business plaintiffs only if they were competitors of the defendant or were
engaged in business dealings with the defendant.]

B.

ABC argues that even if state tort law covers some of Dale and
Barnett's conduct, the district court erred in refusing to subject Food
Lion's claims to any level of First Amendment scrutiny. ABC makes this
argument because Dale and Barnett were engaged in newsgathering for
PrimeTime Live. It is true that there are "First Amendment interests in
newsgathering." In re Shain, 978 F.2d 850, 855 (4th Cir. 1992) (Wilkinson
J., concurring). See also Branzburg v. Hayes ("without some protection
for seeking out the news, freedom of the press could be eviscerated.").
However, the Supreme Court has said in no uncertain terms that
"generally applicable laws do not offend the First Amendment simply

because their enforcement against the press has incidental effects on its ability to gather and report the news." *Cohen v. Cowles Media Co.*; see also *Desnick*, [ ] ("the media have no general immunity from tort or contract liability").

. . .

The key inquiry in *Cowles* was whether the law of promissory estoppel was a generally applicable law. The Court began its analysis with some examples of generally applicable laws that must be obeyed by the press, such as those relating to copyright, labor, antitrust, and tax. [ ] More relevant to us, "the press may not with impunity break and enter an office or dwelling to gather news." [ ] In analyzing the doctrine of promissory estoppel, the Court determined that it was a law of general applicability because it "does not target or single out the press," but instead applies "to the daily transactions of all the citizens of Minnesota." [ ] The Court concluded that "the First Amendment does not confer on the press a constitutional right to disregard promises that would otherwise be enforced under state law." [ ] The Court thus refused to apply any heightened scrutiny to the enforcement of Minnesota's promissory estoppel law against the newspapers.

The torts Dale and Barnett committed, breach of the duty of loyalty and trespass, fit neatly into the *Cowles* framework. Neither tort targets or singles out the press. Each applies to the daily transactions of the citizens of North and South Carolina. If, for example, an employee of a competing grocery chain hired on with Food Lion and videotaped damaging information in Food Lion's non-public areas for later disclosure to the public, these tort laws would apply with the same force as they do against Dale and Barnett here. Nor do we believe that applying these laws against the media will have more than an "incidental effect" on newsgathering. See *Cowles,* [ ]. We are convinced that the media can do its important job effectively without resort to the commission of run-of-the-mill torts.[5]

ABC argues that *Cowles* is not to be applied automatically to every "generally applicable law" because the Supreme Court has since said that "the enforcement of [such a] law may or may not be subject to heightened scrutiny under the First Amendment." [*Turner I*] (contrasting Barnes v. Glen Theatre, Inc., 501 U.S. 560 [ ] (1991), and *Cowles*). In *Glen Theatre* nude dancing establishments and their dancers challenged a generally applicable law prohibiting public nudity. Because the general ban on public nudity covered nude dancing, which was expressive conduct, the Supreme Court applied heightened scrutiny. [ ] In *Cowles* a generally applicable law (promissory estoppel) was invoked against newspapers who broke their promises to a source that they would keep his name confidential in exchange for information leading to a news story. There,

---

[5] Indeed, the ABC News Policy Manual states that "news gathering of whatever sort does not include any license to violate the law."

the Court refused to apply heightened scrutiny, concluding that application of the doctrine of promissory estoppel had "no more than [an] incidental" effect on the press's ability to gather or report news. [ ] There is arguable tension between the approaches in the two cases. The cases are consistent, however, if we view the challenged conduct in *Cowles* to be the breach of promise and not some form of expression. In *Glen Theatre*, on the other hand, an activity directly covered by the law, nude dancing, necessarily involved expression, and heightened scrutiny was applied. Here, as in *Cowles*, heightened scrutiny does not apply because the tort laws (breach of duty of loyalty and trespass) do not single out the press or have more than an incidental effect upon its work.

C.

For the foregoing reasons, we affirm the judgment that Dale and Barnett breached their duty of loyalty to Food Lion and committed trespass. We likewise affirm the damages award against them for these torts in the amount of $2.00. We have already indicated that the fraud claim against all of the ABC defendants must be reversed. Because Food Lion was awarded punitive damages only on its fraud claim, the judgment awarding punitive damages cannot stand.

. . .

■ NIEMEYER, CIRCUIT JUDGE, concurring in part and dissenting in part:

[Judge Niemeyer dissented only from the portion of the opinion denying recovery for fraud (and hence for punitive damages). He argued that Food Lion had relied to its detriment on the ABC employees' misrepresentations.]

. . .

Applicants for employment, even at-will employment, present themselves representing by implication: (1) that they want to become employees; (2) that they intend to work indefinitely, until a change in circumstances leads them or their employer to terminate the arrangement; (3) that there is a possibility that they would become long-term employees; and (4) that they will be loyal employees as long as they work, prepared to work at the promotion of their employer's business. ABC's undercover reporters presented themselves to Food Lion, representing all of these matters falsely. . . .

. . .

. . . Food Lion had less of a chance—indeed, no chance—of developing experienced, long-term, and loyal employees because the likelihood of that possibility was misrepresented. If these employees had disclosed their true identities and intentions accurately, Food Lion would never have hired them and incurred expenses to train them on the chance that they would stay because the employees had already determined there was no such chance. . . .

NOTES AND QUESTIONS

1.   What types of undercover newsgathering operations can be undertaken without potential liability after this decision? Can a reporter pose as an employee without breaching the duty of loyalty? Surreptitiously tape without exceeding the scope of consent and thereby becoming a trespasser?

2.   Does the duty of loyalty preclude bona fide employees from giving media information adverse to the interests of the employer?

3.   Consent obtained through misrepresentation normally is ineffective. What policies support the exception recognized in *Desnick* and applied here? Would similar policies support an exception to the employee's duty of loyalty?

4.   What was the "wrongful act" that exceeded the scope of the ABC employees' consent to enter Food Lion's nonpublic areas? Is surreptitious newsgathering itself a "wrongful act"? Would an undercover journalist commit a wrongful act for these purposes by taking notes for a story adverse to the landowner? By making mental notes for that purpose?

5.   Can *Cowles* be properly viewed as a case in which the challenged conduct was "breach of promise and not some form of expression"? The newspapers in that case breached their promise to Cohen by publishing his name. Why is the act of publishing not "some form of expression"?

F. NEGLIGENCE

As we saw in Chapter Six, courts rarely permit liability for harms caused by *publication or broadcast* unless something more than ordinary negligence is shown. In a few cases in which media have been sued for negligently causing harm through their *newsgathering* efforts, courts have been more receptive to negligence-based liability.

Clift v. Narragansett Television. Clift v. Narragansett Television L.P., 688 A.2d 805 (R.I. 1996), held that "everyone, including the press, should be answerable for unprivileged negligent actions that proximately result in suicide." *Clift* involved an unusual set of facts. A mentally ill man who was threatening to kill himself became involved in a stand-off with police. Without informing the police, a reporter for a television station called the man's home and interviewed him on air. A few minutes after the interview, the man killed himself. The man's wife and children brought suit against the television station, alleging various causes of action, including negligence. The trial judge granted summary judgment on the negligence claim in favor of the television station, and the plaintiff appealed.

The Supreme Court of Rhode Island reversed. The court recognized that the case raised "fundamental First Amendment considerations," but stated that those considerations could be adequately addressed by restricting liability to "uncontrollable impulse" cases: defendants may be held liable if their negligence causes a person to suffer delirium or insanity resulting in an "uncontrollable impulse" to commit suicide. The court found that the plaintiff had alleged facts "that suggest that the decedent's suicide resulted from an uncontrollable impulse that was brought about by a delirium or insanity caused by [the reporter's] negligence." As a result, the court reinstated not only the plaintiffs' negligence claim, but also the derivative claims for wrongful death, loss of consortium, and loss of companionship.

The court held that the television station was entitled to summary judgment on plaintiffs' invasion of privacy claims. The decedent's claim did not survive his death, and the family members could claim no invasion based on a single call to which the decedent consented or on the broadcast of the "newsworthy" interview. The court also held that the trial court had properly dismissed plaintiffs' intentional infliction of emotional distress claims. There was no evidence that defendants intended to cause injury nor that they were a substantial factor in bringing it about, a requirement in suicide cases. Moreover, the plaintiffs had alleged no physical symptoms of emotional distress. A dissenting judge would have reinstated the intentional infliction claim; he argued that plaintiffs should not be required to allege physical symptoms in intentional infliction cases.

The Branch Davidian Case. A federal district judge held that media could be liable for deaths and injuries of federal agents if the media negligently alerted the Branch Davidians to an impending raid on the sect's compound near Waco, Texas. A suit filed by agents injured in the raid and survivors of four agents killed in the raid alleged that members of the sect learned from local television and newspaper staffers that federal officers were about to raid the compound. A television station employee allegedly inadvertently tipped off the Davidians by asking directions of a motorist he encountered in the vicinity of the compound just before the raid; the motorist happened to be a member of the sect. The suit also alleged that the newspaper and the television station were negligent in failing to conceal their presence as they drove back and forth on the road in front of the compound in anticipation of a raid they knew was supposed to be a surprise. (An accusation that a newspaper reporter was responsible for tipping off the Davidians was the basis of the libel case WFAA-TV v. McLemore highlighted in Chapter Four.)

Although he acknowledged that there were no precedents holding journalists liable for such negligence, the judge denied the media motions for summary judgment. "It was arguably foreseeable to the newspaper and KWTX that the failure to provide any guidelines or instructions to the reporters sent to the scene could result in the Davidians being alerted to the impending raid." It was a jury question whether the decision of the law enforcement agency to proceed after it knew that the surprise element had been lost meant that any media negligence was not the proximate cause of the harm. Risenhoover v. England, 936 F.Supp. 392

(W.D. Tex. 1996). After their summary judgment motions were denied, the newspaper, the television station, and an ambulance service that allegedly tipped off the media settled for an undisclosed amount.

If negligence ordinarily is not a permissible basis of liability when the harm results from publication, why is it permissible in these newsgathering cases? Are the free speech implications of imposing liability in these cases significantly weaker?

G. DAMAGES

Damages may be awarded for tortious newsgathering even if the information obtained is never published or broadcast. As the preceding cases in this chapter indicate, however, plaintiffs often seek damages for both the newsgathering tort and subsequent disclosure of the information. Whether such damages are recoverable depends on the answers to two questions: (1) does the tort law permit them? (2) does the First Amendment permit them? Courts are in disagreement as to both questions.

1. TORT LAW

In Costlow v. Cusimano, 34 A.D.2d 196 (N.Y. App. Div. 1970), the court held that publication damages are not available in a trespass case. Plaintiffs alleged that their two children suffocated in a refrigerator located at the family's residence; that defendant, hoping to sell an article about the deaths, arrived at the scene and photographed the premises and the bodies of the children; and that the photographs were published, causing plaintiffs intense emotional distress. The court held that since the articles were newsworthy, no claim could be based on their publication. It then held that the only remedies for any trespass to the premises were nominal and punitive damages: "There is no support for plaintiffs' argument that damages for injury to reputation and for emotional disturbance are recoverable on the alleged facts as the natural consequence of the trespass. . . . [D]amages for trespass are limited to consequences flowing from the interference with possession and not for separable acts more properly allocated under other categories of liability."

But in Prahl v. Brosamle, 295 N.W.2d 768 (Wis. Ct. App. 1980), the court disagreed, citing the Restatement (Second) of Torts § 162, which provides, "A trespass on land subjects the trespasser to liability for physical harm to the possessor of the land at the time of the trespass, or to the land or to his things, or to members of his household or to their things, caused by any act done, activity carried on, or condition created by the trespasser . . . " The court interpreted this as extending a trespasser's traditional liability to include nonphysical harm subsequent to the trespass. "The extension to include nonphysical harm from an intrusion of the type involved is reasonable. To allow only nominal damages under the circumstances presented because of lack of physical harm would permit the trespasser to enjoy the benefits of his tort without fully compensating a plaintiff for his loss."

2.   FIRST AMENDMENT CONSIDERATIONS

As noted earlier, courts hold that the First Amendment does not protect tortious newsgathering. There is no unanimity, however, as to whether the First Amendment permits the damages to be increased to take into account harm caused by the subsequent publication.

Dietemann v. Time Inc. In this case, described in the *Sanders* opinion, the Ninth Circuit affirmed an award of $1,000 for intrusion. Time argued that even if an award for damages from the intrusion was proper, the award could not include compensation for harm resulting from the publication because that would violate the First Amendment. The court rejected the argument:

> Defendant relies upon the line of cases commencing with New York Times Co. v. Sullivan, [ ] . . . to sustain its contentions that (1) publication of news, however tortiously gathered, insulates defendant from liability for the antecedent tort, and (2) even if it is not thus shielded from liability, those cases prevent consideration of publication as an element in computing damages.

> As we previously observed, publication is not an essential element of plaintiff's cause of action. Moreover, it is not the foundation for the invocation of a privilege. Privilege concepts developed in defamation cases and to some extent in privacy actions in which publication is an essential component are not relevant in determining liability for intrusion conduct antedating publication. [ ] Nothing in *New York Times* or its progeny suggests anything to the contrary. Indeed, the Court strongly indicates that there is no First Amendment interest in protecting news media from calculated misdeeds. [ ]

> No interest protected by the First Amendment is adversely affected by permitting damages for intrusion to be enhanced by the fact of later publication of the information that the publisher improperly acquired. Assessing damages for the additional emotional distress suffered by a plaintiff when the wrongfully acquired data are purveyed to the multitude chills intrusive acts. It does not chill freedom of expression guaranteed by the First Amendment. A rule forbidding the use of publication as an ingredient of damages would deny to the injured plaintiff recovery for real harm done to him without any countervailing benefit to the legitimate interest of the public in being informed. The same rule would encourage conduct by news media that grossly offends ordinary men.

Dietemann v. Time Inc., 449 F.2d 245 (9th Cir. 1971).

A very different view was expressed in Pearson v. Dodd, 410 F.2d 701 (D.C. Cir. 1969). In that case, aides to Senator Thomas Dodd secretly removed documents from his files, made copies of them, and then delivered them to newspaper columnists Drew Pearson and Jack Anderson, who published them. Dodd claimed invasion of privacy and conversion. Assuming that the senator's aides committed tortious intrusions, the court nonetheless concluded that no liability attached to the defendant even though they received the documents "knowing" they "had been removed without authorization:"

> ... [I]njuries from intrusion and injuries from publication should be kept clearly separate. Where there is intrusion, the intruder should generally be liable whatever the content of what he learns. An eavesdropper to the marital bedroom may hear marital intimacies, or he may hear statements of fact or opinion of legitimate interest to the public; for purposes of liability that should make no difference. On the other hand, where the claim is that private information concerning plaintiff has been published, the question of whether that information is genuinely private or is of public interest should not turn on the manner in which it has been obtained. Of course, both forms of invasion may be combined in the same case.

> Here we have separately considered the nature of appellants' publications concerning appellee, and have found that the matter published was of obvious public interest. The publication was not itself an invasion of privacy. Since we have also concluded that appellants' role in obtaining the information did not make them liable to appellee for intrusion, their subsequent publication, itself no invasion of privacy, cannot reach back to render that role tortious.

In *Dietemann* and *Pearson*, the courts seemed to assume that publication damages were recoverable unless the First Amendment barred them. Those cases were invasion of privacy cases rather than trespass cases; is that a sufficient reason for assuming that the tort law would permit recovery of publication damages?

Recall that the majority in *Shulman*, the California traffic accident case, held that although the broadcasters' intrusion was actionable, no liability could be imposed for the disclosure of private facts resulting from the intrusion. In the *Sanders* case, the telepsychic case, the award for intrusion was $635,000 and the court noted that "damages from the intrusion were increased by the fact that the intrusion was broadcast." The court rejected ABC's argument that the award could not include damages resulting from the broadcast, but First Amendment issues were not before the court in that case. *Bartnicki*, the case involving the broadcast of the surreptitiously recorded phone conversation, established that at least under some circumstances, publication of tortiously obtained information may enjoy First Amendment protection so long as the publisher is not the tortfeasor. Which is the better view?

Food Lion. If publication damages are recoverable in cases involving tortious newsgathering, that might give some plaintiffs a way to circumvent the constitutional obstacles they would face if they sued for the publication itself. This was a consideration in the *Food Lion* case:

> In its cross-appeal Food Lion argues that the district court erred in refusing to allow it to use its non-reputational tort claims (breach of duty of loyalty, trespass, etc.) to recover compensatory damages for ABC's broadcast of the PrimeTime Live program that targeted Food Lion. The publication damages Food Lion sought (or alleged) were for items relating to its reputation, such as loss of good will and lost sales. The district court determined that the publication damages claimed by Food Lion "were the direct result of diminished consumer confidence in the store" and that "it was [Food Lion's] food handling practices themselves—not the method by which they were recorded or published—which caused the loss of consumer confidence." [ ] The court therefore concluded that the publication damages were not proximately caused by the non-reputational torts committed by ABC's employees. We do not reach the matter of proximate cause because an overriding (and settled) First Amendment principle precludes the award of publication damages in this case, as ABC has argued to the district court and to us. Food Lion attempted to avoid the First Amendment limitations on defamation claims by seeking publication damages under non-reputational tort claims, while holding to the normal state law proof standards for these torts. This is precluded by Hustler Magazine v. Falwell [discussed here in Chapter Six].

> Food Lion acknowledges that it did not sue for defamation because its "ability to bring an action for defamation [ ] required proof that ABC acted with actual malice." [ ] Food Lion thus understood that if it sued ABC for defamation it would have to prove that the PrimeTime Live broadcast contained a false statement of fact that was made with "actual malice," that is, with knowledge that it was false or with reckless disregard as to whether it was true or false. See New York Times Co. v. Sullivan. It is clear that Food Lion was not prepared to offer proof meeting the *New York Times* standard under any claim that it might assert. What Food Lion sought to do, then, was to recover defamation-type damages under non-reputational tort claims, without satisfying the stricter (First Amendment)

standards of a defamation claim. We believe that such an end-
run around First Amendment strictures is foreclosed by *Hustler*.

. . .

Food Lion argues that *Cowles*, supra, and not *Hustler*
governs its claim for publication damages. According to Food
Lion, *Cowles* allowed the plaintiff to recover—without satisfying
the constitutional prerequisites to a defamation action—
economic losses for publishing the plaintiff's identity in violation
of a legal duty arising from generally applicable law. Food Lion
says that its claim for damages is like the plaintiff's in *Cowles*,
and not like Falwell's in *Hustler*. This argument fails because
the Court in *Cowles* distinguished the damages sought there
from those in *Hustler* in a way that also distinguishes Food
Lion's case from *Cowles*:

> Cohen is not seeking damages for injury to his reputation
> or his state of mind. He sought damages . . . for breach of a
> promise that caused him to lose his job and lowered his
> earning capacity. Thus, this is not a case like *Hustler* . . .
> where we held that the constitutional libel standards apply
> to a claim alleging that the publication of a parody was a
> state-law tort of intentional infliction of emotional distress. [ ]

Food Lion, in seeking compensation for matters such as loss
of good will and lost sales, is claiming reputational damages
from publication, which the *Cowles* Court distinguished by
placing them in the same category as the emotional distress
damages sought by Falwell in *Hustler*. In other words, according
to *Cowles*, "constitutional libel standards" apply to damage
claims for reputational injury from a publication such as the one
here.

Food Lion also argues that because ABC obtained the
videotapes through unlawful acts, that is, the torts of breach of
duty of loyalty and trespass, it (Food Lion) is entitled to
publication damages without meeting the *New York Times*
standard. The Supreme Court has never suggested that it would
dispense with the Times standard in this situation, and we
believe *Hustler* indicates that the Court would not. In *Hustler*
the magazine's conduct would have been sufficient to constitute
an unlawful act, the intentional infliction of emotional distress,
if state law standards of proof had applied. Indeed, the Court
said, "generally speaking the law does not regard the intent to
inflict emotional distress as one which should receive much
solicitude." *Hustler* [ ]. Notwithstanding the nature of the
underlying act, the Court held that satisfying *New York Times*
was a prerequisite to the recovery of publication damages. That
result was "necessary," the Court concluded, in order "to give

adequate 'breathing space' to the freedoms protected by the First Amendment." [ ]

In sum, Food Lion could not bypass the *New York Times* standard if it wanted publication damages. The district court therefore reached the correct result when it disallowed these damages, although we affirm on a different ground.

Food Lion, Inc. v. Capital Cities/ABC Inc., 194 F.3d 505 (4th Cir. 1999). Note that the trial court avoided the constitutional issue by denying publication damages on the ground of proximate cause. The court of appeals avoided the proximate cause issue by denying publication damages on First Amendment grounds. Which approach is better?

CHAPTER IX

SUBPOENAS AND SEARCHES

Journalists and other researchers and interviewers may possess information that would be useful to the litigants in a civil case, the prosecution or defense in a criminal trial, a grand jury, or a legislative committee. In the absence of some special protection, those who gather information may be subpoenaed to testify and turn over physical evidence such as notes, tapes, computer drives, and photos. Their premises may be searched and their computers seized pursuant to a properly issued warrant. They often resist these attempts to compel disclosure, particularly when they believe the disclosure would violate an obligation of confidentiality.

To resist such compelled disclosures, reporters ("reporter" is used here as shorthand; the person subpoenaed may be an editor, a broadcaster, a blogger or website operator, a photographer, or even a biographer or historian) sometimes claim a privilege like those that protect communications to physicians, clergy, and attorneys.

Maryland recognized a reporter's privilege by statute in 1896, and since then a large majority of the states have enacted privilege statutes. For many years these statutes—and perhaps informal accommodations between the press and the authorities—seem to have averted most confrontations over compulsory disclosure.

In the late 1960s and early 1970s, the number of confrontations multiplied, primarily because the U.S. Department of Justice began to subpoena reporters frequently. Because there was no federal privilege statute, reporters were forced to articulate First Amendment objections to these subpoenas. The issue reached the Supreme Court in 1972 in the three cases decided as *Branzburg v. Hayes*.

Through most of the twentieth century, it was comparatively easy to decide who was eligible for the "reporter's privilege." There were occasional disputes as to freelancers and scholars, but generally the claimants were employees of newspapers, magazines, and television outlets. In the twenty-first century, the eligibility question became more troublesome as more individuals not affiliated with conventional media asserted that they too were journalists and should get the benefit of the privilege.

The jurisprudence protecting journalists from compelled disclosure is exceedingly complex. Sometimes protection is based on the First Amendment, sometimes on a statute or state constitutional law, and sometimes on the common law. Another important variable is the nature of the disclosure sought—confidential or nonconfidential, published or unpublished, personal observation or second-hand account. Another is the type of proceeding in which disclosure is sought—grand jury investigation, criminal prosecution, criminal defense, civil litigation, or other proceeding. Yet another is whether the reporter (or his or her employer) is a party to the proceeding in which disclosure is sought. Should a reporter be forced to betray the confidence of a whistleblower who exposes corruption in government? To disclose the source of a false and defamatory gossip item? To testify as to what he or she saw at the site of a disaster? To give testimony that might exonerate a criminal defendant? To reveal, as a defendant in a libel case, the source of the defamatory material? These variables may be treated differently from state to state, and even from one federal circuit to another.

A. REPORTER'S PRIVILEGE: THE CONCEPT

The arguments against compelled disclosure by reporters are rarely spelled out in "shield" statutes or in cases applying them. Lawyers for reporters who had no statutory protection were forced to articulate those arguments, however, when they first asked the Supreme Court to find protection in the First Amendment.

Branzburg v. Hayes (Together with In re Pappas and United States v. Caldwell)

Supreme Court of the United States, 1972.
408 U.S. 665.

[This was a consolidation of separate cases involving demands on three reporters by grand juries. One was a federal grand jury, and there was (and still is) no federal shield statute. The others were state grand juries, one in Massachusetts, which had no shield statute, the other in Kentucky, whose statute was held inapplicable to the particular disclosures sought.

One of the reporters, Branzburg, was involved in two cases. In the first, he had written a newspaper article about persons supposedly using a chemical process to change marijuana into hashish. In response to a subpoena, he appeared before a grand jury but refused to identify the individuals he had observed. The judge rejected his claims of privilege and ordered him to answer. The Kentucky Court of Appeals denied relief, construing the Kentucky shield statute to protect the identity of a person who supplied information to a reporter in confidence, but not of a person whose activities the reporter had observed personally.

Branzburg's second case arose out of a later story he wrote after interviewing drug users and observing them smoke marijuana. Subpoenaed again by the grand jury, he filed a motion to quash, arguing that he should not be required even to enter the grand jury room because "[o]nce Mr. Branzburg is required to go behind the closed doors of the Grand Jury room, his effectiveness as a reporter in these areas is totally destroyed." The trial court issued an order protecting him from revealing "confidential associations, sources or information" but requiring that he "answer any questions which concern or pertain to any criminal act" he had personally observed. The Kentucky Court of Appeals again denied relief.

In *Pappas,* a Massachusetts television reporter recorded and photographed statements of local Black Panther Party officials during a period of racial turmoil. He was allowed to enter the party's headquarters to cover an expected police raid in return for his promise to disclose nothing he observed within. He stayed three hours, no raid occurred, and he broadcast no story. He was summoned before the county grand jury but refused to answer any questions about what had taken place while he was there. When he was recalled, he moved to quash the second summons. The motion was denied by the trial judge, who noted the absence of a statutory newsman's privilege in Massachusetts and denied the existence of a constitutional privilege. The Supreme Judicial Court of Massachusetts affirmed.

In the third case, Caldwell had been assigned by The New York Times to cover the Black Panther Party and other black militant groups. He was subpoenaed to testify before a federal grand jury in connection with alleged crimes by the militants, including mail fraud and threats to assassinate the President. The district court denied his motion to quash the subpoena but issued a protective order limiting the questioning to information given to Caldwell for publication and prohibiting questions that would require him to reveal confidential associations, sources, or information. Caldwell still refused to testify on the ground that requiring him to appear in secret before the grand jury would destroy his working relationship with the Black Panthers. He was held in contempt, but the court of appeals reversed, holding that he had a First Amendment privilege to refuse to appear before the grand jury in the absence of some special showing of necessity.]

■ Opinion of the Court by JUSTICE WHITE. . . .

II.

. . . Although the newsmen in these cases do not claim an absolute privilege against official interrogation in all circumstances, they assert that the reporter should not be forced either to appear or to testify before a grand jury or at trial until and unless sufficient grounds are shown for believing that the reporter possesses information relevant to a crime the grand jury is investigating, that the information the reporter has is unavailable from other sources, and that the need for the information is sufficiently compelling to override the claimed invasion of First Amendment interests occasioned by the disclosure. Principally relied upon are prior cases emphasizing the importance of the First Amendment guarantees to individual development and to our system of representative government, decisions requiring that official action with adverse impact on First Amendment rights be justified by a public interest that is "compelling" or "paramount," and those precedents establishing the principle that justifiable governmental goals may not be achieved by unduly broad means having an unnecessary impact on protected rights of speech, press, or association. The heart of the claim is that the burden on news gathering resulting from compelling reporters to disclose confidential information outweighs any public interest in obtaining the information.

We do not question the significance of free speech, press, or assembly to the country's welfare. Nor is it suggested that news gathering does not qualify for First Amendment protection; without some protection for seeking out the news, freedom of the press could be eviscerated. But these cases involve no intrusions upon speech or assembly, no prior restraint or restriction on what the press may publish, and no express or implied command that the press publish what it prefers to withhold. No exaction or tax for the privilege of publishing, and no penalty, civil or criminal, related to the content of published material is at issue here. The use of confidential sources by the press is not forbidden or restricted; reporters remain free to seek news from any source by means within the law. No attempt is made to require the press to publish its sources of information or indiscriminately to disclose them on request.

The sole issue before us is the obligation of reporters to respond to grand jury subpoenas as other citizens do and to answer questions relevant to an investigation into the commission of crime. . . .

It has generally been held that the First Amendment does not guarantee the press a constitutional right of special access to information not available to the public generally. [ ]. In Zemel v. Rusk, [381 U.S. 1 (1965)], for example, the Court sustained the Government's refusal to validate passports to Cuba even though that restriction "render[ed] less than wholly free the flow of information concerning that country." Id. at 16. The ban on travel was held constitutional, for "[t]he right to speak and publish does not carry with it the unrestrained right to gather information." [ ][22]

Despite the fact that news gathering may be hampered, the press is regularly excluded from grand jury proceedings, our own conferences, the meetings of other official bodies gathered in executive session, and the meetings of private organizations. Newsmen have no constitutional right of access to the scenes of crime or disaster when the general public is excluded, and they may be prohibited from attending or publishing

---

[22] "There are few restrictions on action which could not be clothed by ingenious argument in the garb of decreased data flow. For example, the prohibition of unauthorized entry into the White House diminishes the citizen's opportunities to gather information he might find relevant to his opinion of the way the country is being run, but that does not make entry into the White House a First Amendment right." 381 U.S. at 16–17.

information about trials if such restrictions are necessary to assure a defendant a fair trial before an impartial tribunal. . . .

It is thus not surprising that the great weight of authority is that newsmen are not exempt from the normal duty of appearing before a grand jury and answering questions relevant to a criminal investigation. At common law, courts consistently refused to recognize the existence of any privilege authorizing a newsman to refuse to reveal confidential information to a grand jury. . . .

The prevailing constitutional view of the newsman's privilege is very much rooted in the ancient role of the grand jury that has the dual function of determining if there is probable cause to believe that a crime has been committed and of protecting citizens against unfounded criminal prosecutions. . . . Because its task is to inquire into the existence of possible criminal conduct and to return only well-founded indictments, its investigative powers are necessarily broad. . . .

A number of States have provided newsmen a statutory privilege of varying breadth, but the majority have not done so, and none has been provided by federal statute. Until now the only testimonial privilege for unofficial witnesses that is rooted in the Federal Constitution is the Fifth Amendment privilege against compelled self-incrimination. We are asked to create another by interpreting the First Amendment to grant newsmen a testimonial privilege that other citizens do not enjoy. This we decline to do. Fair and effective law enforcement aimed at providing security for the person and property of the individual is a fundamental function of government, and the grand jury plays an important, constitutionally mandated role in this process. On the records now before us, we perceive no basis for holding that the public interest in law enforcement and in ensuring effective grand jury proceedings is insufficient to override the consequential, but uncertain, burden on news gathering that is said to result from insisting that reporters, like other citizens, respond to relevant questions put to them in the course of a valid grand jury investigation or criminal trial.

This conclusion itself involves no restraint on what newspapers may publish or on the type or quality of information reporters may seek to acquire, nor does it threaten the vast bulk of confidential relationships between reporters and their sources. Grand juries address themselves to the issues of whether crimes have been committed and who committed them. Only where news sources themselves are implicated in crime or possess information relevant to the grand jury's task need they or the reporter be concerned about grand jury subpoenas. Nothing before us indicates that a large number or percentage of *all* confidential news sources falls into either category and would in any way be deterred by our holding that the Constitution does not, as it never has, exempt the newsman from performing the citizen's normal duty of appearing and furnishing information relevant to the grand jury's task.

The preference for anonymity of those confidential informants involved in actual criminal conduct is presumably a product of their desire to escape criminal prosecution, and this preference, while understandable, is hardly deserving of constitutional protection. It would be frivolous to assert—and no one does in these cases—that the First Amendment, in the interest of securing news or otherwise, confers a license on either the reporter or his news sources to violate valid criminal laws. Although stealing documents or private wiretapping could provide newsworthy information, neither reporter nor source is immune from conviction for such conduct, whatever the impact on the flow of news. Neither is immune, on First Amendment grounds, from testifying against the other, before the grand jury or at a criminal trial. The Amendment does not reach so far as to override the interest of the public in ensuring that neither reporter nor source is invading the rights of other citizens through reprehensible conduct forbidden to all other persons. . . .

Thus, we cannot seriously entertain the notion that the First Amendment protects a newsman's agreement to conceal the criminal conduct of his source, or evidence thereof, on the theory that it is better to write about crime than to do something about it. . . .

There remain those situations where a source is not engaged in criminal conduct but has information suggesting illegal conduct by others. Newsmen frequently receive information from such sources pursuant to a tacit or express agreement to withhold the source's name and suppress any information that the source wishes not published. Such informants presumably desire anonymity in order to avoid being entangled as a witness in a criminal trial or grand jury investigation. They may fear that disclosure will threaten their job security or personal safety or that it will simply result in dishonor or embarrassment.

The argument that the flow of news will be diminished by compelling reporters to aid the grand jury in a criminal investigation is not irrational, nor are the records before us silent on the matter. But we remain unclear how often and to what extent informers are actually deterred from furnishing information when newsmen are forced to testify before a grand jury. The available data indicate that some newsmen rely a great deal on confidential sources and that some informants are particularly sensitive to the threat of exposure and may be silenced if it is held by this Court that, ordinarily, newsmen must testify pursuant to subpoenas, but the evidence fails to demonstrate that there would be a significant constriction of the flow of news to the public if this Court reaffirms the prior common-law and constitutional rule regarding the testimonial obligations of newsmen. Estimates of the inhibiting effect of such subpoenas on the willingness of informants to make disclosures to newsmen are widely divergent and to a great extent speculative. It would be difficult to canvass the views of the informants themselves; surveys of reporters on this topic are chiefly opinions of predicted informant behavior and must be viewed in the light of the professional self-interest of the interviewees.[33] Reliance by the press on confidential informants does not mean that all such sources will in fact dry up because of the later possible appearance of the newsman before a grand jury. The reporter may never be called and if he objects to testifying, the prosecution may not insist. . . . Moreover, grand juries characteristically conduct secret proceedings, and law enforcement officers are themselves experienced in dealing with informers, and have their own methods for protecting them without interference with the effective administration of justice. . . .

Accepting the fact, however, that an undetermined number of informants not themselves implicated in crime will nevertheless, for whatever reason, refuse to talk to newsmen if they fear identification by a reporter in an official investigation, we cannot accept the argument that the public interest in possible future news about crime from undisclosed, unverified sources must take precedence over the public interest in pursuing and prosecuting those crimes reported to the press by informants and in thus deterring the commission of such crimes in the future.

We note first that the privilege claimed is that of the reporter, not the informant, and that if the authorities independently identify the informant, neither his own reluctance to testify nor the objection of the newsman would shield him from grand jury inquiry, whatever the impact on the flow of news or on his future usefulness as a secret source of information. More important, it is obvious that agreements to conceal information relevant to commission of crime have very little to recommend them from the standpoint of public policy. . . . Such conduct deserves no encomium, and we decline now to afford it First Amendment protection by denigrating the duty of a citizen, whether reporter or informer, to respond to grand jury subpoena and answer relevant questions put to him.

. . .

We are admonished that refusal to provide a First Amendment reporter's privilege will undermine the freedom of the press to collect and disseminate news. But this is not the lesson history teaches us. As noted previously, the common law recognized no such privilege, and the constitutional argument was not even asserted until 1958. From the beginning of our country the press has operated without constitutional protection for press informants and the press has flourished. The existing

---

[33] In his Press Subpoenas: An Empirical and Legal Analysis, Study Report of the Reporters' Committee on Freedom of the Press 6–12, Prof. Vince Blasi discusses these methodological problems. Prof. Blasi's survey found that slightly more than half of the 975 reporters questioned said that they relied on regular confidential sources for at least 10% of their stories. Id. at 21. Of this group of reporters, only 8% were able to say with some certainty that their professional functioning had been adversely affected by the threat of subpoena; another 11% were not certain whether or not they had been adversely affected. Id. at 53.

constitutional rules have not been a serious obstacle to either the development or retention of confidential news sources by the press.

It is said that currently press subpoenas have multiplied, that mutual distrust and tension between press and officialdom have increased, that reporting styles have changed, and that there is now more need for confidential sources, particularly where the press seeks news about minority cultural and political groups or dissident organizations suspicious of the law and public officials. These developments, even if true, are treacherous grounds for a far-reaching interpretation of the First Amendment fastening a nationwide rule on courts, grand juries, and prosecuting officials everywhere. . . .

. . .

The privilege claimed here is conditional, not absolute; given the suggested preliminary showings and compelling need, the reporter would be required to testify. Presumably, such a rule would reduce the instances in which reporters could be required to appear, but predicting in advance when and in what circumstances they could be compelled to do so would be difficult. Such a rule would also have implications for the issuance of compulsory process to reporters at civil and criminal trials and at legislative hearings. If newsmen's confidential sources are as sensitive as they are claimed to be, the prospect of being unmasked whenever a judge determines the situation justifies it is hardly a satisfactory solution to the problem. For them it would appear that only an absolute privilege would suffice.

We are unwilling to embark the judiciary on a long and difficult journey to such an uncertain destination. The administration of a constitutional newsman's privilege would present practical and conceptual difficulties of a high order. Sooner or later, it would be necessary to define those categories of newsmen who qualified for the privilege, a questionable procedure in light of the traditional doctrine that liberty of the press is the right of the lonely pamphleteer who uses carbon paper or a mimeograph just as much as of the large metropolitan publisher who utilizes the latest photocomposition methods. . . . The informative function asserted by representatives of the organized press in the present cases is also performed by lecturers, political pollsters, novelists, academic researchers, and dramatists. Almost any author may quite accurately assert that he is contributing to the flow of information to the public, that he relies on confidential sources of information, and that these sources will be silenced if he is forced to make disclosures before a grand jury.

In each instance where a reporter is subpoenaed to testify, the courts would also be embroiled in preliminary factual and legal determinations with respect to whether the proper predicate had been laid for the reporter's appearance: Is there probable cause to believe a crime has been committed? Is it likely that the reporter has useful information gained in confidence? Could the grand jury obtain the information elsewhere? Is the official interest sufficient to outweigh the claimed privilege?

Thus, in the end, by considering whether enforcement of a particular law served a "compelling" governmental interest, the courts would be inextricably involved in distinguishing between the value of enforcing different criminal laws. By requiring testimony from a reporter in investigations involving some crimes but not in others, they would be making a value judgment that a legislature had declined to make since in each case the criminal law involved would represent a considered legislative judgment, not constitutionally suspect, of what conduct is liable to criminal prosecution. The task of judges, like other officials outside the legislative branch, is not to make the law but to uphold it in accordance with their oaths.

At the federal level, Congress has freedom to determine whether a statutory newsman's privilege is necessary and desirable and to fashion standards and rules as narrow or broad as deemed necessary to deal with the evil discerned and, equally important, to refashion those rules as experience from time to time may dictate. There is also merit in leaving state legislatures free, within First Amendment limits, to fashion their own standards in light of the conditions and problems with respect to the relations between law enforcement officials and press in their own areas. It goes without saying, of course, that we are powerless to bar state courts from responding in their own way and construing their own constitutions so as to recognize a newsman's privilege, either qualified or absolute.

In addition, there is much force in the pragmatic view that the press has at its disposal powerful mechanisms of communication and is far from helpless to protect itself from harassment or substantial harm. . . .

Finally, as we have earlier indicated, news gathering is not without its First Amendment protections, and grand jury investigations if instituted or conducted other than in good faith, would pose wholly different issues for resolution under the First Amendment. Official harassment of the press undertaken not for purposes of law enforcement but to disrupt a reporter's relationship with his news sources would have no justification. Grand juries are subject to judicial control and subpoenas to motions to quash. We do not expect courts will forget that grand juries must operate within the limits of the First Amendment as well as the Fifth.

III.

[The Court reversed *Caldwell*, rejecting the claim that the Government must show a "compelling need" before a reporter can be forced to appear before a grand jury. The Court affirmed Branzburg v. Hayes and Branzburg v. Meigs on the grounds that Branzburg "had direct information to provide the grand jury concerning the commission of serious crimes." Finally the Court affirmed *In re Pappas*, and held that the reporter was required to testify before the grand jury "subject, of course, to the supervision of the presiding judge as to 'the propriety, purposes, and scope of the grand jury inquiry and the pertinence of the probable testimony.' [ ]"]

■ JUSTICE POWELL, concurring.

I add this brief statement to emphasize what seems to me to be the limited nature of the Court's holding. The Court does not hold that newsmen, subpoenaed to testify before a grand jury, are without constitutional rights with respect to the gathering of news or in safeguarding their sources. Certainly, we do not hold, as suggested in Mr. Justice Stewart's dissenting opinion, that state and federal authorities are free to "annex" the news media as "an investigative arm of government." The solicitude repeatedly shown by this Court for First Amendment freedoms should be sufficient assurance against any such effort, even if one seriously believed that the media—properly free and untrammeled in the fullest sense of these terms—were not able to protect themselves.

As indicated in the concluding portion of the opinion, the Court states that no harassment of newsmen will be tolerated. If a newsman believes that the grand jury investigation is not being conducted in good faith, he is not without remedy. Indeed, if the newsman is called upon to give information bearing only a remote and tenuous relationship to the subject of the investigation, or if he has some other reason to believe that his testimony implicates confidential source relationships without a legitimate need of law enforcement, he will have access to the court on a motion to quash and an appropriate protective order may be entered. The asserted claim to privilege should be judged on its facts by the striking of a proper balance between freedom of the press and the obligation of all citizens to give relevant testimony with respect to criminal conduct. The balance of these vital constitutional and societal interests on a case-by-case basis accords with the tried and traditional way of adjudicating such questions.*

In short, the courts will be available to newsmen under circumstances where legitimate First Amendment interests require protection.

---

* It is to be remembered that Caldwell asserts a constitutional privilege not even to appear before the grand jury unless a court decides that the Government has made a showing that meets the three pre-conditions specified in the dissenting opinion of Mr. Justice Stewart. To be sure, this would require a "balancing" of interests by the court, but under circumstances and constraints significantly different from the balancing that will be appropriate under the court's decision. The newsman witness, like all other witnesses, will have to appear; he will not be in a position to litigate at the threshold the State's very authority to subpoena him. Moreover, absent the constitutional pre-conditions that Caldwell and that [the] dissenting opinion would impose as heavy burdens of proof to be carried by the State, the court—when called upon to protect a newsman from improper or prejudicial questioning—would be free to balance the competing interests on their merits in the particular case. The new constitutional rule endorsed by [the] dissenting opinion would, as a practical matter, defeat such a fair balancing and the essential societal interest in the detection and prosecution of crime would be heavily subordinated.

■ JUSTICE DOUGLAS, dissenting in United States v. Caldwell [and the other two cases].

. . .

It is my view that there is no "compelling need" that can be shown which qualifies the reporter's immunity from appearing or testifying before a grand jury, unless the reporter himself is implicated in a crime. . . .

■ JUSTICE STEWART, with whom JUSTICE BRENNAN and JUSTICE MARSHALL join, dissenting.

The Court's crabbed view of the First Amendment reflects a disturbing insensitivity to the critical role of an independent press in our society. The question whether a reporter has a constitutional right to a confidential relationship with his source is of first impression here, but the principles that should guide our decision are as basic as any to be found in the Constitution. While Justice Powell's enigmatic concurring opinion gives some hope of a more flexible view in the future, the Court in these cases holds that a newsman has no First Amendment right to protect his sources when called before a grand jury. The Court thus invites state and federal authorities to undermine the historic independence of the press by attempting to annex the journalistic profession as an investigative arm of government. Not only will this decision impair performance of the press' constitutionally protected functions, but it will, I am convinced, in the long run harm rather than help the administration of justice.

I respectfully dissent.

I.

The reporter's constitutional right to a confidential relationship with his source stems from the broad societal interest in a full and free flow of information to the public. . . .

A.

In keeping with this tradition, we have held that the right to publish is central to the First Amendment and basic to the existence of constitutional democracy. [ ]

. . .

No less important to the news dissemination process is the gathering of information. News must not be unnecessarily cut off at its source, for without freedom to acquire information the right to publish would be impermissibly compromised. Accordingly, a right to gather news, of some dimensions, must exist. . . .

B.

The right to gather news implies, in turn, a right to a confidential relationship between a reporter and his source. This proposition follows as a matter of simple logic once three factual predicates are recognized: (1) newsmen require informants to gather news; (2) confidentiality—the promise or understanding that names or certain aspects of communications will be kept off the record—is essential to the creation and maintenance of a news-gathering relationship with informants; and (3) an unbridled subpoena power—the absence of a constitutional right protecting, in *any* way, a confidential relationship from compulsory process—will either deter sources from divulging information or deter reporters from gathering and publishing information.

It is obvious that informants are necessary to the news-gathering process as we know it today. If it is to perform its constitutional mission, the press must do far more than merely print public statements or publish prepared handouts. Familiarity with the people and circumstances involved in the myriad background activities that result in the final product called "news" is vital to complete and responsible journalism, unless the press is to be a captive mouthpiece of "newsmakers."

It is equally obvious that the promise of confidentiality may be a necessary prerequisite to a productive relationship between a newsman and his informants. An officeholder may fear his superior; a member of the bureaucracy, his associates; a dissident, the scorn of majority opinion. All may have information valuable to the public discourse, yet each may be willing to relate that information only in confidence to a reporter whom he trusts, either because of excessive caution or because of a reasonable fear of reprisals or censure for unorthodox views. The First Amendment concern must not be with the motives of any particular news source, but rather with the conditions in which informants of all shades of the spectrum may make information available through the press to the public. [ ]

    . . .

Finally, and most important, when governmental officials possess an unchecked power to compel newsmen to disclose information received in confidence, sources will clearly be deterred from giving information, and reporters will clearly be deterred from publishing it, because uncertainty about exercise of the power will lead to "self-censorship." [ ] The uncertainty arises, of course, because the judiciary has traditionally imposed virtually no limitations on the grand jury's broad investigatory powers. [ ]

After today's decision, the potential informant can never be sure that his identity or off-the-record communications will not subsequently be revealed through the compelled testimony of a newsman. A public-spirited person inside government, who is not implicated in any crime, will now be fearful of revealing corruption or other governmental wrongdoing, because he will now know he can subsequently be identified by use of compulsory process. The potential source must, therefore, choose between risking exposure by giving information or avoiding the risk by remaining silent.

The reporter must speculate about whether contact with a controversial source or publication of controversial material will lead to a subpoena. In the event of a subpoena, under today's decision, the newsman will know that he must choose between being punished for contempt if he refuses to testify, or violating his profession's ethics and impairing his resourcefulness as a reporter if he discloses confidential information.

. . .

II.

Posed against the First Amendment's protection of the newsman's confidential relationships in these cases is society's interest in the use of the grand jury to administer justice fairly and effectively. The grand jury serves two important functions: "to examine into the commission of crimes" and "to stand between the prosecutor and the accused, and to determine whether the charge was founded upon credible testimony or was dictated by malice or personal ill will." [ ] And to perform these functions the grand jury must have available to it every man's relevant evidence. [ ]

Yet the longstanding rule making every person's evidence available to the grand jury is not absolute. The rule has been limited by the Fifth Amendment, the Fourth Amendment, and the evidentiary privileges of the common law. . . .

Such an interest must surely be the First Amendment protection of a confidential relationship that I have discussed above in Part I. As noted there, this protection does not exist for the purely private interests of the newsman or his informant, nor even, at bottom, for the First Amendment interests of either partner in the news-gathering relationship. Rather, it functions to insure nothing less than democratic decisionmaking through the free flow of information to the public, and it serves, thereby, to honor the "profound national commitment to the principle that debate on public issues should be uninhibited, robust, and wide-open." New York Times Co. v. Sullivan [ ]

In striking the proper balance between the public interest in the efficient administration of justice and the First Amendment guarantee of the fullest flow of information, we must begin with the basic proposition that because of their "delicate and vulnerable" nature, NAACP v. Button, 371 U.S., at 433, and their transcendent importance for the just functioning of our society, First Amendment rights require special safeguards.

A.

This Court has erected such safeguards when government, by legislative investigation or other investigative means, has attempted to pierce the shield of privacy inherent in freedom of association. In no previous case have we considered the extent to which the First Amendment limits the grand jury subpoena power. . . .

. . .

Thus, when an investigation impinges on First Amendment rights, the government must not only show that the inquiry is of "compelling and overriding importance" but it must also "convincingly" demonstrate that the investigation is "substantially related" to the information sought.

Governmental officials must, therefore, demonstrate that the information sought is *clearly* relevant to a *precisely* defined subject of governmental inquiry. [ ] They must demonstrate that it is reasonable to think the witness in question has that information. [ ] And they must show that there is not any means of obtaining the information less destructive of First Amendment liberties. [ ]

. . .

Accordingly, when a reporter is asked to appear before a grand jury and reveal confidences, I would hold that the government must (1) show that there is probable cause to believe that the newsman has information that is clearly relevant to a specific probable violation of law; (2) demonstrate that the information sought cannot be obtained by alternative means less destructive of First Amendment rights; and (3) demonstrate a compelling and overriding interest in the information.

This is not to say that a grand jury could not issue a subpoena until such a showing were made, and it is not to say that a newsman would be in any way privileged to ignore any subpoena that was issued. Obviously, before the government's burden to make such a showing were triggered, the reporter would have to move to quash the subpoena, asserting the basis on which he considered the particular relationship a confidential one.

B.

The crux of the Court's rejection of any newsman's privilege is its observation that only "where news sources themselves are implicated in crime or possess information *relevant* to the grand jury's task need they or the reporter be concerned about grand jury subpoenas." [ ] But this is a most misleading construct. For it is obviously not true that the only persons about whom reporters will be forced to testify will be those "confidential informants involved in actual criminal conduct" and those having "information suggesting illegal conduct by others." [ ] As noted above, given the grand jury's extraordinarily broad investigative powers and the weak standards of relevance and materiality that apply during such inquiries, reporters, if they have no testimonial privilege, will be called to give information about informants who have neither committed crimes nor have information about crime. It is to avoid deterrence of such sources and thus to prevent needless injury to First Amendment values that I think the government must be required to show probable cause that the newsman has information that is clearly relevant to a specific probable violation of criminal law.

. . .

NOTES AND QUESTIONS

1.   Note that four members of the Court would recognize a privilege in these cases, and a fifth, Justice Powell, seems to indicate that he might do so under other circumstances. Is there a majority for the proposition that compulsory disclosure raises First Amendment issues? That there is a First Amendment privilege that must be balanced case-by-case against the need for disclosure? What is the disagreement between Justices Powell and Stewart? Does Justice Powell's decision to write separately imply that Justice White and the three others who join his opinion are ruling out the possibility of a privilege under any circumstances?

2.   The purpose of the privilege claimed by the reporters and endorsed by the dissenters is to assure sources that their confidences will be kept. Do sources rely on the applicable privilege law in deciding whether to disclose to reporters? Do they ascertain for themselves what the law is? Do they rely on reporters' promises of confidentiality, without regard to the law of privilege?

3.   If the privilege works because the source relies on it in deciding whether to disclose, or because the reporter relies on it in deciding whether to promise confidentiality, it will be effective only to the extent that it enables the decision-maker—whether source or reporter—to predict in advance whether the reporter can be ordered to disclose. Does the qualified privilege proposed by Justice Stewart permit such a prediction to be made with reasonable confidence?

4.   Suppose empirical evidence showed that the existence or absence of a reporter's privilege had little effect on sources' willingness to cooperate with reporters, but that reporters usually would go to jail rather than comply with disclosure orders. In that event, a privilege would have little effect on the flow of information to the public, but would avoid sending reporters to jail for adhering to what they believe are professional obligations. Is that a sufficient reason for recognizing a privilege?

5.   The Supreme Court decision of course had no effect on the 17 state shield statutes already in existence. In 2015, the National Law Journal reported that forty-nine states and the District of Columbia had shield laws. Tony Mauro, Formerly Jailed Journalists Push for Federal Shield Law, Ntl. L. J., June 2, 2015. Although more than 100 bills to enact a shield law have been filed at the federal level, none has passed both houses of Congress. Many bills failed because the media could not agree as to the terms of such legislation.

B. How the Privilege Works

Perhaps surprisingly, many state and federal courts read the dissenting and concurring opinions in *Branzburg* as creating a federal constitutional privilege. With little encouragement from the Supreme Court, a large body of constitutional reporter's privilege law evolved.

For a time, circuit courts appeared to have reached a consensus that *Branzburg* created a constitutionally based privilege. That broad consensus was challenged in McKevitt v. Pallasch, 339 F.3d 530 (7th Cir. 2003). In an opinion rejecting a claim of privilege by journalists subpoenaed in a criminal case, Judge Richard Posner said decisions that ignore *Branzburg,* or read its dissenting and concurring opinions to "audaciously declare that *Branzburg* actually created a reporter's privilege," are questionable. How much judicial support remains for a federal constitutional reporter's privilege is unclear, as you will see in the cases discussed below.

Nevertheless, almost all jurisdictions recognize some form of reporter's privilege—statutory, common law, or constitutional. The enthusiasm with which the privilege is embraced varies from one jurisdiction to another. At one extreme, the Florida courts have made the privilege all but absolute (except as to reporters who are actual eyewitnesses to crime). Although they describe the privilege as qualified, they rarely find sufficient reason to override it. At the other extreme, the Massachusetts Supreme Judicial Court has gone only so far as to hold that "it was not improper for the judge to consider the investigative purpose of and the public interest in [the reporter's] use of confidential sources" in deciding not to compel the reporter to testify. Sinnott v. Boston Retirement Board, 524 N.E.2d 100 (Mass. 1988).

Defeating a Qualified Privilege. When a reporter's privilege is recognized, it is rarely absolute. The party seeking disclosure can overcome the privilege by making specified showings. When the privilege is statutory, the statute may state what has to be shown to defeat it. When the privilege arises from common law or the First Amendment, it is a "qualified" privilege along the lines suggested in Justice Stewart's dissent in *Branzburg.* One widely accepted version states that "disclosure may be ordered only upon a clear and specific showing that the information is highly material and relevant, necessary or critical to the maintenance of the claim, and not obtainable from other available sources." Gonzales v. National Broadcasting Company, Inc., 194 F.3d 29 (2d Cir. 1999). Some courts condense this three-part test into two parts, omitting the first element on the ground that it is subsumed by the second. See, e.g., Zerilli v. Smith, 656 F.2d 705 (D.C. Cir. 1981).

Initially many journalists thought anything less than an absolute privilege would be too unreliable to be useful, but many courts applied the tests rigorously enough to protect confidences in most cases. Whether the test has three parts or two, it is clear that "materiality and relevance" in the usual evidentiary sense is not enough: there must be some specific showing of need to outweigh the sacrifice of First Amendment values that disclosure entails. The court is unlikely to see sufficient need for disclosure when the evidence sought would be only cumulative. But suppose the evidence sought would corroborate testimony that otherwise might be discounted?

For a criminal defendant, any bit of evidence that might create a reasonable doubt could be dispositive. The California Supreme Court said "a criminal defendant must show a *reasonable possibility* the information will materially assist his defense." The court said this would include not only evidence tending to exculpate, but also evidence establishing a lesser offense, mitigating circumstances, or impeachment evidence. See Delaney v. Superior Court, 789 P.2d 934 (Cal. 1990).

Alternative Sources. The required showing that the information cannot be obtained from sources other than the reporter is interpreted with varying degrees of rigor. For example, the Illinois Supreme Court held that the requirement had not been met when a prosecutor unsuccessfully sought testimony of three potential leakers despite the fact several others had not been questioned. "We think it clear that the statute requires more than a showing of inconvenience to the investigator before a reporter can be compelled to disclose his sources. . . ." In re Special Grand Jury Investigation, 472 N.E.2d 450 (Ill. 1984). However, when the potential sources included "a very substantial list of employees," the undisclosed source could have been "anyone from an office boy to a top officer," and the reporter was unwilling to provide any information to narrow the field, the court held that requiring exhaustion of alternative sources would impose too great a burden on the party seeking disclosure. See Carey v. Hume, 492 F.2d 631 (D.C. Cir. 1974).

Defeating the Privilege in Libel Cases. Attempts to defeat the privilege appear to succeed more often in cases where the reporter, or the reporter's employer, is a defendant in a libel case. In such cases, the materiality of the information is often obvious: If the plaintiff can prove that the source was not credible, or that the defendant is invoking the privilege to conceal the fact that it fabricated the defamatory allegation, the plaintiff has important evidence on the issue of actual malice. The need for the disclosure may be equally obvious: The actual malice standard requires the plaintiff to prove that the defendant had serious doubts as to the truth of its publication. To the extent that the disclosure might illuminate the defendant's state of mind, it must go to the heart of the plaintiff's case, and must be evidence that is not likely to be available elsewhere.

On the other hand, compelled disclosure in libel cases also poses special risks. If the privilege can be easily overcome by filing a libel suit, it does little good to uphold the privilege in other contexts. This has emerged as a significant threat to Internet anonymity and, in response, several courts have refused to order disclosure until they are satisfied that the libel suit is not merely a device for uncovering a source.

Courts have crafted several different tests to determine when revelation of the identity of an anonymous speaker is justified. Most tests have at least two components. The first requires the plaintiff to provide the anonymous speaker with notice of the libel suit and an opportunity to file a motion to quash in order to protect his identity. Courts have held that plaintiffs can satisfy this component by posting notice of the suit in the forum where the Doe defendant allegedly posted his defamatory statement. See Doe v. Cahill, 884 A.2d 451 (Del. 2005). Once a motion to quash is filed, the plaintiff must show that the libel suit is viable before a court will order disclosure of defendant's identity. Courts have framed this second component in various ways, ranging from requiring plaintiffs to show merely a "good faith basis" for the libel claim to requiring a showing of evidence sufficient to avoid summary judgment. See Dendrite International, Inc. v. Doe, 775 A.2d 756 (N.J. Super. Ct. App. Div. 2001). In addition to these two components, some courts require an explicit ad hoc balancing of the plaintiff's reputational interests against the defendant's right to speak anonymously. For discussion of the variety of standards employed in such cases, see Lyrissa Lidsky, Anonymity in Cyberspace: What Can We Learn from John Doe? 50 B.C. L. Rev. 1373 (2009).

In libel cases, the threat of contempt is not the only risk facing the reporter who refuses to disclose. Because the reporter in this situation is a litigant (or a person subject to the control of a litigant), the court can impose sanctions for nondisclosure that would not be available against a nonparty reporter. These include striking defenses, default judgment, and attorney's fees.

Some state shield statutes make special provision for libel cases. For example, the statutory privilege in Rhode Island does not apply to "the source of any allegedly defamatory information in any case where the defendant, in a civil action for defamation, asserts a defense based on the source of such information." When a newspaper resisted disclosing its source while invoking the defense that it had published the defamatory material in good faith in reliance on the source, the Rhode Island Supreme Court held that neither the statutory privilege nor a First Amendment or common law privilege was available. The court said it was unrealistic to demand that a libel plaintiff exhaust other possible means of discovering the sources relied on by the newspaper before being allowed to seek the information directly from the defendant. See Capuano v. Outlet Co., 579 A.2d 469 (R.I. 1990).

California, through statutory and constitutional privileges, gives reporters absolute protection from contempt, but these provisions do not protect them from the other sanctions that may be imposed on parties to litigation. To fill this gap, the California courts recognize a qualified constitutional privilege in addition to the absolute privileges against contempt. See Mitchell v. Superior Court, 690 P.2d 625 (Cal. 1984).

Despite all these protections, the Ninth Circuit, applying California law, upheld an order requiring the national tabloid Star to disclose confidential sources in a libel suit by celebrity Rodney Dangerfield, on the grounds that the celebrity would not be able to establish actual malice without knowing whether the confidential sources existed and whether they were credible, especially where there were no alternative sources and the celebrity had deposed all of the nonconfidential sources identified by the tabloid. See Star Editorial, Inc. v. District Court, 7 F.3d 856 (9th Cir. 1993).

In a libel case brought by the head coach of the University of Alabama football team against *Sports Illustrated* magazine, the Eleventh Circuit refused to compel the journalists' testimony about the identity of their confidential source even though the identity was "vital" to the coach's claim. The court held that the coach had not shown that the identity was unavailable from alternative sources because the case involved only four key witnesses, one of whose testimony would almost certainly reveal the identity of the confidential source without need for the journalist-defendants to do so. Price v. Time, Inc., 425 F.3d 1292 (11th Cir. 2005).

Defeating an Absolute Privilege. Even if the privilege is in terms absolute, it may have to yield when it conflicts with other constitutional rights. The most frequent conflict is with the Sixth Amendment rights of compulsory process and fair trial.

In the most famous clash between the privilege and a defendant's fair trial interests, the New Jersey Supreme Court held that a criminal defendant's constitutional right to compel testimony and production of documents prevailed over the shield statute, even though the statute created an absolute privilege with no provision for defeasance. See Matter of Farber, 394 A.2d 330 (N.J. 1978). But "in recognition of the strongly expressed legislative viewpoint favoring confidentiality," the court directed that in similar cases in the future the defendant would have to show a "reasonable probability or likelihood that the information sought by the subpoena was material and relevant to his defense, that it could not be secured from any less intrusive source, and that the defendant had a legitimate need to see and otherwise use it."

Is it proper for a court to convert an absolute privilege into a qualified one to save it from unconstitutionality? If the court had held that the statute was unconstitutional because it gave the defendant no opportunity to secure the information, but that a qualified First Amendment privilege existed, would the result have been any different? For an argument that a court should honor the absolute privilege even if it means that the state cannot prosecute the accused, see Alfred Hill, Testimonial Privileges and Fair Trial, 80 Colum. L. Rev. 1173 (1980).

Invoking the Privilege. Courts have rejected the proposition that reporters should not be compelled to appear even to invoke the privilege. Reporters must respond, either by appearing or by moving to quash the subpoena. Usually the reporter must supply some information to lay the foundation for the privilege. Sometimes an affidavit setting out the basis for the reporter's objections to disclosure is sufficient to support the motion to quash. On other occasions, courts have insisted that the reporter testify as to the circumstances from which the claim of confidentiality arises. Other courts have allowed the privilege to be invoked only on a question-by-question basis.

Waiving the Privilege. Like other privileges, a reporter's privilege can be waived. Some reporters have been spared the burden of litigating a privilege claim by sources who agreed to waive the obligation of confidentiality. Still others have been spared from going to jail by sources who agreed to waive confidentiality after the privilege claim was rejected by the courts.

This does not necessarily mean the reporter *must* disclose if the source waives. Attorney-client and physician-patient privileges are viewed as "belonging" to the client or patient, and can be waived by them. Reporter's privilege, however, is treated as belonging to the reporter. See United States v. Cuthbertson, 630 F.2d 139 (3d Cir. 1980), which held that the privilege can only be waived by the reporter.

On the other hand, once the source has destroyed confidentiality, the claim of privilege is weakened. In jurisdictions that recognize a qualified privilege, destruction of confidentiality may tip the balance in favor of disclosure even though the privilege is not considered waived.

Occasionally courts hold that reporters have inadvertently waived any claim of privilege by disclosing part of the information sought. This pitfall can be avoided by objecting to all disclosure before making any; after the objection is overruled, the reporter cannot be said to have voluntarily waived the privilege.

In Camera Review. Judges sometimes demand to inspect *in camera* the material claimed to be privileged. Such demands can create difficult choices for reporters. If *in camera* inspection is properly ordered, the reporter can be held in contempt for refusing to comply even though the material might ultimately have been found privileged and thus shielded from further disclosure. See In re Selcraig, 705 F.2d 789 (5th Cir. 1983). But if the information in question is confidential, its surrender to the judge may itself be a breach of the reporter's promise to the source. Demands to submit to in camera inspection usually are subjected to at least some of the requirements the privilege imposes on compulsory disclosure generally.

Suppose the reporter is willing to go to jail rather than disclose, but believes the judge, after inspecting the material, will not require disclosure. Can the reporter turn the material over (or testify) *in camera* without giving up the right to go to jail to prevent public disclosure? Should a judge agree to an *in camera* inspection in which his or her only choices are to hold the material nondisclosable or give it back to the reporter and hold the reporter in contempt?

Consequences of Noncompliance. What happens if the privilege claim is rejected and the reporter still refuses to disclose? As noted above, when the reporter (or his or her employer) is a party to the proceeding in which disclosure is sought, failure to comply with a discovery order may result in striking a claim or defense, default judgment, or an award of attorney's fees.

When the reporter is not a party, contempt is usually the only sanction available. Typically, the sanction is civil contempt—the reporter is committed to jail until he or she complies with the disclosure order. Occasionally the reporter is sentenced to a specific term (or fine) for criminal contempt. The defendant in a criminal contempt case has the same constitutional rights as any other criminal defendant.

If it appears that the reporter will remain in jail indefinitely rather than comply, some courts hold that the sanction becomes penal rather than coercive, and thus subject to maximum sentence provisions of the criminal contempt law. In Rosato v. Superior Court, 51 Cal.App.3d 190 (Cal.App. 1975), after four reporters and editors had served fifteen days in jail, the court held a hearing, determined that they would not testify, sentenced them to five-day terms for criminal contempt (with credit for time already served), and released them.

Can reporters avoid subpoena problems by routinely destroying notes or erasing tapes or recordings? There is no universal answer. If the material is not available to be subpoenaed, neither is it available for future journalistic uses, or for use by the reporter or his or her employer as evidence in libel suits or other legal proceedings. Even if it would not have been helpful to the media defendant, the suspicions aroused when the jury is told that notes are routinely destroyed may do more harm than the evidence would have done. See generally Betty Holcomb, Should Reporters Torch Their Notes? Colum. Journalism Rev., Jan./Feb. 1986.

In any event, material must not be destroyed after litigation is commenced or after the reporter learns that litigation is likely. Such destruction may be a crime, and a jury may be instructed that it can infer that the destroyed material must have contained evidence supporting the plaintiff's claims. In one libel case, an employee's destruction of documents was held to be evidence supporting a finding of actual malice. See Brown & Williamson Tobacco Corp. v. Jacobson, 827 F.2d 1119 (7th Cir. 1987).

Violating Confidences. In *Branzburg* the reporters argued, and the dissenting justices agreed, that respecting confidentiality "is essential to the creation and maintenance of a news-gathering relationship with informants." Does that argument leave any room for media to break their promises of confidentiality when their journalistic judgment tells them they should? In *Cohen v. Cowles Media Co.*, we saw one case in which media did so. Is the First Amendment argument that the newspapers made in that case consistent with the rationale for a reporter's privilege?

Since the *Cohen* case, other instances of "burning sources" have come to light. A reporter for the Cincinnati Enquirer wrote a series accusing a Cincinnati-based company, Chiquita Brands International, of bribing government officials in South America. The company accused the reporter of illegally accessing its voice-mail system and, as part of a plea bargain, the reporter identified the source who had assisted him. The source was convicted of four misdemeanor counts of attempting unauthorized access to computer files, and sued the Enquirer for breaking its promise of confidentiality. The trial court dismissed the suit on the ground that Ohio law provided absolute immunity from tort liability for anyone providing information to a prosecutor or grand jury. The court of appeals affirmed. Ventura v. Cincinnati Enquirer, 396 F.3d 784 (6th Cir. 2005). The Enquirer fired the reporter, paid Chiquita more than $10 million, and published a front page apology renouncing the series. Chiquita eventually paid a $100,000 penalty and agreed to a cease and desist order in response to an SEC finding that its employees had paid a $30,000 bribe to a Colombian official. See Chiquita to Settle Regulatory Charges, L.A. Times, October 4, 2001.

C. WHO IS A REPORTER?

As Justice White predicted in *Branzburg*, recognition of a reporter's privilege makes it "necessary to define those categories of newsmen who qualified for the privilege." He was "unwilling to embark the judiciary on a long and difficult journey" to resolve that issue, but courts that do recognize a privilege have employed several approaches. The Second Circuit, noting that historians, biographers, sociologists, and other academic researchers may rely on confidences much as reporters do, suggested that a scholar's privilege might be recognized "where a serious academic inquiry is undertaken pursuant to a considered research plan in which the need for confidentiality is tangibly related to the accuracy or completeness of the study." In re Grand Jury Subpoena, 750 F.2d 223 (2d Cir. 1984). In a later case, the same court said the privilege should not be limited to news media but should be available if the person seeking to avoid disclosure had "the intent to use material—sought, gathered or received—to disseminate information to the public and such intent existed at the inception of the newsgathering process." See von Bulow v. von Bulow, 811 F.2d 136 (2d Cir. 1987).

As noted in a newsgathering context in Chapter Eight, with the advent of the digital age, blogging, and citizen journalism, privilege claims by persons who do not fit the conventional mold of "reporter" have become more numerous and more difficult.

O'Grady v. Superior Court

California Court of Appeal, 2006.
139 Cal. App. 4th 1423.

■ RUSHING, P.J.

[Jason O'Grady operated "O'Grady's PowerPage," an "online news magazine" devoted to news and information about Apple Macintosh computers and compatible software and hardware. O'Grady published 15 to 20 items per week on PowerPage. PowerPage and another website called Apple Insider published several articles about a rumored new Apple product called Asteroid or Q97, including technical details and Apple's marketing and manufacturing plans. Apple filed a "Doe" suit against 25 unidentified persons for misappropriation of trade secrets and requested a court order permitting Apple to serve subpoenas on PowerPage and Apple Insider to obtain the identities of the Does.

O'Grady and the pseudonymous publisher of Apple Insider, sought a protective order to block the subpoenas on the ground that the information Apple sought came from confidential sources and was protected by the California Constitution, the California evidence code, and the First Amendment. The trial court denied the protective order, and the website operators applied to the court of appeal for a writ compelling the trial judge to issue the protective order. After rejecting Apple's argument that the controversy was not ripe because no subpoenas had actually been served, the court turned to the petitioners' privilege claims.]

IV. California Reporter's Shield

Article I, section 2, subdivision (b) of the California Constitution provides, "A publisher, editor, reporter, or other person connected with or employed upon a newspaper, magazine, or other periodical publication . . . shall not be adjudged in contempt . . . for refusing to disclose the source of any information procured while so connected or employed for publication in a newspaper, magazine or other periodical publication, or for refusing to disclose any unpublished information obtained or prepared in gathering, receiving or processing of information for communication to the public." Evidence Code section 1070, subdivision (a), is to substantially the same effect. Petitioners assert that these provisions, sometimes known as the California reporter's shield, preclude compelled disclosure of their sources or any other unpublished material in their possession. Apple argues that petitioners may not avail themselves of the shield because (1) they were not engaged in legitimate journalistic activities when they acquired the offending information; and (2) they are not among the classes of persons protected by the statute.

. . .

Apple contends that petitioners failed to carry their burden of showing that they are entitled to invoke the shield. [ ] In particular,

Apple asserts, petitioners failed to establish that they acquired the information in question while "engag[ing] in legitimate journalistic purposes," or "exercis[ing] judgmental discretion in such activities." [ ] According to Apple, petitioners were engaged not in "legitimate journalism or news," but only in "trade secret misappropriation" and copyright violations. The trial court seemed to adopt this view, writing that "Mr. O'Grady took the information and turned around and put it on the PowerPage site with essentially no added value."

We decline the implicit invitation to embroil ourselves in questions of what constitutes "legitimate journalis[m]." The shield law is intended to protect the gathering and dissemination of *news,* and that is what petitioners did here. We can think of no workable test or principle that would distinguish "legitimate" from "illegitimate" news. Any attempt by courts to draw such a distinction would imperil a fundamental purpose of the First Amendment, which is to identify the best, most important, and most valuable ideas not by any sociological or economic formula, rule of law, or process of government, but through the rough and tumble competition of the memetic marketplace.

Nor does Apple supply any colorable ground for declaring petitioners' activities not to be legitimate newsgathering and dissemination. Apple asserts that petitioners merely reprinted "verbatim copies" of Apple's internal information while exercising "no editorial oversight at all." But this characterization, if accepted, furnishes no basis for denying petitioners the protection of the statute. A reporter who uncovers newsworthy documents cannot rationally be denied the protection of the law because the publication for which he works chooses to publish facsimiles of the documents rather than editorial summaries. The shield exists not only to protect editors but equally if not more to protect newsgatherers. The primacy Apple would grant to editorial function cannot be justified by any rationale known to us.

Moreover, an absence of editorial judgment cannot be inferred merely from the fact that some source material is published verbatim. It may once have been unusual to reproduce source materials at length, but that fact appears attributable to the constraints of pre-digital publishing technology, which compelled an editor to decide how to use the limited space afforded by a particular publication. This required decisions not only about what information to include but about how to compress source materials to fit. In short, editors were forced to summarize, paraphrase, and rewrite because there was not room on their pages to do otherwise.

Digital communication and storage, especially when coupled with hypertext linking, make it possible to present readers with an unlimited amount of information in connection with a given subject, story, or report. The only real constraint now is time—the publisher's and the reader's. From the reader's perspective, the ideal presentation probably consists of a top-level summary with the ability to "drill down" to source materials through hypertext links. The decision whether to take this approach, or to present original information at the top level of an article, is itself an occasion for editorial judgment. Courts ought not to cling too fiercely to traditional preconceptions, especially when they may operate to discourage the seemingly salutary practice of providing readers with source materials rather than subjecting them to the editors' own "spin" on a story.

    . . .

Apple contends that petitioners have failed to show that they are among "the types of persons enumerated in the [shield] law." [ ] The law extends to "[a] publisher, editor, reporter, or other person connected with or employed upon a newspaper, magazine, or other periodical publication. . . ." (Cal. Const., art. I, § 2, subd. (b).) In seeking to place petitioners outside this description, Apple does not address the actual language of the statute. It simply asserts that (1) the shield law has been "repeatedly amended to include new forms of media," but "has never been enlarged to cover posting information on a website"; (2) "[p]ersons who post such information . . . are not members of any professional community governed by ethical and professional standards"; and (3) "if Petitioners' arguments were accepted, anyone with a computer and Internet access could claim protection under the California Shield and conceal his own misconduct."

These arguments all rest on the dismissive characterization of petitioners' conduct as "posting information on a website." We have already noted the pervasive misuse of the verb "post" by Apple and allied amici. [ ] Here they compound the problem by conflating what occurred here—the open and deliberate publication on a news-oriented Web site of news gathered for that purpose by the site's operators—with the deposit of information, opinion, or fabrication by a casual visitor to an open forum such as a newsgroup, chatroom, bulletin board system, or discussion group. Posting of the latter type, where it involves "confidential" or otherwise actionable information, may indeed constitute something other than the publication of news. But posting of the former type appears conceptually indistinguishable from publishing a newspaper, and we see no theoretical basis for treating it differently.

Beyond casting aspersions on the legitimacy of petitioners' enterprise, Apple offers no cogent reason to conclude that they fall outside the shield law's protection. Certainly it makes no attempt to ground an argument in the language of the law, which, we reiterate, extends to every "publisher, editor, reporter, or other person connected with or employed upon a newspaper, magazine, or other periodical publication." [ ] We can think of no reason to doubt that the operator of a public Web site is a "publisher" for purposes of this language; the primary and core meaning of "to publish" is "[t]o make publicly or generally known; to declare or report openly or publicly; to announce; to tell or noise abroad; also, to propagate, disseminate (a creed or system)." [ ] Of course the term "publisher" also possesses a somewhat narrower sense: "One whose business is the issuing of books, newspapers, music, engravings, *or the like,* as the agent of the author or owner; one who undertakes the printing or production of copies of such works, and their distribution to the booksellers and other dealers, or to the public. (Without qualification generally understood to mean a *book-publisher* or (in the *U.S.*) also a newspaper proprietor.)" [ ] News-oriented Web sites like petitioners' are surely "like" a newspaper or magazine for these purposes. Moreover, even if petitioners' status as "publishers" is debatable, O'Grady and Jade have flatly declared that they are also editors and reporters, and Apple offers no basis to question that characterization.

D.   Covered Publications

We come now to the difficult issue, which is whether the phrase "newspaper, magazine, or other periodical publication" [ ] applies to Web sites such as petitioners'. Again, Apple offers little if any argument concerning the construction to be given this language, beyond the general notion that it should not extend to petitioners.

As potentially applicable here, the phrase "newspaper, magazine, or other periodical publication" [ ] is ambiguous. The term "newspaper" presents little difficulty; it has always meant, and continues to mean, a regularly appearing publication printed on large format, inexpensive paper. The term "magazine" is more difficult. Petitioners describe their own sites as "magazines," and Apple offers no reason to take issue with that characterization. The term "magazine" is now widely used in reference to Web sites or other digital publications of the type produced by petitioners. Thus a draft entry in the Oxford English Dictionary defines "e-zine" as "[a] magazine published in electronic form on a computer network, esp. the Internet. [ ] Although most strongly associated with special-interest fanzines only available online, *e-zine* has been widely applied: to regularly updated general-interest web sites, to electronic counterparts of print titles (general and specialist), and to subscription-only e-mail newsletters." [ ]

. . .

However, even were we to decide—which we do not—that Web sites such as petitioners' cannot properly be considered "magazines" for purposes of the shield law, we would still have to address the question whether they fall within the phrase "other periodical publications."

. . .

Here it might be suggested that the shield law only applies to "periodical publications" *in print,* because that was a common feature of newspapers and magazines at the time the law was enacted. Yet there is no apparent link between the core purpose of the law, which is to shield the gathering of news for dissemination to the public, and the characteristic of appearing in traditional print, on traditional paper. Indeed, the shield law manifests a clear intention *not* to limit its reach to print publications by also protecting "person[s] connected with or employed by a radio or television station." [ ] Apple alludes to the absence of any similar explicit extension to digital publications such as petitioners', but this consideration is far from compelling. No one would say that the evening news on television, or an hourly news report on radio, is a "newspaper, magazine, or other periodical publication." The broadcast media represent a radical departure from the preexisting paradigm for news sources. Because no one thought of those media as "publications," an explicit extension was necessary to ensure their inclusion. Petitioners' Web sites are not only "publications" under various sources we have noted but also bear far closer resemblance to traditional print media than do television and radio. They consist primary of text, sometimes accompanied by pictures, and perhaps occasionally by multimedia content. Radio consists entirely of sounds, and television consists almost entirely of sounds and pictures. While television could be used to deliver text, it almost never is.

For these reasons the explicit inclusion of television and radio in the shield law does not imply an exclusion of digital media such as petitioners'. . . .

. . .

It does not appear that petitioners' Web sites are published in distinct issues at regular, stated, or fixed intervals. Rather, individual articles are added as and when they become ready for publication, so that the home page at a given time may include links to articles posted over the preceding several days. This kind of constant updating is characteristic of online publications but is difficult to characterize as publication at "regular intervals." . . .

[M]any familiar print publications universally viewed as "periodicals" (or "periodical publications") do not appear with absolute regularity. The New Yorker Magazine is considered a periodical and a magazine (a subset of periodicals) even though it publishes 47, not 52, issues a year. [ ] Similarly, the New York Review of Books is "[p]ublished 20 times a year, biweekly except in January, August, and September, when monthly." [ ]

Given the numerous ambiguities presented by "periodical publication" in this context, its applicability must ultimately depend on the purpose of the statute. [ ] It seems likely that the Legislature intended the phrase "periodical publication" to include all ongoing, recurring news publications while excluding non-recurring publications such as books, pamphlets, flyers, and monographs. The Legislature was aware that the inclusion of this language could extend the statute's protections to something as occasional as a legislator's newsletter. [ ] If the Legislature was prepared to sweep that broadly, it must have intended that the statute protect publications like petitioners', which differ from traditional periodicals only in their tendency, which flows directly from the advanced technology they employ, to continuously update their content.

We conclude that petitioners are entitled to the protection of the shield law, which precludes punishing as contempt a refusal by them to disclose unpublished information.

V. Constitutional Privilege

Petitioners also assert that the discovery sought by Apple is barred, on the present record, by a conditional privilege arising from the state and federal guarantees of a free press. The gist of the privilege is that a newsgatherer cannot to be compelled to divulge the identities of confidential sources without a showing of need sufficient to overbalance the inhibitory effect of such disclosure upon the free flow of ideas and information which is the core object of our guarantees of free speech and press. This argument raises two subsidiary questions: (1) Is such a privilege available to petitioners? (2) If so, has Apple made a sufficient showing to overcome it?

. . .

Before turning to the relevant factors we must of course decide whether petitioners are reporters, editors, or publishers for purposes of this privilege. Our answer to this question is anticipated by the preceding discussion of the California reporter's shield. Whereas we there had to construe relatively specific statutory language, we are concerned here with broad constitutional principles. In that light, we can see no sustainable basis to distinguish petitioners from the reporters, editors, and publishers who provide news to the public through traditional print and broadcast media. It is established without contradiction that they gather, select, and prepare, for purposes of publication to a mass audience, information about current events of interest and concern to that audience.

[Having concluded that the qualified First Amendment privilege was applicable, the court then held that the balancing test required by that privilege favored the petitioners, primarily because Apple had not shown that it had exhausted alternative avenues of investigation. It ordered the trial court to grant the petitioners' motion for a protective order.]

NOTES AND QUESTIONS

1. Would the reasoning of this decision apply to postings that are less clearly journalism, such as publishing gossip on a celebrity "paparazzi" site or posting negative reviews of a competitor?

2. In rejecting Apple's suggestion that the privilege should be confined to those who exercise "editorial oversight," the court asserts that the privilege cannot be denied to those who uncover newsworthy documents and post

them verbatim. If that is true, does it mean that the privilege is available to anyone who posts newsworthy information, without regard to whether the poster or the site is engaged in anything resembling journalism?

3.   The California shield law's definitions of reporter are narrower than those in some states. The Delaware statute, for example, might have made it easier to extend the privilege to PowerPage and Apple Insider. It defines "reporter" as "any journalist, scholar, educator, polemicist, or other individual" who spends at least 20 hours a week in "obtaining or preparing information for dissemination with the aid of facilities for the mass reproduction of words, sounds, or images in a form available to the general public. . . ." Del. Code tit. X § 4320 (1974).

4.   The proposed federal shield bill that died in the Senate in 2013, the Free Flow of Information Act, contained the following definition:

> The term "covered journalist"—
>
> (I)   means a person who—
>
>> (aa) is, or on the relevant date, was, an employee, independent contractor, or agent of an entity or service that disseminates news or information by means of newspaper; nonfiction book; wire service; news agency; news website, mobile application or other news or information service (whether distributed digitally or otherwise); news program; magazine or other periodical, whether in print, electronic, or other format; or through television or radio broadcast, multichannel video programming distributor . . . or motion picture for public showing;
>>
>> (bb) with the primary intent to investigate events and procure material in order to disseminate to the public news or information concerning local, national, or international events or other matters of public interest, engages, or as of the relevant date engaged, in the regular gathering, preparation, collection, photographing, recording, writing, editing, reporting or publishing on such matters by—
>>
>>> (AA) conducting interviews;
>>>
>>> (BB) making direct observation of events; or
>>>
>>> (CC) collecting, reviewing, or analyzing original writings, statements, communications, reports, memoranda, records, transcripts, documents, photographs, recordings, tapes, materials, data, or other information whether in paper, electronic, or other form;
>>
>> (cc) had such intent at the inception of the process of gathering the news or information sought; and

(dd) obtained the news or information sought in order to disseminate the news or information to the public; or

(II) means a person who—

(aa) at the inception of the process of gathering the news or information sought, had the primary intent to investigate issues or events and procure material in order to disseminate to the public news or information concerning local, national, or international events or other matters of public interest, and regularly conducted interviews, reviewed documents, captured images of events, or directly observed events;

(bb) obtained the news or information sought in order to disseminate it by means of a medium set out in subclause (I)(aa) of this section; and

(cc) either—

(AA) would have been included in the definition in subclause (I)(aa) of this section for any continuous one-year period within the 20 years prior to the relevant date or any continuous three-month period within the 5 years prior to the relevant date;

(BB) had substantially contributed, as an author, editor, photographer, or producer, to a significant number of articles, stories, programs, or publications by a medium set out in subclause (I)(aa) of this section within 5 years prior to the relevant date; or

(CC) was a student participating in a journalistic medium at an institution of higher education . . . on the relevant date;

. . .

(B) Judicial discretion. In the case of a person that does not fit within the definition of "covered journalist" described in subclause (I) or (II) of paragraph (A)(i), a judge of the United States may exercise discretion to avail the person of the protections of this Act if, based on specific facts contained in the record, the judge determines that such protections would be in the interest of justice and necessary to protect lawful and legitimate news-gathering activities under the specific circumstances of the case.

113 SB 987.

D. APPLYING THE PRIVILEGE IN LEAKS CASES

The *O'Grady* case is one of many in which the purpose of the subpoena is to learn the source of a leak—an unauthorized disclosure of closely held information. Such cases tend to produce especially intense controversies. Leaks are a fact of life in newsgathering and in government, and they are an important antidote to excessive secrecy. However, they can also be illegal, and if so, the reporter with information stemming from a leak has evidence of a crime. The qualified reporter's privilege is often ineffective in leaks cases because the reporter is likely to be the only person whose testimony can bring the leaker to justice; a test based on need and exhaustion of alternative sources will be easily met in almost every case.

Subpoenas and Leaks Prosecutions in the D.C. Circuit. One high-profile leaks case illustrates some of the difficulties such cases pose. That case involved a leak by then-Vice President Dick Cheney's Chief of Staff, Lewis Libby, about the identity of a CIA agent named Valerie Plame. In the investigation of who had leaked Plame's identity to the press, the Justice Department subpoenaed Time magazine, its reporter Matthew Cooper, and then-New York Times reporter Judith Miller. Cooper and Time cooperated with one subpoena addressing specific conversations they had had with Libby after Libby stated that he had no objection. Cooper and Time refused to cooperate with a subsequent, more general subpoena, and Miller refused to cooperate with all subpoenas. Time, Cooper, and Miller were held in civil contempt of court. Miller spent 85 days in jail for refusing to disclose Libby's identity. The journalists appealed, but the District of Columbia Circuit upheld the contempt citations. The reporters claimed that both a First Amendment privilege and a federal common law privilege had emerged since *Branzburg* was decided. The appellate court, however, unanimously affirmed the ruling of the trial court and held the reporters in contempt. All three judges on the panel agreed that if there was a privilege of any kind, it had been overcome. The court divided 2–1 against recognition of a common law privilege. In re Grand Jury Subpoena, Judith Miller, 438 F.3d 1141 (D.C. Cir. 2006).

Judge David Tatel dissented on this point. Judge Tatel would have recognized a federal common law privilege tailored specifically to leaks cases. Pursuant to the proposed privilege, courts would weigh not only the government's need for information and the exhaustion of alternative sources but would also weigh the harm caused by the leak and the value of the leaked information to the public. Another judge criticized this proposed privilege for its lack of analytical rigor as well as its usurpation of what is essentially a legislative function. See id. (Henderson, J., concurring).

Although the three-judge panel in the case produced four separate opinions (the court's opinion and three concurrences), the full court of appeals rejected the reporters' petition for rehearing en banc, 405 F.3d 17 (D.C. Cir. 2005). Cooper and Miller both testified after Libby consented. Their testimony, together with that of Tim Russert of NBC, helped convict Libby of lying to investigators when he denied that he had told the reporters about Plame. Libby was sentenced to 30 months in prison. President George W. Bush commuted the prison sentence, but left intact Libby's conviction and a $250,000 fine. See Scott Shane and Neil A. Lewis, Bush Spares Libby from Prison Term, N.Y. Times, July 3, 2007. The only person who served jail time was Miller. The outed CIA agent recounted the harm the leak caused in a 2008 book. Valerie Plame Wilson and Laura Rozen, Fair Game: How a Top CIA Agent Was Betrayed by Her Own Government (2008). She sued Libby and other officials in the Bush Administration for violating her civil rights by identifying her to the press, but a federal district court dismissed her suit and the D.C. Circuit affirmed. See Wilson v. Libby, 535 F.3d 697 (D.C. Cir. 2008).

Subpoenas and Leaks Investigations in the Fourth Circuit. Under President Barack Obama, the Justice Department prosecuted more government officials for leaking classified information than it had in any previous administration. The Obama administration initiated at least eleven Espionage Act prosecutions against government officials accused of leaking national security information. One case was against Jeffrey Sterling, a former member of the CIA's Iran Task Force. The government suspected Sterling of being the source for an account in James Risen's book "State of War" concerning a botched CIA attempt to sabotage Iranian nuclear research.

The government subpoenaed Risen, contending that his testimony was essential to prove the case against Sterling. A district judge quashed the government's subpoena insofar as it required Risen to identify his source, U.S. v. Sterling, 818 F.Supp.2d 945 (E.D. Va. 2011), but the Fourth Circuit reversed. U.S. v. Sterling, 724 F.3d 482 (4th Cir. 2013).

Citing *Branzburg*, the court held: "There is no First Amendment testimonial privilege, absolute or qualified, that protects a reporter from being compelled to testify by the prosecution or the defense in criminal proceedings about criminal conduct that the reporter personally witnessed or participated in, absent a showing of bad faith, harassment, or other such non-legitimate motive, even though the reporter promised confidentiality to his source." The court rejected the argument that Justice Powell's *Branzburg* concurrence had "tacit[ly] endorsed" the dissenting opinion of Justice Stewart. The court further noted that the Supreme Court "has never varied from" *Branzburg*'s holding since it was decided, and thus it was the only court authorized to recognize a reporter's privilege springing from the First Amendment.

The court concluded that Risen "has 'direct information . . . concerning the commission of serious crimes.' [ ] Indeed, he can provide the *only* first-hand account of the commission of a most serious crime indicted by the grand jury—the illegal disclosure of classified, national security information by one who was entrusted by our government to protect national security, but who is charged with endangering it instead." The court also concluded that the there was no evidence that the government subpoenaed Risen's testimony in bad faith or for purposes of harassment. Instead, the government was "seek[ing] to compel evidence that Risen alone possesses—evidence that goes to the heart of the prosecution."

The court refused to recognize a reporter's privilege rooted in federal common law, again citing *Branzburg* as clear authority on the issue. The court concluded: "If Risen is to be protected from being compelled to testify and give what evidence of crime he possesses, in contravention of every citizen's duty to do so, we believe that decision should rest with the Supreme Court, which can revisit *Branzburg* and the policy arguments it rejected, or with Congress, which can more effectively and comprehensively weigh the policy arguments for and against adopting a privilege and define its scope."

Judge Roger Gregory, dissenting, argued that Risen's testimony should have been shielded by both a qualified First Amendment privilege and a federal common law privilege tailored specifically to the context of national security leaks. In order to overcome the qualified privilege, the government would have to show that the subpoenaed information was "highly material and relevant, necessary or critical to the maintenance of the claim, and not obtainable from other sources." To this inquiry, the judge would add in national security cases "consideration of two additional factors: the harm caused by the public dissemination of the information, and the newsworthiness of the information conveyed." Consideration of these additional factors would allow the privilege to be overridden in "matters of national security" in the face of "pressing governmental interests."

Applying this test in *Sterling*, the judge would have quashed the government's subpoena seeking Risen's testimony. After summarizing the evidence against Sterling in detail, the judge concluded that the government had failed to show a compelling interest in obtaining Risen's testimony regarding his confidential sources, because this testimony would be superfluous in light of the other strong evidence available to the government. Moreover, the information was available from other means.

Turning to the newsworthiness and harm inquiries, the judge found the information published by Risen concerning "the United States intelligence community's efforts concerning the development of the Iranian nuclear program" to be highly newsworthy. Indeed, Risen's book suggested that the efforts were so misguided that they "may have helped Iran advance its nuclear program." Globally, the information "portends to inform the reader of a blundered American intelligence mission in Iran," an especially important topic in the wake of the U.S. invasion of Iraq based on flawed intelligence information.

The judge, however, did not assess the harm caused by the leak of the classified information but instead would have remanded to the district court, because "the Government has not clearly articulated the nature, extent, and severity of the harm resulting from the leak. Without such evidence, it is impossible for a reviewing court to determine whether the First Amendment interest in presenting newsworthy information to the public—if indeed the district court finds the information newsworthy—is outweighed by the consequences of the leak." The judge conceded that this balancing might be difficult, but "[t]he First Amendment interest in informed popular debate does not simply vanish at the invocation of the words 'national security.'" (citing *United States v. Morison*, 844 F.2d 1057, 1081 (4th Cir. 1988) (Wilkinson, J., concurring)).

Risen's seven-year battle not to testify ended after Attorney General Eric Holder announced prosecutors would end attempts to compel his testimony. Matt Apuzzo, *Times Reporter Will Not Be Called to Testify in Leak Case*, N.Y. Times, Jan. 12, 2015. Jeffrey Sterling was sentenced to three and half years in prison.

In the two cases summarized above, both the D.C. Circuit and the Fourth Circuit Court of Appeals rejected the notion that *Branzburg* created a constitutional reporter's privilege, over strong dissents from Judge Tatel and Judge Gregory, respectively, who both argued for a modified balancing test in national security leaks cases. Does the modified balancing test tip the scales toward the Government's interest in protecting classified information or against it? To what extent would application of the modified balancing test lead to enhanced protection of confidential sources in leaks cases? To what extent would it allow federal judges to usurp the role of the legislative and executive branches?

Alternatives to Press Subpoenas in Leaks Cases. In some leaks investigations conducted during the Obama administration, the Justice Department was able to avoid subpoenaing reporters by secretly obtaining press telephone records and computer communications.

In one 2013 investigation the Associated Press learned that the Justice Department had secretly subpoenaed and obtained telephone records from twenty of its phone lines over a period of two months. According to the Associate Press report, the records:

> [L]isted outgoing calls for the work and personal phone numbers of individual reporters, for general AP office numbers in New York, Washington and Hartford, Conn., and for the main number for the AP in the House of Representatives press gallery. It was not clear if the records also included incoming calls or the duration of the calls.

Mark Sherman, *Gov't Obtains Wide AP Phone Records in Probe*, Assoc. Press, May 13, 2013. Attorney General Eric Holder defended the seizure as necessary to the investigation of a leak of national security information, and his deputy attorney general contended that informing AP in advance of the subpoena would have threatened the investigation. Critics of the seizure pointed out that journalists' phone records potentially reveal not only the identities of confidential sources but also that surveillance has a broad chilling effect on all sources. According to the AP's president and chief executive officer, the disclosures caused a palpable effect: "Officials who would normally talk to us, and people we would talk to in the normal course of news gathering, are already saying to us that they're a little reluctant to talk to us; they fear that they will be monitored by the government." Ravi Somaiya, Head of the A.P. Criticizes Seizure of Phone Records, N.Y. Times, May 19, 2013.

Also in May 2013, the Washington Post reported that the FBI had obtained a search warrant for the contents of the personal email of Fox News correspondent James Rosen in 2010. (James Risen and James Rosen are two separate journalists.) The search warrant issued based on an assertion that the government had probable cause to believe the reporter had violated the Espionage Act by soliciting a State Department official to leak classified information. Ann E. Marimow, A Rare Peek Into a Justice Department Leak Probe, Wash. Post, May 19, 2013. Although the government has prosecuted leakers of government information under the Espionage Act, it has not previously prosecuted a journalist for soliciting such leaks. Attorney General Eric Holder explained to a House judiciary committee that the government did not necessarily plan to proceed against Rosen; instead, the allegations of aiding and abetting allowed the government to sidestep the federal Privacy Protection Act's prohibition against government searches of newsrooms in criminal investigations. Ann E. Marimow, Justice Department's Scrutiny of Fox News Reporter James Rosen in Leak Case Draws Fire, Wash. Post, May 20, 2013.

New Media and Government Surveillance. "New media" companies like Google, Facebook, and Yahoo! have faced a different set of issues involving government surveillance and their role in enabling it. In early June 2013, Glenn Greenwald, a blogger for The Guardian newspaper, published portions of leaked documents detailing the National Security Agency's sweeping electronic surveillance program. See Glenn Greenwald, NSA Collecting Phone Records of Millions of Verizon Customers Daily, The Guardian, June 6, 2013. [Note: The Guardian is a British newspaper that also publishes a U.S. edition online.] The leaked documents confirmed the existence of two different surveillance programs. One program covered domestic telephone communications "metadata." Metadata includes the phone numbers of the parties to the call as well as "location data, call duration, unique identifiers, and the time and duration of all calls" collected on an "ongoing, daily basis."

The other program covered internet communications involving citizens outside the United States. The Washington Post and Guardian exposed a component of the internet surveillance program known as PRISM. See Barton Gellman & Laura Poitras, U.S., British Intelligence Mining Data from Nine U.S. Internet Companies in Broad Secret Program, Wash. Post, June 6, 2013. As part of the PRISM program, the

NSA and FBI obtain "audio and video chats, photographs, emails, documents, and connection logs" from major internet companies, such as Google. Data include the "live communications and stored information" of Internet users residing outside the United States and the Americans with whom they communicate. Glenn Greenwald, NSA Prism Program Taps In To User Data of Apple, Google and Others, The Guardian, June 6, 2013. The NSA's surveillance of Internet communications, unlike its surveillance of phone calls, includes the content of communications. Moreover, under a 2008 amendment to the Foreign Intelligence Surveillance Act of 1978, the NSA can obtain the data based merely upon a "reasonable belief" that one of the parties to the communications is outside the United States.

Faced with the revelation of the surveillance programs, United States government officials testified that the programs had thwarted a significant number of terrorist attacks. Donna Cassata, NSA Director Defends Sweeping Surveillance Program, Says Plot Against Wall Street Thwarted, Associated Press, June 18, 2013. The Department of Justice also charged Edward Snowden, who leaked the details of the surveillance programs to the media, with espionage and sought his extradition to the United States.

Several lawsuits were filed challenging the constitutionality of the surveillance programs under both the First and Fourth Amendments. On May 7, 2015, the U.S. Court of Appeals for the Second Circuit held that the NSA's "bulk telephone metadata collection program" was not authorized by §215 of the Patriot Act, which provided only for the collection of business records "relevant to an authorized investigation." American Civil Liberties Union v. Clapper, 785 F.3d 787 (2d Cir. 2015). The court objected to the government's expansive definition of the term relevant. The court noted:

> "Relevance" does not exist in the abstract; something is "relevant" or not in relation to a particular subject. Thus, an item relevant to a grand jury investigation may not be relevant at trial. In keeping with this usage, § 215 does not permit an investigative demand for any information relevant to fighting the war on terror, or anything relevant to whatever the government might want to know. It permits demands for documents "relevant to an authorized investigation." The government has not attempted to identify to what particular "authorized investigation" the bulk metadata of virtually all Americans' phone calls are relevant.

The court characterized the government as arguing, in effect, that all telephone metadata is relevant because "there is only one enormous 'anti-terrorism' investigation and that any records that might ever be of use in developing any aspect of that investigation are relevant to the overall counterterrorism effort." The court, however, did not determine whether the telephone surveillance program was also unconstitutional, at least in part because Congress was contemporaneously debating whether to reauthorize § 215 of the Patriot Act. The court vacated the district court's holding that the metadata collection was legal but did not enjoin the program because it was set to (and did) expire on June 1, 2015.

On June 2, 2015, Congress passed the USA FREEDOM Act, which replaced § 215 and gave the NSA authority until November 29, 2015, to continue collecting metadata while transitioning to a surveillance program that would require the government to make more specific records requests to the phone companies in order to receive metadata. Uniting and Strengthening America by Fulfilling Rights and Ensuring Effective Discipline Over Monitoring Act of 2015, Pub. L. No. 114–23, 129 Stat. 268. Upon passage of the Act, President Barack Obama announced he intended to act "expeditiously to ensure our national security professionals *again* have the full set of vital tools they need to continue protecting the country." Statement by President Obama on the USA FREEDOM Act, available at https://www.whitehouse.gov/the-press-office/2015/06/02/statement-president-usa-freedom-act (emphasis added). The FBI then petitioned the Foreign Intelligence Surveillance Court (FISC) to re-initiate its authority to collect data. Advocacy groups moved to intervene, but a federal judge on the FISC issued an opinion and order that allowed reimplementation of the bulk metadata collection program. He determined that "[i]n passing the USA FREEDOM Act, Congress clearly intended to end bulk data collection of business records and other tangible things. But what it took away with one hand, it gave back—for a limited time—with the other." In other words, the Act authorized bulk data collection during the 180-day "transition period" until November 29, 2015. The judge also concluded that the Second Circuit's ACLU v. Clapper decision, discussed above, was "not binding on the FISC." The judge wrote: "To a considerable extent, the Second Circuit's analysis rests on mischaracterizations of how this program works and on understandings that, if they had once been correct, have been superseded by the USA FREEDOM Act." Opinion and Order, In re Application of the Federal Bureau of Investigation for an Order Requiring the Production of Tangible Things, Docket No. BR 15–75, Foreign Intelligence Surveillance Court, June 29, 2015. The judge also rejected arguments that the bulk metadata collection violated the Fourth Amendment, citing prior FISC determinations to that effect. The NSA's authority to collect telephone metadata in bulk expired in November of 2015. The NSA may request specific telephone metadata records pursuant to the USA FREEDOM Act. The PRISM program remains unaffected by the USA FREEDOM Act.

One troubling facet of the government's mass surveillance programs is that the government often orders the intermediaries who turn over the information about subscribers to remain silent about their roles in the surveillance process. Google also filed a motion for declaratory judgment with the Foreign Intelligence Surveillance Act Court, contending that Google had a First Amendment right to publish details of the orders it receives from the court. Google also petitioned the Department of Justice to allow it to reveal how many FISA orders it receives and how many accounts those orders cover. John Cassidy, Google and the N.S.A. Spying Apparatus, New Yorker, June 20, 2013. In 2015 Twitter brought a similar suit in federal district court in California. Complaint for Declaratory Judgment, 28 U.S.C. §§ 2201 and 2202, Twitter v. Holder, No 14–cv–4480, (N.D. Cal. Oct. 7, 2014).

Prior to The Guardian's revelations, Amnesty International had challenged the constitutionality of the FISA Amendments, but the Supreme Court dismissed the case for lack of standing. Clapper v. Amnesty Int'l USA, 133 S.Ct. 1138 (2013). Amnesty International argued that its members include lawyers, journalists, and researchers engaged in international communications, and that it was objectively reasonable that the government would acquire their communications pursuant to FISA's surveillance provisions. They also contended that the risk of surveillance forced them to take burdensome measures to protect the confidentiality of their international communications. The district court granted summary judgment on standing grounds, but the Second Circuit reversed stating that Amnesty International had shown "present injuries in fact—economic and professional harms—stemming from a reasonable fear of future harmful government conduct." Justice Alito, writing for a 5–4 majority, reversed and remanded. The Court held: "respondents lack Article III standing because they cannot demonstrate that the future injury they purportedly fear is certainly impending and because they cannot manufacture standing by incurring costs in anticipation of non-imminent harm." The Court labeled as "speculative" the respondents' fears that the government would obtain their communications, ruling that their assertion of harm rested on a "highly attenuated chain of possibilities." The court further stated that "[a]llegations of a subjective 'chill' are not an adequate substitute for a claim of specific present objective harm or a threat of specific future harm" to establish standing. Justice Breyer, in a dissent joined by Justices Ginsburg, Sotomayor, and Kagan, asserted that the respondents' harm "is as likely to take place as are most future events that commonsense inference and ordinary knowledge of human nature tell us will happen." Do these assumptions still hold true?

E. APPLYING THE PRIVILEGE TO NON-CONFIDENTIAL MATERIALS

The typical case is one in which the source has authorized the reporter to use the information provided but insisted that his or her identity be kept confidential, or that the information itself be kept confidential. But often media organizations also resist disclosure of material that was not obtained in confidence. These problems arise most frequently in connection with subpoenas for reporters' notes, unpublished photos, or portions of video or audio tapes not broadcast. Media lawyers tend to refer to all of these loosely as "outtakes cases."

The analogy to other privileges, such as attorney-client, breaks down in these cases because those typically apply only when the information is given in confidence. More importantly, the rationale advanced by the reporters in *Branzburg*—that compelled disclosure will cause sources to cease talking to reporters—is not fully applicable because no promise of confidentiality to a source is at issue.

Some statutes by their terms protect only confidences, but many others explicitly cover nonconfidential materials. For example, the Maryland shield statute applies to notes, outtakes, photos, video and sound tapes, and film, as long as they have not been disseminated to the public. Other statutes seem to protect the reporter from being compelled to testify about even published material. The New Jersey statute, for example, protects "[a]ny news or information obtained in the course of pursuing [the reporter's] professional activities whether or not it is disseminated." It has been construed to prevent the reporter from being asked in court to verify the accuracy of quotes in a published story. In re Schuman, 552 A.2d 602 (N.J. 1989). What First Amendment interests might be jeopardized by requiring a reporter to give such testimony, or to produce originals of published photographs?

The following case holds, consistent with circuit precedent, that a First Amendment privilege applies to nonconfidential materials; however, the court denies the privilege to a film-maker who fails to maintain independence from his sources.

Chevron Corp. v. Berlinger

U.S. Court of Appeals, Second Circuit, 2011.
629 F.3d 297.

■ LEVAL, CIRCUIT JUDGE:

[Joseph] Berlinger created a documentary film, entitled *Crude*, about a litigation being conducted in the courts of Ecuador at Lago Agrio (the "Lago Agrio litigation") over allegations of environmental damage in Ecuador from petroleum exploration and extraction operations conducted by an affiliate of petitioner Chevron Corp. The district court directed Berlinger to produce to the petitioners the videotape footage constituting the outtakes of the film.

Petitioners . . . are: 1) Chevron, which is a defendant in the Lago Agrio litigation, as well as a plaintiff in an arbitration in the Hague against Ecuador protesting the Lago Agrio litigation, and 2) Rodrigo Pérez Pallares (Pérez) and Ricardo Reis Veiga (Reis), attorneys employed by Chevron, who are defendants in criminal proceedings in Ecuador based on their actions in connection with the environmental litigation. They sought the disclosure for use in those criminal proceedings.

Berlinger contends the district court abused its discretion in ordering production of the outtake footage. He argues that his investigative journalism recorded in the raw footage is protected from such compelled disclosure by the press privilege. He therefore asks that we overturn the district court's order.

We reject Berlinger's contention. Given all the circumstances of the making of the film, as reasonably found by the district court, particularly the fact that Berlinger's making of the film was solicited by the plaintiffs in the Lago Agrio litigation *for the purpose of telling their story,* and that changes to the film were made at their instance, Berlinger failed to carry his burden of showing that he collected information for the purpose of *independent* reporting and commentary. Accordingly, we cannot say it was error for the district court to conclude that petitioners had successfully overcome Berlinger's claim of privilege.

BACKGROUND

. . . In 1993, a group of residents of the Oriente region of Ecuador brought a class action suit in [federal district court in New York, alleging that a Texaco subsidiary polluted Ecuador's rain forests and rivers. While the class action, referred to as the *Aguinda* action, was pending, Texaco performed environmental remedial work pursuant to an agreement with the Government of Ecuador, which then agreed to release Texaco from all liability. Meanwhile, the federal district court in New York dismissed the *Aguinda* litigation on *forum non conveniens* grounds in 2001, and the Second Circuit affirmed.

In 2003, [a second class action was brought] against ChevronTexaco in Lago Agrio, Ecuador (the "Lago Agrio Litigation"). Plaintiffs asserted claims for, among other things, violations of an Ecuadorian environmental law enacted in 1999. [Defendants contended that the Government of Ecuador had previously released these claims.]

In 2005, Steven Donziger, one of the lead counsel for the plaintiffs in the Lago Agrio Litigation, solicited award-winning producer and filmmaker Joseph Berlinger to create a documentary depicting the Lago Agrio Litigation from the perspective of his clients. Berlinger recounted that:

> "During the summer of 2005, a charismatic American environmental lawyer named Steven Donziger knocked on my Manhattan office door. He was running a class-action lawsuit on behalf of 30,000 Ecuadorian inhabitants of the Amazon rainforest and was looking for a filmmaker *to tell his clients' story*." [emphasis added]

For the next three years, Berlinger shadowed the plaintiffs' lawyers and filmed "the events and people surrounding the trial," compiling six hundred hours of raw footage.

In 2006, while the Lago Agrio Litigation was pending, Rafael Vincente Correa Delgato was elected President of Ecuador on a platform of economic and social reform. [He urged prosecution of the former attorneys for Chevron/Texaco involved in procuring the release from liability in the Aguinda litigation. Chevron subsequently sought international arbitration in the Hague and asked for dismissal of the Lago Agrio litigation. The Chevron attorneys faced criminal prosecution in Ecuador.]

In 2009, Berlinger released his documentary, entitled *Crude,* [which depicts the Lago Agrio litigation, the oil pollution allegedly caused by the Texaco subsidiary and the serious health problems, including deaths, the pollution allegedly caused. The film contained a number of scenes indicating that Berlinger slanted the film towards plaintiffs' version of events at Donziger's direction. One scene indicated that Berlinger altered scenes at the direction of Donziger. Another scene showed Donziger describing his use of "pressure tactics" to influence an Ecuadorean judge and stating that "[t]his is something you would never do in the United States, but Ecuador, you know, this is how the game is played, it's dirty." Yet another scene showed Donziger with President Correa, in a manner that suggested that the President was clearly on plaintiffs' side and was willing to use his office to advance plaintiffs' cause, perhaps in violation of international law.

Chevron and attorneys Pérez, and Reis, who were facing criminal prosecution in Ecuador petitioned the federal district court in New York] to direct Berlinger to disclose all footage shot or acquired in the making of *Crude* for use by Chevron in the Lago Agrio litigation and the treaty arbitration, and for use by Pérez and Reis in the prosecutions brought against them in Ecuador. In support of their applications, they contended that, because Berlinger had free access to plaintiffs' counsel and shot footage when plaintiffs' counsel were in court chambers and dealing with [a] supposedly neutral court expert, the footage excluded from the film would show improper influence by Plaintiffs' counsel on the court and the court's expert. The Lago Agrio plaintiffs moved to intervene in opposition and were permitted to do so. Upon consideration of the submissions of the parties, the district court granted the petitions, ordering disclosure of the outtakes.

. . .

Berlinger appealed and moved for a stay of the district court's order. On June 8, 2010, a motions panel of this court stayed enforcement of the order until otherwise ordered by the panel assigned to hear the merits of the appeal.

DISCUSSION

We review the district court's factual findings for clear error, and its order directing production of the *Crude* footage for abuse of discretion. [ ]. Identification of the correct legal standard raises a pure question of law, as to which we exercise plenary review. [ ].

Berlinger contends the district court abused its discretion in rejecting his claim of press privilege and consequently ordering him to produce his outtakes. We disagree.

This circuit has long recognized a qualified evidentiary privilege for information gathered in a journalistic investigation. See, e.g., Gonzales v. NBC, 194 F.3d 29 (2d Cir. 1999); [ ]. The privilege for such information is intended to protect the public's interest in being informed by "a vigorous, aggressive *and independent* press," [ ], by limiting the circumstances in which litigants may obtain access to press files through court-ordered discovery. The protection accorded by the privilege, although not absolute, [ ] is at its highest when the information sought to be protected was acquired by the journalist through a promise of confidentiality. Forcing the press to breach a promise of confidentiality threatens its ability in the future to perform its public function by impairing its ability to acquire information for publication. [ ]. But the privilege is not limited to circumstances where the sources of information have been promised confidentiality. We have observed, even where there was no issue of betrayal of a promised confidence, that "wholesale exposure of press files to litigant scrutiny would burden the press with heavy costs of subpoena compliance, and could otherwise impair its ability to perform its duties—particularly if potential sources were deterred from speaking to the press, or insisted on remaining anonymous, because of the likelihood that they would be sucked into litigation." *Id.* at 35. We have noted, furthermore, that unrestricted litigant access to press files would create socially wasteful incentives for press entities "to clean out files containing potentially valuable information lest they incur substantial costs" of subpoena compliance, and would risk "the symbolic harm of making journalists appear to be an investigative arm of the judicial system, the government, or private parties." *Id.*

A person need not be a credentialed reporter working for an established press entity to establish entitlement to the privilege. *See Branzburg*, 408 U.S. at 705, [ ]. Nonetheless, in collecting the information in question, the person must have acted in the role . . . favored by the public interest that motivates the privilege—the role of the *independent* press.

. . .

For determining the existence, or in any event the strength, of the press privilege, all forms of intention to publish or disseminate information are not on equal footing. While freedom of speech and of the press belongs to virtually anyone who intends to publish anything (with a few narrow exceptions), all those who intend to publish do not share an equal entitlement to the press privilege from compelled disclosure. Those who gather and publish information because they have been commissioned to publish in order to serve the objectives of others who have a stake in the subject of the reporting are not acting as an independent press. Those who do not retain independence as to what they will publish but are subservient to the objectives of others who have a stake in what will be published have either a weaker privilege or none at all.

This distinction is perhaps best understood through an illustrative example. Consider two persons, Smith and Jones, who separately undertake to investigate and write a book or article about a public figure in national politics. Smith undertakes to discover whatever she can through her investigations and to write a book that reflects whatever her investigations may show. Jones has been hired or commissioned by the public figure to write a book extolling his virtues and rebutting his critics. Smith unquestionably presents a stronger claim of entitlement to the press privilege (which is not to say the privilege might not be overcome, depending on the circumstances). Jones, who was commissioned to write a book promoting a particular point of view regardless of what her investigations may reveal, either possesses no privilege at all or, if she possesses the privilege, holds one that is weaker and more easily overcome.

The privilege is designed to support the press in its valuable public service of seeking out and revealing truthful information. An undertaking to publish matter in order to promote the interests of another, regardless of justification, does not serve the same public interest, regardless of whether the resultant work may prove to be one of high quality. It is not the policy of the law to exempt such undertakings from the obligation to produce information relevant to a dispute before a court of law.

Applying these principles here, we believe that the district court's findings adequately justified its denial of the press privilege. Although the court did not explicitly state a finding that Berlinger failed to show his independence, its findings that (1) Donziger "solicited Berlinger to create a documentary of the litigation from the perspective of his clients," and (2) "Berlinger concededly removed at least one scene from the final version of *Crude* at their direction," essentially assert that conclusion. It was reasonable for the court to conclude on the basis of these findings that Berlinger's claim of privilege was overcome.

Our ruling in no way passes judgment on the value of Berlinger's film. We rule merely that the district court's factual findings were not clearly erroneous, and that those findings justified a conclusion that, given all the circumstances, Chevron overcame his claim of entitlement to withhold the outtakes under the press privilege. Our ruling likewise does not imply that a journalist who has been solicited to investigate an issue and presents the story supporting the point of view of the entity that solicited her cannot establish the privilege. Without doubt, such a journalist can establish entitlement to the privilege by establishing the independence of her journalistic process, for example, through evidence of editorial and financial independence. But the burden is on the person who claims the privilege to show entitlement, and in this instance, Berlinger failed to persuade the district court that he undertook the task with independence.

Berlinger argues that the district court's order must be overturned because Chevron failed to establish that the *Crude* outtakes contain information of likely relevance to a significant issue in the foreign proceedings which is not reasonably available from other sources. He asserts that some of the information in the footage is plainly irrelevant to the foreign proceedings, and that some of it is available from other sources because film crews employed by Chevron filmed many of the proceedings he filmed.

This argument, however, proceeds from the incorrect premise that our description in *Gonzales* of the showing necessary to overcome the privilege of an independent press entity would apply regardless of whether the press entity claiming the privilege's protections acted with independence. *Gonzales* said no such thing. Our statement that a civil litigant may obtain nonconfidential materials from "a nonparty press entity" if it establishes "the materials at issue are of likely relevance to a significant issue in the case, and are not reasonably obtainable from other available sources" described the showing necessary to overcome the privilege claimed for an independent press undertaking. In that case, NBC had secretly filmed footage of Louisiana police conducting traffic stops on a highway in order to determine whether the police were motivated by bias and engaged in racial profiling. . . . Because the fact of NBC's independence was uncontested, our discussion assumed that the press entity was acting with independence; we did not address the analysis that would control in the event that the independence of the subpoenaed press entity were questioned.

A person (or entity) that undertakes to publish commentary but fails to establish that its research and reporting were done with independence from the subject of the reporting either has no press privilege at all, or in any event, possesses a privilege that is weaker and more easily overcome. We need not decide in this case whether the consequence of the failure of the claimant of the privilege to establish independence means it has a weaker privilege or no privilege at all. It is sufficient to rule that given Berlinger's failure to establish his independence from the Lago Agrio plaintiffs, the district court did not abuse its discretion in ordering the production notwithstanding Berlinger's claim that some of the footage was either irrelevant to the proceedings or could have been obtained from other sources.

. . . .

We hereby vacate the stay order which we entered on June 8, 2010, and affirm in full the district court's ruling of May 10, 2010. The material produced under the district court's order shall be used by the petitioners solely for litigation, arbitration, or submission to official bodies, either local or international. The case is remanded to the district court for all purposes.

NOTES AND QUESTIONS

1. The "outtakes" privilege recognized by the Second Circuit would protect journalists from having to turn over their materials absent a litigant's showing "that the materials at issue are of likely relevance to a significant issue in the case, and are not reasonably obtainable from other available sources." Gonzales v. National Broadcasting Co, 194 F.3d 29 (2d Cir. 1998). Can you articulate the reasons that the showing necessary to overcome the privilege is less stringent in outtakes cases than in cases involving confidential sources?

2. Would the absence of a privilege protecting nonconfidential sources encourage litigants to engage in "fishing expeditions" to discover potentially relevant information in press files? Are there factors other than the existence of the privilege that might deter this behavior? Not all courts have accepted the argument that a First Amendment privilege ought to apply to nonconfidential sources. In McKevitt v. Pallasch, 339 F.3d 530 (7th Cir. 2003), the Seventh Circuit criticized cases that extend the privilege to nonconfidential sources based on "concern with harassment, burden, using the press as an investigative arm of government, and so forth," noting that "these considerations were rejected by *Branzburg* even in the context of a confidential source." The Seventh Circuit questioned "what possible bearing the First Amendment could have on the question of compelled disclosure" when the information sought comes from a nonconfidential source. The court noted, however, that courts could still protect reporters by ensuring that "a subpoena duces tecum directed to the media, like any other subpoena duces tecum, is reasonable in the circumstances, which is the general criterion for judicial review of subpoenas." Under this approach, could a court take into account the fact that the media, particularly broadcasters, are subpoenaed more frequently than many other types of businesses?

3. If burdens imposed by compulsory disclosure of outtakes raise free speech concerns, would similar concerns be raised if comparable burdens were imposed by other legal requirements (e.g., FCC regulations requiring preservation of outtakes, or discovery rules requiring employees to spend time responding to libel suits)?

4. If production of outtakes has the adverse First Amendment consequences discussed above, should media feel free to turn them over voluntarily?

5.   Professor RonNell Andersen Jones contends that the Supreme Court should revisit the privilege issue from the perspective of the anonymous-speech rights of the confidential source. The Supreme Court has recognized a qualified constitutional right to speak anonymously, and that right is implicated by subpoenas of reporters or others to reveal their confidential sources. Putting right to speak anonymously at the center of the privilege inquiry in confidential-source cases would reduce the need to define who is a reporter and more squarely focus the inquiry on the "wider array of First Amendment values implicated by the situation." The privilege envisioned by Professor Jones could be asserted by either source or reporter, and the right would be overcome upon "a showing that the subpoena was issued in good faith, is directly and materially relevant to a core claim or defense, and seeks information that is unavailable from any other source." RonNell Andersen Jones, Rethinking Reporter's Privilege, 111 Mich. L. Rev. 1221 (2013). Would a privilege rooted in the anonymous-speech rights of the confidential source lead to the privilege being overcome more or less often than a privilege rooted in the newsgathering rights of the press (and the information flow interests of the public)?

1. REPORTER AS EYEWITNESS

Reporters are rarely able to avoid testifying when they are eyewitnesses to crimes or other activities that become the subject of legal proceedings.

For example, the Florida Supreme Court held that a qualified First Amendment reporter's privilege "extends to both confidential and nonconfidential information gathered in the course of a reporter's employment" but "does not apply to eyewitness observations or physical evidence, including recordings, of a crime." See State v. Davis, 720 So.2d 220 (Fla. 1998). Likewise, the Florida shield statute "applies only to information or eyewitness observations obtained within the normal scope of employment and does not apply to physical evidence, eyewitness observations, or visual or audio recording of crimes." See Fla. Stat. § 90.5015(2). As a result, no privilege is available in Florida to a reporter who witnesses a police search and arrest, Miami Herald Publishing Co. v. Morejon, 561 So.2d 577 (Fla. 1990), or for outtakes depicting an arrest, CBS, Inc. v. Jackson, 578 So.2d 698 (Fla. 1991).

Similarly, a federal district court held, in Pinkard v. Johnson, 118 F.R.D. 517 (M.D. Ala. 1987), that a First Amendment privilege protected the notes of a reporter who attended a public meeting, but that no privilege attached to the reporter's observations at that meeting.

When the reporter has witnessed the commission of a crime, the courts may hold the privilege inapplicable even when the observation occurred pursuant to a promise of confidentiality. See, e.g., U.S. v. Criden, 633 F.2d 346 (3rd Cir. 1980). Should this reservation apply when the only crime the reporter has witnessed is an illegal leak?

F. SEARCH WARRANTS

Newsroom Searches. The protections of the preceding sections may be circumvented if authorities are free to obtain warrants to search newsrooms and seize notes, memoranda, photos, tapes, or other evidence described in the warrants. After a Supreme Court decision holding that such searches were permissible, the practice seemed to pose a serious threat to confidential relationships and editorial autonomy for some time. Congress and many state legislatures quickly passed laws restricting newsroom searches, however, and the threat dissipated.

The problem erupted when investigators searched the offices of the campus newspaper at Stanford. Police believed that Stanford Daily photographers had taken photographs that would aid in identifying persons who had assaulted policemen during a violent campus demonstration. The police obtained a search warrant and served it on the Daily. The affidavits accompanying the request for the warrant indicated no reason why a subpoena might not have sufficed.

After the search, the Daily brought an action under 42 U.S.C. § 1983 against the chief of police and other local officials for a determination that the search had violated the Daily's First, Fourth, and Fourteenth Amendment rights. The district judge granted declaratory relief, concluding that no search warrant could be issued against any person not suspected of a crime unless a subpoena was shown to be impracticable. Where the object of the search was a newspaper, the judge ruled that a warrant could issue only "where there is a *clear showing* that (1) important materials will be destroyed or removed from the jurisdiction; *and* (2) a restraining order would be futile." The court of appeals adopted the trial judge's opinion and affirmed.

The Supreme Court reversed 5–3, with Justices Stewart, Marshall, and Stevens dissenting. Zurcher v. Stanford Daily, 436 U.S. 547 (1978). Justice White, for the majority, first rejected a Fourth Amendment claim that search warrants could not be directed at any third parties, i.e., persons not themselves suspected of criminal activity. He then turned to the narrower argument that the First Amendment forbade searches directed at the press:

> The District Court held, and respondents assert here, that, whatever may be true of third-party searches generally, where the third party is a newspaper, there are additional factors derived from the First Amendment that justify a nearly *per se* rule forbidding the search warrant and permitting only the subpoena *duces tecum.* The general submission is that searches of newspaper offices for evidence of crime reasonably believed to be on the premises will seriously threaten the ability of the press

to gather, analyze, and disseminate news. This is said to be true for several reasons: First, searches will be physically disruptive to such an extent that timely publication will be impeded. Second, confidential sources of information will dry up, and the press will also lose opportunities to cover various events because of fears of the participants that press files will be readily available to the authorities. Third, reporters will be deterred from recording and preserving their recollections for future use if such information is subject to seizure. Fourth, the processing of news and its dissemination will be chilled by the prospects that searches will disclose internal editorial deliberations. Fifth, the press will resort to self-censorship to conceal its possession of information of potential interest to the police.

But the Court held that these risks required no greater protection than that provided to all by the Fourth Amendment proscription against unreasonable searches and seizures. Even if the materials sought to be seized might be protected by the First Amendment, that meant only that the requirements of the Fourth Amendment must be applied with "scrupulous exactitude." Nothing in the Fourth Amendment barred searches of newspaper offices. They were subject to the same procedures, including the approval of "neutral magistrates." Few searches of newspaper premises had occurred recently. "This reality hardly suggests abuse; and if abuse occurs, there will be time enough to deal with it. Furthermore, the press is not only an important, critical, and valuable asset to society, but it is not easily intimidated—nor should it be."

The media turned to the legislatures for relief and within a few months they received it. Congress passed The Privacy Protection Act of 1980, 42 U.S.C. § 2000aa, that applies to state as well as federal searches. It forbids any official from searching or seizing documentary materials or "any work product material possessed by a person reasonably believed to have a purpose to disseminate to the public a newspaper, book, broadcast, or other similar form of public communication...." Documentary materials include photos, film, tapes, discs, and punch cards. Work product includes notes and drafts, but also mental impressions, conclusions, opinions, or theories of the person who prepared, produced, authored, or created the material.

The statute does not apply where the person possessing the materials is a suspect in the offense to which the materials relate. Documentary materials other than work product may be seized if necessary to prevent death or serious injury or to prevent the material from being destroyed, or if the subject has failed to produce them in response to a subpoena duces tecum after exhausting all appellate remedies. The statute also contains exceptions for national security information and child pornography.

State statutes restricting searches were passed in California, Connecticut, Illinois, Nebraska, New Jersey, Oregon, Texas, Washington, and Wisconsin. Searches by state authorities are controlled by these statutes to the extent that they are more restrictive than the federal statute, and some are. The Texas statute, for example, bans all newsroom searches except for weapons, drugs, or other contraband. Tex. Code Crim. Proc. § 18.01.

Despite these prohibitions, law enforcement officers still raid newsrooms occasionally. In 2010 prosecutors and police, apparently unaware of the federal statute prohibiting newsroom searches, executed a search of the newsroom of The Breeze, the student newspaper at James Madison University. The officers sought evidence in connection with a campus block party that resulted in arrests, property damage, and injuries. They confiscated 926 photos and threatened to confiscate all computers and files. A settlement eventually resulted in the students allowing the prosecutor to keep 20 photos that contained information unavailable from any other source, the return of the rest of the photos to the newsroom, a $10,000 payment to The Breeze for legal fees, an apology from the prosecutor, and the prosecutor's promise to only use subpoenas in any future requests for evidence from a news organization.

Also in 2010, agents raided the home of Gizmodo editor Jason Chen. Gizmodo, an Internet site owned by Gawker Media, had published articles about a new Apple iPhone. Members of the Rapid Enforcement Allied Computer Team, a collaboration between law enforcement agencies and computer businesses like Apple, said they were seeking evidence to decide whether to file charges against the individual who sold the iPhone prototype to Chen. The search warrant was eventually withdrawn and Gizmodo and Chen agreed to release a small portion of documents pursuant to a properly issued subpoena.

Both of these searches are reported in Newsroom Searches Occurring Despite Law, Reporters Committee for Freedom of the Press, Summer 2010, available at www.rcfp.org.

When authorities undertake newsroom searches in violation of the federal statute, they may be liable to the news organization for attorney's fees even when the damages are nominal. For example, the Minneapolis Star Tribune and a local television station won $80,000 in attorney's fees for an illegal knock-and-enter search by the FBI, even though the search did not preclude them from using the photos and film seized or even cause them to miss deadlines. See Sandra Davidson Scott, Police Are Still Storming Newsrooms With Search Warrants, Editor & Publisher, Sept. 17, 1994.

Some journalists have expressed concern that the Foreign Intelligence Surveillance Act (FISA), 50 U.S.C. §§ 1801–1811, might trump the Privacy Protection Act, permitting the government to spy on journalists and discover their sources. FISA, as expanded in 2001 by the

PATRIOT Act, created a special court with powers to issue secret warrants authorizing officials to perform wiretaps and searches. The court cannot grant such an order for the sole purpose of investigating activities protected by the First Amendment, but investigators need only show that national security is a "significant purpose" in order to obtain a FISA warrant. Because proceedings of the FISA court are secret, a journalist whose source is revealed in the course of a FISA inquiry might never learn of the breach. See Confidential Sources and Information: FISA warrants, The First Amendment Handbook, The Reporter's Committee for Freedom of the Press, available at www.rcfp.org.

Computer Records. Law enforcement investigations today often include seizure of computers or computer hard drives. What legal principles, if any, protect news media computers or hard drives from such actions is largely unsettled. The Fourth Amendment prohibition against unreasonable search and seizure is little help because the Supreme Court has held that a demand to furnish physical evidence to a grand jury is not a seizure. See U.S. v. Dionisio, 410 U.S. 1 (1973).

In 2006, the Pennsylvania attorney general, conducting a grand jury investigation apparently implicating some public officials, subpoenaed computer hard drives of Lancaster Newspapers. He said he was looking for Internet histories, including specific Internet addresses and cached Web pages.

The newspapers offered to permit agents of the attorney general to examine the hard drives in the newspaper offices in the presence of newspaper employees. The attorney general insisted on taking possession of the hard drives, though he offered to make copies and return them so the newspapers would have access to the information on them. The trial judge ordered the newspapers to turn the drives over to the attorney general but provided that a technology expert in the attorney general's office would examine them and extract only the Internet histories, and that the expert would not pass that information along to his boss until it was reviewed by the judge to make sure it did not include anything not relevant to the investigation.

The newspapers sought emergency review, invoking the federal statute restricting newsroom searches, the Pennsylvania shield statute, and the First Amendment. They conceded that specific records could be subpoenaed, but contended that turning over entire hard drives would encompass much information, including possibly confidential sources, not related to the investigation.

The Pennsylvania Supreme Court held that the procedure ordered by the trial judge "is not sufficient to address the potential chilling effect referenced by the newspapers, as the unavoidable effect is that the essential 'filing cabinets' of the newspapers are transferred to the custody and control of the executive branch of government." The court said such a transfer could only take place pursuant to a properly issued search warrant and suggested that the judge might appoint a neutral expert to analyze the drives and report the contents to the court. See In re Twenty-Fourth Statewide Investigating Grand Jury, 907 A.2d 505 (Pa. 2006).

Telephone Records. One way to identify sources is to obtain reporters' telephone records from the phone company. Phone companies are accustomed to receiving subpoenas for their customers' records and often do not resist. Such subpoenas pose special dangers for media; they may not even be aware that the subpoena has been issued and once the prosecutor or other requester has the records, he or she may be able to learn about sources for stories unrelated to the one that led to the investigation. Similar dangers arise from subpoenas seeking customers' email records from Internet service providers.

Although the courts acknowledge these dangers, media still have had little success in preventing such subpoenas. New York Times Co. v. Gonzales, 459 F.3d 160 (2d Cir. 2006), offers an example of recognition of the dangers and refusal to block the subpoena. The prosecutor seeking the records was Patrick Fitzgerald, who was also special counsel in the *Miller* case, and one of the reporters whose records were sought was Judith Miller, but the case was unrelated to the Plame leak investigation.

The court held that whatever protection reporters would have against subpoenas issued to them directly also protects their third-party telephone records, and that the reporters can use declaratory judgment procedure to establish that a subpoena issued to the telephone company should be quashed. The court held that the federal common law reporters' privilege recognized in the Second Circuit would apply if the reporters themselves had been subpoenaed, and therefore it was applicable to a subpoena issued to the telephone company as well.

The majority held that the privilege had been overcome, however. The Justice Department convinced the court that the reporters' telephone records were critical to a grand jury investigation of a leak that allegedly tipped off two Islamic charities that the government planned to seize their assets and search their offices. The court said the reporters were the only witnesses, other than the leaker, who could identify the source of the leak, and the leak was a serious matter because it might imperil the safety of officers attempting to execute the search.

Judge Robert Sack, dissenting, noted that there was no evidence that the government had even examined its own phone records to see if those might reveal which government employees had talked to Times reporters, and the only evidence of necessity was the prosecutor's affidavit that the government had exhausted alternative means of obtaining the information. "The government thus takes the position that it is entitled to obtain the Times' telephone records in order to determine the identity of its reporters' confidential sources because it has satisfied itself that the applicable standard has been met," Sack wrote.

Justice Department guidelines, as amended in 2015, specify that "the use of certain law enforcement tools, including subpoenas, court orders issued pursuant to [provisions of the Electronic Communications Privacy Act], and search warrants to seek information from, or records of, non-consenting members of the news media" should be treated as "extraordinary measures, not standard investigatory practices." The guidelines set forth standards proscribing when such extraordinary measures may be employed and procedures that must be followed before use, including authorization by the Attorney General or other senior official. The amended guidelines are codified in 28 C.F.R. § 50.10 (2015).

These guidelines apply only to federal prosecutors. Thus, the guidelines do not inhibit state officials or private litigants who seek to learn the identity of sources by subpoenaing the reporter's telephone and travel records. Does the First Amendment furnish a basis for refusing to comply? This issue was raised in a libel suit by the Philip Morris Companies against ABC News over the network's reports that the company added extra nicotine to cigarettes. In an apparent attempt to learn the identity of a former tobacco industry manager who appeared in silhouette in the reports, the company obtained 13 subpoenas aimed at tracing the movements of the correspondent and producer during the period they were researching the programs. After first ordering ABC to turn over the records, the judge vacated the order pending further discovery, which he said might show that the tobacco company had no compelling need for the information. See Philip Morris Cos. v. ABC Inc., 23 Med. L. Rptr. 2434 (Va. Cir. Ct. 1995). Should subpoenas of this sort be analyzed as if they were requests for the journalists to name their sources?

In drafting legislation involving search warrants or telephone records, how broadly should the group to be protected be defined? Would the same definition be appropriate for shield legislation?

CHAPTER X

ACCESS TO INFORMATION

"[W]ithout some protection for seeking out the news, freedom of the press could be eviscerated," Justice White wrote in Branzburg v. Hayes, the reporter's privilege decision. For most journalists and most news organizations, barriers to the seeking out of news are the most frequent source of contact (and perhaps frustration) with the law. By far the largest body of media law is that dealing with access to records, meetings, institutions, courtrooms, disaster sites, and private premises where news is being made. Most of this law is statutory or administrative and takes the form of freedom of information acts, open meetings statutes, and rules of courts and legislatures. Moreover, much of access law is state law, which means that its texture and variety are difficult to capture in a casebook.

The First Amendment plays only a limited role in access disputes. Although the Supreme Court has recognized a constitutional right of access, it has done so almost exclusively in the context of disputes over access to judicial proceedings and judicial records. Because this body of law has developed more or less independently of the rest of access law, and because the Supreme Court has not extended its principles to other access questions, we treat courtroom access separately in the next chapter. After reading that chapter, however, you should consider whether constitutional rights to gather news about judicial proceedings might not also apply to some of the matters discussed in this chapter.

Access laws emerged out of a broad consensus that citizens in a democracy are entitled to know what their governments are up to. Giving citizens unfettered access to government documents and processes, however, threatens other important values, such as privacy, national security, and administrative efficiency. Historically, many of the major developments in access law have come about as the result of statutes enacted to address specific privacy issues.

This chapter considers primarily access to *public* information and institutions in control of the government, while giving some attention to the rapidly expanding array of statutes and regulations that limit access to information about private citizens, whether held by the government or others. Although government information is an important news source for the media, it should also be noted that reporters often rely on broadly available, commercial information sources and are subject to the same laws that affect access by other citizens when they do. For example, many larger media organizations access public records through individual government websites or commercial service providers. Similarly, many journalists rely on information in Internet-based people searches or credit reports to identify and locate sources.

In this chapter, we first examine the law governing access to public records and public meetings, which is primarily statutory. We then consider First Amendment-based claims of access to public institutions such as prisons. Next, we address claims of access to accident and other news scenes, where the relevant law is usually common law. We then turn to the impact of criminal law on access. Finally, we examine questions that arise when access is offered to some but not others. Throughout these sections, note how here too the definition for the word journalist can become important.

A. ACCESS TO RECORDS

1. FREEDOM OF INFORMATION ACT

James Madison wrote in 1822 that "[a] popular Government, without popular information, or the means of acquiring it, is but a Prologue to a Farce or a Tragedy; or perhaps both. Knowledge will forever govern ignorance: And a people who mean to be their own Governors, must arm themselves with the power which knowledge gives."

As long as legislatures were the preeminent sources of law in the country, persons concerned with government actions could keep track of the process. With the New Deal, however, many administrative agencies and organizations emerged. Congress empowered most to promulgate their own internal rules, to issue substantive regulations, to enforce laws, to adjudicate some controversies, and take other actions of great importance to citizens. The sheer number of regulations and orders being promulgated made it difficult to keep track of the process. In addition, some of the agencies were not open about their operations.

In 1946 Congress passed the Administrative Procedure Act to require all administrative agencies to follow certain procedures in the adoption of regulations and in their adjudicative hearings. Congress also sought to make the internal rules and procedures of agencies more readily available to the public. The APA stated that all public records could be inspected by "persons properly and directly concerned" with the subject matter unless the records were held to be confidential "for good cause." But "good cause" was a simple standard that allowed federal agencies sufficient discretion to circumvent even the minimal inspection principle. As a result, this first effort at openness was not notably successful.

In 1967 Congress responded to growing criticism by adopting the first version of the Freedom of Information Act. The 1967 Act required notice of agency actions, including organization, procedures, and policies, as well as final opinions rendered, and permitted "any person" to request records from "each agency." The Act also provided nine categories of information that were exempt from disclosure. These exemptions soon proved so broad that requesters believed an agency could force any record into one of the exemptions. The 1967 Act also lacked an effective enforcement mechanism. The culture of secrecy in Washington that was aroused by the Cold War remained largely untouched by the FOIA.

In 1974, with the Watergate scandal still lingering, Congress passed a bill amending the FOIA and easily overrode President Gerald Ford's veto. As amended, the FOIA (codified at 5 U.S.C. § 552) applies to all federal government agencies except Congress, the courts, the government of the District of Columbia, and courts martial or the military during wartime. The Act requires each agency to publish in the Federal Register a description of its organization and a list of its personnel through whom the public can obtain information. Each agency must also explain the procedures by which it will furnish information, and must make available to the public staff manuals and internal instructions that affect members of the public, final opinions in adjudicated cases, and current indexes. Records must be segregated so that agencies cannot classify entire categories of records as exempt.

Under the FOIA, "any person" may request information from an agency and the agency must supply it unless the information fits within one of the exemptions. FOIA's exemptions from disclosure include (1) materials "to be kept secret in the interest of national defense or foreign policy" in accordance with an Executive order; (2) materials "related solely to the internal personnel rules and practices of an agency"; (3) certain materials "specifically exempted from disclosure by statute"; (4) certain trade-secret and commercial information (5) certain "inter-agency or intra-agency memorandums or letters"; (6) certain "personnel and medical files and "similar files the disclosure of which would constitute a clearly unwarranted invasion of personal privacy"; (7) certain "records or information compiled for law enforcement purposes"; (8) records of bank examinations; and (9) geological information relating to oil and gas wells. See 5 U.S.C. §§ 552(b)(1)–(b)(9).

In describing the FOIA, the Supreme Court has explained that "disclosure, not secrecy, is the dominant objective of the Act" and has asserted that, as a result, "exemptions have been consistently given a narrow compass." Department of the Interior v. Klamath Water Users Protective Ass'n, 532 U.S. 1, 7–8 (2001). FOIA establishes a presumption in favor of disclosure of agency records: the burden is on the agency to prove that the information it wishes to withhold falls under a claimed exemption. Moreover, if exempt material can be segregated from the rest of the record, the government agency responding to the FOIA request must make available the segregated material not subject to an exemption.

If an agency denies a FOIA request, the requester may request an administrative appeal, and must do so before pursuing a judicial remedy. However, few administrative appeals are successful: In 2007 only three percent resulted in full disclosure of the records requested, and ten percent resulted in partial disclosure. Coalition of Journalists for Open Government, An In-Depth Analysis of FOIA Performance from 1998–2007. (The Coalition ceased operations in 2008).

Despite this unpromising record, the FOIA provides several remedies to assist enforcement. Federal courts may order agencies to disclose and may award reasonable attorney fees and litigation costs to successful litigants, 5 U.S.C. § 552(a)(4)(E), and government officials who "arbitrarily and capriciously" withhold requested records are subject to disciplinary legal actions, though such actions are rare. 5 U.S.C. § 552(a)(4)(F).

The FOIA generates millions of requests and hundreds of lawsuits each year. The Supreme Court has decided numerous FOIA cases, most of them not involving media. Even the media cases are too numerous for full treatment here; a few illustrative examples must suffice.

National Archives and Records Administration v. Favish

Supreme Court of the United States, 2004.
541 U.S. 157.

■ KENNEDY, J., delivered the opinion for a unanimous Court.

This case requires us to interpret the Freedom of Information Act (FOIA), 5 U.S.C. § 552. FOIA does not apply if the requested data fall within one or more exemptions. Exemption 7(C) excuses from disclosure "records or information compiled for law enforcement purposes" if their production "could reasonably be expected to constitute an unwarranted invasion of personal privacy." § 552(b)(7)(C).

In Department of Justice v. Reporters Comm. for Freedom of Press, 489 U.S. 749 (1989), we considered the scope of Exemption 7(C) and held that release of the document at issue would be a prohibited invasion of the personal privacy of the person to whom the document referred. The principal document involved was the criminal record, or rap sheet, of the person who himself objected to the disclosure. Here, the information pertains to an official investigation into the circumstances surrounding an apparent suicide. The initial question is whether the exemption extends to the decedent's family when the family objects to the release of photographs showing the condition of the body at the scene of death. If we find the decedent's family does have a personal privacy interest recognized by the statute, we must then consider whether that privacy claim is outweighed by the public interest in disclosure.

I

Vincent Foster, Jr., deputy counsel to President Clinton, was found dead in Fort Marcy Park, located just outside Washington, D. C. The United States Park Police conducted the initial investigation and took color photographs of the death scene, including 10 pictures of Foster's body. The investigation concluded that Foster committed suicide by shooting himself with a revolver. Subsequent investigations by the Federal Bureau of Investigation, committees of the Senate and the House of Representatives, and independent counsels Robert Fiske and Kenneth Starr reached the same conclusion. Despite the unanimous finding of these five investigations, a citizen interested in the matter, Allan Favish, remained skeptical. Favish is now a respondent in this proceeding. . . .

. . . Favish filed the present FOIA request in his own name, seeking, among other things, 11 pictures, 1 showing Foster's eyeglasses and 10 depicting various parts of Foster's body. Like the National Park Service, the Office of Independent Counsel (OIC) refused the request under Exemption 7(C). [Favish brought suit in the District Court for the Central District of California, and the court granted partial summary judgment to OIC.]

. . . [T]he court held, first, that Foster's surviving family members enjoy personal privacy interests that could be infringed by disclosure of the photographs. It then found, with respect to the asserted public interest, that "[Favish] has not sufficiently explained how disclosure of these photographs will advance his investigation into Foster's death." Any purported public interest in disclosure, moreover, "is lessened because of the exhaustive investigation that has already occurred regarding Foster's death." Balancing the competing interests, the court concluded that "the privacy interests of the Foster family members outweigh the public interest in disclosure." [ ]

[After two appeals, the Ninth Circuit Court of Appeals affirmed the trial court's order to disclose four photos that the trial court determined were not within Exemption 7(C).]

. . .

II

It is common ground among the parties that the death-scene photographs in OIC's possession are "records or information compiled for law enforcement purposes" as that phrase is used in Exemption 7(C). This leads to the question whether disclosure of the four [disputed] photographs "could reasonably be expected to constitute an unwarranted invasion of personal privacy."

[Justice Kennedy, after considering Favish's arguments against extending Exemption 7(C) to the photographs of Vince Foster, concluded that the exemption applies to the contested materials. He explained that "[b]urial rites or their counterparts have been respected in almost all civilizations from time immemorial" and noted that "[t]he outrage at seeing the bodies of American soldiers mutilated and dragged through the streets [in Iraq] is but a modern instance of the same understanding of the interests decent people have for those whom they have lost." Accordingly, "[f]amily members have a personal stake in honoring and mourning their dead and objecting to unwarranted public exploitation that, by intruding upon their own grief, tends to degrade the rites and respect they seek to accord to the deceased person who was once their own." Justice Kennedy also invoked the "well-established cultural tradition acknowledging a family's control over the body and death images of the deceased," an interest that "has long been recognized at common law." Finally, the Court cited several cases and the Restatement (Second) of Torts § 652D Illus. 7 for the proposition that a family has a privacy interest in controlling photos of a deceased relative.]

III

Our ruling that the personal privacy protected by Exemption 7(C) extends to family members who object to the disclosure of graphic details surrounding their relative's death does not end the case. Although this privacy interest is within the terms of the exemption, the statute directs nondisclosure only where the information "could reasonably be expected to constitute an unwarranted invasion" of the family's personal privacy. The term "unwarranted" requires us to balance the family's privacy interest against the public interest in disclosure. See *Reporters Committee*, [ ].

FOIA is often explained as a means for citizens to know "what the Government is up to." *Id.*, [ ]. This phrase should not be dismissed as a convenient formalism. It defines a structural necessity in a real democracy. The statement confirms that, as a general rule, when documents are within FOIA's disclosure provisions, citizens should not be required to explain why they seek the information. . . . The information belongs to citizens to do with as they choose. Furthermore, as we have noted, the disclosure does not depend on the identity of the requester. As a general rule, if the information is subject to disclosure, it belongs to all.

When disclosure touches upon certain areas defined in the exemptions, however, the statute recognizes limitations that compete with the general interest in disclosure, and that, in appropriate cases, can overcome it. In the case of Exemption 7(C), the statute requires us to protect, in the proper degree, the personal privacy of citizens against the uncontrolled release of information compiled through the power of the state. The statutory direction that the information not be released if the invasion of personal privacy could reasonably be expected to be unwarranted requires the courts to balance the competing interests in privacy and disclosure. To effect this balance and to give practical meaning to the exemption, the usual rule that the citizen need not offer a reason for requesting the information must be inapplicable.

Where the privacy concerns addressed by Exemption 7(C) are present, the exemption requires the person requesting the information to establish a sufficient reason for the disclosure. First, the citizen must show that the public interest sought to be advanced is a significant one, an interest more specific than having the information for its own sake. Second, the citizen must show the information is likely to advance that interest. Otherwise, the invasion of privacy is unwarranted.

We do not in this single decision attempt to define the reasons that will suffice, or the necessary nexus between the requested information and the asserted public interest that would be advanced by disclosure. On the other hand, there must be some stability with respect to both the specific category of personal privacy interests protected by the statute and the specific category of public interests that could outweigh the privacy claim. Otherwise, courts will be left to balance in an ad hoc manner with little or no real guidance. [ ]. In the case of photographic images and other data pertaining to an individual who died under mysterious circumstances, the justification most likely to satisfy Exemption 7(C)'s public interest requirement is that the information is necessary to show the investigative agency or other responsible officials acted negligently or otherwise improperly in the performance of their duties.

The Court of Appeals was correct to rule that the family has a privacy interest protected by the statute and to recognize as significant the asserted public interest in uncovering deficiencies or misfeasance in the Government's investigations into Foster's death. It erred, however, in defining the showing Favish must make to substantiate his public interest claim. It stated that "[n]othing in the statutory command conditions [disclosure] on the requesting party showing that he has knowledge of misfeasance by the agency" and that "[n]othing in the statutory command shields an agency from disclosing its records because other agencies have engaged in similar investigations." [ ] The court went on to hold that, because Favish has "tender[ed] evidence and argument which, if believed, would justify his doubts," the FOIA request "is in complete conformity with the statutory purpose that the public know what its government is up to." [ ] This was insufficient. The Court of Appeals required no particular showing that any evidence points with credibility to some actual misfeasance or other impropriety. The court's holding leaves Exemption 7(C) with little force or content. By requiring courts to engage in a state of suspended disbelief with regard to even the most incredible allegations, the panel transformed Exemption 7(C) into nothing more than a rule of pleading. The invasion of privacy under its rationale would be extensive. It must be remembered that once there is disclosure, the information belongs to the general public. There is no mechanism under FOIA for a protective order allowing only the requester to see whether the information bears out his theory, or for proscribing its general dissemination.

We hold that, where there is a privacy interest protected by Exemption 7(C) and the public interest being asserted is to show that responsible officials acted negligently or otherwise improperly in the performance of their duties, the requester must establish more than a bare suspicion in order to obtain disclosure. Rather, the requester must produce evidence that would warrant a belief by a reasonable person that the alleged Government impropriety might have occurred. In United States Dep't of State v. Ray, 502 U.S. 164 (1991), we held there is a presumption of legitimacy accorded to the Government's official conduct. [ ] The presumption perhaps is less a rule of evidence than a general working principle. However the rule is characterized, where the presumption is applicable, clear evidence is usually required to displace it. [ ] United States v. Chemical Foundation, Inc., 272 U.S. 1, 14–15 [ ] (1926) ("The presumption of regularity supports the official acts of public officers and, in the absence of clear evidence to the contrary, courts presume that they have properly discharged their official duties"). Given FOIA's prodisclosure purpose, however, the less stringent standard we adopt today is more faithful to the statutory scheme. Only when the FOIA requester has produced evidence sufficient to satisfy this standard will there exist a counterweight on the FOIA scale for the court to balance against the cognizable privacy interests in the requested records. Allegations of government misconduct are " 'easy to allege and hard to disprove,' " [ ] so courts must insist on a meaningful evidentiary showing. It would be quite extraordinary to say we must ignore the fact that five different inquiries into the Foster matter reached the same conclusion. As we have noted, the balancing exercise in some other case might require us to make a somewhat more precise determination regarding the significance of the public interest and the historical importance of the events in question. We might need to consider the nexus required between the requested documents and the purported public interest served by disclosure. We need not do so here, however. Favish has not produced any evidence that would warrant a belief by a reasonable person that the alleged Government impropriety might have occurred to put the balance into play.

The Court of Appeals erred in its interpretation of Exemption 7(C). The District Court's first order in March 1998—before its decision was set aside by the Court of Appeals and superseded by the District Court's own order on remand—followed the correct approach. The judgment of the Court of Appeals is reversed, and the case is remanded with instructions to grant OIC's motion for summary judgment with respect to the four photographs in dispute.

NOTES AND QUESTIONS

1.   What evidence must a requester produce to show the government agency performed its duties negligently? How can the requester obtain this information? Is requiring the requester to produce evidence of governmental negligence or impropriety consistent with FOIA's placement of the burden on the agency to justify nondisclosure? Would a tip from an insider suffice?

2.   Does whether a disclosure would amount to an unwarranted invasion of privacy depend on the purpose for which the request for information is made? Can a court determine whether a claimed invasion of privacy would be "unwarranted" without knowing what the requester expects the information to show?

3.   Would family members have a legitimate privacy interest in preventing the release of a detailed written report on the final moments of a relative's life? Would it matter how the relative died? In New York Times Co. v. National Aeronautics & Space Admin., 782 F.Supp. 628 (D.D.C. 1991), the court withheld audio from the last moments of the Challenger space shuttle explosion under Exemption 6. "What the astronauts said may not implicate privacy interests," the court wrote, "[b]ut how the astronauts said what they did, the very sound of the astronauts' words, does constitute a privacy interest." The court differentiated the "substantial" privacy interest in the "intimate detail" of the audio and the substantive written transcript of the astronauts' words provided by NASA.

4.   Considering family members' privacy interests in death, the Ninth Circuit held that a prosecutor who gave an autopsy photo of a two-year-old child to news media violated the decedent's mother's constitutional right of privacy. Conceding that previous autopsy-disclosure cases involved the common law right of privacy or privacy exceptions in the FOIA, the court concluded that survivors' privacy rights are also constitutionally protected:

> A common law right rises to the level of a constitutional right if it is "deeply rooted in this Nation's history and tradition, and implicit in the concept of ordered liberty." [ ] The *Favish* Court considered our history and traditions, and found that "th[e] well-established cultural tradition acknowledging a family's control over the body and death images of the deceased has long been recognized at common law." [ ] For precisely the same reasons, we conclude that this right is also protected by substantive due process.
>
> The long-standing tradition of respecting family members' privacy in death images partakes of both types of privacy interests protected by the Fourteenth Amendment. First, the publication of death images interferes with "the individual interest in avoiding disclosure of personal matters" [ ] Few things are more personal than the graphic details of a close family member's tragic death. Images of the body usually reveal a great deal about the manner of death and the decedent's suffering during his final moments—all matters of private grief not generally shared with the world at large.
>
> Second, a parent's right to control a deceased child's remains and death images flows from the well-established substantive due process right to family integrity.
>
> [ ] The interest of parents "in the care, custody, and control of their children . . . is perhaps the oldest of the fundamental liberty interests" [ ] A parent's right to choose how to care for a child in life

reasonably extends to decisions dealing with death, such as whether to have an autopsy, how to dispose of the remains, whether to have a memorial service and whether to publish an obituary. Therefore, we find that the Constitution protects a parent's right to control the physical remains, memory and images of a deceased child against unwarranted public exploitation by the government.

But because this constitutional right was not clearly established at the time that the prosecutor released the autopsy photo, qualified immunity protected him from liability under 42 U.S.C. § 1983. See Marsh v. County of San Diego, 680 F.3d 1148 (9th Cir. 2012). How will this case likely affect the media?

5.   In *Favish* the Court refers to its decision in Department of Justice v. Reporters Committee for Freedom of the Press, 489 U.S. 749 (1989), which held that Exemption 7(C) permitted withholding the contents of an FBI "rap sheet" concerning four members of a suspected "organized crime" family. There, the Court wrote: "we hold as a categorical matter that a third party's request for law enforcement records or information about a private citizen can reasonably be expected to invade that citizen's privacy, and that when the request seeks no 'official information' about a Government agency, but merely records that the Government happens to be storing, the invasion of privacy is 'unwarranted.'" What arguments might Favish's attorney have made for distinguishing the *Reporters Committee* decision?

6.   Could a corporation avoid disclosure of potentially embarrassing information by invoking Exemption 7(C)? The U.S. Supreme Court held that corporations do not have a right of personal privacy for purposes of Exemption 7(C) of the FOIA. In an 8–0 decision written by Chief Justice Roberts, the Court wrote:

> We reject the argument that because 'person' is defined for purposes of FOIA to include a corporation, the phrase 'personal privacy' in Exemption 7(C) reaches corporations as well. The protection in FOIA against disclosure of law enforcement information on the ground that it would constitute an unwarranted invasion of personal privacy does not extend to corporations. We trust that AT & T will not take it personally.

562 U.S. 397, 131 S. Ct. 1177 (2011).

———

Personnel and Medical Files. The exemption most often invoked to protect privacy interests is Exemption 6, for "personnel and medical files and similar files the disclosure of which would constitute a clearly unwarranted invasion of personal privacy." Litigation under this exemption tends to focus on what constitutes a "similar file" and whether the privacy invasion resulting from disclosure would be "clearly unwarranted." Exemption 6 is not limited to medical and personnel records but extends "to cover detailed Government records on an individual which can be identified as applying to that individual." United

States Department of State v. Washington Post Co., 456 U.S. 595 (1982) (holding that Exemption 6 shielded from disclosure information held by the State Department about whether certain Iranian nationals held valid U.S. passports).

In deciding whether a particular disclosure would cause an unwarranted or clearly unwarranted invasion of privacy, courts engage in a balancing of the privacy interest and the public interest in disclosure—a process that to the media often seems like the substitution of a judge's news determination for that of an editor.

In Forest Service Employees for Environmental Ethics v. U.S. Forest Service, 524 F.3d 1021 (9th Cir. 2008), for example, the U.S. Court of Appeals for the Ninth Circuit Court of Appeals held that the U.S. Forest Service was not required to release the names of agency personnel who had responded to a wildfire that killed two Forest Service employees. Four federal agencies investigated the wildfire, including the Forest Service itself. A watchdog organization filed an FOIA request for the Forest Service investigation's report. The Forest Service provided the report but redacted the names of 23 employees who had responded to the fire, citing Exemption 6. Six of these employees were later disciplined for their actions in responding to the fire. The watchdog organization filed suit seeking an unredacted copy, but the District Court found that Exemption 6 applied to the redacted information. The Ninth Circuit agreed.

In balancing the privacy and public interest under Exemption 6, the court stressed that none of the employees was accused of official misconduct; thus "neither the employees' status as civil servants nor the Forest Service's disciplinary decision strip them of their privacy interests." Indeed, the court found this to be true despite the fact that an unredacted copy had been leaked to the family of one of the deceased firefighters. The court also emphasized that the employees had a privacy interest "in avoiding the 'embarrassment, shame, stigma, and harassment' that would arise from their public association" with the underlying tragedy. The court presumed that the employees would not want to discuss their roles with "the media, curious neighbors," or the watchdog organization, since they had not "spoken out in the five years since the incident occurred." Moreover, simply being associated with the incident would risk "embarrassment" of the employees "in their official capacities and in their personal lives." On the other side of the equation, the court found that release of the employees' names would not significantly advance the public interest. The organization sought the information in order to conduct its own investigation of the tragedy, but the court found that the organization already had three reports by separate federal agencies available. In light of the information that was already publicly available, the court found that the employees' privacy interests trumped "the public's marginal interest in conducting another investigation of the [Forest Service's] response to the tragedy."

More recently, the website Gawker made a FOIA request to the Federal Bureau of Investigation asking for certain information concerning the FBI's investigation into the surreptitiously recorded sex tape that Gawker had published featuring professional wrestler and reality television star Hulk Hogan. There, using Exemption 6, the court found that the names of Hulk Hogan's ex-wife, current wife, and children should remain redacted in investigative documents: Gawker had not shown to the court's satisfaction that the public's need to know the information outweighed the individuals' privacy interests in keeping their names unreported. Gawker Media v. FBI, 2015 U.S. Dist. LEXIS 149755 (M.D. Fla. Nov. 4, 2015).

Fees and Fee Waivers. The FOIA allows agencies to collect "reasonable standard charges for document search, duplication, and review" when material is requested for commercial purposes. When information is sought by a news media representative for noncommercial purposes the agency may charge for duplication only. Documents are to be furnished at reduced cost or at no charge "if disclosure of the information is in the public interest because it is likely to contribute significantly to the public understanding of the operations or activities of the government and is not primarily in the commercial interest of the requester."

The fee waiver provision is a significant source of friction between the media and government agencies. Reporters complain that the language invites agencies to deny fee waivers on the basis of their own assessment of the public's interest in the information.

Congress amended FOIA to expand the definition of "news media" eligible for fee waivers in 2007. Under the expanded definition, "any person or entity that gathers information of potential interest to a segment of the public, uses its editorial skills to turn the raw materials into a distinct work, and distributes that work to an audience" is entitled to a fee waiver. See 5 U.S.C. § 552(a)(4)(A)(ii).

A few years later, a nonprofit organization—one the court described as an "advocate[ ] for economic freedom and opportunity by educating the public about the threat posed by improvident federal regulations, spending, and cronyism"—requested a fee waiver, suggesting that it was news media. The D.C. Circuit found that such an organization might qualify because it was a group that gathered information and then supplied it to the public through a website. "[T]here is no indication that Congress meant to distinguish between those who reach their ultimate audiences directly and those who partner with others to do so," the court wrote. The D.C. Circuit differentiated between that type of website-focused "news media" publisher and an individual who does not regularly produce journalistic work:

> [A] requester seeking news-media status generally must
> demonstrate more than an intention to engage in an isolated
> episode of journalistic activity. As we have explained, the news-
> media provision covers a certain kind of person or entity, not a
> certain kind of request, and we therefore doubt that a requester
> could qualify based on even a firm plan to undertake journalistic
> activity on a purely one-off basis.

Cause of Action v. FTC, 799 F.3d 1108 (D.C. Cir. 2015). Does such a
decision create fee waiver potential for all website or Internet publishers?
Where might a line, if any, be drawn?

FOIA "Misuse" and Delay. Some observers have argued that the
FOIA is misused and that such misuse contributes significantly to the
costs and delays associated with FOIA requests. In a 1982 article, written
prior to his appointment to the Court, then-Professor Scalia called FOIA
"the Taj Mahal of the Doctrine of Unanticipated Consequences, the
Sistine Chapel of Cost Benefit Analysis Ignored." Antonin Scalia, The
Freedom of Information Act Has No Clothes, Regulation, Mar./Apr. 1982.

In the first years following passage of the FOIA in 1967, its principal
users were historians and journalists and the costs of administering the
FOIA were estimated at only $50,000 annually. More current numbers
are staggering in comparison. In 2014 federal agencies responded to
714,000 FOIA requests at a total cost to the agencies of $461 million in
processing and appeals. FOIA fees did not begin to cover that total; the
agencies took in only a little more than $4 million in fees that same year.
Office of Information Policy, "Summary of Annual FOIA Reports for
Fiscal Year 2014," May 2015, available at www.justice.gov. Also, unlike
FOIA's early years, a majority of FOIA requests come from "commercial
use" requesters. See Coalition of Journalists for Open Government,
"Frequent Filers: Businesses Make FOIA Their Business," July 3, 2006.
These numbers have created a backlog at many federal agencies; in 2014
the government reported that nearly 160,000 FOIA requests were
backlogged, a jump of more than 60,000 from the previous year. The
Department of Homeland Security had the vast majority of those
backlogged requests that year, more than 100,000.

Suing an unresponsive agency does not offer much of a solution to
the problem. FOIA litigation typically takes years to resolve. Moreover,
with special regard to journalism industry requesters, officials often can
avoid disclosure, practically though not literally, by delaying the release
of information until it is no longer newsworthy.

In 2007 Congress passed the OPEN Government Act in an attempt
to reform some of FOIA's flaws. The Act requires agencies to respond to
FOIA requests within 20 days; if they fail, they cannot collect search fees
or copying fees. 5 U.S.C. § 552(a)(4)(A)(vii). It provides for award of
attorneys fees to those who litigate successfully to gain access to
documents. Agencies must provide reasons for redacting information,

and they must provide "tracking" information so that requesters can monitor the agency's response to document requests. 5 U.S.C. § 552(a)(7).

In 2009 Congress again attempted to reform FOIA by creating the Office of Government Information Services (OGIS), which is charged with mediating disputes over the federal government's interpretation of FOIA. Congress allocated $1.4 million to the OGIS in the 2010 budget year, but critics questioned whether it could effectively coordinate the 97 federal agencies that have a statutory obligation to respond to FOIA requests. See Miranda Fleschart, New Office Opens to Mediate Federal Public Records Disputes, 34 News Media & the Law 16, Winter 2010. In 2014 OGIS reported that it had mediated an average of approximately 500 disputes per year, a significant percentage of which focused on the two privacy exemptions, Exemptions 6 and 7(C). Office of Government Information Services, Building a Bridge Between FOIA Requesters and Federal Agencies, March 2015, www.ogis.archives.gov.

Despite concerns about backlogs, delays, and costs associated with FOIA, thousands of requests, including many by the press, are routinely granted. The very existence of the statute probably induces many officials to disclose even without a formal request.

Access to Electronic Records. With the widespread computerization of government records, FOIA requests have raised many important new issues. The Electronic Freedom of Information Act Amendments of 1996 provided that agencies must make reasonable efforts to search computerized files when responding to FOIA requests and required that agencies provide materials responsive to a FOIA request in electronic format where feasible (thereby facilitating subsequent use of that information by the requester). The law also required agencies to make records "likely to be subject to subsequent requests" available for public inspection and copying, unless the materials are published and offered for sale. In addition, the law specifies that agencies must maintain a general index of these records and make that index available on a web site or other electronic database. Electronic Freedom of Information Act Amendments of 1996, Pub. L. No. 104–231, 110 Stat. 3048 (codified at 5 U.S.C. § 552).

The Electronic FOIA was widely ignored, however. Ten years after its passage, the National Security Archive found that only 21 percent of the agencies had complied with requirements that they post on their websites basic information, such as opinions, orders, policy statements, and rules interpretations. Only 17 percent posted required information on how to file an FOIA request, and many failed to provide indexes to their records or provided erroneous links and phone numbers. For the full report, see Agencies Violate Law on Online Information, available at http://nsarchive.gwu.edu/NSAEBB/NSAEBB216/index.htm (last visited March 12, 2016).

FOIA and "Mosaic" Theory. Government agencies have claimed that FOIA exempts disclosure of information otherwise available to the public where the information, when added to other publicly available information, might fall within a FOIA exemption. The idea is that the "mosaic" comprised of the bits and pieces of publicly available information plus the information released by the agency might compromise national security or privacy or otherwise be exempt. Professor Christina Wells explains that:

> In response to FOIA requests involving national security, government officials find mosaic theory particularly useful because it allows them to argue that information not evidently posing a threat to national security should nevertheless be considered appropriately classified or exempt. Their reasoning is that otherwise apparently innocuous information can be pieced together with other information to form part of a larger, more dangerous picture. Thus, the information, though admittedly innocuous in isolation, *could* prove to be dangerous and must be withheld. Accordingly, mosaic theory is an attempt to expand the government's ability to withhold information under existing law.

Christina E. Wells, CIA v. Sims: Mosaic Theory and Government Attitude, 58 Admin. L. Rev. 845, 853–54 (2008).

Mosaic theory gives the government a powerful argument for withholding information that should otherwise be released under the FOIA. Mosaic theory's potential for allowing the federal government to circumvent FOIA is compounded by the practice of intelligence agencies refusing to explain, even in camera to a federal district court judge, why the unclassified information should not be released. Instead, the government claims that simply explaining the "mosaic" would compromise national security. As Professor Wells has observed, "[i]nvocation of mosaic theory thus creates a vacuum of knowledge that effectively paralyzes judicial assessment of the government's claims." Moreover, the federal government invokes mosaic theory in contexts other than FOIA, including as a justification for "closing deportation hearings, indefinitely detaining non-citizens, restricting dissemination of non-classified information, and secretly searching certain kinds of records, including library and Internet records."

The mosaic theory in part led the Ninth Circuit in 2007 to refuse to release two President's Daily Brief documents, briefings prepared by the Central Intelligence Agency, from the Lyndon Johnson administration decades before. "[N]othing prevents the CIA from relying on the common sense premise that the impact of disclosing protected documents must be evaluated not only based upon the information appearing within the four corners of the document," the court wrote, "but also with regard to what secrets the document could divulge when viewed in light of other information available to interested observers." Berman v. CIA, 501 F.3d 1136 (9th Cir. 2007).

a.   ACCESS TO INFORMATION AND NATIONAL SECURITY

In the first few years after the terrorist attacks on the United States on September 11, 2001, federal courts appeared highly deferential to government claims that documents were exempt on national security grounds. See, e.g. American Civil Liberties Union v. United States Dep't of Justice, 265 F. Supp. 2d 20 (D.D.C. 2003) (holding that the Department of Justice was able to shield statistics on the number of times it utilized surveillance and investigatory methods of the Patriot Act under Exemption 1 of FOIA); Coastal Delivery Corp. v. U.S. Customs Service, 272 F. Supp. 2d 958 (C.D. Cal. 2003) (holding that the U.S. Customs Services could withhold information on seaport inspections under Exemption 2 on the grounds that terrorists could use the information of such inspections to their advantage). But cf. Gordon v. Federal Bureau of Investigation, 390 F. Supp. 2d 897 (N.D. Cal. 2004) (holding that a general statement that information may be sensitive security information was not enough to meet the burden necessary to withhold documents regarding no-fly lists) and American Civil Liberties Union v. Department of Defense, 339 F. Supp. 2d 501 (S.D.N.Y. 2004) (stating that raising national security concerns could not justify unlimited delays in responding to FOIA requests.)

Ten years after the attacks, the Supreme Court heard a FOIA case involving a request for "data and maps used to help store explosives at a [Washington state] naval base." The Court decided that the particular exemption at issue, one protecting internal rules and practices, was inapplicable. However, the Court offered the Navy some alternatives to keep the information out of public hands, advising the Navy that it might classify the documents as secret while the FOIA request was pending, or that it might use Exemption 7's protection for "law enforcement purposes." In concurrence, Justice Alito specifically addressed terrorism concerns:

> [S]teps by law enforcement officers to prevent terrorism surely fulfill "law enforcement purposes." Particularly in recent years, terrorism prevention and national security measures have been recognized as vital to effective law enforcement efforts in our Nation. Indeed, "[a]fter the September 11th attacks on America," the priorities of the Federal Bureau of Investigation "shifted dramatically," and the FBI's "top priority became the prevention of another terrorist attack." [ ] Today, "[t]he FBI's number one priority continues to be the prevention of terrorist attacks against the United States." [ ] If crime prevention and security measures do not serve "law enforcement purposes,"

then those charged with law enforcement responsibilities have little chance of fulfilling their duty to preserve the peace.

Milner v. Dep't of the Navy, 562 U.S. 562 (2011).

A high-profile example of judicial deference in cases involving Exemption 1, the exemption that protects matters deemed secret by executive order in the interest of national defense, was decided by the D.C. Circuit in Judicial Watch, Inc. v. U.S. Dep't of Defense, 715 F.3d 937 (D.C. Cir. 2013). The case involved a FOIA request for post-mortem images of Osama bin Laden, taken during and after the American special forces raid in Pakistan. The Central Intelligence Agency withheld the images, asserting that it had properly classified them Top Secret pursuant to the substantive criteria and procedures specified in an executive order. The CIA supported its summary judgment motion with affidavits from high-level officials stating that release of the photos would harm national security interests. A federal district court granted summary judgment to the CIA, and the Court of Appeals for the District of Columbia Circuit affirmed. The D.C. Circuit gave weight to the CIA's determination that release of the photos could incite violence against Americans and thus create "exceptionally grave harm" to national security; the CIA's predictions of violence were not "speculative," but crossed the threshold criterion of being "logical" or "plausible." See also Center for Constitutional Rights v. Central Intelligence Agency, 765 F.3d 161 (2d Cir. 2014) (holding that requested records of a Guantanamo detainee, the so-called "twentieth hijacker," were exempt from disclosure under Exemption 1).

On the other hand, the Second Circuit rejected a Department of Justice attempt to withhold a legal memorandum concerning targeted killings of United States citizens by drone strikes under Exemptions 1, 3, and 5. In New York Times Co. v. U.S. Dep't of Justice, 752 F.3d 123 (2d Cir. 2014), the government asserted that the memorandum qualified for Exemption 1. The Second Circuit reversed the district court and held that releasing a redacted version of the document would not jeopardize national security interests because the drone strike program already "ha[d] been publicly acknowledged at the highest levels of the Government." It also ruled that "[w]hatever protection the legal analysis might once have had has been lost by virtue of public statements of public officials at the highest levels and official disclosure of [a] DOJ White Paper [addressing the legality of the drone strikes]." Finally, the court held that the DOJ's disclosures had waived any deliberative process or attorney-client privileges that might have applied.

Related Exemptions Motivated by the War on Terror. The war on terror affected more than judicial interpretations of existing FOIA exemptions. Congress passed the Homeland Security Act of 2002, 6 U.S.C.A. § 133 (West Supp. 2003), which makes "critical infrastructure information" voluntarily submitted by businesses to federal agencies exempt from disclosure under the FOIA. The Act grants businesses immunity from civil liability if the information reveals wrongdoing and also makes it a crime for a federal employee to disclose the information. Senator Patrick Leahy called this provision the "most severe weakening of the Freedom of Information Act in its 36-year history" and characterized it as "a big business wish list gussied up in security garb." See Reporters Committee for Freedom of the Press, "Homefront Confidential: How the War on Terrorism Affects Access to Information and the Public's Right to Know" (Spring 2003), www.rcfp.org. By 2015, however, only a small number of cases had interpreted the statute and most courts simply mentioned it in the context of state freedom-of-information requests.

Congress also carved out another exemption to shield photos of abuse against detainees in U.S. custody in Iraq and Afghanistan from release under the FOIA. The U.S. Court of Appeals for the Second Circuit had initially ordered release of the abuse photos in 2008. See ACLU v. Department of Defense, 543 F.3d 59 (2d Cir. 2008). The Justice Department first announced that it would comply, but President Obama reversed that decision on the grounds that release of the photos would inflame public opinion in the Muslim world and endanger U.S. troops. See Jeff Zeleny & Thom Shanker, "Obama Reversal on Abuse Photos," N.Y. Times, May 13, 2009. A few days later Congress added an exemption to the Homeland Security Appropriations Bill allowing the withholding of the detainee photos upon certification by the Department of Defense that their release would endanger lives. President Obama then signed the bill into law. See Miranda Fleschert, "Obama signs law blocking release of detainee torture photos," Oct. 29, 2009, www.rcfp.org.

State Secrets. The war on terror reanimated a long-standing debate about the proper scope of the state secrets doctrine. Under this doctrine, the federal government seeks to have litigation pending in the federal courts dismissed because the discovery process would require the disclosure of classified government materials.

In 2009 Attorney General Eric Holder announced that the Department of Justice would invoke the doctrine only in circumstances in which disclosure of information "reasonably could be expected to cause significant harm to the national defense or foreign relations of the United States." Eric Holder, Office of the Attorney General, Memorandum for Heads of Executive Departments and Agencies, Policies and Procedures Governing Invocation of the State Secrets Privilege at 1 (Sept. 23, 2009), available at http://www.justice.gov/sites/default/files/opa/legacy/2009/09/23/state-secret-privileges.pdf (last visited March 12, 2016).

Despite the Holder memorandum, the federal government subsequently invoked the state secrets privilege in litigation involving claims associated with the federal government's use of extraordinary rendition, indefinite executive detention, or "coercive interrogation techniques." See Mohamed v. Jeppesen Dataplan, Inc., 614 F.3d 1070 (9th Cir. 2010) (en banc). In a 6–5 decision, the court held that the state secrets doctrine prevented the litigation from proceeding.

b.   OPEN GOVERNMENT: PROMISES AND RESPONSES

As in the example noted above regarding state secrets, government officials can sometimes alter course with regard to openness. Journalists have suggested that this was strikingly clear during the Obama presidency generally.

At the beginning of his administration, President Obama issued a memorandum to the heads of executive departments and agencies directing them to undertake initiatives to make the federal government more "transparent," "participatory," and "collaborative." See President Barack Obama, Memorandum of January 21, 2009, Transparency and Open Government, 74 Fed. Reg. 4685 (Jan. 26, 2009). As part of this open government initiative, the Obama administration instructed agencies to apply a presumption against invoking FOIA exemptions. See President Barack Obama, Memorandum of January 21, 2009, The Freedom of Information Act, 74 Fed. Reg. 4683 (Jan. 26, 2009). Previously, the Department of Justice had defended a federal agency's refusal to share government information with the public whenever a plausible legal basis for the secrecy claim existed. Under the new FOIA policy, "all agencies should adopt a presumption in favor of disclosure, in order to renew their commitment to the principles embodied in FOIA, and to usher in a new era of open government." The President's memorandum also instructed agencies to "use modern technology to inform citizens about what is known and done by the government."

In March 2009 Attorney General Eric Holder issued interagency guidelines on the invocation of FOIA exemptions in which he reaffirmed the presumption of disclosure outlined in the President's January memorandum, insisting that "an agency should not withhold information simply because it may do so legally." See Attorney General Eric Holder, Memorandum for Heads of Executive Departments and Agencies, The Freedom of Information Act (FOIA), Mar. 19, 2009.

In addition to these measures, the Obama administration revised the rules governing classified information. Barack Obama, Memorandum of May 27, 2009, Classified Information and Controlled Unclassified Information, 74 Fed. Reg. 26277 (June 1, 2009); see also Carrie Johnson, "Review of Government Secrecy Ordered," Washington Post, May 28, 2009. Executive Order 13526 § 1.1(4)(B) revised the federal government's system of classifying government information, again expressing a presumption in favor of disclosure and against classification. Classified information had to be listed for automatic declassification within a specific time frame or upon the occurrence of a specific event; the default rule calls for declassification within ten years generally and 25 years for "sensitive" information. Id. at § 1.5. Nonetheless, open government advocates complained that the Obama administration repeatedly failed to put its words into action. By 2013, one report suggested that fear was the pervading emotion among administration employees with regard to their interactions with journalists:

> In the Obama administration's Washington, government officials are increasingly afraid to talk to the press. Those suspected of discussing with reporters anything that the government has classified as secret are subject to investigation, including lie-detector tests and scrutiny of their telephone and e-mail records. An "Insider Threat Program" being implemented in every government department requires all federal employees to help prevent unauthorized disclosures of information by monitoring the behavior of their colleagues.

Committee to Protect Journalists, "Leak Investigations and Surveillance in Post-9/11 America" (Oct. 2013), available at www.cpj.org.

The sense among journalists by the end of the Obama administration was that government secrecy had in fact increased, not decreased. See, e.g., Denver Nicks, Study: Obama Administration More Secretive Than Ever, Time (March 17, 2014). In 2015 the Washington Post suggested that the quieting of government officials and agencies had extended beyond Washington. As an example, it pointed to a reporter who had faced federal and state roadblocks in her attempt to investigate a Florida tuberculosis outbreak, suggesting that such barriers were widespread:

> [the reporter's] experience is shared by virtually every journalist on the government beat, from the White House on down. They can recite tales with similar outlines: An agency spokesman—frequently a political appointee—rejects the reporter's request for interviews, offers partial or nonresponsive replies, or delays responding at all until after the journalist's deadline has passed.

Paul Farhi, "Access denied: Reporters say federal officials, data increasingly off limits," Washington Post, March 30, 2015.

The Post article noted that the vast majority of journalists who were surveyed agreed that "[t]he public is not getting all the information it needs because of barriers agencies are imposing on journalists' reporting practices." The story contrasted the situation in 2015 with the greater openness journalists who covered presidential administrations had experienced in the 1970s and 1980s.

Government officials quoted in the article in turn blamed journalists' increasing levels of inexperience and their claims to need information quickly. New media, the officials suggested, made it increasingly difficult to respond as immediately and as accurately as journalists would like, especially regarding complex issues the journalists may not fully understand.

2. STATE OPEN RECORDS ACTS

Every state has its own access-to-information statute. Some states even protect access rights in their constitutions. In November 2004 Californians voted overwhelmingly in favor of a ballot measure making access to government meetings and the writings of government officials a constitutional right. Although the measure preserved existing limits on the right of access, it provides that existing statutes must be interpreted to maximize access. The measure also requires that government officials justify the need for future limitations on access rights. Florida voters approved an even stronger amendment to the Florida constitution. The amendment requires the legislature to pass new exemptions to Florida's public-records or sunshine laws by a two-thirds vote. Fl. Const., Art. I, § 24.

Many state access statutes are patterned after the FOIA, but some follow a quite different model. For example, the Texas Public Information Act, Tex. Govt. Code § 552, uses a quite different enforcement mechanism. Unlike the FOIA, which places most of the burdens of enforcement on the requester, the Texas statute gives the primary enforcement responsibility to the state attorney general. When a request is received, the agency has ten days in which to either comply or seek the attorney general's determination that it need not comply. If it fails to do either, the information is presumed to be disclosable and the agency cannot subsequently contest that issue unless it can make a "compelling demonstration" that the information should not be disclosed. If the agency refuses to comply with the attorney general's determination that the information is disclosable, either the requester or the attorney general may seek a writ of mandamus to compel disclosure. As a practical matter, most disputes are resolved by the ruling of the attorney general and hundreds of such decisions have created a body of precedent that enables the attorney general to answer many requests merely by citing previous decisions. As with the federal FOIA, when the parties disagree some disputed rulings head to court. In 2015 the Texas attorney general successfully convinced a state appeals court that individuals' birthdates were protected from disclosure under the Public Information Act as "confidential by law" because of identity theft concerns and common law privacy-related decisions. Paxton v. City of Dallas, 2015 Tex. App. Lexis 5228 (Tex. App. May 22, 2015).

Even where the state statute is modeled on the FOIA, it may be construed to require disclosure of more (or less) than the FOIA requires. See, for example, Kerr v. Koch, 15 Media L. Rptr. 1579 (N.Y. Sup. Ct. 1988). There, a reporter for the Daily News demanded appointment calendars identifying luncheon and dinner guests of the mayor of New York, whether official or private, under New York's Freedom of Information Law. The mayor invoked an exemption for material that if disclosed would constitute an unwarranted invasion of personal privacy.

The court ordered disclosure: "In an administration that has been sorely afflicted by scandals of one sort or another, it seems quite proper to know the friends of the City's Chief Magistrate and his association with them, especially where a diary of those associations is represented by an appointments calendar kept on the premises of the agency of the Mayor."

State freedom-of-information statutes can also reflect changing times and attempts to expand or contract access in response. In Illinois, the FOIA-like state statute suggests initially that requesters "are entitled to full and complete information regarding the affairs of government" and that "all records" are presumed open. It then lists more than forty exemptions, including one preventing the release of exam scoring keys and another the names of children involved in park district programs. 5 ILCS 140/1 et seq.

Crime-Related Information and State Access Laws. In Newtown, Connecticut, twenty-six people, most of them children, were killed in a mass shooting at an elementary school in 2012. The Associated Press requested 911 calls made by those at the school during the shooting, arguing that the tapes should be made available under the state's FOIA. Police refused until a court ordered that the tapes be released; the court found that the tapes did not fit any of the Connecticut exemptions, including one that prevented the release of law enforcement-related information. Sedensky v. Freedom of Information Commission, 2013 WL 6698055 (Conn. Super. Ct. Nov. 26, 2013). The request for the 911 calls led to failed attempts to change the Connecticut freedom-of-information statute to exempt crime-related calls for assistance. 2014 Legis. Bill Hist. CT S.B. 388. In response to the shooting, the state legislature had already modified its FOIA law to include an exemption for "[a]ny record created by a law enforcement agency . . . consisting of a photograph, film, video or digital or other visual image depicting the victim of a homicide, to the extent that such record could reasonably be expected to constitute an unwarranted invasion of the personal privacy of the victim or the victim's surviving family members." Conn. Gen. Stat. § 1–210. The 911 calls did not fit the exemption.

Newer technology—including police body cameras and other recordings of police interactions made by the police themselves—has led to similar disagreements between open government advocates and police. In Chicago in 2015, for example, a state trial court judge ordered the release of a police car dashboard video showing an officer shooting an unarmed teenager sixteen times. The city had tried to keep the tape sealed, but the court found in favor of the journalist who had submitted a freedom-of-information request. Jason Meisner & Jeremy Gorner, Chicago Forgoes Appeal After Judge Orders Release of Video of Fatal Police Shooting, Chicago Tribune, Nov. 20, 2015. The police union joined the city in its objection to the release of the footage and news reports suggested that some of the victim's family members did not want the tape released to the public.

By 2016 some states had passed legislation restricting access to police body camera recordings and a majority of states were considering such restrictions. Reporters Committee for Freedom of the Press, Guide: Access to Police Body-Worn Camera Video, http://www.rcfp.org/ bodycams, updated searchable map (last visited Dec. 29, 2015). In response to these legislative moves, the access clinic at Yale Law School released a scholarly paper arguing that police-recorded videos of public interactions should generally be released to the public as a form of public oversight of police interactions, arguing that such videos were public records like any other. Media Freedom & Information Access Clinic, Police Body Cam Footage: Just Another Public Record, December 2015. The paper specifically criticized New York's "overbroad exemptions" that protected police personnel records and California's "overly broad investigatory records exemptions," both of which could exempt police body camera footage from disclosure. It credited Washington State's access law, one that the report's authors suggested had limited exemptions that could allow access to police-related footage.

Another recent crime- and privacy-related issue for freedom-of-information laws concerns mugshots or booking photographs, traditionally considered public records and therefore accessible by media and otherwise. Case examples from federal courts best highlight the tension between public access to the information and privacy interests of the arrestee; by late 2015 a circuit split had developed in the federal system. In 2011 the Eleventh Circuit had held that a booking photo implicated enough personal privacy to be exempted from disclosure, maintaining that such an image was a "vivid symbol of criminal accusation" capturing the person "in the vulnerable and embarrassing moments immediately after being accused, taken into custody, and deprived of most liberties." Karantsalis v. United States Department of Justice, 635 F.3d 497 (11th Cir. 2011). The Sixth Circuit had earlier held that such a photograph should be released, explaining that there is good reason the public should see certain mugshots:

> For example, release of a photograph of a defendant can more clearly reveal the government's glaring error in detaining the wrong person for an offense than can any reprint of only the name of an arrestee. Furthermore, mug shots can startlingly reveal the circumstances surrounding an arrest and initial incarceration of an individual in a way that written information cannot. Had the now-famous videotape of the Rodney King beating in Los Angeles never been made, a mug shot of Mr. King released to the media would have alerted the world that the arrestee had been subjected to much more than a routine traffic

stop and that the actions and practices of the arresting officers should be scrutinized.

Detroit Free Press v. United States Department of Justice, 73 F.3d 93 (6th Cir. 1996).

In late 2015, however, the Sixth Circuit signaled a possible shift toward privacy and away from access. It agreed to hear a later case involving a booking photograph (and the same parties) en banc. Detroit Free Press v. United States Department of Justice, 2015 U.S. App. Lexis 20224 (6th Cir. Nov. 20, 2015). In the earlier three-judge opinion, the panel had written that it was "constrained" to hold that such photographs be released because of the 1996 holding, but "urge[d] the full court to reconsider the merits" of the 1996 case. The court seemed especially concerned with the release of the photographs while criminal proceedings were ongoing. 796 F.3d 649 (6th Cir. 2015).

The DPPA and the Media. Like the federal FOIA, most state open records statutes do not inquire as to the purpose for which information is sought—if it is available to media, it is also available to direct marketers, business rivals, and even potential criminals. In a few instances, however, public outcry has led to legislative attempts to discriminate among different types of requesters.

In 2000 Congress passed the Driver's Privacy Protection Act, 18 U.S.C. § 2721, which forbade any person from disclosing information from such records except for law enforcement and other specified purposes. Journalistic purposes were not among those for which release of the information was authorized, although states were permitted to disclose records for any use provided that citizens were given an opportunity to "opt out" of such disclosure. After several states challenged the Act, the Supreme Court held that the DPPA did not violate the Tenth Amendment's reservation of power to the states or federalism principles. Reno v. Condon, 528 U.S. 141 (2000).

Even before the Supreme Court heard oral argument, Congress amended the Driver's Privacy Protection Act to restrict access even further. The new amendments forbade states from releasing personally identifiable information from motor vehicles and driver's license records for marketing, or for any other purpose not specifically authorized in the 1994 statute, without first obtaining "the express consent of the person to whom such personal information pertains." As a result, the majority of states that had acted under the 1994 law to permit use of the records for marketing and journalism, among other purposes unless an individual registered his or her *objection* thereby "opting out" of disclosure, were required to amend their laws to prohibit such uses unless each individual gives *consent* or "opts in." See 18 U.S.C. § 2721–27255 (2006).

In 2015 the U.S. Court of Appeals for the Seventh Circuit broadly held that the media have no constitutional right to obtain or publish even newsworthy information from motor vehicle records. Dahlstrom v. Sun-Times Media, 777 F.3d 937 (7th Cir. 2015). Recall that in *Dahlstrom*, police officers sued the Chicago Sun-Times for violating the Drivers Privacy Protection Act by obtaining and publishing their heights, weights, eye colors, hair colors, and birth dates. The information appeared in an article questioning whether a homicide investigation lineup in which the officers participated was set up to prevent identification of a politically connected suspect. The Chicago Sun-Times cited the Chicago Police Department and the Illinois Secretary of State as its sources. The Sun-Times moved to dismiss the officers' complaint on the grounds that the paper had not published "personal information" as defined by the DPPA, "or, alternatively, if the DPPA bars Sun-Times from publishing this truthful information of public concern, the statute violates the First Amendment[ ]." A district judge rejected the motion, and the Sun-Times appealed to the Seventh Circuit. The federal appeals court concluded that the published information was indeed "personal information" as defined by the DPPA because the information "falls squarely within the universe of information that 'identifies' an individual." The officers did not object to the publication of their pictures, because their photos had been provided to the Sun-Times by the Chicago Police Department.

The court further concluded that the DPPA's prohibition against obtaining such information did not violate the First Amendment because it was merely a prohibition on access to information in government hands. Quoting Houchins v. KQED, a case excerpted later in this chapter, the court wrote: "There is no constitutional right to have access to particular government information, or to require openness from the bureaucracy." Thus, the court determined that the DPPA's prohibition on obtaining personal information easily passed rational basis scrutiny.

The statute's prohibition on publication of information obtained from motor vehicle records was another matter. The court observed that statutes that prohibit publication of information "by virtue of the source, rather than the subject matter" are typically content-neutral, but the DPPA also defined the prohibited disclosures based both on the source of the information and on its content. Nonetheless, the court concluded that the statute was content-neutral because the statute was unrelated to governmental agreement or disagreement with the speaker's message and because it allowed publication of the identical information from other sources. Thus, the statute determined that the constitutionality of the DPPA's prohibition on publication should be judged by intermediate scrutiny.

The court conceded that strict scrutiny would apply if the published information had been lawfully obtained, but the court concluded that the Sun-Times had acted unlawfully in obtaining the information because the "Sun-Times's acquisition of the Officers' personal information invaded their established rights under the DPPA." The court rejected the Sun-Times' argument that it acquired the information through "perfectly routine, traditional journalism," although the facts are not clear whether the Sun-Times did anything more than simply request the information from the Illinois Secretary of State who willingly handed it over.

Applying intermediate scrutiny, the court determined that the DPPA's prohibition on disclosure furthered two important government interests unrelated to the suppression of free expression: "first, the interest in removing an incentive for parties to unlawfully obtain personal information in the first instance; and second, the interest in minimizing the harm to individuals whose personal information has been illegally obtained." The court found that prohibition of disclosure would deter unlawful acquisition and would also further the interest in protecting citizens' privacy, though the court also opined that the disclosed information was of little public importance, given that the Sun-Times published photos of the officers as they appeared in the disputed criminal lineup.

The court also found that the DPPA prohibition on disclosure was narrowly tailored to deter unlawful acquisition and protect privacy. The court reached this conclusion based on the fact that the prohibition "is content neutral, it permits publication of the same information gathered from lawful sources, it imposes no special burden upon the media, and it has a scienter requirement ("knowingly") to provide fair warning to potential offenders." The statute listed fourteen exceptions that would allow disclosure in contexts in which public safety concerns were unlikely to be present. The court ended its opinion by asserting that its reach was limited: "We hold only that, where members of the press unlawfully obtain sensitive information that, in context, is of marginal public value, the First Amendment does not guarantee them the right to publish that information." The court affirmed the district court's denial of the Sun-Times' motion to dismiss and remanded for further proceedings. The Court of Appeals denied rehearing and rehearing en banc.

The United States Supreme Court also upheld the constitutionality of a state statute restricting access to information based on the purpose of the request in Los Angeles Police Dept. v. United Reporting Publishing Corp., 528 U.S. 32 (1999). In 1996 the California legislature had amended its Government Code to prohibit use of arrest records "to sell a product or service to any individual or group of individuals." Cal. Govt. Code § 6254(f). The statute was challenged by a company that had been furnishing the names and addresses of arrestees to clients for commercial purposes. The Supreme Court held, 7–2, that the government had no obligation to provide access to anyone under the First Amendment. Justice Stevens, dissenting, contended that "the State's discriminatory ban on access to information—in an attempt to prohibit persons from exercising their constitutional rights to publish it in a truthful and accurate matter—is . . . invalid."

Several states also have "citizens-only" freedom of information laws that grant access to public records only to citizens of the state. In McBurney v. Young, 133 S. Ct. 1709 (2013), the Supreme Court resolved a circuit split by holding unanimously that a state's refusal to provide the benefits of its FOIA laws to residents of other states did not violate the Privileges and Immunities Clause of the Fourteenth Amendment or the Dormant Commerce Clause. The Court concluded that the rights implicated were not "fundamental." In reaching this conclusion, the Court also cited Houchins v. KQED and held that "[t]here is no constitutional right to obtain all the information provided by FOIA laws." The opinion noted that FOIA laws are relatively new and that the nation long functioned without them. The opinion also held that the state's "citizens-only" access law did not violate the Dormant Commerce Clause, because it did not prohibit access to, nor impose burdensome regulation upon, an interstate market; it merely limited the benefits of its access law "to those who fund the state treasury and whom the State was created to serve."

Additional Statutory Restraints on Access to Public Records. The FOIA and similar state statutes prescribe the records that *must* be disclosed. Officials are free to disclose others at their discretion unless, as indicated above, some other law forbids it. At the federal level, another example of such a prohibition is the Privacy Act, 5 U.S.C. § 552a. It forbids release of personal records that the government routinely accumulates on individuals (e.g., Social Security records) unless disclosure is required by the FOIA or permitted by one of several specific exceptions in the Privacy Act (e.g., disclosure to a court or congressional committee). The restrictions of the Privacy Act impose limits on what government officials may disclose, but do not prescribe punishment for media that publish information improperly made public by the government.

One example of a clash between state and federal law involved state freedom-of-information interests and student privacy concerns embodied in the Family Educational Rights and Privacy Act (FERPA), 20 U.S.C. §1232g. There, the Chicago Tribune, investigating an admissions scandal, had requested information from University of Illinois student applications that would include the names of the applicants' parents and other related admissions information. The University refused the FOIA request, suggesting that the state FOIA exempted disclosure of documents protected by federal law and that FERPA protected admissions records. The trial court decided that FERPA did not "specifically prohibit Illinois from doing anything" with regard to the request and granted summary judgment for the newspaper. Chicago Tribune v. University of Illinois Board of Trustees, 781 F. Supp. 2d 672

(N.D. Ill. 2011). On appeal, the Seventh Circuit refused jurisdiction and vacated the lower court's decision. In doing so, however, it noted the clash between the "substantial public interest in the information" the Tribune had asked for and the "substantial public interest . . . in protecting the legitimate privacy of students and their families." 680 F.3d 1001 (7th Cir. 2012). The Tribune did not refile its claim in state court.

FERPA was not considered in a later decision that forced Michigan State University to reveal the names of student-athletes listed as suspects in police incident reports on campus. "The disclosure of the names of the student-athletes who were identified as suspects in the reports," the court wrote with regard to an ESPN FOIA request, "serves the public understanding of the operation of the University's police department." The trial court, therefore, had not abused its discretion when it ordered that the names be released. ESPN v. Michigan State University, 2015 Mich. App. Lexis 1606 (Mich. Ct. App. Aug. 18, 2015). The Michigan Supreme Court thereafter refused to hear an appeal. 872 N.W.2d 498 (Mich. 2015).

Statutory restrictions on access to public records often arise in response to a specific news event, as seen in the Newtown shooting example from Connecticut. In Florida, when NASCAR driver Dale Earnhardt was killed in a crash at the Daytona Speedway in 2001, media invoked the Florida open records act in an attempt to obtain the autopsy photos. The requests set off a fury among racing fans who objected to the disclosures, and the Florida legislature quickly passed a bill providing that requesters other than family must obtain a court order to gain access to autopsy photos and videos. In deciding whether to give access, courts must consider "whether such disclosure is necessary for the public evaluation of governmental performance; the seriousness of the intrusion into the family's right to privacy and whether such disclosure is the least intrusive means available; and the availability of similar information in other public records. . . ." Earnhardt Family Protection Act, Fl. Stat. Ch. 406.135 (2001). A Florida trial court upheld the law, and the appellate court affirmed. See Campus Communications, Inc. v. Earnhardt, 821 So. 2d 388 (Fla. Dist. Ct. App. 2002). The Florida Supreme Court denied review of the case, 848 So. 2d 1153, and the U.S. Supreme Court denied certiorari. 540 U.S. 1049 (2003). See also Fla. Stat Ann. § 406.135(2) (2006) (making autopsy photos and videos exempt from public records law while in medical examiner custody).

In contrast, privacy interests of the dead were rejected as a basis for withholding investigative records in Blethen Maine Newspapers, Inc. v. Maine, 871 A.2d 523 (Me. 2005). The Supreme Judicial Court of Maine held that the attorney general was required to release investigative records of sexual abuse by priests who were deceased at the time of the records request. The court rejected arguments that the privacy interests of the priests precluded disclosure, particularly in light of the substantial public interest involved. However, the court stated that the names of living people mentioned in the records should be redacted before release.

Telephone Records. A new set of freedom-of-information issues is posed by smart phone technology that creates records of calls and electronic messages. Records of calls made from an official's cellular phone could reveal wrongdoing or suspicious associations; they could also reveal the unlisted phone numbers of the official, family members, informants, or other officials. Courts disagree as to whether records of calls made (as opposed to contents of the calls) are disclosable. In New Jersey, such calls are presumptively exempt from disclosure under the New Jersey Right-to-Know statute and are disclosable only upon a showing that the public need outweighs the privacy interests. See North Jersey Newspapers Co. v. Passaic County, 601 A.2d 693 (N.J. 1992). See also Rogers v. Superior Court, 19 Cal. App. 4th 469 (Cal. App. 1993), holding that records of phone calls made from and received on city council members' cellular phones, home offices, and hotel rooms were exempt from disclosure.

The Georgia Supreme Court held, over two dissents, that records of calls made from cellular phones are disclosable even if they reveal unlisted numbers. Such disclosures would not be sufficiently offensive to be actionable under the tort law of privacy, the court reasoned, and the privacy exception in the Georgia Open Records Act requires an analogous analysis. See Dortch v. Atlanta Journal and Constitution, 405 S.E.2d 43 (Ga. 1991); see also DR Partners v. Board of County Comm. of Clark County, 6 P.3d 465 (Nev. 2000) (finding no expectation of privacy since commissioners knew billing records of their calls were public record).

A more recent freedom-of-information request in Washington State asked for all records, including text messages, sent by a state prosecutor from his personal cell phone that he had also used occasionally for work. After failing to receive the texts she wanted, the requester sued, arguing that a judge should review the texts to determine which were appropriate for release. The trial court held that the texts were not public records; the intermediate level appellate court decided that they were. Washington's highest court granted review and held that only the records that a state employee "prepares, owns, uses, or retains on a private cell phone within the scope of employment" are public records and, therefore, accessible through the state public records act. The court ordered that the prosecutor obtain a transcript of his text messages, produce those that are work-related, and file an affidavit that the others are personal and not relevant under the open records law. Nissen v. Pierce County, 357 P.3d 45 (Wash. 2015).

Courts continue to struggle with the issue of when information created by public employees on their personal smart phones should be accessible by the public. As late as 2015 one California court suggested that the issue remained "in flux." Bertoli v. City of Sebastopol, 233 Cal. App. 4th 353 (Cal. App. 2015).

B. ACCESS TO GOVERNMENTAL MEETINGS

1. FEDERAL LAW

The Sunshine Act. Unlike the FOIA, which preceded most state open records laws and became the model for many, the federal Sunshine Act was a late arrival and was modeled on the highly successful Florida Sunshine Act, Fla. Stat. § 286.011. The federal Sunshine Act, 5 U.S.C. § 552b, was passed in 1976 at the urging of the Florida congressional delegation. The statement of purpose accompanying the Act declares that "the public is entitled to the fullest practicable information regarding the decision-making processes of the Federal Government." The Act sought to "provide the public with such information while protecting the rights of individuals and the ability of the Government to carry out its responsibilities."

Essentially, the act provides that all federal agencies headed by boards of two or more persons appointed by the President— approximately fifty agencies—must hold "every portion of every meeting" open to the public (subject to specific exemptions). Adequate advance notice must be given of each meeting. Even if a meeting is closed because it falls within one of the ten exemptions provided by the Act, the agency must make public a transcript or minutes of all parts of the meeting that do not contain exempt material. Meetings may be closed only after a publicly recorded vote of a majority of the full membership of the agency.

The exemptions apply where the agency "properly determines" that a portion of its meeting "is likely to" result in the disclosure of specified information. The exemptions are similar to those of the FOIA. In addition, the Sunshine Act exempts discussions relating to censure or accusations of crime, discussions of proposed agency action that could be frustrated if revealed in advance, and information about an agency's participation in litigation.

The Federal Advisory Committee Act. This statute, 5 U.S.C. App. § 1, provides yet another access tool, containing both an open-records and an open-meetings provision. It covers committees and task forces set up by Congress, the President, or a federal agency, but does not cover a group "composed wholly of full-time officers or employees of the Federal Government."

The open-records provision of the FACA adopts by reference the exemptions contained in the FOIA. In another respect, however, it is broader than the FOIA, requiring advisory committees to make public reports and working papers even without a request. See Food Chemical News v. Department of Health and Human Services, 980 F.2d 1468 (D.C. Cir. 1992).

The reach of the statute was limited by a decision involving then-Vice President Dick Cheney. In re Cheney, 406 F.3d 723 (D.C. Cir. 2005). The question was whether the Federal Advisory Committee Act covered a federal energy task force that Cheney headed. The task force included executives of energy companies as well as federal officials. The court determined that it was not an "advisory committee" because the outsiders attending committee meetings had "neither a vote nor a veto over the advice the committee renders to the President." The court's definition of "advisory committee" was highly influenced by separation-of-powers concerns: "In light of the severe separation-of-powers problems in applying FACA on the basis that private parties participated in, or influenced, or were otherwise involved with a committee in the Executive Office of the President, we must construe the statute strictly. We therefore hold that such a committee is composed wholly of federal officials if the President has given no one other than a federal official a vote in or, if the committee acts by consensus, a veto over the committee's decision."

Legislative Bodies. The federal open meetings acts, like most state open meetings statutes, do not govern meetings of legislative bodies. Most state constitutions require open legislative sessions, but each house usually is free to make its own rules for meetings of its committees. Sessions of the U.S. House of Representatives have been open since the First Congress, but Senate sessions were closed until 1794. The Senate's practice provoked what may have been America's first open-government campaign, led by Philip Freneau, the famed editor of the *National Gazette*. See Gerald L. Grotta, Philip Freneau's Crusade for Open Sessions of the U.S. Senate, 48 Journ. Q. 667 (1971). The Senate continues to hold occasional closed sessions, usually for discussions of treaties or nominations.

The Senate or House may close their sessions for any purpose by majority vote, though they have done so infrequently. Senate committee meetings may be closed only for certain enumerated reasons, including discussions about national defense or foreign affairs, committee personnel matters, trade secrets, or matters required to be kept confidential by law, and to protect the identities of informers or the privacy or reputation of individuals. In the House, committee hearings may be closed when the testimony involves national security or "may tend to defame, degrade, or incriminate any person." House committee meetings other than hearings may be closed for any purpose by majority vote. Most Senate and House committee meetings that are not closed may be televised and otherwise broadcast.

2. STATE LAWS

The most important body of law governing access to meetings of governmental entities is that created by the state open meetings laws.

Every state has such a statute. Usually the statute provides that all meetings of governmental bodies shall be preceded by public notice and shall be open to the public, then sets forth detailed exceptions, definitions of such terms as "meeting" and "governmental body," notice requirements, and provisions for enforcement. Typical exceptions are for discussions of pending or anticipated litigation, land acquisitions, and personnel matters. Definitions of "meeting" are often quite broad, usually covering any gathering of a quorum of the members of the governing body and sometimes even conversations between any two of its members. State open meetings statutes normally cover local as well as state agencies, and thus apply to the meetings of thousands of boards, councils, commissions, and departments.

Here, advances in technology become important. If it is held that emails exchanged between members of a governing body about public matters do not constitute "meetings," for example, email can be used to circumvent open meetings laws. In 2004 the Virginia Supreme Court determined that the exchange of emails between city council members and members-elect was not a meeting because the emails "did not involve virtually simultaneous interaction" but were instead akin to "traditional letters sent by ordinary mail." Beck v. Shelton, 593 S.E.2d 195 (Va. 2004). A Washington State appellate court reached the opposite conclusion, however. In Wood v. Battle Ground School District, 27 P.3d 1208 (Wash. Ct. App. 2001), the court indicated that emails sent between school board members would constitute a meeting where the "active exchange of information and opinions . . . , as opposed to the mere passive receipt of information, suggests a collective intent to deliberate and/or to discuss Board business." Id. at 1218. But see Rangra v. Brown, 566 F.3d 515 (5th Cir. 2009), which suggests that government officials may have a First Amendment interest in the secrecy of their emails in some circumstances.

Enforcement of open meetings laws varies. In general, the most effective statutes are those that invalidate any action taken in violation of the openness requirements. The least effective are those whose enforcement depends on criminal prosecution of officials who do not comply; prosecutors tend to be unenthusiastic about devoting their time and resources to resolving disputes between their fellow officials and the press. A provision awarding attorneys' fees to persons who successfully challenge the improper closure of a meeting is often effective. See Daxton R. Stewart, Let the Sunshine In, or Else: An Examination of the "Teeth" of State and Federal Open Meetings and Open Records Laws, 15 Comm. L. & Pol'y 265 (2010) (evaluating tools for enforcement of access laws, including alternative dispute resolution procedures).

C. ACCESS TO INSTITUTIONS

When the press seeks to report on conditions in public institutions, such as mental hospitals or prisons, a new set of issues arises. From the press point of view, neither access to records nor access to meetings is sufficient; the reporters and photographers want to see conditions for themselves and talk to the inmates personally. From the government's point of view, concerns arise that are not present in access-to-records or access-to-meetings disputes—concerns relating to security, maintenance of discipline, and protection of the privacy of persons who are largely unable to protect it themselves. Perhaps because there were no statutory solutions to these issues, it was in this context that the press first advanced constitutional arguments for access.

In 1974 the Supreme Court decided two companion cases in which the press sought to enter prisons after the warden had imposed limitations on that access. In Pell v. Procunier, 417 U.S. 817 (1974), a regulation of the California Department of Corrections provided that "media interviews with specific individual inmates will not be permitted." Saxbe v. Washington Post Co., 417 U.S. 843 (1974), involved a similar ban by the federal prison system.

Justice Stewart, writing for the Court in both cases, noted that "this regulation is not part of an attempt by the State to conceal the conditions in its prisons or to frustrate the press investigation and reporting of those conditions." Reporters could visit the institutions and "speak about any subject to any inmates whom they might encounter." Interviews with inmates selected at random were also permitted, and both the press and the public could take tours through the prisons. "In short, members of the press enjoy access to California prisons that is not available to other members of the public." Indeed, the only apparent restriction was the one being challenged.

> The First and Fourteenth Amendments bar government from interfering in any way with a free press. The Constitution does not, however, require government to accord the press special access to information not shared by members of the public generally. It is one thing to say that a journalist is free to seek out sources of information not available to members of the general public, that he is entitled to some constitutional protection of the confidentiality of such sources, cf. Branzburg v. Hayes, and that government cannot restrain the publication of news emanating from such sources. Cf. N.Y. Times v. United States. It is quite another thing to suggest that the Constitution imposes upon government the affirmative duty to make available to journalists sources of information not available to members of the public generally. That proposition finds no support in the words of the Constitution or in any decision of this Court. Accordingly, since § 415.071 does not deny the press

access to sources of information available to members of the general public, we hold that it does not abridge the protections that the First and Fourteenth Amendments guarantee.

Four Justices dissented. Writing in *Saxbe,* Justice Powell, joined by Justices Brennan and Marshall, asserted that the government was not protecting privileged or confidential information. It "has no legitimate interest in preventing newsmen from obtaining the information.... Quite to the contrary, federal prisons are public institutions. The administration of these institutions, the effectiveness of their rehabilitative programs, the conditions of confinement that they maintain, and the experiences of the individuals incarcerated therein are all matters of legitimate societal interest and concern."

Citizens, the dissenting Justices reasoned, could not undertake to learn this information for themselves. "In seeking out the news the press therefore acts as an agent of the public at large." Justice Powell could not "follow the Court in concluding that *any* governmental restriction on press access to information, so long as it is nondiscriminatory, falls outside the purview of First Amendment concern.... At some point official restraints on access to news sources, even though not directed solely at the press, may so undermine the function of the First Amendment that it is both appropriate and necessary to require the Government to justify such regulations in terms more compelling than discretionary authority and administrative convenience."

Justice Powell concluded that the total ban on interviews impaired "a core value of the First Amendment," but that it would be permissible to adopt narrower rules, such as rules that barred interviews with prisoners being disciplined or that limited the number of interviews that might be held with any one person.

Justice Douglas, joined by Justices Brennan and Marshall, also dissented.

A few years later, the Supreme Court returned to the prison question in a slightly different context.

Houchins v. KQED, Inc.

Supreme Court of the United States, 1978.
438 U.S. 1.

[A suicide occurred at the Alameda County Jail at Santa Rita, California. KQED, licensee of a television station in nearby San Francisco, reported the story and quoted a psychiatrist as saying that conditions at the Little Greystone building were responsible for the illnesses of his patient-prisoners at the jail. In an earlier proceeding, a federal judge had ruled that the conditions at Greystone constituted cruel and unusual punishment. Houchins, the county sheriff, refused to admit a camera crew KQED sent to get the story and to photograph the facilities, including Greystone. At the time, no public tours of the jail were permitted.

KQED and the NAACP filed suit under 42 U.S.C. § 1983 claiming violation of their First Amendment rights. The NAACP claimed that information about the jail was essential to permit public debate on jail conditions in Alameda County. The complaint requested preliminary and permanent injunctions to prevent the sheriff from "excluding KQED news personnel from the Greystone cells and Santa Rita facilities and generally preventing full and accurate news coverage of the conditions prevailing therein."

Shortly after suit was filed, the sheriff announced a program of monthly tours. The press received advance notice, and several reporters, including one from KQED, went on the first tour. Each tour was limited to 25 persons and did not include Little Greystone. Cameras and tape recorders were barred, though the sheriff did supply photographs of some parts of the jail. Tour members "were not permitted to interview inmates, and inmates were generally removed from view."

KQED argued that the tours were unsatisfactory because advance scheduling prevented timely access and because photography and interviewing were barred. The sheriff defended his policy on grounds of "inmate privacy," the danger of creating "jail celebrities" who would "undermine jail security," and the concern that unscheduled tours would "disrupt jail operations."

The district judge issued a preliminary injunction barring the sheriff from denying access to "responsible representatives" of the news media "at reasonable times and hours" and "from preventing KQED news personnel and responsible representatives of the news media from utilizing photographic and sound equipment or from utilizing inmate interviews in providing full and accurate coverage of the Santa Rita facilities." He found that a more flexible policy was "both desirable and attainable" without danger to prison discipline. The court of appeals, in three separate opinions, rejected the sheriff's argument that *Pell* and *Saxbe* controlled, and affirmed the injunction.]

■ MR. CHIEF JUSTICE BURGER announced the judgment of the Court and delivered an opinion, in which MR. JUSTICE WHITE and MR. JUSTICE REHNQUIST joined.

The question presented is whether the news media have a constitutional right of access to a county jail, over and above that of other persons, to interview inmates and make sound recordings, films, and photographs for publication and broadcasting by newspapers, radio, and television.

. . .

II.

Notwithstanding our holding in Pell v. Procunier, supra, respondents assert that the right recognized by the Court of Appeals flows logically from our decisions construing the First Amendment. They argue that there is a constitutionally guaranteed right to gather news under *Pell* [ ] and *Branzburg* [ ]. From the right to gather news and the right to receive information, they argue for an implied special right of access to government controlled sources of information. This right, they contend, compels access as a *constitutional* matter. . . .

III.

We can agree with many of the respondents' generalized assertions; conditions in jails and prisons are clearly matters "of great public importance." [ ] Penal facilities are public institutions which require large amounts of public funds, and their mission is crucial in our criminal justice system. Each person placed in prison becomes, in effect, a ward of the state for whom society assumes broad responsibility. It is equally true that with greater information, the public can more intelligently form opinions about prison conditions. Beyond question, the role of the media is important; acting as the "eyes and ears" of the public, they can be a powerful and constructive force, contributing to remedial action in the conduct of public business. They have served that function since the beginning of the Republic, but like all other components of our society media representatives are subject to limits.

The media are not a substitute for or an adjunct of government, and like the courts, they are "ill-equipped" to deal with problems of prison administration. [ ] We must not confuse the role of the media with that of government; each has special, crucial functions each complementing—and, sometimes conflicting with—the other.

The public importance of conditions in penal facilities and the media's role of providing information afford no basis for reading into the Constitution a right of the public or the media to enter these institutions, with camera equipment, and take moving and still pictures of inmates for broadcast purposes. This Court has never intimated a First Amendment guarantee of a right of access to all sources of information within government control. Nor does the rationale of the decisions upon which respondents rely lead to the implication of such a right.

. . .

[*Branzburg*] offers even less support for the respondents' position. Its observation, in dictum, that "news gathering is not without its First Amendment protections," [ ] in no sense implied a constitutional right of access to news sources. That observation must be read in context; it was in response to the contention that forcing a reporter to disclose to a grand jury information received in confidence would violate the First Amendment by deterring news sources from communicating information.

[ ] There is an undoubted right to gather news "from any source by means within the law," [ ] but that affords no basis for the claim that the First Amendment compels others—private persons or governments—to supply information.

. . .

The right to *receive* ideas and information is not the issue in this case. [ ] The issue is a claimed special privilege of access which the Court rejected in *Pell* and *Saxbe,* a right which is not essential to guarantee the freedom to communicate or publish.

IV.

The respondents' argument is flawed, not only because it lacks precedential support and is contrary to statements in this Court's opinions, but also because it invites the Court to involve itself in what is clearly a legislative task which the Constitution has left to the political processes. Whether the government should open penal institutions in the manner sought by respondents is a question of policy which a legislative body might appropriately resolve one way or the other.

. . .

Petitioner cannot prevent respondents from learning about jail conditions in a variety of ways, albeit not as conveniently as they might prefer. Respondents have a First Amendment right to receive letters from inmates criticizing jail officials and reporting on conditions. See Procunier v. Martinez, 416 U.S. 396 (1974). Respondents are free to interview those who render the legal assistance to which inmates are entitled. See id., at 419. They are also free to seek out former inmates, visitors to the prison, public officials, and institutional personnel, as they sought out the complaining psychiatrist here.

Moreover, California statutes currently provide for a prison Board of Corrections that has the authority to inspect jails and prisons and *must* provide a public report at regular intervals. . . .

Neither the First Amendment nor Fourteenth Amendment mandates a right of access to government information or sources of information within the government's control. Under our holdings in *Pell* [and *Saxbe*], until the political branches decree otherwise, as they are free to do, the media have no special right of access to the Alameda County Jail different from or greater than that accorded the public generally.

[Reversed and remanded. Justices Marshall and Blackmun took no part in the decision of the case.]

■ MR. JUSTICE STEWART, concurring in the judgment.

I agree that the preliminary injunction issued against the petitioner was unwarranted, and therefore concur in the judgment. In my view, however, KQED was entitled to injunctive relief of more limited scope.

The First and Fourteenth Amendments do not guarantee the public a right of access to information generated or controlled by government, nor do they guarantee the press any basic right of access superior to that of the public generally. The Constitution does no more than assure the public and the press equal access once government has opened its doors. Accordingly, I agree substantially with what the opinion of The Chief Justice has to say on that score.

We part company, however, in applying these abstractions to the facts of this case. Whereas he appears to view "equal access" as meaning access that is identical in all respects, I believe that the concept of equal access must be accorded more flexibility in order to accommodate the practical distinctions between the press and the general public.

When on assignment, a journalist does not tour a jail simply for his own edification. He is there to gather information to be passed on to others, and his mission is protected by the Constitution for very specific reasons. "Enlightened choice by an informed citizenry is the basic ideal upon which an open society is premised. . . ." *Branzburg* [ ] (dissenting opinion). Our society depends heavily on the press for that enlightenment. . . .

That the First Amendment speaks separately of freedom of speech and freedom of the press is no constitutional accident, but an acknowledgment of the critical role played by the press in American society. The Constitution requires sensitivity to that role, and to the special needs of the press in performing it effectively. A person touring Santa Rita jail can grasp its reality with his own eyes and ears. But if a television reporter is to convey the jail's sights and sounds to those who cannot personally visit the place, he must use cameras and sound equipment. In short, terms of access that are reasonably imposed on individual members of the public may, if they impede effective reporting without sufficient justification, be unreasonable as applied to journalists who are there to convey to the general public what the visitors see.

Under these principles, KQED was clearly entitled to some form of preliminary injunctive relief. At the time of the District Court's decision, members of the public were permitted to visit most parts of the Santa Rita jail, and the First and Fourteenth Amendments required the Sheriff to give members of the press *effective* access to the same areas. The Sheriff evidently assumed that he could fulfill this obligation simply by allowing reporters to sign up for tours on the same terms as the public. I think he was mistaken in this assumption, as a matter of constitutional law.

The District Court found that the press required access to the jail on a more flexible and frequent basis than scheduled monthly tours if it was to keep the public informed. By leaving the "specific methods of implementing such a policy . . . [to] Sheriff Houchins," the Court concluded that the press could be allowed access to the jail "at reasonable times and hours" without causing undue disruption. The District Court also found that the media required cameras and recording equipment for effective presentation to the viewing public of the conditions at the jail seen by individual visitors, and that their use could be kept consistent with institutional needs. These elements of the Court's order were both sanctioned by the Constitution and amply supported by the record.

In two respects, however, the District Court's preliminary injunction was overbroad. It ordered the Sheriff to permit reporters into the Little Greystone facility and it required him to let them interview randomly encountered inmates. In both these respects, the injunction gave the press access to areas and sources of information from which persons on the public tours had been excluded, and thus enlarged the scope of what the Sheriff and Supervisors had opened to public view. The District Court erred in concluding that the First and Fourteenth Amendments compelled this broader access for the press.

Because the preliminary injunction exceeded the requirements of the Constitution in these respects, I agree that the judgment of the Court of Appeals affirming the District Court's order must be reversed. But I would not foreclose the possibility of further relief for KQED on remand. In my view, the availability and scope of future permanent injunctive relief must depend upon the extent of access then permitted the public, and the decree must be framed to accommodate equitably the constitutional role of the press and the institutional requirements of the jail.

■ MR. JUSTICE STEVENS, with whom MR. JUSTICE BRENNAN and MR. JUSTICE POWELL join, dissenting.

. . .

For two reasons, which shall be discussed separately, the decisions in *Pell* and *Saxbe* do not control the propriety of the District Court's preliminary injunction. First, the unconstitutionality of petitioner's policies which gave rise to this litigation does not rest on the premise that the press has a greater right of access to information regarding prison conditions than do other members of the public. Second, relief tailored to the needs of the press may properly be awarded to a representative of the press which is successful in proving that it has been harmed by a constitutional violation and need not await the grant of relief to members of the general public who may also have been injured by petitioner's unconstitutional access policy but have not yet sought to vindicate their rights.

. . .

In *Pell* [ ], the Court stated that "newsmen have no constitutional right of access to prisons or their inmates beyond that afforded the general public." But the Court has never intimated that a nondiscriminatory policy of excluding entirely both the public and the press from access to information about prison conditions would avoid constitutional scrutiny. Indeed, *Pell* itself strongly suggests the contrary.

. . .

The decision in *Pell,* therefore, does not imply that a state policy of concealing prison conditions from the press, or a policy denying the press any opportunity to observe those conditions, could have been justified simply by pointing to like concealment from, and denial to, the general public. If that were not true, there would have been no need to emphasize the substantial press and public access reflected in the record of that case. What *Pell* does indicate is that the question whether respondents established a probability of prevailing on their constitutional claim is inseparable from the question whether petitioner's policies unduly restricted the opportunities of the general public to learn about the conditions of confinement in Santa Rita jail. As in *Pell,* in assessing its adequacy, the total access of the public and the press must be considered.

Here, the broad restraints on access to information regarding operation of the jail that prevailed on the date this suit was instituted are plainly disclosed by the record. . . . Petitioner's no-access policy, modified only in the wake of respondents' resort to the courts, could survive constitutional scrutiny only if the Constitution affords no protection to the public's right to be informed about conditions within those public institutions where some of its members are confined because they have been charged with or found guilty of criminal offenses.

II.

The preservation of a full and free flow of information to the general public has long been recognized as a core objective of the First Amendment to the Constitution. It is for this reason that the First Amendment protects not only the dissemination but also the receipt of information and ideas. . . .

In addition to safeguarding the right of one individual to receive what another elects to communicate, the First Amendment serves an essential societal function. Our system of self-government assumes the existence of an informed citizenry. . . . It is not sufficient, therefore, that the channels of communication be free of governmental restraints. Without some protection for the acquisition of information about the operation of public institutions such as prisons by the public at large, the process of self-governance contemplated by the Framers would be stripped of its substance.[22]

---

[22] Admittedly, the right to receive or acquire information is not specifically mentioned in the Constitution. But "the protection of the Bill of Rights goes beyond the specific guarantees to protect from . . . abridgment those equally fundamental personal rights necessary to make the express guarantees fully meaningful. . . . The dissemination of ideas can accomplish nothing if otherwise willing adherents are not free to receive and consider them. It would be a barren marketplace of ideas that had only sellers and no buyers." Lamont v. Postmaster General, 381 U.S. at 308 (Brennan, J., concurring). It would be an even more barren marketplace that had willing buyers and sellers and no meaningful information to exchange.

For that reason information-gathering is entitled to some measure of constitutional protection. See, e.g., *Branzburg* [ ]; *Pell* [ ]. As this Court's decisions clearly indicate, however, this protection is not for the private benefit of those who might qualify as representatives of the "press" but to insure that the citizens are fully informed regarding matters of public interest and importance.

[Justice Stevens argued that in the prison context, unlike other contexts such as executive sessions of official bodies, there was no interest in confidentiality.] While prison officials have an interest in the time and manner of public acquisition of information about the institutions they administer, there is no legitimate, penological justification for concealing from citizens the conditions in which their fellow citizens are being confined.

. . .

Some inmates—in Santa Rita, a substantial number—are pretrial detainees. . . . Society has a special interest in ensuring that unconvicted citizens are treated in accord with their status.

In this case, the record demonstrates that both the public and the press had been consistently denied any access to the inner portions of the Santa Rita jail, that there had been excessive censorship of inmate correspondence, and that there was no valid justification for these broad restraints on the flow of information. An affirmative answer to the question whether respondent established a likelihood of prevailing on the merits did not depend, in final analysis, on any right of the press to special treatment beyond that accorded the public at large. Rather, the probable existence of a constitutional violation rested upon the special importance of allowing a democratic community access to knowledge about how its servants were treating some of its members who have been committed to their custody. An official prison policy of concealing such knowledge from the public by arbitrarily cutting off the flow of information at its source abridges the freedom of speech and of the press protected by the First and Fourteenth Amendments to the Constitution.

. . .

NOTES AND QUESTIONS

1.   Why would Justice Stewart allow access at times other than those at which the public can enter the jail? What would he do if the sheriff were to stop the public tours?

2.   The district court enjoined the sheriff from excluding KQED, but did not give a remedy to other members of the public. Is that impermissible? In an omitted portion of his dissent, Justice Stevens wrote: "[E]ven though the Constitution provides the press with no greater right of access to information than is possessed by the public at large, a preliminary injunction is not invalid simply because it awards special relief to a successful litigant which is a representative of the press."

3.   Two years after *Houchins*, the Court decided a case that Justice Stevens interpreted as repudiating *Houchins* insofar as the latter held that the First Amendment does not guarantee a right of access to information within the government's control. The case was Richmond Newspapers, Inc. v. Virginia, a courtroom access case which is discussed in the next chapter. He interpreted *Richmond Newspapers* as holding "that the First Amendment protects the press and public from abridgment of their rights of access to information about the operation of their government, including the Judicial Branch. . . ." Consider a re-evaluation of *Houchins* after reading all of the subsequent courtroom access cases discussed in the next chapter.

4.   Can prison officials prevent inmates from using telephone, mail, or visitation privileges to communicate with reporters? In Procunier v. Martinez, 416 U.S. 396 (1974), the Supreme Court upheld a district court decision striking down rules regulating the correspondence of California prisoners, in part because of the First Amendment rights of the recipients of the prisoner's letters: "Whatever the status of a prisoner's claim to uncensored correspondence with an outsider, it is plain that the latter's interest is grounded in the First Amendment's guarantee of freedom of speech. And this does not depend on whether the nonprisoner correspondent is the author or intended recipient of a particular letter, for the addressee as well as the sender of direct personal correspondence derives from the First and Fourteenth Amendments a protection against unjustified governmental interference with the intended communication."

Inmate Interviews. Many prisons restrict news media interviews with prisoners. *Houchins* indicates that prisons do not have an obligation to arrange for interviews with specific inmates at the request of the media. Can prisons prevent interviews with inmates whose speech is likely to be especially objectionable? The Supreme Court held that inmates have only those First Amendment rights "consistent with incarceration," and courts give deference to regulations on access when there is a rational connection between the regulations and "legitimate penological interests." Turner v. Safley, 482 U.S. 78 (1987). However, the First Amendment forbids suppression based on the content of an inmate's speech.

These principles were tested in Hammer v. Ashcroft, 512 F.3d 961 (7th Cir. 2008), a case involving a Bureau of Prisons policy restricting media interviews with death row inmates. Prison officials apparently adopted the policy in response to the broadcast of a "60 Minutes" interview with Timothy McVeigh, who was later executed for murdering 168 people in the bombing of the Alfred P. Murrah federal building in Oklahoma City. After the McVeigh interview, Senator Brian Dorgan publicly criticized the Bureau of Prisons for allowing the interview and wrote the director of the Bureau to demand prohibition of all future interviews with death row inmates. Shortly afterwards, the Bureau adopted a new policy banning face-to-face interviews with inmates on death row and allowing only 15-minute telephone interviews. Then-Attorney General John Ashcroft held a press conference to announce the changed policy. The Attorney General announced that the policy change was designed to "restrict a mass murderer's access to the public podium." In justifying the policy, he also stated: "I'm concerned about irresponsible glamorization of a culture of violence, and that concern has shaped our approach to these issues profoundly."

David Hammer, a federal prisoner on death row who had previously granted face-to-face media interviews, sued the government, alleging violation of his First Amendment rights. The district court granted summary judgment for the government, but a Seventh Circuit panel reversed. The government argued that the ban on face-to-face interviews was necessary to preserve security by preventing death row inmates from becoming jailhouse celebrities.

The Seventh Circuit looked closely at the timing of the policy—coming on the heels of the McVeigh interview—and the contemporaneous statements made by the Attorney General. See Hammer v. Ashcroft, 512 F.3d 961 (7th Cir. 2008). The panel found that Hammer had raised a genuine issue as to whether the policy "was motivated by a desire to prohibit a disagreeable viewpoint or to advance prison security." But a majority of the court en banc held that "[i]t is not clear why one bad motive would spoil a rule that is adequately supported by good reasons." See Hammer v. Ashcroft, 570 F.3d 798 (7th Cir. 2009) (en banc). Chief among those reasons was to prevent inmates from becoming celebrities, which the court said might give them a form of satisfaction that undermined the goal of punishing them.

The panel also found summary judgment inappropriate because it was not clear whether the new policy "leaves open sufficient alternate routes of access to the media and whether there are reasonable alternatives to the ban on face-to-face interviews." One of the alternatives the government cited was inmates' freedom to make phone calls to news media. But Hammer said that was not a satisfactory alternative because another Bureau policy forbade news media from using personal information from one inmate about another inmate who refuses to be interviewed. The en banc majority held that this restriction was rational. Writing for the majority, Judge Easterbrook reasoned that "[t]elling tales about fellow inmates may make them angry (if the tales are defamatory) or may make yet other inmates envious (if the tales are flattering). In either event, disorder may follow."

———

Access to Executions. In 1996 media groups covering an execution by lethal injection at California's San Quentin prison complained that all they were allowed to see was a motionless prisoner lying strapped to a gurney. The intravenous tubes were already in place before the curtain shielding him from view was drawn aside, and the fatal drug was administered from a location out of view and out of hearing. After watching the immobilized prisoner through a window for a few minutes, the witnesses were informed that he was dead.

The district court subsequently enjoined California prison officials from enforcing the policy that prevented media representatives from observing executions in their entirety. The judge said they must be allowed an uninterrupted view from the time the condemned enters the execution chamber until he or she is pronounced dead. See California First Amendment Coalition v. Calderon, 88 F. Supp. 2d 1083 (N.D. Cal. 2000). The Ninth Circuit affirmed, finding that the public enjoys a First Amendment right to view executions from the moment the condemned is escorted into the execution chamber, including initial procedures that are inextricably intertwined with the process of putting the condemned inmate to death. The court found that the prison regulations under review in the case impermissibly restricted that right. See California First Amendment Coalition v. Woodford, 299 F.3d 868 (9th Cir. 2002).

In a somewhat related access case, the Virginia Supreme Court in 2015 reviewed a freedom-of-information request for technical information relating to executions and set a high bar for such requests. There, the requester had asked for electric chair wiring, design, and instruction-related information, execution chamber design plans, and related materials. The court ordered that the trial court reviewing the request give "substantial weight" to the prison's concerns about security and safety, suggesting that testimony from the prison expert about threats from inside and outside the prison would suffice. It also held that execution manuals that contained certain protocols were exempt from disclosure. Virginia Department of Corrections v. Surovell, 776 S.E.2d 579 (Va. 2015).

D. ACCESS TO MILITARY OPERATIONS

The technical capacity to provide live television coverage from battle zones has raised new issues involving access to military operations. During the 1970s, a number of military leaders contended that front-line reporting contributed to the weakening of public support for U.S. involvement in Vietnam. Consequently, when the United States began military operations on the island nation of Grenada in 1983, reporters were excluded for two days, after which a limited group was flown to the island by military aircraft. A lawsuit contesting the exclusion was dismissed for mootness, and the dismissal was upheld on appeal. Flynt v. Weinberger, 762 F.2d 134 (D.C. Cir. 1985).

The Pool System and the Persian Gulf War. Nonetheless, the outcry over the military's total exclusion of the press led the Defense Department to adopt a "pool" system. Under this system, media organizations chosen by the Department were allowed to select specific reporters to be transported to cover the early stages of military operations. These reporters would then "pool" their information, sharing it with other reporters who had not been selected.

The first real test of the pool system was in the 1991 Persian Gulf War, during which the Pentagon outraged the media by carefully controlling and ultimately manipulating their coverage of the war. With the approval of the White House, the Pentagon limited all coverage of combat to press pools escorted by military personnel. The military, rather than the press, determined where the pools would be taken. Reporters and photographers who tried to strike out on their own were subject to detention and disaccreditation, although by the end of the war some correspondents were able to reach battle sites on their own. Media copy was subject to review by military censors for security purposes. Pentagon guidelines said censors were not to delete material because it criticized or embarrassed the military, but correspondents complained that censors occasionally deleted material in violation of the guidelines, and transmission of copy was often delayed until its news value had passed.

Most news of the progress of the war came from briefings by high-ranking military officers in Washington and Riyadh. Briefings emphasized dramatic military videos of "smart" bombs precisely seeking out and destroying inanimate military targets. Although it later became clear that ninety percent of the bombs dropped on Iraq were less accurate "dumb" bombs, some of which struck civilian targets, the results of those bombings generally were not shown. One field commander showed reporters videotape of helicopters attacking Iraqi troops, but the military subsequently refused to make public that and other footage showing human targets. The military also refused to provide sound tracks of the voices of pilots and others reacting to combat.

Media complaints about the restrictions received little support from the public or the courts. Media groups challenged the Pentagon rules limiting access to pool representatives, but the complaint was dismissed. See The Nation Magazine v. Department of Defense, 762 F. Supp. 1558 (S.D.N.Y. 1991). The district court wrote that some First Amendment right of access to military operations might be found in the Supreme Court's decisions concerning access to courtrooms, parks, and prisons, but that it would have to be carefully crafted to protect the legitimate interests of the military. By the time of the decision, the war had ended and the Pentagon said any future rules would be tailored to the specific circumstances of that operation. The court said "prudence dictates that we leave the definition of the exact parameters of press access to military operations abroad for a later date when a full record is available."

———

After the 1991 Persian Gulf War, negotiations between the Pentagon and major news organizations produced a new set of Pentagon rules for future military operations. These new rules state that pools "are not to serve as the standard means of covering U.S. military operations," and that reporters and photographers will be provided access to all major military units. Field commanders are to allow journalists to ride on military vehicles and aircraft whenever feasible. Military public affairs officers are not to interfere with independent reporting and are to be given the resources needed to facilitate timely transmission of pool and independent reports. The only guideline not agreed to by the media was one giving the military the right to review articles and broadcasts to prevent disclosure of information that could endanger the safety of troops or the success of a military mission. News organizations said they would challenge that restriction if and when the Pentagon sought to implement it.

Journalists and news organizations charged that the Defense Department largely ignored the 1992 agreement on media coverage during the war in Afghanistan ten years later. Despite the fact that the agreement was "to be followed in any future combat situation involving American troops," Stanley Cloud, who participated in negotiating that agreement as Washington bureau chief for Time, wrote that "in the early stages, at least, much of the fighting took place in secret, far beyond journalists' eyes and ears. Once again, reporters from the freest country on earth were begging the Defense Department for permission to cover a war firsthand." Journalists were excluded from military operations entirely for the first six weeks of the war, and then forced to rely on press pools for the next month. Reporters alleged that they were threatened by U.S. troops, denied access to military personnel, and subjected to censorship. In December 2002, U.S. Marines locked reporters in a warehouse to prevent them from covering American troops killed or injured by a stray bomb.

The Defense Department did not deny these charges, but rather asserted that, in the words of Assistant Secretary Victoria Clarke, "[w]e are in a whole new world here. We're trying to figure out the rules of the road." The Pentagon apologized for the detention of U.S. journalists, ended pool coverage, and a few months later allowed reporters to accompany U.S. ground troops in combat, but only on condition that they submitted their reports to military censors.

Two organizations challenged the Pentagon's restrictions on coverage in Afghanistan. One was Getty Images News Services Corp., which supplies images to many publications. Getty alleged that it had been inappropriately excluded from press pools when they existed and from press flights arranged by the Defense Department to the detention center at Guantanamo Bay Naval Base. The district court granted the Defense Department's motion to dismiss, largely on the basis that the Department had already rectified much of the treatment of which Getty complained. The court was highly deferential to the Defense Department and the needs of the military, but it did note, citing to Sherrill v. Knight, excerpted later in this chapter, that the Department needed to adopt and follow "reasonable" standards for determining which press outlets were included on the flights to Guantanamo. "Although the Court is reluctant to interfere significantly in the military's conduct of its affairs, the First and Fifth Amendments seem to require, at a minimum, that before [determining] which media organizations receive the limited access available, DOD must not only have some criteria to guide its determinations, but must have a reasonable way of assessing whether the criteria are met." See Getty Images News Services Corp. v. Department of Defense, 193 F. Supp. 2d 112 (D.D.C. 2002).

Hustler publisher Larry Flynt also challenged restrictions on Afghanistan war coverage. The appellate court's decision is below.

Flynt v. Rumsfeld
U.S. Court of Appeals, District of Columbia Circuit, 2004.
355 F.3d 697.

■ SENTELLE, CIRCUIT JUDGE:

Larry Flynt and L.F.P., Inc. (the company that publishes Hustler magazine) (collectively "Flynt" or "appellants") sued Donald H. Rumsfeld, Secretary of Defense, and the United States Department of Defense ("DOD") seeking, *inter alia,* injunctive relief against interference with its exercise of a claimed First Amendment right of the news media to have access to U.S. troops in combat operations, and claiming that DOD's delay in granting Hustler's reporter access to U.S. troops in Afghanistan infringed that right. They further argued that DOD's Directive controlling media access to military forces facially violates this same constitutional right. The District Court dismissed Flynt's as-applied constitutional claims for lack of ripeness and standing, and refused to exercise its discretion under the Declaratory Judgment Act to declare the pertinent DOD Directive facially unconstitutional. This appeal followed. Because we find that no such constitutional right exists, we will affirm the District Court's decision on other grounds. [The Court of Appeals also held that appellants had standing and that the claim was ripe, based on the denial of immediate access to accompany troops.]

I.   Background

A.   Hustler's attempts to gain access

Shortly after the September 11, 2001, terrorist attacks, the United States military began combat operations in Afghanistan in support of the global war on terrorism. On October 30, 2001, Flynt wrote a letter to the Honorable Victoria Clarke, Assistant Secretary of Defense for Public Affairs, requesting that Hustler correspondents "be permitted to accompany ground troops on combat missions and that said correspondents be allowed free access to the theater of United States military operations in Afghanistan and other countries where hostilities may be occurring as part of Operation Enduring Freedom.". . . . [O]n November 15, Clarke sent Flynt a fax stating that access to ground operations was not immediately possible because " . . . the only U.S. troops on the ground in Afghanistan are small numbers of servicemen involved in special operations activity." Clarke explained that "[t]he highly dangerous and unique nature of their work makes it very difficult to embed media" with ground troops, but also stated that there had been "extensive" media access to other aspects of military operations.

Specifically, "[s]cores of reporters and photographers have covered the [air] strikes, witnessed the humanitarian drops and interviewed dozens of [soldiers]." Clarke then provided Flynt with contact information for the Fifth Fleet Public Affairs Officer so that Hustler could have similar access.

[Flynt did not contact the Fifth Fleet Public Affairs Officer but instead filed this lawsuit. He then sent another letter to Clarke requesting access. She responded by sending a letter describing what types of access were available at that point and explaining that media access decisions were controlled by Department of Defense Directive 5122.5. (This directive stems from the agreement discussed earlier.) Ultimately, in May of 2002, a Hustler reporter did obtain access to troops searching for al Qaeda operatives.]

B. The Directive

As stated above, DOD decisions regarding media access to combat troops are guided by Department of Defense Directive 5122.5. . . . At issue in this case is Enclosure 3, entitled "Statement of DOD Principles for News Media." This enclosure begins with the command that "[o]pen and independent reporting shall be the principal means of coverage of U.S. military operations." It then outlines the manner in which such coverage should occur. It allows for media pools, limited numbers of press persons who represent a larger number of news media organizations and share material, but states that pools are not to be the "standard means of covering U.S. military operations." Rather, pools are only to be used when space is limited or areas to be visited are extremely remote. It also directs that "field commanders should be instructed to permit journalists to ride on military vehicles and aircraft when possible." . . .

II. Analysis

This court reviews *de novo* the District Court's dismissal of a complaint for lack of subject matter jurisdiction. [ ]. In our review, we assume the truth of the allegations made and construe them favorably to the pleader. [ ] We review the District Court's decision to withhold declaratory relief for an abuse of discretion. [ ]

A. Appellants' Claims

As a threshold matter, it is important to clarify the right appellants seek to protect. In candor, it is not at all clear from appellants' complaint below or briefs in this court precisely what right they believe was violated or contend the courts should vindicate. After some pressing, at oral argument it became clear that they claimed a right, protected under the First Amendment, in their own words, to "go[ ] in [to battle] with the military." This right is different from merely a right to cover war. The Government has no rule—at least so far as Flynt has made known to us—that prohibits the media from generally covering war. Although it would be dangerous, a media outlet could presumably purchase a vehicle, equip it with the necessary technical equipment, take it to a region in conflict, and cover events there. Such action would not violate Enclosure 3 or any other identified DOD rule.

With that distinction made, appellants' claim comes more sharply into focus. They claim that the Constitution guarantees to the media—specifically Hustler's correspondent—the right to travel *with* military units into combat, with all of the accommodations and protections that entails—essentially what is currently known as "embedding." Indeed, at oral argument appellants' counsel stated that the military is "obligated to *accommodate* the press because the press is what informs the electorate as to what our government is doing in war."

. . .

C.   Facial Challenge

. . .

The facial challenge is premised on the assertion that there is a First Amendment right for legitimate press representatives to travel with the military, and to be accommodated and otherwise facilitated by the military in their reporting efforts during combat, subject only to reasonable security and safety restrictions. There is nothing we have found in the Constitution, American history, or our case law to support this claim.

To support the position that there is such a constitutional right, appellants first point to cases that discuss the general purposes underlying the First Amendment. See New York Times Co. v. United States [ ] ("[t]he press was protected so that it could bare the secrets of government and inform the people.") (Black, J., concurring); [ ]. These cases, however, say nothing about media access to the U.S. combat units engaged in battle.

Appellants also cite cases that allow facial challenges to statutes or regulations that vest public officials with unfettered discretion to grant or deny licenses to engage in expressive activity, such as City of Lakewood v. Plain Dealer Publishing Co., 486 U.S. 750 (1988), and Shuttlesworth v. City of Birmingham, 394 U.S. 147 (1969). This is not, however, a "license" decision. This appeal challenges regulations controlling *access* to government information and activity, not governmental limitation of expression. The Supreme Court has noted the difference. See, e.g., Los Angeles Police Dept. v. United Reporting Publ'g Corp. (distinguishing government limits on access to information in its possession from a government restriction on disseminating information one already possesses).

Likewise, this Court has held that "freedom of speech [and] of the press do not create any per se right of access to government . . . activities simply because such access might lead to more thorough or better reporting." JB Pictures, Inc. v. Dep't of Defense. Appellants admit they face a "dearth of case law concerning press access to battles." From this unenviable position, they ask us to look to Richmond Newspapers, Inc. v. Virginia, for guidance.

In *Richmond Newspapers*, a plurality of the Supreme Court held that a constitutional right of public access to criminal trials existed based on a long history of such access in the United States and in England at the time our organic laws were created. [ ] According to appellants, *Richmond Newspapers* established that the First Amendment may be interpreted to provide for a right of access to government operations, and that access is not limited to criminal trials. They assert that we must apply a *Richmond Newspapers* analysis to the facts of this case. We disagree.

In Center for National Security Studies v. Department of Justice, we held that there was no First Amendment right for plaintiffs to receive the identities of INS detainees and material witnesses who were detained in the wake of the September 11 attacks. Indeed, we made it clear that "[n]either the Supreme Court nor this Court has applied the *Richmond Newspapers* test outside the context of criminal judicial proceedings or the transcripts of such proceedings." [ ] For emphasis, we added that "neither this Court nor the Supreme Court has ever *indicated* that it would" do so. [ ]. Instead, we noted that in all areas other than criminal proceedings, the Supreme Court has applied the general rule of Houchins v. KQED, not the exception of *Richmond Newspapers*. [ ] *Houchins* held that the press have no First Amendment right of access to prisons, and in doing so stated that the First Amendment does not "mandate[ ] a right of access to government information or sources of information within the government's control." *Houchins,* [ ]. To summarize, neither this Court nor the Supreme Court has ever applied *Richmond Newspapers* outside the context of criminal proceedings, and we will not do so today.

Appellants argue that we did, however, use the *analysis* underlying the *Richmond Newspapers* decision in *JB Pictures Inc.* [ ] In that case, several media and veterans organizations challenged a Department of Defense policy. That policy shifted ceremonies for deceased service members arriving from overseas from Dover Air Force base to locations closer to the service members' homes. It also gave the families of deceased military personnel the authority to limit press access to those ceremonies. Contrary to appellants' assertion, the extent of our *Richmond Newspapers* discussion in that case is contained in one sentence: "[i]t is obvious that military bases do not share the tradition of openness on which the Court relied in striking down restrictions on access to criminal court proceedings in . . . *Richmond Newspapers*." [ ]. Thus *J.B. Pictures* not only does not support wholesale adoption of a *Richmond Newspapers* analysis in every case involving requests for access to government activities or information, it rejects such a rule.

Even if we were to apply a *Richmond Newspapers* test, which again, we do not, it would not support appellants' facial challenge to the Directive. As an initial matter, the history of press access to military units is not remotely as extensive as public access to criminal trials. Without going into great historic detail, it is sufficient that in *Richmond Newspapers* the Supreme Court relied on the "unbroken, uncontradicted history" of public access to criminal trials. . . .

No comparable history exists to support a right of media access to U.S. military units in combat. The very article cited by appellants for the proposition that media have traditionally had broad access to soldiers in combat does not support this position. *See* John E. Smith, From the Front Lines to the Front Page: Media Access to War in the Persian Gulf and Beyond, 26 Colum. J.L. & Soc. Probs. 291, 292–305 (1993). Beginning with the American Revolution, war reporting was primarily in the form of private letters from soldiers and official reports that were sent home and published in newspapers. [ ] Indeed, the rise of the professional war correspondent did not begin until at least the time of the Civil War. [ ] In addition, it is not entirely clear that in any of our early wars the media was actively embedded into units, which is the right appellants seek. In sum, even if we were to attempt a *Richmond Newspapers* analysis and consider the historical foundations of a right of media access to combat units, appellants' claim would fail miserably.

Even if *Richmond Newspapers* applied in this context, and even if there was a historical basis for media access to troops in combat, the Directive would still not violate the First Amendment. *Richmond Newspapers* expressly stated that "[j]ust as a government may impose reasonable time, place, and manner restrictions" in granting access to public streets, "so may a trial judge . . . impose reasonable limitations on access to a trial." [ ]. These limitations could be based on the need to maintain a "quiet and orderly setting," or "courtrooms' . . . limited capacity." [ ] The Directive appellants challenge is incredibly supportive of media access to the military with only a few limitations. . . . The restrictions contained in the Directive are few, including: special operations restrictions; limited restrictions on media communications owing to electromagnetic operational security concerns; use of media pools when the sheer size of interested media is unworkable, such as at the beginning of an operation; and expulsion for members of the media who violate the ground rules. [ ] Appellants have offered no reason to conclude that these restrictions are unreasonable. Even if *Richmond Newspapers* did apply, appellants' argument would fail.

. . . In no way did the District Court abuse its discretion in refusing to grant declaratory relief.

D.   As-applied Challenges

We now turn to the as-applied challenges. As explained above, the constitutional right appellants assert does not exist, so the as-applied claim could only survive if this otherwise constitutional Directive was applied to them in some unconstitutional way. It was not. At no time has Flynt ever claimed that he, or Hustler, was treated differently under the Directive than any other media outlet. Nor has he claimed that the Directive is some sort of a sham that was not followed.

. . .

Because we hold that there is no constitutionally based right for the media to embed with U.S. military forces in combat, and because we further hold that the Directive was not applied to Flynt or Hustler magazine in any unconstitutional manner, the District Court's judgment is affirmed.

NOTES AND QUESTIONS

1.   What would be the implications of recognizing a constitutional right to accompany troops into battle? Would the right only apply where there had been a formal declaration of war?

2.   Does the fact that there is less likely to be an identifiable battlefront in modern warfare make press claims for access more or less viable?

3.   For a discussion of war coverage issues, see David A. Anderson, Freedom of the Press in Wartime, 77 U. Colo. L. Rev. 49 (2006).

————

"Embedding" and Public Support for Military Operations. The media's coverage of battle may undermine public support for military operations and risk unwittingly aiding the enemy, but it may also galvanize public support for military operations and expenditures. Although the court in Flynt v. Rumsfeld found no constitutional right of the media to accompany active units into battle, the Pentagon voluntarily chose to allow media "embedding" during the 2003 U.S.-led invasion of Iraq. Reportedly concerned about foreign propaganda concerning the conduct of the invasion, then-Secretary of Defense Donald Rumsfeld allowed journalists to be assigned to field units and cover virtually every aspect of the military action. More than 700 U.S. and foreign journalists were "embedded" with military units and their live reports became a mainstay of electronic coverage of the war.

Critics subsequently noted that some embedded journalists became too involved in the stories they were reporting and too attached to their units (reporting, for example, on "our movements" and "our casualties"), suffered a higher percentage of casualties than soldiers, and provided coverage that tended to focus on details concerning specific unit activities (rather than on broader strategic and policy issues). Moreover, embedded journalists were required to sign an agreement that restricted their reporting about ongoing missions, prohibited reporting on the specific results of missions even after they were completed or cancelled, required them to comply with "embargoes" on stories, and acknowledged that the embedded assignments could be terminated at any time and for any reason. See Andrew Bushell and Brent Cunningham, "Being There," Colum. Journ. Rev., Mar./Apr. 2003.

But the coverage put a face on a distant war, was popular with the public, and gave a greater impression of accountability through journalists' first-hand observations and broad access to combat troops. Moreover, despite a few highly publicized breaches of security, the vast majority of reporting apparently did little to compromise military tactics. See a collection of articles under the series title, The Real-Time War, Colum. Journ. Rev., May/Jun. 2003.

Images of Military Coffins. Another case arising out of access restrictions during the 1991 Persian Gulf War was JB Pictures, Inc. v. Department of Defense, 86 F.3d 236 (D.C. Cir. 1996). In that case, the D.C. Circuit upheld the Defense Department policy banning the press and public from witnessing the arrival of war dead at Dover Air Force Base, the military's only East Coast mortuary. Until 1991, the return of the bodies of soldiers killed in action overseas had been a public event accompanied by ceremonies open to the press and public. Shortly before Operation Desert Storm, the defendant effectively shifted these events to sites closer to the families of the deceased and gave these families veto power over press coverage: "Media coverage of the arrival of the remains at the port of entry or at interim stops will not be permitted but may be permitted at the service member's duty or home station or at the interment site, if the family so desires." Preexisting access to other events at Dover, such as the departure of personnel, was continued.

Plaintiff media and veterans' organizations argued that this was viewpoint discrimination because it allowed the war to be portrayed in a more favorable light. The court disagreed, noting that the policy was applied uniformly "to all members of the press and public, regardless of their views on war or the United States military." Plaintiffs had argued that the policy was not viewpoint-neutral because "the return of war dead is an event necessarily laden with anti-war implications." Instead, the court wrote that "[o]ne has only to think of Pericles's famous speech honoring the first Athenians killed in the Peloponnesian War, or the Gettysburg Address, to recognize that one cannot easily pigeonhole the meaning of a return of soldiers killed in battle."

The court further found that even if the restrictions had the potential for "differential effects," they would not necessarily be invalid in light of "the law's permissive treatment of restrictions on access to government operations not historically open to the public." The court stated that even under a balancing test the plaintiffs' access claims would fail. The Dover policy imposed only a "relatively modest" burden on newsgathering since the "basic facts" regarding war casualties could still be obtained and reported.

Finally, the court found that the Dover policy was "amply" justified by two government interests. The first was the reduction of hardship on the families of the deceased who no longer felt the need to travel long distances to Dover. The second was the "interest in protecting the privacy of families and friends of the dead, who may not want media coverage of the unloading of caskets at Dover. . . . [W]e do not think the government hypersensitive in thinking that the bereaved may be upset at public display of the caskets of their loved ones."

The policy barring photos of military coffins was not followed consistently during the Clinton Administration, but the Pentagon reinstituted it at the beginning of the 2003 Iraq war. An attempt in Congress to instruct the Pentagon to allow such photography failed. The Senate defeated, 54–39, an amendment to a military spending plan that would have instructed the Defense Department to work out a new policy permitting news media to cover the arrival of coffins from war zones. Senator John McCain, one of those who supported the amendment, said "I think we ought to know the casualties of war." The Bush Administration said the ban was necessary to protect the privacy of dead soldiers' families.

The ban on photographs of coffins of war dead was finally lifted in early 2009. Secretary of Defense Robert Gates said photos of coffins arriving at Dover Air Force Base would be permitted if the families of the dead consent. Gates said there was a division of opinion within the Pentagon, but the Army, which accounts for most of the war dead, pushed to permit photos. See Elisabeth Bumiller, Defense Chief Lifts Ban on Picture of Coffins, N.Y. Times, Feb. 27, 2009. More than two-thirds of families initially consented to photo coverage. See Documenting the Return of War Dead at Dover, American Journalism Rev., June/July 2009.

E. CRIMINAL LAW RESTRICTIONS ON ACCESS

Although many of the restrictions on access to information provide for criminal as well as civil penalties, criminal penalties are used only infrequently. However, in some situations, such as disaster sites, criminal law is the primary means of controlling access.

City of Oak Creek v. Ah King
Supreme Court of Wisconsin, 1989.
436 N.W.2d 285.

[An airliner crashed in what the court called a "non-public area" of a publicly owned airport, General Mitchell Field. The General Mitchell Field Media Guide for Airport Emergencies provided that "no representatives of the media will be permitted to enter non-public/restricted areas of the airport without an authorized escort."

Immediately after the crash local law enforcement authorities ordered the crash site secured and stationed officers on streets leading to the site with instructions to keep out all unauthorized persons.

Ah King was a television cameraman who, in a car with others from his station, followed an emergency vehicle through a police roadblock and parked on East College Avenue near the airport. Oak Creek city detective Virgil White, stationed at the roadblock, followed the car and ordered the occupants to leave. As they walked back toward the roadblock, Ah King jumped over a fence separating the street from the airport, ran to the top of a hill, and began taking pictures of the crash site. Detective White pursued Ah King and ordered him to leave the restricted area. Ah King said he would not leave unless he was arrested, which the officer then did. Detective White testified that there were "No Trespassing" signs on the fence Ah King jumped over, and that about five spectators were standing outside the fence.

Ah King was convicted of violating a municipal ordinance prohibiting disorderly conduct, which was defined in relevant part as conduct tending "to cause or provoke a disturbance." The court first held that the statute applied to Ah King because his repeated refusal to obey the detective's order in the presence of other persons was likely to provoke a disturbance, and that the statute was not unconstitutionally vague.]

■ CECI, JUSTICE:

. . .

The appellant advances two principal arguments why news gatherers as surrogates for the general public should have a right of access to emergency sites. First, the appellant argues that the first amendment to the United States Constitution protects the right to gather information. Second, the appellant argues that art. 1, sec. 3 of the Wisconsin Constitution protects the right of the press to gather information.

We will first address the appellant's first amendment argument. It has generally been held that the first amendment does not guarantee the press a constitutional right of special access to information not available to the public generally. [*Branzburg*]; Zemel v. Rusk, 381 U.S. 1, 17 (1965).

The right to speak and publish does not carry with it the unrestrained right to gather information. [ ] Therefore, in *Zemel,* the United States Supreme Court sustained the government's refusal to validate passports to Cuba even though that restriction rendered less than wholly free the flow of information concerning that country. [ ] The Court noted:

> There are few restrictions on action which could not be clothed by ingenious argument in the garb of decreased data flow. For example, the prohibition of unauthorized entry into the White

House diminishes the citizen's opportunities to gather information he might find relevant to his opinion of the way the country is being run, but that does not make entry into the White House a First Amendment right. [ ]

Similarly, in *Branzburg,* the United States Supreme Court stated that "[n]ewsmen have no constitutional right of access to the scenes of crime or disaster when the general public is excluded. . . ." [ ] "Despite the fact that news gathering may be hampered, the press is regularly excluded from grand jury proceedings, our own conferences, the meetings of other official bodies gathered in executive session, and the meetings of private organizations." [ ]

[The court cited *Pell* and *Houchins* for the proposition that the First Amendment does not give the press a "right of special access" to information not available to the public. The court then held that Richmond Newspapers Inc. v. Virginia was inapplicable because it dealt with access to courtrooms by press and public alike, whereas Ah King "is seeking to obtain a special access to the scene of an airplane crash beyond the public's right to access simply because he is a 'news gatherer' as opposed to an 'ordinary citizen.' "]

The dissent concedes that the United States Supreme Court has not recognized a constitutional protection for news gatherers' access to an accident scene, yet the dissent notes that in certain circumstances the Court has recognized that particular institutions have allowed the press greater access than the public to serve as a surrogate for the public. [ ] It is interesting to note the particular facts of the two cases the dissent cites as support for its proposition. In *Richmond Newspapers,* as described above, the Court dealt with the issue of the right of access to courtrooms. In [*Saxbe*] the Court was dealing with the right of access to prisons. The dissent fails to note that there is a difference between an institution allowing news gatherers priority of access on its own accord, in a setting in which the institution may closely control and monitor access, and this court mandating access in an emergency situation. Even the appellant concedes that "[a] right of access to trials does not necessarily imply a right of access to emergency scenes."

Our interpretation of the preceding United States Supreme Court cases leads us to the conclusion that under the first amendment, the appellant has an undoubted right to gather news from any source by means within the law.[4] However, the appellant does not have a first amendment right of access, solely because he is a news gatherer, to the

---

[4]   The dissenting justices obviously misread this court's decision when they opine that "the majority opinion concludes that the federal constitution does not protect the media's right to gather information." [ ] As we have just indicated, "under the first amendment, the appellant has an undoubted right to gather news from any source by means *within* the law" (emphasis added). See *Houchins* [ ], citing *Branzburg* [ ].

scene of this airplane crash when the general public has been reasonably excluded.

The appellant's second argument is that art. 1, sec. 3 of the Wisconsin Constitution provides a basis for a news gatherer's right of access to the scene of an airplane crash beyond the general public's right of access. The appellant, however, has failed to offer any precedent which would support his contention. In addition, on the basis of the record before us, we are not inclined to recognize such a right because news gatherers were not denied access to the crash site of Midwest Express Flight 105 on September 6, 1985.

While the appellant was disregarding Detective White's orders and penetrating into the nonpublic restricted area of the airport, other news gatherers were assembling in the airport director's office at the airport, pursuant to the General Mitchell Field Media Guide. At 4:30 p.m., the airport director held a briefing which lasted approximately 15 minutes. Immediately thereafter, the director took media representatives directly to the crash site to take photographs or film the scene. Therefore, given the fact that news gatherers were given access to the scene of this airplane crash, we are not inclined to rule on the issue of whether a news gatherer has a right of access to the scene of an airplane crash under the Wisconsin Constitution beyond that of the general public's right of access.

Furthermore, the needs and rights of the injured and dying should be recognized by this court as having preference over newly created "rights" that the dissenting justices would give to a "news gatherer" who is simply concentrating on trying to beat out his competition and make his employer's deadline. As the circuit court so aptly noted in its memorandum decision, in an emergency situation "[t]he injured and dying are entitled to receive the immediate and full attention of rescue workers. Law enforcement personnel should not be required to needlessly occupy themselves with persons who have a personal interest not related to restoration of order or with rescue attempts. The defendant, here, chose to disregard the government's efforts to establish order, set himself and his interest above the law, diluted law enforcement efforts to assist those in need, and by so doing elevated his own interest and concerns above the welfare of the persons involved in the tragic accident and the government's efforts in its law enforcement concerns."

. . .

The decision of the circuit court is affirmed.

■ SHIRLEY S. ABRAHAMSON, JUSTICE (dissenting).

The state has a significant interest in keeping people away from the site of an accident or crime to expedite assisting victims, to preserve evidence or to protect the public from injury. This state interest, however, is not at issue in this case. The record shows that the defendant was not interfering with or obstructing emergency personnel and that neither he nor other observers were in danger.

The issue in this case is whether the defendant's refusing to obey an officer's command to leave the accident scene constitutes the offense of disorderly conduct as defined in the Oak Creek ordinance. I conclude it does not. Moreover, I conclude that this court should acknowledge that a representative of the news media may function as a proxy for the public in certain situations where public access is limited.

I.

[The dissent argued that Ah King's conduct did not violate the statute because it was not disruptive.]

II.

. . .

The majority opinion does not, in my opinion, adequately address the defendant's argument regarding the rights of news gatherers to access to an accident scene.

The defendant does not argue that the government must always allow news gatherers access to an accident scene. Rather the defendant asks this court to hold that governmental personnel must give news gatherers access to a position at an accident from which they can observe emergency personnel in action unless exclusion of news gatherers from all locations is required to enable emergency personnel to perform their tasks. The defendant argues that this standard accommodates two important objectives: It enables the media to inform the public about the accident and governmental operations while it prevents news gatherers from jeopardizing people's lives, health or property.

While the United States Supreme Court has not explicitly recognized a constitutional protection for news gatherers' access to an accident scene, the Court has recognized that media representatives serve as surrogates for the public. Chief Justice Warren Burger, writing in Richmond Newspapers, Inc. v. Virginia, [ ] about the right of the public and the press to attend criminal trials observed:

> Instead of acquiring information about trials by firsthand observation or by word of mouth from those who attended, people now acquire it chiefly through the print and electronic media. In a sense, this validates the media claim of functioning as surrogates for the public.

Chief Justice Burger recognized in the *Richmond Newspapers* case that government authorities have allowed priority access to news gatherers in situations where public access is limited by circumstances. The Chief Justice wrote: "While media representatives enjoy the same right of access as the public, they often are provided special seating and priority of entry so that they may report what people in attendance have seen and heard." [ ]

In [*Saxbe*], Justice Potter Stewart, writing for the court, acknowledged that sometimes the press is given greater access to information than the public. The Justice observed that "members of the press are accorded substantial access to the federal prisons in order to observe and report the conditions they find there. Indeed, journalists are given access to the prisons and to prison inmates that in significant respects exceeds that afforded to members of the general public."

This court has itself institutionalized procedures for accommodating media personnel—procedures which do not provide similar rights to private individuals. Chapter 61 of the Supreme Court Rules, entitled Rules Governing Electronic Media and Still Photography Coverage of Judicial Proceedings, concludes with the caveat, "The privileges granted by this chapter to photograph, televise and record court proceedings may be exercised only by persons or organizations which are part of the news media." [ ]

I conclude that, in determining the scope of news gatherers' access to accidents, the court can and should take into consideration the media's role as the "eyes and ears" of the public at large. [ ] Time, place and manner restrictions on access to the site of an accident which are properly applicable to the general public may not be appropriate when applied to the media.

For the reasons set forth I do not join the majority opinion.

I am authorized to state that Chief Justice Heffernan and Justice Bablitch join this dissent.

NOTES AND QUESTIONS

1.   Could Ah King have been charged with trespassing?

2.   The justices also disagreed as to whether Ah King had violated the statute. The majority said the photographer's refusal to obey the officer's order was not in itself disorderly conduct, but became so because of the presence of other people and the importance of crowd control under the circumstances. The dissent said any threat of disruption was speculative and therefore could not support the conclusion that his conduct was disorderly under the statute.

3.   In an omitted section of their opinion, the dissenters noted that other news gatherers who also were taking pictures within the police boundary were not challenged by the police. According to the lawyer who represented Ah King, this evidence was introduced to show that other media representatives were engaging in the same conduct even closer to the site without causing any disruption. Would it also support an argument that the ordinance could not be enforced against Ah King because it was not enforced against others? Must the police arrest all or none?

4.   Can a journalist assert a newsgathering defense against criminal liability for receiving and transporting child pornography via the Internet? In U.S. v. Matthews, a freelance journalist defended against such charges by claiming he was engaged in an investigation to show that law enforcement officials were not effectively policing the distribution of Internet child pornography. The American Civil Liberties Union filed an amicus brief arguing that journalists need a constitutional right to police Internet pornography because law enforcement agencies historically have misunderstood the nature of the Internet and are usually either indifferent or overzealous in the prosecution of Internet pornography. The district court doubted the freelancer's story, but said even if his motives were purely journalistic, the First Amendment would provide no defense. The Fourth Circuit affirmed. See United States v. Matthews, 209 F.3d 338 (4th Cir. 2000). Matthews, supported by the ACLU and the Reporters Committee for Freedom of the Press, argued that the First Amendment protects the use of child pornography for educational or other legitimate purposes, including journalism. They contended that *New York v. Ferber*, discussed more fully in Chapter Two, implied that child pornography statutes should be analyzed on a case-by-case basis to prevent impermissible applications that would violate the free speech rights of adults. But the court held that *Ferber* "rejected even the possibility of a broad First Amendment defense like that proposed by Matthews." The court cited *Branzburg* and *Cohen* as refuting the Reporters Committee's argument that strict application of the statute would violate a First Amendment right to gather news.

F. DISCRIMINATORY ACCESS

Many access disputes involve discrimination against types of media, particularly broadcasting, and types of reporting tools, such as cameras and audio recording devices. This discrimination against categories of news gatherers is one of the issues addressed within this section. (One special variety of categorical discrimination, exclusion of cameras from courtrooms, is considered in Chapter Eleven.)

But media are often the beneficiaries of discriminatory access. Their representatives routinely are granted entry to press rooms and press galleries, news conferences, conventions, and disaster sites from which the public is excluded, and often get free admission to sports and entertainment events for which others must pay.

This favored treatment requires that some line be drawn between those who are "press" and those who are not, and that process may invite discrimination against particular individuals. Some of these issues are explored in the following case.

1. DISCRIMINATION AGAINST INDIVIDUALS

Sherrill v. Knight

United States Court of Appeals, District of Columbia Circuit, 1977.
569 F.2d 124.

[Sherrill, Washington correspondent for The Nation, had credentials for the House and Senate press galleries, but was denied a White House press pass. Under the procedure in effect at the time, once an applicant showed congressional credentials, residence in Washington, and an editor's verification of the reporter's need to report from the White House regularly, the pass was issued unless the Secret Service objected. Here, it was ultimately learned, the Secret Service had recommended against issuing the pass on the ground that Sherrill posed a security risk because he had assaulted the press secretary to the governor of Florida and also faced assault charges in Texas. In Sherrill's suit to obtain a press pass, the district court had ordered the Secret Service to formulate "narrow and specific" standards for judgment and to institute certain procedures for handling such requests. The Secret Service appealed.]

■ McGOWAN, CIRCUIT JUDGE.

. . .

We agree with the District Court that both first and fifth amendment concerns are heavily implicated in this case. We conclude, however, that neither of these concerns requires the articulation of detailed criteria upon which the granting or denial of White House press passes is to be based. We further conclude that notice, opportunity to rebut, and a written decision are required because the denial of a pass potentially infringes upon first amendment guarantees. Such impairment of this interest cannot be permitted to occur in the absence of adequate procedural due process.

III.

Appellants argue that because the public has no right of access to the White House, and because the right of access due the press generally is no greater than that due the general public, denial of a White House press pass is violative of the first amendment only if it is based upon the content of the journalist's speech or otherwise discriminates against a class of protected speech. While we agree with appellants that arbitrary or content-based criteria for press pass issuance are prohibited under the first amendment, there exist additional first amendment considerations ignored by appellants' argument.

These considerations can perhaps be best understood by first recognizing what this case does *not* involve. It is not contended that standards relating to the security of the President are the sole basis upon which members of the general public may be refused entry to the White House, or that members of the public must be afforded notice and hearing concerning such refusal. The first amendment's protection of a citizen's right to obtain information concerning "the way the country is being run" does not extend to every conceivable avenue a citizen may wish to employ in pursuing this right. Nor is the discretion of the President to grant interviews or briefings with selected journalists challenged. It would certainly be unreasonable to suggest that because the President allows interviews with some bona fide journalists, he must give this opportunity to all. Finally, appellee's first amendment claim is not premised upon the assertion that the White House must open its doors to the press, conduct press conferences, or operate press facilities.

Rather, we are presented with a situation where the White House has voluntarily decided to establish press facilities for correspondents who need to report therefrom. These press facilities are perceived as being open to all bona fide Washington-based journalists, whereas most of the White House itself, and press facilities in particular, have not been made available to the general public. White House press facilities having been made publicly available as a source of information for newsmen, the protection afforded newsgathering under the first amendment guarantee of freedom of the press, see [*Branzburg* and *Pell*], requires that this access not be denied arbitrarily or for less than compelling reasons. [ ] Not only newsmen and the publications for which they write, but also the public at large have an interest protected by the first amendment in assuring that restrictions on newsgathering be no more arduous than necessary, and that individual newsmen not be arbitrarily excluded from sources of information. [ ]; [ ].

Given these important first amendment rights implicated by refusal to grant White House press passes to bona fide Washington journalists, such refusal must be based on a compelling governmental interest. Clearly, protection of the President is a compelling, "even an overwhelming," interest. . . . However, this standard for denial of a press pass has never been formally articulated or published. Merely informing individual rejected applicants that rejection was for "reasons of security" does not inform the public or other potential applicants of the basis for exclusion of journalists from White House press facilities. Moreover, we think that the phrase "reasons of security" is unnecessarily vague and subject to ambiguous interpretation.

Therefore, we are of the opinion that appellants must publish or otherwise make publicly known the actual standard employed in determining whether an otherwise eligible journalist will obtain a White House press pass. We do agree with appellants that the governmental interest here does not lend itself to detailed articulation of narrow and specific standards or precise identification of all the factors which may be taken into account in applying this standard. It is enough that the Secret Service be guided solely by the principle of whether the applicant presents a potential source of physical danger to the President and/or his immediate family so serious as to justify his exclusion. [ ] This standard is sufficiently circumspect so as to allow the Secret Service, exercising expert judgment which frequently must be subjective in nature, considerable leeway in denying press passes for security reasons. At the same time, the standard does specify in a meaningful way the basis upon which persons will be deemed security risks, and therefore will allow meaningful judicial review of decisions to deny press passes. We anticipate that reviewing courts will be appropriately deferential to the Secret Service's determination of what justifies the inference that an individual constitutes a potential risk to the physical security of the President or his family.

IV.

In our view, the procedural requirements of notice of the factual bases for denial, an opportunity for the applicant to respond to these, and a final written statement of the reasons for denial are compelled by the foregoing determination that the interest of a bona fide Washington correspondent in obtaining a White House press pass is protected by the first amendment. This first amendment interest undoubtedly qualifies as liberty which may not be denied without due process of law under the fifth amendment.[22] The only further determination which this court must make is "what process is due," [ ]. We think that notice to the unsuccessful applicant of the factual bases for denial with an opportunity to rebut is a minimum prerequisite for ensuring that the denial is indeed in furtherance of Presidential protection, rather than based on arbitrary or less than compelling reasons. [ ] The requirement of a final statement of denial and the reasons therefor is necessary in order to assure that the agency has neither taken additional, undisclosed information into account, nor responded irrationally to matters put forward by way of rebuttal or explanation. This requirement also will avoid situations such as occurred in the case before us, where an applicant does not receive official written notification of his status until more than five years after the status decision is made.

Having determined that appellants' failure to articulate and publish an explicit and meaningful standard governing denial of White House press passes for security reasons, and to afford procedural protections to those denied passes, violates the first and fifth amendments, we affirm that portion of the District Court's judgment requiring notice, opportunity to be heard, and a final written statement of the bases of denial. We remand that portion of the District Court's judgment requiring appellants to develop "narrow and specific standards" for press

---

[22] A related and perhaps equally compelling *property* interest may also be said to require the procedural protections of the fifth amendment. . . . However, because appellee's first amendment liberty interest independently requires the standards and procedural protections set forth in this opinion, we do not reach the question of whether appellee also has a property entitlement of constitutional magnitude.

pass denials in order that this requirement may be modified in accordance with this opinion.

NOTES AND QUESTIONS

1.   What were the First Amendment bases for the reporter's attack? The Fifth Amendment bases?

2.   If the government is limited in its ability to discriminate among persons similarly situated, what justifies the court's passing observation upholding the President's discretion to grant interviews to selected journalists? Is this because the President is involved? Could the same rule be justified for the Attorney General? The local army base commander? The press officer at the Supreme Court?

3.   After this decision, the Secret Service adopted the following standard:

> In granting or denying a request for a security clearance made in response to an application for a White House press pass, officials of the Secret Service will be guided solely by the principle of whether the applicant presents a potential source of physical danger to the President and/or the family of the President so serious as to justify his or her exclusion from White House press privileges. 31 CFR § 409.1.

Procedural regulations give a rejected applicant notice and an opportunity to respond, and a personal appearance before a Secret Service official if requested. If that official sustains the denial, those regulations also require written notification setting forth "as precisely as possible and to the extent that security considerations permit, the factual basis for the denial in relation to the standard set forth in § 409.1." If these regulations had been in effect when Sherrill first applied, what difference would they have made?

In Uniontown Newspapers, Inc. v. Roberts, 839 A.2d 185 (Pa. 2003), a newspaper sought access to telephone records for which a state legislator had requested reimbursement. The legislator told the newspaper that he would release the records if it assigned a different reporter to examine them. The newspaper declined and continued to seek access to the records. The legislator then released them to a radio station, stating that he was refusing to give the records to the newspaper because it was biased. Finally, the legislator offered to give the records to the newspaper if its "counsel absolved him of wrongdoing in connection with them." The newspaper and the reporter sued for right of access to the records. They also alleged that the legislator had violated their rights to equal protection by granting selective access to the records and that he had retaliated against them for exercising their First Amendment rights in violation of 42 U.S.C. § 1983.

Although the Pennsylvania Supreme Court rejected the claim that there was a right of access to the legislator's telephone records, the court held that the newspaper and reporter had alleged cognizable violations of their rights under 42 U.S.C. § 1983. Specifically, the court found a cognizable equal protection claim based on the reporter's claim that "he was denied access to records given to other similarly situated reporters, based on his membership in a class of reporters whose speech offended appellee." The court cited *McBride*, mentioned above, for the proposition that the newspaper and the reporter had made out a prima facie case under Section 1983 based on the legislator's retaliation against them for exercising their First Amendment rights. The dissenting judge argued that the reporter had failed to state a cause of action because there was "no state action involved in a legislator's release of his protected telephone records; and reporters with hurt feelings are not a protected class. The reporter, who works for a newspaper, which buys ink by the barrel, surely has a more effective avenue of recourse than Section 1983."

The cases holding content-based retaliation unconstitutional were ignored in Baltimore Sun v. Ehrlich, 437 F.3d 410 (4th Cir. 2006), which upheld a governor's order prohibiting all executive officials of the state from talking to disfavored reporters. The circuit court reasoned that ordering executive officials not to talk to disfavored reporters was no different than giving preferential treatment to favored reporters: "whether the disfavored reporters number two or two million, they are still denied access to discretionarily afforded information on account of their reporting." Moreover, the court concluded that the "adverse impact" on the reporters' First Amendment rights was *de minimis.*"

The reporters did not allege that the governor had violated their right of access to executive branch officials. Instead, they invoked a line of cases holding that even otherwise lawful acts by public officials may be unconstitutional if they would chill the exercise of First Amendment rights by a person of ordinary firmness. The court held that the reporters had not shown that their coverage of the executive branch was chilled. Would they have fared better with a straightforward claim that they were being unconstitutionally punished for what they had published?

In Borreca v. Fasi, 369 F. Supp. 906 (D. Hawaii 1974), the mayor of Honolulu denied Borreca, a reporter for a local paper, access to press conferences because he had been "irresponsible, inaccurate, biased, and malicious in reporting on the mayor and the city administration." The newspaper sued to gain admission for Borreca. In an action under 42 U.S.C. § 1983, the judge enjoined the mayor from preventing Borreca from attending press conferences "on the same basis and to the same extent that other news reporters attend" them.

If the mayor discontinued press conferences and instead invited all local reporters except Borreca to his office, could anything be done? Suppose two other reporters were also excluded? Is there a difference between inviting one reporter and excluding ten, and inviting ten and excluding one? Are political considerations likely to inhibit this kind of conduct?

Can physical limitations on the size of a meeting hall or office justify limited invitations to the press? Suppose that the mayor decided to hold a meeting in his or her small office with room for only three visitors. Does *Sherrill* suggest any limitations on who may be invited? Or on the mayor's power to decide to meet in a small office?

2.   DISCRIMINATION AMONG TYPES OF MEDIA

A decision to give the press special access that is not available to the public generally requires some definition of "the press," and that may exclude communicators who believe they have an equally strong claim to special treatment. Also, as Justice Stewart observed in *Houchins,* some of those who are defined as "press" will demand access not only for themselves and their pens and notepads, but for their cameras and tape recorders. When those devices are excluded, the broadcasting media are likely to argue that they are being discriminated against by being denied the opportunity to use the tools that make their medium most effective.

While the definition for "press" is explored in Chapter Eight in the context of newsgathering and in Chapter Nine in the context of subpoenas, related matters are considered here in access-centered ways.

a.   DEFINING "PRESS"

The Atlanta federal penitentiary had a regulation permitting interviews with inmates by "representatives of the news media whose principal employment is to gather or report news for a radio or television news program of a station holding a Federal Communications Commission license." The self-producer of a show called "Let's Tell It Like It Is," which aired on the Atlanta cable system's public access channel, wished to interview an inmate for his program. The warden denied permission on the ground that the producer was not a member of the press for purposes of the regulation.

The self-producer sued for declaratory judgment that the regulation was unconstitutional, but the district court and court of appeals agreed that it was not. The latter rejected his First Amendment argument on the ground that neither the press nor the general public had any constitutional right to interview prisoners under *Pell* and *Saxbe.* As to his equal protection clause claim, the court said the case involved no claim of constitutional magnitude, no suspect class, and no invidious discrimination that would require strict scrutiny. Thus, the regulation was valid as long as it was rationally related to the prison's objectives. The regulation met this test because:

> In clear terms the regulation recognizes the need for the prison
> to maintain security and order within the prison and allow

limited access for interviews by insuring that the representatives of the news media are responsible persons employed by and responsible to recognized media organizations. This permits the prison facility to identify those persons who are not likely to pose any threat to security without the facility having to conduct extensive individual investigations of each applicant. Thus, it provides the public with an objective and accurate news presentation by a person whose profession is gathering and reporting news without the likelihood of breaching the prison's security.

Jersawitz v. Hanberry, 783 F.2d 1532 (11th Cir. 1986).

Is the court's treatment of the producer's First Amendment claim consistent with *Sherrill* and the other cases in the preceding sections of this chapter? Could the regulation survive if it were subjected to the tests applied in those cases?

More recent questions about the definition of "press" arise in the context of the Internet. In 1996 the Executive Committee of Correspondents, which oversees accreditation to the House and Senate press galleries, refused to accredit Victor Schreibman, publisher of the online Federal Information News Service (FINS), to the Senate periodical gallery. The Committee justified its refusal on the basis that FINS was distributed without charge and paid Schreibman no salary. Schreibman claimed, however, that the refusal was based on the fact that FINS was published via the Internet; he noted that the Committee had accredited him in 1993, 1994, and 1995 as a correspondent for the Electronic Public Information Newsletter, which was distributed in print. Schreibman's suit against the Committee was dismissed as presenting a nonjusticiable question, because the court found that the accreditation of journalists to the Congressional press galleries was within Congress' discretion and that the members of the Committee, acting under delegated authority from Congress, were immune from suit under the Constitution's speech and debate clause. See Schreibman v. Holmes, 1997 WL 527341 (D.D.C. 1997), aff'd, 203 F.3d 53 (D.C. Cir. 1999).

While the suit was pending, the Committee did accredit its first correspondent from Slate Magazine, which had an entirely online circulation, and the Committee later accredited correspondents from other Internet publications. The step was noteworthy not only because it appeared to respond to claims that the Committee was treating online publications differently than the print or broadcast press, but also because accreditation to a congressional press gallery is a prerequisite for obtaining a White House press pass.

Statutes and regulations that give the press preferential treatment tend to define it based on form rather than function. The wisdom of "defining the press in terms of format, method of distribution, or form of organization" has been questioned on the ground that "there is little correlation between those forms and the purposes for which it might make sense to give preferential treatment to some media." See David A. Anderson, Freedom of the Press, 80 Tex. L. Rev. 429, 436, 441 (2002). In the cases above, were the journalists who sought press passes serving these purposes?

b.   EXCLUDING CAMERAS

Exclusion of cameras from courtrooms is considered in the next chapter. The other class of events from which cameras are regularly excluded is executions. The media have had little success in challenging this exclusion. In 1994 NBC petitioned the North Carolina courts for permission to televise the execution of a prisoner who wanted his execution to be shown on the Donahue show. The North Carolina courts refused and the Supreme Court rejected a petition from Donahue and NBC. See Lawson v. Dixon, 512 U.S. 1215 (1994).

In Rice v. Kempker, 374 F.3d 675 (8th Cir. 2004), the Eighth Circuit held that the First Amendment "does not protect the use of video cameras" at executions. New Life, a religious group, sought a declaratory judgment that the Missouri Department of Corrections media policy, which prohibited videotaping or recording executions, violated the First Amendment. The group hoped to sway public opinion against the death penalty by publicly showing videotapes of executions. The court stated:

> Seeking to persuade this Court to go where no court previously has gone, New Life relies on a two-step argument. The first step New Life asks us to take is to rule that the First Amendment [ ] requires executions to be open to the public. New Life then argues that prohibitions on videotaping are impermissible burdens on its constitutional right of access to executions. We find no need to engage in this two-part inquiry and instead address the issue directly and hold that the First Amendment does not protect the use of video cameras or any other cameras or, for that matter, audio recorders in the execution chamber.

The court did not find it necessary to decide whether there is a constitutional right of access to executions but stated that even if there were such a right, "videotaping and the use of cameras would not be necessary to vindicate [it]."

Finally, the court opined that even if the Department of Corrections policy burdened First Amendment rights, it would still be upheld as "a content-neutral time, place, and manner restriction on speech." The Department's safety and security concerns were substantial governmental interests, and the media policy did not prevent dissemination of information about executions. See also Garrett v. Estelle, 556 F.2d 1274 (5th Cir. 1977) (holding that there is no First Amendment right to attend or film executions).

c.   EXCLUDING AUDIO TAPING

Some states have banned certain reportorial aids for all reporters. Thus, the heads of both houses of the Maryland legislature barred reporters from attending sessions with "tape-recording devices." This was challenged by reporters, who claimed that "speed and accuracy are essential attributes of media news services" and that recorders will ensure accuracy. Their claims were rejected in Sigma Delta Chi v. Speaker, Maryland House of Delegates, 310 A.2d 156 (Md. 1973). Conceding that newsgathering was entitled to some First Amendment protection, the court unanimously denied that banning tape recorders infringed such a right—plaintiffs were not prevented from carrying out their usual duties and the recorders were usable anywhere in the State House except in the chambers. Greater accuracy, although desirable, did not merit constitutional protection.

The court also rejected a due process claim that the restriction interfered with reporters' opportunity to earn a livelihood by diminishing the value of their product, "oral news." The reporters relied on Nevens v. City of Chino, 233 Cal. App. 2d 775 (Cal. App. 1965), in which a similar ban had been upset on the grounds that because the recorders were silent and unobtrusive, their exclusion unreasonably deprived reporters of the means to make an accurate record of what transpired. The California court analogized the ban to an attempt to prohibit the use of "pen, or pencil and paper." The Maryland court thought the analogy inappropriate: while "the removal of pen and paper might frustrate *all* effective communication, the prohibition against tape recorders is a mere inconvenience." There was no due process violation in rules that "may tend to exalt the preservation of order and decorum in the legislative chambers over increased efficiency of the press."

Finally, the reporters claimed that they were denied equal protection of the laws because press members were singled out by the ban. The court countered that the rules barred everyone, public and press, from bringing tape recorders into the chambers. The ban was against the equipment, not a class of persons.

Other states have taken the opposite approach. See Feldman v. Town of Bethel, 106 A.D.2d 695 (N.Y. App. Div. 1984), upholding the award of damages to a reporter who was arrested for using a tape recorder at a town board meeting. The use of the recorder in an unobtrusive manner was protected by state law.

If one were to find a limited First Amendment right to gather news using whatever tools or aids the reporter wishes, what considerations might overcome that incipient right other than those suggested here? What about the contention that tape recorders destroy the free give-and-take of the legislative debate by freezing the words and intonations used by the speakers? Is that good or bad? Is this related to the trend toward greater openness in the legislative process? Does pool video alter the equation? What about an argument that tape-recorded words will be accepted as accurate by those who hear them no matter how many witnesses testify that the speaker used different words—and that tapes may be altered so that false inferences would be drawn?

The frailty of the distinction between "pen and paper" reporters and those who use other tools is revealed in cases involving sketching as a substitute for photography. These cases, along with other aspects of access to judicial proceedings, are considered in the next chapter.

G. THE FIRST AMENDMENT AS A BARRIER TO ACCESS

As we have seen in this chapter, the courts generally reject First Amendment claims of a right of access; they leave it to the state and federal legislatures to balance the public interests in disclosure against other interests such as privacy and security. But in a few instances courts have entertained the possibility that the First Amendment might *prevent* disclosure.

A panel of the Fifth Circuit held that punishing city council members for violating a state open meetings statute by exchanging emails about city business could violate *the officials'* First Amendment rights. See Rangra v. Brown, 566 F.3d 515 (5th Cir. 2009). The case involved an elected city council member who sent an email to three colleagues discussing selection of an engineer for a water project and also asking that a council meeting be scheduled. Rangra sent a "reply-all" email suggesting a different engineer. The district attorney obtained an indictment of Rangra and the council member who sent the original email, alleging that since four council members constituted a quorum, the exchange constituted an illegal meeting under the Texas Open Meetings Act.

The district attorney eventually dismissed the charges, but Rangra filed a federal civil rights suit seeking a declaration that such prosecutions would be unconstitutional. The district court rejected Rangra's claim, relying on Garcetti v. Ceballos, 547 U.S. 410 (2006), in which the Supreme Court held that public employees enjoy no First Amendment protection when they speak in connection with their official duties. But the Fifth Circuit distinguished elected officials from other public employees, holding that "the First Amendment's protection of elected officials' speech is robust and no less strenuous than that afforded to the speech of citizens in general." Because the statute restricted the government officials' emails only when they concerned public business, it was content-based and the state therefore was required to prove that the statute pursued a compelling interest which the law was narrowly tailored to further.

The Fifth Circuit initially granted a motion for en banc review of the panel's decision, but dismissed the appeal as moot after Rangra left office. 584 F.3d 206 (5th Cir. 2009). The attorney who unsuccessfully represented Rangra then recruited a number of other local officials to challenge the law again in a new suit, but the district court again held that the Texas Open Meetings Law was neither vague nor overbroad, was content neutral, and satisfied both intermediate and strict scrutiny. Asgeirsson v. Abbott, 773 F. Supp. 2d 684 (W.D. Tex. 2011). The Fifth Circuit upheld limits in the Texas Open Meetings Law against First Amendment challenge in that case on appeal. 696 F.3d 454 (5th Cir. 2012).

In the following case, the Supreme Court accepted the argument that a First Amendment right of petition-signers to remain anonymous might trump a state law requiring disclosure.

Doe v. Reed
Supreme Court of the United States, 2010.
561 U.S. 186.

■ CHIEF JUSTICE ROBERTS delivered the opinion of the Court.

The State of Washington allows its citizens to challenge state laws by referendum. Roughly four percent of Washington voters must sign a petition to place such a referendum on the ballot. That petition, which by law must include the names and addresses of the signers, is then submitted to the government for verification and canvassing, to ensure that only lawful signatures are counted. The Washington Public Records Act (PRA) authorizes private parties to obtain copies of government documents, and the State construes the PRA to cover submitted referendum petitions.

This case arises out of a state law extending certain benefits to same-sex couples, and a corresponding referendum petition to put that law to a popular vote. Respondent intervenors invoked the PRA to obtain copies of the petition, with the names and addresses of the signers. Certain petition signers and the petition sponsor objected, arguing that such public disclosure would violate their rights under the First Amendment.

The course of this litigation, however, has framed the legal question before us more broadly. The issue at this stage of the case is not whether disclosure of this particular petition would violate the First Amendment, but whether disclosure of referendum petitions in general would do so. We conclude that such disclosure does not as a general matter violate the First Amendment, and we therefore affirm the judgment of the Court of Appeals. We leave it to the lower courts to consider in the first instance the signers' more focused claim concerning disclosure of the information on this particular petition, which is pending before the District Court. . . .

III [A]

The compelled disclosure of signatory information on referendum petitions is subject to review under the First Amendment. An individual expresses a view on a political matter when he signs a petition under

Washington's referendum procedure. In most cases, the individual's signature will express the view that the law subject to the petition should be overturned. Even if the signer is agnostic as to the merits of the underlying law, his signature still expresses the political view that the question should be considered "by the whole electorate." [ ]. In either case, the expression of a political view implicates a First Amendment right. The State, having "cho[sen] to tap the energy and the legitimizing power of the democratic process, . . . must accord the participants in that process the First Amendment rights that attach to their roles." [ ]

Respondents counter that signing a petition is a legally operative legislative act and therefore "does not involve any significant expressive element." [ ] It is true that signing a referendum petition may ultimately have the legal consequence of requiring the secretary of state to place the referendum on the ballot. But we do not see how adding such legal effect to an expressive activity somehow deprives that activity of its expressive component, taking it outside the scope of the First Amendment. Respondents themselves implicitly recognize that the signature expresses a particular viewpoint, arguing that one purpose served by disclosure is to allow the public to engage signers in a debate on the merits of the underlying law. [ ]

Petition signing remains expressive even when it has legal effect in the electoral process. But that is not to say that the electoral context is irrelevant to the nature of our First Amendment review. We allow States significant flexibility in implementing their own voting systems. [ ] To the extent a regulation concerns the legal effect of a particular activity in that process, the government will be afforded substantial latitude to enforce that regulation. Also pertinent to our analysis is the fact that the PRA is not a prohibition on speech, but instead a disclosure requirement. "[D]isclosure requirements may burden the ability to speak, but they . . . do not prevent anyone from speaking." Citizens United v. Federal Election Comm'n, [558 U.S. 310 (2010)] (internal quotation marks omitted).

We have a series of precedents considering First Amendment challenges to disclosure requirements in the electoral context. These precedents have reviewed such challenges under what has been termed "exacting scrutiny." See, e.g., Buckley v. Valeo, 424 U.S. 1, 64 (1976) . . .

That standard "requires a 'substantial relation' between the disclosure requirement and a 'sufficiently important' governmental interest." [ ]. To withstand this scrutiny, "the strength of the governmental interest must reflect the seriousness of the actual burden on First Amendment rights." [ ]

B

Respondents assert two interests to justify the burdens of compelled disclosure under the PRA on First Amendment rights: (1) preserving the integrity of the electoral process by combating fraud, detecting invalid signatures, and fostering government transparency and accountability; and (2) providing information to the electorate about who supports the petition. [ ] Because we determine that the State's interest in preserving the integrity of the electoral process suffices to defeat the argument that the PRA is unconstitutional with respect to referendum petitions in general, we need not, and do not, address the State's "informational" interest.

The State's interest in preserving the integrity of the electoral process is undoubtedly important. "States allowing ballot initiatives have considerable leeway to protect the integrity and reliability of the initiative process, as they have with respect to election processes generally." [ ] The State's interest is particularly strong with respect to efforts to root out fraud, which not only may produce fraudulent outcomes, but has a systemic effect as well: It "drives honest citizens out of the democratic process and breeds distrust of our government." . . .

But the State's interest in preserving electoral integrity is not limited to combating fraud. That interest extends to efforts to ferret out invalid signatures caused not by fraud but by simple mistake, such as duplicate signatures or signatures of individuals who are not registered to vote in the State. [ ] That interest also extends more generally to promoting transparency and accountability in the electoral process, which the State argues is "essential to the proper functioning of a democracy." [ ] Plaintiffs contend that the disclosure requirements of the PRA are not "sufficiently related" to the interest of protecting the integrity of the electoral process. [ ] They argue that disclosure is not necessary because the secretary of state is already charged with verifying and canvassing the names on a petition, advocates and opponents of a measure can observe that process, and any citizen can challenge the secretary's actions in court. [ ] They also stress that existing criminal penalties reduce the danger of fraud in the petition process. [ ]

But the secretary's verification and canvassing will not catch all invalid signatures: The job is large and difficult (the secretary ordinarily checks "only 3 to 5% of signatures," [ ], and the secretary can make mistakes, too, [ ] Public disclosure can help cure the inadequacies of the verification and canvassing process.

Disclosure also helps prevent certain types of petition fraud otherwise difficult to detect, such as outright forgery and "bait and switch" fraud, in which an individual signs the petition based on a misrepresentation of the underlying issue. [ ] The signer is in the best position to detect these types of fraud, and public disclosure can bring the issue to the signer's attention.

Public disclosure thus helps ensure that the only signatures counted are those that should be, and that the only referenda placed on the ballot are those that garner enough valid signatures. Public disclosure also promotes transparency and accountability in the electoral process to an extent other measures cannot. In light of the foregoing, we reject plaintiffs' argument and conclude that public disclosure of referendum petitions in general is substantially related to the important interest of preserving the integrity of the electoral process.

C

Plaintiffs' more significant objection is that "the strength of the governmental interest" does not "reflect the seriousness of the actual burden on First Amendment rights." [ ] According to plaintiffs, the objective of those seeking disclosure of the R–71 petition is not to prevent fraud, but to publicly identify those who had validly signed and to broadcast the signers' political views on the subject of the petition. Plaintiffs allege, for example, that several groups plan to post the petitions in searchable form on the Internet and then encourage other citizens to seek out the R–71 signers. [ ]

Plaintiffs explain that once on the Internet, the petition signers' names and addresses "can be combined with publicly available phone numbers and maps," in what will effectively become a blueprint for harassment and intimidation. [ ] To support their claim that they will be subject to reprisals, plaintiffs cite examples from the history of a similar proposition in California, [ ] and from the experience of one of the petition sponsors in this case [ ].

In related contexts, we have explained that those resisting disclosure can prevail under the First Amendment if they can show "a reasonable probability that the compelled disclosure [of personal information] will subject them to threats, harassment, or reprisals from either Government officials or private parties." [*Buckley*]. The question before us, however, is not whether PRA disclosure violates the First Amendment with respect to those who signed the R–71 petition, or other particularly controversial petitions. The question instead is whether such disclosure in general violates the First Amendment rights of those who sign referendum petitions.

The problem for plaintiffs is that their argument rests almost entirely on the specific harm they say would attend disclosure of the information on the R–71 petition, or on similarly controversial ones. [ ] But typical referendum petitions "concern tax policy, revenue, budget, or other state law issues." [ ]. Voters care about such issues, some quite deeply—but there is no reason to assume that any burdens imposed by disclosure of typical referendum petitions would be remotely like the burdens plaintiffs fear in this case.

Plaintiffs have offered little in response. They have provided us scant evidence or argument beyond the burdens they assert disclosure would impose on R–71 petition signers or the signers of other similarly controversial petitions. Indeed, what little plaintiffs do offer with respect to typical petitions in Washington hurts, not helps: Several other petitions in the State "have been subject to release in recent years," plaintiffs tell us, [ ] but apparently that release has come without incident. [ ]

Faced with the State's unrebutted arguments that only modest burdens attend the disclosure of a typical petition, we must reject plaintiffs' broad challenge to the PRA. In doing so, we note—as we have in other election law disclosure cases—that upholding the law against a broad-based challenge does not foreclose a litigant's success in a narrower one. [ ] The secretary of state acknowledges that plaintiffs may press the narrower challenge in Count II of their complaint in proceedings pending before the District Court. [ ]

[Affirmed.]

[In separate concurring opinions, Justice Stevens, Breyer, Sotomayor, and Ginsburg expressed doubt that an as-applied challenge could succeed because in their view any burdens imposed on speech by disclosure of the signers' names would be inadequate to justify a holding that the First Amendment required secrecy. Justice Alioto thought the plaintiffs would have a strong case for relief against the statute as applied to the Referendum 71 petition because they would be able to cite evidence of widespread intimidation and harassment accompanying a ballot proposition in California to ban gay marriage. Only Justice Scalia argued that the plaintiffs lacked any cognizable First Amendment interest. "Our Nation's longstanding traditions of legislating and voting in public refute the claim that the First Amendment accords a right to anonymity in the performance of an act with governmental effect."]

■ JUSTICE THOMAS, dissenting.

Just as "[c]onfidence in the integrity of our electoral processes is essential to the functioning of our participatory democracy," [ ] so too is citizen participation in those processes, which necessarily entails political speech and association under the First Amendment. In my view, compelled disclosure of signed referendum and initiative petitions under the Washington Public Records Act (PRA), Wash. Rev. Code § 42.56.001, et seq. (2008), severely burdens those rights and chills citizen participation in the referendum process. Given those burdens, I would hold that Washington's decision to subject all referendum petitions to public disclosure is unconstitutional because there will always be a less restrictive means by which Washington can vindicate its stated interest in preserving the integrity of its referendum process. I respectfully dissent. . . .

NOTES AND QUESTIONS

1.   Judging by the precedents cited in the opinion, the "exacting scrutiny" applied by the majority seems to be roughly equivalent to what courts have called "strict scrutiny" in other contexts.

2.   If the public's interests in what their elected officials are saying (as in *Rangra*) or in who is seeking a referendum (as in *Reed*) are not interests that require First Amendment protection, would it be anomalous to hold that the interests of the public officials or the petition signers in resisting disclosure *do* require First Amendment protection?

3.   In what other contexts might those who resist disclosure claim a First Amendment right to communicate privately or anonymously?

CHAPTER XI

ACCESS TO JUDICIAL PROCEEDINGS

Courtrooms and judicial records are at least as important as sources of news as the governmental meetings and records considered in the preceding chapter. We consider them separately in this chapter for several reasons. First, statutory access schemes covering governmental meetings and records invariably exempt judicial proceedings and records, making many of the access mechanisms discussed in the preceding chapter unavailable. Second, some of the conflicts that arise in this area implicate not only the First Amendment, but also the Sixth Amendment ("In all criminal prosecutions, the accused shall enjoy the right to a speedy and public trial, by an impartial jury of the State and district wherein the crime shall have been committed. . . ."). Finally, the litigation over access to judicial proceedings differs from other media access litigation in both quantity and quality. There is more of it, it is primarily constitutional rather than statutory, and the constitutional principles being developed in this area may not be fully applicable to nonjudicial access questions.

In Chapter Two we saw the courts' efforts to protect criminal defendants' fair trial rights by restricting potentially prejudicial trial publicity. The *Sheppard* opinion was widely interpreted as a mandate to restrict news coverage before and during trials. In Nebraska Press Association v. Stuart, however, the Supreme Court made it extremely difficult for courts to protect fair trial rights by imposing direct restrictions on the press. Although that case did not rule out the possibility that a prohibition against publication of prejudicial information might be permissible in some situations, the prerequisites it established are so demanding that "gag orders" against the press have become infrequent.

Courts responded by restricting what trial participants could tell the press. Trial judges issued orders restricting comment by attorneys and sometimes by parties and witnesses. Bar associations promulgated rules limiting what attorneys were allowed to say. Even those strategies have limits. The free speech rights of attorneys and other participants limit the extent to which they can be silenced. See *Gentile*. Moreover, the effort to control their disclosures was often ineffective. In sensational cases, the press invariably obtained information of the sort that the rules were designed to suppress. Information that police or prosecutors previously would have announced publicly now was leaked to the press and published without attribution. Defense lawyers responded to leaks of information adverse to their clients by leaking favorable information, and they sometimes initiated publicity battles themselves. Occasionally these episodes led to acrimonious battles in which judges attempted to force reporters to identify lawyers who had leaked information in violation of the rules. However, as we saw in Chapter Nine, these efforts to compel disclosure often fail. As violations of the rules became commonplace, attorneys frequently ignored them, even holding news conferences at which they discussed matters forbidden by the disciplinary rules.

The ineffectiveness of attempts to restrict trial participants and the constitutional barriers to restricting publication left one obvious avenue open to judges seeking to prevent prejudicial publicity: deny the press access to the pretrial proceedings that often are a major source of such information. Nebraska Press Association v. Stuart had mentioned that possibility with apparent approval. Not surprisingly, the constitutionality of such closures was the next major area of litigation over press coverage of judicial proceedings. In the cases below, most of which were decided in the 1980s, the Supreme Court recognized that both the press and public have a constitutional right to attend criminal trials and some types of pre-trial proceedings in criminal cases. In this line of cases, the Supreme Court held the constitutional right of access to criminal trials may be overcome only in rare cases. Not only must the party seeking closure demonstrate an "overriding interest", but the closure order must also contain detailed findings that will allow an appellate court to conclude that it was narrowly tailored to achieve that interest. These decisions left lower courts to discern whether the constitutional right of access recognized by the Court applied to other types of proceedings or judicial records and what types of interests might be described as "overriding." Thus, courts were forced to decide whether juvenile delinquency cases or mental competency hearings were open to the public as well as whether concerns over pretrial publicity or protecting the privacy of litigants, witnesses, and jurors were sufficient to overcome the presumption of openness of trial proceedings in individual cases. The challenges faced by lower courts in extending the Supreme Court's access jurisprudence became particularly acute in the wake of the terrorist attacks of September 11, 2001, as courts addressed cases in which the overriding interest asserted to justify restrictions on access to judicial proceedings was national security.

This chapter begins with the cases defining the scope of the right of constitutional access to courtrooms. Because courts tend to view the issue of television coverage (and sometimes still photography) differently from the issue of pen-and-paper coverage, we deal first with issues arising from conventional coverage and then with issues involving cameras. The chapter then addresses whether the principles governing access to courtrooms apply to access to jurors and witnesses. Finally, the chapter discusses common law and constitutional rights of access to judicial records and addresses the difficultly of determining what, exactly, is a "judicial record."

A. ACCESS TO COURTROOMS

1. CRIMINAL PROCEEDINGS

Gannett Co. v. DePasquale. The first courtroom closure case to reach the Supreme Court was Gannett Co. v. DePasquale, 443 U.S. 368 (1979). A judge in New York barred the press and public from a pretrial hearing to determine whether confessions in a murder case should be suppressed because they were involuntary. The publisher of the local newspaper challenged the closure on both First Amendment and Sixth Amendment grounds. The Court rejected the Sixth Amendment argument because that amendment guarantees a public trial to the defendant, not to the public. The Court did not decide whether the First Amendment created a right of access to the proceeding but held that even if it did, the trial judge could properly determine that the right was outweighed in the circumstances of the case by the defendant's right to a fair trial. Justices Blackmun, Brennan, White, and Marshall dissented, arguing that the Sixth Amendment gives the public a qualified right of access to judicial proceedings and the accused had failed to make a showing of potential prejudice sufficient to overcome this qualified right.

The decision provoked outrage in the press and uncertainty among the lower courts at a time when many closures were being challenged. The next term the Court agreed to review another courtroom closure case. Although this case involved closure of the trial itself, rather than pretrial proceedings, it had implications for the latter as well, as we shall see in Press-Enterprise Co. v. Superior Court (II), infra.

a. TRIALS

Richmond Newspapers, Inc. v. Virginia
Supreme Court of the United States, 1980.
448 U.S. 555.

[Stevenson was charged with murder. The first trial produced a conviction, but it was reversed because of improperly admitted evidence. The second and third ended in mistrials. At the beginning of Stevenson's fourth trial, his counsel moved to exclude the press and public, apparently primarily to prevent jurors from being influenced by news coverage of the trial. A state statute authorized the trial court "in its discretion, to exclude from the trial any persons whose presence would impair the conduct of a fair trial." The prosecutor did not object and the judge closed the courtroom, giving several reasons, including "the rights of the defendant" and the possibility that the presence of spectators would distract the jury. Appellant's reporters left but later in the day the newspaper unsuccessfully moved to vacate the closure order. The trial proceeded the next day behind closed doors and at the close of the prosecution's evidence the court struck the evidence, discharged the jury, and acquitted the defendant. The Virginia Supreme Court denied the newspaper's appeal.]

Chief Justice Burger announced the judgment of the Court and delivered an opinion in which Justice White and Justice Stevens joined.

The narrow question presented in this case is whether the right of the public and press to attend criminal trials is guaranteed under the United States Constitution.

. . .

II.

We begin consideration of this case by noting that the precise issue presented here has not previously been before this Court for decision. In [*Gannett*], the Court was not required to decide whether a right of access to trials, as distinguished from hearings on *pretrial* motions, was constitutionally guaranteed. . . .

A.

The origins of the proceeding which has become the modern criminal trial in Anglo-American justice can be traced back beyond reliable historical records. . . . [T]hroughout its evolution, the trial has been open to all who cared to observe. [The opinion traced the history and development of criminal trials, concluding that they were marked by "presumptive openness" in both England and colonial America.]

B.

. . .

. . . The early history of open trials in part reflects the widespread acknowledgement, long before there were behavioral scientists, that public trials had significant community therapeutic value. Even without such experts to frame the concept in words, people sensed from experience and observation that, especially in the administration of criminal justice, the means used to achieve justice must have the support derived from public acceptance of both the process and its results.

When a shocking crime occurs, a community reaction of outrage and public protest often follows. [ ] Thereafter the open processes of justice serve an important prophylactic purpose, providing an outlet for community concern, hostility, and emotion. Without an awareness that society's responses to criminal conduct are underway, natural human reactions of outrage and protest are frustrated and may manifest themselves in some form of vengeful "self-help," as indeed they did regularly in the activities of vigilante "committees" on our frontiers. . . .

. . .

In earlier times, both in England and America, attendance at court was a common mode of "passing the time." [ ] With the press, cinema, and electronic media now supplying the representations or reality of the real life drama once available only in the courtroom, attendance at court is no longer a widespread pastime. Yet "[i]t is not unrealistic even in this day to believe that public inclusion affords citizens a form of legal education and hopefully promotes confidence in the fair administration of justice." [ ] Instead of acquiring information about trials by firsthand observation or by word of mouth from those who attended, people now acquire it chiefly through the print and electronic media. In a sense, this validates the media claim of functioning as surrogates for the public. While media representatives enjoy the same right of access as the public, they often are provided special seating and priority of entry so that they may report what people in attendance have seen and heard. This "contribute[s] to public understanding of the rule of law and to comprehension of the functioning of the entire criminal justice system. . . ." Nebraska Press Assn. v. Stuart, [ ] (Brennan, J., concurring).

C.

From this unbroken, uncontradicted history, supported by reasons as valid today as in centuries past, we are bound to conclude that a presumption of openness inheres in the very nature of a criminal trial under our system of justice. This conclusion is hardly novel; without a direct holding on the issue, the Court has voiced its recognition of it in a variety of contexts over the years. . . .

Despite the history of criminal trials being presumptively open since long before the Constitution, the State presses its contention that neither the Constitution nor the Bill of Rights contains any provision which by its terms guarantees to the public the right to attend criminal trials. Standing alone, this is correct, but there remains the question whether, absent an explicit provision, the Constitution affords protection against exclusion of the public from criminal trials.

III. [A.]

. . .

The Bill of Rights was enacted against the backdrop of the long history of trials being presumptively open. Public access to trials was then regarded as an important aspect of the process itself; the conduct of trials "before as many of the people as chose to attend" was regarded as one of "the inestimable advantages of a free English constitution of government." [ ] In guaranteeing freedoms such as those of speech and press, the First Amendment can be read as protecting the right of everyone to attend trials so as to give meaning to those explicit guarantees. "[T]he First Amendment goes beyond protection of the press and the self-expression of individuals to prohibit government from limiting the stock of information from which members of the public may draw." First National Bank of Boston v. Bellotti, 435 U.S. 765, 783 (1978).

Free speech carries with it some freedom to listen. "In a variety of contexts this Court has referred to a First Amendment right to 'receive information and ideas.'" [ ] What this means in the context of trials is that the First Amendment guarantees of speech and press, standing alone, prohibit government from summarily closing courtroom doors which had long been open to the public at the time that amendment was adopted. "For the First Amendment does not speak equivocally.... It must be taken as a command of the broadest scope that explicit language, read in the context of a liberty-loving society, will allow." [ ]

It is not crucial whether we describe this right to attend criminal trials to hear, see, and communicate observations concerning them as a "right of access," cf. Gannett, supra, at 573 (Powell, J., concurring); [*Saxbe* and *Pell*],[11] or a "right to gather information," for we have recognized that "without some protection for seeking out the news, freedom of the press could be eviscerated." *Branzburg* [ ]. The explicit, guaranteed rights to speak and to publish concerning what takes place at a trial would lose much meaning if access to observe the trial could, as it was here, be foreclosed arbitrarily.[12]

B.

The right of access to places traditionally open to the public, as criminal trials have long been, may be seen as assured by the amalgam of the First Amendment guarantees of speech and press; and their affinity to the right of assembly is not without relevance. From the outset, the right of assembly was regarded not only as an independent right but also as a catalyst to augment the free exercise of the other First Amendment rights with which it was deliberately linked by the draftsmen. "The right of peaceable assembly is a right cognate to those of free speech and free press and is equally fundamental." [ ] People assemble in public places not only to speak or to take action, but also to listen, observe, and learn; indeed, they may "assembl[e] for any lawful purpose." [ ] Subject to the traditional time, place, and manner restrictions, [ ] streets, sidewalks, and parks are places traditionally open, where First Amendment rights may be exercised, [ ]; a trial courtroom also is a public place where the people generally—and representatives of the media—have a right to be present, and where their

---

[11] [*Pell*] and *Saxbe* are distinguishable in the sense that they were concerned with penal institutions which, by definition, are not "open" or public places. Penal institutions do not share the long tradition of openness, although traditionally there have been visiting committees of citizens, and there is no doubt that legislative committees could exercise plenary oversight and "visitation rights." *Saxbe* [ ] noted that "limitation on visitations is justified by what the Court of Appeals acknowledged as 'the truism that prisons are institutions where public access is generally limited.'..." [ ]

[12] That the right to attend may be exercised by people less frequently today when information as to trials generally reaches them by way of print and electronic media in no way alters the basic right. Instead of relying on personal observation or reports from neighbors as in the past, most people receive information concerning trials through the media whose representatives "are entitled to the same rights [to attend trials] as the general public." *Estes v. Texas*, 381 U.S. at 540, 85 S.Ct. at 1631.

presence historically has been thought to enhance the integrity and quality of what takes place.

C.

. . .

We hold that the right to attend criminal trials[17] is implicit in the guarantees of the First Amendment; without the freedom to attend such trials, which people have exercised for centuries, important aspects of freedom of speech and "of the press could be eviscerated." *Branzburg,* [ ].

D.

Having concluded there was a guaranteed right of the public under the First and Fourteenth Amendments to attend the trial of Stevenson's case, we return to the closure order challenged by appellants. The Court in *Gannett* made clear that although the Sixth Amendment guarantees the accused a right to a public trial, it does not give a right to a private trial. [ ] Despite the fact that this was the fourth trial of the accused, the trial judge made no findings to support closure; no inquiry was made as to whether alternative solutions would have met the need to ensure fairness; there was no recognition of any right under the Constitution for the public or press to attend the trial. In contrast to the pretrial proceeding dealt with in *Gannett,* supra, there exist in the context of the trial itself various tested alternatives to satisfy the constitutional demands of fairness. See, e.g., Nebraska Press Association v. Stuart, [ ]; Sheppard v. Maxwell, [ ]. There was no suggestion that any problems with witnesses could not have been dealt with by their exclusion from the courtroom or their sequestration during the trial. [ ] Nor is there anything to indicate that sequestration of the jurors would not have guarded against their being subjected to any improper information. All of the alternatives admittedly present difficulties for trial courts, but none of the factors relied on here was beyond the realm of the manageable. Absent an overriding interest articulated in findings, the trial of a criminal case must be open to the public.[18] Accordingly, the judgment under review is reversed.

---

[17] Whether the public has a right to attend trials of civil cases is a question not raised by this case, but we note that historically both civil and criminal trials have been presumptively open.

[18] We have no occasion here to define the circumstances in which all or parts of a criminal trial may be closed to the public. [ ] [O]ur holding today does not mean that the First Amendment rights of the public and representatives of the press are absolute. Just as a government may impose reasonable time, place, and manner restrictions upon the use of its streets in the interest of such objectives as the free flow of traffic, see, e.g., Cox v. New Hampshire, 312 U.S. 569 (1941), so may a trial judge, in the interest of the fair administration of justice, impose reasonable limitations on access to a trial. "[T]he question in a particular case is whether that control is exerted so as not to deny or unwarrantedly abridge . . . the opportunities for the communication of thought and the discussion of public questions immemorially associated with resort to public places." Id., at 574. It is far more important that trials be conducted in a quiet and orderly setting than it is to preserve that atmosphere on city streets. [ ] Moreover, since courtrooms have limited capacity, there may be occasions when not every person who wishes to attend can be accommodated. In such situations, reasonable

Reversed.

■ JUSTICE POWELL took no part in the consideration or decision of this case.

■ JUSTICE WHITE, concurring.

This case would have been unnecessary had *Gannett* [ ] construed the Sixth Amendment to forbid excluding the public from criminal proceedings except in narrowly defined circumstances. But the Court there rejected the submission of four of us to this effect, thus requiring that the First Amendment issue involved here be addressed. On this issue, I concur in the opinion of The Chief Justice.

■ JUSTICE STEVENS, concurring.

This is a watershed case. Until today the Court has accorded virtually absolute protection to the dissemination of information or ideas, but never before has it squarely held that the acquisition of newsworthy matter is entitled to any constitutional protection whatsoever. An additional word of emphasis is therefore appropriate.

Twice before, the Court has implied that any governmental restriction on access to information, no matter how severe and no matter how unjustified, would be constitutionally acceptable so long as it did not single out the press for special disabilities not applicable to the public at large. [Discussing *Saxbe* and *Houchins*] Today, however, for the first time, the Court unequivocally holds that an arbitrary interference with access to important information is an abridgment of the freedoms of speech and of the press protected by the First Amendment.

. . .

■ JUSTICE BRENNAN, with whom JUSTICE MARSHALL joins, concurring in the judgment.

[Deciding when the First Amendment requires access to a courtroom] is as much a matter of sensitivity to practical necessities as it is of abstract reasoning. But at least two helpful principles may be sketched. First, the case for a right of access has special force when drawn from an enduring and vital tradition of public entree to particular proceedings or information. [ ] Such a tradition commands respect in part because the Constitution carries the gloss of history. More importantly, a tradition of accessibility implies the favorable judgment of experience. Second, the value of access must be measured in specifics. Analysis is not advanced by rhetorical statements that all information bears upon public issues; what is crucial in individual cases is whether access to a particular government process is important in terms of that very process.

---

restrictions on general access are traditionally imposed, including preferential seating for media representatives. [ ]

To resolve the case before us, therefore, we must consult historical and current practice with respect to open trials, and weigh the importance of public access to the trial process itself.

II.

[Justice Brennan agreed with Chief Justice Burger that open trials were the practice, historically and currently, throughout the country.]

III.

Publicity serves to advance several of the particular purposes of the trial (and, indeed, the judicial) process. Open trials play a fundamental role in furthering the efforts of our judicial system to assure the criminal defendant a fair and accurate adjudication of guilt or innocence. [ ] But, as a feature of our governing system of justice, the trial process serves other, broadly political, interests, and public access advances these objectives as well. To that extent, trial access possesses specific structural significance.

The trial is a means of meeting "the notion, deeply rooted in the common law, that 'justice must satisfy the appearance of justice.' " . . .

Secrecy is profoundly inimical to this demonstrative purpose of the trial process. Open trials assure the public that procedural rights are respected, and that justice is afforded equally. Closed trials breed suspicion of prejudice and arbitrariness, which in turn spawns disrespect for law. Public access is essential, therefore, if trial adjudication is to achieve the objective of maintaining public confidence in the administration of justice. [ ]

But the trial is more than a demonstrably just method of adjudicating disputes and protecting rights. It plays a pivotal role in the entire judicial process, and, by extension, in our form of government. Under our system, judges are not mere umpires, but, in their own sphere, lawmakers—a coordinate branch of *government*. While individual cases turn upon the controversies between parties, or involve particular prosecutions, court rulings impose official and practical consequences upon members of society at large. Moreover, judges bear responsibility for the vitally important task of construing and securing constitutional rights. Thus, so far as the trial is the mechanism for judicial factfinding, as well as the initial forum for legal decisionmaking, it is a genuine governmental proceeding.

It follows that the conduct of the trial is preeminently a matter of public interest. [ ] More importantly, public access to trials acts as an important check, akin in purpose to the other checks and balances that infuse our system of government. "The knowledge that every criminal trial is subject to contemporaneous review in the forum of public opinion is an effective restraint on possible abuse of judicial power," [ ] an abuse that, in many cases, would have ramifications beyond the impact upon the parties before the court. Indeed " '[w]ithout publicity, all other checks are insufficient: in comparison of publicity, all other checks are of small account.' " [ ]

Finally, with some limitations, a trial aims at true and accurate factfinding. Of course, proper factfinding is to the benefit of criminal defendants and of the parties in civil proceedings. But other, comparably urgent, interests are also often at stake. A miscarriage of justice that imprisons an innocent accused also leaves a guilty party at large, a continuing threat to society. Also, mistakes of fact in civil litigation may inflict costs upon others than the plaintiff and defendant. Facilitation of the trial factfinding process, therefore, is of concern to the public as well as to the parties.

Publicizing trial proceedings aids accurate factfinding. "Public trials come to the attention of key witnesses unknown to the parties.". . .

Popular attendance at trials, in sum, substantially furthers the particular public purposes of that critical judicial proceeding. In that sense, public access is an indispensable element of the trial process itself. Trial access, therefore, assumes structural importance in our "government of laws" [ ].

IV.

. . . What countervailing interests might be sufficiently compelling to reverse this presumption of openness need not concern us now, for the statute at stake here authorizes trial closures at the unfettered discretion of the judge and parties. Accordingly, Va. Code 19.2–266 violates the First and Fourteenth Amendments, and the decision of the Virginia Supreme Court to the contrary should be reversed.

[Justice Stewart, concurring in the judgment, stated: "Whatever the ultimate answer . . . may be with respect to pretrial suppression hearings in criminal cases, the First and Fourteenth Amendments clearly give the press and the public a right of access to trials themselves, civil as well as criminal." Justice Blackmun, also concurring in the judgment, argued that the right of public access to trials should be found in the Sixth Amendment, as he had urged in *Gannett,* but agreed, "as a secondary position, that the First Amendment must provide some measure of protection for public access to the trial." Justice Rehnquist dissented on the grounds that the Constitution did not contain "any provision" that "may fairly be read to prohibit what the trial judge in the Virginia state court system did in this case. Being unable to find any such prohibition in the First, Sixth, Ninth, or any other Amendments to the United States Constitution, or in the Constitution itself, I dissent."]

NOTES AND QUESTIONS

1. To the extent that the decision turns on the tradition of open courtrooms, it provides little support for a First Amendment right of access to other proceedings or institutions that either have little history or

traditionally have been closed. How many of the Justices would find a right of access even in the absence of a tradition of openness?

2.   Are Justice Brennan's reasons for concluding that public attendance furthers the public purposes of trials any less applicable to attendance at other types of governmental meetings?

3.   Chief Justice Burger and Justices Stewart and Stevens were in the majority in both *Gannett* and *Richmond Newspapers*. Do their opinions here succeed in distinguishing the two cases?

Closure of Trial During Testimony of Minor Victims of Sexual Offenses. The next Supreme Court case on access to trials was Globe Newspaper Co. v. Superior Court, 457 U.S. 596 (1982). *Globe Newspaper* involved a Massachusetts statute that had been interpreted to require that the courtroom be closed during the testimony of minor victims of sexual offenses. A majority concurred in an opinion by Justice Brennan striking down the statute. Even though trials involving sexual offenses or other sensational aspects had frequently been closed, the "history of openness" criterion of *Richmond Newspapers* was satisfied. The critical question was not the historical openness of a particular type of trial but rather the "state interests assertedly supporting the restriction." To deny access, "it must be shown that the denial is necessitated by a compelling governmental interest, and is narrowly tailored to serve that interest."

Although the Court found that the state's interest in safeguarding the physical and psychological well-being of minors was a compelling state interest, it did not justify *mandatory* closure. Trial judges must determine case-by-case whether closure is necessary based on factors such as the age of the victim, the victim's maturity, "the nature of the crime, the desires of the victim, and the interests of parents and relatives." The Court noted that the case at hand involved victims whose names were already in the public record; the victims were 16 and 17 and may have been willing to testify in public.

The Court also found that the state's interest in encouraging victims to come forward was insufficient to justify closure, because the state presented no support for the claim that automatic closure would achieve that result. The Court doubted the connection because the statute barred public attendance in court but did not bar press access to the transcript or prevent the press from learning and reporting on what occurred in the closed courtroom by other means. Even if the state's interest was effectively advanced by automatic closure, "it is doubtful that the interest would be sufficient to overcome the constitutional attack, for that same interest could be relied on to support an array of mandatory closure rules designed to encourage victims to come forward." To assert that closure would get more victims of all crimes to come forward and encourage more candid testimony would run contrary to "the very foundation of the right of access recognized in *Richmond Newspapers*."

Chief Justice Burger, joined by Justice Rehnquist, dissented on the merits. They stressed the lack of a history of openness in this type of case and that the statute need not be "precisely tailored so long as the state's interest overrides the law's impact on First Amendment rights and the restrictions imposed further that interest." Because the statute only barred access during the victim's testimony and rationally served the state's overriding interest in avoiding serious psychological damage, they would have upheld the statute. They also feared the effect on parents of learning that their child might have to undergo an in camera hearing before it could be known whether the trial would be closed during the child's testimony. The statute had a "relatively minor incidental impact on First Amendment rights and gives effect to the overriding state interest in protecting child rape victims. Paradoxically, the Court today denies the victims the kind of protection routinely given to juveniles who commit crimes."

Justice Stevens dissented on the ground that the order under review was too abstract for decision.

Voir Dire. The questioning of prospective jurors is an important part of criminal trials, but judges sometimes believe that voir dire can be closed, even if the rest of the trial has to be open, in the interest of protecting prospective jurors' privacy or encouraging them to answer probing questions candidly. In Press-Enterprise Co. v. Superior Court, 464 U.S. 501 (1984) (Press-Enterprise I), a black defendant was charged with the rape and murder of a white teenage girl in California. When a newspaper sought access to the voir dire, the state objected on the ground that juror responses would lack the candor needed in such a case. The trial judge closed all but three days of the six-week voir dire. When the newspaper sought the transcript of the voir dire, both the state and the defense objected on the ground that this would violate the jurors' right to privacy because they had answered sensitive questions under an "implied promise of confidentiality." After the trial was over, the judge continued to refuse to release the transcript.

The Supreme Court unanimously reversed. Chief Justice Burger observed that the "primacy of the accused's right is difficult to separate from the right of everyone in the community to attend the *voir dire* which promotes fairness." The standard created, building upon language from the *Globe* case, was:

> The presumption of openness may be overcome only by an overriding interest based on findings that closure is essential to preserve higher values and is narrowly tailored to serve that interest. The interest is to be articulated along with findings specific enough that a reviewing court can determine whether the closure order was properly entered.

The trial judge made no findings nor considered whether alternatives to closure might have worked. The Court recognized that when interrogation touches on "deeply personal matters" a juror may have a compelling interest in privacy. Such concern might be met by informing jurors in advance that they may request a meeting in chambers with the judge and counsel and a court reporter if something potentially embarrassing comes up during voir dire. If necessary, that part of the transcript might be sealed, but the rest would be open.

Nevertheless, in exceptional circumstances, courts continue to approve the closing of voir dire. In U.S. v. King, 140 F.3d 76 (2d Cir. 1998), the court approved the trial judge's closure of voir dire to promote candor by prospective jurors in a racially charged criminal trial involving boxing promoter Don King. The judge found that jurors' knowledge that their answers might be reported in the press "may so inhibit or chill truthful responses that [the] accused is denied the fair trial to which he is entitled." A 2–1 majority distinguished *Press-Enterprise I* on the ground that it was concerned merely with protecting the privacy interests of jurors, while the interest in the *King* case was the defendant's right to a fair trial. The majority said the trial judge's findings were sufficient to support closure. "[T]his is that unusual case where the fairness of a trial, or at least the voir dire phase, that is usually promoted by public access is seriously at risk of being impaired unless some modest limitation of access is imposed." The dissenter wrote:

> These findings hardly distinguish this case from many high-profile cases tried in federal district courts across this country every year. Were mere notoriety to be deemed a sufficient basis for courtroom closure, the broad presumption of openness established by the Supreme Court in *Press-Enterprise I* would soon lose all force. Indeed, it is precisely in those cases involving controversial or notorious defendants that the public—and its media proxies—are likely to take an interest in criminal proceedings. It would be perverse to enshrine a constitutional right of public access to criminal proceedings, and then to enforce that right only in cases in which the public has no interest.

The same court later made clear that encouraging jurors to be candid can justify closing voir dire only in unusual circumstances. In the trial of Martha Stewart for securities law violations, the trial judge conducted part of the voir dire in chambers and excluded the press on the ground that some prospective jurors might not give full and frank answers for fear that their responses would be publicly disclosed. The judge believed that U.S. v. King authorized her to do so. But the Second Circuit said, "In *King*, the voir dire explored the racial views of potential jurors; given the prevailing national consensus concerning the evils of racism, the district judge recognized that potential jurors were unlikely to admit openly to harboring racist views. No similarly sensitive or contentious lines of questioning were here identified by the district court." See ABC, Inc. v. Stewart, 360 F.3d 90 (2d Cir. 2004).

Federal courts sometimes allow courts to empanel anonymous juries in cases that raise serious concerns about jury safety. Statutory authorization comes from 28 U.S.C. § 1863. In U.S. v. Dinkins, 691 F.3d 358 (4th Cir. 2012), for example, the Fourth Circuit held that a trial court did not abuse its discretion in empaneling an anonymous jury in a case involving the murder of a witness. The court explained that anonymity is a matter of degree, and a jury "is considered to be 'anonymous' when a trial court has withheld certain biographical information about the jurors either from the public, the parties, or both." The court set the standard for empaneling an anonymous jury as follows:

> a district court may empanel an anonymous jury only in rare circumstances when two conditions are met: (1) there is strong reason to conclude that the jury needs protection from interference or harm, or that the integrity of the jury's function will be compromised absent anonymity; and (2) reasonable safeguards have been adopted to minimize the risk that the rights of the accused will be infringed.

A non-exhaustive list of factors that might justify empaneling an anonymous jury included:

> (1) the defendant's involvement in organized crime, (2) the defendant's participation in a group with the capacity to harm jurors, (3) the defendant's past attempts to interfere with the judicial process, (4) the potential that, if convicted, the defendant will suffer a lengthy incarceration and substantial monetary penalties, and (5) extensive publicity that could enhance the possibility that jurors' names would become public and expose them to intimidation or harassment.

U.S. v. Ross, 33 F.3d 1507 (11th Cir. 1994). To minimize any potential prejudicial inferences the jury pool members might make, a trial judge may tell the jury that anonymity will protect them from unwanted publicity. See U.S. v. Lafond, 783 F.3d 1216 (11th Cir. 2015) (allowing a judge to empanel an anonymous jury in a murder trial of gang members based on safety concerns), cert. denied, 136 S. Ct. 213 (2015). If there is a constitutional right to a public trial, why have the appellate courts reviewed trial courts' decisions to empanel anonymous juries for abuse of discretion?

Is juror candor a more "overriding" interest than juror privacy? Recall that the objective of encouraging jurors' candor was also asserted in *Press Enterprise I*. Is candor the ultimate reason for protecting jurors' privacy? Is the defendant's right to a fair trial the ultimate reason for encouraging candor?

b.   PRETRIAL PROCEEDINGS

In *Richmond Newspapers* the Court seemed to draw a sharp line between the criminal trial itself and pretrial hearings. In the following case the Court returned to the question of a First Amendment right of access to pretrial proceedings.

Press-Enterprise Co. v. Superior Court (II)

Supreme Court of the United States, 1986.
478 U.S. 1.

[Robert Diaz, a nurse, was charged with murdering 12 patients by administering a lethal drug. He exercised his right under California law to have a preliminary hearing, rather than grand jury proceedings, to determine whether he should be made to stand trial. He moved to exclude the press and public under a statute that gave him an unqualified right to have a closed hearing. The hearing lasted 41 days and Diaz was bound over for trial on all charges. After the hearing ended, the prosecution and the Press-Enterprise moved to release transcripts of the closed hearing. Diaz objected and the California courts refused to release the transcripts. Later, Diaz waived his right to jury trial and the trial court released the transcript. The Supreme Court held that this did not moot the case because the issue was likely to recur and otherwise was likely to evade review.]

■ CHIEF JUSTICE BURGER delivered the opinion of the Court.

We granted certiorari to decide whether petitioner has a First Amendment right of access to transcripts of a preliminary hearing growing out of a criminal prosecution.

. . .

. . . The California Supreme Court concluded that the First Amendment was not implicated because the proceeding was not a criminal trial, but a preliminary hearing. However, the First Amendment question cannot be resolved solely on the label we give the event, i.e., "trial" or otherwise, particularly where the preliminary hearing functions much like a full scale trial.

In cases dealing with the claim of a First Amendment right of access to criminal proceedings, our decisions have emphasized two complementary considerations. First, because a "'tradition of accessibility implies the favorable judgment of experience'" [ ] we have considered whether the place and process has historically been open to the press and general public.

. . .

Second, in this setting the Court has traditionally considered whether public access plays a significant positive role in the functioning of the particular process in question. [ ] Although many governmental processes operate best under public scrutiny, it takes little imagination to recognize that there are some kinds of government operations that would be totally frustrated if conducted openly. A classic example is that "the proper functioning of our grand jury system depends upon the secrecy of grand jury proceedings." Douglas Oil Co. v. Petrol Stops Northwest, 441 U.S. 211, 218 (1979). Other proceedings plainly require public access. In *Press-Enterprise I,* we summarized the holdings of prior cases, noting that openness in criminal trials, including the selection of jurors, "enhances both the basic fairness of the criminal trial and the appearance of fairness so essential to public confidence in the system." [ ]

These considerations of experience and logic are, of course, related, for history and experience shape the functioning of governmental processes. If the particular proceeding in question passes these tests of experience and logic, a qualified First Amendment right of public access attaches. But even when a right of access attaches, it is not absolute. [ ] While open criminal proceedings give assurances of fairness to both the public and the accused, there are some limited circumstances in which the right of the accused to a fair trial might be undermined by publicity.[2] In such cases, the trial court must determine whether the situation is such that the rights of the accused override the qualified First Amendment right of access. . . .

IV. [A.]

The considerations that led the Court to apply the First Amendment right of access to criminal trials in *Richmond Newspapers* and *Globe* and the selection of jurors in *Press-Enterprise I* lead us to conclude that the right of access applies to preliminary hearings as conducted in California.

First, there has been a tradition of accessibility to preliminary hearings of the type conducted in California. Although grand jury proceedings have traditionally been closed to the public and the accused, preliminary hearings conducted before neutral and detached magistrates have been open to the public. Long ago in the celebrated trial of Aaron Burr for treason, for example, with Chief Justice Marshall sitting as trial judge, the probable cause hearing was held in the Hall of the House of Delegates in Virginia, the court room being too small to accommodate the crush of interested citizens. United States v. Burr, 25 F. Cas. 2 (CC Va. 1807) (No. 14,692). From *Burr* until the present day, the near uniform practice of state and federal courts has been to conduct preliminary hearings in open court.[3] As we noted in *Gannett,* several states following the original New York Field Code of Criminal Procedure published in 1850 have allowed preliminary hearings to be closed on the motion of the

---

[2]   Similarly, the interests of those other than the accused may be implicated. The protection of victims of sex crimes from the trauma and embarrassment of public scrutiny may justify closing certain aspects of a criminal proceeding. [ ]

[3]   The vast majority of States considering the issue have concluded that the same tradition of accessibility that applies to criminal trials applies to preliminary proceedings. [ ]

accused. [ ] But even in these states the proceedings are presumptively open to the public and are closed only for cause shown. Open preliminary hearings, therefore, have been accorded " 'the favorable judgment of experience.' " [ ]

The second question is whether public access to preliminary hearings as they are conducted in California plays a particularly significant positive role in the actual functioning of the process. We have already determined in *Richmond Newspapers, Globe,* and *Press-Enterprise I* that public access to criminal trials and the selection of jurors is essential to the proper functioning of the criminal justice system. California preliminary hearings are sufficiently like a trial to justify the same conclusion.

In California, to bring a felon to trial, the prosecutor has a choice of securing a grand jury indictment or a finding of probable cause following a preliminary hearing. Even when the accused has been indicted by a grand jury, however, he has an absolute right to an elaborate preliminary hearing before a neutral magistrate. [ ] The accused has the right to personally appear at the hearing, to be represented by counsel, to cross-examine hostile witnesses, to present exculpatory evidence, and to exclude illegally obtained evidence. [ ] If the magistrate determines that probable cause exists, the accused is bound over for trial; such a finding leads to a guilty plea in the majority of cases.

It is true that unlike a criminal trial, the California preliminary hearing cannot result in the conviction of the accused and the adjudication is before a magistrate or other judicial officer without a jury. But these features, standing alone, do not make public access any less essential to the proper functioning of the proceedings in the overall criminal justice process. Because of its extensive scope, the preliminary hearing is often the final and most important step in the criminal proceeding. [ ] As the California Supreme Court stated in San Jose Mercury-News v. Municipal Court, 638 P.2d 655 (Cal. 1982), the preliminary hearing in many cases provides "the sole occasion for public observation of the criminal justice system." [ ]

Similarly, the absence of a jury, long recognized as "an inestimable safeguard against the corrupt or overzealous prosecutor and against the compliant, biased, or eccentric judge," Duncan v. Louisiana, 391 U.S. 145, 156 (1968), makes the importance of public access to a preliminary hearing even more significant. "People in an open society do not demand infallibility from their institutions, but it is difficult for them to accept what they are prohibited from observing." [*Richmond Newspapers*]

Denying the transcripts of a 41-day preliminary hearing would frustrate what we have characterized as the "community therapeutic value" of openness. [ ] Criminal acts, especially certain violent crimes, provoke public concern, outrage, and hostility. "When the public is aware that the law is being enforced and the criminal justice system is functioning, an outlet is provided for these understandable reactions and emotions." [ ] In sum,

> "The value of openness lies in the fact that people not actually attending trials can have confidence that standards of fairness are being observed; the sure knowledge that *anyone* is free to attend gives assurance that established procedures are being followed and that deviations will become known. Openness thus enhances both the basic fairness of the criminal trial and the appearance of fairness so essential to public confidence in the system." Press-Enterprise I, 464 U.S., at 508. (emphasis in original).

We therefore conclude that the qualified First Amendment right of access to criminal proceedings applies to preliminary hearings as they are conducted in California.

B

Since a qualified First Amendment right of access attaches to preliminary hearings in California [ ], the proceedings cannot be closed unless specific, on the record findings are made demonstrating that "closure is essential to preserve higher values and is narrowly tailored to serve that interest." [ ] If the interest asserted is the right of the accused to a fair trial, the preliminary hearing shall be closed only if specific findings are made demonstrating that first, there is a substantial probability that the defendant's right to a fair trial will be prejudiced by publicity that closure would prevent and, second, reasonable alternatives to closure cannot adequately protect the defendant's fair trial rights. [ ]

The California Supreme Court, interpreting its access statute, concluded "that the magistrate shall close the preliminary hearing upon finding a reasonable likelihood of substantial prejudice." [ ] As the court itself acknowledged, the "reasonable likelihood" test places a lesser burden on the defendant than the "substantial probability" test which we hold is called for by the First Amendment. [ ] Moreover, the court failed to consider whether alternatives short of complete closure would have protected the interests of the accused.

In *Gannett* we observed that:

> "Publicity concerning pretrial suppression hearings such as the one involved in the present case poses special risks of unfairness. The whole purpose of such hearings is to screen out unreliable or illegally obtained evidence and insure that this evidence does not become known to the jury. Cf. Jackson v. Denno, 378 U.S. 368. Publicity concerning the proceedings at a pretrial hearing, however, could influence public opinion against a defendant and inform potential jurors of inculpatory information wholly inadmissible at the actual trial." [ ]

But this risk of prejudice does not automatically justify refusing public access to hearings on every motion to suppress. Through voir dire, cumbersome as it is in some circumstances, a court can identify those jurors whose prior knowledge of the case would disable them from rendering an impartial verdict. And even if closure were justified for the hearings on a motion to suppress, closure of an entire 41-day proceeding would rarely be warranted. The First Amendment right of access cannot be overcome by the conclusory assertion that publicity might deprive the defendant of [the right to a fair trial]. And any limitation " 'must be narrowly tailored to serve that interest.' " [ ]

The standard applied by the California Supreme Court failed to consider the First Amendment right of access to criminal proceedings. Accordingly, the judgment of the California Supreme Court is reversed.

■ JUSTICE STEVENS, with whom JUSTICE REHNQUIST joins as to Part II, dissenting.

. . .

[Justice Stevens stated that although "a proper construction of the First Amendment embraces a right of access to information about the conduct of public affairs," the risk to the defendant's right to fair trial in this instance outweighed "the countervailing interest in publishing the transcript of the preliminary hearing sooner rather than later."]

. . . [W]e have always recognized the legitimacy of the governmental interest in the secrecy of grand jury proceedings, and I am unpersuaded that the difference between such proceedings and the rather elaborate procedure for determining probable cause that California has adopted strengthens the First Amendment claim to access asserted in this case.

II

The Court nevertheless reaches the opposite conclusion by applying the "two complementary considerations" [ ] of "experience and logic" [ ]. In my view, neither the Court's reasoning nor the result it reaches is supported by our precedents.

The historical evidence proffered in this case is far less probative than the evidence adduced in prior cases granting public access to criminal proceedings. In those cases, a common law tradition of openness at the time the First Amendment was ratified suggested an intention and expectation on the part of the Framers and ratifiers that those proceedings would remain presumptively open. Thus, in [*Richmond Newspapers*] The Chief Justice explained that "[w]hat is significant for present purposes is that throughout its evolution, the trial has been open to all who cared to observe." "[T]he historical evidence demonstrates conclusively that *at the time when our organic laws were adopted*, criminal trials both here and in England had long been presumptively open." [ ] (emphasis added). . . .

In this case, however, it is uncontroverted that a common law right of access did not inhere in preliminary proceedings at the time the First Amendment was adopted, and that the Framers and ratifiers of that provision could not have intended such proceedings to remain open. As Justice Stewart wrote for the Court in [*Gannett*]:

> "[T]here exists no persuasive evidence that at common law members of the public had any right to attend pretrial proceedings; indeed, there is substantial evidence to the contrary. By the time of the adoption of the Constitution ... pretrial proceedings, precisely because of the ... concern for a fair trial, were never characterized by the same degree of openness as were actual trials. ..."

. . .

In the final analysis, the Court's lengthy historical disquisition demonstrates only that in many States preliminary proceedings are generally open to the public. . . . The recent common law developments reported by the Court are relevant, if at all, only insofar as they suggest that preliminary proceedings merit the "beneficial effects of public scrutiny." [*Cox Broadcasting*] The Court's historical crutch cannot carry the weight of opening a preliminary proceeding that the State has ordered closed; that determination must stand or fall on whether it satisfies the second component of the Court's test.

If the Court's historical evidence proves too little, the "value of openness," [ ] on which it relies proves too much, for this measure would open to public scrutiny far more than preliminary hearings "as they are conducted in California" (a comforting phrase invoked by the Court in one form or another more than 8 times in its opinion). In brief, the Court's rationale for opening the "California preliminary hearing" is that it "is often the final and most important step in the criminal proceeding"; that it provides " 'the sole occasion for public observation of the criminal justice system' "; that it lacks the protective presence of a jury; and that closure denies an outlet for community catharsis. [ ] The obvious defect in the Court's approach is that its reasoning applies to the traditionally secret grand jury with as much force as it applies to California preliminary hearings. A grand jury indictment is just as likely to be the "final step" in a criminal proceeding and the "sole occasion" for public scrutiny as is a preliminary hearing. Moreover, many critics of the grand jury maintain that the grand jury protects the accused less well than does a legally-knowledgeable judge who personally presides over a preliminary hearing. [ ] Finally, closure of grand juries denies an outlet for community rage. When the Court's explanatory veneer is stripped away, what emerges is the reality that the California preliminary hearing is functionally identical to the traditional grand jury. . . .

The Court's reasoning—if carried to its logical outcome—thus contravenes the "long-established policy that maintains the secrecy of the grand jury proceedings in the federal courts" and in the courts of 19 States. . . .

In fact, the logic of the Court's access right extends even beyond the confines of the criminal justice system to encompass proceedings held on the civil side of the docket as well. . . . Despite the Court's valiant attempt to limit the logic of its holding, the ratio decidendi of today's decision knows no bounds.

By abjuring strict reliance on history and emphasizing the broad value of openness, the Court tacitly recognizes the importance of public access to government proceedings generally. Regrettably, the Court has taken seriously the stated requirement that the sealing of a transcript be justified by a "compelling" or "overriding" governmental interest and that the closure order be "narrowly tailored to serve that interest." . . . The cases denying access have done so on a far lesser showing than that required by a compelling governmental interest/least restrictive-means analysis, [ ] and cases granting access have recognized as legitimate grounds for closure interests that fall far short of those traditionally thought to be "compelling" [ ].

The presence of a legitimate reason for closure in this case requires an affirmance. The constitutionally-grounded fair trial interests of the accused if he is bound over for trial, and the reputational interests of the accused if he is not, provide a substantial reason for delaying access to the transcript for at least the short time before trial. By taking its own verbal formulation seriously, the Court reverses—without comment or explanation or any attempt at reconciliation—the holding in *Gannett* that a "reasonable probability of prejudice" is enough to overcome the First Amendment right of access to a preliminary proceeding. It is unfortunate that the Court neglects this opportunity to fit the result in this case into the body of precedent dealing with access rights generally. I fear that today's decision will simply further unsettle the law in this area.

I respectfully dissent.

NOTES AND QUESTIONS

1. What is the status of *Gannett* after this case?

2. Does this sequence concerning access to the courtroom suggest any doubt about the cases denying access to prisons and jails?

3. Is the balancing analysis prescribed by this case the same as that set out in *Press-Enterprise I?* In *Globe Newspaper?* Is Chief Justice Burger suggesting that some different analysis might be appropriate if the interest asserted is something other than the defendant's right to a fair trial?

4. The importance of the preliminary hearing procedure in California, emphasized by the majority in *Press-Enterprise II,* was diminished

significantly in 1990 by passage of a voter initiative that made the procedure less attractive to defendants and denied them the option in some cases.

5.   In dissent, Justice Stevens noted that many states have reformed their grand jury proceedings to grant defendants procedural rights, such as the right to cross-examine hostile witnesses and to present exculpatory information. Does the public have a right to attend these "reformed" grand jury proceedings because they more closely resemble criminal trials?

"A Tradition of Openness." Note that side-bar and in-chambers conferences are often closed. Is this because they are not characterized by a "tradition of openness"? What role does this requirement play? What about new types of proceedings that have no history of either openness or closure? What if the history is one of closure, but the court believes openness would be beneficial? Most of these questions remain unanswered. It does appear, however, that the requirement is not to be taken too literally. In El Vocero de Puerto Rico v. Puerto Rico, 508 U.S. 147 (1993), the Court struck down a rule closing preliminary hearings unless the defendant requests an open hearing. Puerto Rico pointed out that the tradition of openness cited in *Globe Newspaper* and *Press-Enterprise II* had never existed in Puerto Rico. The Court said what matters is not the experience of any one jurisdiction, but "the established and widespread tradition of open preliminary hearings among the States."

Some courts have even applied the *Press-Enterprise II* analysis in settings that bear little resemblance to courtrooms. The Ninth Circuit held that *Press-Enterprise II* creates a limited right of access to horse roundups on federal land. A photojournalist sought an injunction requiring the Bureau of Land Management to allow her to observe and photograph the gathering of wild horses on BLM property. The district court denied relief, but the court of appeals reversed and remanded "to conduct the analysis that *Press-Enterprise II* requires."

> First, the district court must determine whether the public has a right of access to horse gathers by considering whether [they] have historically been open to the general public and whether public access plays a positive role in the functioning of gathers. Second, if the district court determines that a right of access exists in this case, it must determine whether the BLM has overcome that right by demonstrating an overriding interest that the viewing restrictions are essential to preserve higher values and are narrowly tailored to serve those interests.

The government argued that *Press-Enterprise II* applies only to judicial proceedings in criminal cases, but the court cited numerous other cases applying it to various administrative and civil proceedings. See Leigh v. Salazar, 677 F.3d 892 (9th Cir. 2012).

Few courtroom closures survive the constitutional scrutiny demanded by Supreme Court precedent, even in situations where the reasons for closure seem tenable. In two New York cases, for example, judges closed courtrooms to conceal the identity of undercover drug agents. The New York

Court of Appeals upheld the closing in one case because the officer testified that she regularly operated in a specific area near the courthouse and would return to work that very day. In the other case, the court said the closing was unjustified because the officer's description of the territory he worked was more general ("the Bronx area") and his reasons for requesting closure were "unparticularized impressions of the vicissitudes of undercover narcotics work." See People v. Martinez, 624 N.E.2d 1027 (N.Y. 1993). Are there any types of situations in which closure ought to be presumptively justified?

Lower courts have not always faithfully applied the stringent constitutional standards that govern courtroom closure. In Presley v. Georgia, 558 U.S. 209 (2010), a defendant fought all the way to the Supreme Court to have his right to a public trial upheld in a per curiam decision, even though the Supreme Court had clearly recognized the right for a quarter of a century. In *Presley*, a trial court ordered courtroom closure during voir dire of prospective jurors, explaining that "it's up to the individual judge to decide what's comfortable." The defendant's uncle was the only member of the public who wished to be present during *voir dire* in the case, and the judge ejected him not only from the courtroom but from the whole sixth floor of the courthouse because prospective jurors might be in the hallway.

The judge did not articulate any "overriding interest" in closure beyond a generic risk that the uncle might sit near prospective jurors, nor did he consider alternatives to closure. Nonetheless, the Georgia Court of Appeals and the Georgia Supreme Court upheld closure. The Georgia Supreme Court found that "the trial court certainly had an overriding interest in ensuring that potential jurors heard no inherently prejudicial remarks from observers during voir dire," and held that the trial court was not required *sua sponte* to consider alternatives to closure, such as holding the voir dire in a bigger courtroom so that the public and prospective jurors need not be seated together.

The U.S. Supreme Court reversed, holding that a criminal defendant's "Sixth Amendment right to a public trial extends to the voir dire of prospective jurors." The Court reminded lower courts that the high burden of justifying closure lies with the trial court and not with the criminal defendant: "Trial courts are obligated to take every reasonable measure to accommodate public attendance at criminal trials." Given that few litigants have the persistence or resources to appeal their cases all the way to the U.S. Supreme Court, what signal does *Presley* send to a trial judge who wishes to order closure of a criminal proceeding? See Daniel Levitas, Scaling Waller: How Courts Have Eroded the Sixth Amendment Public Trial Right, 59 Emory L.J. 493 (2009) (observing that appellate courts have upheld courtroom closures even when trial courts have not applied the appropriate constitutional standards to justify closure nor made the requisite findings prior to closure).

c.   TERRORISM CASES

After September 11, 2001, the government claimed a need to conduct numerous criminal proceedings in secret. The government not only sought to exclude the press and public from courtrooms, but in some cases held suspects incommunicado and kept secret the fact that they had been arrested.

In one case an Algerian named Mohamed Kamel Bellahouel, who had come to the U.S. as a student, married an American citizen, and overstayed his visa, was imprisoned in Miami because he had apparently been seen with three of the September 11 hijackers. He filed a petition for habeas corpus in federal district court. For more than a year, there was no public record that the case even existed—all pleadings were sealed, every hearing was conducted in a closed courtroom, and no mention of the case was made on any docket. After eighteen months, a local reporter discovered the existence of the case when a clerk at the Eleventh Circuit inadvertently allowed Bellahouel's name to appear briefly on the court's argument calendar. The case remained sealed even after the reporter published a story about it. When Bellahouel petitioned the Supreme Court for certiorari, the case was docketed as "M.K.B. v. Warden," large portions of the petition for review were redacted from the public record, and the lower courts were not identified. A coalition of twenty-three media and public interest groups moved to intervene in the Supreme Court proceeding to protest the secrecy, but their motion was denied. The Court denied Bellahouel's petition for certiorari. 540 U.S. 1213 (2004).

If the Constitution permits a person to be held incommunicado without charges, counsel, or a hearing, is it plausible to argue that a tradition of openness compels media access? Will the outcome of access challenges depend on the resolution of issues as to the rights of the detainees? Note that the Supreme Court has held that neither U.S. citizens nor aliens can be denied the right of habeas corpus even if they are "enemy combatants," and that citizens, at least, have a due process right to contest their detention. See Hamdi v. Rumsfeld, 542 U.S. 507 (2004), and Rasul v. Bush, 542 U.S. 466 (2004). The Court also held that the special military commissions set up to try the Guantanamo detainees lacked requisite congressional authorization or authorization under the laws of war. Hamdan v. Rumsfeld, 548 U.S. 557 (2006). In response to the decision, Congress passed the Military Commissions Act of 2006. The stated purpose of the Act was "[t]o authorize trial by military commission for violations of the law of war, and for other purposes." In Boumediene v. Bush, 553 U.S. 723 (2008), the Supreme Court declared the Act's suspension of habeas corpus unconstitutional. The Court ruled that detainees at Guantanamo Bay were entitled to individual hearings in federal court to determine if they met the criteria for detention as terrorists. The first to appear in federal court after the decision was Ahmed Khalfan Ghailani, who was charged with participating in a conspiracy that included the 1998 bombings of the United States embassies in Kenya and Tanzania. At trial, he was acquitted on 279 of 280 charges, partly because some of the evidence against him was excluded because it was obtained through torture. The outcome of the case fueled further debate about whether terrorists should be tried in civilian courts. Max Fishers, Lessons of a Nearly-Lost Terrorist Trial, The Atlantic Wire, Nov. 18, 2010, available at http://www.thewire.com/politics/2010/11/lessons-of-nearly-lost-terrorist-trial/22219/.

The Moussaoui Case. The case of the only person charged in U.S. courts as an actual participant in the September 11 attacks proceeded almost entirely in secret for 20 months. Even the defendant's own pro se pleadings were placed under seal. Eventually the Fourth Circuit ordered the government to review the entire file and make public nonclassified material that could be released without prejudice to national security or foreign relations concerns. United States v. Moussaoui (4th Cir. 2003) (unpublished opinion). Only then did the public learn that Zacarias Moussaoui's defense was that he had nothing to do with the attacks and could not have been scheduled to be among the hijackers, as the government contended, because he was scheduled to participate in later attacks outside the U.S., and that he was seeking the testimony of other captured Al Qaeda operatives who he claimed could confirm that he was not a participant. See Jerry Markon, Moussaoui Says He Was to Aid Later Attack, Wash. Post, May 14, 2003. Much of the file remained sealed, however, and the documents released were often heavily redacted.

The district judge ruled—in secret—that Moussaoui was entitled to take the deposition of one captured Al Qaeda suspect because there was a strong possibility that the witness would provide "material favorable testimony on the defendant's behalf—both as to guilt and potential punishment." In 2006 Moussaoui was sentenced to life in prison. One of the rare open proceedings in the case occurred when the government's appeal of that order was argued in the Fourth Circuit. The court bifurcated the argument, opening to the press and public only the portion relating to the court's jurisdiction, the government's separation of powers arguments, and the scope of the court's power to compel testimony. The court also ordered release of a redacted version of the transcript of the secret portion of the argument. When it acted on this appeal, the Fourth Circuit did not reach the merits, holding that the appeal was premature until the district court attempted to require the government to give Moussaoui access to the witness and the government refused. See United States v. Moussaoui, 333 F.3d 509 (4th Cir. 2003).

Moussaoui eventually pleaded guilty. During the trial to determine his sentence, media representatives filed a writ of mandamus to compel the judge to provide transcripts of bench conferences and same-day access to documentary exhibits. The U.S. Court of Appeals for the Fourth Circuit denied access to exhibits not yet published to the jury or "concealed from the public for reasons of national security," but required access to exhibits "fully published to the jury." The court found no First

Amendment or common law right to contemporaneous access to bench conferences or transcripts of them before the end of trial. In re Associated Press, 2006 WL 752044, 172 Fed. Appx. 1 (4th Cir. 2006).

Another access issue in the *Moussaoui* case was whether the trial court should release the audiotape of the "Cockpit Voice Recorder" of Flight 93, one of the airplanes highjacked by terrorists on September 11, 2001. The prosecution entered the audiotape into evidence during the sentencing phase of the *Moussaoui* trial. At the request of the government and survivors of the victims, the trial court held "that the privacy rights of the victims and the concerns of family members about public disclosure of the audiotape outweigh any right of the public to have access to the recordings" but ordered the release of a written transcript. United States v. Moussaoui (E.D. Va. 2006).

Portions of the first trials of persons captured in Afghanistan were closed, but most of the proceedings, which were conducted by military tribunals at Guantanamo Bay, Cuba, in 2004, were open to the press on condition that the reporters agree to a five-page list of ground rules that included a promise not to publish anything that the presiding officer decided should be kept secret.

Secret Dockets. The practice of maintaining dual docketing systems, one public and one sealed, is not limited to terrorism cases and is allegedly widespread in both state and federal courts. See, e.g., Tony Mauro, Judicial Conference Urges End to "Secret" Dockets, Nat'l L.J., Mar. 19, 2007, at 3.

The practice persists despite decisions holding it unconstitutional. The Second Circuit held that an extensive secret docketing system used in Connecticut state courts for many years violated the First Amendment. See Hartford Courant Co. v. Pellegrino, 380 F.3d 83 (2d Cir.2004). The newspaper alleged that thousands of cases were routinely sealed, concealing among other cases divorce proceedings involving public figures such as General Electric chairman Jack Welch. The Second Circuit noted that "docket sheets provide a kind of index to judicial proceedings and documents, and endow the public and press with the capacity to exercise their rights guaranteed by the First Amendment." Because it was not clear whether the court administrators named in the newspaper's suit had authority to open the files, the court remanded the case to determine whether the practice of sealing was purely administrative or was mandated by judicial order. See also United States v. Valenti, 987 F.2d 708 (11th Cir. 1993) (holding secret dockets unconstitutional).

The Judicial Conference of the United States in 2009 adopted a policy that would require federal district courts to reveal the existence of sealed cases by including on their online lists of cases at least a docket number and a name, such as "Sealed v. Sealed," for every case filed. Earlier, the Judicial Conference had advised courts that they should end the practice of saying "no such case exists" when asked about sealed cases. The recommendations of the Judicial Conference are non-binding but are usually incorporated into local court rules. See Federal Courts Back Off Super-Sealing, The News Media and the Law, Spring 2009, at 31.

For analytical purposes, we sometimes separate matters that are possibly inseparable. In this chapter we have seen closed judicial proceedings and attempts to keep secret their very existence. In Chapter Ten we observed denial of access to certain public records, increased classification of information, and attempts to prevent disclosure of even nonclassified information. In Chapter Nine we saw attempts to prevent information from being leaked by compelling reporters to identify the leakers. From the government's point of view, these are all part of the same effort to combat terrorism and govern effectively. What is their aggregate effect on open government?

2. CIVIL TRIALS

The Supreme Court has not decided whether there is a constitutional right of access to civil trials, but lower courts have assumed that the First Amendment right to attend civil trials is at least as strong as the right to attend criminal trials. The leading case recognizing a qualified First Amendment right of access to civil trials is Publicker Industries, Inc. v. Cohen, 733 F.2d 1059 (3d Cir. 1984). Other federal courts agree that the logic of *Richmond Newspapers* applies and that a First Amendment right of access to civil trials exists. See, e.g., Westmoreland v. CBS, 752 F.2d 16 (2d Cir. 1984); Rushford v. New Yorker Magazine, 846 F.2d 249 (4th Cir. 1988); Brown & Williamson Tobacco Corp. v. Federal Trade Commission, 710 F.2d 1165 (6th Cir. 1983); In re Continental Illinois Securities Litigation, 732 F.2d 1302 (7th Cir. 1984); Newman v. Graddick, 696 F.2d 796 (11th Cir. 1983).

The California Supreme Court held unanimously that the precedents established in criminal cases from *Richmond Newspapers* through *Press-Enterprise II* are generally applicable to civil cases as well. Concluding that the U.S. Supreme Court would recognize a First Amendment right of access to civil proceedings, the court interpreted the California open court statute to require that before substantive civil proceedings can be closed or transcripts sealed, the judge must give public notice of the proposed closure and

> must hold a hearing and expressly find that (i) there exists an overriding interest supporting closure and/or sealing; (ii) there is a substantial probability that the interest will be prejudiced absent closure and/or sealing; (iii) the proposed closure and/or sealing is narrowly tailored to serve the overriding interest; and (iv) there is no less restrictive means of achieving the overriding interest.

NBC Subsidiary (KNBC-TV), Inc. v. Superior Court, 980 P.2d 337 (Cal. 1999). The case involved the trial of various claims by Sondra Locke against Clint Eastwood. The trial judge had excluded the media and public from the courtroom during all proceedings that were conducted outside the presence of the jury, and he refused to provide transcripts of those proceedings until the end of the trial. He said these steps were necessary to prevent jurors from being prejudiced by inadmissible matters in the highly publicized dispute arising out of business dealings between the two actors. The judge rejected media arguments that they had a First Amendment right of access to the proceedings and transcripts. But the California Supreme Court said "the public has an interest, in all civil cases, in observing and assessing the performance of its public judicial system, and that interest strongly supports a general right of access in ordinary civil cases."

Immigration Hearings. Deportation hearings and other cases involving immigration laws are administrative proceedings handled in special courts. After September 11, hundreds of aliens were taken into custody. Then-Attorney General Ashcroft issued additional "security procedures" for the handling of these cases in U.S. Immigration Courts. On September 21, 2001, Chief Immigration Judge Michael Creppy issued an order closing all hearings in cases deemed by the INS to be of "special interest" because of their possible connection to terrorism. Persons detained in such cases were to see "no visitors, no family, no press," and Immigration Court officials were ordered to avoid "disclosing any information" about a case, including even whether a particular case existed on the docket, to anyone outside the Immigration Court. Memorandum from Michael Creppy to All Immigration Judges [and] Court Administrators re: Cases Requiring Special Procedures (Sept. 21, 2001). Immigration judges began opening some proceedings on a case-by-case basis after a few weeks, but many remained closed.

The chief judge's secrecy order was challenged by media groups in Michigan and New Jersey. The district courts held the order unconstitutional in both cases and enjoined its enforcement, but on appeal the circuit courts split. In the Michigan case, the Sixth Circuit held that even though immigration hearings are administrative proceedings conducted by the executive branch, they "exhibit substantial quasi-judicial characteristics" and therefore are properly analyzed under *Richmond Newspapers* rather than *Houchins*. The court held that deportation hearings traditionally have been open, and that openness "undoubtedly plays a significant positive role in this process." It held that media had a First Amendment right of access that could be defeated only if the closure could survive the form of strict scrutiny specified in *Globe Newspaper*] and *Press-Enterprise II*.

The Sixth Circuit accepted the government's argument that it had a compelling interest in preventing disclosure of even bits and pieces of information about suspected terrorist activities. But it held the directive unconstitutional because the hearing in question had been closed without specific findings of a need to do so, and because case-by-case determination offered a narrowly tailored alternative to Creppy's blanket secrecy order. Detroit Free Press v. Ashcroft, 303 F.3d 681 (6th Cir. 2002).

The Third Circuit rejected this reasoning in the New Jersey case. It agreed that *Richmond Newspapers* provided the correct framework for analysis, but held that neither the history prong of that test nor the logic prong supported the claim of a First Amendment right of access to deportation hearings. North Jersey Media Group, Inc. v. Ashcroft, 308 F.3d 198 (3d Cir. 2002).

Despite evidence that Congress had made deportation hearings presumptively open since the end of the nineteenth century, and that Justice Department regulations had made them generally open since 1964, the Third Circuit said "the tradition of open deportation hearings is too recent and inconsistent to support a First Amendment right of access." The court acknowledged that its own precedent recognized such a right even in the absence of a history of openness at common law, but said those should be limited to the criminal context.

Analyzing the other prong of the test, the Third Circuit said access would advance the general goals of openness, but expressed skepticism about the usefulness of that argument. The court said it found no case in which the logic test operated to *deny* access. Whenever courts find the history prong satisfied, the court said, they usually find also that logic supports openness.

The court said this analysis should include not only the benefits of openness, but also the disadvantages. In this case, the benefits were outweighed by the risks to national security that open hearings might pose. The court cited an FBI official's assertions that even minor pieces of apparently innocuous information, such as name and address of a subject and time and place of arrest, "might allow a terrorist organization to build a picture of the investigation." Information revealed by open hearings might allow terrorists to see which methods of illegal entry into the United States work and which do not, determine what the government does and does not know about terrorist activities, and allow them to shift activities to as-yet-undiscovered terror cells. The court admitted that these were speculative, but said the logic prong of the *Richmond Newspapers* test is unavoidably speculative because it focuses on what the effects of openness will be.

Because the court held that there was no First Amendment right of access to the hearings, it saw no need to decide whether case-by-case adjudication offered a narrowly tailored alternative. A dissenting judge argued that both history and logic supported a First Amendment right of access, and that "national security interests can be accommodated on a case-by-case basis."

3. JUVENILE PROCEEDINGS

Delinquency Proceedings. These are often closed, either by statute or at the discretion of the judge. The original theory was that publicity was likely to interfere with the rehabilitation of the offender. In recent years, however, there has been increasing skepticism about the rationale for treating juveniles differently from adults, at least when they are charged with serious crimes. Some states allow judges to open juvenile proceedings at their discretion, and others allow juveniles charged with serious offenses to be transferred to the adult criminal justice system, where they enjoy no special secrecy provisions. See, e.g., State ex rel. St. Louis Post-Dispatch LLC v. Garvey, 179 S.W.3d 899 (Mo. 2005) (holding that a statute excluding the public from juvenile proceeding does not apply where a juvenile is charged with conduct that would be a serious felony if he were tried as an adult).

Before the decisions in *Globe Newspaper* and *Press-Enterprise II,* there seemed to be little doubt that closure of juvenile proceedings was constitutional. Even if the First Amendment created a qualified right to attend such proceedings, the state was likely to be found to have compelling interests in closure:

> Publication of the youth's name could impair the rehabilitative goals of the juvenile justice system. Confidential proceedings protect the delinquent from the stigma of conduct which may be outgrown and avoids the possibility that the adult is penalized for what he used to be, or worse yet, the possibility that the stigma becomes self-perpetuating, thereby making change and growth impossible. Publication of a delinquent's name may handicap his prospects for adjustment into society, for acceptance by the public, or it may cause him to lose employment opportunities. Public proceedings could so embarrass the youth's family that they withhold their support in rehabilitative efforts. . . . Publicity sometimes serves as a reward for the hardcore juvenile delinquent, thereby encouraging him to commit further antisocial acts to attract attention. [ ] Further, the legislative goals of expunging the juvenile's delinquency record are vitiated if the same information could at any subsequent time be obtained freely from newspaper morgues.

In re J.S., 438 A.2d 1125, 1129 (Vt. 1981). This view still commands substantial judicial support. Without actually deciding the matter, the First Circuit expressed doubt that the standards established by *Globe Newspaper* and *Press-Enterprise II* are applicable to juvenile proceedings. It said the assumption that "the First Amendment right of public access does apply to some degree to juvenile proceedings [is] a highly dubious assumption, particularly in light of the long, entrenched, and well-founded tradition of confidentiality regarding juvenile proceedings and the compelling rehabilitative purposes behind this tradition." Nevertheless, the court refused to hold that the federal Juvenile Delinquency Act requires closure of juvenile hearings even though it states that "neither the name nor picture of any juvenile shall be made public in connection with a juvenile delinquency proceeding. . . ." The court said "the Act does not mandate across-the-board closure for all juvenile proceedings, but merely authorizes closure, or any other measures designed to ensure confidentiality, to be determined on a case-by-case basis." Public dissemination of the juveniles' pictures could be prevented by banning cameras from the proceedings and their names could be kept secret by identifying them only through initials or pseudonyms. The court asserted that "this interpretation fully comports with the purpose and language of the statute as a whole, and is far preferable to a strained construction of the Act that mandates complete closure and thus triggers First Amendment concerns." See United States v. Three Juveniles, 61 F.3d 86 (1st Cir. 1995).

Similarly, state law is often interpreted to at least give the judge discretion to open the proceeding. In Wideman v. Garbarino, 770 P.2d 320 (Ariz. 1989), for example, a state constitutional provision requiring that preliminary examining trials for juveniles be held "in chambers" was interpreted to give the juvenile judge discretion to admit news media. In Associated Press v. Bradshaw, 410 N.W.2d 577 (S.D. 1987), the court held that a statute providing that the juvenile judge "may" admit news media representatives created a qualified right of access that could not be denied "unless specific supportive findings are made which demonstrate that closure is essential to preserve higher values and the order must be narrowly tailored to serve that interest."

As the statute mentioned above suggests, courtrooms are one place where the press often enjoys access on more favorable terms than the general public. In trials of unusual public interest, specific seats or sections of the courtroom often are reserved for the press, and occasionally closed circuit television is arranged for additional press representatives who cannot be admitted to the courtroom. Recall that Chief Justice Burger in a footnote in his *Richmond Newspapers* opinion characterized such preferential arrangements as "reasonable restrictions on general access."

Custody Proceedings. Among the types of proceedings that traditionally have not been open are child custody hearings. Closure occasionally is challenged when prominent people are involved. In a case involving the child actor Macaulay Culkin and his siblings, the court reversed a trial judge's decision to open the courtroom. See P.B. v. C.C., 223 A.D.2d 294 (N.Y. App. Div. 1996). A 4–1 majority, concluding that the controlling statutory consideration was "the best interest of the children," focused on the fact that of the six minor children, only two had achieved any degree of fame. Reports on the case had already involved allegations of alcohol and drug abuse and domestic violence. Affidavits suggested that most children "use denial as a healthy defense to an acrimonious separation, and that intense media scrutiny would likely cause a child to revert to more destructive alternative defenses." Also, the children had already been "subjected to derision and embarrassment by their peers, and have suffered educational and emotional difficulties as a result of this spectacle."

An added concern was that, although it was not possible to know in advance what would be elicited at trial, "witnesses at trial might constrain themselves from providing the court with the pertinent details for fear that their testimony might be exploited by the press." Closing the courtroom when this fear presented itself would be too late: "The best efforts of a well-intentioned judge cannot adequately protect against devastating revelations or allegations which may be adduced in the course of rapidly unfolding examination and cross-examination in a hotly contested and acrimonious litigation."

The dissenter thought the presumption in favor of open proceedings had not been overcome.

Conditional Access. Judges sometimes offer reporters admission to otherwise closed proceedings provided they agree not to report certain matters. The Illinois Supreme Court has upheld such a procedure. In two hearings involving children alleged to be the victims of parental abuse, the judge refused to admit reporters unless they signed a pledge not to reveal the identity of the victims. The Illinois Juvenile Court Act gave news media, but not the public, a right to attend such proceedings.

The court rejected the newspaper's argument that both the statute and the First Amendment gave the press a right to report anything it learned in the proceeding. The majority distinguished Oklahoma Publishing Co. v. District Court, which involved delinquency proceedings, on the ground that the state has a stronger interest in protecting the privacy of juvenile victims than alleged delinquents. It distinguished *Smith v. Daily Mail* on the ground that the name of the juvenile there was not obtained from attendance at a proceeding closed to the public. Two dissenting justices found the distinctions unpersuasive and viewed the condition imposed by the trial judge as an impermissible prior restraint. See In re a Minor, 595 N.E.2d 1052 (Ill. 1992).

Should this be analyzed under principles applicable to courtroom access generally, prior restraint, or unconstitutional conditions? Or is it merely a question of the scope of preferential media treatment?

4. COURTROOM PHOTOGRAPHY AND BROADCASTING

In all of the preceding material in this chapter, the assumption has been that the media seek access only for pen-and-paper reporting. When they seek to photograph or broadcast courtroom proceedings, the access question usually is treated quite differently.

Judicial hostility to courtroom photography traces back more than half a century. In the aftermath of the Lindbergh kidnapping case in which media excitedly covered the trial of a man convicted of kidnapping the famous aviator's one-year-old son, the American Bar Association adopted Canon 35 in 1937. Together with amendments in 1952 and 1963, this ethical stricture bans radio and television broadcasting and still cameras from courtrooms. In 1979 an ABA committee proposed that Canon 3A(7), the successor to Canon 35, be amended to allow televising of trials at the judge's discretion. The ABA rejected the recommendation, but many states eventually adopted it.

In Estes v. Texas, 381 U.S. 532 (1965), the defendant had been indicted in the Texas state courts for "swindling"—inducing farmers to buy nonexistent fertilizer tanks and then to deliver to him mortgages on the property. The nature of the charges, and the large sums of money involved, attracted nationwide interest. Texas was one of two states that then permitted televised trials. Over defendant's objection, the trial judge permitted televising a two-day hearing before trial. Estes was convicted.

The Supreme Court, 5–4, reversed the conviction. In his majority opinion, Justice Clark concluded that the use of television involved "such a probability that prejudice will result that it is deemed inherently lacking in due process" even without any showing of specific prejudice. He was concerned about the impact on jurors, judges, parties, witnesses, and lawyers.

Justice Harlan, who provided the crucial fifth vote for reversal, joined the majority opinion only to the extent that it applied to televised coverage of "courtroom proceedings of a criminal trial of widespread public interest," "a criminal trial of great notoriety," and "a heavily publicized and highly sensational affair." In such cases he worried about the impact on jurors.

In Chandler v. Florida, 449 U.S. 560 (1981), the Court unanimously rejected the view that televising a criminal trial over the objections of the defendant automatically rendered the trial unfair. The defendants had argued that the impact of television on the participants introduced potentially prejudicial but unidentifiable aspects into the trial. The majority, in an opinion by Chief Justice Burger, first concluded that Estes did not stand for the proposition that broadcasting was barred "in all cases and under all circumstances." Because of Justice Harlan's narrow basis for concurring in that case, the ruling in Estes should apply only to cases of widespread interest. (On this point, two Justices insisted that *Chandler* overruled *Estes* and should say so.)

The majority said the risk of prejudice from press coverage of a trial was not limited to broadcasting. "The risk of juror prejudice in some cases does not justify an absolute ban on news coverage of trials by the printed media; so also the risk of such prejudice does not warrant an absolute constitutional ban on all broadcast coverage." A case attracts attention because of its intrinsic interest to the public. The "appropriate safeguard" against prejudice in such cases "is the defendant's right to demonstrate that the media's coverage of his case—be it printed or broadcast— compromised the ability of the particular jury that heard the case to adjudicate fairly." The Court also observed that the changes in technology since *Estes* supported the state's argument that it should now be permitted to allow television in the courtroom. Because the defendants in *Chandler*—two former city policemen accused of burglarizing a restaurant—showed no adverse impact from the televising, the convictions were upheld.

State Courts. When *Estes* was decided, most states forbade courtroom photography. Now virtually all permit it under some circumstances. In most states assent of the trial judge is required; in some a criminal defendant has the power to prevent it. Some distinguish between still photography and television, permitting the former but not the latter.

The advent of the Court TV cable network, a channel that later became TruTV, demonstrated the popularity of televised trial proceedings. That popularity reached a peak with the 1995 murder trial of former football star O.J. Simpson, which millions of viewers watched avidly. But that case also touched off something of a backlash against televised trials. Many thought the televising of that trial influenced the behavior of the judge and lawyers, made celebrities of even minor witnesses, and turned the trial into an entertainment spectacle. California had permitted broadcast coverage of all state court proceedings since 1984, but after the Simpson trial the governor and a majority of the state's judges called for a ban on television coverage of trials. The California Judicial Council rejected the proposals for a complete ban, but adopted rules forbidding televising of jury selection, bench conferences, spectators, and conversations between counsel and clients or witnesses. Guidelines require judges to consider the security and dignity of the court, privacy rights of participants, and potential impact on jurors before authorizing coverage. Judges need not give reasons for denying or authorizing coverage. See Maura Dolan, State Panel Puts Partial Ban on Court Cameras, L.A. Times, May 18, 1996. California's reaction was not universal, however. In many states judges continued to allow broadcasting, and in some the rights of the electronic media to cover trials were expanded. Court TV claimed that it televised

33 trials during the nine months of the Simpson trial without any complaint from the judges involved.

The New York Court of Appeals held that New York's statutory ban on cameras in the courtroom does not violate freedom of the press under either the state or federal constitutions. Courtroom Television Network v. State, 833 N.E.2d 1197 (N.Y. 2005). The court reasoned that the ban on cameras restricted only "what means can be used in order to gather news" rather than the "openness of court proceedings." Although the court denied that strict scrutiny of the ban was warranted, it stated that "the statute is narrowly tailored to serve the governmental interests at issue, namely insuring that criminal defendants receive fair trials, that witnesses are forthcoming in their testimony, that the trial court has control of the courtroom and that the integrity of the trial is maintained." The court declined to "circumscribe the authority constitutionally delegated to the Legislature to determine whether audio-visual coverage of courtroom proceedings is in the best interest of the citizens of the state." Cf. Morris Communications v. Griffin, 620 S.E.2d 800 (Ga. 2005) (reversing a trial court's denial of a newspaper's request to take still photos at a murder trial, where the trial court had articulated no ground for exclusion).

Federal Courts. There is still substantial resistance to televising trials in the federal courts. In criminal proceedings, the use of cameras is prohibited altogether. Rule 53 of the Federal Rules of Criminal Procedure provides, "The taking of photographs in the court room during the progress of judicial proceedings . . . shall not be permitted." This rule is enforced even when a criminal defendant wishes to have the proceedings broadcast. See United States v. Hastings, 695 F.2d 1278 (11th Cir. 1983). The defendant, a federal judge charged with bribery, and numerous media intervenors argued that the defendant had a right under the First and Sixth Amendments to have the trial videotaped for broadcast. But the court held that despite the defendant's assent, the prohibition was justified by other interests, such as maintenance of decorum and prevention of any appearance of unfairness that might result.

Federal guidelines allow judges to use electronic sound recording equipment to record proceedings in district courts and authorize the sale of tapes made by this equipment to the public. In a case involving the bombing of the Alfred P. Murrah federal building in Oklahoma City, which killed 168 people, District Judge Richard Matsch designated a court reporter to use mechanical stenography to make the official record but also decided to use sound recording equipment as a backup. Speakers connected with the sound system in the courtroom were also placed in an adjacent courtroom to enable the public and members of the press who could not find seating in the courtroom to listen to the proceedings.

During an April 1996 hearing, tapes were taken from the courtroom while the hearing was still being conducted and were sold to members of the press as they were completed. Shortly after the hearing, members of the press requested that the sound feed from the adjacent courtroom be extended into a nearby press room so that they could make their own recordings. Both the government and defendant Nichols argued that the court should stop the sale of audio tapes and deny an extension of the sound feed. The judge granted both requests, noting that "the ready access to the sound recordings has resulted in the functional equivalent of a broadcast of the court proceedings in violation of Rule 53." He noted that the sound recording system was not being used to make the official record; if it were, production and sale of audio tapes would be required to provide access to the official record. United States v. McVeigh, 931 F. Supp. 753 (D. Colo. 1996). The Court of Appeals rejected a media challenge to this ruling. See 119 F.3d 806 (10th Cir. 1997).

In civil proceedings, the question of access by cameras is controlled by the local rules in each district. The Judicial Conference of the United States once urged district courts to ban all broadcasting. In 2010 the Conference agreed to a pilot program to televise some trials as long as the faces of witnesses and jurors are concealed. U.S. Judges Agree to Pilot Study of Cameras in Court, Associated Press, Sept. 15, 2010. An earlier pilot program in the 1990s had authorized six district courts and two courts of appeals to experiment with courtroom photography in civil cases. That program seemed to go smoothly, but when it expired at the end of 1994, the twenty-seven judges in the Judicial Conference voted down a proposal to make it permanent by a margin of about 2–1. Some of the judges were said to have been influenced by the fact that most of the broadcast images were merely used as background for a reporter's commentary and did not let viewers actually see any significant portion of the proceedings for themselves. See Linda Greenhouse, U.S. Judges Vote Down TV in Courts, N.Y. Times Sept. 21, 1994.

Judges sometimes express fear that unless broadcasting is banned completely, judges, criminal defendants, or parties in civil litigation will be unable to resist pressure from media to consent to it against their better judgment. As to judges, does the strength of this argument depend on whether they are elected? As to parties, is there any more reason to spare them this decision than other difficult tactical choices (such as the decision to publicly air the dispute by litigating)?

Sketching. In states in which cameras are banned, and in the federal courts, television news directors have resorted to using artists who sketch courtroom scenes. Sweeping bans against the practice have been rejected. United States v. Columbia Broadcasting System, Inc., 497 F.2d 102 (5th Cir. 1974). Another case invalidated a restriction on sketching even when it was aimed at preventing jurors from being publicly identified. The judge had told prospective jurors he would attempt to keep their identities concealed. When he saw artists sketching, he ordered them to submit their sketches to him for review. Analyzing the matter as a prior restraint, the Arizona Supreme Court invalidated the order on First Amendment grounds. The record did not show sufficient support for a prior restraint. Of the one hundred fifty jurors questioned, "several" expressed fear of being identified but none of these was on the final panel. Using the three-part approach of the *Nebraska Press* case, the court concluded that the danger was not significant or imminent enough to justify the censorship; less restrictive measures (e.g., voir dire) would have sufficed; and the sketch order was likely to have very limited success in meeting the judge's concern. See KPNX Broadcasting Co. v. Superior Court, 678 P.2d 431 (Ariz. 1984).

Appellate Proceedings. Restrictions on photography and broadcasting rest in part on concerns about possible adverse effects on witnesses and jurors. These worries obviously have no application to appellate proceedings, and there has been some tendency to open these to cameras. Each U.S. court of appeals is now free to decide for itself whether to allow photography and broadcasting of appellate arguments in civil cases. The Ninth Circuit announced that it would entertain requests for electronic coverage of all appellate proceedings except direct criminal appeals and extradition proceedings. Requests must be made seven days in advance, counsel may object, and coverage is to be permitted only if the panel unanimously agrees. The panel has the power to refuse, limit, or terminate coverage to protect the rights of parties or the dignity of the court.

The Supreme Court posts audio recordings of oral arguments on its website at the end of each week's arguments, but reporters are not allowed to carry cameras or audio recording equipment into the courtroom. Supreme Court to Post Audio of Every Argument Online, Associated Press, Sept. 29, 2010.

Some courts routinely make available audio recordings of oral arguments. The Texas Supreme Court posts links to audio recordings of arguments within a few hours of oral argument in most cases. See http://www.supreme.courts.state.tx.us/oralarguments/audio.

B. ACCESS TO JURORS AND WITNESSES

These cases raise two distinct sets of questions. One is whether the media have any right of access to jurors or witnesses. The other is whether jurors or witnesses have a right to speak to the media. Because restrictions are more often challenged by the media than by jurors or witnesses, most of the cases speak (directly, at least) only to the first question. The Supreme Court decisions we encountered in the previous section are the cases cited most frequently in these cases.

A different set of precedents might be relevant if the issue were the First Amendment rights of witnesses and jurors. We saw in *Gentile v.*

State Bar that attorneys do not forfeit their First Amendment rights when they participate in judicial proceedings. Because the participation of jurors and witnesses is usually involuntary, one might suppose that their right to speak would be protected at least as fully as that of lawyers. The only Supreme Court case addressing the question is Butterworth v. Smith, 494 U.S. 624 (1990), which held that a reporter's First Amendment right to disclose what he knew about a matter under investigation by a grand jury did not vanish when he was called before the grand jury as a witness. Does that decision support a juror's right to disclose what transpired during deliberations? If a witness or a juror invokes a First Amendment right to disclose, should the issue be analyzed under Gentile v. State Bar, Nebraska Press Association v. Stuart, or some other framework?

Identifying Jurors. Jurors' identities have traditionally been public, and under the *Richmond Newspapers* series of cases attempts to keep them secret generally have been unsuccessful, at least as to those actually selected as jurors.

The Third Circuit held that the public has a presumptive constitutional right of access to the names of jurors and prospective jurors prior to the empanelment of the jury. In that case, the district judge had attempted to empanel an anonymous jury and to conduct voir dire exclusively through questionnaires until the pool of prospective jurors was reduced to forty; the judge had made no specific findings on the record to justify these actions. United States v. Wecht, 537 F.3d 222 (3d Cir. 2008).

The Seventh Circuit likewise questioned a district court's plan to keep juror names secret until they reached a verdict in the high profile criminal trial of former Illinois governor Rod Blagojevich. United States v. Blagojevich, 612 F.3d 558 (7th Cir. 2010). The court asserted: "Neither the Supreme Court nor this circuit has decided under what circumstances, and after what procedures, jurors' names may be kept confidential until the trial's end." The court nonetheless found the pre-trial release of the names potentially appropriate based upon the federal "common-law right of access by the public to information that affects the resolution of federal suits" and the Jury Selection and Service Act, 28 U.S. § 1861. The Act states that juror names are to be made available after jurors are sworn in absent a determination that the "interests of justice" require confidentiality. Because the trial judge had neither held a hearing nor made findings on the record, the court held that empaneling an anonymous jury was impermissible under the circumstances. The court subsequently amended its original decision to clarify that a trial judge "must find some unusual risk to justify keeping juror's names confidential; it is not enough to point to possibilities that are present in every criminal prosecution." 612 F.3d 558 (7th Cir. 2010). Shortly thereafter, the trial court conducted the Seventh Circuit-mandated hearing and again refused to release the jurors' names based in part on privacy concerns and the risk of outside interference. 743 F. Supp. 2d 794 (N.D. Ill. 2010).

The Fourth Circuit held that the trial judge may not be required to release names and addresses of members of the venire before the jury is selected and seated, but once that occurs the names of both those seated and those not chosen become part of the public record of the case. "If the district court thinks the dangers of a highly publicized trial are too great, it may always sequester the jury; and change of venue is always possible as a method of obviating pressure or prejudice." In re Baltimore Sun Co., 841 F.2d 74 (4th Cir. 1988).

Even when circumstances justify an anonymous jury, the judge may not prohibit the media from revealing jurors' identities if they learn them from independent newsgathering. In a criminal case against former Louisiana Governor Edwin Edwards and others, the district judge granted the government's motion to empanel an anonymous jury to guard against harassment or intimidation of the jurors. The judge ordered the media "not to attempt to circumvent this Court's ruling preserving the jury's anonymity." The Fifth Circuit noted that the judge had authority to protect the identities of the jurors and to forbid the media from attempting to learn them by obtaining confidential court documents. But insofar as the order attempted to forbid them from attempting to identify the jurors through independent investigation, it could not survive the scrutiny required by Nebraska Press Association v. Stuart. See United States v. Brown, 250 F.3d 907 (5th Cir. 2001).

In trials of suspected Mafia figures where possible retaliation against jurors is feared, or in cases where jurors might be subject to public pressure, judges sometimes keep the names and addresses of jurors secret even from the parties. Is this practice subject to challenge by media on the ground that it denies access to information that historically has been available? How palpable must the risk be before the state's interest in secrecy becomes compelling?

Interviewing Jurors. The other major access problem involving jurors arises from judges' desire to protect jurors from harassment, pressure, or embarrassment in post-verdict interviews. In some jurisdictions, lawyers connected with the case are forbidden from questioning jurors about their deliberations, or are permitted to do so only with court approval. In others, attorneys have uninhibited access to jurors after verdict. In cases of high public interest, reporters often wish to interview jurors for many of the same reasons attorneys do—for example, to learn why they decided as they did.

But judges may be concerned that disclosures about jury deliberations will affect the candor of future jurors. In United States v. Cleveland, 128 F.3d 267 (5th Cir. 1997), after a six-week, high-visibility criminal trial and eight days of deliberation, the trial judge instructed the jurors that they could not be interviewed "concerning the deliberations of the jury" without an order from the court. A media challenge to the order was rejected. The court defined "deliberations of the jury" as referring only to "discussions about the case occurring among jurors within the sanctity of the jury room" and not the juror's "general reactions" to the trial proceedings itself. The order was narrowly tailored to meet a threat to the administration of justice—"namely, the threat presented to freedom of speech within the jury room by the possibility of post-verdict interviews."

It seems clear now that a blanket order banning all contact with jurors by the press cannot survive the scrutiny called for by *Press-Enterprise II*. In Journal Publishing Co. v. Mechem, 801 F.2d 1233 (10th Cir. 1986), at the conclusion of a controversial civil rights trial involving the Albuquerque police chief and several other officers, the judge admonished the jurors as follows:

> You should not discuss your verdict after you leave here with anyone. If anyone tries to talk to you about it, or wants to talk to you about it, let me know. If they wish [to] take the matter up with me, why, they may do so, but otherwise don't discuss it with anyone.

The court of appeals held the order impermissibly overbroad:

> It contained no time or scope limitations and encompassed every possible juror interview situation. It would have been constitutionally permissible for the court routinely to instruct jurors that they may refuse interviews and seek the aid of the court if the interviewers persist after they express a reluctance to speak. [ ] It could have told the jurors not to discuss the specific votes and opinions of noninterviewed jurors in order to encourage free deliberation in the jury room. [ ] But the court could not issue a sweeping restraint forbidding all contact between the press and former jurors without a compelling reason.

Narrower admonitions along the lines of those suggested in the *Mechem* case have been upheld. See, e.g., United States v. Harrelson, 713 F.2d 1114 (5th Cir. 1983). There, the trial judge concluded that one request made after a known refusal to be interviewed was enough to allow and that more—repeated requests—were too many. "We cannot say," the court wrote, "that in so concluding he abused his discretion." A juror who later changed his or her mind was "always free to initiate an interview. The court's order does no more than forbid nagging him into doing so."

However, a judge cannot forbid even repeated requests to jurors for interviews "in the absence of any finding by the court that harassing or intrusive interviews are occurring or are intended." United States v. Antar, 38 F.3d 1348 (3d Cir. 1994).

In the face of reports that tabloids were offering jurors in the O.J. Simpson case money in exchange for their first-person stories, the California legislature enacted a statute defining such payments as jury tampering. The statute made it a misdemeanor to offer or accept such payment prior to or within 90 days after discharge of the jury. Any payment in violation is forfeited to a Victims Restitution Fund. See Cal. Penal Code § 116.5.

Witnesses. Can judges order witnesses not to talk to the media? In Sheppard v. Maxwell, the Court suggested that trial judges had a duty to control the extrajudicial statements of witnesses. On the other hand, Butterworth v. Smith held that a newspaper reporter called as a witness before a grand jury had a First Amendment right to disclose what he knew about a matter under investigation, and that decision does not suggest that nonjournalist witnesses would have any lesser rights. There are few cases addressing the First Amendment rights of witnesses. It is not clear whether their rights should be analyzed by analogy to those of attorneys (see Gentile v. State Bar), those of the media (see Nebraska Press Association v. Stuart), or those of jurors (as described in the preceding section).

The willingness of some media to pay witnesses for information or first-person accounts raises a new set of legal questions. In the O.J. Simpson murder prosecution in 1995, potential witnesses accepted money for telling their stories to television programs. Both the prosecution and the defense expressed concern that the practice would call into question the credibility of witnesses. The prosecution decided not to use a witness whose testimony placed Simpson near the murder scene at about the time of the crime because of fears that her credibility would be impugned by the fact that she had received $5,000 for telling her story to the TV tabloid show Hard Copy.

In response to these incidents, the California legislature passed legislation making it a crime for a person who "reasonably should know" that he or she will be a witness from accepting money for information relating to the case until after final judgment in the case. Violation was punishable by six months in jail and a fine equal to three times the amount of compensation accepted. A companion provision in the civil code authorized prosecutors to seek injunctions against enforcement of contracts to pay witnesses.

A media coalition challenged the legislation and a district judge held it unconstitutional. See California First Amendment Coalition v. Lungren, 1995 WL 482066 (N.D. Cal. Aug. 10, 1995). Citing Simon & Schuster Inc. v. New York State Crime Victims Board, the judge held that the statutes were content-based regulations and therefore were invalid unless they were necessary to serve a compelling state interest and were narrowly drawn to achieve that end. She relied on Cox Broadcasting v. Cohn for the proposition that witnesses' stories are "at the core of protected expression," and on Nebraska Press Association v. Stuart for the proposition that the statutes imposed a prior restraint on witness speech. She said these two propositions should be kept in mind in applying the test from *Simon & Schuster*. She rejected the state's argument that *Gentile* and *Nebraska Press* established that the First Amendment rights of trial participants may be restricted in the interest of fair trial. She said both of those decisions require case-by-case evaluation as opposed to the blanket prohibition of the California legislation.

The judge conceded that the state had a compelling interest in insuring a fair trial and that protecting the credibility of witnesses served that interest. However, she said the statutes were unnecessary to protect this interest because the state had other mechanisms to discourage witness fabrications, such as prohibitions on perjury and bribery of witnesses, witness competency requirements in the law of evidence, the oath procedure, and cross-examination. She described these as "non-speech-restrictive safeguards." The state contended that these devices were inadequate because they cannot prevent juries from discrediting or rejecting the testimony of a witness whom they believe has been influenced by payment. But the judge said this amounted only to an argument that it would be inconvenient to counter the jury's perception of bias. The state's argument, that the interest in protecting a defendant's Sixth Amendment interest in a fair trial was more compelling than the interest in providing victim restitution in the *Simon & Schuster* case, was not persuasive because the legislation failed the narrowly tailored test, not the compelling interest test.

Does *Simon & Schuster* provide the right framework for analysis of this case? Does *Gentile* suggest that restrictions designed to protect fair trials need not be as narrowly drawn as other speech restrictions? Do the alternatives mentioned by the district judge address the credibility issue? Is the possibility that payment of witnesses will affect their credibility a real problem? Is it correct (or necessary) to characterize the legislation as a prior restraint?

The state did not appeal the district court decision. This suit did not challenge the California statute, mentioned in the preceding section, forbidding payments to jurors.

C. ACCESS TO JUDICIAL RECORDS AND DISCOVERY MATERIALS

So far we have dealt primarily with efforts of media representatives to attend judicial proceedings and photograph or broadcast them. Many other disputes arise over access to records rather than proceedings— access to transcripts, exhibits, tapes, indictments, search warrants, sentencing reports, settlements, or discovery documents. These disputes have generated a tremendous amount of litigation, only a sample of which can be mentioned here.

Conflicts over access to records are quite diverse. Access to transcripts of courtroom proceedings is closely related to access to the proceedings themselves and tends to be analyzed similarly. Affidavits in support of search warrants or arrest warrants, sentencing reports, court-ordered psychiatric reports, and laboratory reports all have some of the characteristics of judicial records but may not be part of the actual proceeding. At the other extreme, depositions and documents produced during discovery in civil cases are much further removed from the courtroom; they usually are obtained without judicial supervision and they may never be introduced as evidence. Settlement agreements may be worked out with the active intervention of the judge and filed with the court, or they may be simply contracts between the parties. Not surprisingly, the cases reflect this diversity. In attempting to make sense of the decisions, it may be helpful to think about these questions: What is a "judicial record"? Are there arguments against access to particular records that are not present with respect to proceedings?

1. COMMON LAW ACCESS

Before there was any support for a First Amendment right of access to either judicial proceedings or records, the Supreme Court recognized a common law right of access to records in the federal courts. The case was Nixon v. Warner Communications, Inc., 435 U.S. 589 (1978).

During the trial of Watergate conspirator John Mitchell, copies of White House audio tapes were introduced in evidence. Various broadcasting companies sought permission to copy them, both for news purposes and for purposes of marketing the copies commercially. The tapes had been played in open court and transcripts of them had been released and widely published, but the broadcasters argued that the full significance of the conversations could not be appreciated without hearing the inflections and emphasis of President Nixon and others whose voices were captured on the tapes. Nixon objected to their release, and Judge Sirica denied the networks' requests.

The Supreme Court held that there was no constitutional right of access to the tapes. *Richmond Newspapers* had not yet been decided; relying on *Houchins, Saxbe,* and *Pell* (the prison access cases discussed in Chapter Ten) the Court decided that because the public had no access to the tapes, the press had no First Amendment right of access to them.

But the Court did recognize a common law right of access to judicial records arising from the long-standing practice of allowing inspection of court records by anyone wishing to do so. This was only a qualified right, which normally would have to be balanced against Nixon's property and privacy interests, his claims that the tapes were covered by executive privilege, and his argument that it would be "unseemly" for the court to appear to be facilitating commercial exploitation by making the tapes available.

In this case, however, no such balancing was necessary because Congress had recently passed the Presidential Recordings Act, requiring the White House to turn over the originals of the tapes to the Administrator of General Services for screening and eventual release to the public of those deemed by him to be of historical value. Because of this alternative means of serving the public interest in disclosure, the common law right of access to judicial records did not require Judge Sirica to release the tapes. Four members of the Court dissented. Justices Marshall and Stevens would have ordered the tapes released. Justices White and Brennan would have ordered the judge to turn over copies as well as originals of the tapes to the General Services Administration "forthwith." (The GSA made the tapes public in 1980.)

Nixon arguably does not require the states to recognize a common law right of access to court records, and some do not. In Virmani v. Presbyterian Health Services Corp., 515 S.E.2d 675 (N.C. 1999), the court said a North Carolina statute providing for secrecy in medical peer review committees also applied to civil litigation arising from such review, and that the statute trumped any common law right of access. "We do not believe that *Nixon* is controlling authority for the proposition that federal or state common law provides the public a right of access to state courts or their records."

Insofar as the *Nixon* case denied any First Amendment right of access, its authority is questionable in light of the later sequence of courtroom access cases considered in Section A of this chapter. But it has had continuing influence by virtue of its recognition of a common law right of access to judicial records. This at least supports a judge's exercise of discretion to release a record over the objections of a litigant or witness. See, e.g., United States v. Smith, 787 F.2d 111 (3d Cir. 1986). The decision has also influenced state courts to find a right of access to judicial records in their own common law or state constitutions.

2.   FIRST AMENDMENT ACCESS

Although there is some First Amendment right of access to records, its scope is unclear. The issue in *Press Enterprise I* and *Press Enterprise II* was access to transcripts. The Court's decision that the proceedings themselves should have been open necessarily entailed that the First Amendment required release of the transcripts. Those decisions imply a First Amendment right of access to records of open proceedings or proceedings that should have been open.

Nevertheless, trial judges may be able to effectively reverse the presumption of openness with respect to records once a danger to fair trial rights is shown. In a highly publicized political corruption case involving the mayor of Providence, the First Circuit held that a federal district judge may adopt a procedure that automatically seals all papers filed in a case until the judge determines that a specific document poses no undue risk to the defendant's fair trial rights. In re Providence Journal Co., 293 F.3d 1 (1st Cir. 2002). The court agreed that *Press Enterprise II* and *Globe Newspaper* recognized a First Amendment right of access to these records but held that protecting fair trial rights in a case where the dangers of prejudice had been demonstrated is a compelling interest, and under the circumstances of the case "implementation of a general procedure to seal all memoranda temporarily appears narrowly tailored."

Expungement. Some states have statutes providing for the sealing or expungement of records if the defendant is acquitted, no-billed by a grand jury, or meets the conditions of a deferred adjudication. The Ohio Supreme Court upheld the constitutionality of such a statute when it was used to seal the records of a trial after its conclusion. See State ex rel. Cincinnati Enquirer v. Winkler, 805 N.E.2d 1094 (Ohio 2004). The trial had been open, and the records had remained open for five weeks.

> The public's ability to attend a criminal trial is not hindered. The media's right to report on the court proceedings is not diminished. The statute does not restrict the media's right to publish truthful information relating to the criminal proceedings that have been sealed. In addition, the public had a right of access to any court record before, during, and for a period of time after the criminal trial. In fact, the public's access to the records is unrestricted until a decision is made to seal records. The statute ensures fairness by balancing the competing concerns of the public's right to know and the defendant's right to keep certain information private.

Most disputes over access to records involve materials further removed from the question of access to proceedings. For example, media sometimes seek access to physical evidence. In Globe Newspaper Co. v. Commonwealth, 570 S.E.2d 809 (Va. 2002), several newspapers requested access to fluid specimens in a rape-murder case in which the defendant had been executed ten years previously. The newspapers wanted to conduct DNA tests, using more sophisticated methods than were available at the time of trial, to determine whether the defendant was wrongly identified. The court said there was no historical right of access to evidence for the purpose of testing, and creating one would not have a positive effect on the functioning of the judicial process because of the practical problems of supervising such testing and protecting the integrity of the evidence.

The following case involved materials that are arguably the furthest removed: discovery materials obtained by the media as litigants.

Seattle Times Co. v. Rhinehart

Supreme Court of the United States, 1984.
467 U.S. 20.

[Rhinehart and the Aquarian Foundation, a controversial religious group he headed, sued two newspapers for libel, claiming harm to the fundraising and recruitment activities of the foundation. During discovery, the newspapers asked for membership lists and names of financial contributors. The plaintiffs refused to produce this information on the ground that it would violate the members' and donors' freedom of religion and rights of privacy and association. The trial court ordered them to disclose, but issued a protective order forbidding the newspapers from publishing the information, divulging it to other media, or otherwise using it for any purposes other than the litigation.]

■ JUSTICE POWELL delivered the opinion of the Court.

This case presents the issue whether parties to civil litigation have a First Amendment right to disseminate, in advance of trial, information gained through the pretrial discovery process.

. . .

Respondents appealed from the trial court's production order, and petitioners appealed from the protective order. The Supreme Court of Washington affirmed both. 98 Wash. 2d 226, 654 P.2d 673 (1982). With respect to the protective order, the court reasoned:

> Assuming then that a protective order may fall, ostensibly, at least, within the definition of a "prior restraint of free expression", we are convinced that the interest of the judiciary in the integrity of its discovery processes is sufficient to meet the "heavy burden" of justification. The need to preserve that integrity is adequate to sustain a rule like CR 26(c) which authorizes a trial court to protect the confidentiality of information given for purposes of litigation. [ ]⁹

The court noted that "[t]he information to be discovered concerned the financial affairs of the plaintiff Rhinehart and his organization, in which he and his associates had a recognizable privacy interest; and the giving of publicity to these matters would allegedly and understandably result in annoyance, embarrassment and even oppression." [ ] Therefore, the court concluded, the trial court had not abused its discretion in issuing the protective order.

---

⁹ Although the Washington Supreme Court assumed, arguendo, that a protective order could be viewed as an infringement on First Amendment rights, the court also stated: "A persuasive argument can be made that when persons are required to give information which they would otherwise be entitled to keep to themselves, in order to secure a government benefit or perform an obligation to that government, those receiving that information waive the right to use it for any purpose except those which are authorized by the agency of government which exacted the information." [ ]

. . .

III

Most States, including Washington, have adopted discovery provisions modeled on Rules 26 through 37 of the Federal Rules of Civil Procedure. [ ] Rule 26(b)(1) provides that a party "may obtain discovery regarding any matter, not privileged, which is relevant to the subject matter involved in the pending action." It further provides that discovery is not limited to matters that will be admissible at trial so long as the information sought "appears reasonably calculated to lead to the discovery of admissible evidence." [ ]

The Rules do not differentiate between information that is private or intimate and that to which no privacy interests attach. Under the Rules, the only express limitations are that the information sought is not privileged, and is relevant to the subject matter of the pending action. Thus, the Rules often allow extensive intrusion into the affairs of both litigants and third parties. . . .

Petitioners argue that the First Amendment imposes strict limits on the availability of any judicial order that has the effect of restricting expression. They contend that civil discovery is not different from other sources of information, and that therefore the information is "protected speech" for First Amendment purposes. Petitioners assert the right in this case to disseminate any information gained through discovery. They do recognize that in limited circumstances, not thought to be present here, some information may be restrained. They submit, however:

> When a protective order seeks to limit expression, it may do so only if the proponent shows a compelling governmental interest. Mere speculation and conjecture are insufficient. Any restraining order, moreover, must be narrowly drawn and precise. Finally, before issuing such an order a court must determine that there are no alternatives which intrude less directly on expression. [ ]

We think the rule urged by petitioners would impose an unwarranted restriction on the duty and discretion of a trial court to oversee the discovery process.

IV

It is, of course, clear that information obtained through civil discovery authorized by modern rules of civil procedure would rarely, if ever, fall within the classes of unprotected speech identified by decisions of this Court. In this case, as petitioners argue, there certainly is a public interest in knowing more about respondents. This interest may well include most—and possibly all—of what has been discovered as a result of the court's order under Rule 26(b)(1). It does not necessarily follow, however, that a litigant has an unrestrained right to disseminate information that has been obtained through pretrial discovery. . . .

The critical question that this case presents is whether a litigant's freedom comprehends the right to disseminate information that he has obtained pursuant to a court order that both granted him access to that information and placed restraints on the way in which the information might be used. In addressing that question it is necessary to consider whether the "practice in question [furthers] an important or substantial governmental interest unrelated to the suppression of expression" and whether "the limitation of First Amendment freedoms [is] no greater than is necessary or essential to the protection of the particular governmental interest involved." [ ]

A

At the outset, it is important to recognize the extent of the impairment of First Amendment rights that a protective order, such as the one at issue here, may cause. As in all civil litigation, petitioners gained the information they wish to disseminate only by virtue of the trial court's discovery processes. As the Rules authorizing discovery were adopted by the state legislature, the processes thereunder are a matter of legislative grace. A litigant has no First Amendment right of access to information made available only for purposes of trying his suit. Zemel v. Rusk, 381 U.S. 1, 16–17 (1965) ("The right to speak and publish does not carry with it the unrestrained right to gather information"). Thus, continued court control over the discovered information does not raise the same specter of government censorship that such control might suggest in other situations. See In re Halkin, 598 F.2d at 206–207 (Wilkey, J., dissenting).

Moreover, pretrial depositions and interrogatories are not public components of a civil trial. Such proceedings were not open to the public at common law, Gannett Co. v. DePasquale, and, in general, they are conducted in private as a matter of modern practice. [ ] Much of the information that surfaces during pretrial discovery may be unrelated, or only tangentially related, to the underlying cause of action. Therefore, restraints placed on discovered, but not yet admitted, information are not a restriction on a traditionally public source of information.

Finally, it is significant to note that an order prohibiting dissemination of discovered information before trial is not the kind of classic prior restraint that requires exacting First Amendment scrutiny. See [*Gannett*] (Powell, J., concurring). As in this case, such a protective order prevents a party from disseminating only that information obtained through use of the discovery process. Thus, the party may disseminate the identical information covered by the protective order as long as the information is gained through means independent of the court's processes. In sum, judicial limitations on a party's ability to disseminate information discovered in advance of trial implicates the First Amendment rights of the restricted party to a far lesser extent than would restraints on dissemination of information in a different context.

Therefore, our consideration of the provision for protective orders contained in the Washington Civil Rules takes into account the unique position that such orders occupy in relation to the First Amendment.

B

Rule 26(c) furthers a substantial governmental interest unrelated to the suppression of expression. [ ]. . . . The Washington Civil Rules enable parties to litigation to obtain information "relevant to the subject matter involved" that they believe will be helpful in the preparation and trial of the case. Rule 26, however, must be viewed in its entirety. Liberal discovery is provided for the sole purpose of assisting in the preparation and trial, or the settlement, of litigated disputes. Because of the liberality of pretrial discovery permitted by Rule 26(b)(1), it is necessary for the trial court to have the authority to issue protective orders conferred by Rule 26(c). It is clear from experience that pretrial discovery by depositions and interrogatories has a significant potential for abuse. This abuse is not limited to matters of delay and expense; discovery also may seriously implicate privacy interests of litigants and third parties. The Rules do not distinguish between public and private information. Nor do they apply only to parties to the litigation, as relevant information in the hands of third parties may be subject to discovery.

There is an opportunity, therefore, for litigants to obtain— incidentally or purposefully—information that not only is irrelevant but if publicly released could be damaging to reputation and privacy. The government clearly has a substantial interest in preventing this sort of abuse of its processes. [ ] The prevention of the abuse that can attend the coerced production of information under a State's discovery rule is sufficient justification for the authorization of protective orders.[22]

C

We also find that the provision for protective orders in the Washington Rules requires, in itself, no heightened First Amendment scrutiny. To be sure, Rule 26(c) confers broad discretion on the trial court to decide when a protective order is appropriate and what degree of protection is required. The Legislature of the State of Washington, following the example of the Congress in its approval of the Federal Rules of Civil Procedure, has determined that such discretion is necessary, and we find no reason to disagree. The trial court is in the best position to weigh fairly the competing needs and interests of parties affected by discovery. The unique character of the discovery process requires that the trial court have substantial latitude to fashion protective orders.

---

[22] The Supreme Court of Washington properly emphasized the importance of ensuring that potential litigants have unimpeded access to the courts: "[A]s the trial court rightly observed, rather than expose themselves to unwanted publicity, individuals may well forgo the pursuit of their just claims. The judicial system will thus have made the utilization of its remedies so onerous that the people will be reluctant or unwilling to use it, resulting in frustration of a right as valuable as that of speech itself." [ ]

V

The facts in this case illustrate the concerns that justifiably may prompt a court to issue a protective order. As we have noted, the trial court's order allowing discovery was extremely broad. It compelled respondents—among other things—to identify all persons who had made donations over a 5-year period to Rhinehart and the Aquarian Foundation, together with the amounts donated. In effect the order would compel disclosure of membership as well as sources of financial support. The Supreme Court of Washington found that dissemination of this information would "result in annoyance, embarrassment and even oppression." [ ] It is sufficient for purposes of our decision that the highest court in the State found no abuse of discretion in the trial court's decision to issue a protective order pursuant to a constitutional state law. We therefore hold that where, as in this case, a protective order is entered on a showing of good cause as required by Rule 26(c), is limited to the context of pretrial civil discovery, and does not restrict the dissemination of the information if gained from other sources, it does not offend the First Amendment.

The judgment accordingly is affirmed.

■ JUSTICE BRENNAN, with whom JUSTICE MARSHALL joins, concurring.

The Court today recognizes that pretrial protective orders, designed to limit the dissemination of information gained through the civil discovery process, are subject to scrutiny under the First Amendment. As the Court acknowledges, before approving such protective orders, "it is necessary to consider whether the 'practice in question [furthers] an important or substantial governmental interest unrelated to the suppression of expression' and whether 'the limitation of First Amendment freedoms [is] no greater than is necessary or essential to the protection of the particular governmental interest involved.' " . . . I agree that the respondents' interests in privacy and religious freedom are sufficient to justify this protective order and to overcome the protections afforded free expression by the First Amendment. I therefore join the Court's opinion.

NOTES AND QUESTIONS

1.   Why is the protective order in this case "not the kind of classic prior restraint that requires exacting First Amendment scrutiny"? The passage that Justice Powell cites in support of this (from his concurring opinion in Gannett Co. v. DePasquale) said that excluding the press from the courtroom "denies access to only one, albeit important, source," while a classic prior restraint, such as the one in Nebraska Press v. Stuart, prohibits publication irrespective of the source. Is this answer persuasive?

2.   What implications, if any, does *Rhinehart* have for a First Amendment right of access to materials other than discovery documents?

3.   Is *Rhinehart* applicable to situations in which media who are not parties to the litigation (a) seek access to discovery materials, or (b) claim a right to publish such materials? Note that neither the Supreme Court nor the Washington Supreme Court explicitly endorsed the argument that litigants might be considered to have waived their right to publish material they obtained through discovery. Does that preclude a reading of *Rhinehart* that limits it to disclosure of discovery materials by *parties*?

4.   In an omitted portion of the opinion, the Court further discussed In re Halkin, 598 F.2d 176 (D.C. Cir. 1979), which held that a similar protective order was a "paradigmatic prior restraint" requiring close scrutiny under the First Amendment, and In re San Juan Star Co., 662 F.2d 108 (1st Cir. 1981), which held that such orders need only meet "a standard of 'good cause' that incorporates a 'heightened sensitivity' to the First Amendment concerns at stake." In *Halkin* the right to disclose was claimed by a party to the underlying litigation; in *San Juan Star* it was claimed by a nonparty newspaper that intervened. The Supreme Court did not mention this difference and indicated that it viewed the two decisions as being in conflict. Does this imply that *Rhinehart* should be read to apply to nonparty media disclosures of discovery materials?

The *Rhinehart* case is subjected to close analysis in Robert C. Post, Management of Speech: Discretion and Rights, 1984 S. Ct. Rev. 169.

3.   ACCESS TO SPECIFIC TYPES OF DOCUMENTS

In most cases seeking access to documents, media claim both a common law and First Amendment right of access. When courts find a right at common law, they usually decline to address the First Amendment issue. When they find no right under either theory, they often apply similar analyses to both. It is therefore difficult to separate the cases into common law and First Amendment categories. It is equally difficult to categorize types of documents as generally open or generally closed.

One question that runs through many of these cases is whether the materials at issue are judicial records. If the court determines that materials are not judicial records, there appears to be no right of access under either the common law or the First Amendment, although they may be disclosable under freedom of information statutes. Recall from Chapter Ten that judicial records are exempt from the FOIA and most state open records statutes. Rejecting the claim that the documents sought are judicial records may destroy that exemption. In Daily Gazette Co. v. Withrow, 350 S.E.2d 738 (W. Va. 1986), a civil rights action against a sheriff was settled and the parties agreed to keep the settlement terms confidential. In the absence of any claim that the settlement was a judicial record, the state supreme court held that public officials have a common law duty to keep a public record of settlements of lawsuits arising from their official actions, and that such a record is disclosable under the state freedom of information statute.

a.   DOCUMENTS RELATED TO CRIMINAL PROCEEDINGS

Probable cause affidavits, search warrants, arrest warrants, plea bargains, sentencing reports, and grand jury records are often sought by media because of the details they provide about the crime or the accused. They have few of the characteristics of court records, however, and unless they are introduced in court, they are not necessarily disclosable.

In Times Mirror Co. v. United States, 873 F.2d 1210 (9th Cir. 1989), the court held that the First Amendment right of access recognized in *Press-Enterprise II* does not apply to search warrants, at least while the investigation is continuing, because historically they have not generally been public. Further, the court noted that making them available would not serve a positive role in the proceeding for many of the same reasons that grand jury proceedings are kept secret. See also Baltimore Sun Co. v. Goetz, 886 F.2d 60 (4th Cir. 1989); Times Mirror Co. v. United States, 873 F.2d 1210 (9th Cir. 1989); Seattle Times v. Eberharter, 713 P.2d 710 (Wash. 1986); and Newspapers of New England, Inc. v. Ware Clerk-Magistrate, 531 N.E.2d 1261 (Mass. 1988), all denying access to search warrants while investigations were continuing. Once the prosecution is completed, however, the common law right of access may require that search warrants be disclosed. See In re Application of Newsday, Inc., 895 F.2d 74 (2d Cir. 1990); see also In re Application of New York Times Co., 585 F. Supp. 2d 83 (D.D.C. 2008) (applying the "experience and logic test" of *Press-Enterprise II* and holding that there is a First Amendment qualified right of access to search warrant materials after investigation has concluded).

Even if there is a presumptive right of access to such materials, it may be overcome by other interests. The Eighth Circuit recognized a First Amendment right of access to search warrants and supporting affidavits, but held that it may be overcome by the need to protect the privacy and reputational interests of persons who were targets of the search but were not indicted. See Employees of McDonnell Douglas Corp. v. Pulitzer Publishing Co., 895 F.2d 460 (8th Cir. 1990). In Utah v. Archuleta, 857 P.2d 234 (Utah 1993), the Utah Supreme Court held that the media presumptively had a right of access to probable cause statements, affidavits in support of search warrants, and witness subpoenas that had been filed with the trial court. This right was based on the First Amendment, the state constitution, and the common law. But "the documents sought contained sensitive and inflammatory information that was not necessarily accurate or admissible" and therefore posed a substantial threat to the fair trial rights of a defendant in a "highly publicized and gruesome case" of torture, rape, and murder.

The media in the Utah case also sought to inspect and copy exhibits that were introduced at the preliminary hearing, including the autopsy report; photos of the victim's body; fluid, tissue, hair samples, and bone fragments taken from the victim; various instruments used to torture and kill the victim; bloody clothing; and fingerprints. The court said there was no First Amendment right of access to these because there was no history of the public being allowed to examine such exhibits and allowing them to do so would not play a significant positive role in the functioning of the judicial process. For similar reasons the court found no common law or state constitutional right of access.

Plea agreements generally must be disclosed, perhaps because they are usually dispositive and normally come after the major threats to the defendant's fair trial rights have passed. The Ninth Circuit held that the presumption of openness recognized by the Supreme Court in the two *Press-Enterprise* cases and in *Globe Newspaper* is applicable to plea agreements. The court explained that these have historically been open and because most criminal cases end with plea agreements, denying access to them "would effectively block the public's access to a significant segment of our criminal justice system." The Oregonian Publishing Co. v. U.S. District Court, 920 F.2d 1462 (9th Cir. 1990).

Sentencing reports are more problematic, possibly because they often include unverified or privacy-invading information. See, e.g., United States v. Corbitt, 879 F.2d 224 (7th Cir. 1989), holding that there is no First Amendment right to such reports and finding the common law right outweighed by the privacy interests of the defendant and his associates. But see United States v. Kaczynski, 154 F.3d 930 (9th Cir. 1998), holding that the common law required disclosure of results of a psychiatric exam because the public interest in mental state and motivations of the "Unabomber" outweighed his privacy interests.

Grand Juries. Rule 6(e) of the Federal Rules of Criminal Procedure requires that hearings on, and records pertaining to, "matters affecting a grand jury proceeding" be closed or sealed "to the extent necessary to prevent disclosure of matters occurring before a grand jury." Most states have similar rules. Grand jury proceedings are invariably secret, and the indictments that a grand jury issues often are sealed until the person named is arrested. Thereafter the indictment usually becomes part of the public record of the case, but the testimony upon which it rests remains secret. If the grand jury does not indict, there apparently is no right of access to the testimony and documents that it considered unless a statute or rule authorizes disclosure. See Daily Journal Corp. v. Superior Court, 979 P.2d 982 (Cal. 1999), rejecting media demands for grand jury evidence to enable the public to determine whether Merrill Lynch had "bought its way out" of a tenable criminal prosecution for its role in the bankruptcy of Orange County by agreeing to a civil settlement.

Even if there is no First Amendment right of access, courts may have discretion to disclose grand jury records if there is no rule forbidding it. In Arizona v. Mecham, the court, exercising its discretion under state law in an unreported decision, ordered disclosure of the transcripts of grand jury proceedings that led to the indictment of the governor. The court pointed out that neither the prosecution nor the defendants objected to the disclosure, the criminal proceedings had been concluded, much of the grand jury testimony had already been disclosed at trial, and the case was one of great public interest. The court also pointed out, however, that the case was unique, involving the only governor in the nation's history to simultaneously face a felony charge, impeachment proceedings, and a recall election. For these reasons, the court wrote: "this Order is not to be considered as precedent for future requests for public disclosure of Grand Jury transcripts."

Does grand jury secrecy require that all proceedings ancillary to the grand jury's work (and related documents) be secret too? That question surfaced in connection with the Whitewater special prosecutor's investigation of Monica Lewinsky's relationship with President Clinton. Several witnesses who were subpoenaed in that investigation resisted on grounds of executive privilege or attorney-client privilege, and President Clinton moved to have the special prosecutor held in contempt for leaking grand jury testimony to the press. On order of the chief judge of the district court for the District of Columbia, all hearings on these matters were closed to the press and public and all transcripts, pleadings, and other documents were sealed.

Major newspapers, magazines, and networks complained that hearings on the privilege claims and contempt allegations were not grand jury proceedings and should be open as a matter of common law and First Amendment law. They asked for advance notice of hearings on privilege or contempt matters, an opportunity to be heard before such hearings were closed, and public docketing of all motions and orders. The chief judge rejected all the media requests, and the D.C. Circuit upheld her decision in most respects. See In re Motions of Dow Jones & Co., 142 F.3d 496 (D.C. Cir. 1998).

The court of appeals noted that the media did not question the constitutionality of Rule 6(e) and said this rule applies to ancillary proceedings because those will nearly always pose a danger of revealing "matters occurring before a grand jury." The media pointed out that Chief Judge Sirica conducted a famous public hearing on President Nixon's refusal to comply with a grand jury subpoena to turn over the Watergate tapes, but the court said that example "proves too much" because the transcript of the Nixon hearing shows that it disclosed matters that the media in the present case agreed should not be disclosed under Rule 6(e).

The court said: "Recognizing a First Amendment right to force ancillary proceedings to be conducted without referring to grand jury matters would create enormous practical problems in judicial administration, and there is no strong history or tradition in favor of doing so." As to noting hearings, motions, and orders on the public docket, the court said the judge should do so by using captions that would not reveal the nature of matters before the grand jury.

b. DOCUMENTS RELATED TO CIVIL PROCEEDINGS

Pleadings in civil cases are clearly judicial records and are presumptively open at common law and probably also as a matter of First Amendment law. However, that does not mean they cannot be sealed. In one of the many civil suits arising out of allegations of sexual abuse by Catholic priests, a sharply divided Kentucky Supreme Court held that there was no right of access to allegations that had been stricken as immaterial. Roman Catholic Diocese of Lexington v. Noble, 92 S.W.3d 724 (Ky. 2002). The 4–3 majority said there could be no First Amendment right of access because "there is nothing to indicate that the public and the press historically have had access to sham, immaterial, impertinent, redundant, or scandalous material that is without 'legal effect,' " and that access to the material could "only serve to improperly prejudice the populace in general, and potential jurors in particular, against the Diocese's case." The court held that whether to allow access as a matter of common law was within the trial court's discretion.

Discovery Documents. As the Court noted in *Rhinehart*, most of the fact-finding activity in civil litigation takes place outside the courtroom, in the process of discovery. Although the precise issue in *Rhinehart* was the validity of a protective order restricting a party's use of discovery material, the decision generally has been read to speak to the broader question of public access to discovery material. It has proved to be a powerful obstacle to disclosure, even when the claim for access seems strong.

As to discovery materials that have not been filed in court, there is little basis for either a common law or First Amendment right of access. See, e.g., State ex rel. Mitsubishi Heavy Industries v. Milwaukee County Circuit Court, 605 N.W.2d 868 (Wis. 2000), holding that such documents were not public records and a newspaper therefore had no claim of access to them. States are free to designate these as public records, however, and some have done so. The state that has gone furthest in this regard is Texas. A procedural rule adopted by the Texas Supreme Court in 1990 treats discovery documents and settlement agreements as court records—even if they have not been filed—if they relate to information "concerning matters that have a probable adverse effect upon the general public health or safety, or the administration of public office, or the operation of government." These and all other court records may be sealed only after a public notice is posted and a hearing is held, and then only upon a finding that the interest in openness is outweighed by "a specific, serious, and substantial interest" that cannot be protected by alternative means. Nonparties have a right to intervene to contest the sealing or to unseal the records at any future time. Tex. R. Civ. P. 76a. Less far-reaching rules have been adopted in Florida, New York, and a few other states.

When discovery materials are filed with the court, usually in connection with pre-trial motions, they become court records subject to the common law and First Amendment rights of access. But the courts generally hold that this only means that the party seeking secrecy must show good cause for maintaining confidentiality under Rule 26 of the Federal Rules of Civil Procedure. See Chicago Tribune Co. v. Bridgestone/Firestone Inc., 263 F.3d 1304 (11th Cir. 2001), holding that the trial judge must balance a manufacturer's trade secret interests against a newspaper's claim that disclosure would serve the public's interest in health and safety.

Good cause that existed when a protective order was entered may disappear with the passage of time. In Public Citizen v. Liggett Group Inc., 858 F.2d 775 (1st Cir. 1988), the court held that dismissal of the underlying case, removing any concerns about the defendant's right to a fair trial, was a change in circumstances sufficient to justify modification of a protective order despite the defendant's argument that it had relied on the order in furnishing the material.

Some courts have suggested that a change in the Federal Rules of Civil Procedure now requires the media to justify all requests for access to unfiled discovery documents. Rule 5(d) formerly required that "all discovery materials must be filed with the district court, unless the court orders otherwise." This created a presumption that such materials would be accessible to the public unless the court entered a protective order. Rule 5(d) has been amended, however, to prohibit the filing of certain discovery materials unless they are actually used in the trial or the court orders that they be filed. The Second Circuit, in dicta, suggested that the amendment to Rule 5(d) "provides no presumption of filing all discovery materials, let alone public access to them." See Securities & Exchange Comm'n v. TheStreet.Com, 273 F.3d 222 (2d Cir. 2001). At least one district court has relied on the change in Rule 5(d) and the Second Circuit's dicta to find that the press must show a "legitimate reason" before a court will order third-party access to discovery materials. See New York v. Microsoft Corp., 206 F.R.D. 19 (D.D.C. 2002).

Videotapes of Depositions. Unless a state rule authorizes it, media generally have no right to attend depositions. Transcripts of depositions are discovery documents subject to the disclosure rules and procedures described above. If a deposition is videotaped and the tape is filed in court, some courts have held that it becomes a court record subject to disclosure unless good cause for secrecy is established. See In re Application of CBS, Inc., 828 F.2d 958 (2d Cir. 1987), allowing broadcasters to copy a videotaped deposition given by former Teamsters president Roy L. Williams in a trial in which Williams was identified as an unindicted co-conspirator.

But access to two videotaped depositions given by President Clinton was denied on the ground that they were not judicial records. In the criminal trial of the Whitewater defendant Susan McDougal, Clinton's videotaped deposition was played in open court and the judge made available a transcript but denied requests for permission to copy the tape for broadcast. The testimony and the transcript thereof were admitted in evidence but the videotape itself was not. Relying on *Nixon,* the Eighth Circuit held that the videotape was not a judicial record. See United States v. McDougal, 103 F.3d 651 (8th Cir. 1996). Unlike the tapes at issue in *Nixon,* the videotape was not documentary evidence itself but was merely an electronic recording of a witness's testimony. Even if the videotape were treated as a judicial record, the district judge did not abuse his discretion in applying the common law balancing process suggested by *Nixon.*

The court wrote that the public's interest in having access to the videotape was "only marginal because the testimony has already been made visually and aurally accessible in the courtroom and the transcript has been widely distributed and publicized." As in *Nixon,* there was a potential for "misuse" of the tape, but the court did not say how it might be misused. Noting that the media were denied physical access to the videotape of President Reagan's deposition testimony in the Iran-Contra prosecutions, the court wrote that "there is a strong judicial tradition of proscribing public access to recordings of testimony given by a sitting president. . . ." Without discussing later Supreme Court cases establishing a First Amendment right of access to judicial proceedings, the court decided that the media's First Amendment right of access was satisfied by allowing them to listen to the testimony in the courtroom and to read the transcript of the deposition.

President Clinton also testified by videotaped deposition in Paula Jones' sexual harassment suit against him. After that suit was dismissed on his motion for summary judgment, news organizations asked the judge to unseal the discovery materials in the case. Relying on the decision of the Eighth Circuit in the *McDougal* case, the judge refused to unseal either the video or transcript of it on the ground that it was not a judicial record. See Jones v. Clinton, 12 F. Supp. 2d 931 (E.D. Ark. 1998).

Is there a tenable distinction between videotapes introduced as documentary evidence (e.g., a security camera's tape of a robbery) and a videotaped deposition? Why is the video of the deposition, instead of merely the transcript thereof, shown to the jury? Do those reasons argue for treating the video as evidence?

Settlements. These pose several different types of access problems. If the settlement is no more than a contract between the parties, by which one agrees to dismiss the suit in exchange for something of value from the other, it ordinarily would be no more accessible than any other private contract. Under the Texas rule mentioned above, however, even these agreements may be court records if they meet the public interest standards of that rule. Generally, settlements that are submitted to the court for approval become judicial records subject to the common law and First Amendment rights of access. See Jessup v. Luther, 277 F.3d 926 (7th Cir. 2002).

Frequently the determinative issue is whether good cause for a protective order is established by assertions that secrecy was an essential condition of the settlement. Some courts, however, apply a different analysis. For example, in a personal injury case, the parties reached a settlement, a condition of which was that the entire court file, along with the settlement, was to be sealed. A plaintiff in a different lawsuit against the same company, seeking information for use in his own case, challenged the sealing of the record. The Eleventh Circuit held the sealing impermissible even assuming the settlement would not have been reached but for the judge's agreement to seal the record. The court wrote that "[o]nce a matter is brought before a court for resolution, it is no longer solely the parties' case, but also the public's case. Absent a showing of extraordinary circumstances . . . the court file must remain accessible to the public." Brown v. Advantage Engineering, Inc., 960 F.2d 1013 (11th Cir. 1992). See also Wilson v. American Motors Corp., 759 F.2d 1568 (11th Cir. 1985).

If the sealing order includes not only the settlement agreement, but also discovery materials and records of hearings, motions, affidavits, and other materials that were publicly available when filed, it may be possible to unbundle the documents that are subject to the order and disclose at least the settlement. See, e.g., Shenandoah Publishing House v. Fanning, 368 S.E.2d 253 (Va. 1988), permitting sealing of discovery documents after settlement, but holding that the parties' generalized claims of financial, reputational, and emotional harm were not sufficient to overcome a presumption of openness as to the agreement itself.

NOTES AND QUESTIONS

1.   Do the cases described above reflect principles that can be used to predict outcomes in cases seeking access to judicial records, or are they merely ad hoc decisions?

2.   The common law right of access contemplates case-by-case balancing of the interests in disclosure against the specific reasons for secrecy. The First Amendment right of access depends on the history and experience inquiries mandated by *Richmond Newspapers, Globe Newspaper,* and *Press-Enterprise I* and *II,* and even if those yield the conclusion that there is a First Amendment right of access, it too can be overcome by a sufficient showing of a need for secrecy. Given those sources of indeterminacy, does the First Amendment add anything to the common law right of access? Does either approach leave less to the judge's discretion than the other?

In reflecting upon the materials covered in this chapter, note the large number of variables. The list of reasons for which restrictions on access are imposed includes fair trial rights; efficient operation of the court system; rehabilitation of offenders; privacy of victims, witnesses, and jurors; effectiveness of law enforcement; and judicial dignity and courtroom decorum, to name a few. The interests in disclosure are also diverse, ranging from mere curiosity about the amount of money someone received in a personal injury settlement to discovery of wrongdoing by police and elected officials.

Access can be a matter as simple as allowing reporters to see pleadings or as complex as arranging procedures to allow copying of videotapes. Enforcing restrictions can be as easy as ordering a photographer to leave the courtroom or as difficult as trying to control the speech of a juror long after he or she has been discharged. The variety is far greater than it appears here, because we have condensed, synthesized, and simplified this survey of judicial access issues. For an extensive treatment, see David A. Schulz, Communications Law in the Digital Age, 2010 Update: Developments in the Law of Access, 1028 PLI/PAT 399 (Practising Law Institute 2010).

If the First Amendment creates certain rights of access to judicial proceedings, why doesn't it also guarantee some rights of access to the other governmental sources of news considered in Chapter Ten? In that chapter we saw a number of relatively successful statutory solutions to access problems. Would statutory solutions work in the court context? Would they violate separation of powers principles? If courtroom access questions must be left to judges, are they better decided by application of constitutional and common law principles in access litigation than by judicial rulemaking? These questions have emerged only since the courts began recognizing common law and First Amendment rights of access, and many of them have yet to be resolved.

INDEX

References are to Pages

Damages, 326, 341, 503–04
Data protection statutes, 352–54
Driver's Privacy Protection Act, 584–86
False light theory, 327
FOIA, 562–70
Injunctions barring invasions, 326–27
Intrusions, 363–70, 443–60
Invasion of
    By appropriation, 336–51
    By eavesdropping, 467–84
    By use of name, 305, 338
Newsworthiness or lack of public concern, 298, 301–02, 305–07
Of jurors, 638, 648–50
Privacy Act of 1974, 296, 587
Public figures, 307–09
Public record privilege, 313, 314, 317, 319, 445
Rape victim and, 81, 312–14, 315–26, 648
Rights of survivors, 309–10
Use of names, 305, 338
Warren and Brandeis on, 295
Wiretapping, 467–84

PRIVILEGE
    See also Subpoenas
    Generally, 509–23
Defamation and, 221–23

PROGRESSIVE, THE
Enjoined from publishing, 44–45

PROPAGANDA
Wartime, 22, 612

PUBLICITY
Pretrial, 47–48, 51–52, 53–54, 83, 638
Right of, 336–51, 358

RAPE VICTIMS
Disclosing names of, 81, 312–14, 315–26, 372

REPORTER'S PRIVILEGE
See Subpoenas

RUBENFELD, JED
On First Amendment theory, 16

SCHAUER, FREDERICK
On eclecticism, 18
On tort liability for inciting speech, 389–90

SEARCH WARRANTS
Newsroom searches, 555–58

SHIELD LAWS
See Subpoenas

SHIFFRIN, STEVEN
On First Amendment, 18, 351

SIXTH AMENDMENT
Right to public trial, 639

SOLOVE, DANIEL
On privacy, 351

SON OF SAM LAW
Profits of crime, 94–100

SPECTRUM
Broadband, 175
Electromagnetic, Nature of, 175
Scarcity, 127, 129, 170

STAMP ACT
Tax on newspapers, 100

STATUTES
Communications Act
    And net neutrality, 175–81
    As basis for FCC regulation of obscenity, 112
    Section 312(a)(7), 132–37
    Section 315, 130–32
Copyright Act, 46, 412–13, 414, 415, 416, 420, 436
Retraction, 90, 92, 287–88
Shield laws, 523
SLAPP statutes, 291–93
SPEECH Act of 2010, 290
Telecommunications Act of 1996, 150

STEWART, POTTER
On press access to government information, 619

SUBPOENAS
Anonymous speakers, 272
Eye witnesses, 554
Federal common law privilege, 524, 539, 559
Freelancers, 509
Grand jury, 510–23
In camera review, 528–29
Leaks cases, 538–46
Libel cases, 222–23
Outtakes, 547–54
Privilege statutes, 523
Telephone records, 559–60

SUNSTEIN, CASS R.
On free speech, 10–11, 93–94

TAXATION
Discrimination among media, 100
Of media, 100–08
Stamp Act, 100

TELEPHONE
Access to records, 559–60, 589–90, 624–25
Recording conversations, 467–69

TELEVISION
    See also Broadcasting; Federal Communications Commission
Cable television, 129
Cross-ownership, 138–39
History, 23
UHF and VHF, 129, 138–39

WEST, SONJA
On privacy and autobiographical speech, 304